Rockin' Out

Popular Music in the USA

Reebee Garofalo

University of Massachusetts Boston

Allyn and Bacon

Boston   London   Toronto   Sydney   Tokyo   Singapore

Vice President and Editor-in-Chief, Humanities: Joe Opiela
Editorial Assistant: Kate Tolini
Marketing Manager: Karon Bowers
Production Administrator: Deborah Brown
Editorial-Production Service: Susan McNally
Copyeditor: Pat Carda
Design and Electronic Composition: Denise Hoffman, Glenview Studios
Composition/Prepress Buyer: Linda Cox
Manufacturing Buyer: Suzanne Lareau
Cover Administrator: Linda Knowles

Copyright © 1997 by Allyn & Bacon
A Viacom Company
160 Gould Street
Needham Heights, MA 02194

Internet: www.abacon.com
America Online: keyword: college online

Library of Congress Cataloging-in-Publication Data

Garofalo, Reebee.
    Rockin' out : popular music in the USA / Reebee Garofalo
      p.   cm.
    Includes bibliographical references and index.
    ISBN 0-205-13703-2
    1. Popular music—United States—History and criticism.
  I. Title.
  ML3477.G37   1996   96-33424
  781.64'0973—dc20   CIP

Printed in the United States of America
10 9   01 00

Photo Credits:
AP/World Wide Photos: pages 219, 318, 377, 426, 444, and 458
The Bettmann Archive: pages 21 Corbis-Bettmann, 23, 25, 28, 38, 48, 132 UPI/Bettman, 195 UPI/Bettmann, 208 UPI/Bettmann, 227 UPI/Bettmann, 233 UPI/Corbis-Bettmann, 262 Penguin/ Corbis-Bettmann, 319, 359 UPI/Corbis-Bettmann, 383 Reuters/Bettmann, and 417 Corbis-Bettmann
BMI Archives: pages 52, 54, 58, 75, 77, 81, 82, 90, 104, 106, 110, 113, 117, 119, 127, 137, 142, 156, 162, 166, 168, 178, 186, 192 (inset), 199, 202, 211, 215, 216, 225, 234, 254, 260, 266, 268 both photos, 272, 281, 337, 342, 344, 362, 367, 369, 388, 422, 449 © Chris Cuffaro, 452, and 456
Delta Haze Corporation: page 50
Michael Ochs Archives: pages 99, 123, 129, 158, 159, 164, 190, 192, 197, 221 © Tom Copi, 247, 251, 275, 279, 284, 288, 293, 296, 307, 311, 313, 314, 316, 320, 330, 338, 370, 379, 403, 405, 408, 410, 413, 415, 418, 430, and 463 © Anna Luken

Contents

iii

3   "Good Rockin' Tonight": The Rise of Rhythm and Blues   65

4   Crossing Cultures: The Eruption of Rock 'n' Roll   93

5   The Empire Strikes Back: The Reaction to Rock 'n' Roll   149

Preface

Since its inception, popular music has been a source of pleasure for millions of people all over the world. This, of course, is reason enough for listening to it. But popular music is also a social and political indicator that mirrors and influences the society we all live in. This is the reason for studying it.

Popular music—playing it, listening to it, learning from it, teaching it—has been one of the organizing principles of my life ever since I can remember. It energizes me, provides the soundtrack for significant moments in my life, and helps me to navigate the world around me. In society at large, discussions of popular music's significance can be found everywhere—from family dinners and Saturday night parties to the board room and congressional chambers.

There has also been an increasing interest in popular music courses on college and university campuses. As a teacher of such courses for many years, I have found that the current field of popular music studies is often steeped in debates about culture theory that are needlessly esoteric, if not impenetrable. *Rockin' Out,* in contrast, is intended to introduce a general readership to the body of music that underpins these discussions; it is informed by theory without being engulfed by it. While the book is necessarily encyclopedic, it balances information with interpretation.

Popular music cannot be fully understood simply as a set of musical elements in the traditional sense and then measured against some abstract aesthetic norm of quality. Because aesthetic judgments are themselves culturally determined, in studying popular music, it is important to recognize that the musical text is as much a product of its social and political context as any individual's creativity or talent. While specifics of the music must always frame the discussion, a thorough analysis of popular music requires an understanding of history, economics, technology, politics, and cultural practices. Accordingly, *Rockin' Out* offers a grounded, coherent, social history of U.S. popular music since the invention of the phonograph in 1877. The book locates popular music in a social context and provides an interdisciplinary analysis of its impact.

The question of boundaries—what to include within the parameters of popular music and what to exclude, what to emphasize and what to mention in passing—presents an obvious set of issues for a book like this one. Most histories draw boundaries around popular music and exclude classical music, folk music (as opposed to certain folk revivals), and most jazz (particularly where it aspires to be an art music). I have tended to continue this practice. I have also limited myself to music that has exerted an influence in the United States. Because the enslavement and subsequent oppression of African Americans and the resulting cultural interactions have had such a profound effect on the development of our popular music, my inclination is to view popular music first through the lens of race. Needless to say, this is not the only dimension that I consider important. Other crucial demographic variables include class, age, gender, and ethnicity. Technological advances and the political economy of the music industry have also been important in shaping the development of popular music. Finally, popular music invariably develops in relation to the prevailing political climate in a given era. These, therefore, are the themes that run through this book.

Because the notion of "popularity" has an obvious quantitative dimension, I attach a certain amount of importance to sales data. A record that no one hears has no impact. Accordingly, *Rockin' Out* is peppered with popularity chart listings and references to "gold" and "platinum" records. These benchmarks of commercial success are currently defined in *Billboard,* the leading music trade magazine, as the sale of 500,000 album units and 1 million album units respectively. Being mindful of commercial success guards against the tendency to inflate one's personal preferences to the status of aesthetic principles. At the same time, it is important to note that commercially successful artists and records may or may not be the most influential or artistically important. Historical accounts, musical analyses, critical reviews, and audience reactions are important qualitative indicators that must also be factored into any discussion of popular music.

Because histories such as this one focus on a period in popular music history that has been dominated by various rock styles, they often use "rock" as a generic term for all popular music. The term is a convenient (and, in many ways, appealing) shorthand but it is not without its problems. In the 1960s, the term rock 'n' roll, which had always crossed the racial divide, was shortened to "rock," a refinement suggesting a more mature form of the music. By this time, however, rock clearly signified the music of white artists, primarily those associated with the British Invasion and the counterculture in the United States. It was distinguished from "soul," the term used for the music of African Americans. Given the significant contribution of African American artists to popular music during this period, I am critical of the subsequent use of "rock" as the generic term for contemporary popular music. At the same time, I am aware of the difficulty of avoiding this usage since it appears so frequently in the literature. I would also argue that the verb form, rocking, continues to cross the racial divide as something popular music does rather than what it is.

Given that the emergence of rock 'n' roll is taken as a crucial development in the history of popular music, the opening chapters are devoted to a discussion of the changes that pointed the way to rock 'n' roll. The introductory chapter, "Introduction: Definitions, Themes, and Issues," provides an overview of the defining characteristics of popular music, a discussion of the key issues involved in the transition from Tin Pan Alley pop (the music that dominated the mainstream in the first half of the twentieth century) to the emergence of rock 'n' roll, and a sense of the continuing developments that bring the history to the present. As such, it orients the reader to the broad cultural changes and notable controversies that have shaped U.S. popular music in the twentieth century.

Chapter 1, "Mass Technology and Popular Taste: The Tin Pan Alley Era," begins with the invention of the phonograph because records were one critical element in the advent of rock 'n' roll. It then details the rise of Tin Pan Alley and explores the relationship of Tin Pan Alley to African American music (ragtime, blues, and jazz) and to the mass media (records, radio, and film).

Chapter 2, "Blues and Country Music: Mass Media and the Construction of Race" analyzes the history of grassroots music that developed parallel to Tin Pan Alley, but often beneath its notice. While histories of blues and country music are often dealt with separately, they are paired here to emphasize that both served a similar social function and that there was a considerable amount of cross cultural interplay that occurred outside the separate and unequal marketing structures of the music industry. The device of pairing seemingly disparate musical genres is replicated in Chapter 8 with punk and disco, and again, in Chapter 10 with rap and metal.

The long and winding musical road that led to the emergence of rhythm and blues, the genre that made the most substantive contribution to rock 'n' roll, is the subject of Chapter 3, "'Good Rockin' Tonight': The Rise of Rhythm and Blues." It is a tale of population migrations, structural realignments within the music industry, wartime materials shortages, and technological advances that unexpectedly brought a working-class, African American music to the fore.

Chapters 4 and 5 are companion chapters detailing, respectively, the rise of and reaction to rock 'n' roll. Chapter 4, "Crossing Cultures: The Eruption of Rock 'n' Roll," discusses the ascending styles of fifties rock 'n' roll, including New Orleans rhythm and blues and its Los Angeles independent label connections, electrified Chicago blues, the r&b and country output of Cincinnati, the rhythm and gospel fusion that emerged from the black church, the hybrid sounds of New York doo wop, and country-tinged Memphis rockabilly. Chapter 5, "The Empire Strikes Back: The Reaction to Rock 'n' Roll," chronicles the conservative backlash to rock 'n' roll that prompted a range of strategies designed to limit the music. These included "cover" records, pop diversions from folk to calypso, television promotion, and government-sponsored payola hearings. Surf music emerged from the rubble as one vibrant new sound, whose success was nevertheless linked to the ascendency of white middle-class rockers.

If the 1960s and early 1970s were a time of personal experimentation, cultural expansion, and political advancement for artists and fans, they were paralleled by a period of unprecedented mergers in the music industry. Ultimately, centralization in the industry and divisive political forces in the broader society led to the fragmentation of the music. Chapters 6 and 7 are companion chapters that deal with the ups and downs of music during this period. Chapter 6, "Popular Music and Political Culture: The Sixties," explores the relationship between rock (and its folk rock and psychedelic variants) and rhythm and blues (and its gospel-tinged cousin soul) and the social and political movements that dominated the decade—especially the Civil Rights movement and the counterculture. Chapter 7, "Music Versus Markets: The Fragmentation of Pop," details the corporate consolidation that accompanied a huge expansion of the industry infrastructure and the fragmentation of the music into softer rock and soul styles on the one hand and art rock, heavy metal, and glam on the other.

Beginning with a view of the soft, safe center of corporate pop rock that propelled tried-and-true musical formulas to mass sales, Chapter 8, "Punk and Disco: The Poles of Pop," analyzes the commercial potential and political tendencies of two genres of popular music that were widely viewed as polar opposites. Punk was the beneficiary of the lion's share of critical praise because of its presumed political possibilities. Disco was roundly ignored—or worse, actively despised—even though it came closer to realizing the political goal of uniting disparate groups across lines of class, race, and sexual preference.

Chapter 9, "Music Videos, Superstars, and Mega-Events: The Eighties," explores new developments in the music industry, including a major recession, significant technological advances, and the politicization of popular music with the advent of charity rock. In this period, superstars pointed the way out of the recession for the industry, as advances in satellite transmission facilitated their promotion to a global audience. Interestingly, the same technology that encouraged expansion and concentration in the music industry also created the "mega-events" that disseminated messages of political opposition and solidarity world-wide.

In Chapter 10, "Rap and Metal: Youth Culture and Censorship," rap and metal are paired as the cutting edge expressions of youth culture in the 1980s. The chapter chronicles the rise of each style and the ferocious public reaction that each precipitated. In the context of the conservative Reagan/Bush years, organizations following the lead of the Washington-based Parents Music Resource Center sought to impose the most serious regulations on popular music since the payola hearings of 1959–60. Issues of drug use, suicide, devil worship, sexuality, and violence are explored in detail.

Rockin' Out concludes with a discussion of so-called alternative music and its relationship to the mainstream music industry. Chapter 11 is titled "Alternative to What?" to call attention to the meteoric rise of alternative music from outsider status to mainstream marketing category. It occurred amidst such a flurry of critical press that nobody noticed that the early part of the 1990s was dominated by country music, if anything. In the context of conglomerate mergers of astronomical proportions including unprecedented artists' contracts, the anti-commercial tendencies of alternative music seemed that much more contradictory. Nowhere were these contradictory impulses more apparent than in the Lollapalooza festivals. Lollapalooza—at the same time commercially successful and politically relevant—is a fitting capstone for the 40-plus year history of contemporary popular music.

A book that is the scope of *Rockin' Out* does not fall from the sky. In addition to original research, it draws on my previously published work and the work of countless others. While encyclopedias, journal articles, and book-length studies have, of course, provided me with a wealth of secondary source material, discussions over the years with Bill Adler, William Barlow, Iain Chambers, Jannette Dates, Murray Forman, Simon Frith, Donna Gaines, Andrew Goodwin, Herman Gray, Larry Grossberg, Charles Hamm, Dave Harker, Simon Jones, Steve Jones, Charlie Keil, George Lipsitz, Dick Lourie, Portia Maultsby, Susan McClary, Keith Negus, Richard Peterson, Tricia Rose, Danny Schechter, Larry Shore, Philip Tagg, Robert Walser, Peter Wicke, and many others too numerous to mention have been invaluable in shaping my own positions. In addition, I would like to thank the reviewers for their valuable suggestions: Will Straw, McGill University; David Stuart, Iowa State University; Robert D. West, Kent State University; and David Sanjeck, BMI Archives. Dave Sanjek demonstrated repeatedly that he is one of the most knowledgeable and forthcoming researchers in the field, and also deserves special mention in his capacity as BMI archivist for gracing these pages with a treasure trove of photographs. Finally, the late Rick Dutka occupies a special place in my heart and mind as someone whose knowledge of and love for popular music were as boundless as his political energy and activist spirit.

As to my previous work, echoes of *Rock 'n' Roll Is Here to Pay,* the book with which I am most identified, can certainly be detected in *Rockin' Out.* In this instance, I owe a major debt of gratitude to first author Steve Chapple, whose pioneering contributions to popular music studies helped define the field and pushed me to formulate my views. My chapter on the history of black popular music that appeared in *Split Image,* edited by Jannette Dates and William Barlow, informs the discussions of r&b, soul, and rap that appear in this book. An earlier version of the discussion of popular music and the Civil Rights movement was published in *Radical America.* More detailed versions of my research on mega-events have appeared in *Re-Imaging America,* edited by Mark O'Brien and Craig Little; *Technoculture,* edited by Constance Penley and Andrew Ross; and in my *Rockin' the Boat.* My research on censorship has been published in greater detail in the *Journal of Popular Music Studies* and was funded by a grant from the Massachusetts Foundation for the Humanities and the Massachusetts Cultural Council, and neither group bears any responsibility for my opinions on the subject.

Bringing *Rockin' Out* to press has been a project of mammoth proportions. I am, first, indebted to Susannah Brabant for bringing my proposal to the attention of Bill Barke at Allyn and Bacon, and I am thankful to Bill for being the music lover that he is. By the time I finished the manuscript, my first editor, Steve Hull, had already passed the baton to Joe Opiela who gave me the much needed and appreciated extensions to see the project through to completion. My production team was a joy to work with from the start. Susan McNally coordinated competing needs and schedules with a firm but gentle touch that added a thoroughly enjoyable warmth and sense of humor to her competence and professionalism. Copyeditor Pat Carda's organization of the text was invaluable to me, and the book is markedly better for it. Designer Denise Hoffman came up with page layouts and graphic devices that, to me, complement the tone and voice of the book perfectly. There is also a staff team back at the home office whom I have met only briefly but whom I feel have been pulling for the book nonetheless; they certainly include Sandi Kirshner, Deborah Brown, and Karon Bowers, and probably others whom I haven't met. Clerical assistance from Kate Tolini facilitated communication.

My biggest debt of gratitude goes to my family, who put up with me during the four years it took to complete this project. Deborah Pacini Hernandez and I commuted between Boston and Gainesville, Florida, throughout the preparation of the manuscript. Her children, Radha and Tai, have yet to discover how mellow I can really be without a deadline hanging over my head. Radha has the most eclectic appreciation of music of anyone I know; it is a joy and a learning experience to watch her tastes—indeed, her whole life—unfold. The same goes for Tai whose tastes run more to the cutting edge. Tai also gets the credit for coming up with the name for the book. Debby is not just my partner, but a colleague whose knowledge of popular music has added measurably to my own. Throughout the project she offered perspective, insight, and criticism that were incredibly valuable and emotional support I could not have done without. In addition, she read more variations of individual paragraphs of the manuscript than any human being should ever have had to endure. And in the middle of the project, she even consented to marry me. This preface was written one year later at the tail end of our long-awaited, but very satisfying, honeymoon.

Finally, this book is dedicated with love and respect to my mother and father who have seen me through every trial and triumph of my life. I owe them more than words can say.

Reebee Garofalo
July 1996

Introduction: Definitions, Themes, and Issues

Broadly speaking, there have been two great eras of mainstream popular music in the United States in this century: the era dominated by the writers and publishers of Tin Pan Alley, which began at the turn of the century and continued through the end of World War II, and the era that began with the emergence of rock 'n' roll in the early 1950s and continues to the present day. The term rock 'n' roll is thus used to describe both the particular music that became popular among youth in the 1950s and the paradigm that dominated popular music thereafter. *Rockin' Out* begins with the rise of Tin Pan Alley because all of the technological advances (sound recording, radio broadcasting, and to a lesser extent, film and television) and all the musical styles (blues, jazz, country, rhythm and blues, and Tin Pan Alley pop itself) that contributed to development of rock 'n' roll came to fruition during its reign.

While this book covers more than one hundred years of recorded music, its primary focus is on the second half of the twentieth century. The pivotal moment in this history was the emergence of rock 'n' roll in the 1950s, as the transition from Tin Pan Alley to rock 'n' roll revealed important social and cultural shifts in U.S. society. If the music of Tin Pan Alley was lighthearted and urbane, the rock 'n' roll of the 1950s was heavy-handed

> The rock 'n' roll that emerged in the fifties combined all the elements that would define the broad parameters of popular music in the United States for at least the next forty years.

and urban. While Tin Pan Alley appealed to middle-class sensibilities, rock 'n' roll was decidedly working-class in its orientation. Whereas Tin Pan Alley made no particular age distinctions among its listeners, rock 'n' roll was targeted at youth. Tin Pan Alley was identified with sheet music in the same way that rock 'n' roll was associated with

1

records, and it was this difference that signified the beginning of an inextricable connection between popular music and advanced recording technology. Finally, the music of Tin Pan Alley evolved according to a Euro-American paradigm of music making, even when it incorporated other cultural influences. In contrast, rock 'n' roll turned dramatically toward African American conventions. In short, the rock 'n' roll that emerged in the fifties combined all the elements that would define the broad parameters of popular music in the United States for at least the next forty years.

Into the Twentieth Century: Popular Music and Mass Culture

In its association with sheet music, Tin Pan Alley can be seen as a descendant of a popular culture that dates back to the invention of the printing press in fifteenth-century Europe.[1] When the music of Tin Pan Alley emerged, popular music was distinguished from both folk music and folk culture on the one hand and classical or art music and high culture on the other. These distinctions are a part of our inheritance that came with European colonization.

Prior to the advent of popular culture in Europe, European societies were characterized by a two-tiered system of culture which was composed of folk culture and high culture. While there is ample evidence to suggest that there was considerable interaction between the two; at the time, these different levels of culture were officially considered separate and distinct. Historically, folk culture has been associated with the poor and those lacking formal education—in European feudal societies, the peasantry; after the Industrial Revolution, agricultural workers and the urban proletariat. It was a collective and participatory culture, shared by a particular community of people. The music arising from it was comparatively simple in form and structure, performed by nonprofessionals, and passed along, usually anonymously, in oral tradition. Its production and consumption were noncommercial. At the other end of the European cultural spectrum was high culture, which was associated with the ruling classes—the feudal aristocracy, the capitalist bourgeoisie. Its music was more complicated in form and structure and composed by paid professionals who were commissioned through a system of patronage. Because this music was notated (written down), it required a certain literacy and training for its performance. High culture thus imposed a separation between artists and consumers that was unknown in folk culture. What was a community in folk culture became an audience in high culture. As the official culture of court and church, high culture was considered to be superior to folk culture.

Popular culture insinuated itself between folk culture and high culture as a third cultural category, a hybrid that was distinguishable from both but borrowed freely from each as needed. Tin Pan Alley provides an excellent example of these contradictory tendencies. In attempting to cater exclusively to popular (albeit narrow mainstream) tastes, Tin Pan Alley writers consciously sought to construct an alternative to the cultural dominance of European art music. In the process, these writers incorporated influences, however superficially, from wide range of sources including a number of African American genres. At the same, however, these writers often took their cues from classical music and high culture. As late as 1941, for example, the melody of "Tonight We Love," a popular song by Ray Austin and Bobby Worth was lifted virtually note for note from the first movement of Tchaikovsky's *Piano Concerto No. 1*. Furthermore, in leaning heavily on upper-middle-class themes and images—dining at the Ritz, performing in black tie and tails—Tin Pan Alley writers further (and perhaps unwittingly) allied themselves with the high culture they sought to displace.

The invention of new mass communication technologies—records, radio, film, and eventually, television—inserted yet another distinction into the cultural lexicon, namely the concept of mass culture. The new term indicated cultural dissemination on a scale that increased by orders of magnitude. The question of scale had important implications for qualitative judgments about mass culture. Prior to the advent of mass culture, it was possible to consider popular culture as historically continuous with folk culture,

> In the eyes of most observers, the emergence of mass culture was accompanied by a subtle but important shift in orientation from a culture of the people to a culture for the masses.

either slowly replacing folk cultures as the next stage of development following the Industrial Revolution or as coexisting with rural or industrial folk cultures in the modern era. When viewed in this way, popular culture, like folk culture, was a culture of the people. With the introduction of the mass media, however, the idea of a continuing historical progression came to an abrupt halt. In the eyes of most observers, the emergence of mass culture was accompanied by a subtle but important shift in orientation from a culture *of* the people to a culture *for* the masses. In this deceptively simple change there was a profound transformation of meaning. Mass culture was not seen as the lived culture of an identifiable group of people, which reflected their values and aspirations. It was instead a commodified culture produced by a centralized, corporate culture industry for privatized, passive consumption by an alienated, undifferentiated mass.[4] Thus, although the terms *mass culture* and *popular culture* are often used interchangeably today, most observers tended to distinguish between the two in language that was pejorative and/or politically charged until well into the 1960s. In 1959, for example, Oscar Handlin, among others, argued forcefully against "the misconception that the 'mass culture' of the present is but an extension of the popular culture of the past."[2] Indeed, as late as 1965, Stuart Hall and Paddy Whannel maintained that "the typical 'art' of the mass media today is not a continuity from, but a *corruption of,* popular art."[3]

Rock 'n' roll, of course, could be numbered among the victims of this largely false distinction. As an unabashedly commercial product clearly intended for mass consumption, most critics dismissed the music as inferior and unworthy of serious consideration. To avoid the mass culture stigma, critics and historians in the 1960s who became invested in the cultural importance of rock as the mature form of rock 'n' roll, tended to characterize the music as something other than what it was. Historian Carl Belz, for example, argued that "rock is a part of the long tradition of folk art in the United States and throughout the world."[5] As the music took a turn toward greater sophistication, this characterization underwent further change. Discussions of Bob Dylan's lyrics as poetry and the Beatles' *Sgt. Pepper* as art reflected an attempt by some to "elevate" rock from folk music to art, thereby allying it with high culture. At the time, these efforts to categorize rock represented genuine attempts to understand the place of popular music in the hierarchy of cultural practices. Ultimately, however, there was no getting around the fact that rock was both a popular music and a mass cultural form. In 1981, music sociologist Simon Frith, among others, dismissed both earlier positions of rock as folk and rock as art. "Rock is a commercially made mass music," he asserted, "and this must be the starting point for its celebration as well as its dismissal."[6] Since then, musical practices have been discussed more in terms of the death throes of the modern era and its uneasy segue into postmodernism, a period characterized by, among other things, the collapse of all cultural categories.

Rock 'n' Roll:
The Birth of a New Era

The straightforward commercialism and mass appeal of rock 'n' roll did not set it apart from other popular music. What made rock 'n' roll different was its urban orientation, focus on youth culture, and appeal to working-class sensibilities, and its relationship to technology and African American musical influences and performance styles. As Charlie Gillett argues in his classic study *The Sound of the City,* rock 'n' roll was the first popular genre to incorporate the relentless pulse and sheer volume of urban life into the music itself. In his words, "Rock and Roll was perhaps the first form of popular culture to celebrate without reservation characteristics of city life that had been among the most criticized."[7] Here Gillett was referring to urban sounds that were perceived as "brutal and oppressive." It was in this world of droning machines that post–World War II adolescents "staked out their freedom . . . inspired and reassured by the rock and roll beat."[8]

Gillett's conflation of adolescence and rock 'n' roll highlights the fact that the emergence of the music as a genre coincided with the beginnings of youth culture as a phenomenon. Due to the convergence of a number of social forces in the 1950s, including postwar affluence and a demographic shift in the population toward youth, teenagers became an identifiable consumer group and one that possessed an ample amount of disposable income. The music industry learned, albeit not without considerable resistance, that targeting the musical tastes of this generation could be quite lucrative. As Simon Frith noted:

> The young had always had idols—film stars, sportsmen, singers like Frank Sinatra and Johnny Ray; the novelty of rock 'n' roll was that its performers were the same age as their audience, came from similar backgrounds, had similar interests; and the rise of rock 'n' roll meant a generation gap . . . Rock 'n' roll records and radio shows were aimed exclusively at the young, . . . and by the end of the 1950s most pop records were being bought by the young.[9]

Following the eruption of rock 'n' roll, the music industry identified young people as the primary audience for popular music. This new marketing strategy was later complicated by the fact that the baby boomers who comprised the initial rock 'n' roll audience kept on buying records well into their thirties and forties. Indeed, different generational preferences can be seen as a partial explanation for the fragmentation of popular genres in the 1970s. In the 1980s and 1990s, clear generational differences have resurfaced as rap, metal, and alternative have become the cutting-edge statements of youth culture. In response, many baby boomers have adopted the same critical tone toward this new music that their parents directed at early rock 'n' roll.

If rock 'n' roll was different from other forms of popular music in its unique relationship to youth, its connection to technology was also different. Different media have their own internal logic for such elements as composition, chronology, pacing, gesture, tone, inflection, and so forth. The power of filmmaking, for example, does not lie in the simple reproduction and transmission of an existing written work; rather, it is in exploiting the particular characteristics of the medium—camera angles, lighting, editing etc.—that filmmaking becomes an art form in its own right. The same logic extends to the relationship between music and recording. However, while the artistic possibilities of filmmaking were recognized fairly early in the development of the medium, the incorporation of recording technology into the creation of music—as opposed to its simple reproduction—was slower to take hold. Initially recording was thought of as a documentary process that sought only to preserve the quality of a live performance. Thus, while the success of popular music—even the music of Tin Pan Alley—depended to a large extent on mass communication technologies, these technologies were used in the dissemination of the music rather than its creation.

Unlike earlier forms of popular music, rock 'n' roll incorporated the capabilities of advanced technology into the creative process itself.

Unlike earlier forms of popular music, rock 'n' roll incorporated the capabilities of advanced technology into the creative process itself. Far from valuing the purity of the live performance, rock 'n' roll records consciously used the technical features of echo, editing, overdubbing, and multitracking to distort the reality of the performance. "Technical processes," as musicologist Peter Wicke has said, "became musical opportunities."[10] The emergence of rock 'n' roll, then, was characterized by a progressively more intimate relationship with the technologies used in its production and dissemination. This relationship continued as rock ventured toward art in the 1960s. Following the release of *Sgt. Pepper,* an album so dependent on studio technology that it couldn't be performed live, rock groups spent untold hours in the studio experimenting with technological gimmickry, overdubbing and adding special effects, and mixing each cut to perfection. Disco was further immersed in technological wizardry, becoming almost completely a product of the studio. In live performance, the use of feedback and distortion pioneered by Jimi Hendrix has become institutionalized in heavy metal through the use of voltage regulators, special effects boxes, and vocal distortion devices. Rap has pushed the envelope still further, first by using dual turntables as musical instruments, and then by using samplers, sequencers, and programmable drum machines as essential tools of the trade. To the extent that these creative uses of technology have been accepted as artistically valid, they have pushed the very definition of popular music beyond a traditional European conception of music as a pattern of *notes* toward a conception of music as organized *sound.*

Beginning with early rock 'n' roll advanced technologies were married to musical elements that in themselves separated the music from earlier forms of mainstream popular music along lines of class and race. The prominence of rhythm, immoderate volume, slurred notes, grainy vocals, aggressive attack, and vernacular speech that characterized rock 'n' roll tended to place the music outside the reach of middle-class culture and beyond the purview of musicological investigation. Because the field of musicology derives its main categories of investigation from the "notated" tradition of European art music, there has been a tendency to dismiss most working-class forms of popular music (and certainly rock 'n' roll) as "formulaic" and therefore insignificant. Within the parameters valued by official tastemakers—melody, harmony, structure—rock 'n' roll was found wanting. However, as Richard Middleton has pointed out:

> the formulaic processes operate within parameters relatively highly valued by traditional musicology: harmony, melodic shape, basic rhythm pattern. Variant processes, on the other hand, often take place in parameters little valued by traditional musicology (and much harder to notate): slight pitch inflection or rhythmic variation, timbre and timbre changes, accent, and attack.[11]

The subtlety and sophistication of rock 'n' roll, then, were to be found in features of the music which were outside the frame of reference of the cultural elite.

Analyses of structure, melody, and chord progressions, of course, are not without value. They can offer important insights into the differences existing between popular music and other forms of music, as well as differences among popular genres themselves. Rock 'n' roll and Tin Pan Alley pop, for example, can be distinguished in these terms. However, a surface analysis of these elements alone can not adequately capture the disjuncture that characterized the transition between the two. To get to this level of analysis, it is necessary to examine the full range of cultural practices and performance styles that comprised these respective musical eras. The ascendancy of Tin Pan Alley co-incided with the emergence of a number of African American genres, including ragtime, blues, boogie woogie, and jazz. Certain aspects of these African American genres were appropriated by Tin Pan Alley songwriters who were somewhat open to outside influences. From ragtime to swing one can find a hint of syncopation here, a blue note there. But while grassroots blues and jazz lured listeners toward Africa, mainstream pop interpretations of these genres quickly pulled them back to Europe. Tin Pan Alley appropriations were by and large superficial adaptations—what musicologist Charles Hamm has called "a touch of exotic seasoning"[12]—that were incorporated into an aesthetic framework defined by the European tradition. This, of course, was reassuring to some. It preserved the centrality of Western civilization and kept upstart

By all accounts, the eruption of rock 'n' roll entailed a profound shift in cultural values on the part of mainstream youth, a shift away from Euro-American sensibilities and toward African American ones.

African American artists in check. Conservative culture critic H. F. Mooney, for example, considered it fortunate that the influence of African American music was "limited by compromises with middle class conventions" and delighted in the fact that it was "'polished' . . . so as to conform to the standards of European rendition."[13] Revealing his bias further, Mooney noted "The highest compliment most of the public could pay to big-band jazz between 1928 and 1950 was 'symphonic' or 'advanced'."[14] He went on to describe the pressures on African American artists to tow the line:

> *Middle-class Negroes who desired to "come up," as they put it, during the 1930s and the 1940s responded to the smoothly harmonized arrangements of a white Jimmy Dorsey's watered-down jazz. Duke Ellington himself was influenced by Guy Lombardo's "sweetest music this side of heaven," and brought something of the sound of the Roosevelt Hotel ballroom to Harlem. Commercial orchestras of the period around 1920–50 followed more or less the "safe bet"—the aesthetic aspirations of the middle-class market—as did, indeed, most of the big Negro bands.[15]*

Rock 'n' roll, however, turned this situation on its head. By all accounts, the eruption of rock 'n' roll entailed a profound shift in cultural values on the part of mainstream youth, a shift away from Euro-American sensibilities and toward African American ones. The most important feature of this shift was an increased emphasis on rhythm. In the words of Christopher Small, "rhythm is to the African musician what harmony is to the European—the central organizing principle of the art."[16] Although in the slave cultures of the Americas, this African tradition was complicated by considerable pressure to adopt European ways of music making (indeed the history of African American music is fraught with this tension), rock 'n' roll is clearly descended from the tradition of organizing musical elements around a recurring rhythmic structure. In its early years, rock 'n' roll was often referred to as the Big Beat. With the ascent of rock "n" roll, then, this "central organizing principle" came to define mainstream popular music in a way that had never before been the case.

The orientation toward an African American aesthetic also affected such musical elements as structure, chord patterns, and scales, as well as the more subtle features mentioned earlier. As music historian Iain Chambers has written:

> While the thirty-two bar format is the musical cornerstone of Tin Pan Alley, in the Afro-American tradition it is the twelve bar blues: three chords alternating in a fixed pattern. From the perspective of European classical harmony, this offers an even more rigid and correspondingly "poorer" musical frame than that used by the white popular music industry. The "blues scale" is also sparse: consisting of five rather than the seven notes of the official European scale. This produces a telling disorientation for our ears as the blues singer stretches and slides over those intervals ("blue notes") we are accustomed to expect. Such a sensation of "foreignness" is the most recognisable aural trait of the blues and Afro-American music in pop—the slides, slurs, bent, "dirty" and uncertain notes in the voice, guitar, saxophone and bass. It remains the irreducible testimony of the clash between a legitimised white European-derived tradition and a barely recognised Afro-American one.[17]

While there had been an awareness of African American influences among white jazz musicians and Tin Pan Alley composers, rock 'n' roll pushed performers toward the wholesale adoption of an African American orientation. As Peter Wicke has stated:

> Elvis Presley or Bill Haley were no longer merely taking set pieces from blues and rhythm & blues and imposing them as superficial effects on quite different musical categories. Their popularity was founded precisely on the fact that they were copying Afro-American music with all its characteristic features, including the performance style of black musicians, as closely as possible. What was happening was a complete reversal of the earlier situation. Whereas before white musicians had adapted elements of the Afro-American musical tradition to their own aesthetic ideas, now they were trying to suit their performances to the aesthetics of Afro-American music.[18]

If rock 'n' roll tipped the cultural balance toward an African American aesthetic, it was also a music defined by its hybridity. While Elvis Presley clearly drew on African American performance styles, he was also driven by pop tendencies that were entirely consistent with Tin Pan Alley values. Chuck Berry and Sam Cooke, as well as many doo wop groups, enunciated clearly enough to pass muster with the harshest diction teacher. Indeed, doo wop harmonies and vocal styles defy any attempt to analyze rock 'n' roll solely in terms of race. In short, European cultural standards were never abandoned altogether; rock 'n' roll simply imposed a new cultural formula which favored African American values.

Since the advent of rock 'n' roll, there has been a continuing debate regarding the relative proportions of African American and Euro-American influences in popular music. It was considered a mark of distinction by some critics that many of the San Francisco groups of the late 1960s did not sound like they were emulating African American performance styles. Art rock made its musical statement by looking to classical European influences. The concept of instrumental virtuosity in heavy metal derived from the same source. Punk, which ironically was formed in reaction to the excesses of art rock, stripped the music of whatever African American influences remained. Even disco, in the United States, was marked by the tension between funk and soft soul influences on the one hand and the influence of Eurodisco on the other. Popular music has been re-Africanized in rap, which has concentrated primarily on heavy beats and spoken word rhymes, eschewing melody almost completely. In fact, rap is the only form of U.S. popular music that has become more Afrocentric as it has gained in mainstream acceptance.

Marketing and the Politics of Race, Language, and Gender

If rock 'n' roll represented the triumph of African American culture, it did not automatically follow that African Americans would be the main beneficiaries of the victory. The way in which music actually unfolds as a social practice does not necessarily determine the way in which it reaches the ears of its audience. By the time a creative urge has been fed through the star-making machinery of the culture industry, all the biases of class, race, and gender have been brought to bear on it. Although rock 'n' roll proceeded from an aesthetic impulse that viewed cultural borrowing as both natural and desirable, it developed in a commercial context that was subject to all the foibles and inequities of the larger society. In such a context, the natural process of cultural borrowing can become theft, and artists can be categorized incorrectly or excluded from the marketplace altogether for reasons that have little to do with talent or musical style.

If rock 'n' roll represented the triumph of African American culture, it did not automatically follow that African Americans would be the main beneficiaries of the victory.

The marketing categories of the music industry have often classified performers as much by race as by musical style. The beginnings of this practice date back to the 1920s, when the music industry organized popular music into three categories: "race" (African American popular music); "hillbilly" (white, working-class rural styles); and "popular" (mainstream pop of the type produced by Tin Pan Alley).[19] Initially, *Billboard,* the leading music industry trade magazine, published popularity charts for only that music classified as "popular" by the industry. However, when *Your Hit Parade,* a radio program based on listener preferences, became one of the most popular programs in the country in 1935, it became apparent that the commercial interests of the industry were not being served by only one chart. Thus, by the end of the decade, *Billboard* had inaugurated a popularity chart for "hillbilly" music and in 1942 added a chart entitled "The Harlem Hit Parade." Three years later, the magazine changed this title to "Race Music."

Each marketing category was presumed to be a distinct musical style with its own audience. "The assumed mainstream pop audience," according to David Brackett, "was northern, urban, middle or upper class, and also white. The charts for the marginal musics also assumed an audience—African American for race and r&b [rhythm and blues], rural southern white for hillbilly, folk, and country and western (as these charts were variously designated during the 1940s)."[20] Initially, there was little overlap among the categories, which lent credence to the industry's assumption that these were separate, distinct styles. Indeed, these styles did develop regionally in a country that was segregated and racked by class divisions. It was, in fact, the social and cultural changes associated with World War II that began to render the barriers between marketing categories a bit more porous. As the categories "race" and "hillbilly" began to come to the attention of the mainstream audience, these styles were said to cross over.

The term *crossover* refers to that process whereby an artist or a recording from a secondary or specialty marketing category, such as country and western or rhythm and blues (r&b), achieves hit status in the mainstream market. Although recently the term has been used simply to indicate multiple chart listings in any direction, historically it connoted movement from a marginal category to the mainstream. In writing of the golden years of r&b, music historian Arnold Shaw has noted that

> *The crossover concept was inherent in R&B from the start. In fact, acceptance by the pop market of an R&B disk (Cecil Gant's "I Wonder") generated the first mushrooming of R&B record companies. While these labels produced disks basically for ghetto consumption, they always hoped that the larger white market might be receptive.*[21]

The greater acceptance of African Americans in the mainstream market after World War II not only prompted some changes in music charting practices but also put the industry on the horns of a racial dilemma that has been the subject of heated debate ever since.

As late as 1949, most of the music by African American artists could be found under the heading "Race Music" in record company catalogues. As this music began to cross over to the white market, however, it was decided that a more palatable term was needed. Record companies toyed with labels like ebony and sepia for a while, but these too were obviously distinctions of color, not musical style. Eventually "rhythm and blues" became the accepted term, and from 1949 until 1963 *Billboard* charted the music as such. *Billboard* discontinued its r&b charts from the end of 1963 until the beginning of 1965, presumably because the pop charts were becoming increasingly integrated. During this time, however, the number of African American artists on the pop charts actually declined. Accordingly, the r&b charts were reinstated by the magazine, and in 1969, r&b was replaced with the term "soul". The industry came full circle in 1982 when the soul charts were renamed "black" music. *Billboard* later offered the explanation that "'soul' was too limited a term to define the diversity of musical styles appearing on the chart, and that 'black' was a better tribute to the music's cultural origins."[22] Ultimately, however, this term was as vulnerable to criticism as the term "race music" had been four decades earlier. Thus in 1990, *Billboard* reinstated the r&b category, explaining that it was "becoming less acceptable to identify music in racial terms."[23] And the beat goes on.

Were it not for this artificial separation of the races, popular music history might read quite differently. When Syd Nathan, the founder of King Records, encouraged his r&b and country and western artists to record different versions of the same songs, he understood intuitively that pieces of music do not automatically have a genre, that they can be interpreted in many idioms. Still, in keeping with prevailing industry practices, he marketed his r&b releases only to black audiences and his country records only to white audiences. While Nathan was not limited in his choice of artists or material, he, like many others, accepted the notion that a separation of the races was "the way things were."

These same prevailing industry practices led Leonard Chess, head of Chess Records, to inform Chuck Berry that his demo of "Ida Red" ("Maybellene") had to be re-done because it was too country sounding.[24] In doing so, Chess was telling Berry in no uncertain terms that there was simply no way to market a black man as a country singer. Were it not for that reality, Chuck Berry might well have had a very different career trajectory. R&b artist Jimmy Witherspoon once argued, "Chuck Berry is a country singer. People put everybody in categories, black, white, this. Now if Chuck Berry was white, with the lyrics he writes, he would be the top country star in the world."[25] There have been any number of country versions of Chuck Berry songs, from Hoyt Axton's "Maybellene," Freddy Weller's "Too Much Monkey Business" and "Promised Land," Waylon Jennings' "Brown-Eyed Handsome Man," and Buck Owen's "Johnny B. Goode" to Linda Rondstadt's "Back in the U.S.A.," Emmy Lou Harris' "You Never Can Tell," and Johnny Rivers' "Memphis," but every one has been performed by whites.

Such music marketing practices were briefly challenged when Ray Charles recorded *Modern Sounds in Country and Western Music* (Volume I) and *Modern Sounds in Country and Western Music* (Volume II) for ABC-Paramount in 1962. Through these recordings, Charles proved that an artist does not have to be limited to a single performance style and a song can have more than one genre. He had long felt connections between the blues and country that rendered the rigid separation of markets suspect from a musical point of view. "I really thought that it was somethin' about country music, even as a youngster," Charles once remarked. "Although I was bred in and around the blues, I always . . . felt the closest music, really, to the blues [was country and western]. They'd make them steel guitars cry and whine, and it really attracted me.[26] These LPs turned out to be the two best-selling albums of his career. *Volume I* made the pop charts for fifty-nine weeks and was firmly ensconced in the number one slot for fourteen of them. The album also contained a recording of his best-selling single—Don Gibson's "I Can't Stop Loving You"—which went to number one on all three charts, perhaps the only record by an African American artist ever to do so. Even so, it was not until the end of the decade that another African American artist—Charlie Pride—made the country charts.

The identification of music with race, which has tended to exclude African American artists and others from certain marketing structures in the music industry, makes the task of unearthing an accurate history of U.S. popular music quite difficult and encourages serious underestimates of the degree of cross-cultural collaboration that has taken place. Rockabilly, the country strain of rock 'n' roll in the 1950s, for example, was a legitimate musical movement that integrated blues with country and western styles. It had its own identity, and in singers like Elvis Presley, performers of real originality and talent. While privileged seems far too strong a word to describe the early life circumstances and success of most rockabilly artists, it is impossible to separate their popularity from a racist pattern in which styles pioneered by black artists are popularized, dominated, and even defined by whites as if they were the originators. This pattern is apparent in the history of popular music in the United States, from ragtime to jazz to swing. Rock 'n' roll is neither an exception nor the end of the line. As a result, styles are often described (and defended) in terms which are clearly racial rather than musical. As late as 1984, Nick Tosches insisted that "rockabilly is hillbilly rock-and-roll. It was not a usurpation of black music by whites because its soul, its pneuma, was white, full of the redneck ethos."[27] Arnold Shaw had acknowledged a decade earlier that "it was that to a degree," but he went on to say that "it would probably be more accurate to describe [rockabilly] as the sound of young, white Southerners imitating black bluesmen."[28] The late 1960s were marked by endless debates over whether or not whites could sing the blues. The relative absence of African Americans in heavy metal and whites in rap suggest that racial divisions are still powerful determinants in social and cultural relations.

No Hablamos Español: The Language Barrier

Because of this country's history of slavery, there is a tendency to think of racism, whether in the music industry or society as a whole, as a black/white issue. It should be recognized, however, that discriminatory practices have not been limited to African Americans alone. In many ways, the language barrier has proven to be even more intractable than the race barrier. Latin music, for instance, has always been an important influence in U.S. popular music. In the 1950s, there were a series of popular mambos, rumbas, and cha cha chas. Indeed, from Ritchie Valens to Santana to Los Lobos there has always been a strong Chicano presence in rock, and a recognizable Latin influence in dance styles from disco to hip hop. Even so, the number of Top Forty pop hits sung in Spanish in the United States could probably be counted on one hand. "La Bamba" (by Ritchie Valens and Los Lobos) and Santana's "Oye Como Va" readily come to mind, but precious few others. In fact, one could probably tally all of the non-English Top Forty pop hits on two hands. Four versions of "Volare" appeared on the charts as did "Dominique" by the Singing Nun. Kyu Sakamoto's "Sukiyaki" was covered by Taste of Honey during the disco era. While one might quibble about whether to include Ray Barretto's "El Watusi" or Manu Dibango's "Soul Makossa"(both of which

In many ways, the language barrier has proven to be even more intractable than the race barrier.

are primarily instrumental), the point is clear. Non-English hits in the United States are rare. As a result, artists who might sing in other languages feel compelled to record in English when they approach the U.S. market. In the late 1970s and early 1980s, Spanish balladeer Julio Iglesias, a resident of the United States, was among the best-selling recording artists in the world, but he had never had a hit in this country. The only way he could break into the U.S. market was with two English duets—one with Willie Nelson ("To All the Girls I've Loved Before") and one with Diana Ross ("All of You"), both in 1984. Linda Ronstadt, who achieved U.S. superstardom singing in English, provides an example of this logic in reverse. In 1988, Ronstadt, who is part Mexican, returned to her roots to record *Cancions de mi Padre.* The album never reached the U.S. pop Top Forty, even though it received the 1988 Grammy for Best Mexican/American Performance. Cuban-born Gloria Estefan's Top Ten pop album, *Cuts Both Ways* (1989), included Spanish and English versions of "Don't Wanna Lose You" and "Here We Are," but only the English versions became Top Ten pop hits. The Swedish group ABBA charted fourteen Top Forty hits in the U.S. in the 1970s and 1980s, but all were sung in English. Norway's A-Ha broke into the U.S. market with "Take on Me," a cut with spectacular video animation and sung in English. When French Canadian Celine Dion, a veteran of the Quebec music scene, made a bid for international stardom in 1990, she did so on the basis of her first all-English LP, *Unison.* In 1993, she scored her first number one pop hit in the U.S. with "The Power of Love," which was, of course, sung in English. With the increasing diversity of the U.S. population, this situation is bound to change, but for the moment, language barriers in popular music remain strong.

The Long, Hard Climb: Gender Discrimination

The barriers that women face in the music industry are equally formidable. Historically the images of women in popular songs—from angel and baby to earth mother and sex goddess to bitch and "ho"—have been limiting or belittling, if not flat-out offensive and degrading. Women performers have often been pressured by the industry to assume personas based on these stereotypes. Furthermore, the existence of a double standard regarding intimacy and sexual practices in the United States has made the social dynamics of life on the road more complicated and alienating for women than men. As if these difficulties were not enough, women have had to overcome the obstacles that stand between them and control over the creative processes. Technical processes such as record producing, engineering, mixing, and mastering are still overwhelmingly male-dominated.

> Historically the images of women in popular songs—from angel and baby to earth mother and sex goddess to bitch and "ho"—have been limiting or belittling, if not flat-out offensive and degrading.

While some women were able to achieve a certain status as vocalists in the decades preceding the emergence of rock 'n' roll, no woman ever achieved the status of an Al

Jolson, Bing Crosby, or Frank Sinatra, and it was almost never the case that a woman became successful as an instrumentalist. Whatever status could be achieved, disappeared rapidly with the advent of rock 'n' roll. Indeed, rock 'n' roll actually reduced the presence of women in popular music. In the early 1960s, the women who were marketed as folk madonnas were channeled toward softer vocal styles, and were allowed access only to acoustic instruments. This trend continued among the female singer/songwriters of the 1970s, Bonnie Raitt being a notable exception. Even harder rocking women in the 1960s—from the Crystals and the Ronnettes to Grace Slick, Janis Joplin, and Aretha Franklin—were vocalists who never touched the hardware. While there were certain breakthroughs for women when the punk movement rewrote the rules of access, these gains were offset to some degree in the next decade, by the misogyny displayed in rap and heavy metal.

By the late 1980s, women were fairly well represented in most styles (with the exception of heavy metal) and in the early 1990s, they had finally begun to compete on a roughly equal footing with men for lucrative recording contracts. However, as they have achieved greater acceptance in the popular market, they have had to confront an industry infrastructure that is fully owned and operated by men whose ideas about career development frequently push them to conform to male stereotypes of how female performers should act and sound. In other words, like African Americans and other people of color, women performers must confront norms and social practices which limit their development and chances for success.

Regulating Popular Music

Because popular music always interacts with its social environment, it often serves as a lightning rod for the political controversies that invariably accompany change. The Tin Pan Alley pop that dominated the first half of the twentieth century, for example, was marked by a purposeful blandness and a studied inoffensiveness that, in retrospect, makes it difficult to imagine that anything about it, except its saccharine sweetness, could upset anyone. Still, the moral guardians of the early twentieth century felt that even Tin Pan Alley pop was too depraved for mainstream consumption, let alone the jazz that developed concurrently. As early as 1913, the well-known violinist Maud Powell told the National Federation of Music Clubs that the music of the United States had been

> thrown into disrepute through the unspeakably depraved modern popular song, . . . which consists of brazenly suggestive words to a catchy rag-time accompaniment.
>
> Its effect on young folk is shocking. The vicious song is allowed in the home by parents, who, no doubt, have not troubled themselves to look at the words. As a result the suggestive meanings are allowed to play upon immature minds at the dangerous age. It is from the popular song that the popular suggestive dance sprang. Together and apart they are a menace to the social fabric.[29]

The good Miss Powell went on to state that she was "heartily in favor of a board of censorship for the popular song."[30] Imagine the horror she would have felt had she been exposed to the rumblings of the blues or country music, which surveyed more personal themes in a far more vernacular tone.

Throughout the second half of the twentieth century, popular music has been connected quite explicitly with social change and political controversy. As millions of adults left the intensity of urban life in the 1950s for the new and expansive sprawl called suburbia, rock 'n' roll pulled their offspring back to the sounds of the city. While postwar youth may have found the new sound exciting and engaging, adults found it threatening and loosed criticisms far more damning than Powell's condemnations of Tin Pan Alley pop. Indeed in the late 1950s, a conservative reaction against rock 'n' roll sought to turn back the musical clock by imposing rigid guidelines on radio.

A variation of this same social drama was played out in the 1980s and 1990s, as the custodians of culture became convinced that rap and heavy metal had gone too far and tried to regulate popular music through tactics ranging from a demand for warning labels on sound recordings to outright censorship. In fact, given the pronouncements of a whole range of public figures and elected officials during this period, a compelling case can be made that popular culture—particularly popular music—has become the ideological battlefield upon which struggles for power, values, and identity take place. Clearly then, popular music is potent cultural capital—aesthetically, economically, and politically. Unraveling and analyzing the complexities of its often contradictory social functions is the subject matter of *Rockin' Out*.

A compelling case can be made that popular culture—particularly popular music—has become the ideological battlefield upon which struggles for power, values, and identity take place.

NOTES

1. It should be noted that this discussion concerns cultural development as it occurred in European societies. There are, of course, any number of other societies that developed according to different cultural patterns, but the cultural forms and values of the "New World" were informed by those of the European colonial powers, thus an understanding of cultural development in European societies is relevant to understanding the tensions and complexities of contemporary U.S. culture.

2. Oscar Handlin, "Comments on Mass and Popular Culture," in *Culture for the Millions? Mass Media in Modern Society,* ed. Norman Jacobs (Princeton, N. J.: D. Van Nostrand, 1959), 66.

3. Stuart Hall and Paddy Whannel, *The Popular Arts* (New York: Pantheon Books, 1965), 67–68.

4. This analysis was developed most forcefully by the members of the Frankfurt School, a group of Jewish intellectuals in Germany who were rightly disturbed by Hitler's effective use of the mass media in advancing the cause of fascism in the 1930s and 1940s.

5. Carl Belz, *The Story of Rock,* 2d (New York: Harper Colophon, 1971), 1.

6. Simon Frith, *Sound Effects: Youth, Leisure and the Politics of Rock 'n' Roll* (New York: Pantheon Books, 1981), 54

7.   Charlie Gillett, *The Sound of the City: The Rise of Rock and Roll* (New York: Outerbridge and Dienstfrey, 1970), i.

8.   Ibid.

9.   Frith, *Sound Effects,* 203.

10.   Peter Wicke, *Rock Music: Culture, Aesthetics and Sociology* (Cambridge: Cambridge University Press, 1990), 12.

11.   Richard Middleton, "Reading Popular Music." Unit 16 of Open University course U203 *Popular Culture*. Milton-Keynes: The Open University, 1981, p. 17.

12.   Charles Hamm, *Yesterdays: Popular Song in America* (New York: W. W. Norton, 1983), 358.

13.   H. F. Mooney, "Popular Music Since the 1920s: The Significance of Shifting Taste," in *The Age of Rock,* ed. Jonathan Eisen (New York: Vintage Books, 1969), 10 and 11.

14.   Ibid.

15.   Ibid, 10.

16.   Christopher Small, *Music of the Common Tongue: Survival and Celebration in Afro-American Music* (New York: Riverrun Press, 1987), 25.

17.   Iain Chambers, *Urban Rhythms: Popular Music and Popular Culture* (New York: Macmillan, 1985), 10.

18.   Wicke, *Rock Music,* 16–17.

19.   The use of the terms "race" and "hillbilly" as marketing categories for music was initiated by producer Ralph Peer. The origin of the terms is explained in detail in the next chapter.

20.   David Brackett, "The Politics and Practice of 'Crossover' in American Popular Music, 1963 to 1965," *The Musical Quarterly* (Winter, 1994): 777.

21.   Arnold Shaw, *Honkers and Shouters: The Golden Years of Rhythm and Blues* (New York: Collier Books, 1978), 524.

22.   "Billboard Adopts 'R&B' As New Name for 2 Charts," *Billboard,* 27 October 1990, 35.

23.   Ibid., 6.

24.   See Gillett, *The Sound of the City,* 40 and Chapple and Garofalo, *Rock 'n' Roll is Here to Pay,* 39.

25.   Shaw, *Honkers and Shouters,* 215.

26.   Ben Fong-Torres, "The Rolling Stone Interview: Ray Charles," *Rolling Stone,* 18 January 1973, 18.

27.   Nick Tosches, *Country: Living Legends and Dying Metaphors in America's Biggest Music* (New York: Charles Scribner's Sons, 1985), 55.

28.   Shaw, *Honkers and Shouters,* 497.

29.   "To Censor Popular Songs." *Literary Digest,* (24 May 1913): 1181.

30.   Ibid.

1 Mass Technology and Popular Taste: The Tin Pan Alley Era

In the late 1800s, a previously scattered conglomeration of songwriters and publishers began to converge on the Broadway and 28th Street section of New York City, an area that would come to be called Tin Pan Alley after the tinny output of the upright pianos there. The popular songsters who worked there and who would dominate mainstream popular music until World War II were not particularly interested in the tinfoil cylinder phonograph Thomas Edison demonstrated for the staff of *Scientific American* in 1877. While they might have been aware of its possible use in the reproduction of music, this was not yet a practical consideration for them. Edison himself had placed this use third or fourth on his list of priorities. In his mind, the greatest potential for his machine lay in the reproduction of human speech. Consequently, he hailed his invention as a "talking machine." Along Tin Pan Alley, songwriters and publishers were far more preoccupied with the then leading form of musical reproduction—sheet music—than with Edison's invention. After all, sheet music was their primary source of revenue.

In its formative stages, the "music industry" could in no way be considered synonymous with the "recording industry" as it often is today.

In the late 1800s, middle-class home entertainment centered around that symbol of decorum and upward mobility, the piano. In 1880 alone, two years after Edison had formed the Edison Speaking Phonograph Company, some 45,000 pianos were manufactured in the United States.[1] Over the next thirty years, annual production would increase eightfold, and there would still be those who imported their pianos from Europe. Accordingly, sheet music was the vehicle for the mass dissemination of music, and music publishers were at the center of the music business. It was the publishers who turned the creations of songwriters and lyricists into commercial properties. It was the publishers who hired "song pluggers" and engaged the services of vaudeville stars—often for a hefty sum—to popularize their wares. All of the practices of music publishers (many of which existed in the gray areas of ethical) were aimed at one goal—the sale of sheet music.

Sheet music retailed for thirty to forty cents a copy, and for the major publishers, sales in the hundreds of thousands of copies were not unheard of. Indeed, Charles K. Harris' "After the Ball," written and published in 1892, "quickly reached sales of $25,000 a week" and "sold more than 2,000,000 copies in only several years, eventually achieving a sale of some five million."[2] With potential sales such as these, it is not surprising that music publishers initially regarded the revolution in technology that eventually transformed the way in which popular music was produced and consumed as little more than a way to supplement their earnings.

In its formative stages, then, the "music industry" could in no way be considered synonymous with the "recording industry" as it often is today. At the time, it was, if anything, songwriting and music publishing. Of course, the writers of Tin Pan Alley, from Charles K. Harris, Paul Dresser, and Harry Von Tilzer to George Gershwin, Jerome Kern, and Irving Berlin, took notice of records and eventually pushed record companies to record their songs, but for a variety of reasons—practical, technical, legal, aesthetic, and economic—Tin Pan Alley never embraced records. Thus, while Tin Pan Alley and the recording industry intersected at many points and with increasing frequency over the years, in many ways, they developed as separate industries. This is an important piece of historical data that begins to account for the disjuncture that marked the emergence of rock 'n' roll, a music based on records.

Following the decline of vaudeville in the 1920s, Tin Pan Alley tunesmiths turned to Broadway and Hollywood as natural successors to the promotional power of vaudeville. Even as records promised to become the dominant medium for the mass reproduction of music, Tin Pan Alley continued to identify itself primarily with the "literate" Broadway-Hollywood axis of popular music. In contrast, rock 'n' roll, which was derived from innovations in the oral tradition of African American music and country music, was a product of record companies; it owed its popularity to the existence of records. Just as record companies would come to replace publishing houses as the center of the music industry, rock 'n' roll would push aside Tin Pan Alley pop as the dominant style of popular music. Thus, any social history of these changes in popular music must begin with a discussion of the development of sound recording and the uneven relationship that existed between music publishers and record companies.

Sound Recording: From Cylinder to Disc

When Edison first came up with his tinfoil cylinder phonograph, he envisioned marketing it as an office machine. In order to introduce it to the public, however, he decided to exploit its novelty value. In countless demonstrations in lecture halls, theaters, and

Sheet music sells hundreds of thousands of copies

vaudeville houses, members of the audience were invited to make live recordings. Scores of local vocalists, whistlers, and instrumentalists tried their hand at Edison's amazing "talking machine." Although it was soon found that brass reproduced reasonably well, the poor sound quality of the tinfoil cylinder severely hampered its commercial value. By 1880, Edison's talking machine appeared to be dead in the water; Edison himself dismissed it as "a mere toy, which has no commercial value."[3]

The next steps in development were taken in the laboratories of Edison's fellow inventor, Alexander Graham Bell. Five years of research under the directorship of Charles Sumner Tainter and Chichester Bell yielded a machine they called a graphophone to distinguish it from Edison's phonograph. The graphophone used a floating stylus to cut "hill and dale" grooves into a wax-coated cardboard cylinder. The sound quality of the graphophone was significantly better than the sound quality of Edison's machine. Because at this time recording was a mechanical process rather than an electromechanical process, it was called acoustic recording.

In the late 1880s corporate magnate Jesse Lippincott used nearly $1 million of his inheritance to consolidate the Edison patents and the national sales rights to the graphophone into a company called the North American Phonograph Company. It was to be a national office machine combine with local franchises, but it was clear within months that the phonograph did not have a future as a dictating machine. Mechanical problems and resistance from stenographers (who were mostly men at the time) constantly plagued the business. When Lippincott fell victim to infantile paralysis in the early 1890's, the struggling company was thrown into further disarray. Edward D. Easton's District of Columbia franchise—the Columbia Phonograph Company—would have to await a new direction for the talking machine before going on to become the oldest trademark in the record business.

It was Louis Glass, manager of the Pacific Phonograph Company, North American's West Coast licensee, who pointed the way to the future of the phonograph. In 1889, Glass had equipped some of his dictating machines with a patented, coin-activated mechanism and four sets of stethoscopic listening tubes and placed them in the Palais Royal Saloon in San Francisco. For a nickel per listener per play, patrons could avail themselves of the sounds of a prerecorded "entertainment" cylinder. These "nickel-in-the-slot" machines were so successful that within a year Glass had placed machines in eighteen other locations, some of which began bringing in as much as $1,200 annually. The enterprise not only pointed the way for the North American Phonograph Company but also won for Glass the title of "Father of the Juke Box."

In the genteel home entertainment market, the elegance of the piano and the simplicity of sheet music stood in sharp contrast to the ungainly phonograph with its awkward listening tentacles.

Pay phonographs proved to be very popular in amusement parks, penny arcades, ice-cream parlors, and drugstores, as well as saloons, train stations, and ferry-boat waiting rooms. However, because phonographs retailed for almost $150 and cylinders could not be economically mass-produced, a home entertainment market for prerecorded music did not seem feasible. There may also have been aesthetic considerations militating against the creation of a home-based market. "It was ludicrous in the extreme," recalled one phonograph company executive, "to see ten people grouped about a phonograph, each with a listening tube leading from his ears, grinning and laughing at what he heard."[4] In the genteel home entertainment market, the elegance of the piano and the simplicity of sheet music stood in sharp contrast to the ungainly phonograph with its awkward listening tentacles.

Among the early cylinders that caught on with the mainstream listening audience were those featuring brass bands, instrumental solos on cornet, piccolo, piano, and especially, banjo, comic Irish tales, and so-called coon songs, novelty songs exploiting negative stereotypes of African Americans in caricatured black dialect. As the number of locations for coin-operated phonographs increased, so did the demand for prerecorded cylinders, but even so, a number of factors stood in the way of a natural alliance between Tin Pan Alley and the cylinder-recording companies that had come into being. Because of their limited sound quality, cylinders tended to favor spoken-word and instrumental selections; publishers did not receive royalties from the sale or use of recorded music; and the demand for prerecorded cylinders could not compete with the demand for sheet music. Thus, the companies manufacturing prerecorded cylinders grew independent of Tin Pan Alley.

Within this business, the Columbia Phonograph Company quickly distinguished itself as the leading producer of quality entertainment cylinders. Among the company's earliest popular cylinders were recordings by the United States Marine Band, which included Sousa marches, Strauss waltzes, and such popular Irish favorites as "Little Annie Rooney" and "Down Went McGinty." By 1892, Columbia had issued about one hundred recordings of the Marine Band, which sold for two dollars a cylinder. Second only to the Marine Band in popularity were the recordings of whistling virtuoso John Yorke Atlee, a government clerk who kept the nickels flowing with his renditions of tunes like "The Mockingbird" and "Home Sweet Home." New developments in recording technology had rekindled Edison's interest in the field. By the early 1890s, he was Columbia's main competition. During this period, improvements in sound reproduction came quickly, and within a few years, both Columbia and Edison had introduced affordable phonographs, which led to the creation of a home entertainment market for prerecorded cylinders.

By 1896, Columbia's catalogue of prerecorded cylinders listed thousands of titles, including, in addition to selections by the Marine Band and John Atlee, popular songs by Dan Quinn, who specialized in musical comedy, interpretations of sentimental love ballads by tenor George J. Gasken, and monologist Russell Hunting whose tales of Michael O'Casey became international favorites. Edison boasted George Washington Johnson—if not the first, then certainly the most successful black recording artist at the time—who

Emile Berliner develops the first recording disc

John Philip Sousa, famous for his military marches, led the U.S. Marine Band to popular success during an era when the limitations of recording technology favored the reproduction of brass bands. In the 1890s, Columbia catalogues listed scores of recordings by the Marine Band.

achieved fame and fortune with two hits, "The Whistling Coon" and "The Laughing Song." Competition between the two companies was fierce; in fact, they spent so much time fighting each other that they paid little attention to the development of disc recording, an innovation that would eventually consign cylinders to the dust-filled corners of attics.

Emile Berliner, the German immigrant who developed the flat recording disc that became the industry standard, was not the first to experiment with it. Edison himself had already considered and rejected the idea. Berliner had first perfected a method of engraving sound vibrations on wax-coated zinc discs, which could produce a much louder playback volume than the cylinder machines, in 1887 but did not patent his work until 1896. When he had demonstrated his "gramophone" in 1888 at the Franklin Institute in Philadelphia, the machine had generated little interest, but it was at that meeting that Berliner prophesied the ability to make an unlimited number of copies from a single master, the use of discs for home entertainment on a mass scale, and a system of royalty payments to artists derived from the sale of discs. Thus, it was Berliner who first envisaged the contours of the modern music industry. Undaunted by the lack of interest in his gramophone, he set about the task of pursuing his vision.

Berliner delivered on his first prophecy when he made from the zinc masters negative discs, called "stampers," which were then pressed into ebonite rubber biscuits to produce an exact duplicate, or "record," of the master. A later improvement replaced the rubber discs with shellac-based, 78 rpm pressings, which then became the industry standard until the late 1940s. To realize his second prophecy, Berliner knew that he would need someone with more musical ability than himself to coordinate talent and recording. He turned to Fred Gaisberg, who had been playing that role at Columbia. Indeed, Gaisberg was, in effect, the first artist and repertoire (a&r) man in the infant industry. All it took to convince Gaisberg to jump ship was a single demonstration of the "beautiful round tones" of Berliner's disc.

Berliner then contracted with an enterprising machinist named Eldridge R. Johnson to manufacture the gramophones. Adding improvements of his own, Johnson soon began turning out machines by the hundreds. In 1901, Berliner and Johnson consolidated their interests into the Victor Talking Machine Company and adopted as the company's logo the famous "Little Nipper" (the comely pup listening attentively to his master's voice in front of a record horn). The logo was originally a painting by Francis Barraud that was given to Berliner and Johnson by William Barry Owen, head of British Gramophone Co., Ltd., Victor's European operation. Shortly after the formation of the Victor Talking Machine Company, the major recording companies—Edison, Columbia, and Victor—decided to pool their patents and set about the business of making better records and machines.[5] From this point until the advent of commercial radio following World War I, acoustic recording enjoyed its golden era.

Because recording artists were not yet paid royalties and received no credit on records or in catalogues, they were not tied to a single company. Consequently, Gaisberg had little trouble persuading Columbia's celebrities (Atlee, Gasken, and Hunting) to record for Victor. Indeed, he was not even limited to performers in the United States. Through the efforts of Owen, Gaisberg was soon recording in every music capital in Europe. Because of an elitist bias toward high culture, European art music was considered far superior to U.S. popular music. Accordingly, the British Gramophone catalogue contained songs and arias in every European language (Gaisberg even made recordings at the Imperial Opera in Russia), and many Oriental languages as well. Victor imported these high-priced Red Seal recordings for sale in the United States and then began a domestic Red Label series of their own that featured the stars of the Metropolitan Opera in New York.[6] Producer C. G. Childs placed the jewel in the crown of the new series when he managed to sign Italian tenor Enrico Caruso to an exclusive Victor contract by offering him the unprecedented provision of a royalty on records sold, thereby fulfilling the last of Berliner's 1888 prophecies.

Because of an elitist bias toward high culture, European art music was considered far superior to U.S. popular music.

Priced higher than other records, Victor's Red Label series was clearly intended for the wealthy "carriage trade." Columbia, which by this time had entered the disc business, also featured a grand opera series of its own. However, as early as 1910, as Ian Whitcomb points out in his inimitable style, "it was quite clear to the record companies that the classics only brought in prestige and that the steady income was to be made from sales to the 'Cracker-Barrel Trade,' to the 'Good Old Coon Song—Sousa—Monologue—Sentimental Ballad—Bunch.'"[7]

If the choice of recorded material was an indicator of class differences, the choice of format revealed a rural-urban split. "By the middle of the first decade of the twentieth century," writes C. A. Schicke, "the disc had distinctly succeeded in capturing the buying power of the upper and middle classes and the urban population. The cylinder's stronghold—and mostly Edison cylinders at that—was the poorer, rural market."[8] In both instances, however, the selection of recording artists was made with only the white population in mind. Even so-called coon songs, a staple of the recording companies from the beginning, were almost invariably sung by whites. With the exception of George W. Johnson and the great black vaudevillian Bert Williams, nearly all of "the other leading coon-song and black-dialect vocalists before World War I were white, the best known being Charles Asbury, David C. Bangs, Arthur Collins, Billy Golden, Silas Leachman, Bob Roberts, Len Spencer, Billy Williams, and the 'First Lady of Phonograph Records,' Ada Jones."[9] Indeed, prior to World War I, there was only one African American ensemble that had landed a recording contract, the Syncopated Society Orchestra led by James Reese Europe. Europe organized the Clef Club in New York as a black musicians union

The Clef Club, organized by James Reese Europe, was an African American musicians' union that could supply orchestras of varying sizes on request. In 1914, Europe's own Syncopated Society Orchestra was signed to Victor, becoming the first African American ensemble to secure a recording contract.

of sorts which, according to musicologist Eileen Southern, "could furnish a dance orchestra from three to thirty men upon request at any time, day or night."[10] For special occasions, like their 1912 Carnegie Hall concert, a Clef Club orchestra could number as many as 145 players, including 58 banjos, mandolins, and bandores, 10 pianos, and 5 drum kits. Clef Club ensembles benefited from the dance fads that came into being in the early teens. Because of his association with the cosmopolitan dance team of Vernon and Irene Castle, Europe's Syncopated Society Orchestra was added to the Victor talent roster in 1914 and produced dance records that remained profitable for years.

While it is true that the golden age of acoustic recording drew on and preserved a broad range of musical styles, it also established one of the most troubling aspects of the contemporary music industry, namely, the fragmentation of the audience not only along lines of class but also along the lines of geography and, of course, race. It was also claimed that the existing technology favored lower male voices, which clearly left women with few recording stars of their own. (One can only wonder how those piccolo solos got recorded.) Ada Jones was not simply the "First Lady of Phonograph Records," she was one of the only ladies of phonograph records.

The technological advances of the late nineteenth and early twentieth centuries introduced what later critics of mass culture would see as the historical schism, which marked the transition from active music-making to passive music consumption. In the

The technological advances of the late nineteenth and early twentieth centuries introduced what later critics of mass culture would see as the historical schism, which marked the transition from active music-making to passive music consumption.

popular image of a family gathered around the living-room piano, music is "consumed" through the active participation of all concerned. With the invention of recording, it was no longer necessary to have any musical ability whatsoever to re-create the sound of music. In playing to the earlier image of "family entertainment," the publishing houses of Tin Pan Alley were naturally at odds with the record companies. Like the record companies, however, they had the same social and cultural biases that plagued the rest of society.

Tin Pan Alley Constructs the Mainstream Tradition

Tin Pan Alley centralized the power of the U.S. popular music business at a time when European opera was the hallmark of taste. Although songwriters in the United States often took their cues from European high culture, they soon came to realize that the key to future profitability lay in catering to popular tastes. Unlike older, more traditional music publishing houses that issued a broad range of material, the song factories of Tin Pan Alley produced only popular songs and in so doing "Tin Pan Alley songwriters soon reached a stylistic plateau, a much more homogeneous style than had ever before been the case in the history of song in America."[11] Indeed, Tin Pan Alley actually availed itself of a much narrower range of material than the record companies, and parlayed the undertaking into an overwhelming—and distinctly American—success. "Tin Pan Alley did not draw on traditional music," musicologist Charles Hamm has said, "it created traditional music."[12]

Typical of early Tin Pan Alley fare were graceful waltzes and spirited marches. Familiar tunes from the first category included Harry Von Tilzer's "Bird in a Gilded Cage" (1900), "In the Good Old Summer Time" by George Evans (1902), and Egbert Van Alstyne's "In the Shade of the Old Apple Tree" (1905). All were million sellers. The marches of John Philip Sousa and the Marine Band were perhaps best echoed in popular song by the multitalented George M. Cohan. From "Give My Regards to Broadway" in 1904 to his World War I rally tune "Over There" in 1917, Cohan's up-tempo, lightly syncopated numbers won him enduring popularity.

Ironically, for all its definitive American-ness, Tin Pan Alley was a songwriting enterprise dominated by Jewish Americans, at a time when Jewish immigrants were considered racially different by many. If one had to choose a single artist who epitomized the Tin Pan Alley ethos, it would have to be Irving Berlin, about whom the *Literary Digest,* after praising his work, remarked with surprise: "And Berlin belongs to the Jewish race."[13] Born Israel Baline in 1888 in Russia, Berlin was just four years old when he and his family came to the United States after escaping the Russian pogroms. Like many Jewish immigrants of the time, the family settled in New York's lower East Side where they lived in abject poverty. By the age of eight, Berlin was already earning his own keep selling

newspapers. "At fourteen, he was a singing waiter in the honky tonks of Chinatown and the Bowery, absorbing the rich sounds and rhythms of the musical melting pot."[14] Two years later Berlin landed his first Tin Pan Alley job plugging songs for Harry Von Tilzer's publishing firm.

Irving Berlin lived to be 101 years old and became one of the most prolific songwriters of the twentieth century. Because he could play piano in only one key, he compensated by using a piano with a moveable keyboard that could transpose into other keys.

There, he wrote his first published song, "Marie from Sunny Italy" (1907). This was soon followed by such classics as "Alexander's Ragtime Band" (1911), "A Pretty Girl Is Like a Melody" (1919), "Say It with Music" (1921), "Puttin' on the Ritz" (1929), "Easter Parade" (1933), "Cheek to Cheek" (1935), "Let's Face the Music and Dance" (1936), "I've Got My Love to Keep Me Warm" (1937), and "God Bless America" (1939), which captured the hearts and minds of generations and made Berlin a household name. Until he was unseated by Paul McCartney, Berlin was easily the most successful songwriter in history. "The range of his songs, in content and mood, if not in form," Hamm has said, "is enormous . . . Some take on a bit of the flavor of ragtime, of the blues, of country-western, Latin-American, or jazz."[15] His appropriations of multicultural sounds and rhythms—particularly those of ragtime and jazz—speak volumes about his uncanny ability to interpret diverse influences for the mainstream audience and the systematic cultural distortions that accompanied mainstream popularization.

Tin Pan Alley Incorporates African American Music

The rise of Tin Pan Alley paralleled the emergence of ragtime, and the connections between the two reveal the inequitable pattern of cultural borrowing and economic reward among black and white artists that has characterized much of the history of popular music in this country. It is this pattern that is central to understanding the emergence of rock 'n' roll. Ragtime—as opposed to ragtime songs, which were creations of Tin Pan Alley—was a syncopated, African American piano music with structural ties to European marches. It employed, in the words of Gunther Schuller, "the polymetric . . . approach of the African native forced into the simple 2/4 pattern of European marches."[16] It evolved from a dance called the cakewalk, which was in itself a cultural form with a complicated history that involved blacks imitating whites imitating blacks. In the hands of its most famous practitioner, the African American pianist and composer Scott Joplin, ragtime was a self-conscious art form, a composed music. Joplin himself, Whitcomb has noted, "presented the New Negro."[17] His "Maple Leaf Rag" (1899) remains one of the best-known ragtime compositions.[18]

For Tin Pan Alley, ragtime was a craze to be incorporated into popular song. As such, it is often difficult to separate ragtime songs from other Tin Pan Alley pop. In their affinity for slow march tempos, for example, ragtime songs tended to resemble George M. Cohan's most successful musical theater numbers. It can also be argued that there is a historical and stylistic continuity from the so-called coon songs of minstrelsy to the ragtime songs of Tin Pan Alley, although the latter were clearly less offensive. Irving Berlin turned out dozens of ragtime songs, including "Play Some Ragtime" in 1909, "Stop That Rag," "Dat Draggy Rag," and "Oh, That Beautiful Rag" in 1910, and "Ragtime Violin" and his best-known "Alexander's Ragtime Band" in 1911. Although it is obvious to anyone with ears that "Alexander's Ragtime Band" has barely a trace of syncopation in it, the catchy, well-crafted tune, which balanced "dash and energy," as Gilbert Seldes noted in 1924, with a "bow to negro music"[19] proved to be so popular that Berlin was subsequently billed as the "Father of Ragtime." As Hamm has noted:

> *A pattern was established with the ragtime song that was to recur time and again in the twentieth century: white popular music skimmed off superficial stylistic elements of a type of music originating among black musicians, and used these to give a somewhat different, exotic flavor to white music. Though Scott Joplin and a handful of other black ragtime musicians realized a modest profit from their music, the important money went to the white publishers, performers, and composers of ragtime songs.[20]*

A similar, but far more complicated, pattern characterized Tin Pan Alley's use of blues and jazz. The classic blues appeared at about the same time as ragtime. "But, unlike ragtime," Gunther Schuller has noted, "the blues were improvised and as such were more successful in preserving the original and melodic patterns of African music."[21] Using, as Amiri Baraka [Leroi Jones] has pointed out, a "three-line verse form [that] springs from no readily apparent Western source,"[22] and other African retentions, such as the call-and-response style and the flatted thirds and sevenths ("blue notes") that typify the singing of many West African tribes, the blues are clearly part of the African American musical tradition. Even so, this is not the impression one would have gotten during the so-called blues craze that swept the country in the second decade of the twentieth century.

The so-called blues craze amounted to little more than a rash of blues-flavored popular songs interpreted for a white audience by white vocalists. Early appropriations of jazz created the impression that jazz was actually the product of polite society white dance bands.

In 1912, three so-called blues compositions were published: Hart Wand's "Dallas Blues," Arthur Seals' "Baby Seals' Blues," and "Memphis Blues" by W. C. Handy. There has been considerable debate as to whether or not such compositions fit the strict definition of the blues. Handy, for example, who called himself the "Father of the Blues," was a trained composer. Still, he was as conversant with African American folkloric idioms as he was with musical notation. As Baraka [Jones] has argued: "W. C. Handy, with the publication of his various 'blues compositions,' invented [the blues] for a great many Americans and also showed that there was money to be made from it."[23] Handy had the most success with popular blues-influenced material and published his most memorable compositions, including "St. Louis Blues" (1914), "Joe Turner Blues" (1916), and "Beale Street Blues" (1917), during this period. According to William Barlow, "Handy's sudden success demonstrated [the] commercial potential [of the blues], which in turn made the genre attractive to the Tin Pan Alley song hacks, who wasted little time in turning out a deluge of imitations."[24] These Tin Pan Alley knock-offs were almost invariably performed by white singers. The so-called blues craze, then, amounted to little more than a rash of blues-flavored popular songs interpreted for a white audience by white vocalists.

W. C. Handy was one of the first songwriters to bring a feel for the blues into the world of popular composition. Also a successful businessman, Handy established his own publishing house and record label with his partner Harry Pace.

Early appropriations of jazz created the impression among the mainstream audience that jazz was actually the product of polite society white dance bands. While trying to pinpoint the precise influences and exact beginnings of jazz is an exercise in speculation that goes well beyond the scope of this book, it is safe to say that virtually all music historians acknowledge its African American origins. By the time the term came into popular usage, the style had been fed by a number of musical tributaries (minstrelsy, spirituals, ragtime, and blues, among others) that in themselves contained African as well as European elements. Indeed, many African American jazz musicians were well versed in the European classics. Still, there was an important distinction to be made between the oral tradition of improvisational, "hot" jazz and the written tradition of "sweet" dance music played by white society orchestras like Paul Whiteman's. The discussion is further complicated by the fact that performance styles varied not only regionally but also according to audience composition. Because high-society whites and middle-class blacks tended to shun the rough, hard-driving styles played in honky-tonks and brothels, jazz, as showcased in upscale venues, aspired to a cosmopolitanism not considered important in other places. Even pioneering black ensembles like the King Oliver Band, a formative influence in New Orleans jazz, developed a more polished style as they gained mainstream popularity. As a result, there was an association in the minds of most mainstream listeners between jazz and sweet dance music, a connection which resulted in Paul Whiteman being designated the "King of Jazz." Patterns of racial exclusion in the recording industry and, later, in broadcast radio, skewed public perceptions of jazz even more. In 1917, for example, when Victor decided to take a chance on the new sound, the band they ended up recording was the all-white Original Dixieland Jazz Band. Although the ODJB was heavily influenced by the King Oliver Band, the Oliver ensemble did not record until 1923.[25] Similarly, with few exceptions, radio broadcasts excluded black performers as a matter of policy. To most mainstream listeners, then, jazz, which was what just about all dance music was called at this time, was the music played by white dance bands. Indeed, in the context of the times, even Irving Berlin was regarded as a jazz pioneer, a notion that would be rejected out of hand today.

The Tin Pan Alley songwriter who had the closest association with jazz in reality was George Gershwin. Thoroughly conversant with the European classics as well as with popular styles, Gershwin sought to bridge the gap between art music and popular music. He had a genuine affinity for and personal interest in the music of African Americans. One of the earliest and most familiar fruits of these interests was his "Rhapsody in Blue," written for "jazz band and piano" and originally performed at Aeolian Hall in New York in 1924 by Paul Whiteman's orchestra with Gershwin at the piano. While "Rhapsody" is clearly an extraordinary piece of music for its time, it is obvious in retrospect that it is much more a symphonic piece than a jazz composition. If, as culture critic Gilbert Seldes jested at the time, Gershwin was "a traitor to his class (the Tin Pan Alleyists),"[26] it was not because the siren call of African American culture had lured him too far from his European moorings but because he was a popular artist who attempted a work of "serious" music. Still, Gershwin was clearly more sensitive to and respectful of the subtle nuances of African American music than most of his contemporaries. Almost alone among Tin Pan Alley songwriters, his music found wide acceptance among black as well as white audiences. His "Summertime," originally written for the musical *Porgy and Bess* in 1935, quickly passed into the realm of a jazz classic. Indeed, it was the rare black jazz band that did not include a Gershwin tune in its repertoire.

Gershwin's identification with jazz is all the more incredible given the isolationist stance of Tin Pan Alley as a whole. Like his colleagues, Gershwin had little contact with musical developments outside of New York City. Certainly, he had little connection to the pioneering steps taken in New Orleans or the innovations of the territory bands in the Midwest and Southwest. The fact that he was able to assimilate African American influences in a way that resonated across racial lines says more about his musical instincts and talent than it does about the openness of the industry or society as a whole. In general, the image of "skimming off superficial stylistic elements" was a more accurate description of Tin Pan Alley's use of multicultural sounds.

Tin Pan Alley Consolidates Its Power

The institutionalization of Tin Pan Alley was coincident with the ascendancy of vaudeville. From its modest beginnings at Tony Pastor's Opera House in New York's Bowery, vaudeville had evolved by the turn of the century into a national network of hundreds of venues that were dominated by the Keith-Albee chain in the East and in the West, Martin Beck's Orpheum circuit, which ran from Chicago to the Pacific. "Cleanliness, Courtesy, and Comfort," the slogan of the Keith-Albee theaters, described not only the principles of vaudeville houses but also the character of vaudeville performances. In

1900, the bookings for the majority of these theaters were centralized in the United Booking Office (UBO), a satellite organization of the Vaudeville Managers Association (VMA), which was controlled by Keith and Albee. Artists who were chosen to play the Keith-Albee chain or the Orpheum circuit enjoyed an unprecedented access to a national, mostly white, middle-class audience. Clearly then, those who influenced these artists' choices of material wielded tremendous power in determining what the mainstream public heard, and it was in its ability to influence these choices that Tin Pan Alley excelled.

The success of Tin Pan Alley's writers and publishers was due in equal measure to their distinctive songwriting style and their aggressive marketing strategies. Because popular songs were a staple of vaudeville, the gala shows produced in New York by the likes of F. F. Proctor, Oscar Hammerstein, Flo Ziegfeld, and of course, the Keith-Albee houses

> **The success of Tin Pan Alley's writers and publishers was due in equal measure to their distinctive songwriting style and their aggressive marketing strategies.**

were regular stop-off points for the new Tin Pan Alley publishers. "They made fifty or sixty visits a week," Russell Sanjek has noted, "to pass around copies of their newest songs, buy champaign or beer, give out cigars, recommend tailors—in short, do everything they could to boost their newest publications."[27] "Everything," according to Charles Hamm, included "persuasion tactics" that ranged "from furnishing singers with free copies of new songs, to performing small or large kindnesses for them, to out-and-out payment by the publisher—a flat fee, or in some cases a promise of a percentage of profits from sales of sheet music."[28] It was not unheard of for performers like Al Jolson to be credited as writers of the songs they agreed to push. The practice of "paying for play"—legal at the time and considered a form of intelligent marketing rather than a shady business practice—eventually came to be known as "payola." For the publishers, investments in vaudeville's stars were often returned manyfold in sales. It is ironic that the Alleymen conveniently forgot the venerable history of payola a generation later when they decried the ethics of the practice to discredit a cohort of deejays who had pushed rock 'n' roll and records past mainstream pop and sheet music.

As early as 1909, it should have been clear that records were a force to be reckoned with. According to Russell Sanjek, "In 1909, more than 27 million phonograph records and cylinders were manufactured, having a wholesale value of nearly $12 million."[29] While the larger proportion of their revenues would come from the sale of sheet music for years to come, publishers and a growing number of popular artists felt that there was no reason why this revenue should not be supplemented with revenues from record sales. Thus, in 1909, Victor Herbert, a successful composer of semiserious works, and John Philip Sousa led the charge for a revision of the copyright laws which mandated a royalty of two cents for each cylinder, record, or piano roll manufactured, in addition to the royalties already derived from live performances. Because the U.S. Copyright Act of 1909 used the term *mechanical reproduction,* these new fees came to be known as "mechanicals."

When the printer's union went on a nationwide strike in 1919, mechanical royalties actually sustained the publishing industry for a time.

Shortly after the passage of the act, the recording industry and Tin Pan Alley began to cross paths regularly. It began with the dance fever that swept the country from 1910 to World War I and continued with the growth of musical theater. Such Tin Pan Alley hits as Irving Berlin's "Everybody's Doin' It" and "Alexander's Ragtime Band" and Gilbert and Muir's "Waiting for the Robert E. Lee" were well suited to new dances like the turkey trot, the hesitation waltz, the tango, and the one-step. The dance-crazed public, eager to follow in the footsteps of Vernon and Irene Castle, gobbled up recordings of these songs to practice at home. Signed by Victor to supervise a series of dance records, the unconventional Castles hired as their music director James Reese Europe.

The musical theater market, which further linked Tin Pan Alley and the record companies, became apparent when British Victor made a recording of the songs from *Business As Usual,* a popular musical revue, for American soldiers and native Londoners during World War I. This was followed by recordings of two of Irving Berlin's shows, *Watch Your Step* and *Cheep,* which also sold well. U.S. Victor emulated the success of its British partner by recording the best known stage entertainers in the United States. The success of these recordings led Columbia and Edison to follow suit. The singer who created the strongest bridge between Tin Pan Alley and the world of records was Al Jolson. Jolson's 1919 Columbia recording of Gershwin's "Swanee," which he usually performed live in blackface and white gloves, sold over 2 million records. This figure was equaled by a 1920 Victor recording of "Whispering" and "The Japanese Sandman," two Tin Pan Alley favorites performed by the Paul Whiteman Orchestra. With these successes, popular stage entertainers like George M. Cohan, Al Jolson, Nora Bays, and Sophie Tucker soon found themselves pushing Tin Pan Alley songs on records.

To recover all their codified sources of revenue, the Tin Pan Alley songsters organized the American Society of Composers, Authors, and Publishers (ASCAP) in 1914, five years after the passage of the 1909 copyright act. ASCAP is a "performance rights" organization that recovers royalty payments for the performance of copyrighted music. This was done by issuing a blanket license for the use of any selection in the catalogue to live performance venues such as hotels and nightclubs (and, later, radio and television) and then distributing these royalties to writers and publishers according to a complex formula that favored older and more successful members. Membership in the society was skewed toward writers of show tunes and semiserious works and included Richard Rodgers and Lorenz Hart, Cole Porter, George Gershwin, Irving Berlin, and George M. Cohan. Of the society's 170 charter members, only 6 were black: Harry Burleigh, Will Marion Cook, J. Rosamond and James Weldon Johnson, Cecil Mack, and Will Tyers.[30] While other black writers and composers who were schooled in

M*embership in ASCAP was skewed toward writers of show tunes and semiserious works; the vast majority of black artists were routinely excluded from the society* musical notation (W. C. Handy, Duke Ellington) would be able to gain entrance to ASCAP, the vast majority of black artists were routinely excluded from the society and thereby systematically denied the full benefit of copyright protection. Until 1939, when a rival organization was formed, ASCAP was a closed society with a virtual monopoly on all copyrighted music. As proprietor of the compositions of its members, ASCAP could and did regulate the use of any selection in its catalogue. Thus, the organization, and therefore Tin Pan Alley, exercised considerable power in shaping public taste.

Commercial Broadcasting: A Very Private Enterprise

At the beginning of the 1920s, the outlook for records was rosy. But, while gross revenues hit an all-time high of $106 million in 1921, shrewd observers might have noticed a cloud on the horizon—radio. Two years after the advent of commercial radio broadcasting in 1920, annual record revenues showed a decline. By 1933, the height of the Great Depression, they had plummeted to an all-time low of $6 million.

The scientific properties of radio waves had been known since the latter half of the nineteenth century. In the early 1890s, Heinrich Hertz, the German scientist for whom the measure of the frequencies on the electromagnetic spectrum is named, had demonstrated how to set radio waves in motion, how to detect them, and how they passed through solid objects. It was Guglielmo Marconi who developed and implemented the first practical application of "Hertzian waves" to problems of communication. Initially rebuffed by the Italian government when he sought a patent, Marconi, with the help of his Irish mother, secured a British patent on "wireless" communication in 1896 and, a year later, established the Wireless Telegraph and Signal Company, Ltd. In 1899, he established American Marconi in the United States and set his sights on nothing short of a worldwide monopoly on wireless communication.

In its formative stages, wireless communication was used primarily for telegraphy, and its obvious application for ships in distress was demonstrated dramatically through continuous coverage of the Titanic disaster in 1912. The man who is usually credited with transforming the wireless into a technology for telephony—the basis of radio broadcasting—is Lee de Forest, the inventor of the audion, an early version of the vacuum tube that was capable of generating, modulating, amplifying, and detecting radio energy. Reginald Fessenden, a Canadian who was working in the United States with Edison, actually made the first long-distance telephonic transmission in 1906. While from a technical point of view, this can be considered the birth of broadcasting, Fessenden's transmissions were far less dramatic than de Forest's experimental broadcasts of phonograph music from the Eiffel Tower in 1908 or his 1910 broadcast of Caruso from the Metropolitan Opera in New York. As a result, it is de Forest who is called the "Father of Radio." For all

Marconi invents the wireless, makes broadcasting possible

his brilliance, however, de Forest was a less than astute businessman, and in 1913, his United Wireless Company was bankrupted in a patent suit brought by Marconi.[31]

The commercial development of radio was halted during World War I in order to devote all further research and application to the war effort. A pooling of resources and a moratorium on patent suits during the war years encouraged technical advances that might not otherwise have been possible. Once the war was over, however, it was clear that there was a future for commercial radio and Marconi tried to pick up where he had left off. But, when he began to negotiate for exclusive rights to General Electric's 200,000 watt Alexanderson alternator, the U.S. government intervened.

The Growth of Network Radio

Seeing international communication as a key element in the balance of world power, President Woodrow Wilson noted that a British-dominated monopoly on radio would not be satisfactory. In 1919, the president of American Marconi was forced to tell his stockholders: "We have found that there exists on the part of the officials of the [U.S.] Government a very strong and irremovable objection to [American Marconi] because of

Harnessing patriotism to the profit motive, the operations and assets of American Marconi were transferred to a new entity—the Radio Corporation of America.

the stock interest held therein by the British Company."[32] Harnessing patriotism to the profit motive, Owen D. Young, a General Electric vice president, engineered a "solution," with the active support of the U.S. government. When all was said and done, the operations and assets of American Marconi were transferred to a new entity—the Radio Corporation of America—with Young as the first chairman of its board of directors. RCA was set up as a holding company for the major radio patent holders in the United States. In its first few years of operation, its stock was divided in varying proportions among General Electric (GE) and Westinghouse, which would manufacture radio equipment, American Telephone and Telegraph (AT&T), which would manufacture transmitters and control telephonic communication, and the former stockholders of American Marconi.

With the future of North American radio firmly in U.S. hands, a regular schedule of broadcasting began in the United States. In November 1920, Westinghouse's KDKA went "on the air" from the roof of the company's Pittsburgh factory to broadcast the results of the Harding/Cox presidential election. Within two to three years and with few precedents to guide their development, nearly 600 stations were licensed to operate across the country. Existing legislation, designed primarily to govern maritime telegraphy, did not anticipate the impact of commercialized telephonic broadcasting. Issues such as programming, financing, organization, ownership, networking, interference, and advertising were worked out in practice and over time.

By the mid-1920s, the structures and practices that would dominate radio for the next two decades, including network broadcasting and commercial advertising, were already in place. In 1926, AT&T bowed out of broadcasting and sold its flagship station, WEAF, and other assets to RCA for $1 million. That same year, RCA formed a new subsidiary, the National Broadcasting Company (NBC), the first company founded solely to operate a radio network. In November, a twenty-five station network, fed by WEAF in New York and extending as far west as Kansas City, went on the air with a most ambitious program. Broadcasting from the Grand Ballroom of the Waldorf-Astoria, the program featured the New York Symphony Orchestra conducted by Walter Damrosh and a number of "remote" features, including, among other things, the dance bands of Vincent Lopez, Ben Bernie, George Olsen, and B. A. Rolfe, the Metropolitan Opera star Titta Ruffo, the comedy team of Webber and Fields, and a Will Rogers monologue. The formation of NBC marked the transition from radio as an ancillary corporate enterprise to radio as a profit-generating venture in itself.

By 1926, NBC was operating two semiautonomous networks, the Red Network and the Blue Network. The more powerful Red Network, originating at WEAF (later to become WNBC) in New York, offered broadcasts of news, semiserious works, and light opera. The Blue Network, fed by WJZ (later to become WABC), also in New York, presented what *Variety* referred to as "the new school of entertainment, running more to the popular tune."[33] Both networks were headed by the American Marconi telegraph operator who had been in constant contact with the sinking Titanic, David Sarnoff, "wonder boy of the radio." Now a fast-rising executive at RCA, Sarnoff had envisioned consumer broadcasting as quality entertainment as early as the mid-teens. "I have in mind a plan of development which would make radio a 'household utility,' in the same sense as the piano or phonograph," he wrote in a memo to his superiors in 1916. "The idea is to bring music into the home by wireless."[34] Sarnoff became president of RCA in 1930, the year the company was severed from GE in a government-led antitrust suit and went on to serve as chairman of RCA's board of directors from 1947 until his retirement in 1969.

A rival network had been formed in 1927, after Sarnoff had rejected a proposal by Arthur Judson, a violinist turned artist manager, to supply classical musicians to network radio. Enraged, Judson formed an agency entitled United Independent Broadcasters to book talent and, with financial backing from the Columbia Phonograph Company, began the Columbia Phonograph Broadcasting System. When the competition for advertising and programming got rough, however, Columbia pulled out. The fledgling network was put on a firm financial footing when it received an influx of cash from one of its main advertisers, the owner of La Palina cigars, whose son, William S. Paley, was installed as the network's new president in 1928. At this time, the name of the network was changed to the Columbia Broadcasting System. Within a year CBS was NBC's major competition, and coast-to-coast broadcasting was a reality. Paley and Sarnoff were dominant figures in broadcasting for years, each controlling vast media empires.

Although radio developed in a generally laissez-faire fashion with little interference on the part of the government, its progress was closely monitored through a series of conferences on its development held by the National Alliance of Broadcasters (NAB), which actually recommended an extension of government regulatory powers. These recommendations were embodied in the Radio Act of 1927 and then extended in the Communications Act of 1934, which brought into being the Federal Communications Commission. Still, the law lagged behind the technological advances that had occurred and the patterns of ownership that were embodied in the predominance of network broadcasting. It was, according to Erik Barnouw, "based on a premise that had been obsolete in 1927 and by 1934 was totally invalid: that American broadcasting was a local responsibility exercised by independent station licensees."[35] By 1938, the networks were using 98 percent of the available nighttime wattage. A fourth network, the Mutual Broadcasting System had been formed by the *Chicago Tribune* in 1934, but its chances for expansion were limited. CBS and the Red and Blue networks of NBC had already locked up fifty of the fifty-two clear channels—special frequencies allocated to stations with large transmitters positioned to broadcast over great distances with minimal interference—as well as 75 percent of the most powerful regional stations. In terms of ownership patterns, radio had developed as a very private enterprise indeed. Programming, however, was another matter entirely.

The Advertisers Versus the Programmers

In keeping with the times, those involved in radio, which was introduced at a time when Prohibition had forced the pursuit of certain pleasures underground, thought the new medium should nourish the spirit and raise the nation's general level of culture through programs of news, literature, drama, and concert music. While this belief did little for the fortunes of the popular songsters of Tin Pan Alley or the cultural preferences of huge segments of the U.S. public, for that matter, it did affect the programming decisions of commercial stations. Commercial station

Fortunately for popular music, advertisers like Paley, who catered to "vulgar" popular tastes as a matter of necessity, ended up playing the major role in determining the course of radio programming.

owners were preoccupied with maintaining a sense of propriety and "good taste" in everything from program content to advertising. Direct advertising of a product was permitted only during business hours; at night, only a discreet mention of a program sponsor's name was allowed. When it appeared that such principles might somehow be compromised, "cultured" industry stalwarts like Lee de Forest

> lost no opportunity to cry out in earnest protest against the crass commercialism, the etheric vandalism of the vulger hucksters, agencies, advertisers, station owners—who lacking awareness of their grand opportunities and moral responsibilities to make of radio an uplifting experience, continue to enslave and sell for quick cash the grandest medium which has yet been given to man to help upward his struggling spirit.[36]

As the twenties roared past most nineteenth-century conventions, however, the old guard of broadcasting often found itself locking horns with a new breed of unabashedly commercial advertisers. In many ways Sarnoff and Paley personified the two camps. As a visionary corporate executive, Sarnoff was immersed in the public service aspects of the medium. He viewed radio as an "electronic library," that brought useful information, up-lifting literature, and tasteful music into the home "by wireless." Of course, as an equally good businessman, he was not oblivious to the fact that such services would sell millions of the radio receivers his company manufactured. Paley, on the other hand, came to radio as the advertising manager of his father's cigar factory. His product needed a harder sell, the kind that was considered crass by the old guard. Fortunately for popular music, advertisers like Paley, who catered to "vulgar" popular tastes as a matter of necessity, ended up playing the major role in determining the course of radio programming.

Since the birth of broadcasting, news had been a staple of radio programming, consistent with its instructional mission. Drama added another element to radio's aura of respectability. The bulk of radio programming, however, was music. While the old guard leaned toward concert music, advertisers paid more attention to mainstream popular tastes.

Of course, ever vigilant concerning its economic self-interest, ASCAP recognized from the beginning that the preponderance of radio programming was musical and, early on, notified radio of its intention to include musical broadcasts among its sources of copyright royalties. Commercial advertising—even indirect advertising—had placed musical broadcasts within the public performance provision of the 1909 Copyright Act. Station owners, however, rejected ASCAP's initial request for $5 a day for a blanket license. In fact, the NAB was organized in 1923 specifically to deal with ASCAP's "prohibitive" terms. By the end of 1924, Sanjek notes, "ASCAP income from 199 radio licenses was $130,000, up from the previous year's $35,000 but far from the million predicted when the drive to collect from broadcasters began in the summer of 1922."[37] Dissatisfied with its share of the take, ASCAP complained that radio had not simply killed records and vaudeville, it had killed popular music itself. Publishers and broadcasters thus began an adversarial relationship that continued well into the 1960s.

In 1934, ASCAP's total radio royalties were $850,000, still not the threatened $1 million. By 1937, however, total radio royalties had jumped to $5.9 million. It was the advertisers with their close attention to mainstream popular taste who played a leading role in ASCAP's change of fortune. To draw listeners, and thus increase sales, the advertisers supported "dialect" comedy and popular song programs rather than dramatic series or concerts of classical or semiclassical music.[38] Pepsodent toothpaste (and popular demand), for example, turned Freeman Gosden and Charles Correll, the white creators of the "blackface" comedy series "Amos 'n' Andy," into the highest paid entertainers in all of broadcasting. (As usual, racial parody could be counted on to turn a profit.) Advertisers also provided the listening audience with "live" musical entertainment and skirted the stringent advertising code at the same time, by sponsoring performing artists with corporate names like the Browning King Orchestra, the Cliquot Club Eskimos, the A&P Gypsies, the Ipana Troubadours, and the Gold Dust Twins, Goldy and Dusty.

One of the most interesting national prime-time experiments in popular music was sponsored on NBC by the American Tobacco Company, maker of Lucky Strike cigarettes. Company president George Washington Hill directed the show's featured attraction, B. A. Rolfe and his thirty-five piece orchestra, to play only popular dance music with "no extravagant, bizarre, involved arrangements," and invited listeners to send in their song preferences. With Hill's advertising budget of $20 million, even staid NBC executives "suffered his brash, boorish behavior and joined him at Sunday-morning rehearsals to test the 'foxtrotability' of every selection programmed."[39] The show evolved into the famous *Your Hit Parade*, one of the most popular shows ever to hit network radio. In focusing solely on musical selections that were popular among the listening audience, *Your Hit Parade* conferred a measure of power in determining public taste on the consumer. The show's "listener preference" letters foreshadowed the more scientific methods of rating that today determine programming formats.

The tension between "culture" and straight commercial entertainment in radio programming continued until the economic imperatives of the Great Depression put the advertisers in a position to determine the tone of radio more than the programmers. During the Great Depression, as Erik Barnouw has written, "Destitute families that had to give up an icebox or furniture or bedding still clung to the radio as to a last link with humanity."[40] Such loyalty tipped the balance of power in programming to the side of the advertisers. As a result, radio has tended to follow the popular tastes of consumers. This tendency had quite surprising consequences when rock 'n' roll dawned in the early 1950s.

Hollywood Bolsters Tin Pan Alley

If radio never quite measured up to ASCAP's musical or financial expectations (or so it claimed publicly), the creation of another new medium—"talking" films—held out the promise of even greener pastures for Tin Pan Alley composers.

In 1924, AT&T's Western Electric developed the "vitaphone" process of synchronizing disc recordings with sound, which was purchased by Warner Brothers. Warner's classic 1927 film, *The Jazz Singer,* starring Al Jolson, which is often remembered as the first "talkie," was in fact a

The runaway success of MGM's Broadway Melody, released in 1929, made it clear that mainstream popular music (i.e., Tin Pan Alley compositions) would play a major role in talking films.

One of the most popular entertainers of the early twentieth century, Al Jolson is shown in a scene from The Jazz Singer, performing in blackface. Later in his career he discontinued the practice.

silent film with songs. (The ill-fated Lee de Forest had experimented with sound on film as early as 1906 and had formed the Phonofilm Company in 1925. Unfortunately, this company too went into bankruptcy, this time because of inadequate financing.) GE developed a process for actually photographing sound onto film in 1922, and as usual, David Sarnoff was on the scene to maneuver RCA into the middle of all the action. In 1928, Sarnoff organized a new unit, RCA Photophone, to exploit the process. He also acquired stock in Film Booking Offices of America (FBO), a small film production company, and the Keith-Albee-Orpheum theater chain. After ousting Albee, Sarnoff consolidated FBO and the Keith-Albee-Orpheum theater chain into a single company, Radio-Keith-Orpheum (RKO), which controlled about 12 percent of all first-run outlets in the United States. By 1930, sound had been installed in 83 percent of the country's theaters.

The runaway success of MGM's *Broadway Melody,* released in 1929, made it clear that mainstream popular music (i.e., Tin Pan Alley compositions) would play a major role in talking films. Record companies rushed to record dance and vocal versions of the film's hit songs, "Give My Regards to Broadway," "You Were Meant for Me," "The Wedding Song of the Painted Doll," and, of course, the title song. The major motion picture companies—Warner, United Artists, Fox, Paramount, Universal, and MGM—all planned movie musicals. To secure entertainers with guaranteed appeal, they raided the most popular entertainment medium available to them—network radio. One of the first successful movie musicals, *The Big Broadcast*, even borrowed its theme from radio. Among the artists who journeyed westward in 1932 to film the movie were Kate Smith, the Boswell Sisters, and the Mills Brothers, which makes this film one of the few early Hollywood musicals to utilize African American talent. Another artist featured in the film was the singer who would set the standard for pop vocals until World War II—Bing Crosby. Originally steeped in minstrelsy (he actually appeared on film in blackface), Crosby began his singing career in 1926 as one of the Rhythm Boys in the Paul Whiteman band. Shortly thereafter, the Rhythm Boys were performing and recording independently as a vocal trio featuring Crosby. In 1931, Crosby launched his solo recording career and landed his first radio show. He proved to be so popular that Roy Turk and Fred Ahlert offered him a cut of the royalties on "When the Blue of the Night Meets the Gold of the Day" if he would make it his radio theme song. He recorded with everyone from Al Jolson and Louis Armstrong to Paul Whiteman and Duke Ellington. Hits like "Sweet Leilani" (1937), a pseudo-Hawaiian number written by Harry Owens for the Oscar-winning film *Waikiki Wedding*, and "San Antonio Rose" (1940), a western swing song penned by Bob Wills, fed the mainstream attraction for exotic cultural influences and furthered Tin Pan Alley's superficial treatment of these influences. Following *The Big Broadcast*, Crosby went on to star in over sixty musical films, including *College Humor* and *Going Hollywood* in 1933, *Pennies from Heaven* (1936), and *Holiday Inn* (1942). His recording of Irving Berlin's "White Christmas" from the latter film sold more than 30 million copies and entered the pop charts eighteen years in a row.[41]

Among the major Hollywood studios, Fox was the first to ally itself with a Tin Pan Alley publishing house—De Sylva, Brown, and Henderson. The firm more than pleased its new Hollywood partner when it turned out a string of hit musical comedies, *Good News, Three Cheers, Hold Everything, George White's Scandals,* and *Sunny Side Up,* among others. In turn, Warner Brothers acquired a dozen New York publishing houses. The studio utilized the songwriting team of Harry Warren and Al Dubin to score most of Busby Berkeley's extravaganzas, including *42nd Street, Gold Diggers,* and *Footlight Parade* in 1933, and *Dames* in 1934. Family-oriented Broadway musicals, such as Jerome Kern's *Babes in Toyland* and *The Merry Widow* by Rodgers and Hart, were reproduced for the silver screen in 1934. The indefatigable Irving Berlin, whose fee for a musical film score was $75,000 plus a percentage of gross receipts, contributed hit songs to films like *Mammy* and *Puttin' on the Ritz* (1930), *Top Hat* (1935), *Follow the Fleet* (1936), *On the Avenue* (1937), *Carefree* (1938), and *Second Fiddle* (1939). By 1937, the music publishing houses associated with Hollywood, shared 65 percent of ASCAP's publisher dividends, and continued to do so for the next decade.[42]

Established Tin Pan Alley publishing houses thus consolidated their interests in every medium used to disseminate popular music—sheet music, radio, Broadway plays, Hollywood films, and, to a lesser extent, records. At times, Tin Pan Alley's relationship with the recording industry conflicted with its other interests. Radio and movies, for example, netted Tin Pan Alley a hefty sum but hurt the recording industry. After all, the consumer did not have to buy a record to hear the latest hit; he or she needed only to turn on the radio. Furthermore, movie music remained in demand for only as long as the film was in circulation. "When Hollywood created a glut of as many as six or eight songs in a single production, it led to a superabundance of recorded movie music, which sold pictures but not recordings. A Hollywood-connected publisher could no longer assure record makers that a specific song in a forthcoming film would be the plugged hit."[43] Therefore, what were profitable ventures for the Alley's songwriters and publishers may not have been equally lucrative for recording companies. During the 1920s and 1930s, then, record companies had to look elsewhere to realize the financial potential of their product. It may not be purely coincidental that they exploited the markets for blues and country music at precisely the moment that record sales began to decline.

NOTES

1. Russell Sanjek, *American Popular Music and Its Business: The First Four Hundred Years, Volume II from 1790 to 1909* (New York: Oxford University Press, 1988), 377. Sanjek further states: "The production of pianos and player pianos reached its all-time high in 1899, when more than 365,000 were manufactured, and it continued to average 300,000 annually until just after World War I" (p. 296).

2. Charles Hamm, *Yesterdays: Popular Song in America* (New York: W. W. Norton, 1983), 285. Ian Whitcomb puts the figure at 10,000,000 copies over a twenty-year period. See Ian Whitcomb, *After the Ball: Popular Music from Rag to Rock* (Baltimore: Penguin Books, 1974), 4.

3. Sanjek, *American Popular Music*, 2: 365.

4. Jerrold Northrop Moore, *A Matter of Records: Fred Gaisberg and the Golden Era of the Gramophone* (New York: Taplinger Publishing Co., 1976), 6.

5. It is interesting to note that at this point, the term *gramophone* was dropped from the language in the United States (but not in Europe), and phonograph became the generic term for all record players.

6. As if to compliment the gentility of the series, Johnson then introduced the Victrola, the first console record player, which featured an enclosed turntable, tone arm, and playback horn, and a price tag of $200.

7. Whitcomb, *After the Ball,* 98–99.

8. C. A. Schicke, *Revolution in Sound: A Biography of the Recording Industry* (Boston: Little, Brown and Co., 1974), 67–68.

9. Sanjek, *American Popular Music,* 2: 297.

10. Eileen Southern, *The Music of Black Americans: A History* (New York: W. W. Norton, 1971), 347.

11. Hamm, *Yesterdays,* 290.

12. Ibid., 325.

13. "The Birth of Our Popular Songs." *Literary Digest* (7 October 1916): 892.

14. *Irving Berlin's America,* PBS documentary produced by Joann G. Young, 1986.

15. Hamm, *Yesterdays,* 340.

16. Gunther Schuller, *Early Jazz: Its Roots and Musical Development* (New York: Oxford University Press, 1968), 24.

17. Whitcomb, *After the Ball,* 26.

18. It is interesting to note that Joplin never recorded. The recordings attributed to him were actually made from piano rolls he cut. Given the popularity of player pianos at the beginning of this century, piano rolls became a vehicle for introducing the music of some black artists to mainstream listeners. However, since there are no recordings of Joplin himself, there remains no definitive statement as to the tempo at which he played his compositions.

19. Gilbert Seldes, *The Seven Lively Arts* (1924; reprint New York: A. S. Barnes, 1957), 71.

20. Hamm, *Yesterdays,* 321.

21. Schuller, *Early Jazz,* 38.

22. Leroi Jones [Amiri Baraka], *Blues People* (New York: William Morrow, 1963), 69.

23. Ibid., 148.

24. William Barlow, "Cashing In." In *Split Image: African Americans in the Mass Media,* 2d ed., ed. Jannette L. Dates and William Barlow (Washington, D.C.: Howard University Press, 1993), 31.

25. There is actually a more complicated history here than meets the eye. Apparently, a number of black jazz musicians, including New Orleans trumpeter Freddie Keppard, were asked to record by recording companies. They declined because they feared that if recorded, their styles could be studied and stolen, which speaks to the state of race relations as well as to the relationship of African Americans to technology.

26. Seldes, *The Seven Lively Arts,* 94.

27. Sanjek, *American Popular Music,* 2: 339.

28. Hamm, *Yesterdays,* 288.

29. Russell Sanjek, *American Popular Music and Its Business: The First Four Hundred Years, Volume III from 1900 to 1984* (New York: Oxford University Press, 1988), 23.

30. Southern, *The Music of Black Americans,* 353.

31. For more information on the early history of radio see Gleason L. Archer, *History of Radio to 1926* (New York: American Historical Society, 1938) and Erik Barnouw, *A Tower in Babel: A History of Broadcasting in the United States to 1933* (New York: Oxford University Press, 1966).

32. Archer, *History of Radio,* 178.

33. Ibid., 85.

34. Ibid., 112.

35. Barnouw, *The Golden Web,* 33.

36. Lee de Forest, *Father of Radio* (Chicago: Wilcox and Follett, 1950), 442–43.

37. Sanjek, *American Popular Music,* 3: 81.

38. It should be noted that due to a loophole in the 1909 Copyright Act, novels and plays could be read on the air without infringing copyright. This loophole was not plugged until 1952. Much of the classical music that was performed was already in public domain, thus, no royalty payments were required.

39. Sanjek, *American Popular Music,* 3: 166.

40. Barnouw, *The Golden Web,* 6.

41. Donald Clarke, ed., *The Penguin Encyclopedia of Popular Music* (New York: Viking, 1989), 301.

42. Sanjek, *American Popular Music,* 3: 155.

43. Ibid., 110–11.

2 Blues and Country Music: Mass Media and the Construction of Race

In the creation of their distinctive brand of popular music, the most creative of Tin Pan Alley's songwriters absorbed outside influences like aural sponges. For all their incredible breadth of influences, however, they were in many ways narrowly provincial, products of the urban Northeast and Hollywood. While their music was immensely popular, it reflected white, upper-middle-class sensibilities and was actually known and accepted by a rather limited segment of the population. In the final analysis, as Charles Hamm has noted:

> *Tin Pan Alley songs were for white, urban, literate, middle- and upper-class Americans. They remained practically unknown to large segments of American society, including most blacks . . . and the millions of poor, white, rural Americans of English, Irish, and Scottish stock clustered in the South and scattered across the lower Midwest. These two groups had their own distinctive types of music, oral-tradition music. . . .*[1]

This oral-tradition music—primarily blues and country, which at the time the recording companies categorized as race and hillbilly—developed largely outside the orbit of Tin Pan Alley. It was recording companies, aided in some instances by radio and film, that brought this music to the public. That it remained isolated for so long speaks more to the distribution of cultural power than the artistic value of the music.

As marketing categories, designations like race and hillbilly intentionally separated artists along racial lines and conveyed the impression that their music came from mutually exclusive sources. Nothing could have been further from the truth.

43

Blues and Country:
More Equal than Separate

It is difficult to trace the myriad of cultural inputs that went into the creation of music from the grassroots in the first decades of the twentieth century. At street level, of course, there was considerable cross-cultural contact; it was a part of everyday life. To offer but one example: Polk Brockman owned a furniture store in Atlanta, Georgia. His customers cut across racial lines. In the early 1920s, Brockman, like other furniture store owners, expanded his business to include phonographs. To maximize his sales, then, it was in his interest to be somewhat attuned to the musical tastes of his diverse clientele. As a result, Brockman and others like him—Sam Price in Dallas and Henry C. Spier in Jackson— often served as local talent scouts for record companies.[2] In fact, Brockman had a very lucrative sideline supplying both black and white talent to the OKeh Record Company, an independent label founded by Otto Heinemann. At OKeh, however, black artists were assigned to the label's 14000 Race Series and white artists to its 15000 Hillbilly Series. As marketing categories, designations like race and hillbilly intentionally separated artists along racial lines and conveyed the impression that their music came from mutually exclusive sources. Nothing could have been further from the truth. Across the social divide of segregation, these artists were aware of and influenced by each other's work. In cultural terms, blues and country were more equal than they were separate.

The United States can be justifiably proud of the melding of African and European conventions that produced the blues, if not the circumstances of the music's creation. In its initial usage, the term *blues* was not a racially coded reference. As the description of a mood or feeling, the term dates back to sixteenth-century England. "In the nineteenth century, it was a common expression in the United States," Samuel Charters has reported. "The word was used occasionally in song titles, but as a slang expression, without reference to any Negro musical style."[3]

The evolution of the blues as a fundamentally African American musical genre can be traced back to the shouts, field hollers, and work songs of slavery. These pre-blues forms were a functional expression, rendered in a call-and-response style without accompaniment or harmony and unbounded by the formality of any particular musical structure.[4] Gradually, instrumental and harmonic accompaniment were added, reflecting increasing cross-cultural contact. The "Ethiopian airs" of early minstrelsy "with strange modal harmonies and sharply rhythmic dissonance"[5] and the "Negro spirituals" popularized later in the nineteenth century by the Fisk Jubilee Singers who presented "spirituals in choral versions that were greatly influenced by white singing societies"[6] were early codifications of this evolution.

Multicultural influences also shaped country music. In the words of country music historian Bill C. Malone,

The folk music of the South was a blending of cultural strains, British at its core, but overlain and intermingled with the musical contributions of other ethnic and racial groups . . . the Germans of the Great Valley of Virginia; the Indians of the backcountry; Spanish, French, and mixed-breed elements in the Mississippi Valley; the Mexicans of South Texas; and, of course, blacks everywhere.[7]

As country music evolved into a commercial enterprise, its list of sources broadened to include the influence of German and Swiss yodelers, Italian mandolin players, and Hawaiian string bands.

Even a cursory look at the instrumentation used in blues and country music reveals multiculturalism at work. Of the two most common instruments used in early country music—the fiddle and the banjo—the fiddle was from Europe and the banjo was most probably of African origin. While the fiddle undoubtedly arrived with the earliest colonists, the instrument was soon mastered by others. Black fiddlers, for example, were quite well represented in the antebellum South. From the 1920s on, country fiddlers borrowed heavily from blues and jazz. Syncopated rhythms, improvisational styles, and call-and-response patterns were common in commercial country fiddling. An early form of what we know as the banjo—a four-stringed instrument with a long neck and a skin stretched over a hollow body, referred to as a *banza,* a *banshaw,* a *banjil,*[8] a *banjor,*[9] or a *banjar*[10]—was brought over from West Africa in the late seventeenth century. A fifth, or "drone," string and a fretted neck were added in the 1800s to produce the instrument that became a staple of country music, both hillbilly and blues varieties.

The guitar, another staple of both blues and country music, had been present in this country since the colonial period when it was considered a classical instrument. It became a fixture in country blues accompaniment long before it became a dominant instrument in country music. In fact, it found its way into country string bands through white musicians' fascination with the elaborate fingerpicking styles of black artists, which were characteristic of West African techniques but unknown in European folk music. Like the guitar, the mandolin, which was brought to this country by Italian immigrants and concert musicians, was initially regarded as a polite, upper-class instrument. According to Bill Malone, it found its way into rural areas through the catalogues of Sears-Roebuck and Montgomery Ward. The ukulele and steel guitar were introduced to this country by the Hawaiian string bands that toured the country after Hawaii became a U.S. territory in 1900. The wail of the steel guitar in country music at this time echoed the sounds produced by black guitarists using knife blades, bottlenecks, and other devices.

Neither vocal styles nor choice of material were limited by race. Yodeling, most readily identified with country music, has a more complicated history than one might suspect. Although German in origin, certain pre-blues shouts and hollers were described in John W. Work's *American Negro Songs* as a "fragmentary bit of a yodel, half sung, half yelled."[11] Yodeling became part of American minstrelsy early on. Although it was popularized on record by Jimmie Rodgers, black musicians had also learned the vocal technique. Blues artists who were contemporaries of Rodgers, such as Stovepipe Johnson ("Devilish Blues," 1928) and Tampa Red ("Worried Devil Blues," 1934), can be heard yodeling on record.[12]

Familiar characters and folklore heroes also cut across racial lines. In his irreverent portrait of country music, *Country,* Nick Tosches has argued that the ballad of "Frankie and Johnny," a common tragic theme in blues and country, was written by a black singer named Mammy Lou. The tale of Casey Jones, almost exclusively associated with country music (and later, the Grateful Dead), was also written by an African American, Wallace Saunders. At the same time, black musicians were drawn to old folk tales of British origin. Tosches refers to a black version of "Barbara Allen" in which the Scottish lady is a black boy named Boberick Allen. There are also black versions of "The Maid Freed from the Gallows," "Lord Lovel," and "Lady Isabel and Elf-Knight," three more British ballads that traveled to the United States in the eighteenth century.[13]

By the time the blues and country music were recorded in the 1920s and 1930s, these sorts of cross-pollinations were so common that artists were sometimes listed in the wrong racial category in record company catalogues. Nevertheless, because a separation of the races has been so prominent in U.S. social relations, the official histories of blues and country have treated these styles as separate and distinct and used designations like race and hillbilly to emphasize differences.

"Race" Music: The Popular Sounds of Black America

Although all of what is now called blues was categorized as race music in the 1920s and 1930s, it is necessary for the purposes of this discussion to distinguish between country blues (sometimes referred to as rural blues or, in a more specific context, Delta blues) and city, or classic, blues (also known as urban blues or vaudeville blues). "Classic blues was entertainment," Amiri Baraka [Leroi Jones] has said, "and country blues, folklore."[14] Country blues were intensely personal, highly improvised, and quite irregular in form. The music was usually performed by

One of the most unexpected developments of the post–World War I period was the discovery by recording companies of a significant and untapped African American market for classic blues recordings by black artists.

a single male vocalist with only banjo or guitar accompaniment, if there were any accompaniment at all. As Samuel Charters has noted, country blues styles were "related to the city-blues styles in the arrangement of the lyrics and the harmonic patterns, but the singing styles and the rhythms were from the music of the fields and work gangs."[15] In the cities, the myriad of blues styles were codified into an eight-bar and a sixteen-bar pattern, as well as the twelve-bar form that became the standard for classic blues. Classic blues followed a I, IV, V (tonic, subdominant, dominant) chord progression and were so constructed that each verse of the A/A/B rhyme scheme left enough space for either a vocal or an instrumental response. In this call-and-response pattern, there was considerable room for improvisation, but within a standardized musical framework. There also developed a "pianistic adjunct" to the city blues, which was known as boogie-woogie. It utilized repeated eighth-note figures in the left hand, which left the right hand free for blues improvisation.

Boogie-woogie was a city blues piano style that had been pioneered before World War I in Chicago by Jimmy Yancey, a groundskeeper at Comiskey Park, home of the Chicago White Sox. Chicago also boasted Clarence "Pine Top" Smith, whose "Pine Top's Boogie Woogie" became a staple of the genre, and Earl "Fatha" Hines, a classically trained pianist and veteran of a number of Louis Armstrong ensembles. Hines linked the propulsive left-hand rhythms of the ragtime pianists with melodic figures similar to those of Armstrong's trumpet in the right hand in developing a style which came to be known, naturally, as the "trumpet piano" style. In his sophistication, Hines could be considered the Chicago counterpart of the Harlem "stride" pianists such as James P. Johnson, Willie-the-Lion Smith, Luckey Roberts, and Fats Waller. Eventually, the solo piano styles were overshadowed by orchestral developments in jazz. But, boogie-woogie in particular exerted a significant influence on the piano styles of early rock 'n' roll artists including Fats Domino, Little Richard, Huey "Piano" Smith, and Jerry Lee Lewis.[16]

One of the most unexpected developments of the post–World War I period was the discovery by recording companies of a significant and untapped African American market for classic blues recordings by black artists. The fact that this market was unrecognized says a great deal about U.S. race relations at the time. According to Robert Palmer, "the idea of making recordings by and for blacks hadn't occurred to anyone in a position to do anything about it when the so-called blues craze hit around 1914–15, so [W. C.] Handy's 'blues' and the blues of other popular tunesmiths, black and white, were recorded by whites, many of them specialists in Negro dialect material."[17] It wasn't until 1920, and then quite by accident, that this pattern changed. When a recording session that was to feature Sophie Tucker had to be canceled due to illness, the enterprising black producer/songwriter Perry Bradford, "the shrewdest and most determined of the colored blues writers," convinced executives at OKeh to let him do the session with a black contralto named Mamie Smith. Smith's recording of Bradford's "Crazy Blues"— actually the second Bradford/Smith collaboration for OKeh—shocked and delighted company executives when it began to sell 7,500 copies a week, mostly to black buyers. OKeh thus became the first beneficiary of an incredible, previously untapped market among African Americans. Ralph Peer, the OKeh recording director who assisted at the sessions, dubbed these records "race records."[18] The label stuck and remained the designation for black music by black artists for a black audience until 1949.

Smith's singing style, while oriented toward the classic blues, "was more in the tradition of the vaudeville stage than it was 'bluesy.' "[19] Still, her overwhelming success ushered in an era of classic blues recordings that were sung almost invariably by African American women, Ida Cox, Chippie Hill, Sarah Martin, Clara Smith, Trixie Smith, Victoria Spivey, and Sippie Wallace, among others. Taking their cue from the style of Gertrude (Ma) Rainey, "Mother of the Blues," these women formed "the link between the earlier, less polished blues styles and the smoother theatrical style of the later urban blues singers."[20] All were veterans of traveling tent shows, circuses, carnivals, medicine shows, and later, the black-oriented TOBA (Theater Owners Booking Association) theater circuit, which booked tours in the larger cities throughout the South and Midwest.[21] In contrast to the sparsely accompanied country blues singers who were mostly men, these classic blues women were usually accompanied by "a red hot jazz band" or a "scintillating master of the keyboard."[22] As a group, they projected a polish and professionalism hitherto unknown in the blues. The bulk of their material—"upwards of seventy-five percent" according to one estimate—was sung from the point of view of women.[23]

Easily the most famous classic blues singer of her time was Bessie Smith, the "Empress of the Blues." A protégé of Ma Rainey, she spent years on the road perfecting her craft. Her singing style "combined the emotional fervor of country blues with the vigorous appeal of jazz."[24] After working with Ma Rainey as a chorus girl and then touring with the Rabbit's Foot Minstrels, she developed her own *Liberty Belles* revue and eventually became a vaudeville headliner with her own show, *Harlem Frolics.* Smith performed with some of the best jazz bands of the era, including those of Louis Armstrong and Fletcher Henderson. Signed to a failing Columbia in 1923, she recorded scores of sides (160 of which still survive) over the next decade.

The flamboyant and talented Bessie Smith rose to the pinnacle of classic blues success during the 1920s. Her career crashed along with the stock market at the end of the decade.

Her records sold so well—her "Downhearted Blues" (1923), for example, reportedly sold 780,000 copies in six months—that she was said to have saved the company from bankruptcy. The crowning achievement of her career was the title role in the 1929 two-reel film, *St. Louis Blues,* which was based on the W. C. Handy composition of the same name. That same year she recorded "Nobody Knows You When You're Down and Out"; it was her last big hit before the Great Depression wrecked her career.

The initial success of the various blues recordings encouraged the formation of a handful of black-owned, independent labels such as Black Swan, Sunshine, Meritt, and Black Patti. W. C. Handy and his publishing partner, Harry Pace, started Black Swan in 1921. Mayo (Ink) Williams, who was head of the race series for Paramount, a company owned by the Wisconsin Chair Company, which entered the record business in order to sell phonographs, struck out on his own and formed Black Patti in 1927. However, because these companies lacked sufficient resources for national promotion or for distribution outside their home territories, they were either bought up by the major labels or forced out of the industry. Not a single black-owned label survived the 1920s intact.

During the initial surge of classic blues recordings, country blues were all but forgotten. When the record companies began to test the limits of the new market, however, they discovered a considerable demand for country blues, particularly among southern blacks. Northern industrialization and World War I had caused many blacks to leave the South, which was still largely rural. Black rural musical tastes soon mingled with the urban sounds of the classic blues, creating new opportunities for the record companies. At first, these companies brought country blues performers to northern studios to record in the more sophisticated styles associated with the city blues. Later, they ventured south with mobile units to record local singers. While reaping considerable economic reward from this enterprise, the record companies became the unwitting folklorists of U.S. culture.

While reaping considerable economic reward, the record companies became the unwitting folklorists of U.S. culture.

First into the country blues breach was Paramount. In 1924, the company began its previously mentioned race series under the direction of "Ink" Williams and issued as its first release Papa Charlie Jackson's "Lawdy Lawdy Blues." This record was followed with releases by Arthur "Blind" Blake and Blind Lemon Jefferson, perhaps the most popular country blues singer of the decade. A native of Wortham, Texas, Jefferson was born blind but with a gift for music. While he led a chaotic and dissolute life as an itinerant bluesman, his style influenced just about every country blues artist who followed him. Over the course of four years, Jefferson made seventy-nine recordings for Paramount, including "Black Snake Blues" and a hymn entitled "See That My Grave Is Kept Clean," usually in its Chicago studios and a few for other labels as well. As Charters has noted, many of his recordings "were direct reworkings of old field cries and work songs. He shouted the melody in a long, free rhythmic pattern, and the guitar sang behind the voice in a subtle counterpoint."[25]

Throughout the 1920s and 1930s, OKeh, Columbia, Victor, and Vocalion, a small independent label that tried to capitalize on the race boom, engaged in extensive field recording, thus documenting a crucial period in the development of African American music, a period that might otherwise have been lost forever. The person most associated with commercial field recordings was Ralph Peer, the man who had coined the term "race records" at OKeh. In the 1930s, the Library of Congress entered the field recording business through the efforts and documentary ambitions of John Lomax and his son Alan. As a result of all these field forays, both commercial and noncommercial, dozens of country blues artists—among them, Mississippi John Hurt, Sleepy John Estes, Blind Willie McTell, Son House, Charlie Patton, Leadbelly, and Robert Johnson—were brought to wider public attention. Their diverse, idiosyncratic styles ultimately evolved into a more classic mold with standardized structures, tunes, and even guitar breaks. Just as the pioneering guitar work of Blind Lemon Jefferson is echoed in the playing of Lightnin' Hopkins, Aaron "T-Bone" Walker, and ultimately B. B. King, there is a similar stylistic connection that can be traced from blues artists from the Mississippi Delta, especially Robert Johnson, to John Lee Hooker, Muddy Waters, and Howlin' Wolf.

As a group, the formative influence of these classic and country blues artists on rock 'n' roll is undeniable. It is, therefore, fitting that Ma Rainey, Bessie Smith, Leadbelly, Robert Johnson, and Howlin' Wolf have been inducted into the Rock 'n' Roll Hall of Fame as "early influences." B. B. King, John Lee Hooker, and Muddy Waters have been admitted as rock 'n' roll artists in their own right.

"Hillbilly": The Music of the White Working Class

The first recordings of country musicians were as accidental as Mamie Smith's recording of "Crazy Blues." In fact, they were a byproduct of the quest for black talent that dominated commercial field recordings, and once again it was Ralph Peer who opened the market for the music. In 1923, when Peer visited Atlanta in search of new black artists, Polk Brockman persuaded him to record a man who had been a mainstay of the North Georgia folk scene for some forty years, Fiddlin' John Carson. Although Carson was a veteran fiddle player and had won the Atlanta Old Time Fiddler's Convention numerous times, Peer was unimpressed with Carson's "The Little Old Log Cabin in the Lane" and "The Old Hen Cackled and the Rooster's Going to Crow." It was the sales figures of these recordings that convinced Peer of the commercial value of the music.

At the time, the music was never referred to as country music. Record catalogues used such labels as "old time music" (OKeh), "old familiar tunes" (Columbia), and "songs from Dixie" (Brunswick).[26] The word *hillbilly* had been used since the turn of the century as a catchall (and pejorative) term for southern backwoods culture. In 1925, however, a string band headed by Al Hopkins ventured to the OKeh studios in New York to record six songs for Ralph Peer. When Peer asked the name of the group, Hopkins responded: "Call the band anything you want. We are nothing but a bunch of hillbillies from North Carolina and Virginia anyway."[27] Peer thus listed the name of the band as the "Hill Billies," and the name soon became the generic term for commercial country music. The term, however, just like the term *race music,* was laden with contradictory meanings. According to Bill C. Malone,

> *The first recordings of country musicians were as accidental as Mamie Smith's recording of "Crazy Blues."*

> Hillbilly music was not simply rural; it also came before the American populace as a southern art form. Like the South itself, hillbilly music suffered and profited from a conflicting set of images held by Americans that ranged from stability and enchantment to decadence and cultural degeneracy. The music took shape as a commercial entity during a decade when the South's reputation seemed at a particular low ebb. To many people hillbilly music was just one more example, along with Ku Kluxism, Prohibition, sharecropping, racial violence, and religious bigotry, of the South's retarded and degenerate culture. On the other hand, many people no doubt responded positively to the South as a bastion of traditional values and orthodox religion in a nation given over to rapid and bewildering change.[28]

In the early period of commercial country music, string bands like the Hill Billies predominated, and among the finest bands of this period were Charlie Poole and his North Carolina Ramblers, and the Skillet Lickers. At first, the repertoires of these bands consisted of traditional, anonymous folk tunes, surprisingly few of which were of British origin.[29] Gradually, original composers began to appear, and as the music proved commercially viable, professional songwriters joined their ranks. By the time the Skillet Lickers began to record for Columbia in 1926 "in a wild, raucous, but highly infectious style," their repertoire included "everything from traditional ballads, breakdowns, and rural 'dramas' (humorous skits) to the latest popular hits from Tin Pan Alley."[30] Charlie Poole and the North Carolina Ramblers included such songs from the popular arena as "Goodbye Sweet Liza Jane," "Leaving Home," and "Milwaukee Blues." In fact, Poole's favorite singer was Al Jolson. Even so, it is important to note that the broad range of sources, instruments, and sounds these artists drew on were incorporated into regional styles that were intensely familiar to their listening audiences.

Most of the early commercial performers were working people with day jobs who played country music in their off-hours. A few, like Charlie Poole, toured regularly on the vaudeville circuit, but it was rare for a "hillbilly" performer to have a career in show business that paid the rent. One such performer, Vernon Dalhart (who took his name from the towns of Vernon and Dalhart, Texas, where he had worked as a cowboy), actually entered the business through vaudeville and light opera. A graduate of the Dallas Conservatory of Music, Dalhart began recording for Edison in 1916, specializing in so-called coon songs. In 1924, he convinced Victor to record his "The Wreck of the Old

The Carter Family (from left, Maybelle, Sara, and A. P.) represented "family values" in country music even after Sara and A. P. divorced. Their traditional image corresponded with the trea-sure trove of traditional songs they helped to preserve.

97" and "The Prisoner's Song." These became the first country music recordings to sell in the millions, and they established Dalhart as a country artist of note as well as one of the top-selling recording artists of his time in any category. By 1933, when his recording career ended, he had sold an estimated 75 million records.

In 1927, two of country music's most influential acts—Jimmie Rodgers and the Carter Family (A. P., his wife Sara, and his sister-in-law Maybelle)—were first recorded within days of each other by the tireless Ralph Peer, who had moved to Victor when OKeh was absorbed by Columbia in 1926. If Rodgers represented the archetypal "ramblin' man," the Carter Family projected family stability. (These two polar—and equally marketable—images of country music would be well represented for years to come.) Accordingly, while Rodgers roamed through vaudeville and the blues, the Carter Family explored the traditional folkloric component of country music. The Carter Family recorded for several labels, but principally for Victor, from 1927 until 1941. Sara's clear soprano defined the Carters' vocal sound. Maybelle's unique fingerpicking provided a distinctive instrumental base that incorporated blues licks, an occasional steel guitar, and her signature "thumb-brush" style of picking the melody with her thumb on the bass strings while providing rhythm with a downward stroke of her fingers on the treble strings. A. P., who also sang bass and played some fiddle, collected, wrote, arranged, and copyrighted the Carter repertoire, which was published by Peer's Southern Music Company. Any number of their songs, including "The Wabash Cannonball," "Wildwood Flower," "Keep on the Sunny Side," "Worried Man Blues," and "Will the Circle Be Unbroken," have become country music classics. Although their records did not sell in the millions, the Carter Family kept alive a valuable repertoire of traditional music.

The first real star of country music was Jimmie Rodgers, the "Singing Brakeman." Rodgers learned to play the banjo and guitar at a very early age and dreamed of becoming a popular entertainer. Because his mother died when he was young, he often accompanied his father, a rail crew foreman, on extended journeys to different cities in the South. After a stint with a medicine show at the age of thirteen, Rodgers went to work for his father's crews and quickly learned the language and culture of the railroad men he later immortalized in song. In 1925, he joined a minstrel troupe and toured the South and Midwest as a blackface entertainer. He then moved to Asheville, North Carolina, and performed locally until 1927 when he first recorded for Ralph Peer. For his recording debut, Rodgers chose "The Soldiers' Sweetheart" and "Sleep, Baby, Sleep," two sentimental, traditional songs. Soon realizing that they had a potential star on their hands, Victor executives invited Rodgers to their Camden, New Jersey, studios. There he recorded the first of his twelve blue yodels, so called because they incorporated yodeling into the blues. Popularly known as "T for Texas," this recording became the country music hit of the year and Rodgers' only million seller. While his personal appearances were usually solo, Rodgers used a broad range of players and instrumentation in his

Jimmie Rodgers played the "ramblin' man" to the Carters' stable family image. If the Carters stayed close to home musically, Rodgers' travels encouraged him to incorporate a greater diversity of influences into his music than any other country artist at the time.

recordings, including fiddles, banjos, ukuleles, pianos, and guitars, as well as brass and the one instrument that would become a defining characteristic of certain strains of country music, the steel guitar. On "Blue Yodel No. 9" (some blue yodels were simply numbered), Rodgers was joined by Louis Armstrong on trumpet and Lillian Armstrong on piano. His steel guitarists included Joe Kaipo, a real Hawaiian. Rodgers' blue yodels showcased the cultural diversity that informed his music, and his incorporation of yodeling and Hawaiian guitar into the blues influenced generations of musicians. Nothing corresponding to this particular combination of elements had ever before appeared in country music or the blues. Like some of his blues contemporaries, Rodgers was inducted as an early influence into the Rock 'n' Roll Hall of Fame.

Rodgers' influence on the future of country music was incalculable. Following his success, groups like Roy Hall's Blue Ridge Entertainers and Roy Acuff's Smoky Mountain Boys established the steel guitar as a staple in country music. With the rise of such Texas "hillbillies" as Ernest Tubb, Lefty Frizzell, and Bob Wills, all of whom considered Rodgers to be their inspiration, country music took a turn to the West. The Texan who benefited the most from this "westernization" of country music was Gene Autry, the "Singing Cowboy," who began his career as a Jimmie Rodgers imitator. It was, however, Bob Wills and His Texas Playboys who popularized a brand of music called western swing, which became one of the formative influences on early rock 'n' roll.

Wills, who performed daily from 1934 to 1942 on KVOO in Tulsa, Oklahoma, was an outstanding fiddle player with eclectic tastes in music. In its various incarnations, the group included brass, reeds, drums, and electric guitars, all quite frowned upon in country music at the time. He always demanded a strong rhythmic base and hot improvisational solos from his players. By the end of the 1930s, Wills and his group could play anything from fiddle music to big band jazz with spirit. In 1939, his "San Antonio Rose" became a certified million seller for the group and a national sensation when it was recorded by Bing Crosby the following year.

Neither Rodgers nor the Carter Family toured extensively—the Carters by choice, Rodgers due to a running battle with tuberculosis, the disease that eventually took his life. The careers of both were propelled in large measure by their recordings and radio appearances. Although radio had devastating effects on the recording industry as a whole, early country musicians seem to have benefited from a complementary relationship between radio appearances and record sales.

The Dissemination of Blues and Country: More Separate than Equal

While there were significant markets for jazz and blues on records, African American performers were almost never the beneficiaries of early developments in radio or film. Bessie Smith's starring role in *St. Louis Blues* in 1929 was successful enough to suggest more of the same, and the film's director, Dudley Murphy, followed his initial triumph one year later with *Black and Tan Fantasy,* a film built around a Duke Ellington composition. Shortly thereafter, Ellington himself filmed his entire *Symphony in Black.* In 1933, Murphy shot an operatic film version of Eugene O'Neill's *The Emperor Jones* with the incomparable Paul Robeson in the title role.

> Although radio had devastating effects on the recording industry as a whole, early country musicians seem to have benefited from a complementary relationship between radio appearances and record sales. African American performers were almost never the beneficiaries of early developments in radio or film.

As Thomas Cripps has noted, "Thus, in less than four years Murphy demonstrated the richness which sound film could bring to African American themes."[31] Unlike *St. Louis Blues,* however, these later efforts tended toward an art music mode, which was well within the bounds of mainstream acceptability, but far removed from the tastes of most African Americans. Because sound film raised the stakes for moviemaking, the Great Depression shut most independent black filmmakers out of the business, leaving Hollywood firmly in control and Hollywood seldom cast African Americans in anything but subservient and/or degrading roles.

The situation was even worse on radio. The blues—particularly country blues— were seldom heard on the airwaves. "Radio broadcasts," as Nelson George has noted, "were rarely used to promote the grittier forms of music."[32] In 1932, however, Fats Waller's career received a significant boost when he played a long series of broadcasts, entitled *Fats Waller's Rhythm Club,* over WLW in Cincinnati, Ohio. Two other blues performers, Sonny Boy Williamson (Rice Miller), a singer/harmonica player, and Robert Lockwood, a guitarist, were featured on the King Biscuit Flour Company's *King Biscuit Time,* which was broadcast from Helena, Mississippi, in the early 1940s. Given the population of the Mississippi Delta area, King Biscuit's choice of talent probably added measurably to its sale of flour.

When broadcast at all, African American jazz and dance music were usually relegated to late-night, remote broadcasts from popular nightspots. Both jazz and dance music were popular with mainstream audiences. To white listeners, the race of the performers was probably unknown and, therefore, of little consequence.

> *If you liked swing in the 1920s and 1930s you could pick up live broadcasts of Duke Ellington at the Cotton Club and Chick Webb at the Savoy in Harlem, Earl (Fatha) Hines from Chicago's Grand Terrace, or maybe a late set from some California band from the West Coast Cotton Club. Significantly, these broadcasts weren't aimed at blacks. Broadcasters and advertisers were simply meeting America's demand for big-band music. These bands just happened to be black and popular.*[33]

Occasionally, an extremely talented African American musician could find work in radio as a composer or arranger. One such person was William Grant Still. With a music industry résumé that included positions at W. C. Handy's publishing house and the Black Swan record company, Still was an accomplished composer who had studied at the New England Conservatory as well as with the avant-garde French-born, but U.S.-based, composer Edgar Varése. During the depression, Still worked as an arranger and staff composer at both WCBS and WNBC in New York. His work at WCBS led to commissions from such popular entertainers as Artie Shaw, Sophie Tucker, and Paul Whiteman. Still supplied the arrangements for Whiteman's appearance on "The Old Gold Show" in California. On his return to New York, Still was hired by the "Deep River Hour" on WNBC and became the first African American conductor of a white radio orchestra. As in films, however, the employment of African Americans in radio was contingent on their ability to relate to European conventions and mainstream tastes.

There were a few attempts to air shows that featured well-known African American talent, but these attempts were short-lived. The "Ethel Waters Show," sponsored by Amoco on NBC was quickly canceled when the network's southern affiliates threatened to boycott the program. Fleischman Yeast sponsored the "Louis Armstrong Show" on CBS in 1937, but by this time Armstrong was doing comedy routines and singing Tin Pan Alley pop. Scheduled opposite the popular "Jack Benny Show" on NBC, the program lasted only thirteen weeks.

In contrast, country music was given a considerable boost by broadcasters and film producers. Since the dawn of commercial radio in the early twenties, stations throughout the South and Midwest had broadcast country music. It was Fiddlin' John Carson's popularity on WSB, a station owned by the *Atlanta Journal,* that first convinced Polk Brockman there was a record market for country music. After WBAP in Fort Worth, Texas, broadcast a one-and-a-half hour program of square dance music, in 1923, the "barn dance" format quickly became the most popular showcase for country talent. The first such program of note was *National Barn Dance,* which was introduced in 1924 by the Sears-Roebuck station WLS (World's Largest Store), in Chicago. Combining country and folk material with older pop standards, the program had a broader appeal than most country-oriented shows.

Of course, the country music show that eventually overshadowed all country broadcasts was the *Grand Ole Opry,* which was the brainchild of George D. Hay, a popular columnist for the *Memphis Commercial-Appeal* and a veteran announcer on WLS. In 1925, Hay became the station manager for WSM in Nashville, a station owned by the National Life and Accident Insurance Company. Bypassing the cultural biases of the station owners and the Nashville elite, Hay launched the WSM *Barn Dance,* later renamed the *Grand Ole Opry,* and proved that country music could be an effective tool for selling life insurance to working-class people. Within weeks, the show's appeal was reflected in life insurance sales.

The **Grand Ole Opry eventually went on to become the longest-running show on U.S. radio, a clear indicator of the commercial potential of country music.**

As was common in the early days of commercial country music, the program emphasized instrumental music. Its first major singing star was David Harrison, "Uncle Dave" Macon, a gifted and unpretentious banjo player who had a vast storehouse of folkloric material. The program also introduced one of the first black stars of country music (and radio) to its audience, Deford Bailey, a country harmonica player who proved to be one of the show's most popular artists. In 1928, Bailey made twice as many *Opry* appearances as any other performer.

The entertainer who became the *Opry*'s biggest star was Roy Acuff. Acuff, a singer/fiddler who was raised on a tenant farm in the Smoky Mountains, achieved worldwide fame playing traditional mountain music. The Acuffs were a musical family; Roy's mother played piano and guitar, his father played fiddle, and all had fine singing voices. When near-fatal sunstroke dashed Acuff's hopes for a baseball career with the New York Yankees, his interests turned toward music. In 1932, he toured with Doc Hauer's Medicine Show, hawking Moc-A-Tan Compound in blackface. Later, he appeared with a variety of groups on stations WROL and WNOX in Knoxville, Tennessee. His first recording session in 1936, produced by Art Satherley who would also produce Gene Autry's recordings, yielded two of his biggest hits: "Great Speckled Bird" and "Wabash Cannonball," which became a million seller. Joining the *Grand Ole Opry* in 1938, Acuff soon established the singer, rather than the string band, as the show's main attraction. When the show became a featured segment, sponsored by Prince Albert Tobacco, on the NBC radio network in 1939 (WSM had become a 50,000 watt clear channel in 1932), it was hosted by Acuff. The *Grand Ole Opry* eventually went on to become the longest-running show on U.S. radio, a clear indicator of the commercial potential of country music.

"Barn dance" format showcases country music on radio

Gene Autry was not only the most famous singing cowboy on film, he also made a successful transition to television with his own weekly series in the early 1950s.

As country music began to incorporate a western theme into its image, it was radio that helped to popularize the "singing cowboys." Woodward Maurice, "Tex," Ritter, a native of Murvaul, Texas, who attended the University of Texas and Northeastern Law School, began singing western and mountain songs on KPRC in Houston in 1929. From there, he moved to a featured slot on WOR's *The Lone Star Rangers* in 1932, one of the first western radio shows to originate in New York. Montana Slim (actually a Nova Scotia yodeler named Wilf Carter) held forth on the CBS network in New York during this time. Another well-known western group, the Sons of the Pioneers, which included Roy Rogers, the "King of the Cowboys," had an early-morning radio program on KFWB in Hollywood. (Rogers went on to host his own radio show with his wife Dale Evans in the mid-1940s.) Gene Autry got his start as the Oklahoma Yodeling Cowboy on KVOO in Tulsa, Oklahoma. After recording for Art Satherley, who released the singer on the Sears Conqueror label, Autry made a series of appearances on the *National Barn Dance* in Chicago and then landed his own radio show, *Conqueror Record Time,* on WLS, where he became one of the most popular entertainers in the station's history.

The cowboy image became so prevalent in country music that even performers who did not perform western-related material began to dress in garish western-style garb. For a time, the term *western* even became an alternative to the hillbilly designation used for country music. As Bill C. Malone has pointed out, however,

> *In reality, except for the fabric of usable symbols which surrounded him, the cowboy contributed nothing to American music. The "western" music which became fashionable in the mid-thirties came from other sources. . . . in the Southeast: southern traditional and gospel music, popular music, commercial recordings of all kinds (including blues and jazz), and, crucially, black music. Southwesterners could draw additionally on Mexican, Cajun, German, and what generally was described as "Bohemian" music (that is, the polka-derived styles of people who emigrated to South-Central Texas from what is now Czechoslovakia).*[34]

Hollywood also helped to popularize the image of the singing cowboy. Tex Ritter made *Song of the Gringo* in 1936, one of dozens of cowboy movies to follow. The Sons of the Pioneers and Bob Wills and His Texas Playboys also appeared in several westerns. Other western-style singers, such as Ernest Tubb, made occasional appearances in Hollywood films. By far the most successful of singing cowboys of films was Gene Autry. After a small part in *In Old Santa Fe* in 1934, Autry landed a starring role in an odd thirteen-episode cowboy/science-fiction thriller called *The Phantom Empire.* Following a featured role in *Tumbling Tumbleweeds* in 1935, he went on to star in more than 100 western films, most produced by Republic, which was considered the home of "class" westerns. Autry's best-known early films include *Boots and Saddles* (1937), *Under Western Stars* (1938), and *Carolina Moon* (1940). Autry's success was rivaled only by Roy Rogers, who signed with Republic in 1937.

The cowboy image became so prevalent in country music that even performers who did not perform western-related material began to dress in garish western-style garb.

The Long Road Back for Records

The Great Depression decimated the ranks of the independent specialty labels, as blues, jazz, and country music imprints were sometimes called. Independent, black-owned record companies had almost disappeared even prior to the depression. Paramount had acquired the Black Swan catalogue in 1924, and Columbia had absorbed OKeh in 1926. Although country music continued to benefit from national radio exposure, the sale of 10,000 records was considered a hit. Things were no rosier for the major record companies. Already hurt by radio and confused by Hollywood, the depression almost pulled them under. Edison ceased production altogether in 1930. Columbia, which was already in receivership, was picked up by the American Record Company for a mere $70,000 during the depression. Convinced prematurely that records would be a good promotional vehicle for its film stars, Warner Brothers acquired Brunswick, Al Jolson's label. Sarnoff, as usual, planned for the future and slowly built his empire. In 1929, as vice-president of RCA, he engineered a merger between RCA and Victor records and emerged as president of the new company. At the time of the merger, Victor was one of the only record companies that was still holding its own.

For the record industry, the long road back to prosperity began with a machine that had been laid to rest more than two decades earlier—the jukebox. The nickel-in-the-slot phonograph manufacturers had developed a machine that used discs in 1908, but the machines quickly fell into disuse as phonographs and records moved into homes. A new incarnation of the coin-operated record player appeared in 1927 when the Auto-

The jukebox encourages a resurgence of recorded music

matic Musical Instrument Company (AMI) introduced its Selective Phonograph. Once Prohibition was repealed in 1933, bars and cocktail lounges opened by the thousands. Looking for low-cost entertainment and an additional source of revenue, owners were only too happy to consider the jukebox. A number of other companies, Wurlitzer, Rock-ola, and Seburg, among others, soon entered the business. By 1935, there were 150,000 jukeboxes in operation in the United States, and in that year, they accounted for 40 percent of the record trade.

Prior to the dramatic growth of the jukebox, record companies had taken their production cues from hits created in other entertainment media: vaudeville, Broadway, Hollywood, and radio. During the hard times of the 1930s, however, the jukebox emerged as a major source of public entertainment. It provided a guaranteed market for record companies and a valuable promotional vehicle for recording artists. To be sure they had something for everyone, jukeboxes included a much broader range of musical styles than most radio stations. Thus, the mass audience took on a new role in the determination of public taste. *Billboard* and *Variety,* the major entertainment industry trade magazines, soon began the practice of charting jukebox hits. Once this happened, radio producers began to use the charts as a basis for live music programming, and song-pluggers began to pay more attention to records.

Other technological advances also increased the desirability of records. Broadcast technology had ushered in the era of electronic recording in the mid-1920s. Microphones, vacuum tube amplifiers, and an electromagnetic cutting stylus replaced the acoustic recording horn. The better frequency response of the new technology created a more lifelike sound. No longer did musicians have to crowd around a single recording horn; recording studios became expansive, able to accommodate whole orchestras. Sound reinforcement meant that vocalists no longer had to project; they could croon, a practice soon elevated to a virtual art form by Bing Crosby, who used the microphone as if he were singing to a single listener. By 1925, both Victor and Columbia were issuing electrically recorded discs, but although the technology revolutionized the recording industry, with record sales falling, it did not seem practical to market expensive new electric record players. In 1932, Ted Wallerstein, a veteran record executive who left Brunswick to join Sarnoff at RCA Victor, solved the cost problem when he offered the Duo, Jr., an electric turntable with no tubes or speakers that could be "jacked" into a radio, for a list price of $16.50.

If the Duo, Jr. made hardware affordable, a price cut by Decca, a new label, made records once again available to masses of people. American Decca was formed in 1934 when E. R. Lewis, head of British Decca, bought the rights to Brunswick from Warner Brothers and used what remained of Brunswick's catalogue as a base to found the new company. Jack Kapp, who was creative director at Brunswick, was brought over to head the new label. Within months, he had assembled an impressive roster of talent, including Bing Crosby, the Dorsey Brothers, the Mills Brothers, Guy Lombardo, and Fletcher Henderson. While the talent roster certainly helped Decca, the key innovation that contributed to Decca's success and to the revival of the record market as a whole was the slashing of the price of a record from seventy-five cents to thirty-five cents.

After supplying RCA Victor with the Duo, Jr., Ted Wallerstein began negotiations with William Paley and CBS. Wallerstein judged correctly that CBS, which had been operating without a record division until this time, would benefit from the acquisition of an established trademark, a pressing plant, and the rights to British Columbia recordings in the United States. Thus, he convinced Paley and CBS to purchase the faltering Columbia Records, Victor's main rival, from the American Record Company in 1938 for the seemingly outrageous price of $700,000, ten times its purchase price of a few years earlier. Abandoning RCA to become head of the new CBS record division, Wallerstein lured such talent as Benny Goodman, Duke Ellington, and Count Basie to the label. With the big band era in full swing, this was definitely a timely move.

One of the key players in the talent raids that brought Goodman and Basie to Columbia was John Hammond, a wealthy Vanderbilt on his mother's side, a staunch civil rights activist, an aficionado of African American music, and soon to become Benny Goodman's brother-in-law. Hammond, who accepted the job of producer at Columbia from Wallerstein in 1939 (the first full-time job he had ever held), was already a known quantity in the music industry, having produced Bessie Smith's final recording session

John Hammond was one of the few major label executives who truly believed that African American music should be accorded a place of prominence within U.S. popular culture. He was clearly more attuned than most to the sounds that would eventually transform the character of popular music.

and Billy Holiday's first session within months of each other in 1933. His years as a producer at Columbia spanned generations, and he influenced the careers of artists as diverse as Aretha Franklin, Bob Dylan, and Bruce Springsteen.

Hammond was widely respected among African American musicians (and widely considered to be a wealthy eccentric, if not an outright communist, in the music industry) for his attempts to break down racial barriers. And he put his expertise where his beliefs were. In 1938, Hammond had produced the first Carnegie Hall concert ever designed to showcase the entire history of African American music. Entitled *From Spirituals to Swing,* the concert included music recorded in West Africa, boogie-woogie pianists Albert Ammons, Meade Lux Lewis, and Pete Johnson, blues shouter Big Joe Turner, gospel singers Sister Rosetta Tharpe and Mitchell's Christian Singers, harmonica player Sonny Terry, Big Bill Broonzy, the Kansas City Six, and the Count Basie Orchestra, among others. The sophisticates of the New York jazz scene were finally treated to an evening with the real innovators of the music they professed to love. Hammond was one of the few major label executives who truly believed that African American music should be accorded a place of prominence within U.S. popular culture. In his autobiography, he argued for a "lessening of differences between country and popular music, between folk, rock, jazz, gospel, and other categories."[35] He was clearly more attuned than most to the sounds that would eventually transform the character of popular music.

━━━━━━━━━━━━

With the advent of commercial radio and "talkies" after World War I, record companies found their sales slipping and looked about for new markets, discovering in the process a sizable African American market for blues recordings by black artists as well as an untapped market for so-called hillbilly music. While new labels, such as OKeh, Black Swan, and Black Patti, came into existence, most of these were forced out of business or absorbed by larger companies as record sales continued to fall. It was not until the rebirth of the jukebox, which gave the mass audience more of a voice in public taste, that the record companies made a real financial comeback.

By the end of the depression, Columbia, Victor, and Decca had emerged as the big three in recording. Although they faced virtually no competition, they saw no harm in protecting themselves from the possibility that small new companies would find new grassroots music. Thus, each company established a less expensive subsidiary to cover the grassroots. Victor created Bluebird for its so-called race and hillbilly artists. In 1940, Columbia revitalized OKeh as its specialty label. The more recently formed Decca acquired Gennett, an "old-time" label in the late 1930s. This, then, was the situation as the United States prepared for its entrance into World War II.

━━━━━━━━━━━━

NOTES

1. Charles Hamm, *Yesterdays: Popular Song in America* (New York: W. W. Norton, 1983), 379.
2. William Barlow, "Cashing In," in *Split Image: African Americans in the Mass Media,* 2d ed., ed. Jannette L. Dates and William Barlow (Washington, D.C.: Howard University Press, 1993), 43.
3. Samuel Charters, *The Country Blues* (New York: Rinehart and Company, 1959), 34.
4. Following the failure of reconstruction and the replacement of legal slavery with economic dependence and political disenfranchisement, work songs reappeared with a new intensity and in a more basic style, "and in the next decades a crude blues form developed, still largely unaccompanied, and linked together in irregular, freely improvised patterns. This blues was still more in the realm of sung speech rather than song per se" (Gunther Schuller, *Early Jazz: Its Roots and Musical Development* [New York: Oxford University Press, 1968], 37). This is the music that gradually evolved into what is called the country blues.
5. Charters, *The Country Blues,* 27.
6. Schuller, *Early Jazz,* 36.

7. Bill C. Malone, *Country Music U.S.A.: Revised Edition* (Austin: University of Texas Press, 1985), 4.

8. Christopher Small, *Music of the Common Tongue: Survival and Celebration in Afro-American Music* (New York: Riverrun Press, 1987), 36.

9. Leroi Jones [Amiri Baraka], *Blues People* (New York: William Morrow, 1963), 70.

10. Malone, *Country Music U.S.A.,* 24.

11. John W. Work, *American Negro Songs* (New York: Crown Publishers, 1940), 34.

12. While Rodgers tested what would become his characteristic yodel on "Sleep, Baby, Sleep" in 1927, he was not the first to yodel on record. According to Nick Tosches, that honor probably goes to Riley Puckett, the blind guitarist of the Skillet Lickers, who yodeled on the group's Columbia recording of "Rock All Our Babies to Sleep," three years earlier. Bessie Smith cut a song called "Yodeling Blues" in 1923 but did not yodel on the record. The elusive Emmett Miller may have beat them all to yodeling, but he did not record one until 1925 on "Lovesick Blues." See Nick Tosches, *Country: Living Legends and Dying Metaphors in America's Biggest Music* (New York: Charles Scribner's Sons, 1985), 110–11).

13. Tosches, *Country,* 194.

14. Jones [Baraka], *Blues People,* 105.

15. Charters, *The Country Blues,* 48.

16. Over the course of their careers, boogie pianists appeared everywhere, from dives to fashionable society restaurants. One of their major social functions during the Great Depression was to provide entertainment for "rent parties."

> In Harlem, as in other large ghetto areas of northern cities, the only way that many blacks could cope with the problem of paying the excessive rents charged for their apartments was to give parties where "guests" were invited to contribute toward the rent. It was the job of the pianist "to draw people in"—into the barroom or café or the apartment itself—and the vitality and vigor of his playing was his drawing card. The playing of the best pianists could be heard for a considerable distance away. It was very important that a piano should have the correct "barroom" sound; sometimes it would have to be "doctored," by placing newspapers behind the hammers and putting tin on the felts, in order to obtain the effect wanted.

See Eileen Southern, *The Music of Black Americans: A History* (New York: W. W. Norton, 1971), 404–405.

17. Robert Palmer, *Deep Blues* (New York: Viking Press, 1981), 100.

18. Many observers, myself included, have written disparagingly about the implications of the term *race music.* It is likely, however, that Ralph Peer, the man who created the term, simply took his cue from the African American newspapers in which his company, OKeh Record Company, advertised—the *Chicago Defender* and the *Pittsburgh Courier,* which themselves referred to the members of the African American community as "the race."

19. Jones [Baraka], *Blues People,* 99.

20. Ibid., 89.

21. TOBA stood for Theater Owners Booking Association, but the performers often translated it as "Tough On Black Artists," or more crudely, "Black Asses."

22. Charters, *The Country Blues,* 46.

23. Howard W. Odum and Guy B. Johnson, *Negro Workaday Songs* (Chapel Hill: University of North Carolina Press, 1926), 38.

24. Southern, *The Music of Black Americans,* 398.

25. Charters, *The Country Blues,* 67.

26. Malone, *Country Music U.S.A.,* 39.

27. Ibid., 40.

28. Ibid., 42.

29. One study conducted by Anne and Norm Cohen concluded that between 1922 and 1924 only 2 percent of country performer's repertoires were of British origin. See Malone, *Country Music U.S.A.,* 44.

30. Ibid., 52.

31. Thomas Cripps, "Film," in *Split Image: African Americans in the Mass Media,* 2d ed., ed. Jannette L. Dates and William Barlow (Washington, D.C.: Howard University Press, 1993), 146.

32. Nelson George, *The Death of Rhythm & Blues* (New York: Pantheon Books, 1988), 11.

33. Ibid.

34. Malone, *Country Music U.S.A.,* 152.

35. John Hammond, *On Record* (New York: Penguin Books, 1981), 163.

3

"Good Rockin' Tonight": The Rise of Rhythm and Blues

The military buildup that preceded the United States' entrance into World War II greatly enhanced the country's prospects for a complete economic recovery from the Great Depression. The nation's eventual involvement in the war led in turn to profound social changes. Policies and practices concerning race and gender relations were successfully challenged, and as the country approached full employment, the improved financial status of the average citizen contrasted sharply with the hardship of the depression. In the cultural arena, these social changes and other seemingly unrelated variables, such as population migrations, material shortages, and technological advances, all of which were associated with the war effort, played a major role in determining the course of popular music.

As the military buildup began, thousands of southern blacks and poor whites abandoned the oppressive conditions of sharecropping and tenant farming and moved north and west to find better paying jobs in defense plants. Naturally, they took their music with them. At the same time, hundreds of eastern and midwestern G.I.s were put through basic training in southern military bases where they heard musical styles that had not yet achieved mainstream popularity in the North. In this way, blues and country music received unprecedented exposure. While country music had done well on radio earlier, by the early 1940s there were hundreds of stations across

The sweeping commodification of music that accompanied the development of recording and broadcasting had created possibilities for financial gain that could not have been imagined prior to the advent of mass culture.

the country that broadcast country music. The new audiences must have liked what they heard because Detroit jukebox operators reported that country music records were the most played of their selections, and in Europe, the Armed Forces Radio Network voted

Roy Acuff more popular than Frank Sinatra. It seemed even the enemy recognized his importance. A widely reported war story held that Japanese troops went into battle shouting: "To hell with Roosevelt, Babe Ruth, and Roy Acuff."[1]

Unlike country music, the blues, as a rule, had been excluded from radio in earlier years, but the exodus of more than 1 million African Americans from the South during World War II helped to loosen these restrictive programming policies. Wartime prosperity made these newly emigrated African Americans an identifiable consumer group. In areas with a high concentration of African American immigrants, it was in the interests of radio stations to introduce some programming that would cater to this audience. Gradually, some black-oriented programs, usually slotted late at night, began to appear on a few stations. It was this kind of programming that began to tear down the walls of the so-called race market toward the end of the decade.

In the music industry, economic recovery became the occasion for bitter and prolonged power struggles that revolved around one single question: Who should benefit, and in what proportion, from the profits derived from the use and sale of intellectual property? The key to understanding this question lies in the recognition that the music business in the 1940s had expanded far beyond the legal and organizational machinery that determined how to allocate the fruits of the market economy. The sweeping commodification of music that accompanied the development of recording and broadcasting had created possibilities for financial gain that could not have been imagined prior to the advent of mass culture. Neither the Copyright Act of 1909 nor the Communications Act of 1934 anticipated the complex interrelationships that would develop among the major interests in the music business—writers, publishers, performers, broadcasters, and record companies—let alone the relationships that would develop between these groups and consumers. As a result, these groups often found themselves in the midst of shifting alliances, competing interests, and dramatic cultural changes.

The Publishers and the Broadcasters: ASCAP Versus BMI

Broadcasters and publishers had been at odds ever since ASCAP had made its first demand for a $5-a-day royalty fee in 1922 and the NAB had been formed in reaction to the demand. Throughout the first decade of radio broadcasting, the major publishers had complained about declining profits. In point of fact, they had complained all the way to the bank. In the 1930s, according to Russell Sanjek, "ASCAP income from radio, of which the networks paid about 20 percent, had risen from $757,450 in 1932 to $5.9 million in 1937, and then dropped to $3.8 million the following year. It increased by 12 percent, to $4.3 million, in 1939."[2] That 1939 figure represented about two-thirds of

ASCAP's total income for the year. Radio revenues were clearly substantial and their potential at the start of the 1940s was even greater.

As it had before, the prospect of windfall profits brought out the greed in ASCAP's 1,250 or so members who controlled the performing rights to almost all of the best-known songs in the country. ASCAP's fee for a "blanket license" (permission to broadcast any selection in the ASCAP catalogue) was 5 percent of the total receipts from all sponsored programs, including talk shows and sports broadcasts, which did not use music. Such terms naturally exacerbated the tension between ASCAP and the broadcasters. Their already strained relationship began to go up in flames in the summer of 1940 when ASCAP mailed out new contracts that were intended to take effect when the existing agreement expired on 31 December 1940. The new contracts would have, in effect, doubled ASCAP's revenues. Designed to divide the broadcasters against themselves, the contracts included a sliding-scale fee that ranged from 3 percent for smaller stations to 7.5 percent for the networks. But, ASCAP's divide-and-conquer strategy did not work; instead, the broadcasters closed ranks.

In 1939, anticipating the worst from ASCAP and dissatisfied with its own weak position at the bargaining table, the NAB, which then represented some 600 radio stations, had decided to challenge the ASCAP monopoly by forming a performing rights organization of its own. Some 256 stations raised close to $1.5 million to capitalize Broadcast Music Incorporated (BMI), which was launched on 13 October 1939. "Taking advantage of ASCAP's stringent membership requirements, as well as its relative indifference to the popular and folk music being produced outside of New York and Hollywood," Nat Shapiro has written, "BMI sought out and acquired its support from the 'have not' publishers and writers in the grassroots areas."[3] Blues and country music songwriters and publishers found in BMI an inviting home for their work. By the time ASCAP's existing contract was expired, BMI had become a sizable operation, "turning out about 30 new songs a month under its own print" and acquiring "a number of existing catalogues—those of Hinds, Hayden & Eldridge, M. M. Cole, E. C. Schirmer, Ricordi, and [Ralph Peer's] Southern Music Publishing Co."[4]

With a catalogue of its own in place, the NAB responded to ASCAP's 1940 demands by announcing its intention to boycott the entire ASCAP catalogue. At first, ASCAP was not terribly rattled by the prospect of the boycott. The organization assumed that public demand for the likes of Irving Berlin, Cole Porter, and George Gershwin would soon bring the NAB back into the fold. The NAB held to the belief that there would be no public outcry when ASCAP music went off the air. "The music the people like is the music people hear," opined Neville Miller, president of the NAB, somewhat cynically. "It is likely that no one will notice the difference in character and quality of programs on and after January 1, 1941."[5]

For about ten months in 1941, no ASCAP music was heard on radio. As the broadcasters had predicted, there was no public protest.

For about ten months in 1941, no ASCAP music was heard on radio. In its stead, authentic regional styles, supplemented by melodies in the public domain, were broadcast to a national audience via mainstream outlets. As the broadcasters had predicted, there was no public protest. There were, however, a few key acquisitions by BMI that contributed measurably to the success of the boycott. Ralph Peer, who had moved into the international market, offered a catalogue of Latin popular music; Roy Acuff and Fred Rose (who had been members of ASCAP since 1928) offered Acuff-Rose Music, the first all-country publishing company; and E. B. Marks, an established Tin Pan Alley firm, offered the familiar pop fare that was required for network broadcasts. Although the broadcasters and the publishers came to terms in 1941, they did so only after a federally initiated criminal antitrust action forced ASCAP into a consent decree that regulated its dealings with its clients.

In the beginning, BMI came up with few songs of lasting significance. Still, by the end of 1941, its catalogue contained 36,000 copyrights from fifty-two publishers.[6] What was originally envisioned as a throw-away bargaining tool emerged as a valuable source of music and ASCAP's future primary competition. Moreover, for the first time, the Tin Pan Alley-Broadway-Hollywood monopoly on public taste had been challenged. As writers from grassroots areas received encouragement from BMI, songwriting itself became more decentralized. By the end of the decade, BMI writers like Huddie Ledbetter (Leadbelly), Hank Snow, Arthur "Big Boy" Crudup, Roy Brown, Ivory Joe Hunter, Hank Williams, Ernest Tubb, Johnny Otis, Fats Domino, and Wynonie Harris had begun to play a major role in redefining popular music.

Enter the Deejay:
The Broadcasters Versus the AFM

Less than a year after the settlement of its dispute with ASCAP, the NAB found itself embroiled in another controversy, this time with the American Federation of Musicians (AFM). As a rule, the music heard on radio was performed live and often in formal concert settings with audiences in attendance. Searching desperately for less expensive programming during the Great Depression, however, some radio stations had begun to use records as an alternative to live talent. Although perhaps unrecognized by many at the time, records were a direct challenge to the primacy of live music and one that would change the face of popular music.

The records were played by a new figure in broadcasting, the disc jockey, a term that came to be defined as an individual who was "jockeying or riding a record toward success."[7] Until the advent of the disc jockey, radio had simply been a vehicle for transmitting the substance of other media—newspapers, religious pulpits, concert halls, and vaudeville and the legitimate theater. The disc jockey's, or deejay's, show was unique in its combination of live announcing and "canned" (prerecorded) music. The earliest deejays appeared even before the stock market crash in 1929. There were, for example, three stations in Los Angeles, KGFJ, KMIC, and KPLA, that programmed records almost exclusively. The powerful X stations (those with X in their call letters), which broadcast from across the Mexican border, also relied heavily on records. "Doc" Brinkley, the first country deejay, beamed country music into millions of U.S. homes from the 100,000 watt XER in Mexico. The first black deejay, Jack L. Cooper, sold an incredible amount of Tip Top Bread in the 1930s, while spinning "jump, jam, and jive" records on his pioneering show, *The Negro Hour,* broadcast from WSBC on the south side of Chicago. The first woman deejay on a commercially licensed station was Miss Halloween Martin (named after her birth date). Featured on Marshall Field and Company's *Musical Clock,* a wake-up show on KYW in Chicago, Martin played musical comedy, light classical, pop, and some jazz in between her time and weather announcements.

The archetypal deejay appeared in 1935 when the smooth-talking Martin Block began his show, *Make Believe Ballroom,* on WNEW in New York. Block, "whose facile tongue soon successfully defeated all record hiss or needle noise and made the time between records exciting with spellbinding monologues and irresistible advertising pitches," copied the concept for his program, which was sponsored by the makers of Retardo, a weight-reducing pill, from a Los Angeles deejay named Al Jarvis.[8] Within months the audience for Block's two-and-a-half hour daily broadcasts had expanded to 4 million listeners. Block and Jarvis were more than mere technicians who filled "dead air" with recorded music. Focusing systematically on the most recent releases, they introduced the beginnings of "formula" radio.

As deejays became more and more commonplace, the policy of prohibiting the use of records on radio became harder to enforce.

As deejays became more and more commonplace, the policy of prohibiting the use of records on radio became harder to enforce. Indeed, after the formation of Capitol Records by record-store owner Glenn Wallichs, songwriter Johnny Mercer, and Paramount Pictures executive Buddy De Sylva in 1942, many programs and record companies openly ignored the policy. In a 1969 interview, Wallichs recalled the special consideration Capitol Records offered to deejays: "We typed special labels with their names on both sides, pressed them on expensive lightweights, unbreakable vinylite compound and then had our limited employee force drive around and distribute each personally. It was a service that created a sensation. We made the jock a Big Man, an Important Guy, VIP in the industry."[9]

The same year that Capitol went into operation and became the first record company to send records to deejays free of charge, James C. Petrillo, president of the AFM, stepped up his war on "canned music." Petrillo had risen through the ranks of the Chicago local of the AFM during Prohibition. Reasoning correctly that recorded music would eventually put live musicians on radio out of work, Petrillo had tried a variety of tactics to deal with radio's use of records prior to 1942. He had begun by lobbying the Roosevelt administration to prohibit the use of records on radio. When that failed, he had forced Chicago radio stations to employ union musicians to operate turntables. As neither the musicians nor the record companies received royalties from record broadcasts, Petrillo had also convinced record manufacturers to join forces with the AFM to print on record labels a warning against airing commercial discs.[10]

Two things helped Petrillo in the early days of his struggle. First, there had built up over the years a tacit assumption, fed by the FCC, that "live" programming was somehow more in the public interest than "canned" shows. Second (and possibly aided by this assumption), there had been a number of court decisions in the late 1930s that had prohibited radio from airing records. In 1940, however, a lower court decision restraining WNEW from broadcasting Paul Whiteman's records was reversed on appeal. Judge Learned Hand opined that "the common-law property of orchestra leader and corporation manufacturing phonograph records ended with sale of record, so that radio broadcasting company could not be restrained from using records in broadcasts."[11]

It is not surprising that the musicians held out for as long as they did in their struggle to preserve radio as a live performance medium. Radio provided steady work at a time when the vast bulk of most musicians' income came from live performances.

Not one to get overly bogged down in constraining legalities or past alliances, in 1942 Petrillo turned his wrath on the record companies, the ultimate source of the problem, rather than radio, the immediate offender. If no records were produced, Petrillo reasoned, recorded music could not be broadcast. He then warned the record companies that unless they could prevent radio stations and jukebox operators from playing records, his organization would strike the recording studios, a strategy intended to hurt record production and, at the same time, keep musicians working on radio. When the record companies were unable to comply, Petrillo ordered a ban on recording. No musicians were to enter recording studios in Canada or the United States until the AFM's demands were met.

Having anticipated the strike, the record companies had stockpiled unreleased masters.[12] As a result, they finished the year in reasonably good shape, but the musicians lost millions of dollars. As the demand for new releases far outstripped the supply, however, the musicians prevailed. Decca, which had been severed from its British parent, capitulated after thirteen months, but Victor and Columbia, expecting the government to intervene as it had in the ASCAP-BMI controversy, held out for about two years. The strike ended only when the record companies agreed to pay a royalty on record sales. The royalty was used to finance a performance trust fund for out-of-work musicians. If Petrillo couldn't get radio to stop playing records, at least he could make somebody pay for the privilege. By 1950, when WINS in New York announced, over the objections of the AFM, that from now on it would program records exclusively, the era of live music network radio and the formality of its tuxedoed orchestras had clearly come to an end.

It is not surprising that the musicians held out for as long as they did in their struggle to preserve radio as a live performance medium. Radio provided steady work at a time when the vast bulk of most musicians' income came from live performances. Of course, at the time, live music on radio meant live music performed by white musicians for the most part, which the AFM did not seem to find unusual. Indeed, the AFM itself failed to extend its protection to all musicians equally. In 1944, as Arnold Shaw has pointed out, the "NAACP noted that of 673 locals, 32 were 'colored.' Of the remaining 641 'white' locals, 8 had segregated subsidiary branches while many simply excluded Negro members . . . only 2 locals, those in Detroit and New York, admitted Negroes to full membership."[13]

Another group of musicians that remained outside the purview of the strike were the vocalists. The vocalists were covered by a different union—currently called the American Federation of Television and Radio Artists (AFTRA)—and AFTRA didn't join the strike. Throughout the strike, vocalists continued to record but a cappella. By the time the musicians returned to the studios, the vocalists were in charge. Although the AFM strike probably was not a causal factor, it did mark something of a turning point in the rise of the solo vocalist and the decline of the big bands.

From Big Bands to Solo Singers

As swing music (a danceable amalgam of blues, jazz, and Tin Pan Alley pop) grew in popularity in the mid-1930s, nearly all the big bands had performed, sometimes grudgingly, with vocalists. Dance music was considered to be primarily an instrumental music. Vocalists were paid less than other members of the band and were often limited to one chorus of a tune. In fact, they were sometimes used simply to give instrumental soloists a rest. Audiences, however, enjoyed the vocal numbers, and the singers eventually became popular enough to begin solo careers. Bing Crosby ("Der Bingle," as the German soldiers in World War II called him), of course, had already established himself as the most successful vocalist of the era, totaling more than 300 hits between 1931 and 1954.

Others used their big band experience to launch careers that followed similar—if less spectacular—trajectories. Many were women. Mildred Bailey predated Crosby as a vocalist with the Whiteman band. Ella Fitzgerald started her career with Chick Webb; "A-Tisket A-Tasket" (1938) made her a pop star. Peggy Lee sang with Benny Goodman and Duke Ellington and then moved into songwriting and acting. Beginning as a country singer, Kay Starr launched a solo pop career after a stint with Charlie Barnet. Jo Stafford began with Tommy Dorsey and went on to record numerous pop hits that included folk and country material. Anita O'Day graduated from the Max Miller combo to the Gene Krupa and Stan Kenton bands and then to solo stardom.

The first pop vocalist to engender hysteria among his fans (rather than simple admiration or adoration) was an Italian American who refused to anglicize his name—Frank Sinatra, the "Sultan of Swoon." A song stylist with an unmistakable baritone, Sinatra won the *Major Bowes Amateur Hour* with the Hoboken Four in 1935 and then toured with Bowes for two years. He was even filmed performing in blackface. In 1939, an appearance on WNEW's *Dance Parade* led to engagements with the Harry James and the Tommy Dorsey bands. According to pop legend, his 1942 appearance at the Paramount theater with Benny Goodman uncorked a veritable teen frenzy. At his return engagement two years later, 25,000 screaming bobby-soxers blocked the street in what was referred to as the "Columbus Day Riot." From 1943 to 1945, Sinatra was the top vocalist on NBC's *Your Hit Parade.*

Sinatra was also unique among the pop vocalists of the day in that he was socially engaged. He supported Roosevelt for president and spoke out against racial and religious intolerance. He even excised the word *darky* from his recording of Jerome Kern's and Oscar Hammerstein's "Ol' Man River." In the late 1940s, when he was accused of having both communist and Mafia ties, his career faltered but it was revitalized by his Oscar-winning performance as Maggio in the 1954 film *From Here to Eternity*, a role he allegedly landed through Mafia influence. In the 1950s, Sinatra became a vicious opponent of rock 'n' roll. After that, his political leanings tended to take on the character of whoever occupied the White House.

*F*rank Sinatra's early success marked the transition from big bands fronted by singers to vocalists backed up by big bands.

Sinatra's early success is perhaps the strongest indicator of the ascendancy of the solo vocalist. His buy-out of his contract with Tommy Dorsey in 1942, the same year as the AFM strike, marked the transition from big bands fronted by singers to vocalists backed up by big bands. As rock 'n' roll historian Charlie Gillett has noted, "Records by the big bands dominated the best selling lists in 1937 to 1941. During this period band recordings accounted for twenty-nine of the forty-three records that sold over a million copies each."[14] With the rise of the vocalists, however, the pop market was taken over by such figures as Bing Crosby ("Swingin' on a Star"), Dinah Shore ("I'll Walk Alone," "Anniversary Song," "Buttons and Bows"), and Vaughn Monroe ("Rum and Coca Cola," "Let it Snow, Let it Snow, Let it Snow").

Although there were a number of pop-sounding black vocal acts that scored major hits in the pop market in the postwar 1940s—Nat "King" Cole ("For Sentimental Reasons"), Ella Fitzgerald ("My Happiness"), the Mills Brothers ("Across the Valley from the Alamo"), and the Ink Spots ("The Gypsy")—the period was dominated by Italian American men. In addition to Sinatra, there was Perry Como ("Long Ago and Far Away"), Frankie Laine ("That's My Desire," "That Lucky Old Sun," "Mule Train"), Vic Damone ("I Have but One Heart," "Again," "You're Breaking My Heart"), and later Tony Bennett ("Because of You," "Cold, Cold Heart," "Rags to Riches," "Stranger in Paradise"), Dean Martin ("That's Amore"), and Al Martino ("Here in My Heart").[15] The rich tradition of heart-wrenching emotionality that had long been part of Italian popular song seemed to be quite well suited to American popular styles in the 1940s and 1950s.

If the rise of the solo vocalist pushed the big bands into the background, postwar culture dealt them their death blow. At the end of World War II, initiatives in the mainstream culture encouraged women to leave the jobs they had taken and return to their homes. Visions of domestic bliss and fear of nuclear war forced a middle-class retreat from the frantic energy of swing. It was no longer feasible to support the elaborate production of twenty-piece orchestras as a regular attraction. Ballrooms disappeared, and unable to find steady work, the big bands gradually broke up. By 1947, the big bands were almost gone. As Ian Whitcomb has written,

> [Glenn] Miller died in a wartime plane crash, but Herman, James, and Dorsey had folded their original bands in late 1946, together with Benny Goodman and many others. The straighter, less jazzy bands like Lawrence Welk's and Guy Lombardo's survived (for a specialist and aging public) but the Big Band Era, just over a decade, was finished.[16]

The African American jazz innovators, who had provided much of the impetus for the big band sound, were often conspicuous by their absence. While the better known black bands, Count Basie's and Duke Ellington's, for example, could count on an occasional hit record, such as Basie's recording of "Open the Door, Richard" for Victor, which was a best-seller in 1947, it was clear the big band era had ended. Between 1947 and 1949, sales dropped more than $50 million, which represented more than 20 percent of the dollar volume of the industry. With the passing of the big bands, there was something of a void in popular music, and it was rhythm and blues and, to a lesser extent, country and western that stepped into the breach.

The Major Labels Reclaim Country Music

The population migrations that had begun in the military buildup that had preceded World War II had opened the possibility of nationwide markets for specialty music. These markets had not existed prior to the war, and during the war, the major record companies were unable to exploit them because shellac and vinylite shortages significantly affected the number of records that could be manufactured. Shellac, which was imported from India and was the principal ingredient used in making 78 rpm records, became almost impossible to obtain during the Pacific blockade. Vinylite, a superior material that the record companies had begun using more recently, was rationed because it was used for waterproofing raincoats and other war materials. At the height of the shortage, in order to buy a new record it was often necessary to return an old one so that it could be recycled. Since the mainstream audience alone was capable of absorbing almost all the records that could be manufactured, the major companies concentrated their efforts in the mainstream market. The specialty fields, country to some extent but especially blues, jazz, and gospel, bore the brunt of the cutbacks.

Although the shellac and vinylite shortages had seriously limited the supply of specialty music, cross-cultural contact had, if anything, increased the demand for it. After the war and with the death of the big band era, the major labels tried to rebuild their control over the specialty fields. Naturally, the prospect of national markets for regional music titillated company executives who were concerned about their declining bottom lines. In the context of postwar affluence, however, the categories "race" and "hillbilly" seemed inappropriate, if not downright offensive. Many performers had come to resent being categorized in such demeaning terms. In 1949, "rhythm and blues" became the official designation for what was once called "race music." A few years earlier, the industry had begun to use the designation "country and western" or "country" for what was once called "hillbilly."

In the country and western category, the strategies of the major companies for reclaiming the market proved to be remarkably effective, albeit somewhat dispiriting when viewed today. According to Gillett,

> the companies responded by heavily promoting various songs performed in versions of country and western styles. One tactic was to promote the strong southern accent of most country and western singers as a "novelty," as Capitol did successfully with Tex Williams' "Smoke That Cigarette" in 1947, and as Columbia did for several years with various Gene Autry songs, including "Rudolph, the Red-Nosed Reindeer" (1950). Alternatively, the country and western songs that were closest to the melodramatic or sentimental modes of conventional popular songs were promoted as popular songs—or, more frequently, recorded by popular singers in a style that was halfway between country and pop. [17]

Frankie Laine's "Mule Train" and "High Noon" are good examples of this latter strategy. Because of the effectiveness of their marketing, country and western music was soon firmly back in the hands of the major companies. The one exception to this rule was King Records in Cincinnati, Ohio, which boasted a strong roster of country and western artists like Cowboy Copas, Hawkshaw Hawkins, and Moon Mullican, who, as we shall see, came into regular contact with rhythm and blues and were heavily influenced by the western end of the country music spectrum.

The entry of two new major companies into the music industry during this period contributed to the major companies' firm hold on country and western music. The first entry was MGM Records, which was formed in Hollywood in 1946 as an outlet for the film company's movie soundtracks but soon expanded into other kinds of music. The second entry was Mercury, which began in Chicago in 1947. Founded as a specialty label that focused primarily on polka and rhythm and blues, Mercury operated with the flair of an independent. Only its ownership of a pressing plant and its own distribution system

In the context of postwar affluence, the categories "race" and "hillbilly" seemed inappropriate, if not downright offensive.

A veteran of life on the road, Hank Williams continued along the path pioneered by Jimmie Rodgers. His honky tonk swagger brought country music one step closer to rockabilly.

defined it as a major label. In 1947, the company signed Frankie Laine, who scored two hits that were million sellers for the company, "Mule Train" (1949) and "Cry of the Wild Goose" (1950). Both recordings were in the ersatz country mold. It was, however, MGM that picked up Hank Williams, the biggest country and western star since Jimmie Rodgers.

Williams had begun his singing career at the age of thirteen on KSFA in Montgomery, Alabama. Working in roadhouses and honky tonks for years, he registered his original compositions with Acuff-Rose in Nashville. He first recorded for the independent Sterling label in 1946 but in 1947, switched to MGM. Between 1949 and 1953, the year he died, Williams recorded eleven songs for MGM that sold more than 1 million copies each. Fred Rose also "plugged" Williams' songs to pop producers, and numerous popular artists recorded the tunes as pop country hits, including Frankie Laine, who recorded "Your Cheatin' Heart" and "Tonight We're Settin' the Woods on Fire" as solo vocals and "Hey Good Lookin'" as a duet with Jo Stafford. Stafford did a solo version of "Jambalaya" herself, and Tony Bennett recorded "There'll Be No Teardrops Tonight" and reached first place on the pop chart with "Cold, Cold Heart." Guy Mitchell did "I Can't Help It," and Rosemary Clooney scored with "Half as Much."

Altogether, Williams, who credited as his inspiration a black street singer nicknamed Tee Tot (Rufe Payne), penned about 125 songs. His honest, straightforward lyrics and catchy, well-crafted tunes lent his music to a variety of interpretations and established him as something of a folk poet. Although his producers tended to tone him down on record, his honky-tonk swagger, working-class sympathies, use of "backbeat" (accents on the second and fourth beats of a measure), and hot live performances make him one link in the musical chain that joins Jimmie Rodgers, Texas hillbillies like Bob Wills and Ernest Tubb, and Elvis Presley. Like Rodgers before him, Williams was inducted into the Rock 'n' Roll Hall of Fame as an "early influence" in 1987.

The Independents Promote Rhythm and Blues

While the major labels were able to bring country and western music firmly under their sway, the African American music market proved much more difficult for them to capture. During the big band era, the majors had contented themselves with connections to the most prominent black innovators of the big band sound and had lost touch with other developments in the rich and constantly evolving African American culture. A number of African American musicians were now developing styles that were closer to the blues. As the swing era declined, the music that came to the fore in working-class black communities was rhythm and blues (r&b) described by Amiri Baraka [Leroi Jones] as "huge rhythm units smashing away behind screaming blues singers."[18] Unlike country and western, which the major record companies found could be rather easily domesticated for popular consumption, r&b was viewed as unsuitable for the mainstream because of its insistent rhythms and suggestive content. It was, however, a sound that would soon transform the very concept of popular music.

> Unlike country and western, which the major record companies found could be rather easily domesticated for popular consumption, r&b was viewed as unsuitable for the mainstream because of its insistent rhythms and suggestive content. It was, however, a sound that would soon transform the very concept of popular music.

If there is one artist who signifies the transition from the controlled energy and smooth delivery of the big bands to the unbridled emotion that characterizes rhythm and blues, it is Louis Jordan. Signed to Decca in 1939, Jordan and his group, the Tympani Five (actually seven members), anticipated the decline of the big bands and helped to define the instrumentation for the r&b combos that followed. With a much smaller horn section, rhythm became more pronounced. While Jordan's material was composed and arranged, selections like "Saturday Night Fishfry," "Honey Chile," and "Ain't Nobody Here But Us Chickens" evoked blues images that were not found in most black pop. "Chickens," for example, told the story of a farmer duped by a fox in his henhouse. "Those lyrics," according to George Lipsitz, "had their origins in the culture of . . . slavery. African legends about 'trickster-hero buffoons' provided the basis for slave stories in which animals or lesser gods outwitted stronger opponents."[19] At the same time, Jordan's performances were incredibly engaging, a factor that measurably increased his mainstream acceptance.

Between 1944 and 1949, Jordan furnished Decca with nineteen pop hits. His "G. I. Jive," backed with "Is You Is or Is You Ain't My Baby?" (1944), sold 1 million copies, as did "Choo Cho Ch'Boogie" (1946). The shuffle boogie beat that he used is one of the elements that followed r&b into rock 'n' roll. While, at the time, Jordan's music was described as "jumpin' the blues," he was not alone. Most of the r&b artists of the late 1940s screeched, honked, and shouted with themes that were often too raw for the

mainstream market and thus for the major record companies. Still, the raucous sounds of such artists as Wynonie Harris ("Good Rockin' Tonight"), John Lee Hooker ("Boogie Chillen"), Eddie "Cleanhead" Vinson ("I'm Weak but I'm Willing"), Bullmoose Jackson ("I Want a Bow-Legged Woman"), Joe Liggins and the Honeydrippers ("Honeydripper"), saxophonist Big Jay McNeely ("Deacon's Hop"), drummer Roy Milton ("The Hucklebuck"), and pianist Amos Milburn ("Bad, Bad Whiskey") were a harbinger of sounds to come.

The success of these artists speaks to what Nelson George has referred to as "an aesthetic schism between high-brow, more assimilated black styles and working-class, grassroots sounds" that had existed in the black community for a long time.[20] A number of writers, notably Baraka [Jones], have written at length about class differences between jazz and blues. While jazz was an immensely popular and influential crossover music that introduced elements of the African American tradition into the mainstream, in some ways, it was also a product of the black middle class. Many of its most notable practitioners—Duke Ellington, Coleman Hawkins, and Fletcher Henderson, among others—were college-educated. By the 1930s, jazz was a music that had "moved away from the older *lowdown* forms of blues, . . . [It was] a music that still relied on older Afro-American musical tradition, but one that had begun to utilize still greater amounts of popular American music as well as certain formal European traditions."[21]

The pioneer r&b artists of the 1940s were still close to their blues roots. While they often retained some semblance of the big band sound, their initial popularity in the black community in many ways represented a resuscitation of the blues, or race, market of the 1920s and 1930s. "While the term 'jazz' gave Whiteman equal weight with Ellington, and Bix Beiderbecke comparable standing with Louis Armstrong," George has written, "the term 'race' was applied to forms of black music—primarily blues—that whites and . . . the black elite disdained."[22] In the glow of postwar affluence, the African American working class imposed its tastes on black popular music and the results were electrifying (and electrified).

Suddenly it was as if a great deal of the Euro-American humanist facade Afro-American music had taken on had been washed away by the war. Rhythm & blues singers literally had to shout to be heard above the clanging and strumming of the various electrified instruments and the churning rhythm sections. And somehow the louder the instrumental accompaniment and the more harshly screamed the singing, the more expressive the music was.[23]

Since r&b did not readily lend itself to the bland pop vocal or ersatz country and western production styles of the major labels, company executives decided to ignore the burgeoning African American market. This made it possible for a large number of independent labels to enter the business. For the most part, these labels were hampered by a shortage of materials, a lack of funds, and inadequate distribution systems. Yet, they persevered and new independents came into the business because profits were

substantial when a hit was produced. Modern, a Los Angeles-based company founded in 1945, was able to sell its blues singles for $1.05 in the late 1940s, while the major companies were getting only 78¢ for their pop singles. The most successful of the independent labels that survived the 1940s, particularly those with r&b experience, gained a foothold in the industry that would not be dislodged.

By the early 1950s, more than 100 independent labels were still in operation. The most important of these companies were: Aladdin, Modern, Specialty, and Imperial, which were based in Los Angeles; Atlantic, based in New York; Savoy, based in Newark, New Jersey; King, based in Cincinnati, Ohio; Chess, based in Chicago; and black-owned Duke/Peacock, which was based in Houston. While some of these companies, most notably King, produced country and western music, all of them produced r&b. It was these independent companies along with other important independents founded later (Herald/Ember and a dozen or so other labels in New York, black-owned Vee Jay in Chicago, and Sun in Memphis) that produced r&b first for the black community and, with the aid of jukeboxes and independent deejays, brought the music to the attention of a national audience. Indeed, these few companies produced the bulk of the repertoire that constituted the foundation of rock 'n' roll. Perhaps the best indication of their success in popularizing r&b can be seen in *Billboard*'s 1949 decision to drop the term "race music" in favor of the more descriptive term "rhythm and blues."

King records in Cincinnati could be distinguished from the other independent labels in its ability to produce rhythm and blues and country and western with equal success. No doubt, the particular character of the city, which offered significant outlets for blues, jazz, and country music, contributed measurably to King's good fortune. As early as 1937, Cincinnati's radio station WLW had offered a series of country barn dance programs, which had evolved into the *Midwestern Hayride* by the mid-1940s. The city was also home to WCKY, a 50,000 watt clear channel, that devoted a significant amount of airtime to country music. While African Americans had less access to the airwaves in

Cincinnati than others—Fats Waller's WLW broadcasts in 1932 stand out as a notable exception—the entertainment needs of the city's sizable black population were addressed in live music venues, especially the Cotton Club, which featured the territory bands and jump blues combos that became popular in the late 1940s. The bands of Lucky Millinder, Todd Rhodes, and Tiny Bradshaw were among those that toured the region regularly.

The man who brought the city's divergent musical tendencies together under one recording roof was Syd Nathan. In 1945, Nathan left the department store business to start King Records. From the beginning, he was eclectic in his musical acquisitions and astute, if ruthless, in his business decisions. From WLW's *Midwestern Hayride*, Nathan signed the Delmores, Grandpa Jones, and Hank Penny, as well as the next generation of country singers, including Cowboy Copas, Moon Mullican, Hawkshaw Hawkins, and Wayne Raney. Mullican was a pioneer of country boogie who was known as the "King of the Hillbilly Piano Players." His influence on early rock 'n' roll can be heard in the piano playing of Jerry Lee Lewis and others. At the Cotton Club, Nathan met Lucky Millinder and, knowing that Millinder was under contract to Decca, signed his lead vocalist, Bullmoose Jackson, as a solo artist. At the same time, Nathan hired Millinder's arranger, Henry Glover, as a writer/producer. He also signed the Rhodes and Bradshaw ensembles, as well as vocalist Wynonie Harris, another alumnus of the Millinder band.

Initially, most of the King Record's r&b artists were issued on the Queen label, a subsidiary Nathan had established to separate r&b releases from country releases. There was, however, an innovative wrinkle to this separation that added measurably to the company's profit margin. Nathan, largely for reasons of economic self-interest, encouraged his black and white artists to record each other's material. King was perhaps the only independent record company that had equally strong rosters of r&b and c&w artists. As Henry Glover once told Arnold Shaw:

> King Records was covering R&B with country singers almost from the beginning of my work with Syd Nathan. . . . We were more successful in doing the reverse—covering C&W hits with R&B singers. In '49 . . . Bullmoose Jackson's hit "Why Don't You Haul Off and Love Me" was a cover of a Wayne Raney country hit. And Wynonie Harris' "Bloodshot Eyes"— on R&B charts in '51—was originally a Hank Penny country record . . . when a song happened in one field, Syd Nathan wanted it moved into the other.
>
> You see it was a matter of Cincinnati's population. You couldn't sell Wynonie Harris to country folk, and black folk weren't buying Hank Penny. But black folk might buy Wynonie Harris doing a country tune. And since Syd published most of the tunes we recorded, he was also augmenting his publishing income and building important copyrights. He was a smart businessman and he didn't miss a trick.[24]

Nathan's primary motivation may have been more monetary than artistic, but his action produced a far greater cultural mix than might otherwise have been the case. As Bill Malone has noted, his "encouragement was no doubt instrumental in the decision made by such King artists as the Delmore Brothers and Moon Mullican to record their classic boogie tunes in the early fifties."[25] Of course, the key to the company's success in these crossover ventures was the free hand that Nathan gave Henry Glover in recording both r&b and c&w acts. No producer spanned the two fields more successfully than

The fact that Henry Glover wrote and/or produced many of King's r&b hits marked him as successful. The fact that he consciously sought out country artists with whom to accomplish the same success moves him closer to the status of legendary.

Glover. It was Glover, for example, who produced the r&b and c&w versions of "Why Don't You Haul Off and Love Me." The fact that Glover wrote and/or produced many of King's r&b hits marked him as successful. The fact that he consciously sought out country artists with whom to accomplish the same success moves him closer to the status of legendary. Under Glover's musical direction, the King empire not only maintained a foothold in country music, but became one of the premiere r&b labels as well.

Chess records in Chicago was another instance where the collaboration between Jewish businessmen and black producers was a winning combination. Chess was launched in 1949 by Leonard and Phil Chess, two Jewish immigrants from Poland who had settled in Chicago in 1928. In the 1940s, the Chess brothers owned and operated the Macomba, a night club that presented at one time or another such talent as Louis Armstrong, Lionel Hampton, Billy Eckstine, and Ella Fitzgerald. Struck by the lack of adequate recording facilities in Chicago, the brothers bought into Aristocrat Records in 1947. In 1949, they took over the label and changed its name to Chess, eventually establishing three subsidiaries, Checker, Cadet, and Argo. With a small studio in the back room of its storefront record company, Chess was the quintessential shoestring operation, even distributing records from the trunks of the owners' cars. The lack of financing was reflected in the company's recording technique. "To add echo," Arnold Shaw has written, "inventive Leonard Chess hung an open microphone in their tiny toilet. . . . For tape echo effects and distortion, they suspended a ten-foot section of sewer pipe from the ceiling of their so-called studio."[26] Even with such modest equipment, Chess Records managed to turn out some of the most significant of urban blues recordings and to become later one of the most important rock 'n' roll labels in the country.

One key to Chess' success was the presence of Willie Dixon, a Mississippi native who had been associated with the label as a singer, composer, bassist, talent scout, and producer since its days as Aristocrat. Leonard Chess thought of Dixon as "his right arm." Among the 200 or so songs written by Dixon were "Hoochie Coochie Man," "I Just Want to Make Love to You," "Little Red Rooster," and "Seventh Son." He also contributed in other capacities to any number of hits by Chess artists, including Muddy Waters and Howlin' Wolf.

Delta-born Muddy Waters (nee McKinley Morganfield) was one of Chess' earliest discoveries. A master of slide guitar, Waters had been recorded for the Library of Congress by the Lomaxes before he left Mississippi for good in 1943. After settling in Chicago, he switched to electric guitar in order to compete with the sounds of the city.

Chess records offers Chicago blues style to rock 'n' roll

In the mid-1940s, he was presented by Big Bill Broonzy at Sylvio's. This appearance led to recordings produced by Mayo Williams at OKeh, but these were never released. Waters then switched to Aristocrat, recording, among other songs, "I Can't Be Satisfied" and "I Feel Like Goin' Home." When the Chess brothers formed Chess Records, Waters followed them, recording one of his first hits, the immortal "Rolling Stone." Subsequent recordings included "Got My Mojo Working" (1957) and "Baby Please Don't Go" (1958). Most of the next generation of Chicago blues musicians, including Buddy Guy, Junior Wells, and James Cotton, passed through Waters' band at one time or another. He was also a major inspiration for the white blues revival of the 1960s, which featured such artists as Paul Butterfield, Nick Gravenites, and Mike Bloomfield, who had heard him play at Smitty's Corner in the 1950s. When the Rolling Stones took their name from Waters' early Chess hit, he remarked: "They stole my music, but they gave me my name."[27]

Perhaps the most important of all the new independents was Atlantic Records, which was founded in 1947 by Ahmet Ertegun, the son of a prominent Turkish diplomat, and Herb Abramson, the former recording director for National Records, in Ertegun's one-bedroom Manhattan apartment. Abramson was drafted into the army in 1953 and some time later sold his interest in the company. Jerry Wexler, an r&b reviewer for *Billboard,* picked up where Abramson had left off and went on to become head of artist and repertoire for the company. In 1956, Ertegun's brother, Nesuhi, set up what would become a distinguished jazz division. Both brothers were avid jazz and blues collectors, who had some 30,000 records in their private collection. Perhaps their own privileged position and their love of the music gave them an advantage over some of the other entrepreneurs who entered the business solely as a commercial gambit for the Erteguns attracted outstanding talent, and Ahmet, in particular, enjoyed a reputation for honesty and integrity, particularly in his treatment of black artists, that was unmatched in the business.

After a few inconsequential releases, the fledgling company hit r&b pay dirt in 1949 with Sticks McGhee's "Drinkin' Wine Spo-dee-o-dee." The company's first star was

Ruth Brown began singing in the church. The lure of rhythm and blues, however, led her to Atlantic Records where she became the fledgling label's first big star. Although Atlantic was among the most reputable companies and Brown had a decent contract, years later she sued the label for back royalties and won.

Joe Turner's repertoire was clearly the stuff that rock 'n' roll was made of. By the time the phenomenon took hold, however, he had little inclination to break out of the comfortable r&b niche he already occupied.

Ruth Brown. After her debut release, "So Long," in 1949, which was a Top Ten hit, Brown turned out ten more Top Ten r&b hits over the next five years, including "Teardrops From My Eyes" (1950), "5-10-15 Hours" (1952), "Mama, He Treats Your Daughter Mean" (1953), and "Oh, What a Dream" (1954). She was rewarded for these efforts with a contract that guaranteed her $100,000 over five years. For a time, Atlantic was even nicknamed "the house that Ruth built." Big Joe Turner, perhaps the most celebrated of the blues shouters, was offered a contract in 1950. He also turned out a series of blockbuster r&b hits—"Chains of Love" (1951), "Sweet Sixteen" (1952), and "Honey Hush" (1953). By the early 1950s, Atlantic was the most important r&b label in the country and had a talent roster that included LaVern Baker, Ray Charles, the Clovers, and the Drifters, among others. By 1954, Atlantic's releases began to cross over to the pop charts. Such hits as "Sh-Boom" by the Chords, LaVern Baker's "Tra La La," "Tweedlee Dee," and "Jim Dandy," Joe Turner's "Shake, Rattle, and Roll," and Ruth Brown's "Lucky Lips" made an imprint on rock 'n' roll that was unmistakable.

High Fidelity/Low Overhead

If the abandonment of the specialty fields by the major labels allowed independent labels to enter the business, a number of technological advances helped them to survive after entry. The first of these was magnetic tape, an innovation that was "liberated" from the Nazis during World War II. Although the principle of magnetic recording had been known in the late 1800s, it was the Germans who had perfected it. The German magnetophone used plastic tape that was coated with iron oxide, which could be magnetized by amplified electrical impulses to encode a signal on the material. Playback simply reversed the process. Aside from the obvious technical advantages of editing, splicing, and

better sound reproduction, magnetic tape recording was more durable, more portable, and less expensive than the existing technologies. In the United States, the Minnesota Mining and Manufacturing Company (3M) came up with a tape, which the company marketed under its Scotch tape trademark, that surpassed the sound quality of the German product. At the same time, tape recorder manufacturers reduced recording speeds from thirty inches-per-second (ips) to fifteen ips and then to 7.5 ips without seriously compromising sound qual-ity, thus quadrupling the amount of material that

> **W**ith the advent of portable radios, teenagers, who would soon become an identifiable consumer group, could explore their developing musical tastes in complete privacy.

could be recorded on a standard tape. The advantages of tape were immediately apparent to recording companies and radio stations, and they invested in the technology as soon as it became available.

The transistor, introduced by Bell Laboratories in 1948, was a welcome companion to the new recording technology. The transistor was capable of performing all the functions of the vacuum tube but could do so in a solid environment. For this reason, it could be made smaller, required less power, and was more durable than the vacuum tube, which it soon replaced. With the birth of the transistor came the possibility of miniaturizing the cumbersome tube amplifiers that were essential to electronic record-ing. Smaller, more affordable, longer-lasting recording equipment encouraged decentral-ization in the recording field, which again aided independent production. Indeed, the transistor made truly portable radio receivers possible for the first time. With the advent of portable radios, teenagers, who would soon become an identifiable consumer group, could explore their developing musical tastes in complete privacy.

In the same year that the transistor was unveiled, a team of scientists, who were working at CBS's laboratories under the leadership of Dr. Peter Goldmark and William Bachman, invented high fidelity. This breakthrough, which developed out of their inter-est in classical music, yielded the microgroove, or long-playing, 33 rpm record (the LP), which increased the number of grooves per inch on a standard record from 85 to 300. Years later, Goldmark described the challenge the creation of the LP had presented to the group:

> *First of all, to provide more playing time, it was necessary to change the number of grooves— which then necessitated changing the speed—which, in turn, required offsetting the resulting distortion—which then required offsetting the limitation of frequency response which would have occurred. . . . So we had to change the radius of the stylus. We went from sapphire to diamond. But, in order for the tiny radii not to chew up the record, we had to reduce the pres-sure. . . . Then you had wonderful sound quality, but you didn't have a microphone capable of creating wonderful sounds. . . . We . . . had to . . . develop a new kind of microphone, which turned out to be the condenser microphone . . . [that] the Germans already had invented.*[28]

"In other words," Goldmark concluded, "we had to develop a whole new science."[29]

Technological advances encourage independent production

Shortly after the development of the LP, Columbia's Ted Wallerstein demonstrated its superiority to David Sarnoff and a few other RCA executives in the hope of making it the new industry standard. When the demonstration record played for twenty-three minutes without stopping, the RCA executives realized that Columbia had pulled off a coup of major proportions. Sarnoff, as was his wont, responded with polite approval and promptly directed his technical staff to come up with a similar record that played at a different speed. In what was to become known as the "battle of the speeds"—a battle that pitted Columbia's LP against RCA's newly developed 45—the two firms produced vinylite discs with excellent sound quality and maximum durability. The size of the 45 caught the fancy of jukebox manufacturers and soon became the preferred configuration for singles while the LP became the industry standard for albums. Both 45s and LPs were lighter and less breakable than the shellac-based 78s. Thus, they could be shipped faster and more cheaply than the 78s, which made them well suited to the rapidly changing pop market.

As a result of these technological advances, records emerged as a relatively inexpensive medium when compared to radio, film, and television, which were capital intensive industries that required huge sums of money for the production of a product, elaborate systems for transmission, and/or complex bureaucratic interactions for such things as frequency assignments on the electromagnetic spectrum. It was in part for this

In 1952, records finally surpassed sheet music as a source of revenue in the music industry. At about the same time, radio established its primacy over the jukebox as the number one hit maker.

reason that small independent labels were able to challenge the few giant corporations that had monopolized the music business. Records soon became the staple of all radio programming and the dominant product of the music industry as a whole. Indeed, in 1952, records finally surpassed sheet music as a source of revenue in the music industry. At about the same time, radio established its primacy over the jukebox as the number one hit maker.

Television and the Suppression of FM Broadcasting

It was, ironically, the development of television that opened the door to independent radio (and thus r&b) in the late 1940s by deliberately, if temporarily, sidelining a technological innovation that would have increased the quality of radio transmission measurably—FM broadcasting. Messages can be sent over the airwaves either by modulating, or varying, their amplitude, or size, or by modulating their frequency, or rate of propagation. Because early technical limitations favored the development of amplitude modulation (AM), it was AM radio that was designated standard broadcasting in the United

States. Although it was clear that frequency modulation (FM) broadcasting had certain advantages over AM broadcasting, its entry into the marketplace was intentionally suppressed because it conflicted with the development of television.[30]

Interference from either natural or man-made static or from stations on the same or adjacent frequencies had always been a major problem in broadcasting. Indeed, it had driven David Sarnoff to wish out loud that someone would come up with "a little black box to eliminate [radio] static."[31] Intrigued by the wish, inventor Edwin H. Armstrong, already the recipient of $1 million from RCA for the sale of his superheterodyne radio receiver, retired to his laboratory at Columbia University in 1923 to work on the project. He emerged ten years later with a whole new patented transmission system that utilized an FM signal in the very-high-frequency (VHF) range of the electromagnetic spectrum. Sarnoff was so impressed with the system that he moved Armstrong's operation to the RCA facilities atop the Empire State Building.

In 1935, however, Sarnoff reneged on his commitment to Armstrong's invention. Both television and FM transmission operated best in the VHF range, and Sarnoff, understanding even then that television would one day replace radio as the primary entertainment fixture in the home, made the decision to back the visual medium. Within days of evicting Armstrong, Sarnoff and RCA announced a $1 million research initiative aimed at developing television. Realizing that the development of FM would conflict with the development of television, Sarnoff saw it as necessary to sever his ties to his friend Armstrong. The decision was not personal, just business. Although a series of patent wars, regulatory struggles over frequency assignments, and the imperatives of wartime production would slow the advent of television, the ubiquitous Sarnoff and RCA would be there when it arrived after World War II.

Meanwhile, Armstrong continued with the development of FM and, in 1936, approached the FCC with a plan for allocating spectrum space in the VHF range to his FM radio system. At the same hearing, Sarnoff presented plans for reserving the entire VHF band for television. C. B. Jolliffe, who only weeks earlier had been a ranking FCC executive, acted as counsel to the RCA executive. Not surprisingly, the FCC did not accept Armstrong's plan, but he was given permission to build a 50,000 watt FM transmitter in Alpine, New Jersey, which went on the air in 1939. That same year Armstrong and the newly formed FM Broadcasters Association scored a small victory when the FCC assigned the frequency band that had been reserved for television Channel 1 to FM radio. (This is the reason why television receivers were initially built with no Channel 1.) The outbreak of World War II stalled the further development of television and FM, as RCA diverted its resources into the development of radar and Armstrong contributed his personal services and the use of his FM patents to the war effort.

In 1945, the FCC reassigned FM to a higher frequency band, between television Channels 6 and 7 (88 to 108 megacycles), where it now thrives. At the time, however, the ruling was devastating; it placed FM into a band for which neither transmitters nor receivers existed. Investors in FM promptly withdrew from its further development and looked to television for potentially greater profits. The 430 applications for FM licenses that were pending fell victim to bureaucratic shuffling. Furthermore, the end of the war allowed the pent-up wartime demand for new AM receivers to be assuaged, which at least temporarily satisfied the public need for radio. In the first three quarters of 1946, 6.5 million AM receivers but only 80,000 FM radios were manufactured. In suppressing FM radio to promote the development of television, Sarnoff may have insured the future of RCA's bottom line, but he stalled a medium that had significantly better sound quality, which could only have had positive implications for the transmission of music.

Television became a viable consumer item in the late 1940s. By 1951, there were nearly 16 million television sets in operation in the United States, and RCA was already showing a profit on its initial investment. The development of television was the death knell for network radio because the visual medium quickly attracted most of the national advertising that had been done on network radio. Independent radio, on the other hand, emerged as an effective medium for local advertisers, and it did so at a time when the number of radio stations in the United States had doubled from about 1,000 in 1946 to about 2,000 in 1948. Eventually the most successful independent radio outlets pushed aside the more staid network stations and cemented a reciprocal arrangement with record companies that has defined the music industry ever since: inexpensive programming in return for free promotion.

Independent Radio: Deejays in Your Face

Prior to 1948, radio had been dominated by four national networks that viewed the country as one monolithic listening audience. The prevailing marketing strategy was to create programming that could pull in as broad a slice of this total listenership as possible—hence the term "broadcasting." Such programming naturally tended to favor middle-class, family-oriented fare that was largely the same from network to network. Although a considerable amount of popular music was broadcast, it was usually performed by studio orchestras that adhered strictly to swing era conventions, which made them virtually indistinguishable from one another. With the devastation of network radio (and motion pictures) effected by the growth of television, local radio became the primary vehicle for popularizing the music that was produced by independent record companies and then licensed to BMI, which technically the broadcasters owned. This link between BMI and the broadcasters outraged ASCAP almost as much as the "vulgarity," as ASCAP viewed it, of the music in question. Those publishers associated with ASCAP tried in vain to

As national programming gave way to hundreds of locally programmed stations each appealing to its own audience, the flawless, even-toned, accent-free "radio voice" of the typical announcer soon went the way of studio orchestras.

prove that the popularity of BMI music was due to its privileged status on radio and ardently advocated a return to so-called good music. It never occurred to them that perhaps the audience liked what it was hearing.

As national programming gave way to hundreds of locally programmed stations each appealing to its own audience, the flawless, even-toned, accent-free "radio voice" of the typical announcer soon went the way of studio orchestras. Fast-talking deejays—"personality jocks" as they were called—whose stock-in-trade was their own eccentricity took over. Far from being detached, generic voices, these deejays enjoyed a personal involvement with their listeners. "We were the stars in our hometown," said deejay Diggie Doo. "We went to the churches, we went to the clubs, to the schools, the little kids knew us."[32] These deejays not only talked to their fans, they talked like their fans. From his late night slot on WOV in New York, Jocko Henderson held forth in classic jive: "Eeeee tiddilee yok. Ho, this is the Jock. I'm back on the scene with the record machine. Saying goo bop-a doo, how do you do."[33] While hardly the King's English of an earlier generation of announcers, Jocko's rhymes are often cited as one of the formative influences in rap.

As they replaced the live entertainment personalities who had dominated national radio, these independent deejays became, for a time, pivotal figures in the music industry. Record companies routinely supplied free copies of new releases to them in the hope that they could turn them into hits. Relying on their own inventiveness for popularity, independent deejays often experimented with specialty music as an antidote to the standard pop fare of network radio, and in most cases, the key to their success turned out to be r&b.

R&b radio represented a considerable departure from standard radio practices. As noted earlier, up to this point little black music had been broadcast at all, and there had been few African American announcers. As late as 1947, *Ebony* magazine had reported that out of an estimated 3,000 deejays around the country, only 16 were black.[34] Those who were deejays usually followed the example of Jack L. Cooper, an immensely successful, veteran black announcer from the 1930s who had eschewed all traces of black dialect in the pursuit of his conception of racial pride. According to Nelson George, Cooper's successors "tended to be conservative in their programming choices, leaning as heavily on Count Basie and Sarah Vaughan as on their vowels."[35] In r&b radio, however, there were black and white deejays from the start. While pay scales usually favored white announcers, the tone of r&b radio was set by a new breed of black deejays who viewed themselves as entertainers, not just announcers.

> [B]lack disk jockeys were a much more colorful group of platter-spinners than their white brethren, whose main concern seemed to be with dignity, decorum, and the King's English. Black jockeys tended to take over the manners and mannerisms of black preachers. They were showmen rather than announcers. Their job was to entertain, not just to introduce records. By the early '50s, there were quite a number who had made names for themselves on ghetto stations.[36]

At first, the South was the major center for r&b radio. Among the popular black deejays in this region were "Jockey Jack" Gibson in Atlanta, Georgia, "Professor Bop" in Shreveport and Larry McKinley and Vernon Winslow in New Orleans, Louisiana, "Sugar Daddy" in Birmingham, Alabama, "Spider" Burks in St. Louis, Missouri, Bruce Miller in Winston-Salem, North Carolina, and Nat D. Williams, "Bugs" Scruggs, Larry Dean, and George White in Memphis, Tennessee. Indeed, a number of southern r&b recording artists, Elmore James, Rufus Thomas, Sonny Boy Williamson, Howlin' Wolf, and B. B. King, among others, had careers as deejays before they became performers. B. B. King acquired his initials from his radio moniker, "the Beale Street Blues Boy." There were also white r&b deejays who modeled themselves after the "preacher-emcees," as these popular black deejays were sometimes known. There was Zenas "Daddy" Sears in Atlanta, Bob "Wolfman Jack" Smith in Shreveport and Ken Elliott and Clarence "Poppa Stoppa" Hammon in New Orleans, Bill Gordon and Dewey Phillips in Memphis, and Gene Nobles and John Richbourgh in Nashville.

By the early 1950s, a number of so-called Negro stations in the South had proven to be quite successful. In St. Louis, Spider Burks addressed himself to the city's 328,000 African Americans over station KXLW. WOKJ went out to 107,000 blacks in Jackson, Mississippi. WDIA in Memphis, "America's only 50,000 watt Negro radio station," could broadcast to nearly 10 percent of the country's 12 million African Americans. WSOK in Nashville claimed to have several black stockholders. And, in 1951, WERD in Atlanta became the first totally black-owned radio outlet in the country.

Of course, r&b radio was not limited to the South. It also flourished in those major cities of the North and West that had large concentrations of African Americans. In Los Angeles, a white deejay named Hunter Hancock had been playing jazz on station KFVD since 1943. In 1948, Hancock later recalled, a promo man from Modern records "told me that if I wanted to reach average Negroes, jazz wouldn't do it. Thank God that I had the good sense to listen to him and switched my shows to an exclusive diet of r&b disks."[37] Hancock remained among the top-rated r&b deejays in Los Angeles for twenty years. In the San Francisco Bay area, there was a black r&b deejay named Willie Mays on KSAN, and there were two white r&b jocks—"Jumpin'" George Oxford in Oakland and Phil McKernan (who sired the late Pigpen of Grateful Dead fame)—in Berkeley. In Chicago, Delta bluesman Muddy Waters held forth on WOPA before going on to record for Chess records. There was also a white r&b deejay on WOPA, Big Bill Hill, who sang the blues and sold Cadillacs in his version of highly stylized black speech: "Ah doan ca' if you got gahnashees on yo' gahnashees, ah cain p'choo in a big bread box by fo' o'clock dis aftanoon!"[38] However, Chicago's premiere r&b deejay in the late 1940s was Al Benson, "Yo' Ol' Swingmaster," an African American. At the peak of his popularity, Benson hosted five shows on a number of stations and earned as much as $100,000 a year. According to Arnold Shaw, Benson delivered his radio jive in a Jamaican accent. "Benson killed the King's English," recalled one of Benson's young Milwaukee colleagues, "and I don't know if he did it on purpose or not. Everybody had to see Al if they wanted to sell to the black market in Chicago, whether it was beer or rugs or Nu Nile hair cream. . . . He wasn't pretending to be white. He sounded black . . . and most of us were proud of the fact."[39] He made something of a nationwide, if non-musical, splash in 1956 when, as Passman has noted, "he hired two white men (because he feared violence to himself) to shower five thousand copies of the Constitution on Jackson, Mississippi, to emphasize the Supreme Court's antisegregation ruling."[40]

The Northeast also had its share of r&b deejays. There was George "Hound Dog" Lorenz in Buffalo, New York, and Danny "Cat Man" Stiles in Newark, New Jersey. "Symphony Sid" Torin moved from Boston to WMCA in New York, which was also home for Hal Jackson. New York was, of course, the center for r&b radio in the Northeast. In addition to the white deejays just mentioned, the city also had a raucous contingent of black announcer/entertainers. Willie Bryant, "the Mayor of Harlem," and Ray Carroll broadcast their program, *After Hours Swing Session,* on WHOM, a foreign-language station by day. Jack Walker, "the Pear-Shaped Talker," appeared on foreign-language outlet WOV. Joe Bostic, who started at WBNX, held down a late-night slot for his program, *Harlem Music Shop,* on WINS. Tommy Smalls broadcast from WWRL, and Phil "Dr. Jive" Gordon from WLIB.

As this list of deejays indicates, r&b proved to be popular with white as well as black audiences. Unlike dance halls, record stores, and jukeboxes, the airwaves could not be easily segregated. If white teenagers wanted to turn their radio dials to the local r&b outlet, they were free to do so, and, apparently, that is exactly what they did. The new cross-racial appetite for r&b was soon reflected in record sales. As early as 1952, Dolphin's Hollywood Record Shop, a black retail outlet in Los Angeles, reported that its business was suddenly 40 percent white. The outlet's owners attributed it to independent deejays spinning r&b records. A similar pattern was developing at Mallory's Music in New Orleans and elsewhere. It signaled an impending change in popular music tastes, a change that made Fats Domino's "The Fat Man" (1950), Jackie Brenston's "Rocket 88" (1951), Lloyd Price's "Lawdy Miss Clawdy" (1952), and Joe Turner's "Chains of Love" (1951), "Sweet Sixteen" (1952), and "Honey Hush" (1953)—all recorded for independent labels—popular among both black and white audiences.

The most famous of all the r&b deejays was a classically trained trombonist named Alan Freed, who had grown up in Ohio and in high school had fronted a jazz band called the Sultans of Swing. After short stints on a couple of local stations, Freed began his radio career in earnest in 1946 as the host of *Request Review* on WAKR in Akron, Ohio.

Unlike dance halls, record stores, and jukeboxes, the airwaves could not be easily segregated. If white teenagers wanted to turn their radio dials to the local r&b outlet, they were free to do so, and, apparently, that is exactly what they did.

Alan Freed rides r&b radio to rock 'n' roll fame

When his plans to convert the program to a television show in Cleveland failed, he became depressed, drank heavily, and vented his anger on current trends in popular music, saying that jazz had become too abstract and intellectualized to be "the people's music" and that "the run-of-the-mill, country-affected, pop-hit sound didn't do anything for him."[41] In 1951, his fortunes took a turn for the better. Leo Mintz, the owner of the Record Rendezvous Shop in Cleveland and sponsor of a radio program of the same name on WJW, invited Freed to witness firsthand the strange new pattern of white customers buying records by black artists. Mintz convinced the initially reluctant Freed to take over the *Record Rendezvous* time slot and devote the entire show to r&b. Mintz had, of course, seen the future accurately. Freed bayed like a hound over Todd Rhodes' "Blues for Moon Dog" to introduce the show that became *The Moon Dog House Rock 'n' Roll Party*. His gravelly voice (due to damaged vocal chords from having some polyps cauterized) and colorful announcing style were well suited to his new material. "He was always drunk," said WJW morning man Soupy Sales. "It was late at night, but it was alright, he could handle it."[42] In fact, Freed handled it so well that he was soon hired by WINS in New York, which he turned into the number one popular music station in the city.

Freed is often remembered as the "Father of Rock 'n' Roll." He even claimed rock 'n' roll was a term he had invented. While there is ample evidence to suggest that he was the first to use the expression on radio, the phrase had been around the African American community for years. What is beyond dispute, however, is that the trajectory of Freed's career paralleled the rise and fall of this exciting new trend in popular music almost perfectly. "Anyone who says rock 'n' roll is a passing fad or flash-in-the-pan trend along the music road," Freed once said, "has rocks in his head, Dad!"[43] How right he was. Early in 1956, *Billboard* ran a retrospective piece on popular music trends for the previous year under the headline, "1955—THE YEAR R&B TOOK OVER POP FIELD."

In the 1940s, then, all the forces that would unleash rock 'n' roll were set in motion. The smoldering tension between ASCAP and radio burst into flames and set the stage for the structural realignments that affected the very character of popular music. There were subsequent struggles between radio and the musician's union and within the radio establishment itself (between network and independent stations). The death throes of swing created a void that signaled a culture in flux. Technological advances favoring decentralization allowed small independent record companies and flamboyant local deejays to become major players in the music business. Rivalries between giant record companies and competition between major and independent labels provided the corporate backdrop for the cultural developments that led to the rise of rhythm and blues in the late 1940s and the eruption of rock 'n' roll in the early 1950s.

NOTES

1. Ian Whitcomb, *After the Ball: Pop Music from Rag to Rock* (Baltimore, MD: Penguin Books, 1974), 199.

2. Russell Sanjek, *American Popular Music and Its Business: The First Four Hundred Years, Volume III from 1900 to 1984* (New York: Oxford University Press, 1988), 176. The dramatic increase of ASCAP's revenues from 1932 to 1937 came about when eleven music publishing houses controlled by Warner Brothers and representing 20 to 40 percent of the music played on the radio returned to ASCAP's fold. Dissatisfied with their share of publishing revenues, they had decided to collect their own royalties independently and had left ASCAP in 1935. They returned August 1936, freeing up some 36,000 songs, including works by George Gershwin and Jerome Kern, which had been out of circulation since January of that year.

3. Nat Shapiro, *Popular Music: An Annotated Index of American Popular Songs: Volume 2, 1940–1949* (New York: Adrian Press, 1965), 6.

4. "ASCAP Defied," *Business Week,* 16 November 1940, 50.

5. Minna Lederman, "Music and Monopoly," *The Nation,* 28 December 1940, 656.

6. Bill C. Malone, *Country Music U.S.A.,* rev. ed. (Austin: University of Texas Press, 1985), 179.

7. Arnold Passman, *The Deejays* (New York: Macmillan, 1971), 64.

8. Sanjek, *American Popular Music,* 3: 128.

9. D. Dexter, "1935–1945, Disk Jockey: Origin of the Species," *Billboard,* 27 December 1969, 58.

10. According to the terms of the 1909 Copyright Act, only the underlying composition of a recording could be copyrighted; the recording itself could not. As a result, only writers and publishers received royalties from the broadcast of recorded music.

11. Passman, *The Deejays,* 80. Whiteman and RCA Victor had initiated the suit that led to the lower court decision.

12. Using Ralph Peer's international business connections, the companies had also attempted to record U.S. pop in Latin America, but the attempt failed. In Cuba, the language barrier prevented English-language recordings of broadcast quality. In Mexico, the progressive Mexican musicians' union refused to participate in the strikebreaking strategy.

13. Arnold Shaw, *Honkers and Shouters: The Golden Years of Rhythm and Blues* (New York: Collier Books, 1978), 124.

14. Charlie Gillett, *The Sound of the City: The Rise of Rock and Roll* (New York: Outerbridge and Dienstfrey, 1970), 3.

15. Unlike Sinatra, many Italian American performers anglicized their names. Frankie Lane began life as Frank Paul LoVecchio, Vic Damone as Vito Rocco Farinola, Tony Bennett as Anthony Dominic Benedetto, and Dean Martin as Dino Crocetti.

16. Whitcomb, *After the Ball,* 200.

17. Gillett, *The Sound of the City,* 9.

18. Leroi Jones [Amiri Baraka], *Blues People* (New York: William Morrow, 1963), 168. Rhythm and blues, of course, developed in the blues tradition of African retentions superimposed on a European melodic and harmonic structure. For a more detailed discussion see: Portia K. Maultsby, "Africanisms in African American Popular Music," in *Africanisms in American Culture,* ed. Joseph E. Holloway (Bloomington: Indiana University Press, 1990); Reebee Garofalo, "Crossing Over, 1939–1992," in *Split Image: African-Americans in the Mass Media,* 2d ed., ed. Jannette L. Dates and William Barlow (Washington, D.C.: Howard University Press, 1993).

19. George Lipsitz, *Class and Culture in Cold War America: "A Rainbow at Midnight"* (South Hadley, Mass.: J. F. Bergin, 1982), 195–96.

20. Nelson George, *The Death of Rhythm & Blues* (New York: Pantheon Books, 1988), 10.

21. Jones [Baraka], *Blues People,* 160.

22. George, *The Death of Rhythm & Blues,* 9.

23. Jones [Baraka], *Blues People,* 171.

24. Shaw, *Honkers and Shouters,* 278–79.

25. Malone, *Country Music, U.S.A.,* 209.

26. Shaw, *Honkers and Shouters,* 289.

27. Donald Clarke, *The Penguin Encyclopedia of Popular Music* (New York: Penguin Books, 1989), 1217.

28. Edward Zwick, "An Interview with the Father of Hi-Fi: Dr. Peter Goldmark," *Rolling Stone,* 27 September 1973, 44–45.

29. Ibid., 44.

30. Unable to bend like the AM signal, FM waves move in a straight line; transmission, therefore, suffers from a "line of sight" problem, in that irregular topography and the curvature of the earth prevent transmission over long distances. However, the quality of the signal in terms of frequency response and suppression of interference is far superior to AM transmission.

31. Sanjek, *American Popular Music,* 3:173.

32. *That Rhythm, Those Blues,* PBS documentary produced by George T. Nierenberg, 1988.

33. ABC *20/20,* segment on rap produced by Danny Schechter, 1981.

34. George, *The Death of Rhythm & Blues,* 41.

35. Ibid.

36. Shaw, *Honkers and Shouters,* 509.

37. Ibid., 518.

38. Passman, *The Deejays,* 175.

39. George, *The Death of Rhythm & Blues,* 41.

40. Passman, *The Deejays,* 185.

41. Ibid., 176.

42. Ibid.

43. Steve Chapple and Reebee Garofalo, *Rock 'n' Roll Is Here to Pay: The History and Politics of the Music Industry* (Chicago: Nelson-Hall, 1977), 56.

4 Crossing Cultures: The Eruption of Rock 'n' Roll

Trying to pinpoint the beginning of rock 'n' roll is like trying to isolate the first drop of rain in a hurricane. The uninitiated may claim it began in 1955 when "Rock Around the Clock" by Bill Haley and His Comets became the best-selling record of the year. Others may want to date the phenomenon from the first rock 'n' roll record to make the pop charts, but there is no agreement about just which record that was. Charlie Gillett has said it was Bill Haley's "Crazy Man Crazy" in 1953.[1] Nick Tosches has argued for "Sixty Minute Man," which was recorded by the Dominoes in 1951.[2] Writer Jim Dawson and deejay Steve Propes decided "to go down the long list of great recordings that led up to the rock 'n' roll explosion of 1956 and pick out the milestones which have elements of rock 'n' roll in them—and which influenced the music that followed" and ended up devoting 200 pages to debating among fifty contenders.[3]

Of course, part of the problem in determining the beginning of rock 'n' roll is the fact that rock 'n' roll evolved over time; it was not a one-time event. There is also a problem of definition. Which definition of rock 'n' roll should be used when trying to determine its beginning? There is rock 'n' roll, the musical genre unto itself; there is rock 'n' roll, the seemingly more acceptable term for rhythm and blues; and there is rock 'n' roll, the sexual metaphor. While Haley's "Crazy Man Crazy" fits the first definition well enough, the Dominoes' "Sixty Minute Man" highlights all three definitions. "Sixty Minute Man" was a popular r&b release that crossed over to the mainstream audience. R&b releases that did this were often called rock 'n' roll to obscure their origins. The protagonist in the song is a

> *P*art of the problem in determining the beginning of rock 'n' roll is the fact that rock 'n' roll evolved over time; it was not a one-time event.

legendary lover who "rocks" and "rolls" his partners "all night long," leaving little doubt as to the sexual connotation of the term.

It is ironic that the term used by any number of white r&b deejays to give rhythm and blues a more wholesome veneer in the mainstream market was a slang term for the sexual act common in African American music for years. With this in mind, one might date the start of rock 'n' roll from earlier releases that used the phrase in this way—Li'l Son Jackson's "Rockin' and Rollin'" in 1950, for example, or John Lee Hooker's "Rock 'n' Roll," in the same year. There is also Wynonie Harris' hit recording of Roy Brown's "Good Rockin' Tonight" in 1948 and Sister Rosetta Tharpe's "Rock Me" recorded with the Lucky Millinder Orchestra in 1942. For that matter, one could go all the way back to Trixie Smith's 1922 recording of "My Daddy Rocks Me (With One Steady Roll)." Tosches, taking the exercise to the extreme, has traced the sexual origins of the phrase back to medieval times.

> Rock and Roll. Both verbs came to the English tongue during the Middle Ages, and were soon used as skin-thrill metaphors. "My throbbing heart shall rock thee day and night," wrote Shakespeare in Venus and Adonis. An early nineteenth-century sea chanty included the line, "Oh do, me Johnny Bowker, come rock 'n' roll me over." A lyric found in the ceremonial Fire Dance of Florida's obeah worshippers was, "Bimini gal is a rocker and a roller."[4]

Suffice it to say, lest we get lost in history, that the music that came to be called rock 'n' roll began in the 1950s as diverse and seldom heard segments of the population achieved a dominant voice in mainstream culture and transformed the very concept of what popular music was.

Many contenders for the first rock 'n' roll record

Cultural Diversity: The Roots of Rock 'n' Roll

In an age in which the virtues of multiculturalism constantly push against the limitations of a narrowly Eurocentric worldview, it is quite fashionable to focus self-righteously on the culturally diverse influences that gave birth to rock 'n' roll. Still, while there is no question that rock 'n' roll was profoundly multicultural, an analysis of its characteristics must also account for the proportionate influence of various cultures. Applying too simplistic a formula can easily distort the contributions of participating groups.

Unfortunately, when rock 'n' roll is discussed in terms of cross-cultural influences, it is often described in a way that could be represented by an algebraic formula: r&b + c&w = r&r.

Unfortunately, when rock 'n' roll is discussed in terms of cross-cultural influences, it is often described in a way that could be represented by an algebraic formula: r&b + c&w = r&r. The formula is elegant in its simplicity and not without an element of truth—rhythm and blues and country and western were the primary styles that gave birth to rock 'n' roll—but it suffers from a number of shortcomings that render it less than useful for critical analysis, as Robert Palmer has noted:

> The cliché is that rock & roll was a melding of country music and blues, and if you are talk-ing about, say, Chuck Berry or Elvis Presley, the description, though simplistic, does fit. But the black inner-city vocal-group sound . . . had little to do with either blues or country music in their purer forms.
> The Do Diddley beat . . . was Afro-Caribbean in derivation. The most durable . . . bass riff in Fifties rock & roll . . . had been pinched . . . from a Cuban son record. The screaming, athletic saxophone playing . . .was straight out of Forties big-band swing. . . . Traditional Mexican rhythms entered the rock & roll arena through Chicano artists. . . . Rock & roll proved an All-American, multi-ethnic hybrid, its sources and developing substyles too various to be explained away by "blues plus country" or any other reductionist formula.[5]

Clearly, then, the r&b + c&w formula overlooks too much, including the myriad of influences that comprise rhythm and blues and country and western, not to mention the other stylistic elements that contributed to rock 'n' roll. Also, in looking only at the dimensions of race, ethnicity, and musical culture, issues of class and gender are conve-niently ignored. While rock 'n' roll certainly drew on a wide range of cultural inputs, all of its immediate musical sources were firmly rooted in the tradition of popular working-class styles. In fact, it resulted from a complex interplay of social and cultural forces that can not be reduced to a simple algebraic formula. In attempting to capture this complex-ity, George Lipsitz has located rock 'n' roll at the intersection of urbanization, multicul-turalism, and class:

> Workers drawn to cities by the manpower needs of American industry retained elements from their traditional cultures, but also combined with others to form a polyglot, urban, working-class culture. The social meanings previously conveyed in isolation by blues, country, polka, zydeco, and Latin musics found new expression as they blended in an urban setting. . . . Rock and Roll music accelerated and intensified the interactions among ethnic groups, becoming the most visible expression of the increasing commonality of working-class experience.[6]

A final limitation of the algebraic formula has to do with the relative values of r & b and c & w. Without specifying the relative values of r&b and c&w, it may be inferred that each style contributed equally to the new genre. Such an inference invariably under-values the African American contribution. After rock 'n' roll erupted full-blown into the national pop market in 1956, it presented itself as a refreshingly integrated phenomenon with performers like Bill Haley and Elvis Presley sharing the stage equally with artists like Fats Domino, Little Richard, and Chuck Berry. Accordingly, Steve Perry may paint the early history of rock 'n' roll in racially glowing terms: "From 1955–1958, the roster of popular rock 'n' rollers was more racially equal than at any time before or since.

Chuck Berry, Little Richard, the Coasters, the Platters, Fats Domino, Lloyd Price—major stars all, and on a rough par with the likes of Bill Haley, Jerry Lee Lewis, and Buddy Holly."[7] But this only happened after it had begun to expand to disruptive proportions among mainstream fans. As Greil Marcus correctly points out: "Most of the first rock 'n' roll styles were variations on black forms that had taken shape before the white audience moved in."[8]

The athletic honking saxophone, reminiscent of Illinois Jacquet ("Flying Home") and Big Jay McNeely, found its way into rock 'n' roll through Jackie Brenston's spirited solo on "Rocket 88" in 1951. That classic sound was soon echoed on countless rock 'n' roll records by such towering figures as Lee Allen and Herb Hardesty in New Orleans and King Curtis and Sam Taylor in New York. T-Bone Walker ("Call It Stormy Monday") practically invented electric blues guitar playing in the 1940s on the West Coast.[9] His picking style, which Robert Palmer has described as "clean, with a terse, dry tone, and minimal vibrato and sustain," had an obvious effect on Memphis-based B. B. King ("Three O'Clock Blues," "The Thrill Is Gone"), whose so-called bent notes and single string runs influenced generations of rock guitarists.[10] By merging T-Bone Walker's playing with jazz and pop influences, Chuck Berry created the definitive rock 'n' roll guitar style and, mixed with it, universal odes to teenage life: "School Day," "Rock 'n' Roll Music," "Sweet Little Sixteen," and "Johnny B. Goode." This list of influences does not even include Muddy Waters ("Got My Mojo Working"), who had "electrified" the country blues in Chicago just to be heard above the din in the noisy honky-tonks and juke joints where he performed. Shortly thereafter, Bo Diddley ("Bo Diddley," "Say Man"), another Delta-born Chicago transplant, crossed over into the pop market as a rock 'n' roll star with a distinctive Afro-Caribbean variant of the style. New Orleans boogie pianist Professor Longhair, who described his own playing as a "combination of offbeat Spanish beats and calypso downbeats" and "a mixture of rumba, mambo and calypso," was a major influence on Fats Domino whose successful r&b career was transformed into rock 'n' roll legend with such hits as "Ain't That a Shame," "I'm in Love Again," and "Blueberry Hill."[11]

On the vocal front, the assertiveness of such r&b performers as Joe Turner, Ruth Brown, and LaVern Baker helped to create the rock 'n' roll style. The emotional intensity of Roy Brown ("Good Rockin' Tonight"), for example, was carried to an extreme in the outrageous on-and-off-stage antics of archetypal rock 'n' roll screamer Little Richard ("Tutti-Frutti," "Long Tall Sally," "Rip It Up"). The jazz/gospel fusions of Ray Charles ("Hallelujah, I Love Her So," "I Got a Woman") and the more pop-oriented gospel stylings of such vocalists as Clyde McPhatter ("Treasure of Love," "A Lover's Question") and Sam Cooke ("You Send Me," "For Sentimental Reasons") brought the traditions of the black church into the secular world of rock 'n' roll. The elegant harmonies of urban vocal harmony groups like the Orioles ("Crying in the Chapel"), the Crows ("Gee"), the Chords ("Sh-Boom"), and the Penguins ("Earth Angel") ushered in a whole sub-genre of rock 'n' roll that was known as doo wop. Thus, in the well-intentioned and largely accurate celebration of rock 'n' roll's mongrel character, it is important not to lose sight of the fact that most of its formative influences, as well as virtually all of its early innovators, were African American. Among all of the artists who could have been considered rock 'n' roll musicians prior to 1955, there was only one white act of note—Bill Haley and His Comets.

If the tendency to systematically underestimate the African American contribution to rock 'n' roll is enough to give you pause, a consideration of what rock 'n' roll did to women can stop you in your tracks. The revolution that was rock 'n' roll just about eliminated women from the ranks of the best-selling recording artists. In the years immediately preceding the rock 'n' roll assault on the pop market, female vocalists had accounted for as many as one-third of the best-selling singles in a given

> *If the tendency to systematically underestimate the African American contribution to rock 'n' roll is enough to give you pause, a consideration of what rock 'n' roll did to women can stop you in your tracks.*

year. Of course, these were women in the pop Tin Pan Alley mold who performed suitably inoffensive material, Patti Page ("Doggie in the Window," 1953), Kitty Kallen ("Little Things Mean a Lot," 1954), Rosemary Clooney ("Hey There," 1954), Doris Day ("Secret Love," 1954), and so forth. By 1957, however, only two women appeared on *Cashbox*'s list of the twenty-five best-selling records of the year, Debbie Reynolds ("Tammy") and Jane Morgan ("Fascination"). Not a single rock 'n' roll record in the year-end top twenty-five list was by a woman. The breakdown for the following year was exactly the same unless Connie Francis' recording of "Who's Sorry Now" is counted as rock 'n' roll. Occasionally, female performers did penetrate the weekly best-seller lists with rock 'n' roll material—Baker's "Tweedlee Dee" in 1955 and "Jim Dandy" in 1957 and Brown's "Lucky Lips" in 1957—but, overall, a pattern of overwhelming male domination prevailed.

Clearly, the sexuality that characterized rock 'n' roll's initial burst of energy was a male sexuality. Women did not sing; they were sung about. Most often, they were referred to as babies—"Since I met you baby," "Honeycomb, won't you be my baby," "Be Bop a Lula, she's my baby," "Since my baby left me," "There goes my baby," and so forth. Without any models to make them question the double standard of the day, young male rock 'n' rollers were caught between the macho posturing of the "Sixty Minute Man" with his "Great Balls of Fire" and passionate, even vulnerable, declarations of unconditional romantic love, delivered in teenage idiom. Accordingly, in some instances, a woman could be portrayed as a wild "Party Doll," a promiscuous "Butterfly," or a "Devil in Disguise." Alternatively, she could be a heavenly goddess, "Venus" or "Diana," a "Dream Lover" with "Angel Eyes" sent to earth by a "Little Star" or a "Blue Moon." Either way, she was almost never a mature, down-to-earth person with a real personality. At best, women were treated as totally dependent creatures or ideal, unreal apparitions, perched high atop celestial pedestals.

Structural Changes in the Music Industry

Whatever else may be said about rock 'n' roll, in the early 1950s, the appeerence in the mainstream market of African American artists recording rhythm and blues for independent labels turned all the rules of the music industry—especially those concerning artist and repertoire, recording techniques, marketing strategies, national distribution, and consumer preference—upside down. In 1953, for example the Orioles, a black group originally from Baltimore, recorded "Crying in the Chapel," a sentimental country song, for Jubilee, an independent record label. Although there were already three versions of the song on the best-selling lists at the time, the Orioles' release with its sparse accompaniment, a slight gospel tinge, and wordless falsetto swoops in the background, went to number one on the r&b charts and then crossed over to the pop market.

> *Lead singer Sonny Til's wavering tenor and the sighs and cries of the group were familiar to the black audience, but sounded appealingly strange to the popular music audience. Perhaps aided by the fact that Til didn't sound very "black," the record broke into the white popular music market, thereby establishing a precedent for independently produced records featuring black singers.* [12]

Prior to this, the mainstream market had been dominated by the major labels. It has been estimated that in 1948 and 1949, RCA, CBS, Decca, and Capitol released more than 80 percent of all the weekly Top Ten hits.[13] Company executives were firmly convinced that audiences responded favorably to gentle changes in popular styles, which made the market somewhat predictable. Accordingly, marketing categories were as simple and straightforward as they were narrow and limiting: there was popular music for the national market, country and western for the regional market, and rhythm and blues for the African American market. The advent of rock 'n' roll swept away this conventional wisdom in one fell swoop.

Of course, the major labels had been able to keep their hold on the market in part because they controlled the entire production process. Everything from songwriting, artist and repertoire, arranging, production, and engineering to mastering, pressing, promotion, marketing, distribution, and, in some cases, retail sales, were in-house functions and performed according to a strict division of labor. The independent labels that came to life in the 1940s and 1950s had a far less highly organized system of production. Rock lore is rife with stories of enterprising label owners like Leonard Chess and Sam Phillips who performed all the technical functions of producing and recording and then distributed their records from the trunks of their cars. There were, however, two events that permitted the independent labels to compete successfully for a significant share of the market. First was the creation of a series of poorly capitalized independent radio stations that were desperate for inexpensive programming. These stations had come into existence as the FCC had begun to clear away the backlog of applications for radio licenses

After Sonny Til and the Orioles crossed over into the mainstream market in 1953, the floodgates opened for African American artists produced by independent labels. This new trend in popular music took the established powers of the music industry totally by surprise.

that had been put on hold during World War II. Second was the development of the lightweight "unbreakable" 45 rpm record. Although Jack Gutshall, a Los Angeles distributor, had set up the first national independent distribution system in 1945, it was, for the independents, prohibitively expensive to ship shellac-based 78 rpm records because of their weight and fragility. With the introduction of the 45 rpm record, national distribution became a viable and cost-effective option for independent companies, which promptly began to supply independent radio stations with their music, thus introducing specialty music to the mainstream market.

Following the decline of network radio in the early 1950s, patterns of ownership in independent broadcasting began to change from individual stations to "chains," individually programmed stations that were brought together under one corporate roof. Chain owners were first and foremost businessmen for whom radio was just another investment. Said George Storer, the president of Storer Broadcasting,

> *If the legend still persists that a radio station is some kind of art center, a technical museum, or a little piece of Hollywood transplanted strangely to your home town, then the first official act of the second quarter century [of commercial broadcasting] should be to list it along with the local dairies, laundries, banks, restaurants, and filling stations.* [14]

Of course, these businessmen expected their investments to be profitable, thus programming not only had to be inexpensive but also had to appeal to a wide range of listeners. Although there was a lot of talk about a new youth market, astute businessmen could not help noticing that teenagers constituted only about 12 percent of the population and that they were unavailable as listeners (potential consumers) during school hours. While it was true that teenagers constituted a disproportionately large share of the record-buying public, it was not entirely clear that they paid their way in advertising dollars for other products. It was Todd Storz and Gordon McLendon, both of whom owned radio chains, who found the solution to this dilemma in a new format—Top Forty radio— which placed the forty best-selling records in constant rotation all day long.

There are, of course, numerous stories about how the Top Forty format came into being. One story has the format beginning as a cost-cutting measure at Storz's WTIX in New Orleans in 1953. According to this story, McLendon's KLIF in Dallas followed soon after. [15] A more dramatic story has the format originating in Omaha, Nebraska, when Storz and Bill Stewart, his program director at KOWH, were in a bar drinking and noticed that the patrons kept playing the same song in the jukebox over and over again. When at closing time one of the cocktail waitresses who had been subjected to the song all day walked over to the jukebox and selected it yet again, a new format was born. In the spirit of giving the public what it wants, Storz and Stewart reasoned, why not treat radio like a jukebox and play only the best-selling records. The Top Forty format was essentially *Your Hit Parade* on records; the weekly live broadcast simply became a daily programming concept. As a total "sound," the format integrated jingles, special effects, promotional gimmicks, and hourly news broadcasts into the music that was used. The format proved so successful that it soon dominated pop radio.

In the spirit of giving the public what it wants, Todd Storz reasoned, why not treat radio like a jukebox and play only the best-selling records. The Top Forty format was essentially Your Hit Parade on records.

With the success of Top Forty radio, the deejay became a replaceable element in a total sound formula. Naturally the personality jocks railed against the increasing rationalization. George "Hound Dog" Lorenz, the most popular deejay in Buffalo, left

WKBW because, he said, "[t]his concept of radio programming is helping to kill the single-record business, is lowering radio listenership, and is decreasing a new artist's chances of making it."[16] To many, the inescapable conclusion was that the new format would restrict audience access to new music. While this would be the case over time, there is, paradoxically, ample evidence to suggest that in its initial stages, the format had precisely the opposite effect. As Richard Peterson has explained, "because the charts were based not only on radio airplay but also on jukebox play and record sales, many r&b records as well as some country music records charted. Thus, for the first time, these sorts of records began to receive wide exposure via the radio."[17]

Because the aesthetic that had guided network radio programming had not kept pace with changes in popular taste, the format based on public appeal that had been created by independent chains had the effect, at least in the short run, of broadening the range of musical offerings that could be heard on a given station. Imagine hearing Little Richard's "Long Tall Sally," Patti Page's "Allegheny Moon," Carl Perkins' "Blue Suede Shoes," and Morris Stoloff's "Moonglow and Theme from Picnic" all on the same radio station, indeed, on the same show. It was possible in June 1956, when all four recordings were in the Top Forty simultaneously. In the heyday of rock 'n' roll, there was a greater diversity of music heard on the radio than had ever before been the case.

Sounds of the Cities

The music that became rock 'n' roll issued from city centers in just about every region in the country. It was as disruptive in its degree of decentralization as it was exciting in its unpredictability. While there is always the temptation is to trace the roots of rock 'n' roll to the South, perhaps because of the r&b + c&w formula, in the end, this tendency does not do justice to the geographical dispersion of the music or the variety of cultural inputs. In fact, there is no wholly satisfactory way to chart the course of the music. The one thing that can be said with certainty is that rock 'n' roll was an urban sound. Beyond that, the music often owed its characteristic sound to the magical ingredients of some bewitching musical brew—the distinctiveness of a particular region or city, the exceptional quality of a specific recording studio or record company, a unique vocal or instrumental style, even the creative genius of a particular writer, performer, producer, and/or engineer. One place where all these elements came together was New Orleans.

New Orleans: The Fertile Crescent of Rock 'n' Roll

New Orleans is one of those places where diverse cultural elements periodically come together to produce a distinct sound. The city had been home to people from incredibly varied backgrounds (French, Spanish, African, English, Native American, Cajun, and

Top 40 gives record buyers a voice, but is ultimately too restrictive

Creole) for many years before it was purchased by the United States in 1803. The resulting cultural blend, born of conflict, struggle, and accommodation, gave the city a distinctive cuisine, language, architecture, and musical culture. Known in legend as the birthplace of jazz, New Orleans was the site of a thriving r&b scene in the late 1940s and early 1950s. Thus, as Langdon Winner has noted,

> Rock and roll performers nurtured in this fertile environment had a wealth of musical sources upon which to draw. The fabulous ensemble playing of the black funeral bands, the syncopated "second line" rhythms of Mardi Gras parades, the rugged country blues from the surrounding Mississippi delta, the raucous chords of barrelhouse piano players, the elegant styles of jazz improvisation—all became underlying elements of New Orleans rock.[18]

One of the key figures in the construction of the New Orleans sound was an Italian American jukebox operator named Cosimo Matassa. Matassa was co-owner and chief engineer of J&M Studio, and from the 1940s until the late 1960s, almost every r&b record cut in New Orleans was recorded in one of his studios. Matassa began with a Duo-Presto disc recorder but soon moved up to tape, an Ampex 300 one-track machine, which afforded the possibility of some editing. There was, however, no overdubbing, no multitracking, and no electronic embellishments of any kind in Matassa's productions. His style was simple: He set the knobs at the desired level and let the band play. With this elementary philosophy, as well as brilliant sidemen, unique room acoustics, and some well-placed microphones, Matassa created classic New Orleans rock 'n' roll—heavy on bass and drums, light on horns and piano, with a strong vocal lead—that had independent labels from Aladdin, Imperial, and Specialty in Los Angeles to Chess in Chicago, Savoy in Newark, and Atlantic in New York flocking to New Orleans to record.

Cosimo Matassa's production style was simple: He set the knobs at the desired level and let the band play.

The first label to use Matassa's studio was De Luxe from New Jersey in 1947. It was, in fact, Roy Brown's recording of "Good Rockin' Tonight" (now a rock 'n' roll classic) for De Luxe that first focused national attention on New Orleans. Brown's version of "Good Rockin' Tonight" was outsold by Wynonie Harris' that same year, but Brown's record turned the industry spotlight on New Orleans and Brown himself became a significant influence on the vocal styles of artists from B. B. King and Bobby Bland to Jackie Wilson, the young James Brown, and even Little Richard. Charlie Gillett has said that

> The most impressive quality of Brown's style was his intense involvement in his singing. Whereas the blues shouters were always evidently in control of the sounds they made, Brown's voice was shaped by the passions of despair or exhilaration. Rocking frantically to a boogie beat, or wracked by desolate doubt, he committed all he was to the song's message.[19]

Another essential ingredient in the creation of the New Orleans sound was the city's fine array of session musicians. At the center of this pool of talented sidemen was writer, producer, manager, arranger, trumpet player, and bandleader Dave Bartholomew. The son of a respected Dixieland tuba player and a one-time trumpet player with Duke Ellington, Bartholomew started his own band (really an organization) in New Orleans in the late 1940s. From that point on, Bartholomew maintained a stable of first-rate musicians that included, among others, drummers Charles Williams and Earl Palmer, whose syncopated bass-drum style helped define rock 'n' roll drumming, and saxophonists Herb Hardesty, Red Tyler, and Lee Allen, "the Lester Young of rock." Allen was also a mainstay in the band of Paul Gayten, another noteworthy New Orleans bandleader and session musician.

Bartholomew and his organization found steady work at such clubs as the Dew Drop Inn and Club Tijuana and even had a minor r&b hit with "Country Boy" (1949) on De Luxe, but their most influential performances were as the house band at Matassa's studio. In various permutations, they can be heard as the backup band on Lloyd Price's "Lawdy Miss Clawdy" (1952), Shirley and Lee's "I'm Gone" (1952), the Spiders' "I Didn't Want to Do It" (1954), and Smiley Lewis' recording of "I Hear You Knocking" (1955), with Huey "Piano" Smith providing the piano introduction. Still, Bartholomew's biggest successes were with Fats Domino, for whom he acted as mentor, manager, co-writer, arranger, and producer.

Antoine "Fats" Domino was born in New Orleans in 1928. His first language was French. Taught to play piano by his brother-in-law, Domino quit school at the age of fourteen to work in a bedspring factory where he almost lost a few fingers in an industrial accident and to play in the local clubs at night, which is how he met Dave Bartholomew. Even today, Domino's music can be identified by his warm, inviting French Creole accent, Bartholomew's clear, well-constructed arrangements, and that steady boogie-woogie piano, which dates back to Albert Ammons, Mead Lux Lewis, and Pete Johnson but was influenced most immediately by Professor Longhair. "Domino, he was creative," Matassa noted. "No matter what he does comes through. He could be singing the National Anthem . . . you'd still know by the time he said two words it was him, obviously, unmistakably, and pleasurably him. . . . in fact he just hits an opening chord on his piano and you know it.[20]

Domino began recording at Matassa's studio in 1949. Of the eight sides cut at his first session, "The Fat Man"—a cleaned-up version of Champion Jack Dupree's 1940 drug song "Junker Blues"—was released first. It hit the r&b charts in 1950. The next three releases flopped. On the fifth record, "Every Night about This Time," Domino introduced the piano triplets that became his signature. His rock 'n' roll breakthrough came in 1955 when Pat Boone's version of "Ain't That a Shame" went to number one on the pop charts and Domino's original followed it to number ten, establishing him as a full-fledged rock 'n' roll star with no change in his r&b style. From

Never a sex symbol or a musical iconoclast, Fats Domino managed to transcend to a great degree the racism that cheated so many African American artists and the ageism that plagued Bill Haley's career.

Fats Domino's laid-back New Orleans r&b style brought him a devoted rock 'n' roll following even after he was well into his thirties. With the exception of Elvis Presley (and Pat Boone), he charted more Top Forty pop hits than any other rock 'n' roller.

then on, Domino outdistanced almost all the competition. From 1955 to 1963, when he was well into his thirties, Domino charted thirty-six Top Forty pop hits, more than any other rock 'n' roll artist except Elvis Presley (unless Boone, who had thirty-eight, is counted as a rock 'n' roll artist). In addition to "Ain't That a Shame," eight other of Domino's records entered the Top Ten—"I'm in Love Again" and "Blueberry Hill" in 1956, "Blue Monday" and "Valley of Tears" in 1957, "Whole Lotta Lovin'" in 1958, "I Want to Walk You Home" and "Be My Guest" in 1959, and "Walking to New Orleans" in 1960. Never a sex symbol or a musical iconoclast, Domino managed to transcend to a great degree, the racism that cheated so many African American artists and the ageism that plagued Bill Haley's career.

> Somehow he was rock 'n' roll's safety valve, and all he was putting down was good time New Orleans music. . . . Fat's music had not changed in any way to meet his increased popularity. He was still a rhythm and blues singer whose music just happened to be the roots of rock 'n' roll. What he had in abundance was a natural, mellow infectiousness which was instantly recognizable whether the songs were happy frolics or merely plaintive ballads. Relaxed good humor permeated his records, everything was so simple and danceable.[21]

All of Domino's hits, with the possible exception of "I'm Walkin'," were recorded in Matassa's studio, all were produced and arranged by Dave Bartholomew (indeed, most were cowritten by Bartholomew), and all used some combination of the same session men. While the New Orleans scene certainly seemed to be a prescription for success, for some unknown reason nobody thought to consolidate the package into a New Orleans record label. Matassa made a feeble attempt in 1958 when he founded Rex Records, but the company barely made a ripple outside of New Orleans. "I never did really get into the thing of being a producer as such," said Matassa, who went bankrupt in 1966. "I regret it now of course!"[22] The prodigious output of Matassa's modest studio was licensed to existing out-of-state independent labels. It wasn't until Bartholomew passed the creative baton to a second generation of producers, best exemplified by Allen Toussaint, at the turn of the decade that New Orleans developed any notable labels of its own.

The closest thing New Orleans had to a local label in the initial surge of rock 'n' roll was Ace Records, which was headquartered in Jackson, Mississippi, but centered in New Orleans. Founded in 1955 by Johnny Vincent (Vincent Imbragulio), who had been an artist and repertoire man for Specialty, the company had an immediate success with Earl King's "Those Lonely, Lonely Nights." King's second release, "Well-O, Well-O, Well-O, Baby," had that rocking New Orleans piano groove that had been made famous by Huey "Piano" Smith. Smith and his band, the Clowns, provided Ace with its first pop hit, "(I Got the) Rockin' Pneumonia and the Boogie-Woogie Flu" (1957). The recording featured Bobby Marchan as lead vocalist, Charles Williams on drums, and Lee Allen and Red Tyler on saxes. In 1958, the Clowns hit the Top Ten with "Don't You Just Know It." Following that, their biggest success was as the session band for Frankie Ford's "Sea Cruise." As Langdon Winner has pointed out, with this 1959 hit, "all of the elements of a sound which had been evolving for a decade are carried to their logical extremes. The New Orleans horns finally cook like their lives depend on it. The piano prances along, reaching the very essence of boogie-woogie. The lead vocal finally achieves the perfect mix of pure joke and pure hysteria."[23]

Ace's original recording of this song had featured Huey Smith's vocal, but the company had used Frankie Ford for the vocal in the final release in an attempt to find a teen idol who could compete with such white rock 'n' rollers as Elvis Presley and Ricky Nelson. This practice would become all too common in rock 'n' roll as the years went on. To Ford's credit, he had a genuine feel for r&b, and he delivered the song in a style heavily indebted to Bobby Marchan. This may explain why he was never able to repeat his success. Ace had more luck with a less influential white New Orleans rocker named Jimmy Clanton who was managed by none other than Cosimo Matassa. Between 1958 and 1962, Clanton produced a string of pop hits, including three that made the Top Ten: "Just a Dream," "Go, Jimmy, Go," and "Venus in Blue Jeans." These three, especially the last one, removed him from his New Orleans roots and placed him in the company of such ersatz rockers as Fabian, Frankie Avalon, and Bobby Rydell.

The rest of the music recorded at Matassa's studio by New Orleans musicians was issued by more distant labels. Although Clarence "The Frogman" Henry's "Ain't Got No Home," "But I Do," and "You Always Hurt the One You Love" were issued by Argo, a subsidiary of Chess in Chicago, the bulk of the material went to Los Angeles-based labels, primarily Aladdin, Specialty, and Imperial, and at one time or another, Dave Bartholomew worked for all of them. Aladdin signed Shirley and Lee (Shirley Goodman and Leonard Lee), whose "Let the Good Times Roll" reached number twenty on the pop charts in 1956, even though some deejays thought it was too suggestive to play on the air. Imperial had Smiley Lewis ("I Hear You Knockin'") and the Spiders ("I Didn't Want to Do It"), both of whom were backed by Bartholomew's band. Imperial's founder, Lew Chudd, also signed Fats Domino, who turned the label into one of the most successful independent labels in the country. Art Rupe, the owner of Specialty, was so impressed with Domino that in 1952 he went to New Orleans to find someone who could sing like him and found Lloyd Price. The seventeen-year-old Price was the last performer to show up for Rupe's public audition at Matassa's studio. Taken by Price's rendition of "Lawdy Miss Clawdy," a song he had written for a radio advertisement, Rupe spent the next four or five days putting together a band to record it professionally. Bartholomew rounded up the usual sidemen for the session, including Fats Domino on piano. "Lawdy Miss Clawdy" went to number one on the r&b charts and was followed-up by two more Top Ten r&b hits—"Restless Heart" and "Ain't That a Shame" in 1952 and 1953. Before Price could hit his stride, however, he was drafted into the army. After finishing his tour of duty, he switched to ABC-Paramount and delivered nine Top Forty pop hits, including "Stagger Lee," "Personality," and "I'm Gonna Get Married," which were numbers one, two, and three, respectively, in 1959.

Rupe had barely had time to mourn Price's departure from the label when he found two new artists to replace him, Little Richard and Larry Williams, both of whom are examples of the New Orleans-Los Angeles connection. Williams was a Little Richard soundalike from New Orleans, who came to Rupe's attention when he was still employed as Lloyd Price's valet. Recording in Los Angeles with New Orleans session men, Williams turned out three pop hits, "Short Fat Fanny" and "Bony Maronie" in 1957 and "Dizzy Miss Lizzy" in 1958, and then faded from the scene. By this time, however, Little Richard had become the most colorful figure in all of rock 'n' roll.

Little Richard (nee Richard Penniman) hailed from Macon, Georgia, where he sang and learned to play piano in the Pentecostal church. Forced to leave home when he was fourteen because of alleged homosexual activity, he toured with medicine shows for a while. In 1951 in a radio competition sponsored by Zenas Sears, a white r&b deejay in Atlanta, he won a recording contract with RCA Victor, but the contract led to nothing. At the suggestion of Lloyd Price, Richard sent a demo tape to Art Rupe in Los Angeles but

Perhaps more than any other artist, Little Richard unleashed the energy of early rock 'n' roll. On a number of occasions Richard left the world of music to pursue a higher calling. Fortunately for rock 'n' roll, however, his uncontrollable style and irrepressible spirit always won out in the end.

heard nothing for almost a year. By the time Specialty's new producer, Bumps Blackwell, had decided to give Richard a try, he was already under contract to Peacock but still going nowhere. Rupe bought out the Peacock contract for $600 and sent Richard and Blackwell to New Orleans to record. Naturally, they went to Matassa's studio and used Bartholomew's sidemen. At the tail end of the session, which included nary a rocker, Richard began fooling around with a reportedly obscene song called "Wop Bop Aloo Bop." The song caught Blackwell's ear. He quickly brought in Dorothy La Bostrie, a local songwriter, to clean up the lyrics, and with fifteen minutes of studio time left, "Tutti Frutti" was recorded. It hit number twenty-one on the pop charts in 1956 and instantly established Little Richard as the most outrageous rock 'n' roller of them all.

If Fats Domino was rock 'n' roll's safety valve, Little Richard was the steam that made it blow.

Following the success of "Tutti Frutti," Little Richard turned out eight other Top Forty pop hits for Specialty, including "Long Tall Sally," "Slippin' and Slidin'," and "Rip It Up" in 1956, "Lucille," "Jenny, Jenny," and "Keep a Knockin'" in 1957, and "Good Golly, Miss Molly" and "Ooh! My Soul" in 1958. Each was as unrestrained as the one before it. Richard's outrageous personal appearance was the perfect complement to his uninhibited stage act. The eye-popping costumes, exaggerated pompadour, and heavy mascara defined a rock 'n' roll image with which few could compete. His stage antics would later be rivaled only by Jerry Lee Lewis; his fashion statement (minus the eye makeup) only by Elvis Presley. If Fats Domino was rock 'n' roll's safety valve, Little Richard was the steam that made it blow. In describing the difference between the two, Arnold Shaw has also noted the versatility of the New Orleans sound itself.

> *Fats had a friendly baritone and Little Richard's sound was strident and slam-bam. Fats' Cajun-inflected speech had an appealing musicality; Little Richard was a shouter. For Fats, the band played New Orleans jazz with an after beat while he boogied and barrelhoused at the piano. With Little Richard's crashing piano triplets, the band picked up drive and went "a-womp-bomp-a-loo-bomp a-lomp bomp boom" and "bama lama bama loo."*[24]

Little Richard's career came to an abrupt halt in 1958 when he unexpectedly quit the business to join the ministry. A number of not very convincing explanations have been offered for his sudden change in profession. Rupe blamed the first Russian satellite for Richard's departure. "He thought that the Sputnik was a sign from heaven," said Rupe. "That was it."[25] According to another tale, the engine of an airplane Richard was on caught fire and he promised God he would leave the devil's music behind if he could be saved. Some have suggested more cynically that the artist was attracted to the idea that ministers did not pay income taxes. In any case, on board a ship while on tour in Australia, Richard plucked $8,000 worth of rings from his fingers and tossed them into the sea. "If you want to live with the Lord," he told an Australian reporter, "you can't rock 'n' roll it, too. God doesn't like it."[26] When he returned to the United States, he

Little Richard embodies the uncontrollable energy of rock 'n' roll

enrolled at Oakwood College, a Seventh Day Adventist school in Huntsville, Alabama, paying his entire four-year tuition in advance. Whatever the reason for Little Richard's conversion, it was one of a number of fateful occurrences in the late 1950s that signaled the decline of rock 'n' roll.

Los Angeles: From Jump Blues to Chicano Rock

The independent labels that were formed in Los Angeles in the late 1940s sought to satisfy a market that had been created by the cultural needs of waves of poor white, black, and Chicano migrants who had arrived to work in the shipyards and airplane manufacturing plants that had sprung up to meet wartime needs. Many of the artists who first recorded for these labels were pioneers in the transition from big band jazz to various styles of r&b. The first wave artists—Roy Milton, Amos Milburn, T-Bone Walker, and Charles Brown among others—came from Texas. In Los Angeles, they encountered local jazz cum r&b musicians like Joe Liggins and Johnny Otis who helped to shape their sound. As time went on, and a new wave of immigrants arrived from southern Louisiana, Los Angeles' independent labels began to explore the music of New Orleans. Perhaps they did so because New Orleans' early jazz sound, steeped in blues and boogie, resonated well with the transition from jazz to rhythm and blues that was then occurring. As Johnny Otis once noted,

> In the early 40's a hybrid form of music developed on the West Coast. What was happening in Chicago was another kind of thing altogether. It was all rhythm and blues later, but the Chicago bands, the people that came up from the Delta, came up with harmonicas and guitars—the Muddy Waters and the rest of them. They had a certain thing, and we loved it, and we were influenced by it to a certain degree. But on the Coast, the people who were there, like myself and Roy Milton, T-Bone Walker, and Joe Liggins and the Honeydrippers, we all had big band experience. We all thought in terms of big bands, but when it became impossible to maintain a big band, . . . we didn't break down to just a guitar and a rhythm section. We still tried to maintain some of that sound of the jazz bands. We kept maybe a trumpet, a trombone, and saxes—this was a semblance of brass and reeds, and they continued to play the bop and swing riffs. And this superimposed on the country blues and boogie structure began to become rhythm and blues. And out of rhythm and blues grew rock 'n' roll.[27]

Even before Fats Domino and Little Richard recorded with some "semblance," as Otis called it, of the big band sound, Roy Milton (Specialty), T-Bone Walker (Imperial), Amos Milburn (Aladdin), and Joe Liggins and the Honeydrippers (Exclusive) had developed distinctive regional variants of Louis Jordan's jump blues. Charles Brown, the lead singer for Johnny Moore's Three Blazers, developed a smooth r&b style that was heavily influenced by Nat "King" Cole and Leroy Carr in "Driftin' Blues" (Aladdin, 1948) and "Merry Christmas, Baby" (Modern, 1949). Still, only Johnny Otis was able to make the successful transition to rock 'n' roll. Otis had been part of the West Coast r&b scene since its beginnings. He was, in fact, one of its formative influences. As a teenager in Berkeley, he was the drummer for Count Matthews' West Oakland House Rockers. He then moved to Los Angeles with Harlan Leonard and the Kansas City Rockets. In time, he started his own big band, "seven brass, five reeds, four rhythm" and two vocalists, sometimes three. The band's first recording session yielded its first hit, "Harlem Nocturne" (1945) on Excelsior, a subsidiary of Exclusive, one of the only black-owned labels in Los Angeles at the time. Otis was as much an entrepreneur as he was a musician. In the late 1940s and early 1950s, he was part owner of the Barrel House, an r&b club in Los Angeles; he also had a daily radio show and a weekly television show. His traveling road show, the Johnny Otis Show, a "rhythm and blues caravan," as he called it, featured vocalists Little Esther and Mel Walker, with whom he produced eleven hits for Savoy between 1950 and 1952. He is credited with discovering Hank Ballard, Little Willie John, Jackie Wilson, and Etta James. He also produced the ill-fated Johnny Ace[28] ("Pledging My Love," 1955) for Duke/Peacock, as well as Willie Mae "Big Mama" Thornton, for whom he claimed to have cowritten the original version of "Hound Dog" with Jerry Leiber and Mike Stoller. (Otis claims that Leiber and Stoller cut him out when the song became a hit for Elvis Presley.) Otis finally hit rock 'n' roll pay dirt with "Willie and the Hand Jive" (Capitol, 1958), a novelty song played to the "Bo Diddley" beat, an Afro-Caribbean clave rhythm that Otis said he had learned from Count Matthews twenty years earlier.

> Johnny Otis was clearly a catalyst for African American culture and talent. In his whole life, he has never been anything else, which is why it is sometimes surprising for people to learn that Otis happens to be white.

In his heyday, Otis was clearly a catalyst for African American culture and talent. In his whole life, he has never been anything else, which is why it is sometimes surprising for people to learn that Otis happens to be white, the son of Greek immigrants, Alexander and Irene Veliotes. Otis knows he is white, but he identifies himself as "black by persuasion." When he speaks of African Americans, he uses the pronoun "we," and does so with credibility. "My friend, Johnny Otis, is genetically white, but in all other respects completely black," wrote black musician Preston Love in the preface to *Listen to the Lambs,* a book Otis wrote after the Watts rebellion in 1965. "His life has been that of a black man joined with other black men to combat the outside—the hostile and unjust white establishment."[29]

One of the musicians who worked at the Barrel House was Robert Byrd, who recorded as Bobby Day, Bobby Garrett (lead singer for the Hollywood Flames [aka the Satellites]), and Bob of Bob and Earl (Earl was Earl Nelson of the Flames). In 1957, the Hollywood Flames enjoyed pop success with "Buzz, Buzz, Buzz." That same year, Byrd wrote and recorded "Little Bitty Pretty One" under the name Bobby Day for the Class label. Class was another small subsidiary of Exclusive/Excelsior, which was owned by Otis and Leon René. It was Leon René who wrote "When the Swallows Come Back to Capistrano," which was, in fact, the flip side of "Little Bitty Pretty One." Although

Johnny Otis is a mover and shaker in the African American community

"Swallows" was expected to be the hit, deejays preferred "Little Bitty Pretty One." A nearly identical rival version of the song by Thurston Harris was put out by Aladdin, and selected by Dick Clark for play on American Bandstand. It was Harris' only Top Ten pop hit and outsold Day's original four-to-one. The following year, René wrote another "bird" song for Day. This time nothing stood in his way. "Rockin' Robin" (1958) went to number two on the pop charts and became one of the all-time classic rock 'n' roll records.

Until the year "Rockin' Robin" came out, Los Angeles had produced a number of distinctive performers but never a specific "sound" that was identified with the city. In

Los Angeles had produced a number of distinctive performers but never a specific "sound" that was identified with the city. In 1958, however, Los Angeles' rock 'n' rollers began to move toward styles that drew on Mexican rhythms.

that year, however, Los Angeles' rock 'n' rollers began to move toward styles that drew on Mexican rhythms. "Tequila" (which featured Glen Campbell on guitar) by the Champs, a white instrumental group that included Jim Seals and Dash Crofts (later of Seals and Crofts), remained number one on the pop charts for five weeks in 1958. It was followed by "El Rancho Rock," a rocked-up version of the 1934 Mexican ballad "Alla en El Rancho Grande." There was one artist who might have developed this sound further—Ritchie Valens (Richie Valenzuela), the first Chicano rock 'n' roll star. Recorded for Del-Fi, one of a number of labels owned at various times by Bob Keene, Valens' "C'mon, Let's Go" and "La Bamba," a rock 'n' roll version of the traditional folk song, hit the pop charts in 1958 and 1959. His biggest hit, however, was "Donna," a more mainstream ballad that he wrote for his girlfriend. Valens turned out two more hits for Del-Fi—"That's My Little Susie" and "Little Girl"—before he was killed in the same plane crash that took the lives of Buddy Holly and the Big Bopper. The date of that flight, 3 February 1959, is sometimes eulogized as the day the music died. Valens' death slowed the development of Chicano rock, which only made sporadic inroads into the mainstream from then on.

Ritchie Valens drew on his Chicano heritage to add another cultural source to the musical brew that was rock 'n' roll. Who knows how much farther he might have taken that sound had he not been killed in a plane crash three months before his eighteenth birthday?

Chicago: The Blues Electrified

Chicago was one of the main watering holes for urbanized blues musicians from the Mississippi Delta. The city had received a steady influx of African American migrants from the South for decades and included among its inhabitants were Big Bill Broonzy, Sonny Boy Williamson, Willie Mabon, Jimmy Reed, John Lee Hooker, Muddy Waters, and Howlin' Wolf. With the exception of Broonzy, all of these artists recorded for one or the other of Chicago's two main independent record labels, Chess and Vee Jay. Williamson, Mabon, Waters, and Wolf recorded for Chess, Reed and Hooker for Vee Jay.

According to legend, many of the Chicago blues greats simply walked into Chess Records off the street. Leonard Chess, however, was not one to sit and wait for talent to come to him. He made regular field trips to the South to find bluesmen in their natural habitat. It was on one such trip that he first recorded Howlin' Wolf with Ike Turner on piano and James Cotton on harp. Wolf subsequently joined the Chess stable in Chicago and began a professional rivalry with Muddy Waters that lasted until the day Wolf died. On another southern excursion in 1951, Chess acquired Jackie Brenston's recording of "Rocket 88" with Ike Turner's band and Brenston playing sax and singing lead from Sam Phillips, who later founded Sun Records. The song rocketed to the top of the r&b charts and provided a developing Bill Haley with the inspiration he needed to move in a r&b direction. Indeed, "Rocket 88" is sometimes cited as one of the first rock 'n' roll records.

If there is any question about Chess' pioneering role in advancing the new sound, it becomes moot when the label's next two major performers—Bo Diddley and Chuck Berry—are considered. Like the early bluesmen who recorded for Chess, Bo Diddley (born Ellas Bates but reared as Ellas McDaniel after the family that raised him) came from Mississippi. He is distinguishable from his blues contemporaries in a number of ways, not the least of which is the fact that his first instrument was the violin—not the fiddle, the violin. Although Diddley moved to Chicago as a youngster in 1934, he did not record for Chess until 1955. Between 1955 and 1959, he turned out eight r&b hits, including the classic "Bo Diddley" backed with "I'm a Man" in 1955. In 1956, he set an attendance record at the Apollo theater. In 1959, his "Say Man" crossed over to the pop market, and in that same year his "Crackin' Up" made the pop charts but not the r&b charts, reflecting the beginning of the separation of rock 'n' roll from rhythm and blues.

Diddley was more influential than his chart entries indicate. A tall, heavyset man, he was an imposing figure on stage and usually performed in black with a black Stetson hat and oddly shaped square and triangular guitars. As if to emphasize the Afro-Latin quality of his clave-influenced rhythm, which is often incorrectly identified as the "shave-and-a-haircut" beat, he once appeared on the Ed Sullivan Show accompanied only by a rhythm section (maracas, drums, and a second guitarist). His rhythmic signature, which is now known as the "Bo Diddley beat," was copied by Johnny Otis on "Willie and the Hand Jive," as well as by numerous other rock 'n' rollers. His importance at Chess, as in rock 'n' roll generally, however, was overshadowed by the label's biggest star and possibly the greatest rock 'n' roller of them all—Chuck Berry.

Were it not for the dynamics of racism in U.S. society, Chuck Berry probably would have been crowned king of rock 'n' roll. When Berry, the son of a carpenter from St. Louis, Missouri, walked into the offices of Chess Records on the recommendation of Muddy Waters, his demo of "Ida Red" (backed with "Wee Wee Hours," a blues number) had already been turned down by both Capitol and Mercury because it sounded "too country" for a black man. On the advice of Leonard Chess, Berry gave the tune a bigger beat and changed the title to "Maybellene," a name he took from a hair creme. Said Chess a few weeks before he died,

> I liked it, thought it was something new. I was going to New York anyway, and I took a dub to Alan [Freed] and said "Play this." The dub didn't have Chuck's name on it or nothing. By the time I got back to Chicago, Freed had called a dozen times, saying it was his biggest record ever. History, the rest, y' know? Sure, "Wee Wee Hour," that was on the back side of the release, was a good tune too, but the kids wanted the big beat, cars, and young love. [33]

For his part in popularizing the song, Freed and another deejay named Russ Fratto were credited as cowriters of the song, a practice that eventually contributed to the undoing of rock 'n' roll.

The country-tinged "Maybellene" went to number five on the pop charts in 1955. Still, success did not come quickly, as Berry's songs were far too socially relevant for many. As Charlie Gillett has written,

> [Berry's] next four singles, performed in a blues style and presenting in their themes some strong criticisms of aspects of American life, showed his interests much more obviously. Judges and courts in "Thirty Days," credit and car salesmen in "No Money Down," high culture in "Roll Over Beethoven," and all these and more in "Too Much Monkey Business" were cause for complaint. Since these records were performed in a strong "blues" voice, the songs . . . received relatively little attention from disc jockeys. [34]

"Too Much Monkey Business" was actually a two-sided r&b hit. On the back was "Brown-Eyed Handsome Man." The self-descriptive, thinly veiled racial commentary of this song no doubt added to the deejays' reluctance to push the record to a mainstream audience. Berry is best remembered for the simpler, teen-directed but socially relevant recordings that came later—"School Day" and "Rock & Roll Music" in 1957 and "Sweet Little Sixteen" and "Johnny B. Goode" in 1958. All of these reached the Top Ten on the pop charts. In his writing, Berry had the uncanny ability to relate r&b to white teen culture without disowning his blackness. His "duck walk" and other guitar gymnastics, indeed his comedic yet cool stage demeanor in general, added tremendous visual appeal to his performances without demeaning the substance of his music. "As rock & roll's first guitar hero," Nelson George has written, "Berry, along with various rockabilly

Chuck Berry's career interrupted in the early 1960s

musicians, made that instrument the genre's dominant musical element, supplanting the sax of previous black stars."[35]

Berry's career was interrupted in 1959 when he was arrested for a violation of the Mann Act and sent to prison. After returning from a tour in Mexico with an underage young woman in tow (ostensibly to check hats in his night club), he was arrested for transporting a minor across state lines for immoral purposes. The impulse to discredit rock 'n' roll was shown in a headline of the time, which read "Rock 'n' Roll Singer Lured Me to St. Louis, Says 14 Year Old."[36] It took two trials to convict him. The first was vacated because of the blatant racism of the judge who referred to Berry as "this Negro." The second trial, which ended in 1962, landed him in jail for nearly two years. Berry's songs continued to sell, but his career slipped in the 1960s. He staged a comeback in 1972 with a song as commercially successful as it was puerile—"My Ding-a-Ling," his first and only number one pop hit. Although other heroes of rock 'n' roll may have had more and bigger hits than Chuck Berry, none matched his influence in defining its style.

Chicago's other main independent label was formed in the early 1950s by an African American couple, Vivian Carter and James Bracken; hence its name, Vee Jay. Carter was a deejay, one of the few women deejays at the time, who had won a 1948 talent contest for deejays that had been sponsored by Al Benson. Bracken owned and operated a record store that was named after his wife. The label was a natural outgrowth of its founders' experience in the music business. One key to the company's success was the early installation of Calvin Carter, Vivian's brother, as producer. While not a musician himself, Calvin Carter's social and technical skills and fine ear for harmonies produced "a track record that Phil Spector would be envious of."[37] In 1955, Ewart Abner, who later went on to become the president of Motown, joined Vee Jay. Abner was the deal maker; his fast-and-loose style contributed to the rise and fall of the company.

Vee Jay began as a gospel recording label and included among its artists the Swan Silvertones, the Harmonizing Four, the Highway QCs, and the Staple Singers who later moved to Stax. Like Chess, the company experienced some early success in doo wop, offering both the Spaniels and the El Dorados. However, the company's biggest-selling artist in the 1950s was Delta bluesman Jimmy Reed. Signed to the label in 1955, Reed produced thirteen r&b hits over the next six years, including "Honest I Do" (1957) and "Baby What You Want Me to Do" (1960), which crossed over to the pop Top Forty. He is perhaps best known for "Bright Lights, Big City" (1960), which was covered by a number of rockabilly artists, including Elvis Presley and Jerry Lee Lewis. After eight years of recording for other labels, most notably Modern in Los Angeles, John Lee Hooker joined Vee Jay in 1955. Although a more versatile performer, Hooker was less successful than Reed as an r&b artist. He did become better known in retrospect because of his Newport Folk Festival appearances and recordings, which were influential in the blues revival of the 1960s.

Vee Jay seemed destined for major success when the company signed the Impressions. The original Impressions group included Jerry Butler and Curtis Mayfield, who had met when Butler had joined the gospel choir in the church for which Mayfield's grandmother was pastor. In 1957, Butler and Mayfield joined forces with the core of a group called the Roosters to form the Impressions. The group's audition at Vee Jay in 1958 yielded "For Your Precious Love," which was issued on the label's Abner/Falcon subsidiary (named after Ewart Abner). The song became a Top Twenty pop hit but contributed to the destruction of the group because the record was inadvertently credited to Jerry Butler *and* the Impressions. Butler stayed with Vee Jay as a solo artist with Mayfield collaborating as a writer and arranger, but as recording artists, Mayfield and the rest of the Impressions switched to ABC-Paramount where Mayfield penned a series of gospel-influenced "sermon songs" that rightfully belong to the era of the Civil Rights movement, discussed later in this book. Vee Jay made its mark on rock 'n' roll with hits by Dee Clark ("Hey Little Girl," 1959 and "Raindrops," 1961), Gene Chandler ("Duke of Earl," 1962), and Betty Everett ("The Shoop Shoop Song (It's in His Kiss)," 1964).

> In terms of offering career direction to African American artists and displaying a knack for crossing black music over to a white audience, Vee Jay could have been what Motown became.

In terms of offering career direction to African American artists and displaying a knack for crossing black music over to a white audience, Vee Jay could have been what Motown became. Unfortunately, the company seemed to have a knack for losing many of its best acts. Gene Chandler, for example, signed with Constellation shortly after "Duke of Earl" ran its course. While Vee Jay introduced a number of name artists, including the Four Seasons, Gladys Knight and the Pips, and the Dells, many of these performers had their biggest successes after switching to other labels. Even the Beatles were first issued on Vee Jay in the United States, when Capitol initially passed on them. In 1966, the company unexpectedly folded amidst rumors of fiscal mismanagement.

Cincinnati: The Crossroads of Blues and Country

As a major rail stop situated along the Ohio River, Cincinnati had served for years as a gateway to northern iron and steel mills for blacks and poor whites from the South. As such, it was a crossroads for blues and country music. As noted, it was Syd Nathan's King Records that consolidated these influences into a diverse musical enterprise. Under the able direction of producer Henry Glover, Nathan's policy of encouraging his country and western artists and his rhythm and blues artists to record each other's songs provided early examples of the cultural cross-pollination that would yield rock 'n' roll.

Among King's country artists, the Delmore Brothers had first recorded blues-based country hits like "I've Got the Big River Blues" when they were with RCA. Still, it was Glover who continued their development with a wealth of blues-influenced material that culminated in the country hit "Blues Stay Away from Me" in 1949. Glover's biggest country breakthroughs were with Moon Mullican. Mullican demonstrated his affinity for multicultural sounds early on, scoring country hits with "What Have I Done to Make You Go Away," which was "borrowed" from a Louis Jordan tune, and "New Jole Blon," a takeoff on the French Cajun "Jole Blon." "[U]nder Glover's influence," according to historian John W. Rumble, "Mullican expressed his fascination with black music on levels that few country artists had ever attained."[32] With Glover, Mullican found a blues-boogie groove on "Southern Hospitality" and also recorded hit country versions of Nat King Cole's "Mona Lisa" and Leadbelly's "Good Night Irene."

Ivory Joe Hunter was an African American artist who moved in the other direction. Hunter had recorded a number of early r&b hits, such as "Landlord Blues" and "I Quit My Pretty Mama," for King in the late 1940s. By the time he left the company in 1950, his smooth style had begun to appeal to country music fans as well. He achieved pop crossover success with his biggest hit, "Since I Met You Baby" (1956), on Atlantic and ended his career more than a decade later as one of the few African American artists ever to become a regular on the *Grand Ole Opry*.

King Records eventually made a direct impact on the rock 'n' roll market with the Charms ("Hearts of Stone," 1954), Bill Doggett's combo ("Honky Tonk," 1956), and solo vocalist Little Willie John, who became a consistent hitmaker in the latter half of the 1950s with such Top Forty pop hits as "Fever" (1956), "Talk to Me, Talk to Me" (1958), and "Heartbreak (It's Hurtin' Me)" and an old Tin Pan Alley classic "Sleep" (1960). Needless to say, Henry Glover served as producer for all three acts. However, King's greatest influence on rock 'n' roll was exerted through its subsidiary, Federal, which was set up by Nathan in the early 1950s as part of a production deal with producer Ralph Bass. Bass quickly established a personality for the new label when he signed a number of gospel-influenced vocal harmony groups, including Billy Ward and the Dominoes, the "5" Royales, Hank Ballard and the Midnighters, and the Famous Flames, the group that sang backup for James Brown. These groups joined other African

American performers in challenging the perceived morality gap between gospel music and rhythm and blues, and together, they contributed one of the major strands to that style of rock 'n' roll known as doo wop.

R&B Sanctified: The Gospel Connection

In the late 1940s, as r&b grew in popularity, a fair amount of gospel music was also recorded in major city centers throughout the country. In the Northeast, New York's Apollo label had Mahalia Jackson; Savoy in Newark had James Cleveland; and Gotham in Philadelphia had the Famous Ward Singers. Three other well-known groups—the Dixie Hummingbirds, the Silver Echoes, and the Skylight Singers—recorded for a succession of labels in New York City. In the West, the best-known gospel talent, including the Pilgrim Travelers and the Soul Stirrers, appeared on Specialty. Black-owned Peacock Records, founded by Don Robey in Houston, recorded the Five Blind Boys of Mississippi and the Bells of Joy, among others.[38] There was at the time a sharp distinction between gospel and rhythm and blues, if not in the music industry, then certainly in the African American community. "[R]hythm and blues was felt to be degrading, low," said Robey, "and not to be heard by respectable people."[39] Rhythm and blues artists did not perform in church and gospel singers were expected to steer clear of "the devil's music." In the early 1950s, however, some gospel-trained singers began to move into the secular world of rhythm and blues, retaining a gospel tinge that is best seen in their use of organs, soaring vocals, background choruses, and the call-and-response style. The first group to develop this style was the Dominoes, founded in 1950 by the multitalented Billy Ward. In 1951, the group had three r&b successes on the Federal label—"Do Something For Me," "I Am with You," and "Sixty Minute Man" (featuring Bill Brown's bass), which became a crossover classic that caused no small stir in the gospel community. "Sixty Minute Man" boldly confronted all the controversy associated with the secularization of church music. Subsequent gospel-flavored releases, however, such as the Orioles' "Crying in the Chapel" (covered by June Valli for RCA) and "Shake a Hand" by Faye Adams, may have had a more profound effect than "Sixty Minute Man" because of their ambiguity. Both "Crying in the Chapel" and "Shake a Hand" were released in r&b and country versions, and both lent themselves to various interpretations along the sacred-secular continuum. "Here for the first time you were not sure exactly what ground you were on," r&b historian Peter Guralnick has written. "Were these love songs or devotionals? Was the second person singular you or You? It was an intentional ambivalence that was to persist."[40]

The Dominoes' early successes were due in large measure to the incredible leads of Clyde McPhatter who had been gospel trained. In 1952, McPhatter capped his stay with

> *There was at the time a sharp distinction between gospel and rhythm and blues in the African American community. Rhythm and blues artists did not perform in church and gospel singers were expected to steer clear of "the devil's music."*

the group with "Have Mercy Baby," a number one r&b hit. The following year he left the Dominoes to form his own group, the Drifters. He was replaced by the equally talented Jackie Wilson, who delivered a Top Twenty pop hit in 1956 with "St. Theresa of the Roses" on Decca. In 1957, Wilson went solo, and Billy Ward took over as lead vocalist, scoring two more Top Twenty pop hits for the Dominoes that year with "Star Dust" and "Deep Purple" on Liberty.

McPhatter and the Drifters were signed by Atlantic. Every member of the group had a gospel background, and between 1953 and 1955, the group delivered six Top Ten r&b hits for the company, including "Money Honey" and the double-sided hit "Such a Night"/"Lucille." They also did a stirring version of "White Christmas" with lead vocals by both McPhatter and bass Bill Pinckney. After McPhatter was drafted in 1955, the group went through a number of personnel changes and then disbanded. It was later reformed with new personnel and a totally new sound. McPhatter continued with Atlantic as a solo act after serving in the army and became an immediate r&b and pop sensation with such hits as "Treasure of Love" (1956), "Without Love (There Is Nothing)" (1957), and "A Lover's Question" (1958), which was number six on the pop charts. He continued producing hits well into the 1960s.

It was also Atlantic that produced the most influential gospel-tinged vocalist—Ray Charles Robinson, aka Ray Charles, aka "the Genius." Blinded by glaucoma as a youth,

With musical tastes ranging from Chopin to Nat "King" Cole, Ray Charles was a pioneer of the r&b/gospel fusion that has come to be known as rhythm and gospel. For many, his spirited live performances were, indeed, a religious experience.

Charles attended the St. Augustine School for the Deaf and the Blind where he learned to compose and arrange in Braille and then moved to Seattle. In Seattle, he dropped the Robinson to avoid confusion with Sugar Ray Robinson, who was then the middleweight boxing champion, and became Ray Charles. His musical influences were absolutely catholic, ranging from the Five Blind Boys of Mississippi to Chopin to legendary jazz pianist Art Tatum to jazz pianist cum pop vocal stylist Nat "King" Cole. Before leaving Florida, Charles had even joined a hillbilly band in Tampa and learned to yodel. After cutting some forty sides for Swingtime Records in the late 1940s and early 1950s, including a few r&b hits, he was signed by Atlantic in 1952.

Charles was one artist at that time who did not see a contradiction between gospel and r&b. "Now I'd been singing spirituals since I was three," he has said in his autobiography, "and I'd been hearing the blues for just as long. So what could be more natural than to combine them."[41] After a couple of years of groping for his musical persona, the genius began to hit his stride with a string of original r&b hits in 1954—"Don't You Know," "Come Back Baby," and the gospel-inflected "Hallelujah, I Just Love Her So." Often he mined the gospel repertory directly for new material: "Talkin' 'Bout Jesus" became "Talkin' 'Bout You"; "This Little Light of Mine" became "This Little Girl of Mine"; "How Jesus Died" became "Lonely Avenue." All the elements of his revolutionary jazz-gospel-r&b fusion were present by the time he released "I Got a Woman" (1954), one of his most influential, if not most successful, records. The impact of "I Got a Woman" has been remembered by popular music historians as nothing short of apocalyptic. "The very strategem of adapting a traditional gospel song, putting secular lyrics to it, and then delivering it with all the attendant fanfare of a Pentecostal service was, simply, staggering," Peter Guralnick has said. "It was like a blinding flash of light in which the millennium, all of a sudden and unannounced, had arrived."[42] The style reached its logical conclusion with the release of Charles' Top Ten classic, "What'd I Say" (1959), "a culmination of the gospel blues style that Ray Charles had virtually created, an altogether secular evocation of an actual church service, complete with moaning, groaning, and speaking in tongues, a joyous celebration of an utterly profane love."[43]

By this time, Jackie Wilson had left the Dominoes to pursue a solo career at Brunswick. His first six solo hits, which include "Reet Petite" (1957), "Lonely Teardrops" (1958), and "That's Why (I Love You So)" (1959), were cowritten by Berry Gordy, the founder of Motown. Wilson demonstrated his incredible versatility and vocal range in 1960 when Brunswick presented him with two new songs, "Night," based on "My Heart at Thy Sweet Voice" from the opera *Sampson and Delilah,* and "Alone at Last," taken from Tchaikovsky's "Piano Concerto No. 1." Both hit the Top Ten, and as Wilson has said, "Now they knew I wasn't just a screamer."[44] Wilson was still straddling the narrow line that separated gospel from rhythm and blues in 1967. His last Top Ten pop hit, "(Your Love Keeps Lifting Me) Higher and Higher," projected the same sexual/spiritual ambiguity that made the fusion so exciting in the first place.[45]

Perhaps the most profound gospel "desertion" was Sam Cooke's. Until 1957, Cooke was still at the top of the gospel heap as the lead singer for the Soul Stirrers, a group that could date its origins to 1934. The son of a Chicago Baptist minister, Cooke was singing in the church choir before he was ten. He joined the Soul Stirrers in 1950 and quickly became, according to gospel historian Tony Heilbut, "the greatest sex symbol in gospel history."[46] Still, the lure of the material world was present. In 1956,

Bumps Blackwell, Little Richard's producer at Specialty, which was also the Soul Stirrer's label, offered to "cut" Sam Cooke "pop." His first session yielded eight sides, one of which was "Lovable," which was then released, in a fairly transparent attempt to avoid the wrath of the gospel community, under the name of Dale Cook. Cooke agonized over what musical direction to take, but in the end the decision was made for him, as his outraged followers forced him to leave the Soul Stirrers.

Fearing reprisals from his gospel constituency, Art Rupe, owner of Specialty, released both Cooke and Blackwell from the label and gave them Cooke's masters in return for back royalties. The masters were offered to Bob Keene, who had just launched the Keen label. Blackwell became Cooke's manager as well as the head of artist and repertoire for the new company. Cooke's first Keen release, "You Send Me" (1957), climbed straight to number one on the pop charts; his pop appeal seemed as effortless as the gospel-influenced melismas he used to embellish his vocals. Seven more of his Keen releases entered the Top Forty over the next three years. By the end of the decade, Cooke was one of the hottest musical properties in the popular market. In 1960, RCA, a label with virtually no African American artists that was looking for an answer to the black velvet tones of Columbia's Johnny Mathis, signed Cooke. His talent over-

Like many African American singers who learned their trade in the church, Sam Cooke abandoned gospel for the secular world of commercial pop. He went on to become a major hit maker and a business institution with his own record label and publishing and management companies.

powered the generally pop material supplied by producers Hugo Peretti and Luigi Creatore, and he scored nineteen more Top Forty hits. "Chain Gang" (1960), "Twistin' the Night Away" (1962), "Another Saturday Night" (1963), and "Shake" (1964) all entered the Top Ten.

Cooke went on to become a business institution. In 1959, he took what was a rare step for an African American artist and formed his own publishing company, Kags Music, with his friend and mentor, J. W. Alexander, tenor vocalist for the Pilgrim Travelers. A Kags audit of Keen's royalty statements bankrupted the label and ended Cooke's relationship with Bumps Blackwell. Cooke and Alexander used their earnings from Kags to finance a production company, an artists' management company, and SAR (Sam and Alex) Records, arguably the first soul label. SAR served as a vehicle for another side of Sam Cooke—the writer/producer. SAR issued not only straight gospel recordings by the Soul Stirrers but also more soul-oriented material by Johnny Taylor (later of disco fame), the Sims Twins, who prefigured Sam and Dave, and the Valentinos, featuring Bobby Womack, all of whom were gospel artists who had been turned out.

Meanwhile, a number of full-fledged gospel groups moved into the material world of rhythm and blues. These groups found an outlet for their music in the King subsidiary Federal, which was second only to Atlantic in the successful production of "rhythm and gospel." The Gospel Starlighters gave up spiritual trappings to become the Famous Flames, James Brown's backup group. The echoes of the group's gospel past could be heard on "Please, Please, Please" (Federal, 1956), the group's first recording with Brown and an eventual million seller. The Royal Sons emerged as the "5" Royales, and after recording two Top Ten r&b hits ("Baby Don't Do It" and "Help Me Somebody") for Apollo in 1953, moved to King where the group recorded "Think" in 1957 and the original version of "Dedicated to the One I Love" in 1958. The latter song became a Top Ten pop hit for the Shirelles in 1961. After he had signed the "5" Royales, Syd Nathan changed the name of another group on his talent roster to avoid confusion; thus, the Royals became the Midnighters. The group's first recording under its new name, "Work with Me Annie" (1954), launched the erotic Annie series that rocked the gospel world to its foundations and shocked the rest of the nation in the process.

The Midnighters' lead singer, Hank Ballard, who had been heavily influenced by gospel as a boy, imbued the song with all the suggestiveness its title implied. If there was any doubt about the sexual connotation of the verb *work,* it was more than laid to rest in the two follow-up songs, "Sexy Ways" and "Annie Had a Baby," also released in 1954. All three were heavily censored, and all three were million sellers. "Work with Me Annie" was cited by at least one observer as "the Negro national anthem for 1954," because of its immense popularity.[47] The success of the trilogy spurred a number of decreasingly successful answer songs. The Midnighters themselves followed up with "Annie's Aunt Fanny," which fell flat. The El Dorados cut "Annie's Answer" for Vee Jay, which also fell flat. Even Buddy Holly recorded an Annie song called "Midnight Shift," which never went anywhere. A final bomb was offered by the Midnights (not to be confused with the Midnighters) who made "Annie Pulled a Humbug." There was, however, one answer song that was incredibly popular, Etta James' "Wallflower" (1955), popularly known as "Roll with Me Henry" (a reference to Hank Ballard). The song was so similar to the original "Work with Me Annie" that Ballard was credited as a cowriter along with Johnny Otis and Etta James. When pop singer Georgia Gibbs tried to eliminate all traces of James' eroticism for the mainstream audience by redoing the song as "Dance with Me Henry," Ballard and the Midnighters responded with "Henry's Got Flat Feet (Can't Dance No More)," which effectively ended the two-year affair.

Doo Wop: The Intersection of Gospel, Jazz, and Pop

To the average listener, the gospel-oriented vocal groups were virtually indistinguishable from those groups that employed a style of rock 'n' roll that came to be known as doo wop. Doo wop was the product of urban vocal harmony groups, mostly black and almost invariably male. The style owed as much of a debt to gospel, jazz, and pop as it did to the blues. Typical of the genre was a melodramatic, often gospel-inflected lead tenor who was bracketed by a distinctive bass and a soaring falsetto. Background vocals

> Doo wop was the product of urban vocal harmony groups, mostly black and almost invariably male. The style owed as much of a debt to gospel, jazz, and pop as it did to the blues.

typically consisted of nonsense syllables, such as "Sha-na-na-na sha-na-na-na-na," "Buzz-buzz-a-doodle-lee," "Shoo-doo-shoo-bee-doo," or "Oodly-pop-a-cow pop-a-cow pop-a-cow cow" (or however you choose to spell these syllables). "Doo" and "wop" were the syllables used to name the style, but not until well after the fact. In terms of output, doo wop was the largest single subgenre of rock 'n' roll to come into existence, and according to Greil Marcus, "it was the first form of rock & roll to take shape, to define itself as something people recognized as new, different, strange, *theirs*."[48] Doo wop came from just about every region in the country. While there were a few dozen groups who dominated the genre, hundreds more were destined only for obscurity. Among these were countless "bird groups" (the Ravens, the Orioles, the Larks, the Robins, the Swallows, the Flamingos, the Crows, the Cardinals, the Falcons, the Penguins, the Pelicans, the Jayhawks, and stretching the concept, the Feathers) and a slightly lesser number of "car groups" (the Cadillacs, the El Dorados, the Fleetwoods, the Continentals, the Impalas, the Imperials, even the Edsels).

In addition to its gospel roots, doo wop had roots in two black pop/jazz vocal harmony groups that had achieved mainstream success in the 1930s and 1940s—the Mills Brothers and, to an even greater degree, the Ink Spots, who turned out nearly fifty hits for Decca between 1939 and 1951. Both groups utilized close barbershop harmonies and light rhythms. The Ink Spots' "If I Didn't Care" and "My Prayer" (1939), featuring lead singer Bill Kenny's high tenor and "Hoppy" Jones' talking bass, are, by almost any measure, proto doo wop.

In the late 1940s, a number of young black groups—among them, the Ravens, the Four Tunes, the Four Knights, and the Orioles—tried to emulate, with some innovations and varying degrees of success, the style of these groups. The Ravens pioneered the use of the bass lead, reportedly by accident (the nervous bass vocalist, Jimmy Ricks, came in too strong on "My Sugar Is So Refined" during an appearance at the Apollo). The Ravens then repeated the "mis-take" on a recording of "Old Man River" (1946), which sold 2 million copies. Over the next several years, the group turned out a string of r&b hits, including "I Don't Have to Ride No More" (1950) for National and "Rock Me All Night Long" (1952) for Mercury, both of which achieved Top Ten r&b status.

Shortly after the Ravens' recording of "Old Man River," the Vibranaires came to the attention of Deborah Chessler, an astute manager-songwriter, in Baltimore, Maryland. The group and its manager were truly unique in a number of ways. As Greil Marcus has said, "they made their piece of history—a young Jewish woman and five black men in an utterly segregated American city. . . . Together they found the new sound."[49] After a booking on Arthur Godfrey's talent show in 1948, Chessler took a demo of the group to Jerry Blaine, a former bandleader who had recently founded Jubilee Records. Blaine was clearly moved; he renamed the group the Orioles and fashioned a special subsidiary label for them called It's a Natural. The group's very first recording—"It's Too Soon to Know," a Chessler tune that went Top Ten r&b in 1948—was Marcus' "new sound." Indeed, Marcus has suggested that this recording is a contender for "first rock 'n' roll record."

Blaine then switched the group to the Jubilee label, and they promptly followed their first recording with a string of r&b classics, including "Forgive and Forget" (1950), "Baby, Please Don't Go" (1952), and their biggest hit, "Crying in the Chapel" (1953). Jubilee also had the Four Tunes, a group that had r&b hits with "Marie" and "I Understand" in 1954, and the Cadillacs, a group that crossed over to the pop charts with the up-tempo "Speedo" in 1956. Other groups that tried to duplicate the Orioles' "cool" sound included the Larks ("My Reverie," 1951) on the Apollo label and the Five Keys ("Glory of Love," 1951) on Aladdin. In 1954, the Five Keys were signed by Capitol, and produced three Top Forty pop hits—"Ling Ting Tong" (1954), "Out of Sight, Out of Mind" (1956), and "Wisdom of a Fool" (1957).

One pattern that is noticeable immediately in doo wop is the dazzling array of "one hit wonders," groups that disappear after only one pop hit. There are also a significant number of doo wop groups that had just two pop hits before they were relegated to the revival circuit. This pattern is undoubtedly more a function of the treatment of these artists by their record companies than it is a statement about the talent of the groups. Others groups, for example, the Harptones ("Sunday Kind of Love" [1953, Bruce], "Life Is but a Dream" [1954, Paradise], and "What Will I Tell My Heart?" [1961, Companion]) simply bounced from label to label before fading from the scene. As illustrated in the following chart, the number of one- and two-hit groups is rivaled only by the number of places they came from and the number of different labels they recorded for, and it should be noted that the chart is not even close to exhaustive.

The most interesting thing about these one- and two-hit groups is that, in many instances, they made the recordings that define the style. More than in any other genre, it was individual and unrelated records, rather than the special imprint of a particular artist or producer, that gave doo wop its overall character. As a result, the history of the style often tends to read like a record catalogue. It is, however, a remarkable catalogue. Among the sounds that helped define an era were the Crows' fluid dance rhythm on "Gee," Carl Feaster's jazz scatting on "Sh-Boom," Cleveland Duncan's plaintive cry on "Earth Angel," the elegant balladry of Fred Parris on "Still of the Night" and Lee Andrews on "Tear Drops," the playful macho posturing of Mr. Earl (Carroll) on

The Chords were among the many "one hit wonders" who defined doo wop. Their "Sh-Boom" combines the jazz, pop, and r&b influences of the style and remains one of the most memorable songs of the rock 'n' roll era.

Notable One- and Two-Hit Doo Wop Groups

YEAR	GROUP	CITY	RECORD	LABEL
1953	Spiders	New Orleans	"I Didn't Want to Do It"	Imperial
1953	Spaniels	Chicago	"Baby It's You"	Chance
1954			"Goodnight, It's Time to Go"	Vee Jay
1954	Crows	New York	"Gee"	Rama
1954	Chords	New York	"Sh-Boom"	Cat
1954	Penguins	Los Angeles	"Earth Angel"	Dootone
1955	El Dorados	Chicago	"At My Front Door"	Vee Jay
1955	Nutmegs	Hartford, CT	"Story Untold"	Herald
1956	Six Teens	Los Angeles	"A Casual Look"	Flip
1956	Turbans	Philadelphia	"When You Dance"	Herald
1956	Five Satins	New Haven, CT	"In the Still of the Night"	Ember
1957			"To the Aisle"	Ember
1956	Cadillacs	New York	"Speedo"	Josie
1959			"Peek-A-Boo"	Josie
1956	Heartbeats	New York	"A Thousand Miles Away"	Rama
	became			
1961	Shep and the Limelites		"Daddy's Home"	Hull
1956	G-Clefs	Boston	"Ka-Ding Dong"	Terrace
1961			"I Understand Just How You Feel"	Terrace
1957	Rays	New York	"Silhouettes"	Cameo
1957	Mello-Tones	New York	"Rosie Lee"	Gee
1957	Mello-Kings	New York	"Tonight, Tonight"	Herald
1957	Dubs	New York	"Could This Be Magic"	Gone
1957	Techniques	New York	"Hey Little Girl"	Roulette
1957	Tune Weavers	Boston	"Happy, Happy Birthday Baby"	Checker
1957	Little Joe and the Thrillers	Philadelphia	"Peanuts"	OKeh

YEAR	GROUP	CITY	RECORD	LABEL
1957	Lee Andrews and the Hearts	Philadelphia	"Tear Drops"	Chess
1958			"Try the Impossible"	United Art.
1957	Gladiolas	Lancaster, SC	"Little Darlin'"	Excello
	became			
1960	Maurice Williams & the Zodiacs		"Stay"	Herald
1958	Elegants	New York	"Little Star"	Apt
1958	Danleers	New York	"One Summer Night"	Mercury
1958	Aquatones	New York	"You"	Fargo
1958	Monotones	Newark, NJ	"Book of Love"	Argo
1958	Silhouettes	Philadelphia	"Get a Job"	Ember
1958	Crescendos	Nashville	"Oh Julie"	Nasco
1959	Impalas	New York	"Sorry, I Ran All the Way Home"	Cub
1959	Mystics	New York	"Hushabye"	Laurie
1959	Falcons	Detroit	"You're So Fine"	Unart
1959	Fiestas	Newark, NJ	"So Fine"	Old Town
1959	Tempos	Pittsburgh, PA	"See You in September"	Climax
1960	Paradons	Bakersfield, CA	"Diamonds and Pearls"	Milestone
1960	Safaries	Los Angeles	"Image of a Girl"	Eldo
1961	Cleftones	New York	"Heart and Soul"	Gee
1961	Capris	New York	"There's a Moon Out Tonight"	Old Town
1961	Chimes	New York	"Once in a While"	Tag
1961			"I'm in the Mood for Love"	Tag
1961	Marcels	Pittsburgh, PA	"Blue Moon"	Colpix
1961			"Heartaches"	Colpix
1961	Edsels	Youngstown, OH	"Rama Lama Ding Dong"	Twin
1961	Velvets	Odessa, TX	"Tonight (Could Be the Night)"	Monument

"Speedo," the novelty value of Little Joe Cook's screeching falsetto on "Peanuts" and Fred Johnson's staccato bass on "Blue Moon," and the subtle Latin blush of the Elegants' "Little Star" and the Mystics' "Hushabye."

If there was a center for doo wop, it was definitely New York City. It has been said that Alan Freed had a particular affinity for vocal harmony groups, and perhaps this is why a greater number of groups and labels were centered in and around New York than any other region. Herald/Ember, founded by Al Silver in 1952, generally recorded out-of-state talent, the Nutmegs and the Five Satins from Connecticut and the Turbans and the Silhouettes from Pennsylvania. On the other hand, beginning

> **If there was a center for doo wop, it was definitely New York City.**

in 1952, Rama's founder, George Goldner, tended to recruit directly from New York's streets. After his initial success with the Crows, he launched a subsidiary, Gee (named after the Crows' only hit), which had hits with the Mello-Tones, the Cleftones, and Frankie Lymon and the Teenagers ("Why Do Fools Fall in Love" and "I Want You to Be My Girl" in 1956 and "Goody Goody" in 1957). In 1957, Goldner formed two other labels, Gone and End, that listed Alan Freed as producer. It was Freed who changed the name of the Chesters to Little Anthony and the Imperials. The group's "Tears on My Pillow" (1958) became a Top Ten pop hit on the End label. The group reformed in the mid-1960s and scored two more Top Ten hits on the DCP label—"Goin' Out of My Head" (1964) and "Hurts So Bad" (1965).

The label that had the most luck with vocal harmony groups was Atlantic. The company's first successful group was the Clovers from Washington, D.C. From 1951 to 1954, the group had thirteen consecutive Top Ten r&b hits, including "Don't You Know I Love You" and "Fool, Fool, Fool" (written by Ahmet Ertegun), "One Mint Julep," "Ting-a-Ling," and the original rock 'n' roll versions of "Blue Velvet" and "Devil or Angel," which were later pop hits for Bobby Vinton and Bobby Vee, respectively. The group's first pop hit was "Love, Love, Love" (1956). Its last was "Love Potion No. 9" (1959), a rock 'n' roll classic that was written and produced by Jerry Leiber and Mike Stoller for United Artists after the group had left Atlantic.

The writer/producer team of Leiber and Stoller achieved greatness with two other of Atlantic's vocal groups—the Coasters and the Drifters. The Coasters had begun in Los Angeles as the Robins and had recorded as such with Johnny Otis on Savoy in New Jersey. The group's "Double Crossing Blues" (1950) was a number one r&b hit. Although Leiber and Stoller, who were also originally from Los Angeles, had had their first song-writing successes with Charles Brown ("Hard Times") and Big Mama Thornton ("Hound Dog"), when they met the Robins, they chose the group as the vehicle for their novelty r&b songs ("playlets" as Leiber used to call them) on their new Spark label. Atlantic was sufficiently impressed with such songs as "Smokey Joe's Cafe" and "Riot in Cell Block No. 9" that the company bought the Robins' catalogue from Spark, signed the group to its Atco subsidiary, and hired Leiber and Stoller as independent producers (among the first in the business). Once signed to the New York label, the group changed

Under the tutelage of producers Leiber and Stoller, the Drifters took the vocal harmonies of doo wop to new heights and provided a gateway to the more produced r&b sounds of the early 1960s.

its name to the Coasters to reflect its West Coast origins. The first six releases— "Searchin'" and "Young Blood" (1957), "Yakety Yak" (1958), and "Charlie Brown," "Along Came Jones," and "Poison Ivy" (1959), all playlets written and produced by Leiber and Stoller and punctuated instrumentally by the "yakety sax" of King Curtis, made the pop Top Ten. The Coasters remained major hitmakers until 1961. Another Los Angeles group, the Olympics, came close to duplicating the Coasters' sound with such hits as "Western Movies" (1958, Demon) and "Big Boy Pete" (1960, Arvee).

After the original Drifters broke up, the group's manager, George Treadwell, who owned the name and had years remaining on contracts with the Apollo theater and Atlantic Records, persuaded another group that was known as the Five Crowns and featured Ben E. King on lead to take on the name. Produced by Leiber and Stoller, the new Drifters had immediate success with such hits as "There Goes My Baby" and "Dance with Me" in 1959 and "This Magic Moment" and "Save the Last Dance for Me" in 1960. When King left the group in 1960, he was replaced by the gospel-trained Rudy Lewis, who sang lead on "Up on the Roof" (1962) and "On Broadway" (1963). Lewis would have sung lead on "Under the Boardwalk" (1964), had he not died on the morning of the recording session. The emotionality of the group's performance at that session may well have had something to do with the intensity of the moment. The productions of Leiber and Stoller were so elaborate—often involving dozens of takes and significant editing to achieve the desired effect—that they must be seen as the start of the transition from the innocence and spontaneity (and amateurishness) of classic doo wop to the calculated products of the producer as an artist in his own right. It is this difference that separates the doo wop groups from the vocal harmony groups (chiefly, the "girl groups") of the 1960s.

New York, of course, was not the only place that produced doo wop, even during its formative stages. Both the Spaniels ("Baby It's You," 1953) and the Flamingos ("Golden Teardrops," 1953) started their recording careers with Chance Records in Chicago. The Spaniels then moved to Vee Jay where they recorded their biggest hit, "Goodnight, It's Time to Go," in 1954. Vee Jay also had the El Dorados, a group that scored with "At My Front Door" one year later. The Flamingos also broke through to the pop market on the End label with "Lovers Never Say Goodbye" in 1957. The group's biggest hits came at the end of the decade with "I Only Have Eyes for You" (1959) and "Nobody Loves Me Like You" (1960). Chicago's Chess label had the Moonglows, a group founded in Cleveland by Harvey Fuqua in 1951. The group scored three Top Thirty hits—"Sincerely" (1955), "See Saw" (1956), and "Ten Commandments of Love" (1958)—for Chess in the classic doo wop mold before Fuqua became immersed in Berry Gordy's Motown empire as a writer/producer.

In Cincinnati, King Records also tried to exploit the doo wop sound. In addition to the rhythm and gospel groups on its Federal subsidiary, King had the Charms ("Gum Drop" and "Hearts of Stone," 1954, "Ling Ting Tong," 1955, and "Ivory Tower," 1956) on the company's De Luxe label, which Syd Nathan had purchased from a New Jersey firm in 1953. Unfortunately for King, the company lost the group that went on to become the most successful of all the vocal harmony groups—the Platters. Originally signed to Federal, the group was often used as backup for some of the other acts. When Buck Ram, the group's coach and manager, insisted on $100 a session for background vocals, however, Nathan released them. Ram, who also managed the Penguins, negotiated a near impossible contract that signed both groups to Mercury, a major label, in 1955. The Penguins died without a follow-up to "Earth Angel," but the Platters scored twenty Top Forty pop hits over the next seven years.

Their first two releases for Mercury were Ram tunes: "Only You" went to number five in 1955 and "The Great Pretender" hit number one in 1956. It was the Platters, more than any other group, who carried the torch that had been lit by the Ink Spots two decades earlier. "My Prayer," a number one pop hit in 1956, was a virtual remake of the Ink Spots' 1939 original. Tony Williams' lead vocal paid homage to that of Bill Kenny before him. The Platters mined the past for other material as well. "Twilight Time," a number one hit in 1958, had been cowritten by Ram in 1938 for a group called the Three Suns. In 1958, the Platters also went to number one with Jerome Kern's "Smoke Gets in Your Eyes." "Harbor Lights" (1960), the group's last Top Ten hit, had been first popularized by Rudy Vallee in 1937. The Platters actually sounded more pop than doo wop. Still, their music was accepted as rock 'n' roll.

It is worth noting that most of the doo-wop groups were black. They were joined by a lesser number of white or integrated groups. Among the white doo-wop groups, Italian Americans predominated. The Mello-Kings ("Tonight, Tonight," 1957), according to Charlie Gillett, "succeeded remarkably well in achieving the 'pure' sound of black groups."[50] They were followed by the Elegants ("Little Star," 1958), the Mystics ("Hushabye," 1959), and the Capris ("There's a Moon Out Tonight," 1961). At the periphery of the style were the Royal Teens ("Short Shorts," 1958), featuring Bob Gaudio who went on to join the Four Seasons, and the Regents ("Barbara Ann," 1961), with Guy Villari on lead. The most popular Italian American doo-wop group came from Belmont Avenue in the Bronx. Thus, they called themselves Dion (DiMucci) and the Belmonts. Performed in classic doo-wop style, nonsense syllables and all, "I Wonder Why," the group's first of many releases on Laurie, became a Top Twenty pop hit in 1958. "A Teenager in Love" and "Where or When," the Rodgers and Hart classic, made the Top Ten in 1959 and 1960, respectively. In 1960, Dion left the group to pursue a solo career. By 1963, the handsome tenor had acquired thirteen Top Forty pop hits, a new wife (the inspiration for "Runaround Sue," recorded with the uncredited Del-Satins), and a drug problem that forced him out of the business for the next five years. The Belmonts had two more hits—"Tell Me Why" (1961) and "Come On Little Angel" (1962)—then faded from view.

> **M**ost of the doo-wop groups were black. Among the white doo-wop groups, Italian Americans predominated.

Dion and the Belmonts were one of the first white groups to pick up the torch of doo wop and carry it beyond the 1950s. Italian Americans all, they were true to the style and a testament to the hybridity of the music.

The Dell-Vikings, who met in the service, were the first racially integrated doo-wop group (three black singers and two white in the group's original incarnation) to hit the pop charts. "Come Go With Me" and "Whispering Bells" both entered the Top Ten in 1957. The group then switched from Dot to Mercury and turned out a number of lesser-known hits. Johnny Maestro and the Crests included an Italian American lead (John Mastrangelo), two African Americans (Tommy Gough and Jay Carter), and a Latino (Harold Torres). Honing their craft on the Lexington Avenue subway in New York, the Crests came to the attention of Coed Records for which the group recorded five Top Thirty hits. The best was the first—"Sixteen Candles" in 1958. When the Crests faded, Johnny Maestro disappeared onto the supper club circuit with the Del-Satins, a group that merged with a show band called the Rhythm Method in the 1960s to produce a new group, the Brooklyn Bridge ("The Worst Thing that Could Happen," 1967), with Maestro singing lead.

Second in rarity to racial integration was gender balance. Buck Ram added Zola Taylor to the Platters largely for show. Both the Skyliners ("Since I Don't Have You," 1959) and the Cleftones ("Heart and Soul," 1961) also performed with female vocalists who had no readily distinguishable roles. Certainly, in 1956, Trudy Williams' lead on the Six Teens' "A Casual Look" was a rare occurrence. Female leads were repeated by Margo Sylvia of the Tune Weavers on "Happy, Happy Birthday Baby" in 1957, Barbara Lee on the Aquatones' "You" in 1958, and in 1960, by Kathy Young with the Innocents on "A Thousand Stars." Each of these songs, however, had only a hint of doo wop. The Fleetwoods, a trio from Olympia, Washington, composed of two women and a man, would also have to be positioned at the margins of doo wop; their soft, elegant harmonies on "Come Softly to Me" and "Mr. Blue" in 1959 and "Tragedy" in 1961, were built around an almost seamless male-female blend.

> Second in rarity to racial integration was gender balance.

As for all-female groups, in the heyday of doo wop, there were few. Among the best were the Teen Queens ("Eddie My Love," 1956), the Bobbettes ("Mr. Lee," 1957), the Shepherd Sisters ("Alone," 1957), the Poni-Tails ("Born Too Late," 1958), the Quintones ("Down the Isle of Love," 1958), and the Chantels ("Maybe," 1958). In some ways, especially in the way their songs defined male-female relationships, these groups prefigured the arrival of the early 1960s "girl groups." Interestingly, the producer most associated with the "girl group" phenomenon, Phil Spector, who was also an assistant to Leiber and Stoller, got his first big break as part of a vocal trio with a female lead, the Teddy Bears. "To Know Him Is to Love Him," a song Spector fashioned from the inscription on his father's tombstone, featured Annette Kleinbard's lead and went to number one in 1958. Spector duplicated the soothing vocal sound with the Paris Sisters ("I Love How You Love Me") in 1961 before his production style became completely devoted to his legendary "wall of sound."

Doo-wop was a phenomenon of the 1950s that spilled over somewhat into the next decade. From Jersey City, the Duprees carried on the tradition with "You Belong to Me" in 1962. The Tymes ("So Much in Love" and "Wonderful, Wonderful," 1963) anticipated the soft soul sound that would be associated with their native Philadelphia at the end of the decade. Even in 1965, the Vogues ("Five O'Clock World") from Turtle Creek, Pennsylvania, and the Fortunes ("You've Got Your Troubles") from Britain could be associated, if vaguely, with the style. The Four Seasons could also trace their musical roots to doo wop. Beginning as the Four Lovers in Newark in 1956, the group scored a minor hit with "You're the Apple of My Eye" that same year. As the Four Seasons, the group's first single, "Sherry" (1962), a number one pop hit for Vee Jay, received significant airplay on black radio before a live appearance on American Bandstand revealed a white Italian American vocal harmony group. Even so, the group, which featured the three-octave range of lead singer Frankie Valli (born Francis Castelluccio), turned out twenty-nine chart singles over the next fifteen years in addition to Valli's nine solo hits. Still, as a phenomenon, doo-wop was over in 1961. As if to signal the demise of the style, Little Caesar and the Romans released "Those Oldies but Goodies" that same year. The song went to number nine on the pop charts, and the designation "oldies but goodies" was immediately applied to songs that had been released in the previous decade, including some that had been hits a year earlier.

Rockabilly: The Country Strain

It was, of course, only a matter of time until some young entrepreneur figured out, after the initial surge of rock 'n' roll, that white artists who could merge r&b and c&w with credibility would have enormous sales potential. The person who is usually credited with this discovery is Sam Phillips, who founded Sun Records in Memphis, Tennessee, in 1953. According to Marion Keisker, Phillips' secretary, Phillips once said, "If I could find a white man who had the Negro sound and the Negro feel, I could make a billion dollars."[51] The answer to his prayers was, needless to say, Elvis Presley, the man who was crowned the "King of Rock 'n' Roll." The rest, as rock 'n' roll lore would have it, is history or at least a serviceable version of it.

> *It was only a matter of time until some young entrepreneur figured out that white artists who could merge r&b and c&w with credibility would have enormous sales potential.*

In fact, Presley was not the first major white rock 'n' roll artist to reach the mainstream market with a fusion of r&b and c&w. That distinction belongs to Bill Haley and His Comets. Haley is often separated from Presley in the history of rock 'n' roll because of differences in musical style and public image. The music that Presley and the Sun artists who followed him played was called rockabilly after its amalgam of rocking

African American and so-called hillbilly styles. According to Charlie Gillett, rockabilly differs from Haley's fusion, in that it has "much looser rhythms, no saxophones, nor any chorus singing."[52] Haley's music, in contrast, sounds more arranged, more calculated. Haley related to his country roots through the instrumentation of a jump blues combo; Presley's early Sun sides did not even include drums. If such musical differences are significant, the difference between Haley's public persona and that of the rockabilly artists are even more so.

In the mythology of rockabilly, there is always something appealing about white southern performers, roughly the same age as their fans, who record with pronounced regional accents for independent labels. Presley was the archetype even after he no longer fit the image. Bill Haley had none of these things. Already balding and looking somewhat middle-aged by the time his career took off, he was, in fact, a most unlikely candidate to become a rock 'n' roll sensation. Born in Highland Park, Michigan, and singing with no distinguishable regional accent, Haley's celebrity as a rock 'n' roller seems all the more unlikely in that he was signed by a major label, Decca, and his best-selling record, "Rock Around the Clock," was written by two Tin Pan Alley veterans (Max Freedman and Jimmy DeKnight) who registered the song with ASCAP.

Bill Haley and His Comets drew their inspiration from sources as disparate as Bob Wills and the Texas Playboys and Louis Jordan and the Tympani Five in constructing their country/r&b fusion. Adding outrageous stage antics to the mix, they earned a memorable niche in rock 'n' roll history.

Haley and his group, however, were clearly open to a variety of influences. Indeed, he experimented with various styles for ten years before coming to the attention of the mainstream public, and he once described his early sound as "a combination of country and western, Dixieland, and the old style rhythm and blues."[53] His heroes were Bob Wills and His Texas Playboys, who played western swing, and his band approximated the pivotal sound of Louis Jordan. Haley's producer, Milt Gabler (who had been Jordan's producer in the 1940s), told Arnold Shaw that he had consciously modeled Haley's sound after Jordan's jump beat. "We'd begin with Jordan's shuffle rhythm," said Gabler. "You know, dotted eighth notes and sixteenths, and we'd build on it. I'd sing Jordan riffs to the group that would be picked up by the electric guitars and tenor sax. . . . They got a sound that had the drive of The Tympany Five and the color of country and western."[54]

In the early 1950s, Haley decided that r&b-flavored dance music was the key to his future. He did well with his own versions of Jackie Brenston's "Rocket 88" and "Rock the Joint" by Jimmy Preston. It was just after his "Crazy Man Crazy" hit number fifteen on the pop charts in 1953 that he signed with Decca. There, with Gabler as his producer, he enjoyed his biggest hits, including "Dim, Dim the Lights" (1954), "Burn That Candle" (1955), and "See You Later, Alligator" (1956). With its lyrics cleaned up, his 1954 version of Big Joe Turner's "Shake, Rattle, and Roll," became a classic rock 'n' roll recording and his first million seller. "Mambo Rock," a Top Twenty hit in 1955, was Haley's nod to the Latin dance craze that was then sweeping the nation.

Although it may now seem strange, when Haley's "Rock Around the Clock" was first released in 1954, it fizzled. Because of its Tin Pan Alley parentage, however, the song was selected as the theme for the Hollywood film, *Blackboard Jungle.*[55] Within weeks of the film's release in 1955, the song went to number one on the pop charts. It remained there for the next eight weeks, eventually becoming one of the biggest-selling rock 'n' roll records in history, with sales of nearly 17 million copies. By the time Elvis Presley hit the pop charts, more than a year after "Rock Around the Clock" was first released, Haley was in his thirties and over-the-hill by teenage standards. His star was soon supplanted by the younger rockabilly artists from Memphis—Carl Perkins, Johnny Cash, Jerry Lee Lewis, and of course, Presley himself.

Sam Phillips, the man who brought all these artists to the attention of the record-buying public, had a definite strategy in mind when he launched their careers. While Syd Nathan at King Records encouraged blues and country artists to record each other's songs, he expected his country artists to record country versions of r&b hits and vice-versa. He was not trying to break down racial barriers; he did not care if his white artists had "the Negro sound and the Negro feel" any more than he expected his African American artists to sound "country" (although some of this did happen). He was simply trying to maximize his income. Phillips, on the other hand, may have been just as economically motivated but he deliberately sought to filter the black experience through white performers, thus making it more accessible to the mainstream audience. As Peter Gural-nick has noted, "With Elvis, Phillips apparently found the key because following Elvis' success he had a succession of rockabillites who did just that. All of his major artists were poor whites who had not only lived in constant contact with black people all their lives but had obviously absorbed a great deal of their culture."[56]

Phillips' strategy earned Sun Records a place of mythic proportions in the history of rock 'n' roll, but it also raises all sorts of questions about rip-offs and racism.

Phillips was a former radio engineer who got into the recording business when he started the Memphis Recording Service in 1950. For $2 a side, anyone could walk in and make a record. It did not take Phillips long to realize that he had the only convenient studio around for the Delta bluesmen who played the nearby Beale Street clubs. In the days when Leonard and Phil Chess from Chicago and Saul and Jules Bihari, the founders of Modern/RPM in Los Angeles, were scouring the South with portable machines in search of new talent, Phillips was already recording Howlin' Wolf, B. B. King, Bobby Bland, James Cotton, Little Walter, Little Junior Parker, Elmore James, Walter Horton, and Rufus Thomas, among others. At first, he leased all his masters to Modern and Chess. But after producing such notable r&b hits as Jackie Brenston's "Rocket 88" and Little Walter's "Juke," for Chess and Checker, respectively, he decided to launch a full-fledged record label of his own—Sun Records. In its beginnings in 1952, Sun was devoted almost exclusively to rhythm and blues releases. The label's first r&b hit was Rufus Thomas' "Bear Cat" (1953), the answer song to Big Mama Thornton's "Hound Dog," which went to number three on the r&b charts and occasioned a lawsuit for an infringement of the "Hound Dog" copyright. That same year, a young truck driver whose family had moved to Memphis from Tupelo, Mississippi, stopped in at the Memphis Recording Service and paid $4 to cut two songs for his mother's birthday. The truck driver was Elvis Presley, and a little more than a year later he would profoundly alter the operations of Sun Records and change the face of popular music forever. "When Elvis and Carl Perkins and Johnny Cash come along," Rufus Thomas once said, "just like he catered to black, Phillips cut it off and went to white. No more blacks did he pick up at all."[57]

To a man (and they were all men), the white artists who gravitated toward Sun had grown up dirt poor and in close proximity to African Americans and their culture. Jerry Lee Lewis once explained how he

used to hang around Haney's Big House, that was a colored establishment where they had dances and such. . . . we was just kids, we wasn't allowed in. So we'd slip around to the back and sneak in whenever we could. I saw a lot of 'em there, all those blues players. No, it wasn't anything about us being white, we was just too young. . . . it wasn't no big thing just because it was a colored place. Of course we was about the only ones down there.[58]

Carl Perkins explained his background by noting that he had been

raised on a plantation in the flatlands of Lake Country, Tennessee, and we were about the only white people on it. I played with coloured kids, played football with socks stuffed with sand. Working in the cotton fields in the sun, music was the only escape. The coloured people would sing, and I'd join in, just a little kid, and that was coloured rhythm and blues, got named rock 'n' roll, got named that in 1956, but the same music was there years before, and it was my music.[59]

Elvis Aron Presley was born the only child (a twin brother was born dead) of poor, white Mississippi parents—Vernon and Gladys Presley—on 8 January 1935. When he was ten years old, he placed fifth in a talent contest singing "Old Shep," a sentimental country tune. He learned to play the guitar a year later when he received one as a birthday present. As a teenager in Memphis, Presley attended Pentecostal church services, and in a more secular vein, got turned on to the Delta bluesmen.

I'd play along with the radio or phonograph, and taught myself the chord positions. We were a religious family, going round together to sing at camp meetings and revivals, and I'd take my guitar with us when I could. I also dug the real low-down Mississippi singers, mostly Big Bill Broonzy and Big Boy Crudup, although they would scold me at home for listening to them.

"Sinful music," the townsfolk in Memphis said it was. Which never bothered me, I guess.[60]

It took Phillips more than a year to record Presley commercially, and there are at least two stories about Presley's first recording session for Sun. According to one, Phillips originally intended to work on a couple of sentimental ballads like the ones Presley had cut for his mother's birthday. When nothing gelled, Presley and session men Scotty Moore (guitar) and Bill Black (bass) started fooling around with Big Boy Crudup's "That's All Right." According to Presley, however, "That's All Right" was one of the songs Phillips had suggested. Either way, "That's All Right," backed with Bill Monroe's classic bluegrass tune, "Blue Moon of Kentucky," set in motion a chain reaction that ultimately transformed the pop landscape. Within a day or so, a dub of the recording was sent to Dewey Phillips (no relation to Sam), a Memphis deejay, who liked it so much that he played it thirty times in one night. By the time Sam Phillips had the record pressed, he had orders for 5,000 copies.

From the beginning, Presley presented a marketing dilemma. No one knew exactly what to make of this "hillbilly cat," as he was described by one early billing that managed to capture the tension of his down-home, yet wildly cool persona. "I recall one jockey telling me that Elvis was so country he shouldn't be played after 5 A.M.," said Sam Phillips. "And others said he was too black for them."[61] When Dewey Phillips interviewed Presley on the air, he made it a point to establish that Elvis had attended the all-white Humes High School "because a lot of people listening had thought he was colored."[62] Though Presley's first release combined r&b and c&w (as did all his subsequent Sun releases), he was marketed as country. The record, which was a local hit, appeared only on the Memphis c&w charts.

The professional reaction to Presley's unorthodox style was mixed. After his debut at the *Grand Ole Opry,* he was told to go back to truck driving. He had better luck at the *Louisiana Hayride,* where he became a regular. Invariably, his live performances were electrifying, as country singer Bob Luman recalled.

> This cat came out in red pants and a green coat and a pink shirt and socks, and had this sneer on his face and he stood behind the mike for five minutes, I'll bet, before he made a move. Then he hit his guitar a lick, and he broke two strings. I'd been playing ten years, and I hadn't broken a total of two strings. So there he was, these two strings dangling, and he hadn't done anything yet, and these high school girls were screaming and fainting and running up to the stage, and then he started to move his hips real slow like he had a thing for his guitar. That was Elvis Presley when he was about 19, playing Kilgore, Texas.[63]

Presley recorded a total of ten sides for Sun. Each of the five records had an r&b song backed with a c&w song:

"That's All Right"/"Blue Moon of Kentucky" (1954)
"Good Rockin' Tonight"/"I Don't Care if the Sun Don't Shine" (1954)
"Milkcow Blues Boogie"/"You're a Heartbreaker" (1955)
"Baby Let's Play House"/"I'm Left, You're Right, She's Gone" (1955)
"Mystery Train"/"I Forgot to Remember to Forget" (1955)

In their innocence and seeming spontaneity, these recordings contributed measurably to the construction of the Presley legend, and in their unique blend of cultural influences, they contributed to the definition of the rockabilly style. Still, although each record sold better than the one before it, Presley never reached a mass popular music audience through them. It was not until the heavy-handed Colonel Tom Parker replaced deejay Bob Neal as Presley's manager in 1955 that a developing career was transformed into the stuff that myths are made of.

Parker engineered the sale of Presley's contract to RCA-Victor for the then unheard of sum of $35,000 plus $5,000 in back royalties, which Presley used to purchase his fabled pink Cadillac. His first release for RCA, "Heartbreak Hotel" (1956), featuring Chet Atkins on guitar and Floyd Cramer on piano, went to number one on the pop charts and remained there for the next eight weeks. Later that same year, "Hound Dog"/"Don't Be Cruel," a double-sided hit, reached number one on the pop charts, the r&b charts, and the c&w charts simultaneously, perhaps the first record ever to do so. From that moment on, Elvis Presley enjoyed multiple Top Forty

It was not until the heavy-handed Colonel Tom Parker replaced deejay Bob Neal as Presley's manager in 1955 that a developing career was transformed into the stuff that myths are made of.

pop hits every year until the day he died. Parker's practice of allowing his star to record only songs with publishing rights assigned to Presley Music (BMI) or Gladys Music (ASCAP) restricted Presley's choice of material in later years but added significantly to his income. "When I first knew Elvis," Parker once said with pride, "he had a million dollars' worth of talent. Now he has a million dollars."[64] Under Parker's guidance, Presley's career options mushroomed to include records, TV appearances, movies, and finally Las Vegas club dates.

Following television appearances on the shows of Milton Berle, the Dorsey Brothers, and Steve Allen and just weeks after Ed Sullivan had said he would never book him, Parker landed Presley a coveted $50,000 series of slots on Sullivan's show. Sullivan tried to anticipate the objections of his family audience by ensuring that Presley would be filmed only from the waist up. However, mere cinematic censorship could not contain the popular appeal of "Elvis the Pelvis," as his detractors called him. Presley used one of his Sullivan appearances to debut the title song from his first film, *Love Me Tender*. The song became a number one pop hit and the film catapulted Presley to stardom in yet another medium.

While Presley's star would continue to rise as he became a pop idol, his influence as a seminal figure in the development of rock 'n' roll waned during his 1958 to 1960 stint in the army. Until that time, he had recorded some quality material and turned in more than a few memorable performances at RCA. After "Hound Dog," Leiber and Stoller were brought in to write "Don't" and "Jailhouse Rock," the title song for his third and probably best movie. Writer Otis Blackwell followed up "Don't Be Cruel" with "All Shook Up" in

1957. In 1958, "One Night" (a cleaned-up version of "One Night of Sin," cowritten by Dave Bartholomew for Smiley Lewis) came close to recapturing the excitement of his Sun recordings. At RCA, however, Presley's clear tenor, the stripped-down energy of early rockabilly, and the simplicity and straightforwardness of the Sun sound were overshadowed by vocal swoops from the higher to the lower register, bloated productions (supervised by Chet Atkins), and syrupy background choruses provided by the Jordanaires. This situation encouraged Presley to indulge the pop tendencies that had always been part of his musical aesthetic. After all, the blues and country aura of the Presley myth never adequately captured the range of styles that shaped the singer. The two songs he cut for his mother's birthday in 1953 were "My Happiness" and "That's When Your Heartaches Begin," both stylized ballads that had been popular hits for the Ink Spots. At the time he made his first commercial recordings, his singing idol was Dean Martin. Following military service, Presley reentered popular music through a TV special with Frank Sinatra. His inclination toward pop conventions was already evident in his ardent gushing on "Love Me Tender," which was adapted from the folksong "Aura Lee." It emerged full-blown in a number of the releases he made after his military service, such as "Are You Lonesome Tonight" written in 1926, "Surrender" adapted from "Come Back to Sorrento," and his own reputed favorite, "It's Now or Never," a pop-oriented, Latin-flavored number, based loosely on "O Sole Mio" by Mario Lanza, Presley's favorite opera star.

There has never been a career quite like that of Elvis Presley. All told, he charted 149 Top Forty hits on *Billboard*'s Hot 100 and ninety-two LPs on the album charts—all this with some of the most insipid material ever recorded. If he was able to infuse even his most middle-of-the-road recordings with some measure of exuberance, it did not come through in his films, which became increasingly more vacuous as the 1960s wore on.

Elvis Presley briefly redeemed himself as the quintessential rock 'n' roller in a TV special taped in 1968.

Indeed, Presley turned out some of the worst, although still profitable, films imaginable. Still, the soundtrack albums, as shallow as they were, almost invariably entered the Top Forty. "The fact is, I think, that Elvis was too well suited to success," Peter Guralnick has said. "He was intelligent, adaptable, ambitious, and sure of his goals. . . . He soon settled in fact on a fairly comfortable and formulaic approach which took advantage of his wide-ranging musical background, facility in a number of styles, real talent as a quick study, and almost total lack of taste."[65] He briefly redeemed himself as the quintessential rock 'n' roller in a TV special taped in 1968. "If you're looking for trouble," sneered Elvis into the camera, completely outfitted in black leather and looking his greased-back best, "you've come to the right place." In addition to the obligatory big production numbers, he was joined on stage by such old musical friends as Scotty Moore and drummer D.J. Fontana. In those moments, he recaptured the "young Elvis" pictured on his 1992 memorial postage stamp.[66]

When Sam Phillips sold Presley's contract to RCA, he staunchly defended what, in retrospect, appears to have been a miscalculation of monumental proportions. At the

Presley transforms wide-ranging pop tastes into solid gold

time, Phillips needed the money to capitalize Sun properly, and he thought he had another artist waiting in the wings who would be bigger than Elvis. At first, it seemed that Carl Perkins, the son of a sharecropper, would not disappoint; his "Blue Suede Shoes" entered the *Billboard* pop charts on 10 March 1956 and climbed to number two, making it Sun's best-selling record to date. (It was followed immediately by "Heartbreak Hotel," Presley's debut release on RCA, the record that kept it from hitting pop number one.) "Blue Suede Shoes" is listed in Dawson and Propes' *What Was the First Rock 'n' Roll Record* as a contender "because it kicked up dust in all markets. Occasionally an R&B or country record strayed onto the pop charts, and big pop songs often sloshed over into one of the specialized charts, but Perkins' little paean to fancy footwear was the first to capture them all."[67] It is this kind of cross-genre appeal that lands Perkins in the company of Jimmie Rodgers and Hank Williams.

Like Presley, Perkins was a poor white southerner whose musical influences crossed racial lines. At the top of Perkins' list of sources were the *Grand Ole Opry* and a black sharecropper named Uncle John Westbrook, who lived across the field from him. One of his early rockabilly recordings, "Gone, Gone, Gone," hinted at a fusion of blues and country. "That's what rockabilly music is," he once said, "a country man's song with a black man's rhythm."[68] With the success of "Blue Suede Shoes," it appeared as if Perkins might ride that formula to even greater heights than Presley, but just as he was about to take off commercially, he was nearly killed in a car crash on his way to New York for an appearance on the Ed Sullivan show. Perkins never entered the Top Forty again, and his career never regained its momentum. Still his influence on rock 'n' roll is undeniable. In 1964, the Beatles invited him to a recording session where they recorded three of his songs—"Honey Don't," "Everybody's Trying to Be My Baby," and his adaptation of an old Blind Lemon Jefferson song, "Matchbox."

The rock 'n' roller who did the most to keep Sun operating in the black after Presley's departure and Perkins' misfortune was the uncontrollable Jerry Lee Lewis, who seemed to have a knack for revealing the underside of the fusion that made rockabilly. Typical of rockabillies, Lewis grew up poor amidst that convoluted southern mixture of music and religion, sin and depravity. Nicknamed "the Killer" in his adolescence, Lewis' personal life has been peppered with more than its share of debauchery and violence (two of his six wives died under mysterious circumstances). He quit high school after logging a record twenty-nine Fs and was then expelled from Bible school as well. By the time he was signed by Sun in 1956, he made Elvis look like a Boy Scout. There was, it could be said, a certain consistency between his personal life and his musical life; he rode his piano just as hard as he rode everyone around him. Once forced to take second billing to Chuck Berry at an Alan Freed show, Lewis reportedly closed his set with a frenzied rendition of "Whole Lotta Shakin' Goin' On" as he set fire to the piano. With the crowd boosted to fever pitch, he walked off stage and calmly said to Berry: "Follow *that*, Nigger."[69]

In terms of his music, Lewis came from a long line of hard-rocking piano men, including the boogie woogie greats on the r&b side and artists like Moon Mullican on the country side. With his boogie-powered "pumping piano," as his instrument was billed, Lewis turned out three Top Ten pop hits in a row for Sun, "Whole Lotta Shakin' Goin' On" and "Great Balls of Fire" (1957), and "Breathless" (1958). "Whole Lotta Shakin'" not only went to number three on the pop charts, it topped the c&w and the r&b charts as well. Shortly after "Breathless," however, Lewis left his second wife, and without divorcing her, married his thirteen-year-old cousin, Myra, whose father played bass in Lewis' band. The press, of course, had a field day with Lewis, who was on tour in Great Britain with Myra in attendance. The remaining concerts in Britain were canceled and Lewis returned home to a career in shambles. He hit the pop charts three more times, but like Perkins, he was never a pop headliner again.

While Presley, Perkins, and Lewis were Sun's most notable artists, other white southern artists also passed through the company on their way to stardom or obscurity elsewhere. Warren Smith recorded the memorable (and racist) "Ubangi Stomp" and "So Long, I'm Gone," a minor pop hit, for Sun before settling for a short-lived country career on Liberty. Charlie Rich began as a session musician at Sun and had a minor pop hit with "Lonely Weekends" in 1960. He became a major country star a decade later. Conway Twitty recorded for the label under his real name, Harold Jenkins, but none of his recordings were released. Roy Orbison cut a version of "Ooby Dooby" at Sun before switching to Monument. Johnny Cash started at Sun in 1955. After a few country hits (including "Folsom Prison Blues"), "I Walk the Line" became a Top Twenty pop hit in 1956. A photograph of Cash, Presley, Perkins, and Lewis that year had as its caption "the million dollar quartet." Cash switched to Columbia in 1958 and embarked on a career that included gold and platinum albums, films, and even his own television show.

> The sound Sam Phillips had created—soulful white singers from the grassroots, embellished by tape delay echo and backed by instrumentation (slap bass, electric guitar, pumping piano) that straddled c&w and r&b perfectly—defines one of the major strands of rock 'n' roll.

As the 1950s drew to a close, Sam Phillips began to treat Sun as something of a sideline. Still, the sound he had created—soulful white singers from the grassroots, embellished by tape delay echo and backed by instrumentation (slap bass, electric guitar, pumping piano) that straddled c&w and r&b perfectly—defines one of the major strands of rock 'n' roll. It was Phillips' introduction of the rockabilly style that set the stage for other white rock 'n' rollers who fell at various points along the r&b/c&w continuum and, thus, made possible the search for the "new Elvis" elsewhere.

Impressed by RCA's success with Presley, Capitol decided to take a chance on Vincent Eugene Craddock, better known as Gene Vincent, a former U.S. Navy enlistee from Norfolk, Virginia, who had injured a leg in a motorcycle accident. On Vincent's first release, "Be-Bop-A-Lula" (1956), a song reportedly inspired by the *Little Lulu* comic strip,

Capitol engineers pumped up Vincent's naturally gentle voice with "flutter echo" to achieve "a perverse, gothic performance."[70] Vincent intended the song to be the B side of the record, but "Woman Love" on the flip side was an "overtly sexual record, full of glottal twitches and orgasmic pantings" that was judged hardly suitable for mainstream airplay.[71] Capitol issued nineteen Gene Vincent records before he left the label in 1961. Only two more made the Top Forty in the United States—"Lotta Lovin'" (1957) and "Dance to the Bop" (1958). Although Vincent never hit his stride in the United States, he was revered in Great Britain and, hounded by the IRS, emigrated there in 1959. Eddie Cochran ("Summertime Blues," 1958), another would-be Elvis whose career followed a similar trajectory, joined Vincent for a British tour in 1960. The previous year, Cochran had recorded "Three Stars," a song commemorating the deaths of Richie Valens, the Big Bopper, and Buddy Holly. At the end of his British tour, Cochran was killed instantly as the limousine transporting him, his girlfriend Sharon Sheeley, and Vincent careened off the road while en route to the airport. Sheeley was hospitalized. Vincent suffered another injury to his bad leg and never really recovered from the incident. The British, however, gobbled up Cochran and Vincent recordings just as they had earlier gobbled up Bill Haley and Little Richard recordings earlier.

Buddy Holly was another artist who enjoyed greater success in Great Britain than in the United States. Indeed, some of Holly's songs that were hits in Great Britain—"It's So Easy," for example—did not even chart on this side of the Atlantic. Still, at the time of his death, Holly was probably positioned better than anyone else to follow in Presley's footsteps. Holly was one of a number of Texas-born rockabillies to reach the pop audience. He started performing as part of a country duo, but it was his flair for rock 'n' roll that brought him to the attention of Decca Records in 1955. If Bill Haley, a balding man with a spit curl, could make hits, reasoned Decca, why not a younger man with "coke-bottle" glasses? Unfortunately, Holly was handled poorly by producer Owen Bradley and released from Decca at the end of 1956. Undaunted, Holly returned to his native Lubbock, Texas, where he formed the Crickets and then went to Clovis, New Mexico, to record with Norman Petty. Petty already had a notable rock 'n' roll success brewing with another Texas group, the Rhythm Orchids, for whom he produced "Party Doll" and "I'm Stickin' with You." Bandleaders Buddy Knox and Jimmy Bowen sold the masters to Morris Levy at Roulette Records in New York. Levy released the cuts separately as "Party Doll" by Buddy Knox and "I'm Stickin' with You" by Jimmy Bowen with the Rhythm Orchids. "Stickin'" went to number fourteen and "Party Doll" hit number one, establishing Roulette as a significant rock 'n' roll label and Petty as a producer to watch. The Petty/Holly/Crickets collaboration proved to be worthwhile for all concerned. The first release, "That'll Be the Day" (1957)—actually a revved-up, heavily electrified version of a number Holly had cut for Decca earlier—turned out to be the best and most successful recording any of them ever made. At the time, however, that outcome probably seemed highly unlikely to all of them. The song was turned down not only by Roulette but also by Atlantic, Columbia, and RCA. Ironically, Bob Thiele, a Decca producer, had engineered a contract for the Crickets on Brunswick and a solo deal for Holly on Coral, both Decca subsidiaries after Holly's relationship with Decca was terminated.

Coral was a more conservative label that featured acts like the McGuire Sisters and Lawrence Welk. Releases such as "Early in the Morning" and "Rave On," both in 1958, must have tested the label's limits.

"That'll Be the Day" was finally released on Brunswick and promptly shot straight to number one, remaining in the Top Forty for sixteen weeks. Holly and the Crickets celebrated by recording fifteen more songs in Petty's studio. Their next release, "Peggy Sue," issued on Coral in 1957 and backed with "Everyday," was credited only to Buddy Holly. It was followed one month later by "Oh Boy!" backed with "Not Fade Away," which was credited to the Crickets, on Brunswick. Coral was a more conservative label that featured acts like the McGuire Sisters and Lawrence Welk. It is not surprising, therefore, that Holly's "softer" material was first released on Coral. Subsequent Coral releases such as "Early in the Morning" (recorded without the Crickets) and "Rave On," both in 1958, must have tested the label's limits.

In retrospect, it seems difficult to imagine that anyone could mistake Buddy Holly and the Crickets for a black r&b act. In the 1950s, however, rock 'n' roll was an expression of cultural upheaval that was rife with racial ambiguities. As "country" as "That'll Be the Day" may sound today, it was an r&b hit in 1957. In fact, Holly was the only major rockabilly act who never had a country hit. As incredible as it may seem, Buddy Holly and the Crickets were booked, sight unseen, into the Apollo Theater. Even if owner Frank Schiffman knew who they were, most of the audience did not. "I knew his records," recalled singer Leslie Uggams who saw Holly's Apollo performance. "You thought, 'Hey, another brother out there doing his number.' Then this white guy comes out and everybody says, 'Oh, that's Buddy Holly!' . . . You know, here comes this guy

The fact that Buddy Holly did not fit the description of a teen idol did not prevent him from becoming a rock 'n' roll legend. He and his group, the Crickets, were regular hit makers on the pop and r&b charts. Interestingly, they never had a country hit.

Buddy Holly's unique sound strangely appealing in the r&b market

with these glasses and funny-looking suit and stuff. I said, 'He's white, isn't he?' But he was terrific."[72]

Crossing racial barriers touched Holly's personal life as well. On one of his first trips to New York, he proposed to, and eventually married, Maria Elena Santiago, a Puerto Rican receptionist at Peer-Southern Music. A new wife and the lure of New York precipitated a split between Holly, the Crickets, and Petty. Holly's last recording with the group was "It Doesn't Matter Anymore" (1959), a pop-oriented Paul Anka tune that was recorded in Petty's studio with a full string section. The song hit the pop charts one month after Holly's untimely death.

Another Texas rocker with equally bad vision followed Holly. Roy Orbison's image complemented the pathos he evoked in his lead vocals. Like Holly, Orbison, who usually dressed in black, first recorded in Petty's studio. However, he quickly moved to Sun, RCA, and finally to Monument where he made his biggest hits. "Only the Lonely" (1960), his first Top Ten pop hit, featured a heart-wrenching vocal in a call-and-response style with a hint of Latin flavor. It embodied the diverse cultural influences of rock 'n' roll in classic style. Orbison's incredible vocal range and crystal-clear upper register lent a distinctive sound to the releases that followed—"Blue Angel" (1960), "Running Scared" and "Crying" (1961) and "Dream Baby" (1962). Perhaps because of his unique vocal talents, Orbison was among the few rockabilly artists to ride out the British Invasion. His biggest hit, "Oh, Pretty Woman" (1964), hit number one at a time when the U.S. pop charts were dominated by the Beatles and a host of other British groups.

Somewhat outside the Sun orbit, but well within the boundaries of rockabilly, were the Everly Brothers who were among the most successful of country-influenced rock 'n' rollers. Their close harmonies were characteristic of country music, but their syncopated guitar riffs, positioned as instrumental responses to their vocal leads, suggested possible African American influences. Their father, Ike, was himself a blues-influenced guitar player. In the early 1950s, brothers Don and Phil went to Nashville to sing and write songs for Acuff-Rose. When "Bye Bye Love" (Cadence, 1957) went to number two on the pop charts, they gave Nashville a new profile in rock 'n' roll and launched a career that included twenty-six Top Forty pop hits, including four that went to number one: "Wake Up Little Susie" (1957), "All I Have to Do Is Dream" and "Bird Dog" (1958), and "Cathy's Clown" (1960).

The appeal of country-influenced rock 'n' roll enabled a number of major label country acts to experience success in the pop market. Columbia weighed in with Guy Mitchell and Marty Robbins. Mitchell's "Singing the Blues" (1956) and "Heartaches by the Number" (1959) both went to number one. In 1957, he recorded a song called "Rock-A-Billy" that hit the Top Ten. Robbins broke the top three three times with "A White Sport Coat (and a Pink Carnation)" (1957), "El Paso" (1959), and "Don't

Worry" (1961). Capitol had Sonny James ("Young Love"), Tommy Sands ("Teen-Age Crush"), and Ferlin Husky ("Gone"), all of whom had their biggest hits in 1957. Everly soundalikes, the Kalin Twins (Herbie and Hal), had a number five hit with "When" (1958) on Decca. Patsy Cline ("Walking After Midnight," "I Fall to Pieces," "Crazy"), also signed by Decca, was a straight country artist who crossed over to the pop market on the heels of country rock. Conway Twitty on MGM made the Top Ten three times with "It's Only Make Believe" (1958), "Danny Boy" (1959), and "Lonely Blue Boy" (1960). Don Gibson hit the Top Ten with "Oh Lonesome Me" for RCA in 1958.

Although rockabilly broadened the appeal of certain country artists, it was no kinder to women than the rest of rock 'n' roll. It was not that women could not sing rockabilly. Charlene Arthur and Janis Martin ("the Female Elvis"), who recorded for RCA, and Barbara Pittman, who recorded for Sun, had the force of personality to deliver the goods, but a lack of interest in them, a dearth of good material, weak promotion, and/or outright male hostility kept these women from the attention of the mainstream public.[73] Patsy Cline, like Kitty Wells ("It Wasn't God Who Made Honky Tonk Angels") before her, could get in touch with rockabilly sentiments, but she and the other female vocalists were restrained by the double standard of the culture that nurtured them. When Arthur, Martin, and Pittman went against those constraints, they paid the price of obscurity for their trouble. Except for Capitol's hard-rocking Wanda Jackson, who edged into the Top Forty three times beginning with "Let's Have a Party" in 1960, there was only one other woman of note who could be included in a discussion of rockabilly—the diminutive Brenda Mae Tarpley, known professionally as Brenda Lee. Signed by Decca at the age of eleven, she turned out twenty-nine Top Forty hits between 1960 and 1967, including the suggestive "Sweet Nothin's" and two number one ballads, "I'm Sorry" and "I Want to Be Wanted." Like Orbison, she rode out the British onslaught with dignity (and hits), then returned to more traditional country roots for the remainder of her career.

> **Although rockabilly broadened the appeal of certain country artists, it was no kinder to women than the rest of rock 'n' roll.**

Sam Phillips may have been the first rock 'n' roll producer to look for "a white man with the Negro sound," but he was not the only one. Ace Records tried for this with Frankie Ford, and in 1957, after years of promoting black artists exclusively, Atlantic signed Bobby Darin to the company's Atco subsidiary. Two of his earliest releases on Atco, "Splish Splash" and "Queen of the Hop," hit the Top Ten on both the pop and the r&b charts in 1958. To their credit and the credit of the labels that signed them, these artists had at least some musical connection to the styles they interpreted. Unfortunately, the same cannot be said of the next generation of white rockers. Performers like Frankie Avalon, Fabian, and Bobby Rydell mustered little more in the way of talent than boy-next-door good looks and a feeble Elvis sneer. They had few if any identifiable links to previous rock 'n' roll styles, but youthful attractiveness and some semblance of rhythm enabled them to be successfully marketed as rock 'n' roll singers.

Such a musical development may have been inevitable, but it still served the purposes of those who were terrified by the cultural implications of rock 'n' roll. The energy of early rock 'n' roll had crossed lines of age, class, race, and culture in a country that seldom takes kindly to social upheaval and certainly did not during the conservative 1950s. As soon as rock 'n' roll captured the hearts, minds, and bodies of teenagers across all demographic categories, it was linked by some with every perceived social ill from juvenile delinquency and miscegenation to atheism and communism. Asa Carter, executive secretary of the Alabama White Citizens Council, put the threat that some perceived in rock 'n' roll starkly when he said in 1956, "the obscenity and vulgarity of the rock 'n' roll music is obviously a means by which the white man and his children can be driven to the level with a 'nigra'. . . . If we choose to call it the Communist ideology, I think we hit it fairly on the head."[75] While Carter's position was extreme, rhetoric like this pushed all the emotional buttons of most worried white middle-class parents. If some variant of rock 'n' roll was "here to stay," as Danny and the Juniors had prophesied in 1958, nowhere was it written that social pressures could not alter its character. The rock 'n' roll facelift of the late 1950s was but the most visible manifestation of a much broader reaction to the music.

NOTES

1. Charlie Gillett, *The Sound of the City: The Rise of Rock and Roll* (New York: Outerbridge and Dienstfrey, 1970), 1.

2. Nick Tosches, *Country: Living Legends and Dying Metaphors in America's Biggest Music* (New York: Charles Scribner's Sons, 1985), 32.

3. Jim Dawson and Steve Propes, *What Was the First Rock 'n' Roll Record?* (Boston: Faber and Faber, 1992), xvi–xvii.

4. Tosches, *Country*, 28.

5. Robert Palmer, "The Fifties," *Rolling Stone*, 19 April 1990, 48.

6. George Lipsitz, *Class and Culture in Cold War America* (South Hadley, Mass.: J. F. Bergin, 1982), 214.

7. Steve Perry, "Ain't No Mountain High Enough: The Politics of Crossover," in *Facing the Music*, ed. Simon Frith (New York: Pantheon Books, 1988), 67–68.

8. Greil Marcus, *Mystery Train: Images of America in Rock 'n' Roll* (New York: Dutton, 1975), 166.

9. In *San Antonio Rose: The Life and Music of Bob Wills* (Urbana: University of Illinois Press, 1976), Charles R. Townshend suggests that Walker and his friend Charlie Christian (who was to electric jazz guitar what Walker was to electric blues) were themselves influenced by white, western-swing electric guitarists Bob Dunn, who played for Milton Brown and His Musical Brownies, and Leon McAuliffe, who was a steel guitarist for Bob Wills and His Texas Playboys. In "The Church of the Sonic Guitar," *South Atlantic Quarterly* 90, no. 4 (Fall 1991), Robert Palmer argues that Walker's style is derived from Blind Lemon Jefferson and jazz licks he learned from Christian.

10. Palmer, "The Church of the Sonic Guitar," 652.

11. John Storm Roberts, *The Latin Tinge: The Impact of Latin American Music on the United States* (Tivoli, N.Y.: Original Music, 1985), 136.

12. Gillett, *The Sound of the City*, 42.

13. For a more detailed discussion of the concentration of the music industry during this period, see Richard A. Peterson and David C. Berger, "Cycles in Symbol Production: The Case of Popular Music," *American Sociological Review* (April 1975).

14. Erik Barnouw, *The Golden Web: A History of Broadcasting in the United States, 1933–1953* (New York: Oxford University Press, 1966), 221.

15. Arnold Shaw, *The Rockin' '50s* (New York: Hawthorne Books, 1974), 66.

16. Ibid., 235.

17. Richard A. Peterson, "Why 1955? Explaining the Advent of Rock Music," *Popular Music* (January 1990): 113.

18. Langdon Winner, "The Sound of New Orleans," in *The Rolling Stone Illustrated History of Rock 'n' Roll,* ed. Jim Miller (New York: Rolling Stone Press, 1976), 42.

19. Gillett, *The Sound of the City*, 148.

20. John Broven, *Rhythm and Blues in New Orleans* (Gretna, La.: Pelican Publishing Co., 1988), 29.

21. Ibid., 64.

22. Ibid., 14.

23. Winner, "The Sound of New Orleans," 46.

24. Arnold Shaw, *Honkers and Shouters: The Golden Years of Rhythm and Blues* (New York: Collier Books, 1978), 190.

25. Shaw, *The Rockin' '50s,* 210.

26. Ibid. Since then, Richard has tried to manage the tension between his ministry and his music career. Invariably, his irrepressible rock 'n' roll spirit shows through.

27. Steve Chapple and Reebee Garofalo, *Rock 'n' Roll Is Here to Pay: The History and Politics of the Music Industry* (Chicago: Nelson-Hall, 1977), 233.

28. Johnny Ace was the first major rock 'n' roll fatality. He died playing Russian roulette on tour on Christmas eve in 1954, just before "Pledging My Love" hit the pop charts.

29. Preston Love, preface to *Listen to the Lambs,* by Johnny Otis (New York: W. W. Norton, 1968).

30. Shaw, *Honkers and Shouters,* 278.

31. Malone, *Country Music U.S.A.,* 209.

32. John W. Rumble, "Roots of Rock 'n' Roll: Henry Glover at King Records," *Country Music Journal* (Vol. 14, No. 2, 1992): 38.

33. Michael Lydon, *Rock Folk: Portraits from the Rock 'n' Roll Pantheon* (New York: Dell, 1968), 10.

34. Gillett, *The Sound of the City*, 96–97.

35. Nelson George, *The Death of Rhythm and Blues* (New York: Pantheon Books, 1988), 68.

36. Lydon, *Rock Folk,* 20.

37. Robert Pruter, *Chicago Soul* (Urbana: University of Illinois Press, 1992), 25.

38. Robey also bought Duke Records from founder James Mattis, who was a deejay for WDIA in Memphis, thus forming the Duke/Peacock complex.

39. Shaw, *Honkers and Shouters,* 479.

40. Peter Guralnick, *Sweet Soul Music: Rhythm and Blues and the Southern Dream of Freedom* (New York: Harper and Row, 1986), 26.

41. Ray Charles and David Ritz, *Brother Ray: Ray Charles' Own Story* (New York: DaCapo Press, 1992), 149.

42. Guralnick, *Sweet Soul Music,* 50.

43. Ibid., 66.

44. Shaw, *Honkers and Shouters,* 444.

45. Wilson suffered a heart attack on stage in 1975 and remained in a coma until he died in 1984.

46. Tony Heilbut, *The Gospel Sound: Good News and Bad Times* (New York: Simon and Schuster, 1971), 76.

47. Gillett, *The Sound of the City,* 182.

48. Greil Marcus, "Is This the Woman Who Invented Rock & Roll?: The Deborah Chessler Story," *Rolling Stone,* 24 June 1993, 41.

49. Ibid., 43.

50. Gillett, *The Sound of the City,* 89.

51. Peter Guralnick, *Feel Like Going Home: Portraits in Blues and Rock 'n' Roll* (New York: E. P. Dutton, 1971), 140.

52. Gillett, *The Sound of the City,* 38.

53. Ibid., 30.

54. Shaw, *Honkers and Shouters,* 64.

55. *Blackboard Jungle* was the first Hollywood film to include a rock 'n' roll record in its soundtrack, which might not have happened without the advocacy of its Tin Pan Alley composers. Either *Rebel Without a Cause,* starring James Dean and released that same year, or *The Wild One,* released in 1954 with Marlon Brando in the lead role, would have been equally obvious choices for rock 'n' roll soundtracks, but both films used big-band soundtracks, which tended to contradict their themes of youth rebellion.

56. Guralnick, *Feel Like Going Home,* 140.

57. Peter Guralnick, *The Listener's Guide to the Blues* (New York: Facts on File, 1982), 80.

58. Guralnick, *Feel Like Going Home,* 149–50.

59. Lydon, *Rock Folk,* 32.

60. Gillett, *The Sound of the City,* 36.

61. Peter Guralnick, "Elvis Presley," in *The Rolling Stone Illustrated History of Rock 'n' Roll,* ed. Jim Miller (New York: Rolling Stone Press, 1976), 35.

62. Guralnick, *Feel Like Going Home,* 142.

63. Paul Hemphill, *Nashville Sound.*

64. Guralnick, "Elvis Presley," 36.

65. Ibid., 36, 38.

66. Presley died on 16 August 1977 in Memphis, a bloated, drugged-out caricature of his former self.

67. Dawson and Propes, *What Was the First Rock 'n' Roll Record?* 192.

68. Ibid.

69. Tosches, *Country,* 82.

70. Ibid., 95.

71. Ibid.

72. Ted Fox, *Showtime at the Apollo* (New York: Holt, Rinehart and Winston, 1983), 207.

73. For an excellent discussion of these unsung female rockabillies, see David Sanjek, "Can a Fujiyama Mama Be the Female Elvis? The Wild Wild Women of Rockabilly," in *Sexing the Groove*, ed. Shiela Whitely (New York: Routledge, 1996).

74. Chapple and Garofalo, *Rock 'n' Roll Is Here to Pay*, 246–47.

75. *Rock and Roll: The Early Days*, video documentary produced by Patrick Montgomery, 1985.

5 The Empire Strikes Back: The Reaction to Rock 'n' Roll

By the late 1950s, rock 'n' roll had changed the popular music landscape irrevocably and, in so doing, was signaling the coming of still broader social change. It was the prospect of this change that precipitated unbridled enthusiasm and vicious backlash in equal proportions. Economically, the music had enhanced the fortunes of what seemed to some, untutored writers and artists, upstart independent record companies, and wildly eccentric deejays. In essence, rock 'n' roll had turned the structure of the music business on its head. Aesthetically, the music had encouraged a tilt toward African American sensibilities and working-class styles. Thus, to some, it challenged the existing canons of cultural value and public taste. Socially, the music had threatened to upset the neat separation of the races that had guided, not just the operations of the music industry, but the dynamics of all social interaction to date. Depending upon how one felt about these things, rock 'n' roll was either celebrated as a true democratization of culture or decried as the destruction of Western civilization.

> *E*isenhower was as old-fashioned, conventional, bland, polite, and conservative as rock 'n' roll was youthful, innovative, wild, intrusive, and rebellious.

Given its impact and the conservative political climate in which it developed, it is not terribly surprising that rock 'n' roll became a target for repression. As surely as the 1950s are remembered musically as the decade of rock 'n' roll, they are remembered politically as the Eisenhower era. Two more diametrically opposed images would be hard to find. General, and then President, Dwight D. Eisenhower was as old-fashioned, conventional, bland, polite, and conservative as rock 'n' roll was youthful, innovative, wild, intrusive, and rebellious. By the mid-1950s, the general had developed a weak heart. Rock 'n' roll, in contrast, had nothing if not heart. If Eisenhower could be identified with golf (his favorite sport), rock 'n' roll could only be described as a demolition derby. The general, who had led the Allies during World War II, had become president in 1953 while U.S. troops were fighting Communists in Korea and Senator Joe McCarthy was feverishly manufacturing them at home. The Communists, who had been allies during World War II, had now become the enemy, a necessary condition for the consolidation and expansion of U.S. capitalism. Eisenhower presided over the containment of communism, the operative strategy of this country's postwar foreign policy. His secretary of state promised "massive retaliation" against anyone who violated U.S. turf. After the defeat of French colonialism in Vietnam, Eisenhower's vice president, Richard M. Nixon, pushed to implement the containment policy in that country, a course of action that precipitated cataclysmic political reverberations in the next decade.

As with the official government position on communism, the powers that be also attempted to contain culture within a certain narrow framework of acceptability. Complementing the lackluster Eisenhower persona, the following bland releases were listed in *Billboard* as the ten best-selling records for the year he took office:

1. Song from Moulin Rouge—Percy Faith
2. Vaya Con Dios—Les Paul and Mary Ford
3. Doggie in the Window—Patti Page
4. I'm Walking Behind You—Eddie Fisher
5. You, You, You—Ames Brothers
6. Till I Waltz Again with You—Teresa Brewer
7. April in Portugal—Les Baxter
8. No Other Love—Perry Como
9. Don't Let the Stars Get in Your Eyes—Perry Como
10. I Believe—Frankie Laine

Uninspiring political leaders and insipid popular music ran in tandem with another aspect of American life in the 1950s—mind-numbing conformity. Battle-weary veterans, seeking to forget the ravages of war, aspired to little more than peace, quiet, prosperity, and what they remembered as "family life." In their quest for these things, they sought refuge from the harshness of city life, if not the horrors of nuclear war, in a new, and ultimately desperate, place—suburbia. Entrance to this tranquil environment did not come without a price. Each workday, according to the stereotype of the 1950s, men commuted to city centers as members of David Reisman's "lonely crowd." In the workplace, they became "organization men," mere cogs in the machine of the expanding U.S. economy; their wives stayed at home, usually even more lonely and isolated than they were.

For their teenage children, the claustrophobic atmosphere of the workplace was replaced with the regimentation of school. In its essential features—the compartmentalization of knowledge, the passive reception of information, the pressure to achieve, the competition for grades, and the regulation of behavior by bells—school was preparation for work. It was, in the eyes of many, the job of the school to inculcate the values of rigidity and conformity in future workers and their future mates.

Unfortunately, rigidity and conformity, so desirable in the workplace and the military, conflicted sharply with the demands of the new consumer economy. The Great Depression had ended with the nation's entrance into World War II, but the successful conversion to a peacetime economy depended in part on creating an increased demand for consumer items. The single most important strategy in this effort was (and remains) the pleasure principle: People will buy that which they perceive as increasing their pleasure. The most obvious application of this principle could be seen in the growing use of sexuality to sell products. Thus, there was a contradiction between the social conditioning needed to produce a functioning workforce and the social conditioning needed to produce a model consumer who would be eager to absorb the surplus of manufactured goods. The values encouraged in the Protestant work ethic—discipline, frugality, asceticism, and abstinence—are best represented in a rather rigid, authoritarian, and sexually repressed personality. The ideal consumer, on the other hand, is an impulsive hedonist, given to boundless extravagance and insistent on instant gratification—that is to say, sexually more liberated. For teenagers in the 1950s, the conflict between these types of conditioning was experienced as a conflict between the official values of school/family/church and the reality of their leisure-time activities.[1]

Postwar prosperity enabled enough income to trickle down to teenagers to make them an identifiable consumer group, much to the surprise and joy of manufacturers, who began to produce products aimed specifically at a youth market. These products served to emphasize the growing chasm between teenagers and the adult generation. At the same time, dependence on parents became more and more extended as high school and college and, for some, graduate school postponed entrance into adulthood and financial independence. Just as memories of wartime tragedies and the conditions of alienating work created the need for relaxation and escape in adults, teenagers sought relief from school and parental authority and found it in their leisure choices. Leisure became their alternative world, and rock 'n' roll, its major port of entry. While adults tried to avoid facing the harsh realities of changing social mores and the threat of global thermonuclear war through backyard barbecues and family fallout shelters, teenagers sought to become engaged in their world through the sensuous ritual of dancing, in the celebration of the sounds of urban life, and in multicultural explorations. Thus, in contrast to the vapid, unobtrusive popular

Rock 'n' roll represented everything that white, middle-class parents feared: it was urban, it was sexual, and most of it was black.

music of the adult generation, rock 'n' roll represented everything that white, middle-class parents feared: it was urban, it was sexual, and most of it was black.

As a cultural commodity, rock 'n' roll, like other products, prepared teenagers to be good consumers. (Indeed, the music has since been used to sell other products.) To adults, however, its message seemed to undermine the values of work, a necessary condition for consumption. "Rocking around the clock," not to mention rocking and rolling "all night long" in "sixty minute" intervals, hardly described the lifestyle of the upright citizen or the responsible employee. As a result, rock 'n' roll was frequently denounced by adults as the "devil's music," an NAACP strategy for recruiting young whites, or a communist plot to undermine the moral fiber of the younger generation.

The Established Powers Fight Back

To put the reaction against rock 'n' roll into proper perspective, it is necessary first to assess the degree to which the music actually encroached on the coveted pop terrain. The vintage rock 'n' roll years coincided with a period in which the fortunes of the music industry as a whole nearly tripled; revenues from record sales climbed from $213 million in 1954 to $603 million in 1959. The question is: How much of this expansion can be attributed to rock 'n' roll? While market-share data broken out by musical style is difficult to come by, Charlie Gillett has offered a measure that gives at least some indication of relative proportions. Of the fifty-one records to make the pop Top Ten in 1955, only eight were rock 'n' roll. In contrast, in 1959, thirty-eight of the eighty-nine Top Ten records were rock 'n' roll. This means that rock 'n' roll jumped from 15.7 percent of the pop market in 1955 to 42.7 percent in 1959. In this same period, the total number of Top Ten pop hits produced by major record companies decreased from forty in 1955 to thirty in 1959, while those produced by independent record companies increased from eleven to fifty-nine. In other words, independent record companies went from a 21.6 percent share of the pop market in 1955 to a 66.3 percent share of a pop market that was roughly three times larger in 1959.

The major labels had no one to thank for this situation but themselves. In the late 1940s and early 1950s when countless independent labels came into existence to cash in on the growing demand for r&b, it should have been clear that these new developments in black popular music could be ignored only at your own peril. Rock 'n' roll was one of those rare instances in which ideological blinders prevented the music industry from operating in its own economic self-interest. After it was clear that rock 'n' roll was here to stay, the industry giants responded with strategies that ranged from stances usually associated with ostriches to limited amounts of talent buying and the widespread practice of

Rock 'n' roll was one of those rare instances in which ideological blinders prevented the music industry from operating in its own economic self-interest.

so-called cover records (alternative versions of original recordings). When these tactics did not improve things economically, some of the majors, principally RCA and Columbia, tried to divert audiences from the new sound by promoting alternative forms of music. When all these efforts failed, the established powers of the industry (artists, labels, and most prominently, ASCAP publishers) joined forces with the U.S. government in an attempt to suppress the music which Russell Sanjek has labeled the "War on Rock."[3]

Given Columbia's historical connection to African American music (the company's vaults contained some of the best recordings of Bessie Smith, Robert Johnson, Louis Armstrong, Fletcher Henderson, Duke Ellington, and Count Basie), the label's almost complete lack of response to rock 'n' roll is somewhat surprising. After a reportedly feeble attempt at bidding for Elvis Presley's contract, Mitch Miller, Columbia's artist and repertoire chief, tried his best to ignore the music totally. Although it has been said that Miller despised rock 'n' roll, to his credit, he never joined the chorus of industry malcontents who publicly denounced it. Instead, he devoted his time and energy to perfecting the pop production techniques that were used with artists like Frankie Laine, Jo Stafford, Rosemary Clooney, and Doris Day. These techniques had made Columbia the most successful label in the country.[4]

Early in the 1950s, the emotionally unhinged Johnny Ray could have provided Columbia with a way into rock 'n' roll. His uninhibited stage performances, during which he routinely ripped off his shirt, were at least in part the result of tutelage by LaVern Baker and her manager. Following the phenomenal success of his heart-wrenching, tear-jerking recording of "Cry," which was number one on the pop charts for eleven weeks, Ray was switched from the OKeh subsidiary to the parent Columbia label. However, when ASCAP succeeded in having Ray's successful cover record of the Drifters' "Such a Night" banned from the airwaves in 1954 because of its sexual suggestiveness, Columbia may have thought that a deeper commitment to the performer and his current direction would be more trouble than it was worth. Except for a brief and inexplicable flirtation with the outrageous Screamin' Jay Hawkins ("I Put a Spell on You," 1956) on OKeh, the closest Columbia came to rock 'n' roll was the silken balladry of Johnny Mathis ("It's Not for Me to Say," "Chances Are," "The Twelfth of Never"). Produced in the same style as Columbia's other pop artists, the African American baritone (who was also a world-class athlete) was young enough and hip enough to appeal to the rock 'n' roll audience.

At RCA, Hugo Winterhalter was no better than Miller at producing rock 'n' roll, and artists like Vaughn Monroe, Dinah Shore, and Eddie Fisher were certainly no better at performing it than Columbia's artists.[5] However, in the Sarnoff tradition of covering all bases, RCA came up with a far more enlightened (and lucrative) strategy for dealing with the new sound. Recognizing that rock 'n' roll was not only a force to be reckoned with but also an idiom that required its own talents, RCA simply bought the most promising rock 'n' roll star it could get its hands on—Elvis Presley. It was the smartest move the company ever made. Presley carried the faltering record division for years.

Impressed by RCA's success, a number of other major labels tried to imitate the strategy. Capitol's search for the "new Elvis" yielded Gene Vincent. MGM had no connection to rock 'n' roll until they signed Conway Twitty in 1958. Like Presley before him, Twitty had served a classic, if undistinguished, apprenticeship at Sun Records in Memphis and had then moved on to an equally undistinguished career as a country singer at Mercury. However, at MGM, according to Charlie Gillett, "Twitty assumed a sonorous baritone, apparently satirizing the heavy breathing of Elvis Presley's 'Don't,' a hit earlier in the year."[6] Twitty's country background enabled him to create that delicate balance of country and pop that found acceptance as rock 'n' roll because of the success of rockabilly. His biggest hit, "It's Only Make Believe," "was one of the many records of 1958 that succeeded in absorbing elements of rock 'n' roll into the tradition of melodramatic ballads that popular music arrangers enjoyed working with."[7]

It is, perhaps, not surprising that MGM turned to Twitty. When the major labels decided to make a foray into rock 'n' roll territory, they naturally gravitated toward pop-oriented, country-influenced singers and material. This was a music to which they still had some connection, and given the racial fears that rock 'n' roll conjured up in some people, it was probably considered a safer move. Decca had first set the example by signing Bill Haley in 1953, a move that predated the other major labels by eighteen months. The company, however, couldn't quite bring itself to replicate the pattern. In 1957, Buddy Holly and the Crickets were turned down by Decca, although, as noted in Chapter 4, they were signed by Bob Thiele to two of Decca's subsidiaries, Coral and Brunswick. Coral had been founded in 1949 as an r&b label, but in the early 1950s, it became one of the labels that engaged in a systematic attempt to blunt the crossover appeal of early rock 'n' roll through the practice of issuing cover records.

Covering the Bases

In the 1950s, major companies and some independents tried to capitalize on the growing popularity of r&b among white listeners by producing alternate versions of r&b hits using white artists and styles the companies thought would be more appropriate for and sell well in the mainstream market. In the vast majority of cases, black artists recording for independent labels were the victims of this practice.[8] Cover records not only altered stylistic elements but also often doctored lyrics as well. Bill Haley's 1954 cover of Joe Turner's "Shake, Rattle, and Roll," for example, sanitized the original version by replacing sexual phrases with fashion statements and moving the action from the bedroom to the kitchen. Cover records were often released during the expected chart life of the original, and owing to the superior distribution channels and promotional powers of the majors, frequently outsold the original.

The practice of making cover records began in earnest in 1953 when June Valli recorded "Crying in the Chapel" for RCA. At the time it was released, there were three other versions of the song out, two country and one r&b. The r&b release by Sonny Til and the Orioles had crossed over to the pop market and was enjoying considerable success until it was eclipsed by the Valli cover, which became one of the best-selling records of the year. RCA scored another coup with Perry Como's cover of "Ko Ko Mo," a lively novelty song originally recorded by Gene and Eunice for Combo in 1954, then rerecorded by the same group for Aladdin. This rerecording became an r&b hit and was covered by two independent labels—Checker, using the Flamingos, and Modern, using Marvin and Johnny—that hoped to use the song's novelty value to break into the pop market. Their efforts were thwarted when three major labels also covered the rerecordings. Mercury released a version by the Crew Cuts and Columbia used Tony Bennett, but the RCA recording by Perry Como became the most popular, which gave the electronics giant another ersatz rock 'n' roll hit even before Presley was signed.

Bill Haley's "Shake, Rattle, and Roll" sanitized the original version by replacing sexual phrases with fashion statements and moving the action from the bedroom to the kitchen.

Of all the major companies, Decca and Mercury had the best luck with covers. Bill Haley's "Shake, Rattle, and Roll" cover for Decca went to number seven on the pop charts and became the artist's first gold record. Theresa Brewer and the McGuire Sisters on Decca's Coral subsidiary also made successful cover records. The McGuire Sisters' cover of "Sincerely" by the Moonglows hit number one on the pop charts and became the seventh best-selling pop single of 1955. Brewer's 1956 cover of Fats Domino's "Bo Weevil" went to number seventeen while Domino's only reached thirty-five.

Mercury, which had begun as an independent and had then made the transition to a major, knew the market well. The company used Georgia Gibbs to cover Etta James' "Wallflower" (popularly known as "Roll with Me, Henry") with a cleaned-up version called "Dance with Me, Henry." James' version sold 400,000 copies for Modern, but the Gibbs cover hit the 1 million mark. This was only the beginning for Mercury. The Chicago label really cashed in on cover records with two Canadian groups, the Diamonds and the Crew Cuts. The Crew Cuts systematically pillaged the r&b charts, after their cover version of the Chords' "Sh-Boom" (originally on Atlantic's Cat label) became the fifth best-selling song of 1954. In addition to the previously mentioned "Ko Ko Mo," the group covered the Penguins' "Earth Angel" (Dootone), Nappy Brown's "Don't Be Angry" (Savoy), and the Charms' "Gum Drop" (Deluxe). Between 1956 and 1961, the Diamonds had hits with Frankie Lymon and the Teenagers' "Why Do Fools Fall in Love," the Gladiolas' "Little Darlin'," the Rays' "Silhouettes," and the Danleers' "One Summer Night."

The label that really worked the cover market was Dot Records, an independent with the pretensions of a major.[9] Launched by Randy Wood in Gallatin, Tennessee, in 1951, Dot's posture toward rock 'n' roll has been described as "predatory." Two of Dot's

Pat Boone has served as the lightning rod for all the race-related criticism associated with the practice of cover records. This dimension of his questionable contribution to rock 'n' roll has prevented him from being inducted into the Rock 'n' Roll Hall of Fame.

female acts were quite successful covering a wide variety of rock 'n' roll. The Fontane Sisters recorded "Hearts of Stone" by the Charms, "Seventeen" by Boyd Bennett and the Rockets, "Eddie My Love" by the Teen Queens, and "I'm in Love Again" by Fats Domino. Gale Storm had Top Ten hits with Frankie Lymon and the Teenagers' "Why Do Fools Fall in Love," Smiley Lewis' "I Hear You Knocking," and the Charms' "Ivory Tower," among others. The company also had on its roster the singer who represents the epitome of cultural theft, Pat Boone.

It is not simply the fact that Pat Boone has more covers to his credit than anyone else that makes him the lightning rod for all the criticism of the practice; it is the fact that he built his career by sanitizing the classics. His cover of Fats Domino's "Ain't That a Shame" (1955) was Boone's first number one single; "I Almost Lost My Mind" (1956), originally recorded by Ivory Joe Hunter, was his second. He also cleaned up the Eldorados' "At My Front Door" and the Flamingos' "I'll Be Home." His antiseptic versions of Little Richard's "Tutti Frutti" and "Long Tall Sally" alone would be enough to earn him the unyielding wrath of anyone who professes a love of rock 'n' roll. The "white buck" shoes that became his signature only reinforced the racist implications of his "white bread" delivery. Once he was firmly established in the rock 'n' roll market, Boone retreated into mainstream pop balladry ("Love Letters in the Sand," "April Love," "Moody River") and scored thirty-eight Top Forty hits. He was rewarded in 1957 with his own television show. The fact that anyone could associate him with rock 'n' roll in any way is a good indication of how much the style had been eroded.

In the mythology of rock 'n' roll, the major labels are often portrayed as narrow, rigid companies that tried to insulate the mainstream from the complexities of difference while the independent labels heroically pushed against the limits of public taste out of a love for the music from the grassroots. The truth, of course, is more complex than this. Record companies, whether majors or independents, frequently act in self-contradictory ways that are as likely to involve idiosyncratic choices and dumb luck as carefully crafted business plans or scientific market analyses. The appearance of Haley on Decca and

Presley on RCA, let alone Lloyd Price on ABC-Paramount, certainly complicates the mythology. Given Columbia's aversion to rock 'n' roll, why did the company even bother to take a chance on a performer like Screamin' Jay Hawkins, whose stage act included rising from a burning coffin in full voodoo regalia? Capitol also nurtured an equally outrageous performer named Esquerita for a while. Toward the end of the 1950s, MGM signed two black rock 'n' roll acts—the Impalas ("Sorry (I Ran All the Way Home)," 1959) and Jimmy Jones ("Handy Man" and "Good Timin'," 1960)—to their Cub subsidiary. These are not the acts of companies that are trying to insulate the mainstream. By the same token, few independents entered the business solely for artistic reasons. If the independents had a progressive effect, it is because they were smart enough and flexible enough to respond to an unsated consumer demand that would have required a considerable shift in orientation for the majors. Dot's view of music simply as a product (a view that came to serve as a model for many of the independents that followed) was extreme, but even Dot was sufficiently attuned to the music to sign the Dell-Vikings, whose "Come Go With Me" and "Whispering Bells" (1957) are regarded as vocal harmony classics.

Record companies frequently act in self-contradictory ways that are as likely to involve idiosyncratic choices and dumb luck as carefully crafted business plans or scientific market analyses.

In this more complicated picture, there are also contradictory aspects of the practice of cover records which must be considered. Usually cover records are discussed only in terms of their destructive effects in the cultural arena. Under certain conditions, however, cover records in the 1950s could be beneficial to an artist, or more often, his label. A cover record often exposed a song to a larger audience through record sales and radio play. Such exposure could more than make up for a loss in record sales through an increase in writer's royalties for artists who wrote their own material. When royalty increases did not occur, it was often because independent label owners induced naive artists to sell their publishing rights for a few dollars or to sign them away for the "privilege" of recording. In any case, as teenagers became more familiar with rock 'n' roll and its roots, they became more adept at distinguishing originals from covers and covers became less valuable to the majors as a strategy for dealing with rock 'n' roll.

Pop Diversions: From Kingston Town to the Kingston Trio

One of the things that separated the majors from the independents was the fact that the majors—particularly Columbia and RCA—could rely on their catalogues or subsidies from other corporate divisions when they were not producing hit records. Thus, they could, in many instances, avoid dealing with such messy cultural practices as in rock 'n' roll and cover records. In fact, Columbia and RCA were so reluctant to have anything to do with rock 'n' roll that they were less aggressive than others with cover versions. For a brief time, it appeared as though they might have other, more dignified strategies for dealing with the new music market. Chief among these was an attempt to divert popular tastes toward two other types of music, calypso and popularized folk music.

Beginning in late 1956, RCA and Columbia began promoting U.S. interpretations of calypso, hoping that the new sound would supplant rock 'n' roll, which they viewed as a passing fad. There was, as Gillett has pointed out, a certain logic to the strategy.

> *Given the way major record companies seemed to think and operate, calypso no doubt seemed to them a logical and clever answer to the dilemma of needing to divert their audience's attention from a product that the independent companies were best able to supply. Calypso was a black people's music, as jazz and rhythm and blues before it had been. Further, it had a Latin beat, which had always seemed to fit nicely into North American popular music. . . . Best of all, there were enough novelty songs in calypso with no sensual implications for the companies to escape having to deal with the disturbing content of rhythm and blues.* [10]

Had it not been for the self-serving intervention of the AFM, the majors that decided to promote calypso might well have found they had a "tiger by the tail." In its original Trinidadian form, calypso had long been a highly politicized music that was based on topical social commentary and depictions of male-female relations that routinely brushed with lewdness. However, pressure from the AFM prevented such outspoken calypsonians as Lord Kitchener and the Mighty Sparrow from performing in the United States and left the task of representing West Indian culture to Harry Belafonte. The multitalented Belafonte, who was born in New York, started his singing career as a straight pop vocalist for Jubilee in 1949. In 1955, he was signed by RCA as a folk singer, recording material like "Scarlet Ribbons" and

Beginning his career as a straight pop vocalist, it fell to Harry Belafonte to interpret a depoliticized version of Trinidadian calypso for the U.S. audience. Never one to be a pawn of the music industry, he soon took his considerable talent and progressive political views to the world stage where he continues to champion humanitarian causes.

With coordinated preppy attire and college-oriented humor, the Kingston Trio swept the country with a pop folk repertoire that only hinted at the power of the folk revival yet to come.

"Shenandoah." In 1956, he made the transition to what passed for calypso in the United States with the release of the LP *Calypso*, which stayed on the charts for eighty-four weeks and was firmly ensconced in the number one slot for thirty-one of them. This was an unprecedented chart run. The two hit singles from the album, "Jamaica Farewell" and "Banana Boat" (aka "Day-O"), established the tone and content of U.S. calypso. The sexual innuendo and pointed social commentary of Caribbean calypso was discarded and the novelty value of the sound was emphasized. The result was a series of well-crafted pop arrangements with a Latin rhythmic flavor. In retrospect, such apolitical pop calypso appears to be an ironic career choice for the man who would soon become a leading civil rights activist and an outspoken critic of injustice.

Columbia followed RCA's lead with Terry Gilkyson and the Easy Riders ("Marianne," 1957). Other notable pseudo calypso hits included the Tarriers' "The Banana Boat Song" and Belafonte's "Mama Look-a Boo Boo." In the final analysis, however, U.S. calypso, not rock 'n' roll, was only a fad. Within two years, the sound had segued into popular folk music, a second diversionary strategy by the majors that yielded a new set of players. As noted earlier, before Belafonte took the plunge into calypso, he had recorded pop versions of traditional songs, and, in many ways, his calypso recordings were the Caribbean version of the same tendency. The Tarriers, before boarding the banana boat, had backed Vince Martin on "Cindy, Oh Cindy," another folk-sounding ditty with a vaguely Latin feel. However, it was not until a San Francisco group called the Kingston Trio unleashed their repertoire of popular folk sounds that the music industry realized the potential power of popular folk material. The Kingston Trio came up through the San Francisco folk scene but managed to avoid the left-wing taint that had haunted most folk artists since the McCarthy era. Perhaps their clean-cut image, brightly colored matching shirts, and upscale college humor made it difficult to think of them as politically subversive. As was the practice in folk circles, the Kingston Trio issued their material as LPs, not singles, but no other folk artists had ever before matched their success. Signed by Capitol in 1957, they released eighteen albums that made the Top Twenty, and a number of these remained on the charts for a year or more; five hit the number one spot. Rarer still, some of their LPs generated hit pop singles. "Tom Dooley," for example, from their first album went to number one, which was almost unheard of for folk material.

Soon other, largely forgettable, folk-oriented groups, including the Limeliters, the Highwaymen, and the Journeymen, tried their hands at the pop market. When Columbia had moderate success with the Brothers Four ("Greenfields," 1960), college campuses suddenly became fertile grounds for talent scouts. By the time the folk revival got into full swing, however, with yet another roster of performers, it was allied with the burgeoning Civil Rights movement, and the music industry really did have a tiger by the tail.

Schlock Rock: Enter the White Middle Class

By the late 1950s, the initial rush of rock 'n' roll excitement was over. From a musical point of view, rock 'n' roll was a rather limited science that by then had been sufficiently absorbed into the collective unconscious that singers, songwriters, and producers with no particular feel for the music's roots or subtleties could still turn out commercially viable approximations. This new reality brought forth a new generation of white, middle-class teen idols, whose roots barely scratched the surface of pop. Performers like Paul Anka ("Diana," "You Are My Destiny," "Lonely Boy," "Put Your Head on My Shoulder," "Puppy Love"), Frankie Avalon ("Dede Dinah," "Ginger Bread," "Venus," "Bobby Sox to Stockings"), Annette ("Tall Paul," "O Dio Mio"), Fabian ("Turn Me Loose," "Tiger," "Hound Dog Man"), Bobby Rydell ("We Got Love," "Wild One," "Swinging School"), Connie Francis ("Who's Sorry Now," "My Happiness," "Lipstick on Your Collar," "Everybody's Somebody's Fool"), Freddy Cannon ("Tallahassee Lassie," "Way Down Yonder in New Orleans," "Palisades Park"), and Neil Sedaka ("Oh! Carol," "Stairway to Heaven," "Calendar Girl," "Happy Birthday Sweet Sixteen," "Breaking Up

Whatever higher morality or artistic integrity might have been attributed to the independents in the early days of rock 'n' roll had given way to a singular commercial pop orientation.

Major labels try to divert audience tastes to popular folk music

Is Hard to Do"), as well as many others ushered in a style of music that can only be referred to as "schlock rock."[7]

In the rise of schlock rock, little separated the majors from the independents, save for market superiority. For every Tommy Sands ("Teenage Crush"), Connie Francis, and Sonny James ("Young Love") who recorded for a major label, there was a Charlie Gracie ("Butterfly"), Annette, and Tab Hunter ("Young Love") who recorded for an independent. Warner and Colpix, new Hollywood-related labels, contributed Connie Stevens ("Sixteen Reasons") and James Darren ("Goodbye Cruel World"), respectively. Whatever higher morality or artistic integrity might have been attributed to the independents in the early days of rock 'n' roll had given way to a singular commercial pop orientation.

The major hub for this commercial activity was Philadelphia, the home of three independent labels, Chancellor, Cameo/Parkway, and Swan, that had come into existence following Dot's success with cover records. These three labels transformed local teenagers into archetypal teen idols. Chancellor offered Fabian and Frankie Avalon; Cameo had Bobby Rydell; and Swan signed Freddy Cannon, who actually came from Lynn, Massachusetts, but contractually and aesthetically belonged to Philadelphia. "The focus in Philadelphia in particular was on image," Gillett has noted. "The unsophisticated white southern singers, and the unfashionable black ones, were supplanted by kids who could be the boy-next-door, whose visual appeal was more important than their musical ability."[11]

In a few short years, rock 'n' roll had degenerated from Sam Phillips' dream of a white man who could sing black to a white high-school kid who couldn't sing at all.

In this regard, Chancellor led the pack. According to critic Ed Ward, co-owner Bob Marcucci told *Billboard* in the late 1950s,

> *We now run a school where we indoctrinate artists into show business. We may sign them and spend three months schooling them before they cut their first record. We teach them how to walk, how to talk, and how to act onstage when they're performing. We worked with Frankie Avalon for three months before making "Dede Dinah."*
>
> *It was Frankie who introduced me to Fabian, a sixteen-year-old high school kid who likes to play football. Somehow I sensed that here was a kid who could go. He looks a little bit like both Presley and Ricky Nelson. I figured he was a natural. It's true that he couldn't sing. He knew it and I knew it.*[12]

By the time the rest of the world found out, however, Fabian had racked up eight Top Forty hits. In a few short years, rock 'n' roll had degenerated from Sam Phillips' dream of a white man who could sing black to a white high-school kid who couldn't sing at all.

"Showing a perverse wish to return to the standards of pre-rock 'n' roll days," Gillett has written, "the operators of the new independents scoured the same streets that had spawned the crooners who had been the core of major company rosters."[13] In so doing, they, like the majors, assembled a roster of vocalists who were, for the most part, pale imitations of the pop mainstays of the late 1940s and early 1950s. Once again, they were predominantly Italian American. Fabian (Fabiano Forte), Frankie Avalon (Francis Avalone), Bobby Rydell (Robert Ridarelli), Freddy Cannon (Frederick Picariello), Bobby Darin (Walden Robert Cassotto), Annette (Funicello), Connie Francis (Concetta Franconero), James Darren (James Ercolani), and Connie Stevens (Concetta Ingolia) were all of Italian descent. This is, perhaps, not surprising. At a time when ethnic succession still played a major role in white ethnic intergroup relations, entertainment and sports (as black artists and athletes knew only too well) offered the most promising avenues for upward mobility. It is interesting to note that all of these performers felt compelled to anglicize their names; still, they were not unaware of their heritage. Connie Francis toted up thirty-five Top Forty singles for MGM, but her two albums of *Italian Favorites* (the first of which charted for more than a year and a half) far outdistanced her two *Greatest Hits* LPs. One of Bobby Rydell's best-selling singles was "Volare" (1960). The problem was that this was not rock 'n' roll.

As in the 1940s, Italian American cultural tendencies seemed to work better with styles that were closer to mainstream pop, and among the new white rockers, connections to pop abounded. When Bobby Darin changed his singing style to record Kurt Weill's "Mack the Knife" (1959), Darin's first number one single, it was because he aspired to be the next Frank Sinatra, not the next Elvis Presley. Bobby Rydell was actually discovered at the age of nine by bandleader Paul Whiteman. In addition to his stylistically questionable, but commercially successful, rock 'n' roll hits, Rydell hit pay dirt with "That Old Black Magic" (1961), a Johnny Mercer/Harold Arlen tune from the 1940s. Although there was an obvious, if narrow, connection between Italian Americans and pop/rock crooners, the new pop orientation in rock 'n' roll cannot be reduced to the function of a particular ethnic affiliation. In fact, the production of schlock knew no ethnic boundaries.

By the 1960s, the momentum of schlock rock had produced a second generation of white, teen heartthrobs across ethnic lines who had varying degrees of talent. At the

Frankie Avalon was one of a number of teen idols who turned boy-next-door good looks and a modicum of talent into a full-fledged rock 'n' roll career.

higher end of the scale, Del Shannon ("Runaway," "Hats Off to Larry") evidenced musical roots in the country sound of Hank Williams. Gene Pitney delivered some powerful, if pop-oriented, vocals on such hits as "(The Man Who Shot) Liberty Valence," "Only Love Can Break a Heart," "It Hurts to Be in Love," and "I'm Gonna Be Strong." He also distinguished himself as a writer of considerable note, penning such classics as "Hello Mary Lou" for Ricky Nelson and "He's a Rebel" for the Crystals. Among the less distinctive talents were Bobby Vee ("Devil or Angel," "Rubber Ball," "Take Good Care of My Baby," "Run to Him," "The Night Has a Thousand Eyes"), Brian Hyland ("Itsy Bitsy Teenie Weenie Yellow Polkadot Bikini," "Sealed With a Kiss"), Johnny Tillotson ("Poetry in Motion," "Without You," "It Keeps Right on A-Hurtin'," "Talk Back Trembling Lips"), Bobby Vinton ("Roses Are Red," "Blue on Blue," "Blue Velvet," "There I've Said It Again," "My Heart Belongs to Only You," "Mr. Lonely"), Jay and the Americans ("She Cried," "Only in America," "Come a Little Bit Closer," "Cara Mia"), and

> Gradually, but decisively, strong regional accents gave way to neutral unlocalized voices. Raucous improvised solos were overtaken by lavish strings and orchestral arrangements. The sexual double entendre was replaced by a highly romanticized vision of teenage love and/or angst.

Tommy Roe ("Sheila," " Everybody"). Female entries included Sue Thompson ("Norman") and Little Peggy March ("I Will Follow Him"). Leslie Gore ("It's My Party," "Judy's Turn to Cry," "She's a Fool") would also have to be positioned here, even though she performed one of the first feminist songs, "You Don't Own Me" (1963). Finally, there was the duo Paul and Paula ("Hey Paula"). Individual differences aside, the overwhelming social function of these artists as a group was to put a bland white middle-class face on rock 'n' roll. Gradually, but decisively, strong regional accents gave way to neutral unlocalized voices. Raucous improvised riffs and solos on sax, guitar, or piano were overtaken by lavish strings and orchestral arrangements. The sexual double entendre was replaced by a highly romanticized vision of teenage love and/or angst.

While the second generation of schlock was overwhelmingly white, there was one black superstar, Chubby Checker, whose "The Twist" was the first of a series of dance crazes that swept the country in the early 1960s. A funkier, original version of "The Twist" had been released two years earlier by Hank Ballard and the Midnighters and had sold extremely well in the r&b market. There was, however, little crossover into pop, and nothing hinting at the national fad that Checker triggered with his version. Unlike Ballard, Checker was a pop phenomenon. He was created as an image act in the corporate offices of Cameo/Parkway Records, which was, of course, located in Philadelphia. At the suggestion of Dick Clark's wife, the former Ernest Evans was given a name that sounded vaguely like Fats Domino (Fats = Chubby, Domino = Checker). "The Twist" reached number one on the pop charts twice, once in 1960 and then again in 1962. In fact, it was listed as the best-selling single of all time well into the 1970s.

Attempting to cash in on the craze the twist had set in motion, Cameo/Parkway concocted a seemingly endless series of new dance records, made by both black and

Twist craze opens pop market to African American artists

white artists. Checker followed up with "The Hucklebuck," "Pony Time," "The Fly," and "Limbo Rock." Bobby Rydell contributed "The Fish." The Orlons offered "The Wah Watusi." The Dovells chimed in with the "Bristol Stomp" and the "Hully Gully." Dee Dee Sharp announced that it was "Mashed Potato Time" and then told people to "Do the Bird." She was offered "The Loco-Motion" by Gerry Goffin and Carole King, but when Cameo passed on the song, the writers released a version by their babysitter on the Dimension label. Eva Narcissus Boyd became Little Eva and "The Loco-Motion" became a number one hit.

In its historical context, the twist craze was socially ambiguous. The dance was welcomed enthusiastically into conservative white suburban America even though its leading exponent was African American. Certainly, it anticipated more openly sexual dances like the monkey, the jerk, and the Philly dog. For a brief period, it served as an alternative port of entry to the pop market for African American artists, even as mainstream forces sought to turn back rock 'n' roll. In 1962 alone, Sam Cooke's "Twistin' the Night Away" and Gary 'U.S.' Bonds' "Dear Lady Twist" and "Twist, Twist Senora" broke into the Top Ten, the Isley Brothers followed their classic "Shout" with "Twist and Shout," and Atlantic Records reissued an album of old Ray Charles material as *Do the Twist with Ray Charles,* which hit number eleven on the album charts. In the long run, however, Cameo/Parkway's faddish dance crazes tended to reduce rock 'n' roll to a novelty. As a Philadelphia independent, the company also had a close association with *American Bandstand,* the televised dance party that was primarily responsible for promoting the new teen idols.

Television's Greatest Hits

The program, initially called *Bandstand,* had begun in 1952 as a local Philadelphia broad-cast on WFIL-TV, an ABC network affiliate. The program's first host, Bob Horn, was fired after he was arrested for drunk driving just as the *Philadelphia Ledger,* the owner of WFIL, was waging a vigorous campaign against the practice. Income-tax evasion and an unsubstantiated teenage vice charge added to his career troubles. Looking for a replace-ment, the station asked Dick Clark, a Syracuse University graduate who had begun working there in 1952 as a news announcer, to take over in 1956. Although Clark, "the perpetual teenager," was twenty-seven years old, he looked as young as most of the teenagers who danced on the show, but he carried himself more like a big brother. This distancing served him well in the turbulent years that followed. Under his leadership, *Bandstand* quickly became one of the most important promotional vehicles in the music industry. By 1957, the show had been picked up by ABC-TV for national broadcast and had been renamed *American Bandstand.* As Sanjek has noted, "Within two years, it was being broadcast by 101 affiliates to an audience of 20 million. . . . Because of program policy, [the performers who appeared on *Bandstand*] were invariably white in the early years."[14] As a result, "Dick Clark, the youthful, debonair host with Dentyne smile," was remembered by Arnold Shaw "as the ballast to Alan Freed, representing cool, white rock as Freed was the avatar of hot black rock."[15] Clark has maintained that associating him with only white rock is a cheap shot. "To write that the music we presented was all white bread is a fallacious premise. It's an easy angle," he has said. "It happens to be wrong."[16]

While it may be true, as Clark has pointed out, "that over two-thirds of the people who've been initiated into the Rock & Roll Hall of Fame had their television debuts on *American Bandstand,*"[17] there is no question that the show's Philadelphia location placed the local independents in a particularly good position to display their wares, which they did. Fabian, Frankie Avalon, Bobby Rydell, and Freddy Cannon made regular appear-ances, and it seems unlikely that they would have become as popular as they were with-out such exposure. It is equally clear that Clark positioned himself to benefit from such successes. By the end of the decade, he was financially involved in thirty-three music-re-lated corporations, including three record companies, a management firm, and a pressing plant. His publishing company held the copyright on 162 songs, many of which his show had helped to popularize. While a consummate businessman, Clark's financial entangle-ments often led him to the borders of ethical practice, as his handling of Duane Eddy illustrates.

Born in Corning, New York, Eddy relocated to Phoenix at the age of seventeen to work with producer Lee Hazelwood. Experimenting with echo in the studio, the two cre-ated the "twangy" guitar sound that became Eddy's signature. From 1958 to 1963, Eddy and his group, the Rebels, charted fifteen Top Forty hits, the best known of which are "Rebel-'Rouser" (1958), "Forty Miles of Bad Road" (1959), and "Because They're

Young" (1960). Between 1958 and 1961, Clark played eleven of Eddy's hits some 240 times on *Bandstand.* While Clark has claimed that he simply followed national trends on the show, there is no doubt that his promotion helped to propel the songs to hit status. Throughout this period, Eddy recorded for Clark's Jaime label, he toured under the auspices of Clark's management company, and all of his copyrights were owned by Clark's publishing company. Given this, it is not difficult to imagine how Clark's private holdings could have come into conflict with the promotional aspects of *American Bandstand.* Of course, television had long been used as a promotional vehicle for all kinds of music, including, on occasion, rock 'n' roll. Elvis Presley, Chuck Berry, Carl Perkins, Jerry Lee Lewis, Buddy Holly, and Bo Diddley, for example, had all appeared, albeit infrequently, on the many TV variety shows that then existed. However, these artists did not appear on national television until their musical abilities were proven. In the case of schlock rock, visual appeal itself became the basis for launching a musical career.

While *American Bandstand* may have been the primary culprit in this area, it was not the only one. Annette Funicello had been the *Mickey Mouse Club*'s most popular mouseketeer since 1955. Still, the Disney show was an odd platform for launching a career in rock 'n' roll. Connie Stevens, who played Cricket Blake on the detective series *Hawaiian Eye,* teamed up with Edd "Kookie" Byrnes, the ultra-cool parking attendant on *77 Sunset Strip* who wowed millions of viewers each week with his hair-combing technique, for a duet entitled, naturally, "Kookie, Kookie (Lend Me Your Comb)." The Top Ten single launched short-lived singing careers for both actors. Tommy Sands had the starring role in *The Singing Idol,* a TV play based very loosely on the life of Elvis Presley. Sands' first hit, "Teenage Crush," came from the telecast.

Although most of the teen idols of schlock were cast in something of an Elvis Presley mold, they seldom measured up. There was, however, one television artist who managed to project at least a tenuous continuity with his rockabilly forebears, the soft-spoken, soft-rocking Ricky Nelson. As rock 'n' roll became more mainstream, a less rebellious, more middle-class new "Elvis" was required, and for a time, Nelson filled the bill. Nelson grew up playing himself with his real-life family on a TV sitcom entitled *The Adventures of Ozzie and Harriet*, a show about a so-called normal middle-class, suburban family in the 1950s. In 1957, Verve records hit upon the idea of recording Nelson singing on the show. His mediocre cover of Fats Domino's "I'm Walking" broke into the Top Twenty, while the flip side, "A Teenager's Romance," unexpectedly went to number two. Imperial, which was Domino's label, was so impressed with Nelson's success that the company bought his contract from Verve and set about promoting him as a respectable alternative to Presley. Over the next seven years, Nelson released twenty-five Top Forty hits on Imperial, including "Be-Bop Baby" and "Stood Up" (1957), "Believe What You Say" and "Poor Little Fool" (1958), "It's Late (1959), and "Travelin' Man" backed with "Hello Mary Lou" (1961), and a few more on Decca before he was swamped by the British onslaught.

Although most of the teen idols of schlock were cast in something of an Elvis Presley mold, they seldom measured up.

While there is no question that Nelson's clean-cut image and popular TV series figured heavily in his success as a singer, he was not simply a creation of the media. Unlike most of the teen idols of schlock, he was well rooted in music. His father was a multitalented big band leader in the 1930s with nearly forty hit records to his credit. His mother was the band's vocalist. His backup band included James Burton who went on to join Presley, and most of his own early hits were written by Dorsey and/or Johnny Burnette, two rockabilly writers whose backgrounds were similar to Presley's. Furthermore, he had the capacity to grow as a singer. After his untimely death in 1985, Nelson was eulogized as a country rock singer of some stature. Looking at the early days of his career, however, it is impossible to separate his success from the move to make rock 'n' roll both white and middle class.

The Brill Building: The New Tin Pan Alley

As rock 'n' roll became too popular for the established music industry to ignore, it also attracted a new breed of professional to its ranks—songwriters with a respect for the Tin Pan Alley tradition who could write (and sometimes sing) in teenage idiom. They put another nail in the coffin of early rock 'n' roll even as they tried to professionalize the genre. Paul Anka, a Canadian of Middle Eastern descent, aspired to a career as a professional songwriter and, as a brash teenager, was convinced he could sing as well. After an initial release on a local label in 1956, he took advantage of some indirect professional connections and, while in Los Angeles, pitched his next batch of tunes to Don Costa, a record executive at ABC-Paramount. Costa signed him immediately and produced Anka's first record, the Latin-inflected "Diana" (1957), written for an older babysitter from his childhood years. The song became a number one hit single. With Costa arranging and conducting, Anka continued to do well in the pop market until the British Invasion in 1964 swept away all the reigning popular styles. Undaunted, he segued into the role of adult songwriter, penning "Johnny's Theme" for the *Tonight Show* and the lyrics to "My Way" for Sinatra. "That was the turning point—in '68—for me, as *From Here to Eternity* was for him in '55," Anka once told an interviewer. "Suddenly, after years of sending out songs and demos, I was accepted and recognized as a writer—I mean, for others."[18] Such validation was more important to Anka than his rock 'n' roll career.

Neil Sedaka was a concert pianist who studied at Julliard. Like Anka, he began his career as a professional songwriter, working in constant collaboration with Howard Greenfield, his high-school friend. Sedaka and Greenfield displayed a versatility and a breadth—ranging from "Stupid Cupid" and "Frankie" for Connie Francis to "Since You've Been Gone" for Clyde McPhatter and "I Waited Too Long" for La Vern Baker— that defies easy categorization. His own singing career, however, was defined by a series of trivial teen-oriented songs, with his light tenor double-tracked over a moderate beat. Sedaka and Greenfield, like Anka, turned more toward adult pop following the British Invasion, writing for Peggy Lee, Johnny Mathis, and the Fifth Dimension, among others.

It is easy to associate writers like Anka and Sedaka and Greenfield with the death of rock 'n' roll—they wrote plenty of anemic material and effortlessly made the transition to adult songwriting. At the same time, they were part of a larger and more complicated effort to professionalize rock 'n' roll by restoring a Tin Pan Alley approach to popular music. This effort hearkened back to a division of labor in which writers wrote songs, singers sang them, and artist and repertoire men brought the two together. In this model, corporate executives could feel reasonably assured that the appropriate artist would be matched with a professionally written song. The physical and spiritual center of this new enterprise was the Brill Building at 1619 Broadway, the new uptown location for a new Tin Pan Alley. In cramped quarters, songwriting teams like Gerry Goffin and Carole King, Barry Mann and Cynthia Weil, Howard Greenfield and Neil Sedaka, Jeff Barry and Ellie Greenwich, and Doc Pomus and Mort Shuman pounded out new melodies in much the same way that their Tin Pan Alley forebears

Paul Anka was one teen idol who got more gratification from being a songwriter. He was part of a stable of young writers who found a home near the Brill Building, the Tin Pan Alley of rock 'n' roll.

had decades earlier. This new generation of composers were to rock 'n' roll what Richard Rodgers and Lorenz Hart and George and Ira Gershwin were to the popular music of an earlier time. The results were mixed.

Following the successful pairing of the song "Stupid Cupid" with Connie Francis, Sedaka and Greenfield went to work for Al Nevins and Don Kirschner at Aldon Music, the flagship company of Brill Building pop, which was actually located across the street. Like Sedaka and Greenfield, Aldon's other young writers (which included Goffin/King, Mann/Weil, and even Bobby Darin for a time) displayed consummate skill, real innovation, and genuine sensitivity one minute and a truly incredible flair for the insipid the next. It is difficult to imagine that the same Gerry Goffin and Carole King who wrote "Up on the Roof" for the Drifters and "Natural Woman" for Aretha Franklin also wrote "Her Royal Majesty" for James Darren and "Pleasant Valley Sunday" for the Monkees. How could Barry Mann and Cynthia Weil have turned out both "You've Lost that Lovin' Feeling" for the Righteous Brothers and "Blame It on the Bossa Nova" for Eydie Gorme? Doc Pomus and Mort Shuman were a cut above, but even they cranked out "Turn Me Loose" for Fabian. As contradictory as it seems, the Brill Building writers produced some of best rock 'n' roll of the era as well as some of the worst schlock imaginable.

Aldon's young writers displayed consummate skill, real innovation, and genuine sensitivity one minute and a truly incredible flair for the insipid the next.

The Official Attack on Rock 'n' Roll

As the ascendancy of schlock rock perhaps proves, by the mid-1950s, rock 'n' roll had become the focal point for all of society's fears of miscegenation, sexuality, violence, juvenile delinquency, and general moral decline. In the eyes of many, the danger was not simply that the music was urban, sexual, and black; such music had been around for a long time. The danger was that it was no longer contained on "the other side of the tracks." Rock 'n' roll's biggest sin was to bring styles of music that were considered class- and race-specific into the mainstream and in so doing to redefine our conception of popular music.

The opening salvo of organized opposition began in late 1954, even before the term "rock 'n' roll" had come into widespread usage. Opining that the rash of sexual double entendres entering the mainstream primarily through r&b crossovers were in poor taste, the entertainment trade papers called on the industry to police itself lest other forces do it for them. An editorial in *Variety*, one of the leading trade papers, coined the term "leer-ics" to call attention to the objectionable phrases. The editorial was widely reprinted and generated a considerable public response, allowing *Variety* to congratulate itself for having its finger on the moral pulse of the nation. Fearing reprisals, record companies, ranging from majors like RCA and Decca to independents like King, and radio stations, including prominent black-oriented outlets like WDIA in Memphis, announced campaigns to weed out suggestive lyrics. To keep them honest, Catholic youth organizations in Boston, Chicago, and Minneapolis, and fundamentalist religious groups all over the South supplied lists of objectionable records. As one might expect, such songs as "Sixty Minute Man" and "Work with Me Annie" made all the lists, but even the Everly Brothers' "Wake Up Little Susie" managed to get banned in Boston. Municipalities set up review boards to screen new releases. When all else failed, police confiscated offensive records and jukeboxes.

Finding their concentration on "smutty" lyrics did not stop the music, opponents then changed their tactics. After 1955, according to Linda Martin and Kerry Segrave,

> the anti-rock advocates moved into broader attacks on the music. Attacking with just a sexual brush could only "tar" a few songs. By moving into wider areas of attack the opposition hoped to tar the full spectrum of rock 'n' roll. Henceforth attacks would center more on the poor and abysmal quality of rock music, its supposed effect in creating juvenile delinquency, and the lewdness of performers themselves.[19]

To its credit, the industry was not uniformly in agreement on these matters. "American pop music today, despite the attacks upon it, is in its most vital period," editorialized the outspoken Paul Ackerman in *Billboard*. "It most broadly reflects the diverse elements making up musical America. It is rich and fresh in sound and content."[20] Still, the attacks on rock 'n' roll both within and outside the music industry created a climate that encouraged more official interventions. These interventions came about through a loosely coordinated series of government investigations and legislative actions that culminated in the infamous "payola hearings" of 1959 and 1960. As noted in Chapter 1, payola—the practice of "paying for play," that is, offering financial, sexual, or other personal inducements in return for promotion—was hardly a newcomer to the music business. Song plugging, as the practice was called earlier in the century, had been the lynchpin of industry marketing since the heyday of Tin Pan Alley. As early as World War I, it was estimated that about $400,000 per year was paid to singers for the express purpose of pushing certain songs. Indeed, similar practices have characterized the development of most industries in their formative stages. In the 1950s, however, the focus on payola in the music industry became the operative strategy for neutralizing rock 'n' roll.

Beneath all the high-toned rhetoric lay a massive accumulation of ignorance and racism and a fair amount of unabashed economic and political self-interest.

Acting in concert, if not conspiracy, ASCAP and some of its most notable publishers, the major record companies and some of their biggest stars, and the U.S. government and some of its most tiresome elected officials, waged a protracted public battle for a return to "good music." As most rock 'n' roll material was written by BMI writers, ASCAP, which had been at war with BMI since 1939, was more than happy to join in the fray. For them, the attack on rock 'n' roll was simply an escalation of their continuing efforts to put BMI out of business. For the major labels, the fight was an attempt to halt the expansion of the independents. Forty of the seventy records to make the Top Ten in 1957, for example, were produced by independent labels.[21] To conservative elected officials, jumping on the bandwagon with the likes of Frank Sinatra, Bing Crosby, Steve Allen, Ira Gershwin, and Oscar Hammerstein may have seemed like a sure way of grabbing some quick and memorable headlines. Beneath all the high-toned rhetoric, then, lay a massive accumulation of ignorance and racism and a fair amount of unabashed economic and political self-interest.

What was perhaps most frustrating to society's custodians of good taste and the established powers of the music industry was the fact that they could not understand how rock 'n' roll had gathered such momentum in the first place. For this, they had no one to blame but themselves. By initially ignoring the music in the hope that it was a passing fad, they had allowed it to gain a following that could not be turned around. As it had gained ascendancy, rock 'n' roll had brought with it a number of changes in the way popular music was produced and disseminated, changes that made it much more difficult to contain. Unlike the mainstream pop that had been produced by the major record companies according to a fairly precise division of labor and with fairly clear lines of power and authority, rock 'n' roll was the product of a highly decentralized and disorganized network of independent and very idiosyncratic writers, publishers, performers, producers, and distributors. In the world of rock 'n' roll, a single person often played multiple roles. As the beneficiaries of technological advances that encouraged low-cost, independent production and distribution, the entrepeneurs of rock 'n' roll precipitated major shifts in the economic infrastructure of the music industry. These shifts tended to democratize and decentralize the production of popular music as a *Billboard* study comparing production in 1939 and 1959 illustrated. As Arnold Shaw notes,

> *Whereas the publishers of Top Ten songs in '39 were all located in New York, in '59 they were distributed in eight states. The songwriters now came from eighteen states instead of three. In '39 Top Ten disks were made by only three companies; in '59 by thirty-nine companies. And these companies, instead of all being located in New York, were distributed in ten states.*
> *The conclusion was inescapable: music business had broken out of Broadway, and Tin Pan Alley was gone as a shaper of trends and styles.*[22]

Although the established powers of the industry were certain that they wanted to eliminate rock 'n' roll, they were never sure, given the anarchy of its production, where or how to intervene. In the complex network of flamboyant personalities that produced rock 'n' roll, it was not easy to point to a particular place at which the flow of product could be stopped. Thus, as historian Trent Hill has argued, "one way to read the payola hearings is as an attempt—an attempt that was ultimately successful—to force a greater degree of organization and hierarchical responsibility onto the record industry so that the flow of music/product could be more easily regulated."[23]

ASCAP, which was in effect the organizational agent of Tin Pan Alley, led the charge. In 1953, thirty-three ASCAP members filed a $150 million antitrust suit against BMI, charging it with a conspiracy to dominate the market by keeping ASCAP music off the radio. Sydney M. Kaye, chairman of BMI, promptly pointed out that none of the radio stations that owned stock in BMI had ever received a dividend and that "all broadcasters have so-called blanket licenses from both ASCAP and BMI. . . . They cannot save one penny if they play more BMI and less ASCAP music. Broadcasters have, therefore, no incentive to discriminate against ASCAP music.[24] In sworn testimony, Stanley Adams, the president of ASCAP, could not identify a single station or network that had discriminated against ASCAP. Still, ASCAP continued to attack.

In 1956, under pressure from the Songwriters of America, a group of some 700 ASCAP writers, the Antitrust Subcommittee of the House Judiciary Committee, which was chaired by Congressman Emmanuel Celler, halted their investigation of rigged television quiz shows to initiate a probe into BMI. Officially, the committee was to investigate whether or not the structural relationship between BMI and radio had any influence on the music that was aired. However, Congressman Celler made clear the racial aspects of the investigation when he said: "Well, rock and roll has its place. There is no question about it. It's given great impetus to talent, particularly among the colored people. It's a natural expression of their emotions and feelings."[25] Although the committee heard testimony from a parade of influential ASCAP writers, it could find no evidence of wrongdoing on the part of BMI and referred the matter to the Justice Department.

The next battle occurred in 1958 when ASCAP succeeded in having introduced in the Senate a bill that would have prevented broadcasters from owning any BMI stock. To gather support for the bill, no less a figure than Frank Sinatra wrote:

> My only sorrow is the unrelenting insistence of recording and motion picture companies upon purveying the most brutal, ugly, degenerate, vicious form of expression it has been my misfortune to hear—naturally, I refer to the bulk of rock 'n' roll.
>
> It fosters almost totally negative and destructive reactions in young people. It smells phony and false. It is sung, played and written for the most part by cretinous goons and by means of its almost imbecilic reiterations and sly—lewd—in plain fact, dirty—lyrics, and as I said before, it manages to be the martial music of every sideburned delinquent on the face of the earth. This rancid aphrodisiac I deplore.[26]

Once again, a chorus of ASCAP sympathizers held forth. The Songwriters Protective Association, which was made up of ASCAP members, testified before the Communications Subcommittee of the Senate Committee on Interstate and Foreign Commerce, charged with gathering information relevant to the bill. If there were any doubts about the racial implications of Sinatra's statement, those doubts were certainly erased by Vance Packard who, appearing at the hearing as a paid witness, declared that rock 'n' roll "was inspired by what had been called race music modified to stir the animal instinct in modern teenagers."[27] Even with 1,200 pages of such testimony, however, the bill died in committee.

In 1959, rock 'n' roll's opponents came closer to hitting its nerve center when ASCAP convinced the Legislative Oversight Subcommittee of the House Committee on Interstate and Foreign Commerce to launch a new probe into payola just as the committee's investigation of rigged television quiz shows was coming to an end. Rock 'n' roll's opponents reasoned correctly that radio had been the primary vehicle for popularizing rock 'n' roll and that deejays had become powerful, largely unregulated figures in the process. Curtailing their freedom, opponents argued, could go a long way toward stopping the flow of music. While the committee, which was chaired by Arkansas Democrat Oren Harris, was convened to investigate abuses at all levels of the recording industry, deejays became the main targets of its hearings.

Ignoring all previous evidence, the payola hearings proceeded according to the assumption that no deejay would play a music as inferior and tasteless as rock 'n' roll unless he was handsomely rewarded for it. It never occurred to the committee that the deejays and their fans liked the music. The most damning indictment in the payola hearings was that of Alan Freed. While other deejays also fell victim to the probe, Freed was the most visible symbol of everything that many found threatening about the music and thus the most obvious target. He had played a major role in popularizing r&b

The payola hearings proceeded according to the assumption that no deejay would play a music as inferior and tasteless as rock 'n' roll unless he was handsomely rewarded for it.

among white teenagers to begin with, and he had continued to push original black recordings during the cover-record period. He had also refused to sign a statement saying that he had never received money or gifts to promote records. In fact, Freed had been a controversial figure in the music business since he had turned to r&b in 1951. He had first run afoul of the law when a concert he staged in 1952 at the Cleveland Arena was oversold and had to be canceled. Although he was charged with fraud (the charge was eventually dropped), the real issue had been that the crowd was half black and half white at a time when Cleveland was a segregated city. Freed ran into a similar problem in Boston in 1958 when a concert staged at the Boston Arena degenerated into violence outside the facility. This time Freed was indicted on two charges of inciting a riot. One week after the concert, he was no longer a WINS deejay. He moved to a slot at WABC radio and shortly thereafter also began hosting a dance party on WNEW-TV. In November 1959, after one of his Boston indictments had been dropped and he had pleaded no contest to the other, he was fired from WABC. Two days later, he lost his job at WNEW as well. By the time the payola hearings really took off, Freed's career was already on the ropes. In 1960, he was arrested for accepting $30,000 in payola and two years later was fined and given a suspended sentence. Unemployed and penniless, he was indicted again in 1964 for income tax evasion. He died of uremia the following year, a broken man.

Dick Clark, in contrast, came through the payola hearings without a smudge on his reputation. Clark was no cleaner than Freed, but he represented an acceptability that Freed did not. Clark was also toting up some $12 million in annual billings for ABC, as compared to Freed's $250,000. As a result, ABC-TV issued a statement in support of Clark even after the radio division had fired Freed. Having voluntarily divested himself of the companies that would be most likely to show conflicts of interest, Clark was pronounced "a fine young man" by chairman Oren Harris. If anything, Clark's position within the music industry was strengthened by the hearings.

When all was said and done, the committee had unearthed little. A mail survey by the committee had revealed $263,245 in payola to deejays, but there was no hard evidence to back this figure. Not even comparable to World War I levels of abuse, one could not help but wonder what all the fuss was about. Still, the number of deejays who felt compelled to come forward and confess their sins was reminiscent of the worst aspects of the McCarthy era. Furthermore, as they had during the McCarthy era, reams of public testimony and extensive media coverage helped to create a climate so unfavorable to "down and dirty" rock 'n' roll that the music I have described as schlock rock was encouraged further. Of course, by the time the committee had finished its deliberations, much of the work to contain rock 'n' roll had ceased to be necessary, as a number of the most prominent rock 'n' roll pioneers had already been neutralized in one way or another. Presley had been drafted in early 1958, and by the time he came home from Germany in 1960, his influence in shaping the genre had ended. Indeed, through television appearances with Frank Sinatra and films like *Blue Hawaii* and *Viva Las Vegas,* he had become family entertainment, if not worse. Little Richard had quit rock 'n' roll in the late fifties to join the ministry. Jerry Lee Lewis' career had self-destructed in 1958 when he married his cousin. Buddy Holly had died in a tragic plane crash, which also took the lives of Ritchie Valens and the Big Bopper, in 1959, the same year the committee began its hearings. Later that year, Chuck Berry's arrest for a violation of the Mann Act had effectively removed him from the rock 'n' roll scene.

In the end, the hearings were instrumental in passing a bill that outlawed payola. The most immediate effect of the bill was to impose on radio a tighter, more hierarchical structure that rendered the flow of popular music easier to control. Thus, in effect, mainstream radio was caught between a rock and a hard place. Severely chastised by the committee, which had delivered its racial message in no uncertain terms, and fearful of FCC reprisals that could affect licensing, rock radio became skittish about programming too many black artists. However, there was still a demand for the music, so rock stations could not afford to ignore it completely. In general, they responded by playing as few black artists as they could without losing their listenership.

The number of deejays who felt compelled to come forward and confess their sins was reminiscent of the worst aspects of the McCarthy era.

Surf's Up!

In the early 1960s, as the second generation of schlock rockers pitted their dubious talents against the more complicated phenomenon of the "girl groups" and the emergence of Motown (two developments that will be dealt with in the next chapter), surf music emerged with vocal and instrumental variants. Its trajectory was remarkably short, essentially rising and falling from 1962 to 1964. While, on the one hand, surf music must take its historical place as part of the continuing trend to make rock 'n' roll both white and middle class, it has proven to be a more complex phenomenon than this. Certainly, nowhere is the imagery of white middle-class America more apparent than in surf music, and certainly in the early 1960s surfing became the central metaphor for an easygoing lifestyle based on the unabashed celebration of consumption. As Lillian Roxon has noted, the emergence of surf music "marked the first time in music history that a sport actually had its own music."[28] Its themes dealt primarily with images of affluence—expensive fast cars, attractive women and men at leisure on the beach, and, of course, surfing itself. Still, unlike schlock, which offered rock 'n' roll little more than a backward look to pop song stylists of an earlier era, surf music provided something of a gateway to the 1960s. It offered a vibrant, driving sound worthy of the name rock 'n' roll. As Steve Chapple and I have argued elsewhere:

> **S**urf music should not be confused with the drivel that had issued from Hollywood "beach party" movies a few years earlier.

Surf music brings images of affluence into rock 'n' roll

> The surfing music that appeared in the early sixties should not be seen as just another fad that softened rock 'n' roll. Rather it was a precursor to the psychedelic and underground progressive rock of the sixties. Several of the important people involved in surfing music—especially the Beach Boys . . . and Lou Adler, one of the first producers of Jan and Dean, became central figures in sixties rock. Surfing music represented an authentic West Coast rock 'n' roll culture that differed in one important way from earlier rock 'n' roll produced by urban blacks and Southern rockabillies: it was made by middle-class whites.[29]

Of course, surf music should not be confused with the drivel that had issued from Hollywood "beach party" movies (*Bikini Beach, Muscle Beach Party, Beach Blanket Bingo*) a few years earlier. These movies, which began in 1959 with *Gidget,* starring Sandra Dee and James Darren, and reached their zenith in 1963 with *Beach Party,* starring Annette Funicello and Frankie Avalon, transformed the southern California surf cult into a national fad but naturally trivialized the vitality and discipline of the sport with their focus on bikinis and middle-class teen dilemmas. They do represent, however, one instance in which Hollywood beat the record companies to the punch by nearly four years.

The prototypical surf music group was Dick Dale and the Del-tones from southern California. Working closely with Leo Fender, creator of the first solid-body electric guitars, Dale helped to develop the amplification and reverberation equipment that gave much of surf music its distinctive sound. He and his group were a powerhouse live combo with a dedicated following that had a local hit with "Let's Go Trippin'" in 1961. On the strength of the group's live shows, Capitol offered Dale and the Del-tones a contract with a hefty promotional budget in 1963, but the group failed to deliver any hits. By this time, the group's strong bass lines, sax-based instrumentals, and Dale's harsh vocal style—indeed, the very name of the band—seemed almost anachronistic in the national market. It would be left to other groups, primarily from southern California, to establish the style nationally. A number of these groups were instrumental ensembles. First out of the gate were the Marketts who released "Surfer's Stomp" in 1962. That same year, a British group, the Tornadoes, effected a surf sound on "Telstar," a number one hit. Instrumental surf peaked in 1963 with the release of "Pipeline" by the Chantays, "Wipe Out" by the Surfaris, and "The Lonely Surfer" by session man Jack Nitzsche. The Pyramids scored with "Penetration" in 1964, and by this time, other groups from across the country (the Astronauts from Denver and the Wailers from Seattle to name two) had found their way into the pop market through the surf tag. But 1964 was really the swansong for surf as the British Invasion effectively washed away the entire genre.

In its short life, instrumental surf music was part of a venerable tradition of instrumental rock 'n' roll that began with talented musicians like organist Bill Doggett ("Honky Tonk," 1956), alto sax player Bill Justice ("Raunchy," 1957), who worked as a staff producer at Sun Records, and Bill Black, Elvis Presley's original bass player, who went on to record eight Top Thirty instrumental hits with his own combo. Initially, instrumental rock 'n' roll drew on a wide range of sources. The Champs' "Tequila" echoed the Chicano rhythms of the Southwest. Jazz drummer Cozy Cole broke into the rock 'n' roll market in 1958 with "Topsy (part II)," a revived Basie tune from the late 1930s. It was followed with "Topsy (part I)" and "Turvy (part II)" in 1958. In 1959, Santo and Johnny Farina from Brooklyn had a number one hit with "Sleep Walk," which featured a lilting Hawaiian steel guitar. In 1960, the Viscounts resurrected a version of the jazz classic "Harlem Nocturne" with enough tremolo and echo to qualify it as pure rock 'n' roll.

It was, however, as novelty music that instrumental rock 'n' roll had its greatest successes. In 1959, Johnny and the Hurricanes hit number five with "Red River Rock," a rock 'n' roll version of the traditional "Red River Valley." This was quickly followed by "Reveille Rock" (1959), an adaptation of the Army bugle call, and "Beatnik Fly" (1960), a remake of Burl Ives' "Blue Tail Fly." Kokomo pillaged a Grieg piano concerto to turn "Asia Minor" into a Top Ten rock 'n' roll hit in 1961. That same year, B. Bumble and the Stingers turned "The Flight of the Bumble Bee" into a boogie-woogie piano hit called "Bumble Boogie." The group followed up in 1962 with "Nut Rocker," a rock 'n' roll version of Tchaikovsky's "The Nutcracker." The subtlety and polish of Cozy Cole gave way to the novelty drumming of Sandy Nelson whose adolescent pounding on "Teen Beat"

(1959) and "Let There Be Drums" (1961) anticipates the classic surf drum solo that appeared on "Wipe Out."

There were two groups that dominated the guitar-based sound that eventually came to define instrumental rock 'n' roll—Duane Eddy and the Rebels and the Ventures. Eddy and the Rebels were the most successful, but the Ventures were the most influential. Both, however, contributed to the effort to make rock 'n' roll, instrumental or not, white and middle class. In the hands of Dick Clark, Eddy became another teen idol. The Ventures, the pride of Seattle, established the instrumentation of the classic rock 'n' roll quartet—lead, rhythm, and bass guitars and drums, no horns, no keyboards, just electricity and rhythm. On their debut single, "Walk—Don't Run" (1960), the group evidenced polish and technical precision, without sacrificing excitement and drive. The group also had versatility as its rock 'n' roll version of the Latin standard "Perfidia" in 1960 indicates. Overall, the group enjoyed a longevity that was rare for an instrumental group and recorded more than fifty albums, sixteen of which made the Top Forty. In fact, neither the twist craze nor the turn toward surf music in the early sixties phased the group. Surf even provided the Ventures with a new marketing hook in 1964 as they entered the Top Ten with a surf remake of their rock standard entitled "Walk—Don't Run '64." As rock writer Greg Shaw has noted, however, "surf music was the last hurrah for instrumental rock as a popular genre; after the British Invasion of 1964, vocals again assumed primacy in white rock."[30]

As if to anticipate this development, the Beach Boys became the definitive surf group. The group was a family affair. In the early 1960s, brothers Brian Wilson (keyboards, bass), Carl Wilson (guitar), and Dennis Wilson (drums) teamed up with their cousin, Mike Love (lead vocals), and their Hawthorne, California, neighbor Al Jardine (guitar, bass), to form the most popular self-contained vocal/instrumental combo in town. The only surfer in the group was Dennis, but he convinced Brian and Mike Love to write songs that elevated the sport and its cultural trappings to a metaphor for the American Dream. Their images, like surf music in general, were bound to a kind of affluence that was available to only a narrow segment of the population. In the early 1960s, such images contrasted sharply with those of the burgeoning Civil Rights movement. Seemingly oblivious to their own privilege or the social currents around them, the Beach Boys were hardly apologetic for their music. "We're white and we sing white," the group said.[31] Despite this comment, the group copped the melody line (at least with attribution) for "Surfin' U.S.A.," their first Top Ten single, from Chuck Berry's "Sweet Little Sixteen." In many ways, however, it was fitting that the group should "collaborate" with Berry. After all, barring the suburban focus and a West Coast orientation, the Beach Boys constructed teen anthems in much the same way that

The Beach Boys constructed teen anthems in much the same way that Chuck Berry did. The group's sophisticated close harmonies and elegant counterpoint created a sound that was unique among white U.S. rock groups.

Berry did. The group's sophisticated close harmonies and elegant counterpoint created a sound that was unique among white U.S. rock groups.

The Beach Boys first came to national attention in 1962 when their first release, "Surfin'," which had been a local hit the previous year, reached number seventy-five on the national pop charts. Signed by Capitol that same year, the group hit number fourteen with "Surfin' Safari." The group's biggest year was 1963, which was also the peak of the surfing fad. "Surfin' U.S.A." backed with "Shut Down," "Surfer Girl" backed with "Little Deuce Coup," and "Be True to Your School" backed with "In My Room" all hit the charts between April and November. By 1964, the group's boldly conceived ideology of "Fun, Fun, Fun" was well established, if not quite believable. In pursuit of this ideology, the lyrics of the group's songs "shut down" all challengers on the dragstrip, defended the honor of their high school, and wished aloud that all (attractive) women could be "California Girls." Clearly, the group is vulnerable to the criticism that their

The Beach Boys made no bones about infusing rock 'n' roll with white middle-class themes and images. Without apology, they managed to merge the squeaky cleanliness of Philadelphia schlock with the unbridled energy of a high school garage band.

Beach Boys dominate surf music, score national hits

songs offered primarily male-oriented, sexist imagery. At their worst, they were no better than the Hollywood beach blanket movies. At the same time, however, they were capable of expressing doubt ("When I Grow Up (To Be a Man)"), even insecurity ("Don't Worry Baby"). Even the most tired clichés became invested with a certain freshness and vitality. Although the group's songs were never quite cynical, they managed to convey the sense that propping up false myths was a task that could not be taken too seriously. In this spirit, they delivered all the raunchiness of a high-school garage band but still managed to sound as squeaky clean as the Philadelphia crowd. The job of managing these contradictions—transforming them into hits—fell mostly to Brian Wilson, a largely untutored musical genius and an increasingly tortured soul.

Brian had emerged as the group's main writer, arranger, and producer (a rarity in the heyday of artist and repertoire men at major labels) following the extraordinary success of the group's second album, *Surfin' U.S.A.* Never fitting comfortably into the group's sun and fun image, he preferred the safety of the studio, where his demons could be more easily concealed. He listened to the creations of his idol Phil Spector and became determined to perfect the oceanic version of Spector's "wall of sound" (see chapter 6) based in the group's harmonic virtuosity. Starting with the complicated arrangement and unorthodox harmonies on "I Get Around" (1964), Brian began to push the limits of pop convention. By the time the style was fully developed on "California Girls" (1965), he had also begun testing the limits of his own consciousness with mind-altering drugs. The Beach Boys' *Pet Sounds* LP, released in 1966, experimented with advanced studio techniques well before the Beatles' *Sergeant Pepper* album. After the success of the fully "psychedelic" million-seller "Good Vibrations" in 1966, Brian embarked on what was supposed to be his crowning achievement—a concept LP tentatively titled *Smile.* A short time into the project, however, his behavior became erratic. After he had allegedly destroyed many of the album's vocal tracks in a fit of paranoia, the project became irrevocably stalled. The release of *Sergeant Pepper* was the final blow. Brian suffered a complete breakdown and withdrew from the group. The remaining members released a hastily assembled substitute LP called *Smiley Smile,* which included some fine cuts but failed to reach the Top Forty at all. Although the group continued to produce hits, it never regained the magic of Brian's peak years.

The only other act that came within striking distance of the surf crown was Jan and Dean. Jan (Berry), Dean (Torrence), and Arnie Ginsberg, a high-school buddy not to be confused with the deejay of the same name, had been active since 1959 when their performance of "Jennie Lee" became a Top Ten hit. It was released as "Jan and Arnie" since Dean was in the army at the time. A year later, however, Jan and Dean scored another Top Ten hit with a novelty rocker called "Baby Talk." The two did not really hit their stride, however, until 1963 when "Surf City," written by Jan and Brian Wilson, went to the number one slot. "Surf City" clearly established Jan and Dean as a surf act, a marketing label that the two rode to further chart success with "Drag City" in 1963, and "Dead Man's Curve" and "The Little Old Lady (From Pasadena)" in 1964, among others. Unfortunately, in 1966, Jan played out a variation of the story line from "Dead Man's Curve" in real life when he hit a parked vehicle at 65 mph, killing three passengers and sustaining brain damage himself. The tragedy effectively ended the career of Jan and Dean, but only after the genre itself had already self-destructed.

Because it opened a new chapter in the social relations of class, age, and race (but not gender), rock 'n' roll became a target of attack by those who feared the changes the music signaled. Behind every attack—from cover records to government investigations—was an attempt to reclaim mainstream cultural space for white middle-class values, themes, and images. It can be said that this attempt was at least in part successful as the characteristics that had defined rock 'n' roll in the first place—strong regional accents, hot instrumental solos, and suggestive lyrics—gradually fell by the wayside. In all these changes, the connections between rock 'n' roll and its r&b heritage became more strained, which had the effect of imposing a separation on two genres that had been virtually indistinguishable.

Prior to 1959, rock 'n' roll had effected an extraordinary degree of overlap between the pop charts and the r&b charts. Not only had black artists gained unprecedented access to the popular market through rock 'n' roll, but white artists had sold to the black record-buying public in record numbers. In 1958, for example, more than half the records to make the r&b Top Ten were by white artists.[32] From 1959 on, however, bland, white vocalists like Fabian, Frankie Avalon, and Bobby Rydell were marketed as rock 'n' rollers. Although they achieved considerable success as such, their styles were inappropriate for r&b radio, and as a result, white artists' penetration of the r&b market declined sharply. Black radio returned to a policy of programming more black artists than white. Somewhat paradoxically, the separation of rock 'n' roll and r&b contributed to a resurgence of rhythm and blues as a separate style with crossover potential. After 1959, artists like Wilbert Harrison ("Kansas City"), Barrett Strong ("Money"), Jimmy Jones ("Handy Man," "Good Timin'"), the Shirelles ("Will You Love Me Tomorrow," "Dedicated to the One I Love"), Gary 'U.S.' Bonds ("New Orleans," "Quarter to Three," "School Is Out"), the Crystals ("He's a Rebel"), Gene Chandler ("Duke of Earl"), and the Marvelettes ("Please Mr. Postman") provided a welcome change of pace (and race) in the popular market.

The percentage of black artists crossing over into the popular market remained uncommonly high until the onslaught of British performers in 1964. Seen in this light, not even the Beatles—the very musicians who breathed new life into the music—can be considered apart from the racist attacks on rock 'n' roll. It is, in fact, impossible to understand the magnitude and immediacy of their acceptance in this country without some reference to this theme. At the same time, it would be a gross distortion of history to underplay their unique contribution to the music and the culture of the 1960s. The Beatles were refreshing, talented, and the harbingers of broad cultural and political change.

N O T E S

1. For a more detailed analysis of this, see Steve Chapple and Reebee Garofalo, *Rock 'n' Roll Is Here to Pay: The History and Politics of the Music Industry* (Chicago: Nelson-Hall, 1977), 300–04; and Peter Wicke, *Rock Music: Culture, Aesthetics and Sociology* (New York: Cambridge University Press, 1990), 30–34.

2. Charlie Gillett, *The Sound of the City: The Rise of Rock and Roll* (New York: Outerbridge and Dienstfrey, 1970), 360.

3. Russell Sanjek, "The War on Rock," *Downbeat Music '72 Yearbook* (Chicago: Maher Publications, 1972).

4. This situation was complicated when Frank Sinatra charged Miller with trying to foist BMI material on him while he was still with Columbia in 1956. In response, Miller produced statistics that disproved Sinatra's allegation.

5. Just as Columbia did through its subsidiary OKeh, Victor maintained a presence in the r&b market through its Groove subsidiary, which was founded in 1953. One memorable Groove recording that hit rock 'n' roll pay dirt was the eerie "Love Is Strange" (1957) by Mickey and Sylvia. Mickey was the experienced session guitarist Mickey "Guitar" Baker; Sylvia was Sylvia Robinson who went on to form Sugar Hill Records, the first rap label of note, in the late 1970s.

6. Gillett, *The Sound of the City,* 74.

7. Ibid.

8. For a reasonably exhaustive listing of pop/r&b covers, including label and release date, see Philip Ennis, *The Seventh Stream: The Emergence of Rocknroll in American Popular Music* (Hanover, N.H.: Wesleyan University Press/University Press of New England, 1992), 223–26.

9. Dot achieved the status of a major when it was purchased by ABC-Paramount in 1957.

10. Gillett, *The Sound of the City,* 76.

11. Ibid., 127.

12. Ed Ward, Geoffrey Stokes, and Ken Tucker, *Rock of Ages: The Rolling Stone History of Rock & Roll* (New York: Rolling Stone Press, 1986), 166.

13. Gillett, *The Sound of the City,* 127.

14. Russell Sanjek, *American Popular Music and Its Business: The First Four Hundred Years, Volume III from 1900 to 1984* (New York: Oxford University Press, 1988), 444.

15. Arnold Shaw, *The Rockin' '50s* (New York: Hawthorne Books, 1974), 176.

16. Henry Schipper, "Dick Clark," *Rolling Stone,* 19 April 1990, p. 70.

17. Ibid.

18. Shaw, *The Rockin' '50s,* 197.

19. Linda Martin and Kerry Segrave, *Anti-Rock: The Opposition to Rock 'n' Roll* (New York: DeCapo Press, 1993), 24–25.

20. Shaw, *The Rockin' '50s,* 218–19.

21. Gillett, *The Sound of the City,* 360.

22. Shaw, *The Rockin' '50s,* 267.

23. Trent Hill, "The Enemy Within: Censorship in Rock Music in the 1950s," *South Atlantic Quarterly* (Fall 1991): 677.

24. Sanjek, *The War on Rock,* 18.

25. Ibid., 11, 19.

26. Ibid., 62.

27. Ibid.

28. Lillian Roxon, *Lillian Roxon's Rock Encyclopedia* (New York: Grosset and Dunlap, 1971), 477.

29. Chapple and Garofalo, *Rock 'n' Roll Is Here to Pay,* 52.

30. Greg Shaw, "Instrumental Groups," in *The Rolling Stone Illustrated History of Rock & Roll,* ed. Jim Miller (New York: Rolling Stone Press, 1976), 108.

31. Arnold Shaw, *Black Popular Music in America* (New York: Schirmer Books, 1986), 207.

32. Gillett, *The Sound of the City,* 218.

6 Popular Music and Political Culture: The Sixties

The conservative hegemony and control that rock 'n' roll challenged implicitly in the 1950s gave way to open social and political upheaval in the 1960s. Just as the Beatles marked the decade musically, a myriad of grassroots social and political movements— civil rights, antiwar, black power, student power, the counterculture, and, later, women's liberation—signified a dramatic shift in the political center of gravity toward the left. These changes were firmly grounded in contradictions that had been bubbling just beneath the surface of American life for quite some time.

Throughout the 1950s, the growth of suburbia had been rivaled only by the frenzy of activity euphemistically called "urban renewal." Charges that suburbia could be culturally bankrupt and emotionally deadening and that urban renewal was often little more than neighborhood removal were dismissed as the price of progress. It was expected that each generation of Americans would be heir to a higher standard of living than the generation that preceded it. There were, however, a number of paradoxes in this ever-improving picture. First and perhaps foremost was the "race problem," which was brought into bold relief by the historic Supreme Court school desegregation decision of 1954 (*Brown* v. *Board of Education*). The Court's decision was the most important government intervention in race relations since the previous

Given that rock 'n' roll crossed the lines of class, race, and age, it is ironic, in retrospect, that civil rights activists tended to avoid the music initially because its commercial bent seemed antithetical to the goals of the struggle.

century. Second, while Madison Avenue encouraged disciplined workers to become hedonistic consumers, there still existed throughout the country an almost Victorian attitude toward sexuality. In some ways, rock 'n' roll represented an initial (and partial) response to this paradox. Finally, although the country had entered a period of unprecedented affluence, there still existed a widespread, but largely invisible, poverty.

Those who placed their faith in the security of the American Dream found it shaken to the core when the Soviet Union launched *Sputnik*, the first orbiting space satellite, in 1957. The event had implications for everything from military superiority to the computer revolution still in its infancy. The country entered the era of high technology playing second fiddle to the Soviet Union. Education was seized upon as the key to the future, and there ensued a tremendous expansion of the college and university system nationwide. Because it was envisioned that the society of the future would require an educated labor force, higher education, once the province of the economic and intellectual elite, became available on a mass scale.

Thus, the 1960s dawned as the United States was in the process of reinventing itself. The search for a new image led to the election of the youngest president in the history of the country, John F. Kennedy. He would assemble "the best and the brightest," as his advisers were called, to address all the problems of the country, and he would ask his supporters to give unselfishly of themselves in the restructuring of American values. The momentum of his vision and the political acumen of Lyndon Johnson, his vice president and then successor, yielded a spate of landmark legislation and social programming. It was in this context that young men and women of all classes, races, and ethnic backgrounds entered (and often dropped out of) college in record numbers. The participation of these young people—indeed, their leadership—in rethinking America produced the movements and the tumultuousness that defined the 1960s.

The Civil Rights Movement and Popular Music

The link between the Civil Rights movement, the movement from which all other movements took their cue, and music was first forged through early union songs and spirituals like "Which Side Are You On," "This Little Light of Mine," "Keep Your Eyes on the Prize," "This Land Is Your Land," "Down by the Riverside," and, of course, "We Shall Overcome." Songs like these were, in the words of Bernice Johnson Reagon, the "songs that moved the movement."[1] Given that rock 'n' roll crossed the lines of class, race, and age, it is ironic, in retrospect, that civil rights activists tended to avoid the music initially because its commercial bent seemed antithetical to the goals of the struggle.[2] Still, while civil rights activists may have avoided rock 'n' roll, the Civil Rights movement had an impact on the larger musical culture, including rock 'n' roll, that went far beyond its own internal practices. In fact, it is possible to analyze the impact of the movement on the national consciousness by charting the trajectory of popular music during this period. Consider, for example, the mid-1950s. During this time, a new, activist southern black clergy, led by Reverend Martin Luther King, Jr., began to form political alliances with such secular organizations as the National Association for the Advancement of Colored People (NAACP), the Congress on Racial Equality (CORE), and, later, the Student Non-Violent Coordinating Committee (SNCC). At the same time, as Nelson George has noted, "the music world was witnessing the breaking of a longstanding taboo, as gospel began to fuse with rhythm and blues."[3] Thus, in popular music, as in the struggle for civil rights, the black church became a force to be reckoned with. Prior to the eruption of civil rights as a national issue, there were a number of regional struggles for equal rights. As these regional struggles, which were based primarily in the South, came to national attention, early rock 'n' roll, which was based on southern r&b styles, found a national audience. In Montgomery, Alabama, in 1955, Rosa Parks moved up to the front of a segregated bus and refused to relinquish her seat. At the same time, Fats Domino, Little Richard, and Chuck Berry began to cross over into the mainstream market as heroes of rock 'n' roll. The rebellious tone of early rock 'n' roll mirrored the growing demand for political change in the black community. And just as community-based black activism would change the political face of the nation, so would rock 'n' roll alter the national popular music landscape.

When Chuck Berry released "School Day" in 1957, he had no problem conjuring up images of teachers teaching "the golden rule" even as President Eisenhower sent federal troops to Little Rock to enforce the Supreme Court's school desegregation edict.

With the advent of rock 'n' roll, the form and style of popular music changed dramatically and irrevocably. But these changes were not yet accompanied by analogous changes in lyric content. When Chuck Berry released "School Day" in 1957, he had no problem conjuring up images of teachers teaching "the golden rule" even as President Eisenhower sent federal troops to Little Rock to enforce the Supreme Court's school desegregation edict. Berry may have been a true storyteller in the folkloric sense of the term, but he was also a man of his time. As he would later tell his fans: "I said: 'Why can't I do as Pat Boone does and play good music for the white people and sell as well there as I could in the neighborhood? And that's what I shot for writing 'School Day.'"[4]

The strategy of the early Civil Rights movement, like Chuck Berry's crossover dream, was integrationist; even at its most militant—the lunch-counter sit-ins of 1960 and the freedom rides of 1961—the demand was for social equality. Once that was attained, it was argued, full citizenship and assimilation into the mainstream of American life would follow naturally. Issues like institutionalized racism, white skin privilege, and black self-determination were not yet prominent on the political agenda. Society, it was widely believed, did not need a major overhaul but some intelligent fine tuning. During this period, then, the influence of the Civil Rights movement on rock 'n' roll is not apparent in the content of its lyrics but in the ascendancy of black producers and black-owned record labels and in the appearance of black female vocal groups. There can be no question that the growing Civil Rights movement provided a climate that encouraged these developments.

Civil Rights movement affects developments in popular music

The "Girl Groups" and the Men behind Them

In the early 1960s, as civil rights activity heated up, r&b moved "uptown," to use the term Charlie Gillett coined to describe the more polished, distinctly urban production style that came into being. Uptown r&b had been prefigured in Leiber and Stoller's pioneering work with the Drifters ("There Goes My Baby," "Dance With Me," "This Magic Moment," "Save the Last Dance for Me") in 1959 and 1960, and its crossover potential was immediately apparent. Using varying combinations of elaborate instrumentation, lavish studio production, and advanced recording techniques, the next generation of independent r&b producers, which included Luther Dixon, Phil Spector, and Berry Gordy, were able to deliver the forcefulness and emotional impact of rhythm and blues. In the process, they rekindled the spirit of early rock 'n' roll and brought to the forefront for the first time a score of black female vocal groups, known collectively as the "girl groups," that became overwhelmingly popular. In 1962, thanks primarily to the girl groups, there were more black artists on the year-end singles charts (but not the album charts) than at any time in history. Between 1962 and 1963 alone, for example, the best-seller lists included the Orlons ("The Wah Watusi," "Don't Hang Up," "South Street"), the Crystals ("He's a Rebel," "Da Doo Ron Ron," "Then He Kissed Me"), the Sensations ("Let Me In"), the Chiffons ("He's So Fine," "One Fine Day"), the Essex ("Easier Said Than Done"), the Ronettes ("Be My Baby"), Ruby and the Romantics ("Our Day Will Come"), and the Motown groups Martha and the Vandellas ("Come and Get These Memories," "Heat Wave," "Quicksand") and the Marvelettes ("Please Mr. Postman," "Playboy"). By 1964, Motown's Supremes had come into their own and turned out fifteen hit singles in a row over the next few years. The only significant girl groups that were white were the Angels ("My Boyfriend's Back") and the Shangri-Las ("Leader of the Pack"). Still, as talented as these groups were, it is virtually impossible to separate their artistic appeal from the genius of the producers who molded their sound.

Phil Spector is often regarded as the genius behind some of the most important "girl groups." The "wall of sound" he created for them produced the perfect marriage of technology and rhythm and blues. It remains one of the defining sounds of the early 1960s.

The Shirelles from Passaic, New Jersey, were the prototypical girl group. They first recorded for the independent Tiara label, which had been formed by Florence Greenberg, one of the very few women to own her own record company. The Shirelles' first hit, "I Met Him on a Sunday," was written by the group; it sold so well locally that it was picked up by Decca for national distribution in 1958. Decca had no faith in the group, however, and the group's next records were put out on Greenberg's Scepter label. At Scepter, the group was placed under the tutelage of producer Luther Dixon. Combining a plaintive gospel call-and-response style with the urban sensibilities of uptown r&b, Dixon shepherded the Shirelles through a string of hits from 1960 to 1962. Among these recordings, which are now considered rock 'n' roll classics, were "Will You Still Love Me Tomorrow," "Dedicated to the One I Love," "Mama Said," "Baby, It's You," and "Soldier Boy." By 1962, the commercial appeal of female vocal groups had been proven, and Dixon's production techniques, which had been developed simultaneously by Phil Spector and Berry Gordy, had become a virtual science.

Phil Spector, who produced two of the most important groups, the Crystals and the Ronettes, is the producer whose name is most readily associated with the so-called girl group phenomenon. Like Jerry Leiber and Mike Stoller with whom he apprenticed, Spector was a white man whose vision was to harness the wizardry of studio production and the precision of a professionally written song to the energy and vitality of rhythm and blues. Certainly, there was no better cultural milieu than the unassuming integrationist stance of the early Civil Rights movement to nurture such a vision. Indeed, Spector's first and last hits, "Spanish Harlem" and "Black Pearl," seem to underscore this connection. "Spanish Harlem," a song about a Latina named Rose with "eyes as black as coal," was written by Spector and Leiber within months of Spector's arrival in New York in July 1960. Spector then coproduced the song with Leiber and Stoller for Ben E. King, providing the singer with his first solo hit after leaving the Drifters. In 1969, Spector produced his last Top Twenty hit single for an integrated group called the Checkmates. The song, "Black Pearl," which he had written with Toni Wine, was about a black woman who'd "been in the background too long." "Black Pearl and Rose are fascinatingly similar," David Hinckley has written in the liner notes to the Spector boxed set, *Back to Mono,* "shaded flowers to whom the singer offers sun. That Spector helped bring to life a rose that was Spanish and a pearl that was Black reflects a human rainbow pop music did not always acknowledge so sympathetically."[5]

Spector's artistic vision and his genius for production were matched in equal proportions by his egotism and his paranoia. He controlled every aspect of the production

His singular devotion to his recordings contributed greatly to the perception of Phil Spector as a Svengali-like producer who treated his artists as one more sonic element in the creation of a total sound. This perception encouraged the notion of the girl groups as replaceable entities on the assembly line of pop.

process from start to finish. His resounding financial success (he was a millionaire before his twenty-first birthday) prompted conservative satirist Tom Wolfe to dub him "The First Tycoon of Teen" in an essay of the same name. Describing his recording enterprise, Wolfe noted:

> Spector does the whole thing. He writes the words and the music, scouts and signs up the talent. He takes them out to a recording studio in Los Angeles and runs the recording session himself. He puts them through hours and days of recording to get the two or three minutes he wants. Two or three minutes out of the whole struggle. He handles the control dials like an electronic maestro, tuning various instruments or sound up, down, out, every which way, using things like two pianos, a harpsichord and three guitars on one record; then re-recording the whole thing with esoteric dubbing and over-dubbing effects—reinforcing instruments or voices—coming out with what is known throughout the industry as "the Spector sound."[6]

Spector clearly paid attention to detail, indeed, to every detail. While other companies issued multiple releases simultaneously, Spector labored over and thoroughly promoted only a few records per year. This kind of singular devotion to his recordings contributed greatly to the perception of Spector as a Svengali-like producer who treated his artists as one more sonic element in the creation of a total sound. It was this perception that encouraged the notion of the girl groups as replaceable entities on the assembly line of pop. This notion was further reinforced by the interchangeability of the personnel who comprised the groups that Spector produced. Darlene Love, for example, was and remains a formidable talent. She recorded only two Top Forty hits (both with Spector in 1963) under her own name, "(Today I Met) The Boy I'm Gonna Marry" and "Wait 'Til My Bobby Gets Home." However, she was part of the Blossoms, a group Spector used for background vocals, and a member of Bob B. Soxx and the Blue Jeans, another Spector group that had two Top Forty hits with "Zip-A-Dee Doo-Dah" (1962) and "Why Do Lovers Break Each Other's Hearts" (1963). She also sang lead on two of the Crystals biggest hits in 1962—"He's a Rebel" and "He's Sure the Boy I Love"—even though she was never listed as a member of the group. In short, there exists something of a Darlene Love legacy that has been overshadowed by the producer's signature and the shoddy practice of crediting recordings incorrectly. Love's case is one of the more dramatic examples of this tendency to undervalue the individual talent of the women singers themselves, focusing instead on a consideration of the girl groups as a social phenomenon or their producers' overall sound.[7]

If the discussion of Phil Spector and the groups he produced seems to embody some of the dreams of the early Civil Rights movement, then this discussion cannot be complete without also considering the Brill Building songwriters discussed in Chapter 5. While, at their worst, these writers turned out more than their share of schlock, at their best, they accomplished culturally what the early Civil Rights movement only dreamed of politically: white songwriters and black vocalists incorporating the excitement and urgency of rhythm and blues into the mainstream tradition of professional pop. Nowhere was this marriage more apparent (or better executed) than in the classic hits of the girl groups. Gerry Goffin and Carole King wrote "One Fine Day" for the Chiffons and "Chains" and "Don't Say Nothin' Bad About My Baby" for the Cookies, a trio that was often used for background vocals at Aldon Music. One of the best compositions of the era was their "Will You Love Me Tomorrow," the Shirelles' first number one hit in 1961. If Goffin's lyrics had seemed, up to that point, unusually progressive, he more than compensated a year or so later when he wrote "He Hit Me (It Felt Like a Kiss)," which was written for the Crystals but had to be withdrawn for obvious reasons.

By this time, Phil Spector in partnership with Lester Sill had formed his own company, Philles Records, and he soon became the Brill Building's best customer. Pairing the Crystals with the husband and wife songwriting team of Barry Mann and Cynthia Weil produced "Uptown," a song of uncommon sensitivity and sophistication about urban working-class life, and "He's Sure the Boy I Love," a more teen-directed piece. Between these two releases, Gene Pitney, another writer at Aldon, gave the group "He's a Rebel," their biggest hit. In fact, just about every hit on which Darlene Love sang lead came from the Brill Building. "Why Do Lovers Break Each Others' Hearts" "(Today I Met) The Boy I'm Gonna Marry," "Not Too Young to Get Married," "Wait 'til My Bobby Gets Home," and "A Fine, Fine Boy" drew on the talents of Tony Powers, Jeff Barry, Ellie Greenwich, and Spector himself in different combinations. Barry and Greenwich then worked in collaboration with Spector to produce such tunes as "Da Doo Ron Ron," "Then He Kissed Me," "Heartbreaker," "All Grown Up," "Girls Can Tell," and "Little Boy" for the Crystals and "Be My Baby," "Baby I Love You," "I Wonder," "Keep On Dancing," and "I Wish I Never Saw the Sunshine" for the Ronettes, all of which are from Spector's "wall of sound" period. Spector had a special interest in the Ronettes, eventually marrying the group's lead singer, Veronica Bennett. For them, he teamed up with other top Brill Building songwriting teams to write "Is This What I Get for Loving You?" (with Gerry Goffin and Carole King) and "Walking in the Rain," "You, Baby," "Woman in Love (with You)," and "Born to Be Together" (with Barry Mann and Cynthia Weil). The Spector/Greenwich/Barry team also wrote "Chapel of Love," which became a number one hit for the Dixie Cups.

The production formula for the girl groups remained largely the same, whether the groups were black or white. When George "Shadow" Morton discovered the Shangri-Las, he called on his high-school friends Ellie Greenwich and Jeff Barry to help him write "Leader of the Pack," the group's best-selling single. The song, which tells the story of an impossible relationship that ends in tragedy as the outlaw biker protagonist speeds to self-destruction, was then recorded with the sound of a real motorcycle and a horrifying crash to give it the power of rock 'n' roll. Because gender roles had not yet been challenged, the Shangri-Las, like the other girl groups, were confined to singing about their relationships with men who were "rebels" and "leaders of the pack" rather than singing about women themselves and marketed as much for sexual appeal as for musical abilities. As late as 1968, *Rolling Stone* remembered the Ronettes as

> *tough whorish females of the lower class, female Hell's Angels who had about them the aura of brazen sex. The Ronettes were Negro Puerto Rican hooker types with long black hair and skin tight dresses revealing their well-shaped but not quite Tina Turner behinds. . . . Ronettes records should have been sold under the counter along with girly magazines and condoms.*[8]

The British Invasion marked the beginning of the end for the girl groups. For Spector, however, the dream of a pop/r&b fusion continued. Turning his attention to the Righteous Brothers, a white male duo that was better able to stand up to the onslaught of British groups, Spector once again mined gold at the Brill Building, writing the duo's first and biggest hit, "You've Lost That Lovin' Feelin'" (1964), with Barry Mann and Cynthia Weil, and their second release, "Just Once in My Life" (1965), with Gerry

The Ronettes belted out some of the most memorable songs of the early 1960s. Often, however, a consideration of their talent seemed to be overshadowed by a focus on their sexuality. Too bad the two could not have been appreciated equally.

Goffin and Carole King. The sound that Spector created for the Righteous Brothers was so successful that it commanded a new marketing category of its own—"blue-eyed soul." Other groups like the Young Rascals ("Good Lovin'," "Groovin'") on Atlantic and Mitch Ryder and the Detroit Wheels ("Sock It to Me, Baby") on New Voice also fit this bill. In these instances, the color-blindness of the early Civil Rights movement was reinforced, for here was black-sounding music that was written by whites, produced by whites, performed by whites, and accepted by blacks. Thus, it was a crushing blow to Spector when he was unable to repeat these results with an African American act.

> *The sound that Phil Spector created for the Righteous Brothers was so successful that it commanded a new marketing category of its own—"blue-eyed soul." The color-blindness of the early Civil Rights movement was reinforced, for here was black-sounding music that was written by whites, produced by whites, performed by whites, and accepted by blacks.*

"River Deep—Mountain High" (1966) had all the elements of success: it was written by Spector, Greenwich, and Barry; Spector, as producer, was at the height of his wall of sound powers; and the song was performed by Ike and Tina Turner, one of the hottest r&b acts in the business. At the time, it seemed like "River Deep—Mountain High" couldn't miss; Spector thought of it as his finest song, his crowning achievement. When it flopped, the millionaire boy genius of the music industry quickly became the Howard Hughes of rock.

The girl groups were a short-lived phenomenon for several reasons. Despite their talent and the sophisticated production that accompanied their releases, these artists simply faced too many obstacles: they were, in many ways, a throwback to a 1950s style, they were women, and they were black. After the British Invasion, there were only two girl group releases that ever reached the Top Ten, the Shangri-Las' "I Can Never Go Home Anymore" (1965) and the Chiffons' "Sweet Talkin' Guy" (1966). The Motown blockbuster acts that survived and thrived did so because they transcended the "girl group" label, and they were able to do this because Berry Gordy did not just produce great records, he built long-term careers.

Motown: The Integration of Pop

In the early stages of the Civil Rights movement, it seemed to many that the primary task facing African Americans was assimilation into the mainstream of American life. It was in this context that Motown developed and defined itself. The company soon integrated the pop market with a success unmatched in the history of the music industry. Until its 1988 purchase by MCA and subsequent conglomerate merger with Matsushita (which eventually sold its interest to Seagram), Motown was the largest black-owned corporation in the United States. Its founder, Berry Gordy, was a tough, black, middle-class jazz buff from Detroit, who preferred the world of music to life in the Ford Motor Company. Gordy, who was a regular at local jazz clubs, ran a small jazz record store in

Beginning with a modest studio in Detroit, Berry Gordy built his Motown empire into the largest black-owned corporation in the United States. It opened a new chapter in the treatment of African American artists in the music industry.

the mid-1950s. He was also a prizefighter with a number of wins to his credit. It was his association with Jackie Wilson, a Golden Gloves champion and r&b star, that brought these two strands of his life together. For about three years in the late 1950s, Gordy wrote Wilson's biggest hits, including "Reet Petite," "Lonely Teardrops," "That's Why (I Love You So)," and "I'll Be Satisfied." During this period, Gordy also met Smokey Robinson of the Miracles. After Gordy wrote and produced a Top Thirty hit for Barrett Strong ("Money," 1960) that was issued on a small family-owned label named after his sister Anna and leased to Chess, Robinson convinced him to start his own company. This was the beginning of the Motown empire.

Motown, which was as private and secretive a company as there ever was, embodied the promise of the early Civil Rights movement in that it opened a new chapter in the treatment of African American artists in the music industry. Virtually all of its creative personnel—artists, writers, producers, and session musicians—were African American and all were groomed for long careers. At the same time, from its very beginnings, the company envisioned itself as a crossover label. For years, the company had one white employee, Barney Ales, the vice president for distribution whose relationships with mainstream distributors were crucial to the label's financial health. It was Gordy's job to produce the records that would satisfy their pop needs.

To do this, Gordy, like Spector, evolved a production technique aimed at maximum crossover. Working closely with Smokey Robinson on the label's early releases, he multi-tracked compelling leads and rich gospel harmonies over strong rhythm and horn tracks and the signature bass lines of the legendary James Jamerson. In doing this, Gordy came up with a musical formula that was the perfect metaphor for the early civil rights era: upbeat black pop that was irresistibly danceable and threatening to no one in tone or content. This was the "Motown Sound," or, as the Motown label logo boasted, "The Sound of Young America." Gordy would later comment that any successful Motown hit sold at least 70 percent to white audiences.

> *Berry Gordy came up with a musical formula that was the perfect metaphor for the early civil rights era: upbeat black pop that was irresistibly danceable and threatening to no one in tone or content. This was the "Motown Sound."*

The company was organized as a completely in-house operation totally under the control of Gordy. It included not only the Motown and Tamla labels but also the Hitsville USA studio, Jobete Publishing, and International Talent Management (ITM). ITM provided personal management, including choreographic training by industry veteran Cholly Atkins and lessons on etiquette from local beauty-school owner Maxine Powell, and tour bookings. Remembering Powell, Martha Reeves once recalled: "She taught us how to walk, how to sit proper, and how to get up. She'd have a line of us—the Marvelettes, the Supremes, and the Vandellas all learned together."[9]

To his credit, Gordy built all of his acts from the ground up; he did not simply bleed them for one or two hits, which had been an all too common experience for black artists in the past. As a result, first-generation artists at Motown enjoyed a longevity that was almost unheard of for black artists in the pop market. While other labels may have treated particularly successful groups with such care, Motown approached its whole roster in these terms as just a sample of Motown hits from 1961 to 1966 proves. In this five-year period, Motown acts who had Top Ten pop hits included among others, the Miracles ("Shop Around," "You've Really Got a Hold on Me," "Mickey's Monkey"), the Marvelettes ("Please Mr. Postman," "Playboy," "Don't Mess with Bill"), Mary Wells ("The One Who Really Loves You," "You Beat Me to the Punch," "Two Lovers," "My Guy"), Martha and the Vandellas ("Heat Wave," "Quicksand," "Dancing in the Streets," "Nowhere to Run"), the Temptations ("My Girl," "Beauty Is Only Skin Deep," "(I Know) I'm Losing You"), the Four Tops ("I Can't Help Myself," "It's the Same Old Song," "Reach Out I'll Be There"), Junior Walker and the All Stars ("Shotgun"), and, of course, Marvin Gaye ("Pride and Joy," "How Sweet It Is to Be Loved by You," "I'll Be Doggone," "Ain't That Peculiar"), and Stevie Wonder ("Fingertips—Part 2," "Uptight (Everything's Alright)," "Blowing in the Wind," "A Place in the Sun"). From 1961 to 1971, the company placed well over 100 singles in the pop Top Ten, not to mention hundreds more lesser hits.

Motown really hit its stride in 1964 when the Supremes were assigned to the writer/producer team of Holland-Dozier-Holland. The trio of Florence Ballard, Mary Wilson, and Diana Ross quickly became the jewel in the crown of the Motown empire. Beginning with the release of "Where Did Our Love Go," the Supremes turned out five number one singles in a row, including "Baby Love," "Come See about Me," "Stop! In the Name of Love," and "Back in My Arms Again," no mean achievement for an African American act during the first wave of the British Invasion. By the time Cindy Birdsong (formerly of Patti LaBelle and the Blue Belles) replaced Ballard in 1967, the group had turned out five more number one hits.

It was the company's understanding of the Top Forty radio format, as well as its outstanding artists, that permitted Motown to produce so many hits. On Top Forty radio, records are squeezed in between commercials and fast-talking deejays who sound like used-car salesmen. Understanding the constraints of this AM radio format, Smokey Robinson sought to exercise maximum creativity in a two- to three-minute time frame. In his own words,

> My theory of writing is to write a song that has a complete idea and tells a story in the time allotted for a record. . . . I've just geared myself to radio time. The shorter a record is nowadays, the more it's gonna be played. This is a key thing in radio time, you dig? If you have a record that's 2:15 long it's definitely gonna get more play than one that is 3:15 at first, which is very important.[10]

Still, while there may have been a formula mentality for the structure of a song, the formula did not substitute for creativity. With songwriters like Holland-Dozier-Holland, Norman Whitfield, and Nick Ashford and Valerie Simpson, Motown boasted an in-house staff that could rival the best of the Brill Building writers. A partial listing of their credits more than makes the point: Holland-Dozier-Holland, "Heat Wave" for Martha and the Vandellas; "Where Did Our Love Go," "Baby Love," "Stop! In the Name of Love" and many others for the Supremes; "Baby, I Need Your Loving," "I Can't Help Myself," and "Reach Out, I'll Be There" for the Four Tops; Norman Whitfield, "Pride and Joy" and "I Heard it Through the Grapevine" cowritten for Marvin Gaye, "Girl (Why You Wanna Make Me Blue)," "(I Know) I'm Losing You," and "You're My Everything" for the Temptations; and Nick Ashford and Valerie Simpson, "Ain't Nothing Like the Real Thing" for Marvin Gaye and Tammy Terrell; "Ain't No Mountain High Enough" for Diana Ross.

In his quest for a mainstream audience, Berry Gordy made sure his writers paid heed to the conventional, if unfounded, industry wisdom that controversial issues had no place in the lyric content of popular music.

In his quest for a mainstream audience, Gordy made sure his writers paid heed to the conventional, if unfounded, industry wisdom that controversial issues had no place in the lyric content of popular music. In this self-imposed constraint, Gordy was not alone. Motown took off at a time when the best rock 'n' roll was being composed by Brill

Building songwriters who wrote with intelligence, even wit but, with few exceptions, an utter lack of substance. When these songs were hits, it was usually because of the distinctive performance of the artist. The pop/soul alliance between writer/producers Burt Bacharach and Hal David and song stylist Dionne Warwick, who recorded for Scepter Records, is a good example of this. Warwick's soulful delivery of Bachrach's and David's well-crafted tunes transformed lyric fluff into a thing of such beauty that even the British Invasion couldn't slow them down. From 1963 to 1970, Warwick recorded twenty-two Top Forty hits, including "Anyone Who Had a Heart," "Walk on By," and "I Say a Little Prayer," that never broached a topical issue.

Motown's songs were also well constructed and performances were invariably compelling, "but when it came to lyrics," as Gerri Hershey has said, Berry Gordy "had a larger constituency to consider. . . . Gordy's demographics could countenance no overt militancy."[11] It should not be surprising, then, that socially relevant themes and images were no more to be found in early Motown lyrics than any other genre of pop, rock, or rhythm and blues. Stevie Wonder's 1966 cover of "Blowin' in the Wind"—six years after the founding of the label and well past the initial surge of the Civil Rights movement—was Motown's first "topical" release. Thus, while the climate of the early Civil Rights movement encouraged the success of Motown, the company never became a voice for the cause. At the time, social commentary could be found in the folk arena and, to a lesser extent, in jazz. It is perhaps for this reason that the early 1960s saw the popular folk revival that the major labels had tried unsuccessfully to engineer from the top down just a few years earlier.

Folk Music: The Voice of Civil Rights

It is impossible to analyze the folk revival of this time without mentioning Woodie Guthrie and Pete Seeger. Avowed left-wing activists since the 1930s, Guthrie and Seeger were no strangers to insurgent political movements. Guthrie, an "Okie" who had been radicalized by the events of the Great Depression, wrote some of this country's most enduring folk songs, including "This Land Is Your Land" and "This Train Is Bound for Glory." His influence on folk music is incalculable. It was, in fact, Guthrie's radio show on KFVD in Los Angeles in the late 1930s that helped to create the association between folk music and leftist politics, an association perhaps bolstered by the statement on his guitar: "This machine kills fascists." Seeger was a college-educated, New York radical who saw music as a means for helping to mobilize a mass movement. Together, Guthrie and Seeger formed the Almanac Singers in 1941 and pushed their progressive political message across the country. In the late 1940s and the early 1950s, Seeger experienced the rush of million-selling records as a member of the Weavers. His disaffection with pop success and the specter of McCarthyism, however, forced his career into the background. By this time, Guthrie was seriously debilitated by Huntington's chorea. From the early 1960s until his death in 1967, he was bedridden, and among his constant visitors was the young Bob Dylan, who described himself as something of a Woody Guthrie jukebox.

In folk circles at the time, there was a fiercely argued, if not terribly relevant, distinction between performers who were "authentic" and those who were "commercial."

The Civil Rights movement was a natural outlet for Seeger's creative and political energies. It was Seeger more than anyone who tirelessly popularized the movement's anthem "We Shall Overcome" to a global audience. While he was a folk purist who railed against commercialism in music and seldom basked in the pop limelight himself, his guiding hand was never far from view. "If I Had a Hammer," a song he had written in 1949 with Lee Hays, became a Top Ten hit in 1962 for Peter, Paul & Mary and then again in 1963 for Trini Lopez. The Kingston Trio also scored in 1962 with his "Where Have All the Flowers Gone."

In folk circles at the time, there was a fiercely argued, if not terribly relevant, distinction between performers who were "authentic" and those who were "commercial." For most, Pete Seeger defined authenticity while the Kingston Trio and most of the groups that garnered the Top Forty hits from popularized folk material—the Rooftop Singers ("Walk Right In," 1963), the New Christy Minstrels ("Green, Green," 1963), and the Serendipity Singers ("Don't Let the Rain Come Down," 1964)—were clearly commercial. The distinction, of course, was riddled with inconsistency. Eric Darling, the leader of the Rooftop Singers, had been a member of the Weavers with Seeger. Joan Baez was considered authentic even though she charted twelve Top Forty LPs, six of which were certified million sellers. As activist liberals with commercial success, Peter, Paul & Mary sort of straddled the fence. The one artist who openly challenged the distinction, and ultimately rendered it useless, was the newcomer who had sat at the feet of the ailing Woody Guthrie, the enigmatic Bob Dylan. Born Robert Zimmerman, the son of a middle-class Jewish family, Dylan grew up in Hibbing, Minnesota, listening to a 1950s mixture of rhythm and blues, country and western, rock 'n' roll, and pop. One of his boyhood dreams was to play in Little Richard's band. After knocking around the University of Minnesota for a while and reading Guthrie's autobiography, *Bound for Glory,* the young Zimmerman moved to New York. There, he visited the hospitalized folk legend and began building his own myth as a Guthrie-style folksinger. He also legalized his newly acquired surname and shrouded his earlier life in mystery. He was signed by John Hammond to Columbia in 1962 and, over the next two years, issued three albums of highly unorthodox, self-accompanied acoustic folk to critical raves.

With selections like "Oxford Town" (racism in a Mississippi town) from his second album, *The Freewheelin' Bob Dylan,* and "The Lonesome Death of Hattie Carroll" (the death of a black domestic) from his third, *The Times They Are A'Changin',* Dylan was early on proclaimed a leader in the Civil Rights movement. In 1963, he performed "Only a Pawn in Their Game," his song about the murder of civil rights leader Medgar Evers, at the March on Washington, where he stood next to Martin Luther King, Jr., and shared the stage with such folk luminaries as Pete Seeger, Joan Baez, and Peter, Paul & Mary. That

After sitting at the feet of an ailing Woody Guthrie, the freewheeling Bob Dylan shrouded his past in mystery and set about building his own myth as a Guthrie-style folksinger. The early Civil Rights movement gave him the perfect springboard for success.

same year, Peter, Paul & Mary had Top Ten pop hits with Dylan's "Blowin' in the Wind" and "Don't Think Twice, It's Alright." In two short years, then, Dylan was well along the road to transforming, almost singlehandedly, the lyric content of popular music. It was at this point that he made a musical decision that cost him his authenticity but brought him a mass audience. In 1965, he appeared at the Newport Folk Festival playing an electric guitar (a classic rock Fender Stratocaster, no less), and backed by an electric band (the Paul Butterfield Blues Band). Seeger was livid, and Dylan was booed off the stage.

But, as the song says, "something was happening" and Dylan knew what it was better than his critics. In a world of increasing student activism (Dylan released his first album just as Tom Hayden and a group of radical students were putting the finishing touches on "The Port Huron Statement," which announced the formation of Students for a Democratic Society [SDS]), folk offered an alternative to rock 'n' roll's lyric vacuity, but folk could never supplant the more primal urges that rhythm and blues and rock 'n' roll had turned loose. For this reason, folk could never capture the mass audience. Bridging that gap was Dylan's particular genius. *Bringing It All Back Home,* Dylan's next album, contained one whole side of electric music with uncommonly substantive lyrics that were held up by a hard-driving, straight-ahead rock 'n' roll beat. "Subterranean Homesick Blues," the first cut on the electric side of the album, became his first Top Forty pop hit, and a roar of outrage arose from the folk community. Was Dylan the true seer the folkies had once thought he was or the consummate opportunist they now criticized? It depended on who was asked. Amidst charges that he had sold out not just the Civil Rights movement but the entire American left, Dylan took his own advice about following leaders and turned his back on politics. In this change of direction, he was often contrasted with Phil Ochs whose songs such as "Here's to the State of Mississippi" and "I Ain't Marching Anymore" from his second album, which spanned the Civil Rights and antiwar movements, remained true to the folk protest ideal. Ostracized by the true believers, Dylan soon left his detractors in the dust as he ushered in the era of folk rock. Ochs, in contrast, was tortured by his inability to become "the first left-wing star," a torment that eventually pushed him to take his own life in 1976.

> *Folk offered an alternative to rock 'n' roll's lyric vacuity, but folk could never supplant the more primal urges that rhythm and blues and rock 'n' roll had turned loose. Bridging that gap was Bob Dylan's particular genius.*

The debate over commercial versus authentic performers tended to obscure a far more important issue at the time. From old-timers like Pete Seeger to newcomers like Joan Baez, Bob Dylan, and Peter, Paul & Mary, the best-known artists in folk music were white. Seeger, to his credit, included such African Americans as Odetta, Sonny Terry, and Brownie McGhee in his concerts and on his albums, and gradually, these artists became prominent as voices of the Civil Rights movement. However, they did not come to the attention of a mass public on their own. Indeed, during the initial surge of the folk revival, artists of color who performed folkloric material seldom became well known outside folk circles. Harry Belafonte, an outspoken activist and a director of Martin Luther King's

Southern Christian Leadership Conference (SCLC), was, of course, an obvious exception. In 1960 he recorded a second million-selling live album at Carnegie Hall, this one including Odetta, Miriam Makeba, and the Chad Mitchell Trio. But, Belafonte was already a pop star; his music and his acting/television career seemed curiously separate from his political choices. It was inevitable, given the times, that his commercial success would seem to taint his authenticity. Trini Lopez was also something of an exception. Like Ritchie Valens before him, the "Tex-Mex" pop singer included Mexican and American popular and folk material in his repertoire. His best-selling follow-up to Seeger's "If I Had a Hammer" was "Lemon Tree" (1965), a song that he had adapted from the traditional Latin song "Hojita de Lemon." Buffy Sainte-Marie, a Cree Indian from Canada, might have received greater recognition early on if she had not been forced to take time off in 1963 because of ill health. Although identified as a folksinger, she was really more of a singer/songwriter. At the time, such original compositions as "Now that the Buffalo's Gone" and "My Country 'Tis of Thy People You're Dying" offered her limited audience a profoundly different view of Native Americans than the view expressed by such pop fare as Johnny Preston's "Running Bear" or Larry Verne's "Mr. Custer."

Although a number of African American artists had championed a merger of gospel and r&b styles in the 1950s, it was not until the mid-1960s that the social consciousness of folk music was linked to the popular appeal of the gospel/r&b fusion. The center for this innovation was Chicago and the often underappreciated Curtis Mayfield. Like fellow Chicagoan Sam Cooke, Mayfield had left the gospel choir for the secular world of popular music in the 1950s. After a series of hits with the Impressions—"For Your Precious Love" (1958), "Gypsy Woman" (1961), and "It's All Right" (1963)—Mayfield "got religion" once again. Beginning in 1964, he penned a series of successful folk-sounding but pop-produced "sermon songs" for the group, including "Keep on Pushing" and "Amen" in 1964 and "People Get Ready" in 1965. Through these, he became, in the words of Nelson George, "black music's most unflagging civil rights champion."[12]

Curtis Mayfield started as a talented writer and singer who effected a successful pop gospel fusion in the 1950s with his group the Impressions. The Civil Rights movement provided the inspiration for some of his best music. He went on to become a producer, label chief, and solo artist, scoring Superfly, one of the most successful so-called blaxploitation films of the early 1970s.

Mayfield's fusion had actually been anticipated by the Staple Singers, a family gospel group that started in a Chicago Baptist church in 1950. In the late 1950s, they recorded gospel for Vee Jay with Pop Staples' understated guitar and daughter Mavis' compelling lead vocals. In the early 1960s, the group demonstrated Mayfield's pop feel for the material, recording such spiritual classics as "Will the Circle Be Unbroken?" "Amazing Grace," and "We Shall Overcome" with electric guitar and drums. The Staple Singers did not make the pop charts until they signed with Stax in the 1970s, but even then, gospel-tinged songs like "I'll Take You There," "If You're Ready (Come Go with Me)," and "Touch a Hand, Make a Friend" were prominent among their hits.

Another look at Sam Cooke's career completes Chicago's musical connection to civil rights. Cooke had made a mild but successful foray into social commentary as early as 1960 when "Chain Gang" went to number two on the pop charts. Still, it was not until he heard Bob Dylan's "Blowin' in the Wind" that he felt compelled to relate to the Civil Rights movement more directly. In late 1964, he attempted a pop/folk fusion with "A Change Is Gonna Come." By the time the record was released as a single, however, Cooke had been shot to death under unsavory circumstances. When his friend Malcolm X was assassinated only two months later, on 21 February 1965, "A Change Is Gonna Come" was moving up the charts to Top Forty status; it stands as Cooke's monument to civil rights.

The British Invasion Occupies the Pop Charts

The promise of President John F. Kennedy's New Frontier, as his blueprint for America was called, was dealt a crushing blow when he was assassinated on 22 November 1963. In the aftermath of his death, the national mood was one of defeat and depression. It is noteworthy that in the six months between Kennedy's assassination and the passage of the Civil Rights Act of 1964, the Beatles' upbeat sound captured the cultural life of the nation. "In retrospect," as "gonzo" critic Lester Bangs has written, "it seems obvious that this elevation of our mood had to come from outside the parameters of America's own musical culture, if only because the folk music which then dominated American pop was so tied to the crushed dreams of the New Frontier."[13]

> So dramatic was the Beatles' impact that, from a cultural point of view, there is a tendency to think that the sixties, that is, the cultural era rather than the chronological decade, began in 1964, the year they first hit the U.S. pop charts.

The Beatles transformed popular music just as the issue of civil rights became permanently imprinted on the national consciousness. For both the Beatles and civil rights, the time was right; for both, the results were profound. So dramatic was the Beatles' impact that, from a cultural point of view, there is a tendency to think that the sixties, that is, the cultural era rather than the chronological decade, began in 1964, the year they first hit the U.S. pop charts. It was as if the country had simply been marking time for four years waiting for their arrival. There were many reasons for this perception. First, the Beatles made their American debut at a time when the U.S. music industry was stagnating. While the industry had more than doubled in size between 1955 and 1959, record sales had decreased by 5 percent (to $600 million) in 1960. In 1963, sales were up by only 1.6 percent from the previous year. After 1964, however, the industry enjoyed double digit growth every year until the end of the decade and, including tape sales, more than doubled its revenues (to about $1.6 billion). The Beatles, of course, did not rejuvenate the music business singlehandedly, but other artists paled in the face of their impressive statistics and fresh sound. In 1964 alone, they charted twenty-eight singles and released six best-selling albums. From 1963 to 1968, the group sold an estimated $154 million worth of records worldwide.[14] Not even Elvis in his heyday could compete with numbers like these.

Second, the Beatles eclipsed all other talent so quickly and so completely that many lost sight of the fact that prior to their arrival, the most exciting developments in popular music had been in African American music. Indeed, the Beatles' first album in the United States, *Introducing . . . The Beatles,* which included five Top Ten singles, was released on the black-owned Vee Jay label. It is interesting that neither the Beatles themselves nor most of the other British groups who flooded the United States in the mid-1960s lost sight of this fact. The early sound of the Beatles, the Animals, and the Rolling Stones, among others, was hard-driving rock 'n' roll and much of their inspiration came directly from African American artists. Indeed, many of the Beatles' early recordings were essentially note-for-note reproductions of such African American rock 'n' roll classics as "Roll Over Beethoven" by Chuck Berry, "Long Tall Sally" by Little Richard, "Twist and Shout" by the Isley Brothers, "Money" by Barrett Strong, "Boys" and "Baby it's You" by the Shirelles, "You've Really Got a Hold on Me" by Smokey Robinson and the Miracles, and "Chains" by the Cookies. This is not to suggest that the Beatles could, in any way, be reduced to mere cover artists. The group brought a freshness and originality to popular music that was truly innovative. Their motivation in covering so many African American hits was less to cash in on black culture than to pay tribute to their musical heroes. The Beatles openly credited Chuck Berry, the Miracles, Chuck Jackson, and Ben E. King as formative influences. In fact, they (and even more the Stones and the Animals) introduced a whole generation of white, middle-class Americans to the rich tradition of African American music that had always existed within earshot. Still, it was a fact of American life that, while openly and repeatedly acknowledging their debt to African American music and touring with early rock 'n' roll greats like Little Richard, the Beatles and the other English groups that followed them were more marketable than the African American artists they admired. It was this particular contradiction in America that had created the need for the Civil Rights movement in the first place.

The Beatles were not what they appeared to be. After paying their dues in the rough-and-tumble nightclubs of Hamburg, manager Brian Epstein dressed them up in suits and ties and went to great pains to present them as family entertainment.

Prior to the arrival of the Beatles, British artists had ventured to North American shores only one or two at a time: Lonnie Donegan ("Does Your Chewing Gum Lose Its Flavor (on the Bedpost over Night)") in 1961 and Kenny Ball ("Midnight in Moscow")

At *its worst, the taste for anything British became so indiscriminate that British acts like Chad and Jeremy and Ian Whitcomb had Top Ten pop hits in the United States while remaining completely unknown at home.*

and Mr. Acker Bilk ("Stranger on the Shore") in 1962. When the Beatles first hit the U.S. pop charts in January 1964, their records were issued on six different labels. By February of that year, they had become the country's hottest act although they had yet to step foot on U.S. soil. By mid-April they had twelve singles in the *Billboard Hot 100,* including the top five positions. *Billboard* reported that the group had accounted for nearly 60 percent of all singles sold for a period of about three weeks.

Over the next two years no fewer than two dozen British groups would appear on the U.S. pop charts. At its best, the British Invasion recalled the enthusiasm of early rock 'n' roll and pointed the way to numerous future developments in popular music. At its worst, the taste for anything British became so indiscriminate that British acts like Chad and Jeremy ("Yesterday's Gone") and Ian Whitcomb ("You Turn Me On") had Top Ten pop hits in the United States while remaining completely unknown at home. The assault also overshadowed all other developments in popular music. There was, for example, a Mexican American influence in popular music during this period. "Pop"ularized as "Ameriachi" by Herb Alpert and the Tijuana Brass, one of the best-selling bands of the era, there was also a clear connection to rock and soul. In 1962, Chris Montez, a protégé of Ritchie Valens, scored a Top Ten hit with "Let's Dance" and was signed by Alpert's A&M label. In 1966, he scored four more Top Forty hits. Another Chicano act from Los Angeles, Cannibal and the Headhunters, released the defining arrangement of "Land of 1000 Dances" in 1965, well over a year before Wilson Pickett had a Top Ten hit with the song. A Chicano group from Detroit, ? (Question Mark) & the Mysterians, hit number one with "96 Tears" in 1966. Indeed, from 1965 to 1967, Sam the Sham & the Pharoahs from Dallas, Texas, turned out six Top Forty hits, including "Wooly Bully" (1965) and "Lil' Red Riding Hood" (1966). There was something of a "sound" to this music (like the prominent use of Farfisa organ on many cuts), but it was totally overpowered by the craving for all things British. So great was this hunger that another Tex-Mex-influenced rock band, the Sir Douglas Quintet ("She's About a Mover," 1965), led by a white local, Doug Sahm, from San Antonio, Texas, was actually promoted as a new British group.

The groups identified with the first wave of the British Invasion came from far and wide. There were the Zombies ("She's Not There") from Hertfordshire and the Moody Blues ("Go Now!") from Birmingham. Peter and Gordon ("A World Without Love") came from Scotland. The group Them ("Here Comes the Night," "Gloria") was Irish. The Seekers ("I'll Never Find Another You") were Australian. If it seems odd that the Sir Douglas Quintet came from San Antonio, it is equally ironic that the Nashville Teens ("Tobacco Road") hailed from Weybridge, Surrey. In the minds of many fans, even the Beau Brummels ("Just a Little") from San Francisco were associated with the British onslaught. Mostly, however, the British Invasion came from three cities: Liverpool, Manchester, and London.

The Beatles, of course, came from Liverpool, as did the Searchers ("Needles and Pins"), Gerry and the Pacemakers ("Don't Let the Sun Catch You Crying," "Ferry Cross the Mersey"), Billy J. Kramer and the Dakotas ("Little Children"), and the Swinging Blue Jeans ("Hippy Hippy Shake"). Although Liverpool is a dreary, gray, industrial seaport town located along the Mersey River, there was at the time a flourishing rock 'n' roll culture among its working-class residents that was due to the steady stream of American merchant seamen who brought records over. Once absorbed, rock 'n' roll mingled with British folk styles and achieved pop status in a type of music known as "skiffle." (Skiffle was fleetingly exposed to American audiences in Lonnie Donegan's "Rock Island Line" in 1956.) It was skiffle that John Lennon, Paul McCartney, George Harrison, and Stuart Sutcliffe, who later died of a brain hemorrhage, played as the Quarrymen. This was the musical amalgam that shaped the Beatles and their Merseybeat comrades, but they paid their dues playing rock 'n' roll in the rough-and-tumble nightclubs of the German port city of Hamburg. Hamburg was the crucible that forged their professionalism. By the time they journeyed to Hamburg, the Quarrymen had metamorphosed to Johnny and the Moondogs, then to the Silver Beatles, and at last to simply the Beatles with Pete Best on drums. When they returned home, they were showcased with the best-known Liverpudlian groups at a dingy basement club called the Cavern, which is where they first came to the attention of Brian Epstein, record-store owner cum manager. Like all beat groups, the Beatles had mastered a standard rock 'n' roll repertoire of Chuck Berry, Little Richard, Elvis Presley, and Buddy Holly and the Crickets, as well as such r&b classics as Barrett Strong's "Money" and the Isley Brothers' "Twist and Shout" and material from the girl groups. Unlike many of the groups, however, Lennon and McCartney wrote original songs right from the beginning.

Once under the brilliant tutelage of Epstein, the group, which had been turned down at other labels, was signed by producer George Martin to EMI. Their first single "Love Me Do" (with Ringo Starr replacing Best on drums) went Top Twenty in Great Britain in 1962. "Please, Please Me" hit number two there in 1963. "From Me to You" went all the way to number one that same year. All three of these hits were Lennon-Mc-Cartney tunes. When another Lennon-McCartney original, "She Loves You," became the best-selling single in British history in late 1963, Epstein decided the group was ready to take on the United States. The "fab four" arrived in New York on 7 February 1964, when "I Want to Hold Your Hand" was the number one single in the country. For the next six months, they occupied the number one slot on the U.S. pop charts. Once again, eight of their nine Top Ten hits during this period were Lennon-McCartney tunes. Their first movie, *A Hard Day's Night,* a black and white film by director Richard Lester about a day in the life of the group, opened in August to rave reviews. The soundtrack album of the same name yielded two Top Ten singles—the title song and "Can't Buy Me Love." Beatlemania, as the frenzied reaction to the group was called, was no less dramatic in the United States than it had been in England, and the group quickly established a beachhead for the rest of the British Invasion.

Unlike Liverpool, the city of Manchester turned out some of the most mindless drivel ever associated with the British Invasion, with the exception of Wayne Fontana and the Mindbenders, who spent one glorious week in 1965 at number one with "The Game of Love." Herman's Hermits ("Mrs. Brown, You've Got a Lovely Daughter," "I'm Henry VIII, I Am") pre-sented an alternative to the rock 'n' roll/skiffle fusion of the beat groups that showed just how low a pop interpre-tation of the British music hall tradition could sink. Even so, between 1964 and 1970, the group charted eighteen Top Forty singles and ten albums in the United States. Freddie and the Dreamers ("I'm Telling You Now," 1965) elevated vacuity to an art form, as Freddie Garrity's stage act of flapping both arms while lifting each leg outwardly—a set of moves requiring no skill

Herman's Hermits presented an alternative to the rock 'n' roll/skiffle fusion of the beat groups that showed just how low a pop interpretation of the British music hall tradition could sink.

and less grace—became a dance craze that guaranteed another hit, "Do the Freddie." With close harmonies that set them apart from other Manchester groups, the Hollies improved with age, but the best they could turn out by the end of the first wave of the British assault was "Bus Stop" (1966). When Graham Nash left the group in 1968 to "make records that say something" with David Crosby and Stephen Stills, it was evident that music in the United States was heading in a new direction.

London, which was far more eclectic than either Liverpool or Manchester, offered artists ranging from the jazz-influenced Manfred Mann ("Doo Wah Diddy Diddy," 1964), who was born in South Africa, to Dusty Springfield ("I Only Want to Be with You," "You Don't Have to Say You Love Me"), one of the two women who held her own from the beginning of the British Invasion to the end of the decade. (The other was thirtysomething Petula Clark from Epsom, Surrey, who charted fifteen Top Forty singles, winning Grammies for her first two, "Downtown" and "I Know a Place," both in 1965.) Another London woman who did not fare as well as these two was Honey Lantree, drummer for and namesake of the Honeycombs, a group whose only big hit, "Have I the Right?" (1964), sounded vaguely like the Dave Clark Five, a group from the London suburb of Tottenham. Clark was the drummer for his group but mostly because they didn't have another one. His rudimentary pounding, the defining characteristic of the group's sound, was likened by *Time* magazine to an "air hammer." Beginning with "Glad All Over" and "Bits and Pieces," both Top Ten hits in 1964, the Dave Clark Five brought new meaning to the term "beat" music. The quintet relied on a series of r&b classics for success, as did many other British groups. In 1965, they scored with covers of Chuck Berry's "Reelin' and Rockin'" and Chris Kenner's "I Like It Like That." The group's last Top Ten hit was a remake of Marv Johnson's "You Got What It Takes."

One London group that had the talent and creativity to be truly influential was the Kinks. Under the leadership of writer/vocalist/guitarist Ray Davies, the group took the United States by storm in late 1964 with three original Top Ten hard rockers ("You Really Got Me," "All Day and All of the Night," and "Tired of Waiting for You"). After these, the group seemed to stall. This may have happened because they encountered such problems with the American Federation of Television and Radio Artists (AFTRA) on their first U.S. tour that they could not return for four years or because the group never really had an effective promotional apparatus or because the group's follow-up hits ("A Well Respected Man" and "Dedicated Follower of Fashion"), while brilliant contributions to popular music, were so distinctly British that they were lost on U.S. audiences. Whatever the reason, the Kinks never attained the stature that should have been their due.

The London groups that had the most influence on U.S. music were the white blues revivalists. Blues aficionado Alexis Korner, owner of the London Blues and Barrelhouse Club, had been jamming with visiting African American bluesmen since the mid-1950s. In the early 1960s, Korner went electric and formed Blues Incorporated. At about the same time and at Korner's request, John Mayall moved to London to form the Bluesbreakers. These two ensembles served as catalysts for some of the best blues-based rock Britain has ever had to offer. Among the musicians who passed through the Korner/Mayall brotherhood were John McVie and Peter Green of Fleetwood Mac, Eric Clapton, Jack Bruce, and Ginger Baker who went on to become Cream, Ray Davies of Kinks fame, future members of Pentangle, Free, and Led Zeppelin, and two founders of the British rock band that has outlasted all of them, drummer Charlie Watts and lead singer Mick Jagger of the Rolling Stones.

The Animals from Newcastle, a town every bit as tough as Liverpool, was another influential blues-based group. They had begun as a combo bearing the name of its organizer, organist Alan Price, but the early addition of Eric Burdon as lead singer and the group's wild stage act led to the name change. After the release of their first album, *The Animals* (1964), which included the hit single "The House of the Rising Sun," Burdon's hard, bluesy delivery prompted *Ebony* magazine to devote five pages to the group's funky sound, rare coverage for a white singer. In hindsight, it is possible to say that what appeared to be authenticity at the time was in fact Burdon's obsession with blackness.

Like most British rockers at the time, the Animals and the Rolling Stones included a good deal of African American music in their repertoires. The Rolling Stones did "Walking the Dog" by Rufus Thomas, "Under the Boardwalk" by the Drifters, "Hitchhike" and "Can I Get a Witness" by Marvin Gaye, a number of Chuck Berry tunes, including "Carol," "Talking About You," and "Around and Around," and went into the country blues with Slim Harpo's "I'm a King Bee." The Animals brought back Ma Rainey's "See See Rider" and John Lee Hooker's "Boom Boom," Nina Simone's "Don't Let Me Be Misunderstood," Shirley and Lee's "Let the Good Times Roll," Fats Domino's "I'm in Love Again," Chuck Berry's "Talkin' 'Bout You" and "Around and Around," a number of Ray Charles hits, including "Hallelujah, I Love Her So," "Mess Around," and "Hit the Road, Jack," and Sam Cooke's "Bring It on Home to Me" and "Shake." There were, however, important differences in the ways in which Jagger and Burdon approached the material. In Britain, where social divisions are more clearly expressed in class terms than in the United States, Jagger could pull off his self-mocking delivery of African American styles without the slightest embarrassment at being white. While the Stones displayed the typical British fascination with African American culture, they had a sufficient distance on it that their involvement with the music was primarily aesthetic. Not so for Burdon, for whom blackness loomed as an unattainable personal goal and a never-ending source of frustration.[15]

For the United States, where race tends to dominate the discourse of social division, the revival of African American styles that the British onslaught set in motion had

> **W**hile the Stones displayed the typical British fascination with African American culture, they had a sufficient distance on it that their involvement with the music was primarily aesthetic. Not so for Burdon, for whom blackness loomed as an unattainable personal goal and a never-ending source of frustration.

immediate race-based implications for commercial viability and touched off endless debate about white people singing the blues.[16] It was during this period that the r&b charts were briefly discontinued, at least in part as a result of the integrationist impulse of the early Civil Rights movement. For African American artists, the results were disastrous. In 1962, 42 percent of the songs on the year-end singles charts were by African Americans. In 1966, African Americans declined to 22 percent, the lowest point since the initial surge of rock 'n' roll in the mid-1950s. Only three of the top fifty albums for the years 1964 and 1965 were by black artists. In contrast, nearly one-third of the Top Ten releases for 1964 belonged to British artists; one year earlier there had been none. Among African American artists, only the Motown acts survived the first wave of the British Invasion. They did so not only because of the freshness of the Motown sound, but also because the businessman in Berry Gordy intuitively understood that his interests would best be served by an alliance with popular British acts. It was no coincidence that the Supremes' third album, *A Bit of Liverpool* (1964), showcased cover tunes from British groups, especially the Beatles. In two important telecasts, *T.A.M.I.* (1964) and *TNT* (1965), the Supremes, Smokey Robinson and the Miracles, and Marvin Gaye appeared with British groups Gerry and the Pacemakers and the Rolling Stones.[17] *Ready Steady Go!* a television pop music variety show in Great Britian, devoted an entire episode to the Motown sound in 1965. When Motown launched a tour of Britain featuring a number of the company's best-selling artists that same year, everybody gushed. The Beatles lauded the music at every opportunity. Even the *Sunday Times* was enthusiastic. If there had been any misconceptions about where Berry Gordy sought to position Motown on the pop music continuum, his remarks laid them to rest: "We are very honored the Beatles should have said what they did. . . . They're creating the same type of music as we are and we're part of the same stream."[18]

The politics of class and culture played itself out further in the tension between Liverpool and London or, more specifically, between the Beatles and the Rolling Stones. As revolutionary as the Beatles' music may have sounded, Brian Epstein took great pains to present the group as middle-class family entertainment. Their first U.S. appearance was on the *Ed Sullivan Show*. The press marveled at their wit. Even parents liked them, they were "cute." They wanted only "to hold your hand." The Stones were anything but cute. If Epstein extracted an image of innocence from the Beatles, Andrew Loog Oldham, the Stones' manager and earlier an Epstein employee, cultivated precisely the opposite image for his group. The Rolling Stones took longer to arrive in the United States than the Beatles (the country's thirst for Beatles clones had to be quenched first) but when they did, they were embraced as the menacing, street-toughened alternative to the playful mop-tops. The Stones scowled at the camera; they were surly. Their music was full of disdain, mostly for women. After they played the *Ed Sullivan Show*, Sullivan vowed that

As revolutionary as the Beatles' music may have sounded, Brian Epstein took great pains to present the group as middle-class family entertainment.

they would never return. Of course, neither the Beatles nor the Rolling Stones were quite what they appeared to be. The Beatles came from solidly working-class backgrounds. Prior to their Epstein manicure, they had played Hamburg in slicked-back hair and black leather jackets. In contrast, only two of the Stones—Bill Wyman and Charlie Watts—had working-class backgrounds. Brian Jones, the Stones' first rhythm guitarist who drowned in 1969, was an upper middle-class dropout. Keith Richards attended art school, and Mick Jagger remained a student at the London School of Economics until the group became a going concern. These were no more "street-fighting men" than the Beatles were wholesome, carefree mop-tops. The respective images of each group were based on strategic career choices.

If anything, the Stones were bohemians; the terrain that the group staked out, the tradition they wished to explore, the musical statement they wanted to make was based in the blues. It was down and dirty, replete with exaggerated aggressiveness and overt sexuality. It almost demanded a tough, streetwise, working-class image. Almost a year after the Beatles were presented with MBE (Members of the British Empire) awards by the queen herself at Buckingham Palace (over the loud protests of outraged upper-class conservatives), the Rolling Stones were still cultivating their working-class identities at New York's Academy of Music, a venue that recalled Alan Freed's week-long, walk-in rock 'n' roll shows at the Brooklyn Paramount. For the Beatles, who were steeped in working-class culture and destined to remain within its confines until Epstein's arrival, the wholesome, mop-top image offered a way out of their class-determined fate. Epstein's strategy of scrubbing them clean and dressing them up in suits and ties was, as

The Rolling Stones arrive in New York for the first time in 1964 with Brian Jones (second from left) as rhythm guitarist. In retrospect, the bad boys of sixties rock look more youthful than tough. They have gone on to become one of the longest running, self-contained rock acts in the business.

always, on the mark. Certainly, the Beatles were as well schooled in contemporary African American music as the Stones, but the group's equally strong affinity for skiffle and the British music hall tradition resonated more with another musical phenomenon that was beginning to bloom in the United States—folk rock.

Breaking the Sounds of Silence

Given the folk revival's stringent requirements for authenticity, it would have been difficult for Bob Dylan to trumpet his admiration for the Beatles in 1964. It was, however, precisely his attraction for the group that started him thinking about recording with other musicians and moving in a rock 'n' roll direction. As he later confessed to Anthony Scaduto, his first serious biographer:

> I had heard the Beatles in New York when they first hit. Then, when we were driving through Colorado we had the radio on and eight of the ten top songs were Beatles songs. In Colorado! I Wanna Hold Your Hand, all those early ones.
>
> They were doing these things nobody was doing. Their chords were outrageous, just outrageous, and their harmonies made it all valid. You could only do that with other musicians. Even if you're playing your own chords you had to have other people playing with you. That was obvious. And it started me thinking about other people.
>
> But I just kept it to myself that I really dug them. Everybody else thought they were for the teenyboppers, that they were gonna pass right away. But it was obvious to me that they had staying power. I knew they were pointing the direction where music had to go.[19]

On the other hand, it was not difficult for the Beatles to acknowledge their high regard for Dylan. When the folksinger toured England in May 1964, the Beatles, as well as the Rolling Stones and Eric Burdon, went to see him. According to popular music lore, two important things happened. First, Dylan allegedly turned the Beatles on to marijuana.[20] Hallucinogenic drugs had an obvious influence on their future development, and, therefore, the rest of popular music. Second, Dylan heard the Animals' "House of the Rising Sun" before it was released in the United States. It knocked him out. ""My God, ya oughtta hear what's going down over there," he told a friend when he returned to New York. "Eric Burdon, the Animals, ya know? Well, he's doing *House of the Rising Sun* in rock. *Rock!* It's fuckin' *wild!* Blew my mind."[21] The Animals had, in fact, mined Dylan's first album for their first two recordings, redoing "Baby Let Me Follow You Down" as "Baby, Let Me Take You Home" and then transforming "House" into electric, transatlantic magic. Dylan appreciated its significance immediately. "You see, there was a lot of hypocrisy all around," he told Scaduto, "people saying it had to be folk or rock. But I knew it didn't have to be like that."[22]

Bob Dylan moves folk toward rock, creates new category

Folk Rock: Adding Substance to Form

If the Animals had concocted the alloy that would yield folk rock, it was the Byrds who turned it into a full-fledged genre (marketing category). The Animals had come at folk material from a rock and blues direction. The Byrds were folkies, who, like Dylan, embraced rock. Leader Jim (later, Roger) McGuinn had arrived in Los Angeles through the Chicago folk circuit. Guitarist and vocalist David Crosby was a California-bred folksinger from the start. Chris Hillman picked up the electric bass after laying down his bluegrass mandolin. Together, they evolved a self-conscious sound (defined by McGuinn's electric twelve string Rickenbacker) that was clearly based in a rock aesthetic. Like Dylan's Newport 1965 debacle, the Byrds' sonic conception challenged a number of orthodoxies, as Lillian Roxon has pointed out:

> *Until the Byrds, the very notion of a group of folk singers strengthening their sound with rock devices was unthinkable. Folk was highminded, pure and untouched by sordid commercial values. Rock was something you played for a quick buck. The most important thing the Byrds ever did was to recognize that rock could revitalize folk—with a finished product that was considerably more than the sum of its parts.*[23]

At the beginning of their career, the Byrds drank heavily from the well of Dylan's creativity, recording rock versions of four of his songs on their first album. When the group's version of "Mr. Tambourine Man" (the title song from their debut album) became a number one pop hit in 1965, folk rock became a "thing." Lovin' Spoonful ("Do You Believe in Magic"), Barry McGuire ("Eve of Destruction"), Sonny and Cher ("I Got You Babe"), and Simon and Garfunkel ("Sounds of Silence") all debuted in 1965. Donovan also came into his own with "Sunshine Superman" that year, although he had been dogged by comparisons with Dylan earlier. In Los Angeles, it paid to be Dylan-influenced, as the Turtles discovered when "It Ain't Me Babe" quickly followed the Byrds' "Tambourine Man" up the charts. Cher even offered Dylan to the teenyboppers in 1965 with her version of "All I Really Want to Do," which was also a hit for the Byrds that year.

To say that 1965 was *the* year for folk rock does not mean that folk rock died after 1965; it simply means the electrification of folk in the rock market was more or less taken for granted from that point on. It was well understood by almost everyone that in the mainstream market the social consciousness that folk brought to the table would be folded into a commercialized rock aesthetic, not the other way around. Lillian Roxon correctly chastised *Newsweek* for referring to the Byrds as "Dylanized Beatles when the whole point was that they were Beatlized Dylans."[24] In the marriage of folk and rock, rock was in control, with all the contradictions that such a statement implies. For those artists who could not reconcile themselves to these contradictions, the results could be

Folk rock marries folk consciousness to rock aesthetic

disastrous, as the untimely death of Phil Ochs proves. Others unwittingly expressed their uneasiness in their music. Peter, Paul & Mary's feeble ode to rock, "I Dig Rock and Roll Music" (1967), reveals both their musical discomfort with the genre and their political distrust of its unabashedly commercial bent.

At the time, folk rockers were usually considered to be "thinking musicians," which in the rock market, until the Beatles, was a virtual contradiction in terms. It was not that there had never been topical songs in rock 'n' roll. From Chuck Berry's "Brown-Eyed Handsome Man" to the Crystals' "Uptown," rock 'n' roll had occasionally flirted with the notion of something more, but folk rock offered a steady diet of such material, be it about personal relationships ("All I Really Want to Do") or social commentary ("Sounds of Silence"). In this way, folk rock pointed the way for the singer/songwriters who would go on to capture one strand of the fragmented audience of the 1970s. Perhaps nothing illustrates the transition from one era to the other better than the career of Simon and Garfunkel.

Paul Simon and Art Garfunkel first performed in the late 1950s as Tom and Jerry. Eight years later, when their producer Tom Wilson added drums and electric backing to

The Byrds showed how rock could transform folk. They are pictured in an airport about to begin the journey that would take them eight miles high.

an acoustic recording of "Sounds of Silence" without their permission, their careers took off. The song shot to number one and established Simon and Garfunkel (now performing under their real names) as a folk rock act. After racking up five gold or platinum albums and ten Top Thirty singles (including their number one hit from *The Graduate,* "Mrs. Robinson"), the duo turned the decade with the moving, if sentimental, social commentary of "Bridge Over Troubled Water" from the six-Grammy-Award-winning album of the same name. When they broke up over artistic differences around 1972, both men segued easily into solo soft rock careers, with Simon eventually leaving his former song mate far behind.

In addition to the social consciousness embedded in its songs, folk rock held out the elusive possibility of rock protest. The energy of rock 'n' roll had always been identified with rebellion but never with a cause. Folk rock was different. Here, for the first time, was a mainstream music that could be used explicitly in the service of thoughtful protest and creative opposition. Folk rock thus brought not only the poetic leanings but also the predominantly left-wing political inclinations of folk music to a mainstream audience. In its earliest and most didactic form, there was Barry McGuire's raspy "Eve of Destruction," which rose to the top of the pop charts. Such doomsday fears, however, were met with rejoinders. Within six months, "The Ballad of the Green Berets" by SSgt. Barry Sadler, who was himself a Green Beret, had also risen to the top of the charts.[25] The battle lines that would soon separate the hippies from the hard hats were already being drawn.

Oddly enough, given the tenor of the times and the propensities of its folk roots, a good deal of folk rock had an uncommonly sunny disposition even while President Johnson was committing U.S. forces to Vietnam irrevocably. Two groups in particular—Lovin' Spoonful and the Mamas and the Papas—seemed to offer as large a dose of good old Tin Pan Alley escapism as they did folk protest. Interestingly, both groups came from a common source. John Sebastian, Zal Yanovsky, Cass Elliot, and Dennis Doherty had been a group called the Mugwumps (the name was borrowed from a group of nineteenth-century liberal reformers who had, for the most part, left the Republican Party). When the group split up after one forgettable LP, Sebastian and Yanovsky formed the Lovin' Spoonful and Elliot and Doherty joined John and Michelle Phillips to become Mamas & The Papas. Just as the Mamas and the Papas launched their career with the cheerful "California Dreamin'" in 1966, Lovin' Spoonful began with two unbelievably lighthearted singles "Do You Believe in Magic?" and "You Didn't Have to Be So Nice." The group's carefree "Daydream" (1966) continued the trend. Even the distrustfulness of "Monday, Monday" by the Mamas and the Papas and the cynicism of the group's "Words of Love" were delivered congenially. About the closest either group came to rock grittiness was the Spoonful's "Summer in the City" (1966), which was recorded with street sounds and a real jackhammer to give it a convincingly urban sound.

The energy of rock 'n' roll had always been identified with rebellion but never with a cause.

Even groups that were more given to social commentary than these two sounded fairly lighthearted. Compare, for example, the Byrds' "Chimes of Freedom" with Dylan's original. Dylan's half-spoken/half-sung delivery with sparse acoustic accompaniment sounds almost ominous when it is contrasted with the brightness of McGuinn's electric twelve string and the Byrds' upbeat falsetto harmonies. Indeed, the music may have been more effective than so-called pure folk precisely because of its lightness and wit. Perhaps for all its folkiness, folk rock never lost sight of the sheer delight of rock entertainment, or perhaps its spirit emanated from those innocent "years of hope" before they turned, as Todd Gitlin has said, to "days of rage."[26]

Black (Music) Is Beautiful

If 1965 was a pivotal year for folk rock, it was even more so for the Civil Rights movement. Sam Cooke's posthumous tribute to the early phase of the Civil Rights movement, "A Change Is Gonna Come", ironically coincided with the assassination of Malcolm X. The passage of the Voting Rights Act was significant, but it did little to paper over racial injustice. This was the year that activists marched from Selma to Montgomery, Alabama, to protest racial discrimination and it was the year that rebellion broke out in the Watts neighborhood of Los Angeles, signaling an era of urban unrest. The phrase "black power"—coined by Stokely Carmichael that year and invested with new meaning by the Black Panther Party, which was formed one year later— would soon occupy a prominent place in the American political lexicon. Nina Simone captured the tenor of the times with her 1965 recording of "Mississippi Goddam," which foreshadowed the militancy that was about to erupt just as her "Backlash Blues" anticipated the reaction to it. This transformation in the tenor of the times was reflected in changes in the form, tone, production style, and eventually lyrics of black popular music.

> When southern soul crossed over to the pop market, it was not because the music had changed, it was because black pride had created a cultural space in which unrefined r&b could find mainstream acceptance on its own terms.

As the themes of black pride and black self-determination gradually supplanted the call for integration, Motown's hegemony over black pop was successfully challenged by a resurgence of closer-to-the-roots, hard-driving rhythm and blues recorded in the Memphis–Muscle Schoals region of the South. Chiefly responsible for the popularization of southern soul, as this grittier r&b was called, was a temporary but highly successful collaboration between Atlantic Records and a number of southern studios, most notably Stax-Volt in Memphis, Tennessee, and Fame in Muscle Shoals, Alabama. The fruits of this collaboration captured the spirit of the emerging black militancy in tone rather than content. From 1965 on, artists like Otis Redding ("I've Been Loving You Too Long"), Wilson Pickett ("In the Midnight Hour"), Sam and Dave ("Soul Man"), Arthur Conley ("Sweet Soul Music"), and Percy Sledge ("When a Man Loves a Woman") were the new chart toppers. Their recordings were raw, basic, almost angry and much less "produced" than the cleaner, brighter Motown sound.

Stax-Volt, Motown's chief competitor, was founded around 1960, about the same time as Motown. It was, however, as open and disorganized as Motown was opaque and tightly controlled. Originally, Stax was a white-owned company, named after its founders, Jim Stewart and Estelle Axton. With integrated units like Booker T. and the MGs and the Memphis horns as session musicians, creative functions were as likely to be handled by whites as by blacks. The "Memphis sound" that these musicians spawned was almost invariably the product of cross-racial teamwork. Initially, the credits on all Stax recordings read simply: "produced by the Stax staff." Motown, on the other hand, was clearly a haven for black talent. Even so, Motown is remembered by Nelson George as being "totally committed to reaching white audiences," while Stax aimed its recordings "at r&b fans first, the pop market second."[27]

In many ways, it was the simplicity and straightforwardness of southern soul production that gave the music its claim to authenticity. In the quest for black pride, Motown's lavish use of multitrack studio production to achieve a more "pop" sound seemed out of sync with the search for African roots. Commenting on the difference in style between Stax-Volt and Motown, Otis Redding said:

> Motown does a lot of overdubbing. It's mechanically done. At Stax the rule is: whatever you feel, play it. We cut together, horns, rhythms, and vocal. We'll do it three or four times and listen to the results and pick the best one. If somebody doesn't like a line in the song we'll go back and cut the whole song over. Until last year [1967], we didn't even have a four track tape recorder. You can't overdub on a one track machine.[28]

It is somewhat ironic that it was this largely integrated effort that came to signify black power at its most militant. When southern soul crossed over to the pop market, it was not because the music had changed, it was because black pride had created a cultural space in which unrefined r&b could find mainstream acceptance on its own terms.

Between 1965 and 1967, the Stax roster grew from a dozen or so acts to about 100, with a concomitant expansion in sales. A good deal of the credit for the expansion in sales has to go to Al Bell, a former deejay and Stax's first black executive. Bell, who was hired as head of sales in 1965, opened promotional doors Stax did not know existed. In his outgoing flamboyant style, he was the perfect foil to Jim Stewart's inherent conservatism. "To most of the blacks in the company," music historian Peter Guralnick has said, "Al Bell was a kind of secret hero, the 'Jesse Jackson' of in-house politics."[29] The internal tensions that would eventually prove to be Stax's undoing were not apparent in 1966 when Al Bell toted up sales of 8 million records. At that moment, all was right with the world, and Al Bell was on everybody's A-list at Stax.

Of the many artists who passed through Stax on their way to fame, Wilson Pickett is perhaps most illustrative of the magic of the marriage with Atlantic Records. Signed to

Atlantic in the early 1960s, Pickett was sent by producer Jerry Wexler to Memphis to record with Booker T. and the MGs. The results were immediate. "In the Midnight Hour" (cowritten in typical cross-racial Stax fashion by Pickett and guitarist Steve Cropper) went to number one on the r&b charts in 1965 and also achieved significant crossover to the pop market. Pickett's next song, "634-5789," replicated the same success one year later. When relations between Atlantic and Stax became strained in 1966, Wexler simply sent Pickett over to Fame studios in Muscle Shoals, Alabama, and repeated the same success. Over the next few years, Pickett tallied a couple of dozen more pop hits, hitting the Top Ten with "Land of 1000 Dances" in 1966 and "Funky Broadway" in 1967. Pickett's hits were straight-ahead dance tunes. While the coarse grain of his voice and the rhythmic insistence of southern soul clearly signified the forcefulness of the new black militancy, it would be left to others to combine the passion of southern soul with explicit social consciousness.

Aretha Franklin was one artist who would do just that. After floundering at Columbia for years, she was signed to Atlantic in January 1967 by Jerry Wexler and taken immediately to Muscle Shoals where, after one legendary session, she found her sound. The resulting single, "I Never Loved a Man (The Way I Love You)," became her first of many Top Ten releases for Atlantic. Later that spring, she cut a version of the song that had been Otis Redding's signature tune. "Respect" went straight to number one and was instantly "transformed from a demand for conjugal rights into a soaring cry of freedom."[30] Shortly thereafter, she was crowned "Lady Soul." Aretha herself projected a presence that confirmed the slogan, "Black Is Beautiful." The vocal and emotional range of her early Atlantic releases ("Baby, I Love You," "Natural Woman," "Chain of Fools," and "Think," to name a few) express the fervor of the era dramatically. As Hettie Jones once remarked,

Aretha Franklin earned the title "Lady Soul" as she took the fusion of gospel and r&b to new heights. Her music was as powerful and uplifting as the Civil Rights movement at its best.

Aretha did not pray like Mahalia for the endurance to make it on through, nor make you believe her pain as Billie Holiday had. The statement black artists wished to make had changed, the blues had been transfigured by anger and pride. Aretha's music was a celebration, she was "earthmother" exhorting, preacher woman denouncing, militant demanding, forgotten woman wailing. She was black, she was beautiful, and she was the best. Someone called that time in 1967 the summer of 'Retha, Rap, and revolt'.[31]

An even more dramatic parallel to the trajectory of black politics, can be found in the career of James Brown. In the 1950s, Brown was an ambitious and headstrong r&b artist whose music was intended for, and in many ways confined to, the black audience. At the time of his first Top Ten crossover single, "Papa's Got a Brand New Bag" (1965), he billed himself with some justification as "the hardest working man in show business." By 1968, he was "Soul Brother No. 1." When he came to the attention of the white audience, he did so without compromise. His string of Top Ten pop hits ("I Got You," "It's a Man's Man's Man's World," "Cold Sweat," "I Got the Feelin'") made fewer concessions to mainstream sensibilities than any music in the pop market. Critic Robert Palmer has described it as follows:

With no chord changes and precious little melodic variety to sustain listener interest, rhythm became everything. Brown and his musicians and arrangers began to treat every instrument and voice in the group as if each were a drum. The horns played single-note bursts that were often sprung against the downbeats. The bass lines were broken up into choppy two- or three-note patterns, a procedure common in Latin music but rare in r&b. Brown's rhythm guitarist choked his guitar strings against the instrument's neck so hard that his playing began to sound like a jagged tin can being scraped with a pocketknife. Only occasionally were the horns, organ or backing vocalists allowed to provide a harmonic continuum by holding a chord.[32]

James Brown's performances were unparalleled and got him billing as "the hardest working man in show business." By the late 1960s, his stripped down, rhythmically charged proto-funk echoed the forcefulness of the black power movement.

This was prototypical "funk." In taking every instrument to the limit of its rhythmic capabilities, Brown carried the Africanization of popular music to its logical extreme. It was a musical statement that strongly echoed the cultural nationalism that was developing as part of the new militancy in the African American community. If, by chance, a listener missed the significance of Brown's music for black pride, it became explicit in the lyrics of his 1968 hit single, "Say It Loud—I'm Black and I'm Proud," which became an anthem in the struggle for black liberation.

Against the Grain: The Counterculture

The ascendancy of the black power movement reflected the growing separation between blacks and whites in their struggles for power, identity, and meaning. As the movement for black liberation became more traditionally militant, record numbers of white youths began to experiment with alternatives to middle-class life. The making of the counterculture, as it has been labeled, was based on a rejection of the competitive, achievement-oriented culture surrounding them in favor of free-living, free-loving lifestyles and shared communities of choice. It is noteworthy that the citizens of the counterculture were called "hippies," an inversion of "hipster," a black term from the 1940s and 1950s for urban outsiders. A number of philosophical tendencies and social and political developments framed the counterculture, including a Christian belief in "loving thy neighbor" and a fascination with Eastern religions and music, the mass availability of reliable birth control (the Pill), and the escalation of the war in Vietnam. The one unifying element that held this myriad of forces together was the widespread use of mind-expanding drugs.

The making of the counterculture was based on a rejection of the competitive, achievement-oriented culture in favor of free-living, free-loving lifestyles and shared communities of choice.

By the mid-1960s, statements about drugs had become so clear that conservatives no longer had to identify the Beatles' "Yellow Submarine" as a submarine-shaped barbiturate known as a "yellow jacket," or to transform Peter, Paul & Mary's "Puff the Magic Dragon" into a drug song by changing "puff" into a verb. The Association's "Along Comes Mary" (1966) as a code for marijuana or the Stones' "Jumpin' Jack Flash" (1968) as methedrine were much easier connections. When the Byrds flew "Eight Miles High" in 1966, none of the radio stations that banned the song thought the group was referring to an airplane ride. A year later, there was no question about the function of the pills in the Jefferson Airplane's "White Rabbit" or the "Purple Haze" that swirled around Jimi Hendrix. By this time, all of this was a part of the "Journey to the Center of the Mind" (Amboy Dukes, 1968). Of course, sensational media coverage notwithstanding, not all the drug songs were in favor of drugs. It seemed fitting to many that the first Top Ten antidrug song, "Kicks" (1966), came from Paul Revere and the Raiders; at the time they were the house band for Dick Clark's television program *Where the Action Is.* It was

Mind-expanding drugs are one common element of the counterculture

simply bewildering when Donovan, the "Sunshine Superman" himself, whose "Mellow Yellow" (1966) had initiated a short-lived and highly unproductive banana-smoking craze, suddenly denounced drug use. In that same year, the Rolling Stones spoke to the problem of middle-class prescription drug abuse in "Mother's Little Helper," a song which pointed up the hypocrisy of those who criticized the use of marijuana. Merle Haggard's "Okie from Muskogee" (1969), which chided marijuana-smoking hippies for their anti-American values while extolling the virtues of "white lightening," was as hypocritical as it was humorous. Later, the Stones' "Sister Morphine" and James Brown's "King Heroin" would capture the downside of inner-city addictions, a theme that would become much more prevalent in the 1980s and 1990s. For the counterculture, the focus on mind-expanding drugs seemed to offer the possibility of greater self-awareness and consciousness, which would in turn lead to a world without war, competition, or regimentation.

Blues on Acid: Psychedelic Rock

By the late 1960s, a number of musical strands (folk rock, a home-grown blues revival, and the second wave of the British Invasion) seemed to become emblematic of a larger cultural change going on in the United States. Although there were inputs from major city centers such as New York, Chicago, and Los Angeles, the spiritual Mecca for the counterculture was San Francisco, the site of a burgeoning rock scene that could boast of such groups as the Charlatans, the Jefferson Airplane, the Grateful Dead, Country Joe and the Fish, Quicksilver Messenger Service, Moby Grape, Sopwith Camel, and Big Brother and the Holding Company.

The Jefferson Airplane was the only San Francisco group ever to have Top Ten singles in the 1960s. In 1967, primarily because of the powerful vocals of Grace Slick, "Somebody to Love" and "White Rabbit" moved into the upper reaches of the pop charts. Even before Slick replaced Signe Andersen as lead singer of the group, the Airplane was the first San Francisco band to get a major label contract and the first to get national exposure. Still, it was the Grateful Dead, a group that never registered a Top Ten album or single, more than any other group that embodied all the elements of the San Francisco scene and came, therefore, to represent the counterculture to the rest of the country. The story of the Grateful Dead is one that combines the anticommercial tendencies of disaffected white middle-class youth with the mind-altering properties of lysergic acid diethylamide (LSD, acid), a chemical first synthesized by a Swiss chemist during World War II. After Timothy Leary, a Harvard psychology professor was dismissed from the school in 1962 for his controversial experimentation with the drug, he turned his back on academia and set about convincing the world (or, at least, young people) to "turn on, tune in, and drop out." The attractiveness of this philosophy was immediately apparent to California novelist (and former state wrestling champion) Ken Kesey and his extended family, the Pranksters. Before LSD was declared illegal, Kesey, the Pranksters, and the Grateful Dead (then called the Warlocks), organized the first Trips Festival, one of a number of public LSD gatherings, which has been chronicled by Tom Wolfe in *The Electric Kool-Aid Acid Test.*

The Dead came from a smorgasbord of musical influences. Leader Jerry Garcia had played folk and bluegrass. Ron "Pigpen" McKernan, the son of a white r&b deejay, brought his blues background to bear in his keyboard and harmonica playing. Bassist Phil Lesh had studied classical music. The group's sound was rounded out by Bill Kreutzmann on drums, Bob Weir on guitar, and the later addition of eclectic percussionist Mickey Hart. The band's first LP, *The Grateful Dead* (1967), was a straightforward rock album with a distinctly r&b flavor. Ever open to the beckoning of psychedelia, the Dead went on to become one of the most experimental and improvisatory bands in rock.

One of the most endearing qualities of the band was their undying commitment to a sense of community. Never ones to impose a distance between themselves and their fans, the Dead lived in the Haight-Ashbury district, the heart of the hippie scene. The Haight was dedicated to the provision of free goods and services for all who needed them, including free lodging, free food, free medical care, and free music. The Dead were first among equals in giving unselfishly of themselves to hippie culture, performing "more free concerts than any band in the history of music."[33]

The sense of community that the Grateful Dead created was easily as important as the music they played. From the beginning, they were first among equals in giving of themselves to the counterculture.

It was this sense of community, of contributing to the collective good that made the counterculture, and San Francisco in particular, unique. It was reflected in the way bands now named themselves. Prior to the counterculture, groups invariably used plural nouns to describe themselves (the Temptations, the Rolling Stones). All the San Francisco groups (the Dead, the Airplane, Quicksilver, Big Brother, Moby Grape) and, after 1967, the most important groups from elsewhere (the Who, the Jimi Hendrix Experience, Sly and the Family Stone, Led Zeppelin, Blood, Sweat, and Tears, Cream, Chicago, War) chose either the singular form of a noun or a collective noun for their names. While the plural form of a noun indicates an aggregate of individuals, the singular form or a collective noun describes a single entity, a unified whole, which was far more in keeping with the communal philosophy of the counterculture.

The music that emerged from the psychedelic experience came to be known, logically enough, as acid rock. Efforts to reproduce the effects of the psychedelic experience naturally resulted in a new kind of swirling concert poster art and light shows, attempts to incorporate colorful moving images as an integral part of the music a band was playing. Sometimes, simply the presence of these extra musical elements was enough to categorize music as acid rock. In fact, as Lillian Roxon has noted, "Much of the San Francisco music of that period came out of the blues, but because of the whole psychedelic coloring of that culture, moved out of blues into the wider realms of acid rock."[34] In fact, blues-based rock enjoyed a surge among white rockers throughout the United States during this period. The blues revival had its beginnings in Chicago, where white teenager Paul Butterfield served as the American counterpart to Britain's Alexis Korner. Butterfield jammed with blues greats like Muddy Waters, Howlin' Wolf, and others and eventually formed his own integrated blues band in 1963 with Mike Bloomfield on guitar. By 1965, New York folk-blues artists Danny Kalb, Tommy Flanders, Steve Katz, and Al Kooper had followed suit and formed The Blues Project. Both groups recorded reasonably successful LPs that included classic blues numbers. In Los Angeles, Canned Heat began in 1965 but the group did not get off the ground until "On the Road Again" hit the Top Twenty in 1968. By then, Butterfield had added horns to his group, thus anticipating Katz and Kooper's formation of Blood, Sweat, and Tears.

At first, the music these groups played was largely derivative. If it was connected to the psychedelic experience, it was primarily by virtue of its association with the counterculture ethos. It was the British group Cream that married the authenticity of the blues to the commercial appeal of the new rock aesthetic. Cream was the first of the supergroups (groups that were comprised of top musicians from previously existing groups), in that it brought together drummer Ginger Baker, bassist Jack Bruce, and virtuoso blues guitarist Eric Clapton. Bruce and Baker had played together in the early 1960s as part of the Graham Bond Organization, an organ-based group with jazz and blues influences.

Efforts to reproduce the effects of the psychedelic experience naturally resulted in a new kind of swirling concert poster art and light shows, attempts to incorporate colorful moving images as an integral part of the music a band was playing.

Acid rock often blues-based rock with psychedelic trappings

Clapton had embraced the blues so thoroughly as a member of the Yardbirds that he left the group (and was replaced by Jeff Beck) just as the blatantly commercial "For Your Love" (1965) rocketed to number six. Clapton then joined the more "authentic" Bluesbreakers. The group united Bruce and Clapton until Bruce left to join the more commercial Manfred Mann. Cream became a reality in 1966 when Clapton met Baker at a summer jam and the two decided to recruit Bruce and start a new band.

As the first of the power trios (a configuration that later proved very attractive to heavy metal groups), Cream provided its three members with more room to move than they had ever enjoyed before. In live performance, all three soloed extensively at deafening volumes, and through all the calculated distortion that drove listeners to new musical places, their musicianship was impeccable. The group combined psychedelics and the blues at the production level, defying listeners to figure out how many times Clapton had overdubbed himself. The layers of sound on the group's first LP, *Fresh Cream,* added a new dimension to the music, and yet somehow Skip James' "I'm So Glad" could still be related to its originator. The group's second album, *Disraeli Gears,* yielded a Top Ten Single, "Sunshine of Your Love" in 1967. *Wheels of Fire* went to number one on the album charts before the group disbanded in 1968. Although other British blues groups followed—most notably the Jeff Beck Group, which included Rod Stewart and Ron Wood, and the Spencer Davis Group, which featured Steven Winwood, who went on to form Traffic—Cream set the standard to which all others had to measure up.

Of course, San Francisco attracted its share of white blues enthusiasts as well. Steve Miller was a veteran of the Chicago blues scene who was lured to San Francisco by the

prospect of lucrative recording contracts. His band included fellow Chicagoan Boz Scaggs. Eventually, Mike Bloomfield also left Chicago for the West Coast where he teamed up with drummer Buddy Miles to form the Electric Flag. Janis Joplin, conspicuous as the only white female blues singer, came to the city from Port Arthur, Texas. Paired with Big

Janis Joplin gave her life to rock 'n' roll—literally. The intensity of her bluesy performances mirrored the tumultuousness of her life. In the end hers was a flame that burned out all too soon.

Brother and the Holding Company, Joplin covered Big Mama Thornton's "Ball and Chain" and Irma Franklin's "Piece of My Heart" in 1968. Never one to save herself for the future, Joplin poured everything she had into every performance, but the intensity of her lifestyle took its toll. Having become a symbol of rebellion for millions of white middle-class youth, she died of a heroin overdose in 1970. She would have been proud to see her last album, *Pearl,* which was released posthumously, and its hit single, "Me and Bobby McGee," rise to the top of the pop charts in 1971.

The San Francisco scene peaked, so to speak, during the 1967 Summer of Love. When Los Angeles singer Scott McKenzie advised the young people heading to San Francisco that year to "wear some flowers in your hair," thousands upon thousands did just that. In the minds of the majority of the population, "flower power" became the hippie analog to "black power." Just as the Black Panthers in neighboring Oakland were identified with confrontational male posturing in the extreme and often depicted brandishing twelve-gauge shotguns over the slogan "Power comes from the barrel of a gun," the hippies were shown exploring the gentler, perhaps more female, side of resistance. One of the most memorable images of the counterculture pictured hippies planting daisies in the rifle barrels of the National Guard troops who were deployed to police mass demonstrations.

> "*F*lower power" became the hippie analog to "black power." Just as the Black Panthers were identified with confrontational male posturing in the extreme, the hippies were exploring the gentler, perhaps more female, side of resistance.

Commercializing the Counterculture: The Monterey Pop Festival

The commercial possibilities of the counterculture became apparent when the first Human Be-In Festival drew some 20,000 fans to San Francisco's Golden Gate Park in the spring of 1967. Almost immediately, some hip capitalist rock entrepreneurs from Los Angeles hoping to produce a profit-making festival along the same lines, booked the Monterey fairgrounds for the weekend of June 16 through 18. It was John Phillips of the Mamas and the Papas who convinced them to turn it into an artist-run, nonprofit, but still very commercial, event. Gradually, Phillips' manager Lou Adler took over, and the Monterey International Pop Festival was born. It was the perfect opening event for the Summer of Love.

In the hands of Adler and Phillips, the Monterey Pop Festival took shape as a decidedly West Coast event. About half of the two dozen or so artists who performed at the festival came from Los Angeles (the Byrds, Buffalo Springfield, the Mamas and the Papas, Canned Heat, Scott McKenzie) or San Francisco (Jefferson Airplane, Country Joe and the Fish, the Grateful Dead, Janis Joplin, Big Brother and the Holding Company, Quicksilver Messenger Service, Steve Miller). New York singer/songwriters were represented by Laura Nyro and Simon and Garfunkel, although Nyro's overly laid-back performance earned her a place on the cutting room floor when a film of the festival was made. Although Eric Burdon and the Animals appeared, it was the Who, relative unknowns, that advanced the British Invasion as well as the ideology of the counterculture with a blistering performance of "My Generation." Not surprisingly, there was a dearth of black artists, but those who performed—Otis Redding, Jimi Hendrix, Lou Rawls, and Hugh Masekela—represented a broad range of styles. Even though Smokey Robinson sat on the festival board, not a single Motown act materialized, but then Berry Gordy seldom allowed his artists to participate in anything that he didn't control.

Throughout the weekend, a range of countercultural impulses was on display, everything from the violent spectacle of the Who smashing their equipment to the curious sexuality of Jimi Hendrix making love to his guitar as he set it ablaze.

Whatever its shortcomings, the Monterey Pop Festival was a landmark event. As the first huge rock festival (30,000 fans in attendance), it pointed the way for all others. The event was patronized by the "hip-eoisie" of the counterculture and by the elite of the recording industry, both of whom took it extremely seriously. It launched the U.S. careers of the Who and Jimi Hendrix, and it provided Otis Redding with the ideal springboard for crossover success, which unfortunately ended when he died in a plane crash later in the year. Janis Joplin emerged from the festival as nothing short of a white blues goddess and was promptly signed to a lucrative contract by Clive Davis, president of CBS Records. The flowering San Francisco scene had already earned the Grateful Dead and Jefferson Airplane contracts with Warner and RCA, respectively. Vanguard picked up Country Joe and the Fish, and later, Capitol signed both Quicksilver Messenger Service and the Steve Miller Band, reportedly for the then unheard of sum of $40,000 in advances.

If the Monterey Pop Festival confirmed the creeping commercialization of the counterculture, it also provided a platform for the politics of its adherents. David Crosby introduced the Byrds' "He Was a Friend of Mine," a song about the Kennedy assassination, with a direct challenge to the Warren Commission's official version of the story. "When President Kennedy was killed, he was not killed by one man," Crosby said. "He was shot from a number of different directions by different guns. The story has been suppressed, witnesses have been killed and this is your country."[35] Crosby also waxed eloquent about the joys of acid. His words infuriated McGuinn and marked the beginning of the end of Crosby's association with the Byrds. Undaunted, Crosby sat in with Buffalo Springfield, which included Stephen Stills and Neil Young who were equally outspoken, and laid the groundwork for the supergroup configurations of Crosby, Stills, and Nash and Crosby, Stills, Nash, and Young.

Monterey Pop was, in fact, peppered with artists who had taken an antiestablishment stance in their music for some time. Earlier in the year, Buffalo Springfield had scored a Top Ten hit with "For What It's Worth (Stop, Hey What's That Sound)," a Stephen Stills song protesting the brutal treatment of peaceful demonstrators by police. Country Joe (McDonald) had been performing his anti-Vietnam "I-Feel-Like-I'm-Fixin'-

Monterey Pop Festival combines commerce and politics

to-Die Rag" in various folk and jug band versions since 1965. Together with the Fish, he performed it as rock at rallies and demonstrations long before it was released on record. The Animals' "We Gotta Get Out of This Place" had already become an early anthem protesting the constraints of urban life. The Who's "My Generation" solidified the generation gap.

Lyric content was not the only source of antiestablishment statements. One look at a stoned Mama Cass drinking in Janis Joplin with her eyes made it abundantly clear that applying the label acid rock to music required little more than music and acid. Indeed, throughout the weekend, a range of countercultural impulses was on display, everything from the violent spectacle of the Who smashing their equipment to the curious sexuality of Jimi Hendrix making love to his guitar as he set it ablaze. More bluesy than Clapton, louder than Cream, and more bizarre sexually, on stage, at least, than Jim Morrison of the Doors could ever hope to be, Hendrix was a left-handed, African American expatriate virtuoso guitarist from Seattle who started in his teens as a sideman for acts like Little Richard and the Isley Brothers. After he was lured to London by ex-Animal Chas Chandler, dressed up in "mod" gear, and paired with Noel Redding on bass and Mitch Mitchell on drums, he proceeded to dazzle British audiences with both his technical ability and his image, which Lillian Roxon has described as "the Wild Man of Borneo . . . crossed with all the languid, silken, jewelled elegance of a Carnaby Street fop."[36] In 1968, Eric Clapton described Hendrix's rise to popularity with a racist hipness that was all too common at the time:

> He had the whole combination in England. It was just what the market needed, a psychedelic pop star who looked freaky, and they're also hung up about spades and the blues thing was there. So Jimi walked in, put on all the gear, and made it straight away. It was a perfect formula.[37]

After his first single "Hey Joe" hit the British Top Ten early in 1967, Hendrix brought his trio, known as the Jimi Hendrix Experience, back to the United States. His debut album, *Are You Experienced,* promptly climbed to number five on the charts. After performing at the Monterey Pop Festival, Hendrix and his band toured as the opening act for the Monkees ("Last Train to Clarksville," "I'm a Believer," "Daydream Believer"), a group of white, squeaky clean, mostly nonmusicians who were created by NBC-TV to fill the teen void left by the Beatles' maturity. It seems more than likely that audiences for the Monkees were ill prepared to see Hendrix on stage "doing things to his guitar so passionate, so concentrated and so intense that anyone with halfway decent manners had to look away," as Roxon has said. "By the time it was over he had lapped and nuzzled his guitar with his lips and tongue, caressed it with his inner thighs, jabbed at it with a series of powerful pelvic thrusts. Even the little girls who'd come to see the Monkees understood what this was about."[38]

While Hendrix, who died unexpectedly in 1970, never attracted a substantial black U.S. audience to his music during his lifetime, he was considerably more important

to music than his commercial, psychedelic, oversexed black-man image indicates. He was a fine writer. He pioneered the incorporation of distortion and feedback into the language of popular music. His interpretation of Dylan's "All Along the Watchtower," his only single to break the U.S. Top Twenty, added measurably to the music. "I liked Jimi Hendrix's record of this and ever since he died I've been doing it that way," said Dylan in the liner notes to *Biograph.* "Strange though how when I sing it I always feel like it's a tribute to him in some kind of way." During his lifetime, however, the commercial interests surrounding him kept him tied to the formula that had made him a star even when he wanted to expand his musical horizons. The pressures of the situation drove him not only to chemical excesses but also to his Electric Ladyland studios where he logged some 800 hours of tape exploring fusions of jazz, rhythm and blues, and contemporary rock styles with Miles Davis, John McLaughlin, and other avant-garde jazz notables. None of these tapes was released during Hendrix's lifetime, and it is only recently that black artists and audiences have begun to recover the music with which he was identified.

At Monterey (as in the counterculture generally), psychedelia was the common thread that bound a Scott McKenzie, a Janis Joplin, an Otis Redding, a Jimi Hendrix, and a Ravi Shankar together. Nowhere was the power of this bond more apparent than in the recorded music that was played between performances. That music was the

Beatles' recently released *Sgt. Pepper's Lonely Hearts Club Band. Sgt. Pepper* was the Beatles' masterpiece. Eight months in the making, the album epitomized all the creativity (and the excesses) of the counterculture. As the first concept LP (an album designed as a coherent whole with each song segueing seamlessly into the next) *Sgt. Pepper* established a new plateau in record production. It was an album conceived as a single; it required hundreds of hours of studio time; it utilized special effects so sophisticated the music could not be performed live. Of course, they had flirted with such developments in earlier albums. The release of *Rubber Soul* in 1965 had allowed Lennon and McCartney to show the new level of maturity they had reached in their songwriting. "Nowhere Man" hinted at Lennon's frustration with the group's lack of political engagement. At the same time, Harrison pioneered the use of the sitar in rock on "Norwegian Wood," introducing a sound that would become all too familiar in the psychedelic era. (It was later marketed, somewhat sacrilegiously, as raga rock, referring to the Indian sitar music from which it took its name.) It was also at this point that George Martin went from being an excellent producer to being an indispensable creative force for the group, the "fifth Beatle," as he was now called. *Revolver* (1966), an even more experimental album, continued these trends. Harrison developed his sitar playing further under the tutelage of Ravi Shankar. "Taxman," the first Beatles song to contain an explicit political reference, chastised British government officials by name. George Martin polished every layer of sound to perfection. Released as a single early in 1967, "Penny Lane," backed with "Strawberry Fields," once again confirmed the Beatles' artistry and clearly prefigured the sound of things to come. But all of these merely hinted at the impact that *Sgt. Pepper* would have. In *Sgt. Pepper,* the connection between music and psychedelics came to full fruition. It was not just transparent references like "<u>L</u>ucy in the <u>S</u>ky with <u>D</u>iamonds" or "With a Little Help from My Friends" or the cannabis plants hidden among the flora on the album cover collage; it was the whole sonic presentation of the album from the hurdy-gurdy effects on "Mr. Kite," which were created by cutting a tape of steam organ music into foot-long sections and splicing them back together at random, to the seemingly interminable decay of the final mesmerizing chord on "A Day in the Life." Rounded out with military marching band regalia, *Sgt. Pepper* presented an artful and engaging foray into new musical terrain and represented the spirit of a whole way of life.

Riding the Storm

If the Beatles usually brought out the optimistic, upbeat aspects of the counterculture, the Doors were the avatars of its darker side. John Lennon might have tended toward a hostile surrealism at times, but Doors leader Jim Morrison actually embraced madness and terror in both his art and his life. The Doors had begun as an underground Los Angeles rock band. Morrison had met keyboardist Ray Manzarek in some of his classes when he was a student at UCLA. Manzarek had then recruited guitarist Robby Krieger and drummer John Densmore from the Third Street headquarters of Maharishi Mahesh Yogi, where they practiced transcendental meditation. The group took its name from Aldous Huxley's *The Doors of Perception,* a book about the liberating aspects of drug use.

After knocking around the Los Angeles club scene for a while, the group came to the attention of Jac Holzman, who signed them to his Elektra label in 1967. Their self-titled debut LP was an immediate smash. "Break on Through (To the Other Side)," the album's hard-rocking first single, defined the group's

If the Beatles usually brought out the optimistic, upbeat aspects of the counterculture, the Doors were the avatars of its darker side. John Lennon might have tended toward a hostile surrealism at times, but Doors leader Jim Morrison actually embraced madness and terror in both his art and his life.

music and captured their image perfectly. The final cut, "The End," was an Oedipal fantasy that ran eleven minutes, forty-one seconds and got the group banned from the Whiskey-A-Go-Go before the record was released. What seems incredible is not that such material proved attractive to the Los Angeles underground but that the group became the number one teenybopper band in the country when "Light My Fire" (written by Krieger) rocketed to the top of the charts in 1967. Spreads in teenage magazines that cast Morrison as a teen idol were juxtaposed against a real-life dramatic, on-stage, sex-related bust in New Haven, Connecticut, and warrants for "lewd and lascivious behavior" in Miami. The Doors' teen success spoke volumes about 1950s sexual repression coming undone in strange ways.

The Doors let it all hang out and became wildly successful

Led by poet/vocalist Jim Morrison, the Doors explored the darker side of rock, made headlines for their sex and drug-related escapades, and much to the dismay of parents, became teen idols in the process.

Throughout the late 1960s, as the group's next five albums made the Top Ten, the Doors remained one of the most in-demand acts in rock. Even Ed Sullivan felt compelled to book them, a move he regretted when they defied his censors and included a reference to getting "higher" in their performance of "Light My Fire." Although Morrison's constant brushes with the law served to bolster the group's outlaw image, the intensity of his lifestyle took its toll on all concerned. In 1971, he left the band for a temporary sabbatical in Paris. It became permanent when he died on July 3, most probably from a drug-induced heart attack. Three weeks later, the Doors' final hit single, "Riders on the Storm," began its ascent into the Top Twenty.

For observers of the American scene, the storm had begun several years earlier. In 1968, the Tet Offensive in Vietnam had shattered all hopes of a short stay, let alone the oft promised "imminent victory" for U.S. forces. At home, Martin Luther King, Jr., was assassinated just after the Kerner Commission on Civil Disorders, which had been created to address the issue of increasing urban violence, warned that the country was "moving toward two societies, one black, one white—separate and unequal." Shortly thereafter, Robert Kennedy was murdered just as he was about to make a bid for the presidency. (That night David Crosby wrote "Long Time Coming" lamenting his death.) To some, it seemed that revolution was just around the corner. King's assassination 4 April 1968 provoked violent reactions in over 100 American cities. As the most politically credible black artist at the time, James Brown was courted by the political establishment as ambassador to the streets. On the day King was assassinated, Brown was scheduled to perform at the Boston Garden. Faced with a potentially uncontrollable outburst of sorrow and rage, the city made it possible for the show to be broadcast on public television, which kept Boston cool, at least for one evening. Brown was later flown to Washington, D.C., to appeal to rioting youth there.

Other artists of all styles and personal backgrounds responded to race-related tensions in their own ways. Releases such as "Abraham, Martin, and John" (1968) by Dion and "Everyday People" by Sly and the Family Stone (1969) picked up the "black and white together" theme of the early Civil Rights movement. The difficulties of interracial relationships had already been explored in sixteen-year-old Janis Ian's "Society's Child," released in 1967. The Rascals had taken an increasingly antiracist stance even before the group released "People Got to Be Free" in 1968. Reportedly, they refused a slot on the *Ed Sullivan Show* when Sullivan refused to book a black opening act. Curtis Mayfield and the Impressions continued a series of socially conscious "sermon songs" with "We're a Winner" and "This Is My Country" in 1968 and "Choice of Colors" in 1969. Even Elvis Presley's rather unlikely entry, "In the Ghetto" (1969), went to number three on the pop charts. The Temptations' "Ball of Confusion (That's What the World Is Today)" (1969) captured the

Aretha Franklin's stirring recording of Nina Simone's "Young, Gifted, and Black" captured the spirit of a community that had weathered a torrent of urban violence and provided the musical capstone for a decade of civil rights struggle.

restlessness of the era and the state of the Civil Rights movement after King's death. "The civil-rights struggle was not dead," Nelson George has written, "but its energy was increasingly scattered. The Black Panthers embraced communism. Ron Karenga's U.S. organization advocated an Afrocentric cultural nationalism. . . . Black Power came to mean whatever its user needed it to . . . the assimilationists pressed on."[39] In 1971, the entropy of the movement was clearly reflected in popular music. While John Lennon's exhortation "Power to the People" and The Chi-Lites' "(For God's Sake) Give More Power to the People," represented attempts to recall the heyday of the Black Panthers, Bob Dylan's tribute to the memory of slain black leader George Jackson made clear that the more radical elements in the struggle for black liberation had already been neutralized. Dylan's "George Jackson" was released in the aftermath of the massacre (thirty-three prisoners and ten hostages killed by police bullets) that followed the Attica State Prison uprising, which had begun as a silent vigil protesting Jackson's death. The disillusionment of the period was best expressed in Marvin Gaye's "What's Goin' On" and "Inner City Blues." Still, Aretha Franklin's stirring recording of Nina Simone's "Young, Gifted, and Black" captured the spirit of a community that had weathered a torrent of urban violence and provided the musical capstone for a decade of civil rights struggle.

Meanwhile, the social and political consciousness that the Civil Rights movement had awoken found its way into an increasingly broad range of concerns. For countercultural whites, the issues fell roughly into three categories: the open celebration of sex with or without love; spiritual transcendence; and a call for social change, which was expressed in terms of a revolution in consciousness, a call to arms, a commemoration of particular individuals or incidents, or opposition to the war in Vietnam.

The Beatles' 1964 desire just to "hold your hand" had by 1967 escalated to the Rolling Stones' open call to "spend the night together" (even though they complied with the censors' directive to change the lyric to "spend some *time* together" for their appearance on the *Ed Sullivan Show*). In that year, the social complexity of Janis Ian's conception of intimacy in "Society's Child" was washed away by the Beatles' simpler maxim "All You Need Is Love." Even teenyboppers were included in the new sexual freedom, as they "tumbled to the ground" embracing each other in Tommy James and the Shondells' "I Think We're Alone Now" (1967). There was little doubt as to what was going on in "Itchycoo Park" in 1968. One year later, even the Beatles (Paul, actually) wondered aloud: "Why Don't We Do It in the Road." While the sexual revolution was real enough, it did not liberate men and women equally. There was something about the energy of the Rolling Stones' music that could move both male and female bodies, but many of the group's songs—"Stupid Girl," "Under My Thumb," and, later, "Honky-Tonk Women" and "Brown Sugar"—were downright nasty toward women. Although the National Organization for Women (NOW) was founded in 1966, the best women could do on their own behalf that year was Nancy Sinatra's "These Boots Are Made for Walkin'." Even when Helen Reddy roared "I Am Woman" in 1972, it was less than ferocious, although it was explicitly feminist. In music, women had limited roles; they could be groupies or they could be go-go dancers, which indicates a good deal about their positions in society as a whole. Janis Joplin and Grace Slick held out to their listeners the possibility of a stronger voice for women, but only Aretha Franklin demanded respect. As a group, women declined on the year-end singles charts from an all-time high of 32 percent in 1963 to 6 percent in 1969.

In some ways, the call for social change split the counterculture into two groups: those who favored militant political action (the so-called politicos) and those who favored a strategy of individual consciousness-raising. The popular slogan "The revolution is in your head" reflected the counterculture's preoccupation with self-awareness and consciousness expansion, which sometimes intermingled the call for social change with spiritual transcendence. For some, revolution was an act of self-development, not the overthrow of one political system by another. Nowhere is this definition of revolution better illustrated than in the Beatles' "Revolution" (1968), which rose to number twelve as the flip side of "Hey Jude," the group's best-selling single. In their anti-Maoist rhetoric, Lennon's lyrics represented a rejection of militant political action in favor of individual consciousness-raising, which would then make everything "alright." Criticized by New Left activists, Lennon made a barely perceptible, but highly significant, change in the song when a slower version was included on the so-called *White Album* (1968). Where the single had spoken of "destruction," Lennon had said "count me out." On the album cut, he added "in" to the line, which was then sung as "count me out/in." Confronted with a real dilemma about the value of political action, Lennon could only leave the choice up to the listener. After the Beatles went their separate ways, Lennon tried to connect to grassroots political movements and to assume, in his own way, a more activist stance. There were, for example, the "bed-ins" he staged with Yoko Ono to protest the war in Vietnam and anthems like "Give Peace a Chance" and "Power to the People," which were clearly intended for mass participation. While beautifully expressed in "Imagine" (1971) with the Plastic Ono Band, Lennon's vision was ultimately utopian. For the real "politicos," who were more grounded in the here-and-now of radical transformation, the Doors' "Five to One" (1968), referring to the notion that *our* "numbers" were more powerful than *their* "guns," or the Jefferson Airplane's "We Can Be Together" (1969), which called together those who were "outlaws" in the eyes of their country, had more appeal.

In the summer of 1968, radical activists turned their eyes toward Chicago, which was to be the site of the Democratic National Convention. For radicals, Chicago was to be the occasion to embarrass the government for its repressive policies at home and abroad. With frontrunner Hubert Humphrey cloaking himself in outgoing President Lyndon Johnson's mantle, there was only mild-mannered Senator Gene McCarthy to carry the antiwar banner to the convention. Anticipating little support from within the Democratic Party, a most unlikely group of "co-conspirators" (who were later tried, and acquitted, for inciting a riot) vowed that their constituents would descend on the windy city in great numbers. The "Chicago Eight," as they were called, represented everyone from conscientious objectors and student radicals to yippies and Black Panthers. Todd Gitlin recalls thinking of Chicago as a "grand fusion between radical politics and counterculture— drugs, sex, rock 'n' roll, smash the State."[40] Protesters who came for the music were sorely disappointed. Political stalwart Phil Ochs did his part, but of all the prominent rock bands that were invited, only the MC5 was there to "Kick Out the Jams." Their appearance may have had something to do with the fact that their manager was White Panther leader John Sinclair. Those who came for the mayhem got more than they bargained for. The Chicago police spared no quarter in suppressing all dissent outside the convention hall. The theme music for these confrontations could have been the Rolling Stones' just released "Street Fighting Man" (despite its own disclaimers), if most of the Chicago rock stations had not refused to play it. If there had been any innocence among the demonstrators before the convention, it was lost forever, especially because a good part of the American population seemed to approve of the brutality they saw on their television screens. In the end, McCarthy's bid for the nomination failed, Humphrey ran, and Richard Nixon was elected. In the eyes of those who demonstrated in Chicago, this was simply adding the ultimate political insult to considerable physical injury.

Chicago '68 was a watershed event. For many activists, it confirmed the bankruptcy of the American political system; some withdrew from politics altogether, others became radicalized. Once beyond the pale of electoral politics, radicals explored various paths toward revolutionary change. The resulting sectarianism fragmented the New Left beyond hope as the 1969 SDS National Convention (the organization's last convention) proved. The meeting was torn by bitter factionalism between Progressive Labor Party (PL) delegates and the Revolutionary Youth Movement (RYM)-Weathermen faction and their third world allies, the Young Lords, Brown Berets, and Black Panthers. When a Panther took to the stage to announce that the only position for a woman in the revolution was prone, the new voice of feminism rose to a deafening roar. In the end, the largest and most visionary organization of the New Left was irrevocably shattered. But just as the Weathermen (who took their name from the lyrics to Dylan's "Subterranean Homesick Blues") were gearing up to "bring the war home" by "fighting in the streets," Woodstock offered a fleeting pastoral approximation of the countercultural utopia.

Woodstock and Altamont: Reaching the Heights, Taking the Fall

The Woodstock Music and Art Fair took place in August 1969 on Max Yasgur's 600-acre farm in Bethel, New York. Despite a solid financial base and considerable advanced planning, the festival was a prime example of Murphy's Law—everything that could possibly go wrong did so. The crowd was expected to number 50,000 or so. There were instead seven or eight times that number. Roads were obstructed for miles; there was insufficient food and water, dreadfully inadequate medical and sanitary facilities, and the potential for a security nightmare. And then it began to rain. For all of this, Woodstock was the counterculture's finest hour. It was not just that there was no violence; it was that a spirit of cooperation infused the entire event. The three accidental deaths that did occur were balanced, at least symbolically, by three births. Bad acid was identified from the stage. Wavy Gravy

Roads were obstructed for miles; there was insufficient food and water, dreadfully inadequate medical and sanitary facilities, and the potential for a security nightmare. And then it began to rain. For all of this, Woodstock was the counterculture's finest hour.

and the Hog Farm Commune offered practical guidance and makeshift medical attention and even managed to stretch the food supply to provide "breakfast in bed for 400,000," as Gravy described it. On the last day of the festival, Yasgur was moved to tell "the largest group of people ever assembled in one place" that "you have proven something to the world . . . that half a million kids can get together and have three days of fun and music and have nothing *but* fun and music."[41] With some exceptions, police and local residents described the crowd in terms as glowing as Yasgur's. Here, then, was the counterculture made real, the spontaneous temporary community that was later lionized by Chicago Eight defendant Abbie Hoffman as the "Woodstock Nation."

The symbolism of Woodstock was overpowering, and its music was compelling. Creedence Clearwater Revival and The Band represented good old American rock 'n' roll. Together, they summed up an era of rock styles in much the same way the festival summed up the counterculture. Arriving from England, where the group's groundbreaking rock opera, *Tommy,* had just been released, the Who began with "Touch me, feel me . . ." from *Tommy* and then burst into a memorable performance of "Summertime Blues," which later became a hit single for the group. Roger Daltrey's bare-chested costume with the long white fringes provided one of the most lasting visuals of the event. Ten Years After did a more than credible job of representing the second wave of British blues bands. Also riding the second wave of the British Invasion was Joe Cocker, who had just embarked on his first U.S. tour after the release of his first LP, *With a Little Help from My Friends* (which included Jimmy Page and Steven Winwood). His soulful, spastic performance of the title song at the festival has been imprinted on the national consciousness ever since. The following year, he played to sellout crowds on a tour organized by Leon Russell and billed as Mad Dogs and Englishmen.

San Francisco offered the Jefferson Airplane, Country Joe and the Fish, and Santana. The Jefferson Airplane delivered some of the more political material from their *Volunteers* album. Country Joe and the Fish introduced "I-Feel-Like-I'm-Fixin'-to-Die-Rag" with a rousing version of the "Fish Cheer." Like most of the San Francisco groups, Santana had begun in 1967 as a blues band but because of their Latin roots they quickly outgrew the genre. Their performance of "Soul Sacrifice" at Woodstock introduced them to a new mass audience and earned them a recording contract with Columbia. The self-titled debut album, which was released a month later, rose to number four and included the hit single "Evil Ways." The group's second album, *Abraxas* (1970), went all the way to number one, and acquainted a national audience with a Latin rock version of "Black Magic Woman" and a stunning interpretation of Tito Puente's "Oye Como Va."

The festival also had the expected deficiencies. Aside from Melanie, Grace Slick, and Janis Joplin (none of whom were included in the original film), there was only one other female headliner—Joan Baez. Performing "Joe Hill," a song about the martyred labor organizer, Baez introduced a new generation of rock fans to the music of the labor movement. There were also only three African American acts for three days of morning-to-evening performances—Richie Havens, Jimi Hendrix, and Sly and the Family Stone. As much an anomaly as Hendrix, Havens, a black folkie, opened the festival as the organizers were still putting the finishing touches on logistics. Asked to stall until the next act was ready, the artist ran out of material. He closed his set with "Freedom," a song that he improvised on the spot and felt captured the ethos of the day. Hendrix also delivered a political message of sorts. His searing performance of "The Star-Spangled Banner," which replicated the sounds of "bombs bursting in air" on the guitar as only Hendrix could, turned the national anthem into an antiwar song.

> *Hendrix delivered a political message of sorts. His searing performance of "The Star-Spangled Banner," which replicated the sounds of "bombs bursting in air" on the guitar as only Hendrix could, turned the national anthem into an antiwar song.*

Woodstock comes up short on women and African American performers

Sly (second from left) and the Family Stone created socially relevant music that crossed the boundaries of r&b, jazz, and psychedelic rock as boldly as the group transcended the divisions of race and gender. It was an ambitious project for the late 1960s, and for a while, they pulled it off better than anyone.

The only act that could be considered a black act with a substantial following in the African American community was Sly and the Family Stone. Comprised of black and white, women and men, they managed to marry the funk and rock cultures in a way that no other artists had been able to do. Between 1968 and 1971, Sly and the Family Stone recorded a series of Top Ten pop hits—"Dance to the Music" (1968), "Everyday People" and "Hot Fun in the Summertime" (1969), "Thank You (Falletinme Be Mice Elf Agin)" (1970), and "Family Affair" (1971)—that transcended the confines of musical style, much as the band crossed the boundaries of race and gender. Based in San Francisco, the group was a model of racial and sexual harmony. The group's 1969 LP, *Stand!*, illustrated both the band's growing maturity and Sly's growing militancy. The album contained not only the all-inclusive number one single "Everyday People" but also the bolder title song and the more provocative "Don't Call Me Nigger, Whitey." The group's 1971 LP, *There's a Riot Goin' On,* was considered even more controversial, but by this time, Sly's militance was more than offset by his drug-induced unreliability. Following a number of personnel changes, the group slowly disintegrated. "Family Affair" was the group's last Top Ten pop single.

It was Crosby, Stills & Nash who got the most out of their Woodstock appearance. The supergroup had begun to form in the summer of 1968 when an informal jam at singer/songwriter Joni Mitchell's house in Laurel Canyon turned into serious talk about starting a group. After David Geffen was brought in to help with contractual arrangements (most of the principals were already signed to various labels), the new group, which consisted of David Crosby, Stephen Stills, and Graham Nash, was signed to Atlantic. The self-titled debut album showcased all the talents of the group's members: their obvious writing ability, elegant harmonies, penchant for social commentary, and seasoned

Crosby, Stills, Nash & Young began their career with a well-received appearance at Woodstock. Ironically, they were also among the headliners for Altamont, the event that is remembered as the death of the counterculture.

professionalism. Heralded by critics as the best LP of the year, the album included the seven-minute single they performed at Woodstock, "Suite: Judy Blue Eyes," as well as "Marrakesh Express," Crosby's "Long Time Coming," and "Wooden Ships," which was written by Crosby, Stills, and Paul Kantner of the Jefferson Airplane about the horrors of nuclear war. "Long Time Coming" and "Wooden Ships" were both used on the opening audio track for the *Woodstock* film. At the suggestion of Ahmet Ertegun, Neil Young was recruited for the group's second effort. *Déjà Vu* (1970) was, if anything, received even more warmly by the critics as it climbed to the number one position on the charts. Side two began with "Woodstock," a song that Joni Mitchell had written about the festival for CSN&Y. The quartet also released a single that year that was not included on the album. When the National Guard opened fire on a demonstration at Kent State University in Ohio, killing four students and wounding nine others, the group responded immediately with "Ohio," a protest song that named Nixon as the guilty party. The single was released within weeks of the shooting and quickly became a Top Twenty hit.

One of the things that made Crosby, Stills, Nash & Young attractive to its members was the freedom to work on solo projects throughout the life of the group. As individuals, each member turned out quality music, often using topical material, as in Neil Young's "Southern Man," a warning to Alabama's racist Governor George Wallace, Crosby and Nash's "Immigration Man," Stephen Stills' "Love the One You're with," and Graham Nash's "Chicago," written about the 1968 Democratic National Convention for a benefit for the Chicago Eight. Individually and as a group, Crosby, Stills, Nash & Young represented the creativity and positive political impulses of the 1960s as well as the commercial potential of topical material.

Between Woodstock and Altamont, it seemed like the apocalypse might be approaching. Having promised "days of rage," the Weathermen tore up Chicago's upscale Gold Coast just as Charles Manson and his tribe were emerging from the California desert to kill actress Sharon Tate, reportedly inspired by the Beatles' "Helter Skelter." In Washington, D.C., at the Vietnam Moratorium on November 15, Pete Seeger led three-quarters of a million antiwar activists in a chorus of John Lennon's "Give Peace a Chance." On December 4, Chicago police shot Black Panther Fred Hampton dead in his bed. Two days later, there was California's Altamont.

Altamont might well have turned into a Woodstock-like miracle save for two key differences. First, the concert was held in an area that was a fraction of the size of Max Yasgur's farm. Second, the San Francisco chapter of the Hell's Angels were hired to do security for $500 worth of beer.

Altamont was a free concert that the Rolling Stones had planned as the climax to their 1969 U.S. tour promoting their *Let It Bleed* album. Held at the Altamont Speedway just outside San Francisco, the concert was captured in all its gory detail in a documentary entitled *Gimme Shelter*. There are, in fact, a lot more similarities between Woodstock and Altamont than it is comfortable to remember—an audience numbering in the hundreds of thousands, inadequate food, water, and toilets, shifting sites at the last minute, traffic jams, equal numbers of deaths and births. Altamont might well have turned into a Woodstock-like miracle save for two key differences. First, the concert was held in an area that was a fraction of the size of Max Yasgur's farm. Second, the San Francisco chapter of the Hell's Angels were hired to do security for $500 worth of beer.

Initially lukewarm to the idea of a free concert, the Stones had become more comfortable with it as the tour wore on. It was the group's first tour in the United States since 1966 and Mick Taylor's introduction to the American audience. The concert was originally slated for Golden Gate Park in San Francisco, but the site was then shifted to the Sears Point Raceway, where all the logistical planning and on-site construction were completed. Unfortunately, final negotiations with the owners of the raceway broke down at the eleventh hour. Upscale San Francisco attorney Melvin Belli was brought in to set things straight. He promptly negotiated an alternative deal with the Altamont Speedway, which meant that all the logistics had to be redone and all the staging had to be torn down and reassembled at the new site. The idea of hiring Hell's Angels to do security was not rejected by the Stones for a number of reasons. First, the British Hell's Angels had done security without incident for the free concert the group had staged in London's Hyde Park the previous summer. That concert had attracted some 300,000 fans. Second, the Grateful Dead, however naively, optimistically, or stupidly, had advised the Stones that it would be cool to use the group. The romantic outlaw biker image in mid-1960s films like *Easy Rider* fascinated Americans and the Stones probably felt that using the Angels for security would complement their own outlaw image. However, the British Hell's Angels the Stones knew were pale imitations of their U.S. counterparts, who came armed with knives and lead-filled pool cues, which they used at the slightest provocation.

From the beginning, the concert was marred by bad trips and violence. Instructed to keep people off the stage, Hell's Angels treated the area as if it were a military stronghold. Marty Balin, the Jefferson Airplane's lead singer, was punched unconscious by one of the Angels during the group's performance of "Somebody to Love" when Balin found himself caught between the security force and a group of fans who had climbed onto the stage. The violence continued unabated throughout the day, reaching its apex when a black student named Meredith Hunter was murdered. Hunter, who was brandishing a pistol, was stabbed several times by one of the Angels and then clubbed to death during the Stones' plodding performance of "Under My Thumb." Sporting an orange and black cape and a T-shirt emblazoned with an appropriately prophetic Greek letter *omega* ("the end"), Mick Jagger made feeble attempts to calm the crowd. Nothing could have made it clearer who were the real street-fighting men and who were the rock 'n' roll pretenders, and it was all captured on film.[42]

The violence at Altamont reflected the deterioration of political movements and served notice of the counterculture's impending demise. Within months, New York City construction workers would attack antiwar activists and hippies in the street with the tacit approval of the Nixon administration. With hundreds of Panthers already dead or in jail, Bobby Seale, having just weathered the Chicago Eight debacle, would find himself on trial for murder. The U.S. military would bomb Cambodia illegally, and a state of outright repression would become a public spectacle with the killing of student demonstrators at Kent State and, shortly thereafter, at Jackson State. Their deaths would have the same chilling effect on direct political action that the deaths of Hendrix, Joplin, and then Morrison would have on popular music.

━━━━━━━━━━━

In 1970, Motown made a rare sortie into social commentary when it released Edwin Starr's "War." "War," proclaimed the artist, bellowing the song's title, was worth "absolutely nothing." As the song became a number one pop hit, its message obviously struck a chord among listeners, but it fell on deaf ears among Washington policymakers. Starr's follow-up hit "Stop the War" (1971) also failed to translate into social policy even though it echoed the sentiments of millions of Americans. It was clear that the era was coming to an unsatisfactory end and that the "return to normalcy" would be marked by an enforced decline in urban violence with no alleviation of its root causes and a separation of popular music from political ferment.

━━━━━━━━━━━

NOTES

1. Bernice Johnson Reagon, "Songs That Moved the Movement," *Civil Rights Quarterly* (Summer 1983).

2. At the time, mass culture was considered to be a sign of capitalism at its worst. Thus it was viewed as an irredeemably debased culture, produced only for profit, with no possibility for resistance or opposition rather than as an arena for cultural struggle. By the end of the decade, politically minded people had begun to rethink this position.

3. Nelson George, *The Death of Rhythm & Blues* (New York: Pantheon Books, 1988), 69.

4. *Hail! Hail! Rock 'n' Roll,* film documentary, prod. Taylor Hackford, 1987.

5. David Hinckley, Liner Notes, *Phil Spector Back to Mono (1958–1969),* Phil Spector Records, 7118-2.

6. Tom Wolfe, "The First Tycoon of Teen," *The Kandy-Kolored Tangerine-Flake Streamline Baby* (New York: Farrar, Straus, and Giroux, 1965), 69.

7. Love has gone on to become an accomplished actress, who is perhaps best known for her role as Danny Glover's wife in the *Lethal Weapon* films.

8. Richard Farrar, "Da Doo Ron Ron," *Rolling Stone,* 11 May 1968, p. 18.

9. Jay Grossman, "Let There be Dancing in the Streets," *Rolling Stone,* 23 May 1974, p. 22.

10. Michael Lydon, "Smokey Robinson," *Rolling Stone,* 28 September 1968, p. 21.

11. Gerri Hersey, *Nowhere to Run: The Story of Soul Music* (New York: Penguin Books, 1984), 190.

12. George, *The Death of Rhythm & Blues,* 85.

13. Lester Bangs, "The British Invasion," in *The Rolling Stone Illustrated History of Rock 'n' Roll,* ed. Jim Miller (New York: Random House, 1976), 164.

14. Steve Chapple and Reebee Garofalo, *Rock 'n' Roll Is Here to Pay: The History and Politics of the Music Industry* (Chicago: Nelson-Hall, 1977), 70.

15. Burdon went on to front the African American ensemble War in the late 1960s, an association that lasted through the release of the painfully titled LP *Black Man's Burdon.* The group then left Burdon, going on to record fifteen hit albums of its own.

16. For a developed discussion of white blues controversy, see Chapple and Garofalo, *Rock 'n' Roll Is Here to Pay,* 250–257.

17. These two shows, currently available on a single home video as *Born to Rock* (UPA Productions of America, 1982), also included such African American artists as Chuck Berry, Bo Diddley, Ray Charles, James Brown, the Ronettes and Ike and Tina Turner.

18. Hersey, *Nowhere to Run,* 185.

19. Anthony Scaduto, *Bob Dylan* (New York: Signet Books, 1973), 203–204.

20. Although it is not hard to imagine that they took this occasion to toke up, it seems quite unlikely that they had not encountered the mind-altering substance during their hard day's nights in Hamburg, where they flirted with the German art school scene through the influence of Stuart Sutcliffe's girlfriend Astrid Kirchherr.

21. Scaduto, *Bob Dylan,* 204.

22. Ibid.

23. Lillian Roxon, *Lillian Roxon's Rock Encyclopedia* (New York: Grosset and Dunlap, 1971), 78.

24. Ibid., 187.

25. After Vietnam, Sadler worked as a mercenary, hiring himself out to more than half a dozen battles around the world. In September 1988, he took a bullet in the head in Guatemala City.

26. Todd Gitlin, *The Sixties: Years of Hope, Days of Rage* (New York: Bantam Books, 1993).

27. George, *The Death of Rhythm & Blues,* 86.

28. Jim Delahunt, "Whatever Success I Had Was Through the Help of the Good Lord," *Rolling Stone,* 20 January 1968, p. 13.

29. Peter Guralnick, *Sweet Soul Music: Rhythm and Blues and the Southern Dream of Freedom* (New York: Harper and Row, 1986), 169.

30. Ibid., 332.

31. Hettie Jones, *Big Star, Fallin' Mama* (New York: Viking Press, 1974), 41. The term "Rap" in Jones' quote refers to H. Rap Brown, the militant black leader who's poetic fiery speeches may well have been one of rap music's formative influences.

32. Robert Palmer, "James Brown," in *The Rolling Stone Illustrated History of Rock & Roll,* ed. Jim Miller (New York: Rolling Stone Press, 1976), 136.

33. Roxon, *Lillian Roxon's Rock Encyclopedia,* 210.

34. Ibid., 209.

35. David Crosby, *The Monterey International Pop Festival,* boxed set, Rhino R2 70596.

36. Roxon, *Lillian Roxon's Rock Encyclopedia,* 229.

37. "The Rolling Stone Interview with Eric Clapton," *Rolling Stone.* 11 May 1968, p. 12.

38. Roxon, *Lillian Roxon's Rock Encyclopedia,* 228–229.

39. George, *The Death of Rhythm & Blues,* 98.

40. Gitlin, *The Sixties,* 287.

41. *Woodstock,* film directed by Michael Wadleigh, 1970.

42. *Gimme Shelter,* film directed by David Maysles, Albert Maysles, and Charlotte Zwerin, 1970.

7 Music versus Markets: The Fragmentation of Pop

The 1960s rolled into the 1970s, leaving behind a series of unresolved issues. As a result, the 1970s are often viewed as a decade of retreat. While it is true that the two great movements of the previous decade—the Civil Rights movement and the antiwar movement—were in decline, lasting social and cultural (if not structural) changes did occur. Society was not radically transformed in the manner the New Left wanted but neither did conservatives reestablish the cultural and political hegemony that they had enjoyed in the early 1950s. There were advances in environmental politics (ecology and the anti-nuclear movement) and, particularly, the women's movement. The oppression of poor people, people of color, and women would not disappear, but these constituencies would never again be silent or invisible. Finally, the 1970s called into question all traditional notions of masculinity and femininity.

> The music industry, like the population at large, had been swept up in the political currents of the 1960s, as popular music was used to fuel every impulse from explorations of awakened sexuality and flights of psychedelic fantasy to furious discharges of political spleen. But the industry never lost its footing as an enduring capitalist enterprise.

The music industry, like the population at large, had been swept up in the political currents of the 1960s, as popular music was used to fuel every impulse from explorations of awakened sexuality and flights of psychedelic fantasy to furious discharges of political spleen. But the industry never lost its footing as an enduring capitalist enterprise. Any internal tensions the industry felt were expressed, predictably, in terms of culture versus commerce, music versus markets, the electric version of the authentic-commercial debate of the folk revival. The more astute observers of the scene understood that this contradiction had always been inherent in rock 'n' roll. "From the start," Michael Lydon said in

239

1970, "rock has been commercial in its very essence. . . . it was never an art form that just happened to make money, nor a commercial undertaking that sometimes became art. Its art was synonymous with its business."[1] Just as the radical movements of the 1960s depended, in part, on the affluence provided by the war effort, popular music was bound to the capitalist interests that produced it. Thus, to understand the trajectory of popular music in the 1970s, it is necessary to explore commercial and technological developments that began in the music industry in the late 1960s.

As popular music in the late 1960s began to incorporate blues, jazz, classical, Indian, and electronic sounds, the boundaries separating audiences became somewhat murky. In the late 1960s, for example, because of the technical development of FM rock radio, which led to short-lived experiments in free-form programming, it was not out of the ordinary to hear the Beatles, Stevie Wonder, Janis Joplin, Jimi Hendrix, Pink Floyd, and the Grateful Dead on the same radio program or to find them in the same record collection. At the time, all these artists were included in the umbrella category of progressive rock, which presumably distinguished them from less interesting formulaic pop. A few years later, however, as the industry tried to rationalize production, such a range of artists would be spread over a number of more discrete, less overlapping audiences. It is for this reason that *Rolling Stone*'s Steve Pond remembers the 1970s as a time when rock

> became diffuse, scattered and unfocused, fragmenting into little genres whose fans paid less and less attention to other little genres. In the Seventies, rock had a hundred different focal points: Elton John for popsters; Led Zeppelin for hard rockers; Emerson, Lake and Palmer for the art rockers; Joni Mitchell for the singer/songwriter contingent; David Bowie in the glam rock corner; Stevie Wonder for soul aficionados. Instead of a center, rock had a batch of radio formats.[2]

Keeping its capitalistic roots in mind, the music industry moved to a strategy of trying to target fans with the most disposable income. Thus, the art of marketing became more and more tied to the science of demographics.

The Music Industry: A Sound Investment

By 1973, the music business had become a $2-billion-a-year industry, about as large as the sports and film industries combined. Having learned from their rock 'n' roll mistakes, major record companies no longer resisted the creative impulses of offbeat artists or upstart independent labels. Instead, they happily signed acts directly, made label deals, entered into joint ventures, or contracted for distribution. When the Jefferson Airplane left RCA to set up Grunt records, the group did not hesitate to look to its old label for distribution. Capitol contracted with the

By 1973, the music business had become a $2-billion-a-year industry, about as large as the sports and film industries combined.

Beach Boys to distribute Brother Records. Frank Zappa's Bizarre label, which was distributed by Warner, developed new talent. When he directed Alice Cooper to Warner in the early 1970s, the company was smart enough to listen, and the outrageous metal ensemble became one of the label's best-selling acts. Warner also entered into a lucrative distribution deal with Chrysalis, which had Jethro Tull and Procol Harum. At the same time, distribution deals with Stax and Philadelphia International provided CBS Records with a profitable entree to the soul market.

What had begun in the late 1960s as a period of political awakening with a cultural flourish for the rock 'n' roll audience was, for the music industry, a period of commercial expansion and corporate consolidation. While the industry learned to "go with the flow" to a great extent, the impulse to engineer trends from the top down was never completely extinguished. Sometimes the magic worked, as in the creation of the Monkees and their cartoon cousins the Archies, and sometimes it did not, as in the ill-fated effort to create the "Bosstown Sound," an attempt to replicate the San Francisco experience in Boston that cost MGM an estimated $4 million.

Merger Mania

Even with the occasional failure, Wall Street finally came to view the music industry as a sound investment. Thus, there ensued a period of unprecedented merger activity, not just large record companies gobbling up smaller ones but huge conglomerates, unrelated to music, acquiring properties in the music industry. RCA, CBS, Capitol-EMI, and their related labels, which had long been divisions of multinational electronics firms, simply expanded their holdings. Phillips, the Dutch electronics conglomerate, acquired Mercury and MGM. Gulf and Western bought Paramount. GRT, the tape company, purchased Chess. Omega Equities bought Roulette.[3] By far, the most interesting merger, however, was the one that created the Warner Communications empire.

Warner Brothers Records had been a rather lackluster label that was created in 1958 as a division of the film company. In 1963, the purchase of Frank Sinatra's Reprise label, which was run by Mo Ostin, put the corporation on a firmer footing financially, but its place in the burgeoning youth culture was not secured until promo man Joe Smith, soon to become the company's president, signed the Grateful Dead in 1967. In that year, through a series of merger techniques, the combined labels were bought by the smaller Seven Arts film company, which also acquired Atlantic Records. (At the time it was bought, Atlantic was consolidating its hold over southern soul with Aretha Franklin and the Stax-Volt roster and moving into new terrain with second-wave British acts like Cream.) Warner-Seven Arts, as the newly formed company was called, then ran head first into Steve Ross. Ross had just parlayed his wife's family funeral business into a modest empire that included rental cars and the Kinney parking lot system. It was the subsequent purchase of a talent agency that whetted Ross' appetite for the music business. Within months, his Kinney Corporation, as the conglomerate was called, had bought Warner-Seven Arts and its associated labels. Shortly thereafter, Jac Holzman's Elektra label was added. Elektra had been launched as a folk label in the 1950s, but it became a more attractive property financially after Holzman signed the Doors in 1967. In 1973, David Geffen's Asylum Records was acquired by Ross and amalgamated with Elektra in the following year. Geffen then replaced Holzman at the helm. Asylum had started as a refuge for softer acts such as Joni Mitchell, the Eagles, and Jackson Browne, many of whom Geffen had managed with his partner Eliot Roberts.

By this time, Ross had reorganized the company as Warner Communications. In addition to a couple of dozen associated labels, the corporation had extensive holdings in film and television, *Mad* magazine, sixty-three comic books, and a piece of *Ms.* magazine. Its national record distribution was set up as Warner-Elektra-Atlantic (WEA). In addition to the talent mentioned earlier, the company had Led Zeppelin, Deep Purple, Black Sabbath, the Faces, Crosby, Stills & Nash, Neil Young, Arlo Guthrie, Gordon Lightfoot, Van Morrison, James Taylor, Randy Newman, and the Mothers of Invention. While the committee of record executives that coordinated the music operation—Joe Smith and Mo Ostin from Warner-Reprise, David Geffen from Elektra-Asylum, and Ahmet and Nesui Ertegun from Atlantic—had little contact with Steve Ross, their combined efforts turned him into one of the most powerful men in the recording industry as well as American business as a whole.

By the time gasoline shortages miraculously led to record profits for the oil companies between 1973 and 1974, structural realignments had produced a level of concentration in the music industry that had not been witnessed since the postwar 1940s. The top four record corporations accounted for over 50 percent of all records and tapes sold. CBS and Warner Communications alone took in about 40 percent of the total. The industry had also consolidated vertically. In addition to its own labels, recording studios, pressing plants, national distribution, and publishing division, CBS, Inc., for example, owned the Columbia Record and Tape Club, Pacific Stereo and the Discount Records chain, Fender Guitars, Leslie Speakers, Rhodes Pianos, and Rogers Drums. EMI in Great Britain had an analogous set of holdings. Because of the predominance of electronics corporations in the field, there was a wrinkle to this corporate structure that seemed particularly antithetical to the ideology of popular music at the time. That was the unexpected connection between music and the military. Ever since the invention of the wireless, electronic communication had developed according to its military applications. "Audio is a fairly obscure backwater of electronics," producer Peter Williams has explained. "When people do go out to design a new chip they're not thinking how many recording studios can we sell it to. They're thinking how many missiles can we stick this in. Most electronic development is highly military."[4] The connection between music and the military was driven home dramatically to Keith Richards when he discovered that Decca, the Stones' label, had diverted the profits it made from the sale of Rolling Stones records to precisely this kind of research and development.

> *We found out, and it wasn't years till we did, that all the bread we made for Decca was going into making little black boxes that go into American Air Force bombers to bomb fucking North Vietnam. They took the bread we made for them and put it into the radar section of their business. When we found that out, it blew our minds. That was it. Goddamn, you find you've helped to kill God knows how many thousands of people without even knowing it. I'd rather the Mafia than Decca.*[5]

In the headiness of the late 1960s and early 1970s, such connections were not always apparent. This was the time when rock became art, when it became progressive, indeed, revolutionary. The industry rose willingly to the challenge of accommodating the new aesthetic.

Expanding the Infrastructure: Counterculture as Commodity

Developments in recording technology had a dramatic impact on the production of music. By the late 1960s and early 1970s, high-fidelity stereo records had become the industry standard (with various tape configurations vying for acceptance) and had increased the public desire for high-quality sound. In the search for better sound, the two four-track tape machines that had been used to record *Sgt. Pepper* in 1967 were rendered obsolete by the appearance of eight- and sixteen-track studios. Multi-track recording had immediate consequences for the social relations of musical production. No longer was it necessary for musicians to perform together to make a record. Indeed, a single musician could now play all the instruments.

By the early 1970s, the major record labels had narrowed their focus essentially to the manufacture and sale of records. Virtually all of the creative aspects of music-making were contracted out.

Overdubbing, layering, mixing, and the addition of special effects such as reverb, equalization, and compression removed increasingly important aspects of the creative process from the studio performance and located them in the control room, elevating the producer to an artistic status equal to that of the musicians he produced. As a result, the term "production" in the music industry, as Peter Wicke has astutely pointed out, came to have two related but distinct definitions: "the production of music and the manufacture of records."[6] By the early 1970s, the major record labels had narrowed their focus essentially to the manufacture and sale of records. Virtually all of the creative aspects of music-making were contracted out. "The mechanics of a record company are just that—the mechanics," said Joe Smith in 1974.[7] On the creative end, record companies were involved primarily in talent acquisition, marketing, and promotion. And promote they did. The record companies were quick to pick up on the antiestablishment fervor of the late 1960s and early 1970s in promoting some of the more creative strands of rock that were being labeled progressive rock, a term which resonated nicely with the radical rhetoric of the era. In 1968, CBS introduced an ad campaign that promoted some of its rock acts as "The Revolutionaries." Advertisements were headlined with slogans like "The Man can't bust our music." Warner released a compilation LP called *The People's Album* that was largely a repository for their singer/songwriters and soft rock acts. The album cover art, however, had lettering intended to look like Chinese characters and depicted heroic, banner-waving protesters in Mao jackets, thus suggesting an association with the cultural revolution that was occurring halfway around the world.

The appearance of a whole new industry infrastructure greatly enhanced the promotional power of the record companies. Once experimentation with psychedelic drugs introduced a new visual dimension to live rock performances, a touring circuit of ballrooms and small clubs opened up to showcase the new progressive rock acts. Taking their cue from promoter Bill Graham's Fillmore Auditorium in San Francisco, clubs like the Electric Circus in New York, the Boston Tea Party, the Electric Factory in Philadelphia, the Grande Ballroom in Detroit, and the Kinetic Playground in Chicago embellished rock performances with strobe effects and undulating, amoebalike light patterns that pulsated to the beat of the music. When the psychedelic clubs and ballrooms folded after only a few years, it was largely because the progressive rock market had outgrown such small venues. Established promoters simply moved into arena or stadium-size venues and huge outdoor festivals. They could do so because advances in sound reinforcement technology had opened up the possibility of mass audience events on the scale of Woodstock. By the early 1970s, the Grateful Dead were touring with enough power to provide electricity for "six blocks of tract homes." Traveling with thirty-two tons of equipment, Emerson, Lake, and Palmer brought new meaning to the term "power trio."

A burgeoning rock press and the advent of FM rock radio completes the picture of the music industry's growing infrastructure. Prior to the mid-1960s, popular music was geared toward the Top Forty AM radio format. The format was perfected when programmer Bill Drake, who learned his trade at KYA in San Francisco and KYNO in Fresno, California, developed tight, distinct *sound* for his stations by encouraging his stereotypically fast-talking deejays to eliminate what he termed "dead air." The format reduced the power of deejays by forcing them to adhere rigidly to a limited list of forty or fewer songs that were rotated all day long and liberally interspersed with commercials.

As Smokey Robinson at Motown recognized early on, the unit of pop production for AM Top Forty was the three-minute single. However, the new lyric substance that the folk revival of the early 1960s had brought to popular music and concept LPs like *Sgt. Pepper* did not readily lend themselves to the fast-paced AM radio format. It was at this point that FM rock radio opened up to accommodate this new musical style.

After the postwar decision to reassign FM to the 88–108 MHz band, which rendered one-half million FM receivers instantly obsolete (see Chapter 3), FM radio continued to develop but as a service that was clearly ancillary to AM broadcasting. In the

1960s, however, two FCC rulings transformed the importance of FM for rock. In 1961, the FCC authorized FM "multiplexing," a process of broadcasting two signals simultaneously on a single channel. It is this process that makes possible a stereo broadcast. Although the fifty-seven multiplex stations that existed in 1961 were broadcasting primarily middle-of-the-road and classical music, the multiplexing process itself soon became attractive to a larger audience for whom rock was art. It was the second FCC decision in 1965 that married FM and rock. At this time, the FCC ruled that FM programming in cities with a population greater than 100,000 had to differ from AM programming at least 50 percent of the time. In effect, the ruling forced station owners to divide their AM and FM properties or release their FM

The existing trade magazines—Billboard, Cash Box, Record World— shared AM radio's inability to incorporate new developments in music. They could no more fashion a music journalism that could relate to progressive rock contextually than the counterculture could confront the downside of its own antiprofessionalism.

stations altogether. Station owners promptly decided to use FM to explore new styles of music. Progressive FM rock began more or less simultaneously on the East and West coasts around 1967, although a number of college stations had used the format even earlier. One of its commercial pioneers was "Big Daddy" Tom Donahue who initiated a laid-back, "free form" music show in the 8:00 PM to midnight slot on station KMPX in San Francisco. Within months, Donahue was programming the whole station. He described the format as one that "embraces the best of today's rock and roll, folk, traditional and city blues, raga, electronic music, and some jazz and classical selections."[8] By 1970, there were 668 FM outlets in the United States, and a goodly number of them—WBCN in Boston, WABC and WNEW in New York, WBBM in Chicago, WKNR in Detroit, KSAN in San Francisco, and KMET in Los Angeles, among others—were playing rock.

Born of the counterculture, progressive FM rock radio exhibited a unique blend of culture and politics in its formative stages. Within a few years, the better FM stations even rivaled some AM outlets in commercial success, but as soon as they did, they fell victim to the same corporate pressures toward homogenization that affected AM radio. *Rolling Stone*'s Ben Fong-Torres, who did some moonlighting as a deejay, detailed the process in 1973:

> *The typical FM station goes on with waves of good vibes, building an audience of loyal listeners by playing album cuts unheard on AM, by talking with, instead of to, listeners, and by opening up the station to the community. As the audience builds, however, the ratings, "the numbers," climb, and the station owners suddenly have a marketable commodity. Suddenly the air is filled with increasingly uptight advertisers, administration takes over, and everything is sterilized. Suddenly there are playlists; certain records have to be banned. No more interviews—can't stop the flow of music. No politicizing—remember the Fairness Doctrine. Got to have that license in order to do your thing, you know. Suddenly there's no community out there, but a "share" of the "quarter hour audience." And in the end, FM rock stands naked. It is, after all, just another commercial radio station.[9]*

The rock press followed much the same trajectory. The existing trade magazines—*Billboard, Cash Box, Record World*—shared AM radio's inability to incorporate new developments in music. They could no more fashion a music journalism that could relate to progressive rock contextually than the counterculture could confront the downside of its own antiprofessionalism. It is hardly surprising, then, that dozens of alternative magazines, for example, *Crawdaddy!* in Boston (proving ground for Jon Landau, Peter Guralnick, and Ed Ward) began appearing around 1966 to fill the void. Robert Christgau, Ellen Willis, and Richard Goldstein cut their journalistic teeth at *Cheetah* in New York. Most of the alternative rags, such as San Francisco's *Mojo-Navigator R&R News,* were completely disorganized and folded within months. Some, such as *Creem,* watering hole for Dave Marsh and Lester Bangs, published sporadically but with considerable impact. On 18 October 1967, Jann Wenner launched the magazine that would outlast them all—*Rolling Stone.* From its very beginnings, it ran counter to the antibusiness culture of rock.

Wenner, whom Robert Draper has described as a dedicated and driven journalist, an unabashed and insecure social climber, a fawning stargazer, and a ruthless businessman "who cut a multitude of ethical corners," was a Berkeley drop-out and rock 'n' roll fanatic who found himself immersed in the eruptions of mid-1960s San Francisco.[10] Through the efforts of his friend and mentor, Ralph Gleason, the *San Francisco Chronicle*'s music critic, Wenner landed a job as entertainment editor for the radical *Sunday Ramparts* at a time when the magazine's political leadership had not grasped, to Wenner's satisfaction, the full cultural importance of rock. At the invitation of Chet Helms, manager of the Avalon Ballroom, a psychedelic club in San Francisco, Wenner then joined a group that, by his standards, was taking an interminably long time to start a counterculture magazine called *Straight Arrow.* After attending a few meetings, Wenner stole the group's mailing list and started his own magazine. Cofounder Ralph Gleason christened the magazine *Rolling Stone,* and it was published by Wenner's own company, which he named Straight Arrow. Helms was flabbergasted.

It was Gleason who gave the magazine legitimacy in progressive rock circles. He had been a tireless advocate of the alternative rock scene at a time when few established critics ventured out onto that limb. With Gleason's name on its masthead musicians were willing to grant interviews to the magazine and record companies were willing to buy ads. Forget that 34,000 of the 40,000 copies of *Rolling Stone*'s premiere issue were returned unsold. Within months, the magazine was carrying ads from almost every major record company. Taking both rock and journalism seriously, Wenner managed to attract the best stable of writers of any rock magazine; his first generation of writers included Michael Lydon, Jon Landau, Greil Marcus, Langdon Winner, and Jim Miller, among many others.

In the first issue of *Rolling Stone,* which pictured John Lennon in an army uniform on the cover, as the film in which he appeared, *How I Won the War,* was premiering at

When Jann Wenner launched **Rolling Stone**, he was responding to the tenor of the times. Although he evidenced little tolerance for countercultural inefficiency or movement politics, he genuinely sought to develop a serious journalism for the music he loved.

the San Francisco Film Festival, Wenner told his readers, "*Rolling Stone* is not just about music, but also about the things and attitudes that the music embraces."[11] This hint of a connection to politics seemed to be borne out in Ralph Gleason's piece on racism in television and Michael Lydon's exposé of the Monterey Pop Festival which he criticized as being "done for a cost plus songs, not for a song plus costs."[12]

Rolling Stone, which soon became required reading in the music industry, was considered authoritative from the start, and Wenner never missed an opportunity to distance his publication from all others. The trade magazines, he had opined in his first editorial, were "inaccurate and irrelevant" and fanzines "an anachronism, fashioned in the mold of myth and nonsense."[13] *Cheetah,* he observed elsewhere, was "dull, poorly-conceived and pointless."[14] While the magazine could be influential, as an article on Texas rock that plugged the then unknown albino blues guitarist Johnny Winter and netted him a $600,000 advance from Columbia Records proved, Wenner could also be spiteful. He reportedly refused to grant Simon and Garfunkel favorable coverage because a former girlfriend had taken up with Paul Simon.

Wenner's editorial condemning the Yippie protest at the 1968 Democratic National Convention in Chicago for "using methods and means as corrupt as the political machine it hopes to disrupt" clearly separated him from the more radical political tendencies of his generation. To the outrage of the New Left, Wenner said, "Rock and roll is the *only* way in which the vast but formless power of youth is structured, the only way in which it can be defined or inspected."[15] For the New Left, this kind of mystification of rock was precisely what was wrong with the counterculture. Following the Chicago '68 editorial, the magazine was regularly bombarded with angry letters that denounced it as a capitalist shuck, the ultimate 1960s insult. Wenner tried to redeem himself with a fake to the left in *Stone's* 1969 issue on "The American Revolution," in which he grudgingly editorialized, "These new politics are about to become part of our daily lives, and willingly or not, we are in it," but it was too late.[16] The magazine had long since staked out its relationship to politics. As Robert Draper has said,

> *While the nation buried Martin Luther King, Jr.,* Rolling Stone *published an obituary of . . . Frankie Lymon; while America cried for Robert F. Kennedy, Jann Wenner fired bullets at the new Cream album.* Rolling Stone *responded to the rapid escalation of the Vietnam War with an article showing how soldiers were smoking good weed overseas. Nixon's election—a brutal blow to the counterculture—did not warrant a mention, as the magazine was preoccupied with John Lennon's foreskin.*[17]

By the time of the magazine's fourth anniversary in 1971, Wenner no longer cared about taunts from the left but instead embraced the term "capitalist," trying to invest it with a positive spin. "As long as there are bills to pay, writers who want to earn a living by their craft, people who pay for their groceries, want to raise children and have their own homes," he editorialized, *"Rolling Stone* will be a capitalistic operation."[18] By this time, the magazine was firmly ensconced in its new $7,000-a-month Third Street offices; had already lost some of its best writers, including Marcus and Winner, largely over political differences; and had entered a new phase of corporate expansion with the addition of millionaire computer magnate Max Palevsky to its board of directors. Politics at *Rolling Stone* now meant electoral politics as in Hunter Thompson's "gonzo" coverage of the Nixon-McGovern race in 1972, the magazine's endorsement of Jimmy Carter in 1976, and some good investigative pieces on particular issues throughout the decade. After all, music had always been *Rolling Stone*'s primary mission, and Wenner had reasoned early on that, to realize his vision, the magazine would have to be built on a solid economic foundation, even if that meant distancing it from the political upheaval that provided its context. This was not too high a price for him to pay. He never trusted movement politics any more than he tolerated countercultural inefficiency. What was important to Jann Wenner was the surety that the music he loved was taken seriously and that there was a place for him in the scene.

Creativity and Commerce: Rock as Art

In the new music industry, rock enjoyed a privileged position. Technological advances and journalistic seriousness invested it with the status of art. The signal event for this development had been, of course, the 1967 release of the Beatles' *Sgt. Pepper* album. With 900 hours of studio time required for completion at a then unheard-of price of $100,000, *Sgt. Pepper* became the Sistine ceiling of rock and George Martin, its Michelangelo. Meticulous attention had been paid to every detail of composition, balance, and technical execution. It was, in the modest opinion of guitarist Lenny Kaye, "an artistic statement in a music that was never regarded as art before."[19] Even established academics stood up and took notice. Noted musicologist Wilfred Mellers called it "the most distinctive event in pop's brief history."[20] Clearly the days when the Beatles, or any other rock group, could release six best-selling albums in one year were gone forever. Rock artists now labored over every cut, experimenting with new sounds, adding special effects, and overdubbing to perfection. Joe Smith told a story of how the Grateful Dead said they wanted to "record thirty minutes of air in the summertime, when it's hot and smoggy. Thirty minutes of heavy air. Then we could go to the desert and record thirty minutes of clean air. Then mix the two together, get a good sound, and record over it."[21] The Dead found themselves in trouble with (and in debt to) Warner after they ran up a $120,000 tab in various studios around the country before a single album resulted. But the Dead were not alone in the search for perfection.

In the new music industry, rock enjoyed a privileged position. Technological advances and journalistic seriousness invested it with the status of art.

As the counterculture and the social movements that accompanied it deteriorated in the early 1970s, rock increasingly found refuge in its newly acquired status as art. If rock-as-counterculture had existed outside market relations, then rock-as-art hovered above them. This was, of course, a hopelessly contradictory belief, but it echoed the anti-commercialism of the period and made musicians central to the creative process. Critics friendly to the music began to construct their own versions of *auteur* theory in popular music. "The criterion of art in rock," said Jon Landau, "is the capacity of the musician to create a personal, almost private, universe and to express it fully."[22] This focus tended to carry rock in the direction of European art music, drawing on classical influences, delving into opera, exploring the possibilities of orchestration, and stressing the technical aspects of musicianship. George Martin's training as a classical oboist had doubtless played more than a small role in the appearance of cellos, piccolo trumpets, and classical string quartets on Beatles' records. *Sgt. Pepper* "marked the turning point," Wilfred Mellers has said, "when the Beatles stopped being ritual dance music and became music to be listened to."[23] It was in this sense, then, that rock was said to be the mature form of rock 'n' roll. However, the adjective was laden with extra-musical baggage.

In the context of U.S. race relations, rock's artistic explorations were not simply neutral forays into a broader musical terrain; they mirrored the separation of the races that had begun in the late 1960s. "No one who can hear today," proclaimed *Rolling Stone* editor Ralph Gleason in January 1968, "can possibly find any way in which the Beatles imitate Black musicians."[24] In May of that year, Gleason extolled the virtues of the San Francisco groups for much the same reason:

> *One of the most encouraging things about the whole hippie scene and rock music in San Francisco which grew out of it is that no one is really trying to be anything other than what he is. The white sons of middle class America who are in this thing are not ashamed of being white. They are the first American musicians, aside from the country and western players, who are not trying to sound black.*[25]

These sentiments were later echoed by Eric Clapton, who built his career covering B. B. King guitar licks. "My whole attitude has changed," said Clapton. "I listen to the same sounds and records but with a different ear. I'm no longer trying to play anything but like a white man."[26] Such comments devalued the contributions that black artists made, placing them outside the definition of progressive music and, therefore, beneath the critical attention of the rock press. Progressive rockers headed off in new artistic directions, relating to black music as a touchstone of historical significance rather than a continuing source of artistic inspiration. Black music had provided the foundation; now progressive rock would construct the edifice. By 1971, Motown chronicler Dave Morse was able to observe, rather bitterly, "Black musicians are now implicitly regarded as precursors who, having taught the white men all they know, must gradually recede into the distance as white progressive music, the simple lessons mastered, advances irresistibly into the future."[27] Jon Landau argued that black music "provides rock with the continuity which allows developments like the rise of San Francisco to take place."[28]

Progressive rockers headed off in new artistic directions, relating to black music as a touchstone of historical significance rather than a continuing source of artistic inspiration. Black music had provided the foundation; now progressive rock would construct the edifice.

San Francisco's psychedelic clubs, of course, were one of the places where rock began its advance toward art. When George Hunter formed the Charlatans, one of the progenitors of the San Francisco scene, he was studying electronic music and staging "happenings" at San Francisco State College. The Charlatans' good-time electric folk had less of an impact than the group's vintage gold-rush cowboy fashions and innovative poster art, which had been inspired by turn-of-the-century illustrator Maxfield Parrish. These images found a ready home in the city's psychedelic clubs where designers, sculptors, visual artists, and electronics experts were as important to the "total environment" as the music itself. A more systematic impetus for combining these elements came from British art schools, which had long been a haven for bohemian students who went on to become rock stars. Said Keith Richards, who did a stint at the Sidcup Art School, "I mean, in England, if you're lucky you get into art school. It's somewhere they put you if they can't put you anywhere else."[29] As Peter Wicke has pointed out, a remarkable number of British rock musicians took this path to stardom:

> *John Lennon was registered at the Liverpool College of Art from 1957 to 1959; Pete Townshend studied at London's Ealing Art College at the same time as Ron Wood, later a member of the Rolling Stones, and Freddie Mercury of Queen; Ray Davies of the Kinks was from London's Hornsey Art College; Jeff Beck, guitarist with the Yardbirds, and Eric Clapton were both educated at London's Wimbleton College of Art; and even David Bowie and Adam Ant were art school graduates, from St. Martin's School of Art and Hornsey Art College respectively.[30]*

In their engaging study *Art Into Pop*, Simon Frith and Howard Horne have noted that British art schools promoted a nineteenth-century Romantic notion of (high) art as an autonomous, personal statement operating within (and sometimes resisting) the shifting demands of capitalist culture. The schools thus encouraged an atmosphere of experimentation and self-indulgence that enabled would-be musicians to bring "into music-making attitudes that could never have been fostered under the pressures of professional entertainment."[31] Alongside the fine arts courses, somewhat more practical courses in industrial and fashion design and photography allowed students to investigate the aesthetic dimensions of image and style within modern mass media. For those who were interested and talented, rock offered the potential for bringing all of these elements together in a single, total experience (and held out the possibility of earning a living from it). Pete Townshend, for example, applied what he had learned from avant-garde lecturers in theater, poetry, and film to the Who's stage act, treating it as performance art. In this spirit, the Who experimented with noise and destroyed instruments and sound

The Who were the first pop art band. From Pete Townshend's Union Jack jacket to the use of real radio ads and jingles on record, they pioneered the use of popular signs and symbols as an artistic statement in music.

British art schools become havens for art rock scene

systems. Pop artist Peter Blake (who designed the *Sgt. Pepper* cover) played a key role in determining the image of the Who (badges, medals, targets, the Union Jack on Townshend's jacket), which established the group as the first pop art band. When the Who released the first rock opera, *Tommy*, in 1969, it placed them in an artistic realm that would have been considered a contradiction in terms a few years earlier.

The use of national symbols (the Union Jack on Townshend's jacket, the Stars and Stripes on hippies) for graphic embellishment paralleled the appearance of Campbell Soup cans and comic book images in fine art galleries. While pop art was blurring the distinctions between high art and mass culture, Andy Warhol, its most famous practitioner, was working to neutralize the contradiction between all art and commercial necessity. He saw "commercial art as real art and real art as commercial art."[32] While his position displayed both disturbing cynicism and considerable insight, it also addressed the needs of the music industry.

> By the end of the 1960s LP sleeve designers were roaming across the history of modern art, film and fashion as knowingly (and for much the same reason) as advertising agencies—the sleeves, like the rock posters and group images, at first glimpse the most obvious sign of a high art presence in rock, were, in fact, designed to sell the product.[33]

Warhol became directly involved in rock through his tutelage of the Velvet Underground, a group with a discomforting sound that would become influential in the void that yielded punk. There was a perversely interesting connection between his famous banana cover for the debut Velvet Underground album, which allowed the consumer to peel off the skin revealing the fruit beneath, and his cover design for the Rolling Stones' *Sticky Fingers* (1971), which pictured Mick Jagger's jean-clad mid-section with a real zipper for a fly.

For a time, the move to elevate rock to art was balanced by a sense of humor. When the Beatles acknowledged the Mothers of Invention's *Freak Out* as one of the inspirations for *Sgt. Pepper*, Frank Zappa returned the favor with a complete send-up of *Sgt. Pepper*'s cover art on an album entitled *We're Only in It for the Money*. The Who followed with the tongue-in-cheek *The Who Sell Out*, which simulated a commercial radio broadcast and included ads and jingles, some made up and some real. Pete Townshend's pop art strategy, Frith and Horne have said, was to use "the vitality of commerce itself, the bombardment of sales patter, to both heighten the 'realism' of the Who's music and draw attention to its spuriousness."[34] As the 1960s turned into the 1970s, however, a new generation of British art rockers brought "high seriousness" to full fruition and the music abandoned its sense of humor. "It was the abstract chimera of 'art' surrounding the music of such groups as Yes, Jethro Tull, Genesis, Emerson, Lake & Palmer, and the Moody Blues," contends Iain Chambers, "that continued to exert a disproportional influence on the direction and sense of much pop music, distributing judgment and dividing the musical field into frequently quite rigid divisions."[35] At this point, art rock emerged as a new marketing category which distinguished these groups from other progressive rock acts. There was perhaps a greater tendency to "dignify" the music with classical references in Britain where class distinctions are more sharply felt than in the United States. The Moody Blues kicked off this trend when the group's *Days of Future Past,* which was recorded with the London Festival Orchestra, reached number three on the charts in 1968. They followed up with six gold LPs in a row. With keyboardist John Lord's *Concerto for Group and Orchestra* in 1970, which was recorded at the

> **C**ertainly, art rock was vulnerable to the criticism that it pandered to middle-brow cultural sensibilities in a vain effort to gain acceptance among people who would have regarded the two words as mutually exclusive. At the same time, however, it has to be acknowledged that this music worked.

Royal Albert Hall, Deep Purple was headed in the same direction until guitarist Ritchie Blackmore intervened and changed the group's direction. At their worst, musicologist Rob Walser has said, these classical appropriations reeked of upper-class pretension. In this regard, he has been particularly critical of Emerson, Lake & Palmer:

> [N]eoclassical extravaganzas, such as their rendering of Mussorgsky's Pictures at an Exhibition *(1972), were intended as elevations of public taste and expressions of advanced musicianship. Keith Emerson's attraction to classical resources was unabashedly elitist; he considered ordinary popular music degraded and took on the mission of raising the artistic level of rock.*[36]

Certainly, art rock was vulnerable to the criticism that it pandered to middle-brow cultural sensibilities in a vain effort to gain acceptance among people who would have regarded the two words as mutually exclusive. At the same time, however, it has to be acknowledged that this music worked. If the reaction of the critics was any indicator, it worked artistically; if the response of the fans counted, it worked commercially. Indeed, it worked beyond the wildest fantasies of the record companies. "Emerson, Lake & Palmer have no faults," said the *Cash Box* review of the group's first New York City appearance in 1971.[37] Apparently fans concurred; all of the albums the group released in the 1970s were certified gold.

Emerson, Lake & Palmer was a supergroup that had drawn its members from existing rock bands: keyboardist Keith Emerson from the Nice, an earlier rock/classical fusion group, guitarist Greg Lake from King Crimson, drummer Carl Palmer from the Crazy World of Arthur Brown. Lake's and Palmer's blues orientation provided the group with a hard rock base, but it was Emerson who was the group's guiding force. As a boy he had taken classical piano lessons, which had introduced him to the percussive piano sound of Béla Bartok. Indeed, Bartok's influence colored their self-titled debut album. As the group matured, Emerson took the concept to new heights, typically rushing around amidst a bank of keyboards (at one point a piano, a Moog synthesizer, two electric organs, and other unnamed sound-producing devices) stabbing at them with staccato 32d note runs. Four of the group's next five albums reached the Top Ten. In the mid-1970s,

Art rockers attempt to elevate the level of musical culture

Emerson, Lake & Palmer were among the groups who felt that there was no incompatibility between rock and serious art. Among their defining characteristics were the use of synthesizers and the incorporation of classical influences in their music.

group members took time out for a number of solo projects, including Emerson's failed attempt to record a piano concerto with the London Philharmonic. In 1977, they staged a comeback with the release of two volumes of mostly solo material. *Works, Volume I* and *Works, Volume II* sold well enough, but the seventy-piece orchestra assembled for the group's comeback tour had to be laid off because of poor ticket sales. By this time, disco was making far more efficient use of the synthesizer and punk had stripped rock down to its bare essentials. Art rock extravagance seemed bloated by comparison. Emerson, Lake & Palmer disbanded in 1979, only to regroup at the end of the next decade.

Yes, another art rock group, had actually begun before Emerson, Lake & Palmer. The group, which had several members who were well versed in the classics, had first started recording for Atlantic in 1968 but had then undergone a number of personnel changes. By the time their third LP, *The Yes Album,* was released in 1971, they had edged into the U.S. Top Forty, but the group didn't hit its stride until keyboardist Tony Kaye was replaced by Rick Wakeman, a classically trained pianist from the Royal Academy. The next album, *Fragile* (1972), hit the Top Ten and yielded one of the group's only successful singles of the decade, "Roundabout." Critical response to the album was one of unbridled enthusiasm, and there was no denying the commercial appeal of the music. From *Fragile* on, every Yes album reached the Top Twenty. Wakeman ventured out as a solo artist in the mid-1970s and confirmed the pretentiousness of art rock with such weighty titles as *The Six Wives of Henry the VIII, Journey to the Center of the Earth* (recorded with the London Symphony Orchestra), and *The Myths and Legends of King Arthur and the Knights of the Round Table* (recorded with the English Chamber Choir).

Perhaps because the life of the group was divided into two distinct phases with different cultural referents, Pink Floyd was more eclectic in its influences than either Emerson, Lake & Palmer or Yes. From 1965 to 1968, the group was dominated by writer/guitarist Syd Barrett, a Camberwell Art School student with an unusual flair for combining kinky imagery ("Arnold Layne," the group's debut single about a transvestite, was banned by the BBC) with all the psychedelic trappings of San Francisco. Indeed, they were the first British group to perform with an accompanying light show. By 1968, however, Barrett had succumbed to the psychic perils of LSD experimentation and had been replaced by David Gilmour. *A Saucerful of Secrets,* released that year, was the band's first real introduction to the U.S. audience and marked the ascendancy of bassist Roger Waters as the spiritual center of the group. Under Waters' leadership, the group eschewed Barrett's three-minute forays into psychedelia in favor of long-winded, spacy sonic voyages that were often based on a single chord. This tendency earned them equal measures of critical praise as the quintessence of art in rock and out-of-hand dismissal as the purveyors of psychedelic muzak. The group reached its zenith in 1973 with the release of *Dark Side of the Moon,* one of the darkest and best-selling rock albums ever. Some 566 weeks and 10 million copies after its release, the album still registered on the pop charts. It was during this period that the group introduced its 360° sound system. The system drew on Waters' background as an architecture student at Regent Street Polytechnic and the expertise of the Light/Sound Workshop from Hornsey Art College. Shortly after its introduction the group was playing "concert halls to audiences as hushed as if they were at a classical event."[38] The group continued in this vein throughout the punk era, crowning the decade with *The Wall* (1979), a number one album that yielded their only number one single, the anthemic critique of formal education, "Another Brick in the Wall."

> *U*ltimately, the canon of art rock that emerged, like the canon of the classical music from which much of it drew inspiration, was a social construct. Inclusion in the art rock category was linked to art school training, to the appropriation of classical and other esoteric resources, even to being British.

Ultimately, the canon of art rock that emerged, like the canon of the classical music from which much of it drew inspiration, was a social construct. Inclusion in the art rock category was linked to art school training, to the appropriation of classical and other esoteric resources, even to being British. Using these criteria, Procol Harum with its nod toward Bach on "A Whiter Shade of Pale" in 1967 was an easy entry. The Bach influence was also enough to place Deep Purple in the art rock category at least for a while, even though the group was heading toward the border of the emerging and much less prestigious category of heavy metal. Because hip critics could not find a constructive way of positioning themselves in relation to Led Zeppelin's ultra-macho presentation, they were excluded from the art rock category despite their broad range of influences. Concept LPs and theatrical stage shows that were more intelligent than most allowed Genesis to be categorized as art rock. Ian Anderson's spirited flute playing and religious musings propelled Jethro Tull into the category. The release of the Who's second rock opera, *Quadrophenia,* was enough to continue the group's association with art. On the other hand, few American groups seemed to meet the criteria. Nobody, for example, thought of Chicago as an art rock group even though several of its members had studied in conservatories or had majored in music at college. Perhaps in the eyes of the critics, the group had too many Top Forty hits to be considered serious or perhaps a horn-based group sounded too much like jazz, which was a different kind of art.

There was, in fact, a jazz rock, or fusion, category that emerged in the early 1970s after Miles Davis' *Bitches Brew* (1970) reached number thirty-five on the pop charts. At the time, a gold jazz album was virtually unthinkable. A full-page ad in *Rolling Stone* boasted: "Critics agree Miles Davis has found a new audience. Or is it that Rock has just found Miles Davis."[39] Jazz rock differed from art rock in that entrants into the category were jazz musicians who were enjoying a brief flirtation with the mainstream audience rather than rock musicians who were drawn to jazz influences. There was virtually no overlap between the two categories. John McLaughlin, who played guitar on *Bitches Brew,* reached the mainstream audience with his Mahavishnu Orchestra on *Inner Mounting Flame* (1971) and *Birds of Fire* (1973). He also teamed up with fellow Sri Chimnoy devotee Carlos Santana for *Love Devotion Surrender* in 1973. Another Davis alumnus, Herbie Hancock, scored with the platinum *Headhunters* in 1974 and finished the decade with three more Top Forty albums. While jazz artists like George Benson and Chuck Mangione achieved mainstream success in the late 1970s, their sound is better described as pop jazz than jazz rock. Jazz rock was almost invariably a repository for black or racially integrated groups while art rock remained the exclusive province of white men.

Art rock was also separate from other forms of black music in significant ways. At a time when most black music was still built around the hit single, art rock focused on extended compositions and LP suites. Typically, art rockers sold far more albums than singles. Among the most successful, Emerson, Lake & Palmer registered eight Top Forty albums between 1971 and 1978; Yes, eleven between 1972 and 1983; Jethro Tull, sixteen between 1969 and 1982; Pink Floyd, seven between 1973 and 1983; and the Moody Blues, thirteen between 1968 and 1986. All of these groups routinely tallied Top Ten album entries and gold record certifications, but throughout the 1970s only one of these groups ever had a Top Ten single—the Moody Blues' "Nights in White Satin" hit number two in 1972. Jethro Tull never even hit the Top Forty with a single, and Pink Floyd and Yes made it to the Top Ten singles charts once, but not until the 1980s. By the late 1960s, however, LPs had surpassed singles as a source of revenue in the music industry. By the early 1970s, it was estimated that about 80 percent of the sales dollars (and

Jazz rock briefly enters the mainstream market

therefore the lion's share of promotional budgets) was in albums. Thus, black music was marginalized financially.

There was also an aesthetic/social dimension to this financial separation. Art rock was often a music of ponderous introspection; it underscored the connection between rock and hallucinogenic drugs. At its most ethereal, it was called "head" music. Clearly, this was a music of the mind, not a music of the body. Nourishment for the body—the "ritual dance music" which drew on increasingly distant African resources—was devalued accordingly. Aside from the racist implications of homologies that suggest the superiority of European/art/mind over African/entertainment/body, the marginalization of black music carried with it the virtual disappearance of stylized partner dancing, which remained on the periphery until it resurfaced with a vengeance during the disco craze. In the interim, it was replaced by the broadly interpretative and highly individualized free-form swirling that sometimes accompanied "journeys to the center of the mind."

Sweeter Soul Music

African American artists seldom shrank from their role as entertainers since that role allowed their creativity to shine. In the black community, commercial success was regarded less as a compromise than as a necessity. As differences in material reality and political strategy occasioned a separation of black and white communities in the late 1960s, however, the music press often decried the commercialism of black popular music while praising the artistry of rock, even r&b-based rock. "The soul and R & B strains of Janis Joplin, Rod Stewart, Joe Cocker, and Van Morrison were praised," Iain Chambers has said, "while Ray Charles and Aretha Franklin, not to mention the unredeemable Tamla Motown stable (with the precise exception of the 'progressive' Stevie Wonder), were accused of decaying in the swamps of a commercial jungle."[40] If the music press tended to deprecate black music, radio tended to ignore it entirely. Jerry Wexler, Atlantic's primary rhythm and blues producer, has said that, by 1971, radio stations did not want to "burden" their listeners "with the sound of breaking glass in Watts or the sirens coming from Detroit, which is what r&b music meant at the time, . . . so they took most of it off the radio."[41] Hardly above criticism themselves, Atlantic responded to this situation by changing direction to focus primarily on its British rock acts, just as its former soul partner, Stax, was about to begin its long and torturous descent into bankruptcy, a saga that paralleled the trajectory of the Civil Rights movement itself.

Wexler's comment suggests there was a connection between the decline of r&b on the radio and the political shift that marked the end of the tumultuousness associated

As differences in material reality and political strategy occasioned a separation of black and white communities in the late 1960s the music press often decried the commercialism of black popular music while praising the artistry of rock, even r&b-based rock.

with the 1960s. Certainly by the early 1970s, the Civil Rights movement appeared to have run its course, and civil rights themes declined in popular music. While War scored with "The World Is a Ghetto" in 1972, by 1973, only the Spinners' "Ghetto Child" and Stevie Wonder's "Living for the City" were noticeable in the pop singles market. There was a corresponding decline in the popularity of southern soul, the militant-sounding strain of r&b from the deep South. Arthur Conley, Percy Sledge, and Sam and Dave disappeared from the Top Forty after 1968, and by then, Otis Redding had died. Wilson Pickett lasted until 1972 and then faded from pop view. That same year, Ike and Tina Turner had their last Top Ten hit of the decade. Soul music had not disappeared completely; instead outside social forces altered its character.

As radicalism in the black community was repressed either by the cooptation of key leaders or by the more sinister effectiveness of the FBI's COINTELPRO (Counter-Intelligence Program) operation, there was a fleeting attempt to use the music industry as a proving ground for black capitalism, which was then pushed as an alternative to urban violence. The music industry was quite aware of discrimination within its own ranks. At the 1969 convention of the National Association of Television and Radio Announcers (NATRA), Stan Gortikov, then president of Capitol, had accused the industry of being "too damn white."[42] Earlier that year, at a conference held by the Recording Industry Association of America (RIAA), New York Senator Jacob Javits had expressed the "hope that the industry . . . will move forward . . . by striking a resounding note for black capitalism."[43]

The flurry of rhetoric and action that ensued over the next few years produced some interesting, if paradoxical, results. Having declined on the singles charts from 34 percent in 1968 to 24 percent in 1971, artists of color then accounted for an all-time high of 44 percent of the best-selling singles in 1972. From a dramatic decrease on the album charts to just 12 percent in 1971, they rebounded to 24 percent one year later. During this time, there had been a short-lived and highly controversial breakthrough of sorts for African Americans in Hollywood in the form of black-oriented movies like "Shaft," "Superfly," and "Troubleman" (the so-called blaxploitation films). The soundtracks for these movies were scored by Isaac Hayes, Curtis Mayfield, and Marvin Gaye, respectively. Still, soundtrack albums alone do not account for the substantial presence of African Americans on the pop charts in 1972. There are two other developments that come closer to explaining the dramatic increases: the emergence of a number of African American artists as album-oriented acts and the popularization of softer soul sounds that would provide one of the building blocks for disco.

If there was a dominant black sound that reflected the seemingly quieter mood of the early 1970s, it was Philadelphia soft soul, which was pioneered by the writer-producer team of Kenny Gamble and Leon Huff and producer-arranger Thom Bell who joined forces with Sigma Sound Studios. The three men collaborated in the tripartite administration of Mighty Three Music, the publishing company they formed for their music. Having come of age in Philadelphia in the early 1960s, Gamble, Huff, and Bell were no strangers to a predominantly white music scene. Gamble had sessioned for Leiber and Stoller in New York and had helped to produce Danny and the Juniors' "At the Hop." When he returned to Philadelphia, he formed the Romeos with Thom Bell on keyboards. After Bell was replaced by Huff, Gamble teamed up with Huff to do freelance production projects for Atlantic and other labels. The two scored their first Top Ten hit with the blue-eyed Soul Survivors' "Expressway to Your Heart" on Crimson. Bell worked at Cameo and, when the label folded in 1968, moved to Philly Groove with the Delfonics. There he produced the group's blockbuster hit, "La La Means I Love You." Gamble and Huff quickly followed suit with a series of novelty songs for the Intruders, "Cowboys to Girls" and "(Love Is Like a) Baseball Game." After these, they resuscitated the flagging career of Jerry Butler with a new persona—The Iceman—and smoothed out the rough edges of soul on his "Only the Strong Survive," "Moody Woman," and "What's the Use of Breaking Up." In doing so, they perfected the production style that would be described in *Rolling Stone* as "not as bluesy as the Memphis/Muscle Shoals stuff, not as pop as Detroit."[44]

In the long run, Gamble and Huff infused the market with romantic ballads and stylish dance music more than they rejuvenated the Civil Rights movement with a message of black liberation.

In a five-year period, Gamble and Huff produced thirty million-selling singles, with twenty-two records on the charts in 1968 alone. In 1970, the duo grossed over $1 million. Even so, the two did not hit their stride until 1971. In that year, Gamble and Huff formed Philadelphia International Records (PIR) and made a distribution deal with CBS Records. The deal was important to the team financially because it offered economic self-sufficiency, but it was also important to Gamble personally. Gamble was a nationalist with inclinations toward Islam. He saw PIR as a platform for pushing a message; thus, in the words of Nelson George, "Gamble and Huff contemplated slavery (the O'Jays' mini-epic "Ship A'Hoy"), ecology ("The Air I Breathe"), spiritual enlightenment ("Wake Up Everybody"), corruption ("Bad Luck"), and the male-dominated nuclear family ("Family Reunion")."[45] In the context of the increasingly conservative Nixon-Ford era, however, certain aspects of nationalism (economic self-sufficiency, for example) resonated as well with Nixon's call for black capitalism as with the development of a strong opposition movement. In the long run, Gamble and Huff infused the market with romantic ballads and stylish dance music more than they rejuvenated the Civil Rights movement with a message of black liberation.

Gamble and Huff's two biggest groups—Harold Melvin and the Blue Notes ("If You Don't Know Me By Now," "The Love I Lost") and the O'Jays ("Back Stabbers," "Love Train," "I Love Music," "Use Ta Be My Girl")—were produced throughout the 1970s with what critic Jim Miller called an "urbane glossiness."[46] During the same time, Thom Bell drew on the classical training he had received as a youngster to provide lush orchestral arrangements over a polite rhythmic pulse for the Stylistics ("Betcha By Golly,

Wow," "Break Up to Make Up," "You Make Me Feel Brand New") on the Avco label, and the Spinners ("I'll Be Around," "Could it Be I'm Falling in Love," "The Rubberband Man," "Working My Way Back to You/ Forgive Me, Girl") on Atlantic. By the mid-1970s, MFSB (Mother Father Sister Brother), the massive integrated house band at Sigma Studios, and its back-up vocal trio, The Three Degrees, had become hitmakers in their own right. In 1974, their recordings of "TSOP (The Sound of Philadelphia)" and "When Will I See You Again," were numbers one and two, respectively, on the charts. Together, these groups set the standard in black popular music for the first half of the decade and anticipated one strand of the disco craze that was about to erupt.

Other artists quickly tuned into the new soft soul sound. In Chicago there were the Chi-Lites ("Oh Girl") and the ever-changing Isley Brothers ("That Lady"). Even southern soul yielded the velvety smooth Al Green ("Let's Stay Together," "I'm Still in Love With You"). One of the most striking things about all of the soft soul groups was just how long many of them had been together. The Chi-Lites had formed in 1961. The Isley Brothers had their first hit in 1959. The Spinners had begun in 1957 as Harvey Fuqua's back-up

The Spinners started as Harvey Fuqua's backup group, the Moonglows, in 1957, but didn't achieve major success on their own until the 1970s. In that decade, they straddled the fence between soft soul and disco.

group, the Moonglows. When Fuqua took the group to his new Tri-Phi label in the early 1960s, their name was changed to the Spinners. Personnel changes and moves to Motown and VIP eventually led to the group's 1970s configuration and five gold albums on Atlantic. The O'Jays had begun in Canton, Ohio, as the Triumphs in 1958. The group changed its name in the early 1960s to honor Eddie O'Jay, the Cleveland deejay who showed them the ropes. They had been signed by Imperial, Bell, and Minit before they came to the attention of Gamble and Huff in the late 1960s. At PIR, between 1972 and the end of the decade, they had six gold and three platinum LPs.[47] The fact that it took so many years for these groups to peak says something about their perseverance and speaks to the strength of the forces arrayed against them.

If Philadelphia soul had supplanted its rougher southern variant, it was also clear that the heyday of vintage Motown had ended. The Supremes were performing without Diana Ross, and the Miracles, without Smokey Robinson. David Ruffin and Eddie Kendricks had left the Temptations (in 1968 and 1971, respectively) because of disputes with the record company. The Marvelettes and Martha and the Vandellas were already a thing of the past. After a $22 million lawsuit, Holland-Dozier-Holland, Motown's top producer team, left the label to form their own Invictus imprint. The Four Tops followed them to the new label in 1971. Two years later, Gladys Knight and the Pips moved to Buddah where white singer/songwriter Jim Weatherly supplied them with some of their biggest hits, including their only number one single, "Midnight Train to Georgia."

Still, while Motown may have been down, it was not out, thanks to the Jackson 5. Their first four releases on the label—"I Want You Back," "ABC," "The Love You Save," and "I'll Be There"—all rose to number one on the pop charts in 1970. The next two— "Mamma's Pearl" and "Never Can Say Goodbye" went to number two in 1971. This kind of success with debut releases was almost unheard of. From Berry Gordy's perspective, the success of the Jackson 5 proved that his upbeat pop orientation still worked. To some critics, however, such releases appeared to be a throwback to Motown formula production. "One has the feeling, whether it's true or not," said Jon Landau, "that Berry Gordy passes personal judgment on every single that comes out on his label."[48] For many of the label's veterans, however, Gordy's centralized control, once necessary to the survival of the organization, was artistic constraint. Gordy would have to be dragged, kicking and screaming, toward a new point of view. It was Stevie Wonder and Marvin Gaye, two important exceptions to the initial talent drain at Motown, who accomplished this.

When he turned twenty-one in 1972, Stevie Wonder demanded the royalty payments that had been held in trust for him by Gordy since he was a child. Wonder spent about $250,000 of this money on the production of *Music of My Mind* (1972), which reintroduced him to the white audience as a progressive act. At about the same time, Wonder gained control of his own publishing; he was the first Motown artist to do so. Subsequent progressive albums—*Talking Book* (1972), *Innervisions* (1973), *Fulfillingness' First Finale* (1974), and *Songs in the Key of Life* (1976)—were all top five albums and

Marvin Gaye, Stevie Wonder, War become album-oriented artists

confirmed his position as a crossover star. Gaye spent years trying to convince Gordy to back him as an album artist. He finally succeeded in 1971 when *What's Goin' On* was released. It was followed by *Let's Get It On* (1973). Both of Gaye's albums went Top Ten. Although Motown released smash hit singles by the Jackson 5, the new Temptations, and the solo Diana Ross throughout the 1970s, it was Stevie Wonder and Marvin Gaye who introduced the company to the financial joys of independent production and album-oriented releases.

It was not just the album-oriented releases of Stevie Wonder and Marvin Gaye that did well. War, which had been Eric Burdon's back-up band on MGM until the group went out on their own on United Artists (UA) in 1971, released eight albums between 1972 and 1977, four of which made the Top Ten, all of which were certified gold or platinum. UA tried to take credit for the group's success, pointing to the label's nondiscriminatory policy of promoting black acts no differently from white acts. Jerry Wexler, however, had a different explanation: "The old myth used to be that an r&b record could sell maybe 200,000 copies and, in order to get any real muscle in sales, [it] had to sell pop (to whites). But now I think millions of sales are possible on 'secret service' hits—records that whites may not really be familiar with."[49] Whatever the truth, War's mellow grooves seemed consonant with the tenor of the new times. The group's music ("Slippin' into Darkness" and "The Cisco Kid") tended toward a laid-back rhythmic base with a funky r&b feel.

James Brown adapted to the new political era by singing a new political tune. The political establishment had been wooing Brown since the late 1960s, but the streetwise artist had always seemed to project a clear sense of where his sympathies lay. In 1970, *Rolling Stone* quoted him as saying, "Me and Nixon don't get along. He asked me to go along to Memphis in the campaign. I don't want to be his bullet proof vest. I didn't want to protect him from my people, deceive them. Make them think he's with me and I'm with him."[50] In 1972, however, his loyalties changed. Whether it was Nixon's support for black capitalism or his alleged six-figure contribution to Brown, in that year Brown endorsed Nixon for the presidency, a move that compromised Brown's credibility in the traditionally Democratic black community. Soul Brother No. 1 became, in the eyes of his detractors, Sold Brother No. 1. He had his last pop hits of the decade in 1974, the year Nixon resigned, and did not return to the Top Forty until the film *Rocky IV* propelled "Living in America" to number four in 1986.

Aretha Franklin also faded from the Top Ten charts. She hit the Top Ten for the last time in the 1970s in 1974 with "Until You Come Back to Me (That's What I'm Gonna Do)" and did not achieve that position again until 1985 with "Freeway of Love." It was not that her career dissolved; there were a few lesser hits and some successful albums. Still, between 1976 and 1981, she did not place a single entry in the Top Forty albums or singles. To be sure there were personal problems that affected her recording career, but, perhaps more importantly, in the less militant 1970s, her sound no longer appeared to be the compelling force it once was. Indeed, by the early 1970s a good deal of rhythm and blues seemed to have lost its edge. Almost everywhere, black popular music seemed less feisty than it had been. It wasn't that there was no great black popular music being produced; there was, but it no longer had the insistence of southern soul. The operatic Roberta Flack hit the number one slot three times in three years for Atlantic with singles as soothing as they were beautiful—"The First Time Ever I Saw Your Face" (1972), "Killing Me Softly with His Song" (1973), and "Feel Like Makin' Love" (1974). Her duets with Donny Hathaway were equally delicious. Taking romantic sincerity all the way to self-parody, Barry White, backed by his Love Unlimited female trio and the forty-piece, string-laden Love Unlimited Orchestra, produced hits such as "I'm Gonna Love You Just a Little More Baby" and "Never, Never Gonna Give Ya Up" (1973) and "Can't Get Enough of Your Love, Babe" and "You're the First, the Last, My Everything" (1974). Both Flack and White joined the ranks of successful album artists. Flack had eight gold records to her credit; White had five gold and two platinum.

> *By the early 1970s a good deal of rhythm and blues seemed to have lost its edge. Almost everywhere, black popular music seemed less feisty than it had been. It wasn't that there was no great black popular music being produced; there was, but it no longer had the insistence of southern soul.*

White's saccharine grunting and groaning had actually been anticipated by Isaac Hayes on *Hot Buttered Soul,* which had been released on Stax's Enterprise label in 1969. Hayes' eighteen-minute version of "By the Time I Get to Phoenix" with its extended spoken word intro of murmured declarations of love made the album the best-selling LP in Stax's history and might have provided the company with an entree to the softer sounds of the 1970s if it had not been about to be buried under the pressures of high finance. By the start of the decade Stax had become a multimillion dollar corporation built on practices that were no more disreputable than those of the rest of the industry but no less either. Under the leadership of Al Bell, the company had entered a new period of political engagement with ties to Richard Prior and the Reverend Jesse Jackson.

Sales were fine, and a new distribution deal with CBS provided the company with $6 million in capital advances.

In 1972, the label undertook its most ambitious project, Wattstax, a spectacular benefit concert in Los Angeles to commemorate the 1965 Watts uprising. The concert featured all the Stax stars, and in many ways, it was a success. A feature-length film and a six-sided album resulted from it, and almost $100,000 in charitable contributions were divided among such organizations as the Sickle Cell Anemia Foundation, the Martin Luther King, Jr., General Hospital in Los Angeles, and Jesse Jackson's Operation PUSH (People United to Save Humanity) in Chicago. Without question, the concert underscored the connection between southern soul and black power. At the same time, however, it revealed identity problems and political tensions within the company. Why was Stax promoting a benefit in Los Angeles? What had they done for hometown Memphis? As these questions were being raised within the company, the IRS launched an investigation into the company's business operations and turned up a number of highly unorthodox business expenditures. Over the next few years, Stax—Al Bell in particular—was dogged by a series of grand jury investigations into a variety of money-laundering and kickback schemes. The unceremonious firing of Clive Davis as president of CBS Records in 1973 because of alleged high-level drug improprieties did not help; CBS was distributing Stax at the time. By the time Bell was cleared of all charges against him in 1976, Stax had already closed its doors. Jim Stewart, Stax's conservative white founder, defended his partner's honesty, adding that Bell "got too involved in politics and not enough in the record business."[51] Given what Stax's music signified politically, it may well have been impossible for any black man to avoid doing this. Still, it was clear that the times demanded a new cultural orientation. Philadelphia provided soft soul sounds; white singer/songwriters provided soft rock.

Singer/Songwriters, Soft Rock Solutions, and More

The singer/songwriters of the 1970s were intensely personal—at times intimate, at times introspective, at times confessional. In the aspirations of rock toward art, they represented an attempt to apply lyric poetry to semiautobiographical themes. As a trend in popular music, they were born of the 1960s and edged toward a break with that same era. In them, the introspection of the drug culture manifested itself in a level of self-disclosure that, a decade before, only a psychiatrist would have heard. At the same time, this turning inward signaled a retreat from—or was it a reevaluation of?—the politics of the 1960s.

In the radical movements of the 1960s, personal concerns were often treated as psychological inadequacies that got in the way of revolutionary transformation. It was, of course, women who figured out that this usually meant that men did not have to deal with their own oppressive tendencies at the level of interpersonal relations, which meant, in turn, that the complete liberation of women would be deferred until after the revolution. The articulation of the powerfully simple feminist maxim "the personal is political" rendered all such thinking invalid. Now power relations had to be considered at all levels. Vulnerability was no longer a sign of political weakness; it was an essential ingredient in any trusting relationship. For radicals, of course, this was a tricky proposition. Openness and honesty could undermine revolutionary discipline; the lack of it could destroy the bonds of trust. At its best, a successful resolution of this tension tended toward equalizing power at least among individuals, although frequently positions on all sides were exaggerated beyond parody along the way. At its worst, such thinking was considered soft. And soft was not the stuff that revolutions were made of.

Soft was not the stuff that rock was about at the turn of the decade. Indeed, until the appearance of the singer/songwriters, the words "soft" and "rock" would not have appeared in the same sentence. Hard rock was perceived as male in its loud, aggressive tone and phallic connection to instruments; soft rock represented the female side of the equation.

Soft was also not the stuff that rock was about at the turn of the decade. Indeed, until the appearance of the singer/songwriters, the words "soft" and "rock" would not have appeared in the same sentence. Surprisingly, at a time when most rock was rough, this new music was gentle; when most rock was deafening, its amplification was modest; while rock sought to let it all hang out, its tone was reserved. At the time, hard rock was perceived as male in its loud, aggressive tone and phallic connection to instruments; soft rock represented the female side of the equation. The results were mixed. On the plus side, soft rock was the first style since the advent of rock 'n' roll that allowed women to sing in their own voice and encouraged men to try on new personas. On the minus side, its gentleness could sound mousy and its self-revelations could approach masochism or cliché.

If an appearance of vulnerability is used to define soft rock, then singer/songwriter Joni Mitchell heads the list. Her romantic involvements (with David Crosby, producer of her first album *Songs to a Seagull* [1967], Graham Nash, the inspiration for "Willy" on *Clouds* [1969], and James Taylor, "My Old Man" on *Blue* [1971]) were more widely noted than her music and frequently submerged consideration of her artistry beneath the tabloid tales of her life. Mitchell bore some responsibility for the situation herself, as she devoted much of her considerable talent—a near three-octave range, intricate melodies, and elegant lyrics—to exploring the exquisite pain of her amorous ups and downs. Still, critic Robert Christgau saw the influence of feminism at work, even if Mitchell herself would not have worn the label. Said Christgau, commenting on *Blue:*

> Like her voice, Joni Mitchell's lyrics have always suggested emotional life with startling highs and lows and an attenuated middle. Just because she knows herself, she reveals how dangerous and attractive such a life can be, especially for women. . . . In a male performer such intense self-concern would be an egotistic cop-out. In a woman it is an act of defiance.
>   Not that Mitchell herself has always perceived it that way.[52]

Soft rock opens possible new approaches for women and men

Soft rock risks becoming too introspective, self-absorbed

Signed to Reprise in 1967, Mitchell's first big break came in 1968 when Judy Collins scored a Top Ten hit with her "Both Sides Now." As her career progressed, Mitchell moved from acoustic accompaniment to a soft rock band and switched to Asylum, where she was more protected from prying reporters. While she generated a handful of Top Forty hits—"Big Yellow Taxi," "You Turn Me On, I'm a Radio," "Help Me"—she was first and foremost an album artist (she even painted a number of her own album covers). After turning out eight gold or platinum LPs in the 1970s, she turned toward jazz. She had hoped her crowning achievement of the decade would be a collaboration with jazz bassist Charles Mingus, but he died before recording could commence. *Mingus,* her tribute album, broke her run of gold certifications. She returned to more accessible material in the 1980s and switched labels for the last time to Geffen.

Second only to Mitchell in self-absorption was James Taylor, another singer/songwriter and Mitchell's one-time lover. As a performer, he was unquestionably talented. On stage, he was always polite, if somewhat wooden, the antithesis of in-your-face 1960s rockers. To the trained observer, his overly laid-back demeanor may have suggested the frequent bouts of depression or the heroin addiction that characterized his late teens. To his critics, however, his demeanor exuded the kind of mellowness that Woody Allen was talking about when he said something to the effect that he did not like getting too mellow because he was afraid he would ripen and rot. Robert Christgau once recounted a story of how the late Lester Bangs had wanted to run Taylor through "with a broken-off Ripple bottle," and went on to say, "Me, I only took the poster from his third album and ripped it into four or five pieces. Then I hung the face on my wall and scrawled upon it slogans from imaginary Maoist comic books, e.g.: 'Eat felt-tipped death, capitalist pig!'"[53]

Of course, the response to Taylor would not have been so virulent had he not become so famous. Originally signed to the Beatles' Apple label by Peter Asher, Taylor's self-titled debut album caused little stir even with the appearance of Paul McCartney and George Harrison. It was not until he returned to the United States with Asher in tow as his new manager and switched to Warner that his star began to rise. His first album for the company, *Sweet Baby James* (1970), became one of the defining sounds of the soft rock genre and went platinum to boot. For the next eleven years, Taylor enjoyed nothing less than gold album sales. His 1972 marriage to Carly Simon simply heightened his visibility. Despite Taylor's skill as a songwriter (*Sweet Baby James* contained some of his best material including the title song, "Fire and Rain," and "Country Road"), most of his hit singles were covers of other artists' material—Carole King's "You've Got a Friend" (1971), Marvin Gaye's "How Sweet It Is (To Be Loved By You)" (1975), and Jimmy Jones' "Handy Man" (1977). Taylor also joined Simon and Garfunkel on Sam Cooke's "What a Wonderful World" and hit number five with Carly Simon on Charlie and Inez Foxx's "Mockingbird" in 1974.

Carly Simon had tried to launch a career as a recording artist in the 1960s, but when differences with manager Albert Grossman (also Dylan's manager) scuttled a 1966 Columbia recording session, she spent the next few years regrouping. She signed with Elektra in 1970 and hit the Top Thirty with her self-titled debut album in 1971. The LP's hit single, "That's the Way I've Always Heard It Should Be," hinted at a feminist influence in its exploration of the deadening effects of marriage. The following year, her number one single, "You're So Vain," which was released

> In the end, the independence that Carly Simon projected was more a function of economic privilege than political choice.

just after her marriage to James Taylor, prompted endless queries as to whether Mick Jagger (who sang back-up vocals) or Warren Beatty (a rumored earlier affair) was the subject of the song. If nothing else, the queries placed her square in the middle of the rock aristocracy that framed her experience. In the end, the independence that Simon projected was more a function of economic privilege (she was an heir to the Simon and Schuster publishing empire) than political choice. The album cover photograph for *Hotcakes* (1974) revealed an upper-class coquette rather than a role model for young women. This image was reinforced when her "Nobody Does It Better" (the title song for the James Bond thriller, *The Spy Who Loved Me*) reached number two in 1977.

Carole King was neither consumed by politics nor driven to share the intimate details of her private life with the record-buying public. She never tried to become "one of the boys," but she also never felt compelled to ooze sex. She seemed at home with herself, a calm during the storm. She appeared forthright and genuine, a "natural woman" if you will. She projected contentment at a time when most listeners were suspicious of it in their own lives. She wrote with a personal touch, sang in a conversational tone, and, in 1971, outsold everyone in the music business. But, then, she had been in the business much longer than most of her contemporaries. While most of soft rock's singer/songwriters could trace their roots to the folk revival of the early 1960s, King was a seasoned Brill Building professional before that movement even started. By 1961, before she was out of her teens, she and Gerry Goffin, her lyricist husband, were already collecting royalties on their first major hit, the Shirelles' "Will You Love Me Tomorrow." In 1962, she had her own pop hit as a solo vocalist, "It Might as Well Rain until September." After she and

Goffin were divorced, she and their two daughters moved to the West Coast where she continued to write songs. By the end of the decade, she was both composer and lyricist. A contract with Lou Adler's Ode Records launched her career as a full-fledged singer/songwriter. Her first outing, *Carole King: Writer* (1970), failed to crack the Top Forty, but her second, *Tapestry* (1971), broke all existing records.

Tapestry contained its share of sentimentality, but it was never disingenuous. On an artistic level, all of its elements worked in synergy—King's genius as a songwriter, the understated sensuality of her lightly r&b-inflected piano playing, the warm and friendly voice you could believe in. Another key ingredient was Adler's uncluttered production. *Tapestry* "was a very naked sounding album," he said. "I wanted it to sound like she was in the room playing piano for you."[54] In its first year, *Tapestry* ended up in 5 million rooms. It remained in the Top Forty for sixty-eight weeks and was located at number one for fifteen of them. Within five years, the album had sold 13 million copies, becoming the best-selling record of all time. It also garnered an impressive four Grammies: Album of the Year, Song of the Year ("You've Got a Friend"), Record of the Year (*It's Too Late*), and Best Female Pop Vocalist.

Tapestry was such an outstanding achievement—"a triumph of mass culture," said Christgau—that it would be difficult to fault King for not repeating its success. The album provided her with the means to withdraw from touring almost completely and she did. She adopted a strict no-interview policy, becoming, in the words of Katherine Orloff, "a housewife who writes songs."[55] While she turned out seven more Top Forty albums before the decade was out, by the late 1970s she had moved to Idaho and had limited her live performances to occasional appearances at benefits. Despite the substantial presence of women among the singer/songwriters, life on the road was still largely the province of men.

Although Australian-born Helen Reddy is seldom classified as a singer/songwriter because she was essentially a nightclub singer who introduced material by singer/songwriters into her act, she also wrote, and it was her composition "I Am Woman" (cowritten with Ray Burton) that announced feminism to the mainstream audience in 1972. As a feminist, Reddy took heat from all sides. The obvious connection of "I Am Woman" to feminism angered conservatives and prompted radio to demur from playing it; the easy-listening, pop feel of the song made it odious to radicals. In her own way, Reddy was committed to the women's movement (at one point she even started her own Hollywood Hills consciousness-raising group) but she never strayed far from its more centrist tendencies. She also set her priorities carefully. "I am first and foremost a singer," she told historian Gillian Gaar. "That's how I earn my living. I don't earn my living as a feminist."[56] All the same, Reddy would be the first to admit that the women's movement had an obvious effect on her career, as it did on the other female performers of the era.

In the early 1970s, all the women in rock (and a good many men) were affected by the women's movement to some degree, and whether they were singer/songwriters or not, the women rockers who came into their own during this era—among them, Maria Muldaur, Melissa Manchester, Bonnie Raitt, and Linda Ronstadt—all took a soft rock approach in their music. Maria Muldaur knocked around the acoustic folk scene for years with her husband Jeff of Jim Kweskin's Jug Band before she achieved solo success with the balmy "Midnight at the Oasis" in 1974. Melissa Manchester studied under Paul Simon at the High School of Performing Arts in New York before moving on to middle-level soft rock success on her own.

Linda Ronstadt's sexpot image—one reviewer referred to her as "an impossibly cuddly chicklet"—may have advanced her career on one level, but it tended to overshadow a determined personality and a considerable talent.

Bonnie Raitt always seemed destined for superstardom, but at the beginning of the 1970s, it was still some twenty years away. Her love of blues and proficiency on electric slide guitar—as well as her Quaker upbringing and political activism—set her apart from most of her contemporaries. Still, she did not overwhelm her audiences (in the beginning, she performed sitting down), she communicated with them . . . respectfully. Linda Ronstadt found a pop niche much earlier. She had already experienced major success as the lead singer for the Stone Poneys ("Different Drummer," 1967). She went solo at the end of the 1960s, steadily built her career, and achieved number one status with her album *Heart Like a Wheel* and its hit single "You're No Good," both of which were released in 1974. Ronstadt went on to become one of the most successful solo female vocalists of the decade with nothing but gold and platinum albums to her credit, including two more that were number one—*Simple Dreams* (1977) and *Living in the USA* (1978). Ronstadt combined Carly Simon's penchant for "cheesecake" photographs on her album covers with Joni Mitchell's inability to separate her personal life from her professional life. "I have no self-control," she told an interviewer in 1974. "When I meet somebody I really admire and I trust, which has to be somebody I'm involved with businesswise, I always end up having a sexual relationship with him. Then it blows it."[57] Ronstadt's sexpot image—one reviewer referred to her as "an impossibly cuddly chicklet"—may have advanced her career on one level, but it tended to overshadow a determined personality and a considerable talent.

All of these women had an awareness of themselves as female performers, all of them wrestled with the contradictions of life on the road, and all of them grappled publicly with the difficulties of expressing their sexuality comfortably. The fact that they all were channeled toward soft rock solutions presented a different kind of dilemma. To the extent that soft rock offered a vehicle for more personal communication, it was progressive for women. But to the extent that it looked to acoustic folk as its model, it was regressive in form, and not just for women but for rock as a whole. Many of the men who were categorized as soft rockers or singer/songwriters—from major stars like James Taylor and Paul Simon to lesser known artists like Jonathan Edwards, Jim Croce, Harry Chapin and Mac Davis—were identified with a retreat from rock. "[James] Taylor is leading a retreat," said Christgau in 1972, "and the reason why us rock and rollers are so mad at him is simply because the retreat has been so successful."[58] Artists like British-born Cat Stevens and Canadian Gordon Lightfoot, both of whom began recording in mid-1960s, added to the perception of regression. Influenced by the hippie mysticism of Donovan, Stevens, who was described by one reviewer as "the English James Taylor," came to the attention of the U.S. market in 1971 with the release of *Tea for the Tillerman*, which included the hit single "Wild World." As critic Stephen Holden has noted, "Although his records were pretty, they were quite vacuous."[59] Nine Top Forty albums later, Stevens began to tire of the music business. After his 1979 conversion to Islam, he withdrew from it completely. Lightfoot was a folkie who had written songs for Peter, Paul & Mary, Marty Robbins, and others in the mid-1960s. His seven Top Forty albums between 1971 and 1978, including the number one *Sundown* (1974), set him up for a comfortable recording career in the 1980s, even though his music seemed to be a throwback to an earlier time. Similarly, (Jim) Seals and (Dash) Crofts ("Summer Breeze," 1972) sounded far more reserved than they had when they first started playing with the Champs in 1958. Nevertheless, six gold albums established them as a solid soft rock act. Even more successful were folk-rockers America ("A Horse With No Name," 1972), who had eight Top Forty albums to their credit.

The singer/songwriter category also included some variation, particularly among the critics' choices for the "next Dylan"—David Bromberg, Loudon Wainwright III, John

Prine, Steve Goodman, even the early Bruce Springsteen, and a range of cult-figure types, including Leonard Cohen, the poet, Tom Waits, the beatnik barfly who claimed to have slept through the 1960s, and Randy Newman whose wry humor more than balanced the earnestness of most of others in the field. Many of Newman's compositions were clever dramatic narratives that dealt with such issues as racism and other forms of discrimination ("Sail Away," "Rednecks," "Short People"), but often from the point of view of the perpetrators, which left the listener to grapple with an uncomfortable ambiguity. The narrator on "Rednecks," for example, boasted about "keeping our 'nigras' down" and poked fun at the "smart-ass New York Jew." Newman was too talented to be dismissed out of hand, but one often had to wonder whether his Swiftian irony crossed the line.

Bruce Springsteen can be classified as a singer/songwriter in the same sense that Van Morrison or the solo John Lennon can be. They all composed personal, poetic verse. They also belted it out with incredible intensity; they were hardly soft. Following the breakup of Them, Morrison tasted success on his first solo album *Blowin' Your Mind* (1967), which had the hit single "Brown Eyed Girl." After a dry spell that included the failure of the critically acclaimed *Astral Weeks*, he regained his footing in 1970 with *Moondance* and *His Band and the Street Choir*. The latter of these yielded the single "Domino," which made the Top Ten. At his most confessional, Lennon transformed months of primal scream therapy into singles like "Cold Turkey" and album cuts like "Mother," from his first solo LP, *John Lennon/Plastic Ono Band* (1970), the album that included "Working Class Hero." Springsteen was that working-class hero.

Bruce Springsteen demonstrated that singer/songwriters did not have to be hamstrung by the parameters of soft rock.

There were a number of reasons for promoting Bruce Springsteen as the new Dylan. He was signed to Columbia by the same John Hammond who had brought Dylan himself (not to mention Billie Holiday and Benny Goodman) to the label. Furthermore, on his first two albums—*Greetings From Asbury Park, N.J.* (1973) and *The Wild, the Innocent, and the E Street Shuffle* (1974)—he exhibited Dylan's tendency to fill a song with more words than a line could hold. At the same time, Springsteen, who grew up in the resort towns of the Jersey shore, could evoke images of everyday working-class lives that were as powerful as they were sympathetic. His live shows were raw, brash, and full of energy, often extending to the three-hour range. Songs like "Rosalita" from his second album were absolute showstoppers. More than any other performer, Springsteen demonstrated that singer/songwriters did not have to be hamstrung by the parameters of soft rock. To his followers, he was a legend even before Jon Landau wrote in 1974: "I saw rock and roll's future and its name is Bruce Springsteen."

It was *Born to Run* (1975) that provided Springsteen with the creative and commercial breakthrough he needed to crack the Top Ten, but the breakthrough did not come without a price. Always a disciplined artist and an exacting craftsman, Springsteen

Bruce Springsteen combined working class roots and social consciousness with riveting live performances. Even as a superstar in the age of video he remained essentially a live artist who could project working class solidarity with credibility.

hit a creative block in the midst of *Born to Run,* and Landau was brought in to guide the album to completion. For his work, he shared a coproducer's credit with Springsteen and Mike Appel, Springsteen's manager. On its release, the album was hailed as a rock masterpiece. "Thunder Road," and "Jungleland" became instant rock classics. The LP hit number three and propelled Springsteen to national fame. In the last week of October that year, both *Time* and *Newsweek* pictured him on their covers (perhaps one of the ancillary benefits of having a critic as a producer). At about this time, however, Springsteen began to part ways with Appel over career direction. When the artist insisted on using Landau as the producer for his next album, his manager refused. The ensuing lawsuits kept Springsteen tied up in court for the next year. By the time *Darkness on the Edge of Town* was released in 1978, a number of its cuts, including the title track, "Badlands," and "The Promised Land," were already live performance favorites.

Throughout the remainder of the 1970s, Springsteen matured both musically and politically. He pared down his music, unleashed the fury of his guitar, and created ever more vivid images. In 1979, he took a step that moved him closer to the activism that would characterize his career in the 1980s. As a favor to his friend Jackson Browne, he agreed to headline two shows for No Nukes, a weeklong series of concerts protesting the construction of nuclear power plants in the wake of the Harrisburg, Pennsylvania, Three Mile Island disaster. The concerts were held at Madison Square Garden and sponsored by Musicians United for Safe Energy (MUSE). MUSE represented a coalition of antinuclear groups. Bonnie Raitt was among its active artists. John Hall, formerly of Orleans ("Dance with Me," "Still the One"), was also a central figure and provided the group with its anthem, "Power." Jackson Browne sat on the MUSE Board. Browne had come into his own as a solo vocalist with "Doctor My Eyes" in 1972. In the latter half of the decade, *The Pretender* (produced by Landau) and *Running on Empty* moved him into the Top Ten as an album-oriented artist. As a singer/songwriter he was as self-confessional as any of them, but he had an activist spirit. He joined the antinuclear movement in the mid-1970s and performed for the Clamshell Alliance in New Hampshire and the Alliance for Survival in California. Eventually, he was arrested with demonstrators at California's Diablo Canyon nuclear power plant.

At first glance, No Nukes appeared to be soft rock heaven. Along with Raitt, Hall, and Browne, James Taylor, Carly Simon, and Crosby, Stills, and Nash were on the bill, but the bill also included Springsteen, the Doobie Brothers, and newcomer Tom Petty, not to mention Chaka Khan, Sweet Honey in the Rock, and Gil Scott-Heron. In fact, it was Scott-Heron who had first raised the issue of nuclear power in song. A political singer/songwriter if there ever was one, Scott-Heron had started as a poet and novelist and had then begun to collaborate with musician Brian Jackson to deliver his message in a new medium. He is perhaps best known for his anti-apartheid "Johannesburg" from the album *From South Africa to South Carolina* (1975). The South Carolina half of the title referred to the song "South Carolina (Barnwell)," which protested plans to build a reprocessing plant for nuclear waste in Barnwell. Two years later, he raised the issue even more forcefully in "We Almost Lost Detroit."

The only sellout nights in the No Nukes series were the nights that Springsteen played. On one of those nights, a frustrated Chaka Khan walked off the stage, thinking that the cries for "Broooce" were boos. No Nukes yielded a documentary film and a triple LP that sold moderately well. The California Alliance was even more ambitious. It staged over fifty shows that included Joan Baez, Peter, Paul & Mary, Bob Dylan, Gil Scott-Heron, Bruce Springsteen, Jackson Browne, Minnie Ripperton, Bette Midler, and Stevie Wonder. These artists can claim some small share of the credit for the success of the movement. By 1982, Robin Denselow has noted, "every single station ordered in the USA since 1974 had either been canceled completely or indefinitely postponed."[60]

Women's Music: The Feminist Alternative

Throughout the 1970s, the sexist nature of rock was openly debated in the feminist press. Those who felt that rock was irrevocably sexist gravitated toward softer styles. There were some, however, who felt that rock could be a valuable cultural asset for them. Feminist critic Ellen Willis wrote:

> *Music that boldly and aggressively laid out what the singer wanted, loved, hated—as good rock-and-roll did—challenged me to do the same, and so, even when the content was antiwoman, antisexual, in a sense antihuman, the form encouraged my struggle for liberation. Similarly, timid music made me feel timid, whatever its ostensible politics.*[61]

In 1972, in a concrete attempt to harness the energy of rock in the service of feminism, the Chicago Women's Liberation Rock Band and its East Coast counterpart, the

New Haven Women's Liberation Rock Band, recorded *Mountain Moving Day* for Rounder Records, an independent label. While the creation of the record was an overtly political act, even in circles that were less political, women began to venture into territory that had been exclusively male. A number of regionally known all-female rock bands came and went. Eyes and the Enchanted Forest were too short-lived to make any impact. Ace of Cups never landed a contract. Although Goldie and the Gingerbreads had been popular in Great Britain since the early 1960s, the group was never able to make a dent in the U.S. market. Isis ventured into jazz rock with a full horn section. The Deadly Nightshade recorded *The Deadly Nightshade* (1975) and *Funky and Western* (1976) for RCA and then folded. There was also a group from Berkeley—Joy of Cooking—that showed promise. It was a mixed-gender group, but it was led by two women, electric guitarist Terry Garthwaite and electric keyboardist Toni Brown. Garthwaite and Brown's music was not political in the narrow sense, but it was compelling in that it reflected the experiences of two literate, adult women. With two well-received albums to their credit by 1971 (*Joy of Cooking* and *Closer to the Ground*) it looked as if the group might be the beginning of a nonsexist tradition in commercial rock. Christgau opined: "Many vaguely feminist women have no special connection to rock not out of ideology but simply because it has never really spoken to them. Joy of Cooking can end that."[62] However, after a disappointing third album, *Castles* (1972), the group dissolved. Brown and Garthwaite headed to Nashville to record *Cross Country* as Toni and Terry before embarking on solo careers.

Fanny was the first self-contained, all-female rock band to be signed to a major label and the only one of its generation to hit the Top Forty. The group was started by two sisters from the Philippines, June and Jean Millington, who had formed bands with their female classmates throughout their high-school years. Signed to Reprise in 1969 by Richard Perry, the band faced an almost impossible situation. Within the women's movement, their impolitic name and such double entendre album titles as *Charity Ball* (1971)

For the members of Fanny, becoming a rock band and developing a feminist consciousness were mutually exclusive choices. The group chose to become a rock band and, in so doing, helped eliminate one of the biggest obstacles facing women in music—access to electric instruments.

and *Fanny Hill* (1972) made them something of an embarrassment. A promotional campaign that included "Get Behind Fanny" bumper stickers did not help. In the music business, the band was seen as a novelty group; when their concerts were well received, the sentiment was "not bad . . . for chicks." The fact that the title cut from *Charity Ball* reached the Top Forty was remarkable.

June Millington eventually came to resent the fact that the quality of Fanny's music was measured by the group's ability to play like men. At the time, however, it never occurred to the members of Fanny that the women's movement might be a natural point of reference for them. Feminism "was such a dirty word!" said June Millington.[63] Fanny was thus caught between rock and a hard place. The sector of the music business the band had chosen to enter was so male-dominated there were no female referents, let alone a support network. "You had to prove that you could play like a guy, or play as good as a guy," Millington later recalled. "That's really all there was. The whole attitude, what you wore, the way that you projected, every note that you played, was male territory."[64] In such a milieu, the women's movement could never have presented itself as a refuge. For the members of Fanny, becoming a rock band and developing a feminist consciousness were mutually exclusive choices. The group chose to become a rock band and, in so doing, helped eliminate one of the biggest obstacles facing women in music—access to electric instruments.

Fanny was the model for the Runaways, an all-female rock band made up of four southern California teenagers. Like their predecessors, they were never able to transcend their novelty status (with releases like "Cherry Bomb" written by Kim Fowley, the group's manager, it is hardly surprising), and eventually broke up. Still, the band was the proving ground for Joan Jett and Lita Ford, who would go on to achieve some measure of solo hard rock success in the 1980s. The group's one-time vocalist, Micki Steele, later

Fanny's name and double entendre song titles proved to be something of an embarrassment for the first self-contained, all-female band to make the Top Forty. Cofounder June Millington (lower left), however, went on to a career in women's music, becoming a regular session player at Olivia Records.

surfaced as one of the Bangles. Suzi Quatro, the group's fourth member, also ventured into hard rock with some success during this period. Again, however, the progress she represented was trivialized by her role as Leather Tuscadero on the television series *Happy Days*.

The failure of all-female rock bands and the hostility of the music industry toward women in rock bands in general led to the development of explicitly feminist, mostly folk-oriented alternative music. For the most part, it was music Ellen Willis would have found timid. Women's music, as this new sound came to be called, was institutionalized in 1973 when a group of politically active women from Washington, D.C., started Olivia Records at the suggestion of singer Cris Williamson. Olivia's first release was a single that featured Williamson's "If It Weren't for the Music" backed by Meg Christian's rendition of "Lady" by Carole King/Gerry Goffin. The single sold 5,000 copies through mail order. The revenue it generated was used to relocate the operation to San Francisco and to finance the label's first album, Meg Christian's *I Know You Know* (1975), which sold 70,000 copies. Olivia's second album, Cris Williamson's *The Changer and the Changed*, sold over 250,000 copies. While the album was in preparation, Williamson had invited June Millington, who had left Fanny in 1973, to play. Millington's appearance served as her introduction to a career in women's music; she began touring with Williamson and became a regular session player at Olivia. "I decided to just get into working with other women," she said.[65]

Sales of *The Changer and the Changed* revealed the existence of an untapped feminist market. Other women's labels soon filled the void: Margie Adam launched Pleiades and Kay Gardner founded Wide Woman/Urana. Seeking to avoid the mainstream music industry completely, women's music formed its own subindustry. Olivia established a network of volunteers to distribute its records at concerts, in feminist bookstores, and door-to-door. As other women's music labels came into existence, Olivia's volunteers formed a network called WILD (Women's Independent Labels Distributors) that distributed these labels as well as Olivia's. Festivals like the Michigan Womyn's Music Festival began to attract thousands of feminists annually. In 1978, Roadwork, Inc., a national booking agency, was created to coordinate tour bookings.

Women's music was originally conceived as music by women, for women, and about women. It was, for all intents and purposes, lesbian music. However, lesbians had experienced discrimination not only in society at large but also within the women's movement. Thus, the term "women's music" was used because it was less threatening to the public as a whole. "Women were less likely to be harassed for listening to or performing 'women's music' than 'lesbian music,'" said feminist music historian Cynthia Lont.[66] Because of the women's movement, there was a tendency to think of women's

The male-dominated music industry was sufficiently exclusionary that there were no career paths to positions of power for women; there were no female record company presidents or record producers to serve as role models.

Feminist labels try to create alternative to the music industry

music in separatist terms. Tactically, a separatist orientation was probably necessary, at least in the short run. The male-dominated music industry was sufficiently exclusionary that there were no career paths to positions of power for women; there were no female record company presidents or record producers to serve as role models. As a way of life, however, separatism limited the audience for the music and led to damaging internal tensions within the movement. The experience of Holly Near and Redwood Records is a case in point. In political circles, Near was originally known as an antiwar activist. She started Redwood Records as an outlet for political material after visiting North Vietnam in 1973. Because of her involvement with the women's movement, however, she and the men who recorded for Redwood were stocked in the women's music section in record stores. When she "came out" as a lesbian in 1978 on *Imagine My Surprise* (1978), she was criticized for using Jeff Langley, her long-time piano player, on the album. Political differences of this sort sapped an inordinate amount of time and energy from women's music.

As often happens in situations like these, the marketplace served as the final arbiter. By the 1980s, the market for women's music had become saturated, leaving the alternative industry with no alternative but to expand its audience or die. "Ironically," Gillian Gaar has written, "Olivia now found itself trying to break out of the 'women's music' genre they worked so hard to create."[67] Abandoning its earlier position of using only female musicians, the label responded by launching Second Wave to diversify its roster. The move was less a compromise of principles than a part of the natural evolution of a business. Olivia could be justifiably proud of having helped create a cultural space for postpunk feminists from Tracy Chapman to Two Nice Girls.

From Country Rock to Southern Boogie

In the late 1960s, country rock became yet another term in the growing lexicon of hyphenated rock styles. Country music had long been one of a number of significant influences in popular music. Rockabilly had been a major strand of rock 'n' roll in the fifties and was carried into the 1960s by artists like Roy Orbison and Brenda Lee. Ray Charles' two volumes of pop country and western tunes were his best-selling albums. The late 1960s brought down-home, traditional Nashville sounds into the rock idiom. The artist who kicked off this trend in 1968 utilized clean, unfettered production, accompaniment that was laid back and spare, and sang in a voice sounding uncharacteristically throaty. On first hearing, it would have been difficult to tell that it was Bob Dylan.

Dylan had been on hiatus since *Blonde on Blonde* had been released following his 1966 motorcycle accident. In the interim, Columbia had issued a greatest hits album. By 1968, then, Dylan's new album had been long awaited. When it came, it was totally unlike anything anyone had been expecting. At a time when rock was immersed in technological overindulgence, Dylan's *John Wesley Harding* was as spartan as his earlier acoustic efforts. At a time when the counterculture was as free-spirited and antiestablishment as it could be, *John Wesley Harding* was recorded in Nashville, a bastion of traditional values. Dylan had, once again, thrown his fans a curve, one of his most successful. *John Wesley Harding* rose to number two on the album charts, Dylan's highest position to date. If there were any doubts about the seriousness of his new artistic direction, he laid them to rest with the release of *Nashville Skyline* in 1969, which included the Top Ten hit single "Lay Lady Lay" and a duet with country legend Johnny Cash on "Girl from the North Country." As Bill Malone has written, "Dylan lent respectability to a musical form, and to a body of musicians, that had been perceived as 'corny' or old fashioned."[68]

Nashville soon became the hot "new" recording center, and country rock became a new trend. The top session players in the country music capitol, those "Nashville Cats" the Lovin' Spoonful sang about, began getting so much work that they started their own performing ensemble called Area Code 615. Over the next few years, folk and rock musicians, from Buffy Sainte-Marie to the Nitty Gritty Dirt Band to the Byrds, followed Dylan into country, thus putting an end to its association with socially regressive values. Buffy Sainte-Marie journeyed to Nashville to record *I'm Gonna Be a Country Girl Again,* the title song of which became a hit single in 1972. That same year, the Nitty Gritty Dirt Band recruited country greats Roy Acuff, Doc Watson, Merle Travis, Maybelle Carter, and Earl Scruggs, among others, for a three-record album entitled *Will the Circle Be Unbroken.* Because the artists who traveled to Nashville treated country and western music without condescension, they began to soften the negative view that Acuff and other country performers had of hippies.

Most prominent among Dylan's fellow travelers on the road to country rock at the end of the 1960s were four Canadians and one "good ole boy" from Arkansas who were known collectively as the Band. Guitarist Robbie Robertson, organist Garth Hudson, bassist Rock Danko, and pianist Rich Manuel had been fans of country music from childhood, even though they had been born and raised in Canada. Drummer Levon Helm from Marvell, Arkansas, could not have avoided country music even if he wanted to. One by one, beginning in the late 1950s, these players joined the Hawks, the backup band for rockabilly artist Ronnie Hawkins with whom they toured for years, honing their craft. "There were only three kinds of rock then: rhythm and blues, corny white rock, and rockabilly," said Robertson. "We played rockabilly."[69] They first met Dylan through the efforts of folk blues guitarist John Hammond, Jr. (the son of Dylan's producer). At the time, Dylan was moving toward electric music. Hired as the backup band for his

1965 tour, they withdrew with him to Woodstock, New York, after his accident. There they collaborated—jammed, really—on rock's first significant bootleg, later released by Columbia as *The Basement Tapes.* The Band's official debut album, *Music from Big Pink* (1968), a reference to their Woodstock home, and their second release, *The Band* (1969), introduced a number of country rock classics, including "Long Black Veil," Dylan's "I Shall Be Released," and Robertson's "Up on Cripple Creek," "Rag, Mama, Rag," "Across the Great Divide," and "The Night They Drove Old Dixie Down." This last song became a Top Ten hit for Joan Baez in 1971. Their third, and again critically acclaimed, album, *Stage Fright,* continued in the country rock mold.

In 1973, Dylan and the Band recorded their first official album together. *Planet Waves* was recorded in three days and rose to number one on the album charts almost as fast. Dylan and the Band then embarked on Dylan's first full tour in eight years. The tour was captured on the two-disc LP *Before the Flood.* Since Dylan's contract with Columbia was in limbo at this time, both albums came out on Asylum, a major coup in the eyes of the industry for David Geffen. However, Dylan returned to Columbia for *Blood*

The Band started as a rockabilly outfit and became Bob Dylan's backup band for his first electric tour. Their breakup on Thanksgiving Day, 1976, *was immortalized in* The Last Waltz, *directed by Martin Scorsese, one of the best concert films ever made.*

on the Tracks (1975) and *Desire* (1976). Both of these albums, which went to number one on the charts, would have been introspective enough to land Dylan back in the singer/songwriter category had it not been for the hit single "Hurricane," a political protest song dedicated to boxer Rubin "Hurricane" Carter, whom Dylan believed had been wrongly convicted of murder.

There were a series of groups, mostly from southern California, that picked up on Dylan's turn toward country. The Byrds, having been keenly aware of Dylan's importance when they transformed his acoustic material into folk rock earlier in the decade, again followed his lead. By this time, the group had recruited Gram Parsons. Parsons, a Harvard Divinity School dropout, became a pioneer of country rock. His influence on the Byrds' *Sweethearts of the Rodeo,* which was recorded in Nashville, helped the group to become the first rock band to play the Grand Ole Opry. Although the album did not reach the Top Forty, it was a milestone for country rock.

Parsons left the Byrds when the group planned a tour of South Africa and formed the Flying Burrito Brothers with Chris Hillman and Gene Clarke, two alumni of the Byrds. Although they had only one album that charted, *Last of the Red Hot Burritos,* they played to packed houses and rave reviews, merging rock and country as no other group had done. The group further emphasized the fusion of cultures by performing in striking sequined Nudie suits that were embroidered with marijuana leaves instead of the cactus plants and wagon wheels selected by most country artists. By the time he died from heart failure in the mid-1970s, Parsons was credited with influencing everyone from Emmylou Harris (his protégé) to the Rolling Stones.

When the formation of Crosby, Stills, Nash, and Young left the Buffalo Springfield without Stills and Young, two of the group's remaining members, Richie Furay and Jim Messina, formed the nucleus of another country rock ensemble, known as Poco. Three of their half-dozen or so LPs charted, but the group never matched their solid performances with comparable record sales. By the time their best-selling album *Legend* was released in 1979, none of the original members were still in the group. Furay had fallen on hard times with the intended supergroup configuration of Souther, Hillman, and Furay. Messina had become the second half of Loggins and Messina, a country-inflected pop rock act best known for their light rocker "Your Mama Don't Dance" (1972), which was followed by half-dozen Top Forty LPs. Both men went solo in the late 1970s with Kenny Loggins achieving the greater success with five best-selling solo albums.

Fronting the Stone Canyon Band, Rick (Ricky) Nelson made a country rock comeback with "Garden Party" in 1973. At various points, his new ensemble included members of Poco, Little Feat, and the Eagles, the group that would come to dominate country rock in the 1970s. The Eagles were accomplished writers and vocalists, as well as multi-instrumentalists. Sixteen Top Forty singles and four number one albums in a row attest to that. Indeed, the group's credentials were impeccable; bassist Randy Meisner had been a founding member of Poco, and guitarist Bernie Leadon had played with the

Burritos. Along with drummer Don Henley and guitarist Glenn Frey, who became the group's main writers when Meisner and Leadon departed, all had backed up Linda Ronstadt at one time or another. There was, however, something about the group that was unsettling. When rockers like Creedence Clearwater Revival or the New Riders of the Purple Sage or the Grateful Dead or Neil Young performed country-flavored material, there was a certain southern ethos, a down-home earthiness, in the way they sang. The Eagles were slicker, more polished. The group was certainly talented enough to replicate the sound of country music, but they brought it out of the backwoods and into the big city. The word that most readily comes to mind in describing them is corporate. Somehow, the Eagles placed country rock in a new social context. With *John Wesley Harding,* Dylan had responded to the election of Richard Nixon by reclaiming the music of the heartland for rock 'n' roll. The Eagles were different. From their signature song "Take It Easy" (cowritten by Jackson Browne in 1972), about the joys of an unencumbered life on the road, to the music on *Hotel California* (1976), their seminal statement about the California good life, they used country rock as a vehicle for embracing the hedonism of the 1970s. "The Eagles are the ultimate in California

> *T*he Eagles were certainly talented enough to replicate the sound of country music, but they brought it out of the backwoods and into the big city. The word that most readily comes to mind in describing them is corporate.

The Eagles place country rock in a new social context

The Eagles were consummate musicians and canny self-promoters. In the mid-1970s, they came to dominate country rock with music (and a lifestyle) that was as hedonistic as it was successful.

dreaming," said Christgau, "a fantasy of fulfillment that has been made real only in the hip upper-middle-class suburbs of Marin County and the Los Angeles canyons."[70]

It was not that the group was unaware of politics; there were direct political influences in their lives. Once Linda Ronstadt started dating Jerry Brown, who was then governor of California, she pulled the group into the electoral arena, and Jackson Browne exerted an environmental influence in the latter part of the decade. The very fact the group took its name from Native American folklore suggested an awareness of some kind of transcendence. In the context of the early 1970s, however, the name did not reflect that truth, nor did it ring with irony as it might have a few years earlier. During the culmination of the war in Vietnam and Nixon's final years, the eagle was as likely to represent a bird of prey as a symbol of liberation. Still, the group was politically astute enough to know that with a name like the Eagles, they should have a major album out in 1976, the bicentennial year. *Hotel California,* musically their best effort, commercially their biggest success (15 million copies sold), was the pinnacle of their success. Eventually, the years of "Life in the Fast Lane," as the Eagles termed it, took their toll on the group. "I think the underbelly of success is the burden of having to follow things up," Frey told an interviewer. "We started to run out of gas. Don [Henley] sort of blew his literary nut on *Hotel California.*"[71] The result was the nightmarish three-year effort it took to produce the group's final studio LP, ironically titled *The Long Run.*

The success of country rock paralleled that of its pop/country variants. Glen Campbell and John Denver were the biggest beneficiaries of this trend. Campbell parlayed such songs as "Wichita Lineman" and "Galveston" into major pop stardom in the late 1960s. Between 1968 and 1978, he tallied eleven gold albums, which brought him his own television program. Denver scored fifteen Top Forty albums and placed thirty-two singles in the Hot 100 between 1971 and 1982. A number of his biggest singles—"Take Me Home, Country Roads," "Rocky Mountain High," "Thank God I'm a Country Boy," and "Sunshine on My Shoulder"—suggested country themes, which his jeans-and-flannel image reinforced. Other artists cashed in as well. Canadian Anne Murray placed "Snowbird" in the pop and country Top Ten in 1970, kicking off an eleven-year run as a hitmaker.

As rock artists made a move toward country, a number of country artists were drawn to rock. At the center of this movement were a number of country artists who sought to challenge the conservative hegemony of Nashville. For their insolence, they came to be known collectively as "the outlaws." They wore the label proudly and marketed it to their advantage and RCA's. In 1976 the company released *Wanted: The Outlaws,* a compilation LP with songs by Willie Nelson, Waylon Jennings, Tompall Glaser, and Jessi Colter. The album became the first certified platinum country album.

Nelson and Jennings were the most famous of the so-called outlaws. By the time he began to tire of Nashville's slickness in the mid-1960s, Nelson had toed the country mark for over a decade. He had achieved great success as both a writer—he wrote

"Crazy," Patsy Cline's biggest hit—and a performer. Before the 1960s ended, he had more than a dozen albums to his credit. It was when he moved back to Texas in the early 1970s that he began to change his image, growing his hair long and discarding his western suits and ties in favor of jeans and T-shirts. His new look suited both his laid-back, conversational singing style and his refusal to be pigeonholed for commercial reasons. He first came to the attention of the rock press with *Shotgun Willie* and *Phases and Stages,* which he recorded in the early 1970s. He crossed over to the pop market with *Red Headed Stranger* in 1975, his first of more than thirty albums to make the pop charts. In 1978, he recorded his best-selling album of the decade, *Waylon and Willie.*

Waylon Jennings' country roots had first led him toward rock in 1958 when he joined Buddy Holly on bass. In fact, it was Jennings who gave up his seat to the Big Bopper on the flight that killed the Big Bopper, Holly, and Ritchie Valens. Although RCA's Chet Atkins had tried to fashion Jennings in the mold of a respectable country singer, it was his tough rockabilly past that defined the character he portrayed in the film *Nashville Rebel* in 1966. Throughout the 1960s, Jennings fought hard for artistic freedom; his influences ran as far afield as Dylan and the Beatles. He even had a minor hit with "MacArthur Park" with the Kimberleys in 1969. Jennings, like Nelson and the rest of the outlaws, resisted easy categorization and musical limitations, but he was always respectful of his roots. "The ultimate irony of the Outlaws," Bill Malone has said, "may be that, while drawing upon a diverse array of musical sources and reaching out to new audiences, they did more to preserve a distinct identity for country music than most of their contemporaries who wore the 'country' label."[72]

Malone's comment was directed at artists like Kenny Rogers and Dolly Parton who achieved incredible mainstream success with material that hugged the middle of the pop/country road. Emmylou Harris took a different route. Harris was a truly eclectic performer who managed to stay grounded in tradition even as she explored rock-based material with her versatile (and aptly named) Hot Band. While the group was adept at playing traditional acoustic country, their electric numbers were bold enough to be linked with a more extreme development in country-identified rock, which came to be known as redneck rock or, more politely, southern boogie.

Little distinguishes southern boogie bands—the Allman Brothers, the Marshall Tucker Band, Lynyrd Skynyrd, the Charlie Daniels Band, Molly Hatchett, and ZZ Top—from hard-rock bands other than a truculent identification with the South. Like other hard-rock bands, these groups were based in blues and country, their music was loud and sometimes crude, and they exhibited the same

If Bob Dylan had recovered country for the mainstream rock scene, southern boogie returned rock 'n' roll to the soil.

macho posturing, albeit with a bit of "good ole boy" flair. However, at a time when much of rock had become a pale imitation of its former self, these bands, even with their reactionary tendencies, sounded refreshing. If Dylan had recovered country for the mainstream rock scene, southern boogie returned rock 'n' roll to the soil.

The Allman Brothers were the proto-typical southern boogie band. Except for its identification with the South, there was little that separated southern boogie from hard rock in general. The Allmans' signature sound included rhythm and blues influences and intricate instru-mental harmonies.

The prototypical southern boogie band was the Allman Brothers, which featured brothers Duane and Greg Allman on guitar and keyboards, Dickie Betts on guitar, Berry Oakley on bass, and Jai Johanny "Jaimo" Johanson and Butch Trucks on drums. Duane had been a session player at Fame Studios in Muscle Shoals, backing artists like Aretha Franklin and Wilson Pickett. He was also the second lilting lead guitar on Eric Clapton's *Layla*. At their best, the Allmans were a tight, disciplined unit with intricate instrumental harmonies over a strong percussive base. The group first came to the attention of the national audience with *Idlewild South* (1970). *Eat a Peach* (1972) was the band's first Top Ten album and contains Duane's last recordings. (Duane was killed in a motorcycle accident before the album was completed; a year later, Berry Oakley died in a similar accident.) The band continued after Duane's death, recording their best-selling album, *Brothers and Sisters,* which hit number one on the album charts and yielded the number two hit single "Ramblin' Man" in 1973. That same year, along with two other acts—the Band and the Grateful Dead—the group headlined a single show at Watkins Glen, New

York, that attracted some 600,000 fans, dwarfing even Woodstock in audience size. Although commercial success continued unabated throughout the decade, greatness, that very elusive quality, remained out of reach after the loss of Duane.

The Marshall Tucker Band, which took its name from the owner of the band's rehearsal space, was softer and more laid back than the other southern boogie bands but still in the mold of country rock. Like the Allmans, the group was signed to Phil Walden's Capricorn label. Guitarist Toy Caldwell's playing was often compared to that of the Allman's Dickie Betts. The group toured with the Allmans and, along with other Capricorn acts, did benefits for Jimmy Carter. The Tucker Band was respectable enough to be rewarded with gigs at the White House after Carter's victory, but other southern rockers lived life closer to the edge.

Lynyrd Skynyrd, a phonetical spelling of the name of the high-school gym teacher who suspended the group for wearing long hair, were fiercely proud to be southern. The band's first two albums—arguably their best—were produced by Al Kooper. The first contained "Freebird," a ten-minute tribute to Duane Allman, that became something of a signature song for the group. The second had the group's best-selling single, "Sweet Home Alabama," an explicit defense of the southern way of life in response to Neil Young's "Southern Man." If southern rock had an ideological component, this was it. (It would pop up again in Charlie Daniels' "The South's Gonna Do It Again.") With four gold and four platinum albums by 1980, Lynyrd Skynyrd found a ready audience, if not critical praise, for their music, which was as wild and rowdy as their personal lives. The beginning of the end for the group came in 1977 when a plane crash claimed the lives of lead singer Ronnie Van Zant and band members Steve and Cassie Gaines. The band's natural successor was Molly Hatchett, a group that first entered the Top Twenty in 1979 with the platinum-selling *Flirtin' with Disaster*.

ZZ Top was a Texas-based trio that took southern rock into the 1980s. Their influences ranged from acid rock to the down-home blues of John Lee Hooker and Elmore James. Album titles like *Tres Hombres, Fandango!, Tejas, Deguello,* and *El Loco* suggested a Tex-Mex cultural location. They had flirted with heavy metal as early as 1975 when they included the metal classic "Tush" on *Fandango!*. In the 1980s, when the trio adopted their anonymous bearded look, they attempted a more conscious blues-based metal/pop fusion. When all was said and done, the southern rockers could be distinguished from their hard-rock contemporaries only by geography and, in some cases, personal appearance.

Mad with Power: Heavy Metal

Depending on one's perspective, the softer rock and soul styles of the 1970s represented either a withdrawal from the political engagement of the 1960s, a reevaluation of its efficacy, a foregrounding of music as entertainment, or a new strategy for making the world a better place. In contrast, heavy metal represented an absolute rejection of the peace and love ethos. The music was too intense to be regarded as entertainment, and it was too self-absorbed to worry about making the world a better place. It was the critics' worst nightmare: hard rock taken to the extreme, with no socially redeeming features. Or, so it seemed.

The origins of the genre's name can be traced to a number of sources. It is used in chemistry to describe the heavier elements in the periodic table. In literature, the term has been ascribed incorrectly to the William Burroughs novel, *Naked Lunch*, and correctly to a later novel, *Nova Express*. Most agree that its first appearance in popular music occurred in the line "heavy metal thunder" from Steppenwolf's "Born to Be Wild" (1968), a Top Ten single that became a biker anthem after it was featured in the film *Easy Rider*. In rock journalism, the term is usually credited to the incomparable Lester Bangs, one of the few critics who would touch the music with a less than ten-foot pole.

> *Heavy metal represented an absolute rejection of the peace and love ethos. It was the critics' worst nightmare: hard rock taken to the extreme, with no socially redeeming features. Or, so it seemed.*

By the time heavy metal coalesced into a genre in the early 1970s, it had developed several distinctive elements. Chief among these was sound quality: "The essential sonic element in heavy metal is power, expressed as sheer volume," Deena Weinstein has claimed.[73] "If there is one feature that underpins the coherence of heavy metal as a genre," Robert Walser has noted, "it is the power chord" (a chord that is strummed at deafening volume and held to maximum sustain).[74] The power of heavy metal was intended to overwhelm its listeners, to flood them in a kind of sonic tidal wave. Heavy metal was not a violent break from hard rock; rather, it was a logical extension of hard rock with sufficient variation to defy its detractors' simplistic characterization of it as a wall of noise.

According to Weinstein, the origins of heavy metal lie in blues-based rock and psychedelic music.[75] Walser concurs with Weinstein's analysis but adds classical music to the list of sources.[76] Thus, heavy metal bears the influences of Muddy Waters, Howlin' Wolf, B. B. King, and Chuck Berry at one extreme, and Bach, Beethoven, Mozart, and Vivaldi at the other. As always, genre boundaries are a matter of subjective judgment at the fringes. Black Oak Arkansas occupied the territory between metal and southern boogie. The J. Geils Band played hard blues-based rock but their Boston contemporaries, Aerosmith, moved into heavy metal. Bachman-Turner Overdrive, from Canada, which was formed after guitarist Randy Bachman left Guess Who ("These Eyes," "American Woman"), pushed boogie to the limit on "Takin' Care of Business" and unleashed Who-like power chords on "You Ain't Seen Nothin' Yet" but fell just short of metal in the eyes of most observers. According to Walser, "The sound that would become known as heavy metal was definitively codified in 1970 with the release of *Led Zeppelin II*, Black Sabbath's *Paranoid*, and *Deep Purple in Rock*."[77] The ascension of these three pivotal bands illustrates the diversity of sources that produced the genre.

Heavy metal begins to coalesce as a new category

Metal's immediate acid and blues rock antecedents are what one might expect. From Eric Clapton to Jimmy Page, the lead guitarists who fronted the Yardbirds, marked the path. Clapton had always been a blues aficionado. As a founding member of Cream, he overlaid his taste in blues with the psychedelic experience. Cuts like "Sunshine of Your Love" began to pull together the elements that define heavy metal: pounding bass and drums, blaring guitar, and screeching vocals. Hendrix was a parallel acid/blues influence who added incredible virtuosity to deafening sonic distortion. A number of American groups, including Blue Cheer ("Summertime Blues," 1968) and Steppenwolf also pushed the boundaries of volume and distortion. In metal, these elements were fueled by power chords, which were already evident in the music of the Kinks and the Who. These were the influences that guided Jimmy Page when he sought to extend the work of the Yardbirds in a new configuration.

For American audiences in particular, Led Zeppelin—Jimmy Page (guitar), Robert Plant (vocals), John Paul Jones (bass), and John Bonham (drums)—became the archetypal heavy metal group. Initially billed as the New Yardbirds, Led Zeppelin (reportedly, the Who's immodest drummer Keith Moon quipped that the group's music would go over like a "lead zeppelin," thus the name) filled the void for fans looking for a new intensity in rock. From the release of the group's first self-titled album in 1969, the band was a hit. Each of the eight subsequent albums released before the end of the decade rose to numbers one or two on the pop charts. Aided by the business acumen of manager Peter Grant, the group set concert attendance records all over the United States. They were, however, ignored by the rock press. "[A]cclaim," Plant once said, "always came from the street, never from the written critique."[78]

Black Sabbath followed a similar heavy metal road and enjoyed an equally poor relationship with the press. The group started as Earth, a working-class, hippie blues rock band from Birmingham, England. They changed their name to Black Sabbath after writing a song with that title, which was taken from an old Boris Karloff horror movie. The name change coincided with a move to a louder, more aggressive style and something of a break with the group's hippie past. In their new incarnation, the group paralleled Zeppelin's success and had five platinum albums in a row in less than four years, peaking with *Master of Reality* in 1971. For this feat, they were charged with a "complete lack of subtlety, intelligence, and originality."[79] Continued *Los Angeles Times* critic John Mendelsohn, "Black Sabbath's . . . new songs are as indistinguishable from its old songs as its old songs are from one another."[80]

Complaints that the music was too loud, that you couldn't hear the words, that it all sounded the same sounded like the 1950s and overlooked considerable variation in the music itself.

While Black Sabbath may have been as good a target as any for such condemnation, this type of blanket dismissal was reminiscent of the things parents and critics said about rock 'n' roll when it first emerged. Complaints that the music was too loud, that you couldn't hear the words, that it all sounded the same sounded like the 1950s and overlooked considerable variation in the music itself. Led Zeppelin, for instance, was influenced by everything from U.S. soul music to Celtic mysticism. Zeppelin's first album ran the gamut from sluggish blues to ethereal ballads. Page even played pedal steel on "Your Time Is Gonna Come." *Led Zeppelin III* (1970) balanced the hard-rock riffing on cuts like "Immigrant Song" with a whole side of largely acoustic music. On "Gallows Pole," for example, Page played banjo. A folkish influence continued on the group's fourth album, which featured "The Battle of Evermore," a vocal duet between Plant and folk rocker Sandy Denny for which Page used a mandolin. *Led Zeppelin IV* (1971) also included the group's seminal "Stairway to Heaven," which builds from an acoustic intro to a blistering climax with Plant's piercing tenor soaring over Page's deafening salvo of raw guitar licks.

Deep Purple had an even broader range of influences as well as a strong psychedelic bent and the beginnings of that conscious incorporation of classical virtuosity that would become increasingly important to the genre. The group first hit the Top Ten with

Heavy metal springs from a diversity of musical sources

For many Americans, Led Zeppelin defined heavy metal. Despite a broad range of influences, however, they were not accepted in art rock circles. Instead, they were trashed from the left for their sexism and condemned by the right for their fascination with the occult.

"Hush" in 1968. The use of an organ gave the group a fuller sound than most of their contemporaries and landed them at first in the company of groups like Vanilla Fudge, who described their music as "psychedelic symphonic rock," and Iron Butterfly. Vanilla Fudge interpreted songs like the Supremes' "You Keep Me Hanging On" and the Beatles' "Eleanor Rigby" as if they were being played at a speed slower than most turntables could go, thereby creating in listeners the feeling of a drug-induced effect. Working in a similar way, Iron Butterfly parlayed the droning seventeen-minute "In-A-Gadda-Da-Vida" from their debut album of the same name into Atlantic's best-selling record. Deep Purple evidenced a similar psychedelic connection on *The Book of Taliesyn.* Music from this album was used in the science-fiction drama *2001: A Space Odyssey,* the ultimate filmic acid trip. Classical influences also became evident in Deep Purple's music early on. Both guitarist Ritchie Blackmore and organist John Lord had studied classical music in their youth. The critical and financial success of Lord's *Concerto for Group and Orchestra* (1970) suggested that the group would follow the trajectory of an art rock ensemble, but Blackmore balked, feeling "that the whole orchestra thing was a bit tame. I mean, you're playing in the Royal Albert Hall, and the audience sits there with folded arms, and you're standing there playing next to a violinist who holds his ears every time you take a solo. It doesn't make you feel particularly inspired."[81] Blackmore clearly felt put off by the ambiance of the concert hall; he wanted to make use of classical resources, but in the context of heavy metal.

Blackmore's guitar playing became a hallmark of the precision and virtuosity that defined the next generation of metal guitarists. It shows up clearly on *Machine Head* (1972), Deep Purple's best-selling album, which includes the group's best-known single "Smoke on the Water." In a direct reference to the classical sources the group drew on in the album, Blackmore described the chord pattern for his solo on "Highway Star" as "a Bach progression." After he left Deep Purple to form Rainbow, the liner notes for Rainbow's first LP included the credit: "Inspiration: J. S. Bach." These classical influences would continue. As Robert Walser has pointed out, "A few years later Blackmore even took up study of the cello, and Rainbow's 1981 release featured a very direct use of classical music in its title cut, 'Difficult to Cure,' an instrumental built around the 'Ode to Joy' from the last movement of Beethoven's *Ninth Symphony.*"[82]

By the mid-1970s, there was a whole generation of heavy metal acts that wore the label proudly; they had found their way into the genre through the paths that their predecessors had followed. Some came from psychedelia. For example, Rush, a Canadian group, had begun by playing Cream and Iron Butterfly covers in 1974, using a classic power trio lineup. When Judas Priest released *Rocka Rolla* in 1974, they were a hard acid-rock band. By *Sad Wings of Destiny,* which was released one year later, however, they were squarely in the heavy metal camp. Uriah Heep took a similar road. Ted Nugent made a more gradual break from his psychedelic past as the leader of the Amboy Dukes to a solo career that reached a heavy metal peak with the release of *Cat Scratch Fever* in

1977. Some came from blues-based rock. When Aerosmith was first signed by Columbia in 1972, the group was considered Boston's answer to the Rolling Stones. Lead singer Steven Tyler even looked (and pranced) a bit like Mick Jagger. By the time *Toys in the Attic* made the Top Forty in 1975, the group had begun edging toward the lighter side of heavy metal, a niche that they then occupied successfully throughout the 1980s. Humble Pie, a blues-based rock ensemble aimed at younger fans, was beginning to move toward metal when guitarist Peter Frampton left to become a solo superstar. The James Gang from Cleveland had been aiming at metal with more eclectic influences when guitarist Joe Walsh left for a stint with the Eagles and his own solo career. Bad Company, a group under the tutelage of Zeppelin's manager Peter Grant, played predictable heavy blues-based rock. Although they could emulate Zeppelin's stance on cuts like "Can't Get Enough" and "Ready for Love," they could not match Zeppelin's talent or success.

In the classical realm, there was one guitarist in particular who followed in Blackmore's footsteps and rewrote the book on virtuosity and sophistication, thus helping to usher in the new wave of heavy metal guitarists that dominated the 1980s: Eddie Van Halen. Van Halen and his drummer brother Alex were born in the Netherlands but raised in California, where they were trained to become classical musicians until the lure of rock won out. With Michael Anthony on bass and David Lee Roth on vocals, Van Halen was a high-energy act right from the beginning. Signed by Warner in the late 1970s, the group's debut LP, *Van Halen* (1978), made the Top Twenty. Every subsequent album charted higher than the one before it until the group hit number one in 1985. While Van Halen owed its early success partially to Roth's athletic, overtly sexual (some would say sexist) performances, the group's defining and sustaining force was Eddie Van Halen's pathbreaking guitar style.

> *J*ust as it is important to recognize the range of influences that comprised heavy metal, it is important to recognize that these influences were utilized in the service of the blustering, sexist, hard-rock scene that provided its context.

Like many of his contemporaries, Van Halen was drawn to hard rock through the blues. It was the combination of the emotionality of the blues feel, the aggressiveness of hard rock, the discipline of his classical training, and his sophisticated knowledge of music theory that enabled him to propel metal guitar playing to new heights. According to Walser, Van Halen's solo on the appropriately titled "Eruption" from the group's debut album heralded the arrival of the new virtuosity in heavy metal. Walser describes the solo as "one minute and twenty-seven seconds of exuberant and playful virtuosity, a violinist's precise and showy technique inflected by the vocal rhetoric of the blues and rock and roll irreverence. Here and elsewhere, Van Halen's guitar playing displays an unprecedented fluidity."[83] As a result, *Guitar Player* magazine chose Van Halen as the best rock guitarist for five years in a row.

Just as it is important to recognize the range of influences that comprised heavy metal, it is important to recognize that these influences were utilized in the service of the blustering, sexist, hard-rock scene that provided its context. Perhaps the best example is

Zeppelin's "Whole Lotta Love," a rip-off of Willie Dixon's "You Need Love," which appeared on *Led Zeppelin II*. While the thundering rhythm underpinning Plant's insistent shrieking vocals and Page's chugging guitar and buzzsaw fills laid out the parameters of classic metal, the song itself illustrates why most critics were so antagonistic to the music. "I have felt over the past year and a half a steadily increasing disaffection with rock's male chauvinism," wrote Robert Christgau shortly after the song's release. "I am acutely uncomfortable with songs of cock-pride (Led Zeppelin's "Whole Lotta Love," for instance)."[84] For a number of groups (and critics), Plant's macho posturing and Page's phallic guitar thrusts defined heavy metal.

There was only one American band that could rival Led Zeppelin in its unique combination of macho swagger, commercial success, and critical disdain: Grand Funk Railroad, a group that began in Flint, Michigan. Grand Funk played raw, basic rock that was not terribly distinctive and, as often as not, out of tune. There were dozens of antecedents for their brand of rock, and they added little to the corpus of this music other than a few tunes by guitarist Mark Farner. The fact that the group achieved any success at all is surprising; the fact that they became one of the top five rock bands in the world in their heyday is astounding. Grand Funk tallied eleven gold albums in a row—eight of them Top Ten—peaking with *We're an American Band* and a number one single of the same name in 1973. It is all the more incredible that the band achieved this status with virtually no radio play and an almost total lack of press coverage. The only possible explanation is that near-unanimous condemnation conferred on the group the ultimate in outsider status. It was hyped to the fullest by the group's manager Terry Knight.

The lack of critical recognition for the genre meant that most acts had to support their albums with grueling tours. These live shows tended to be ear-splitting spectacles of testosterone-drenched rock that aroused aggression more than sexuality. As a result, the audiences for metal concerts were predominantly young, white, working-class men, engaging in rites of male bonding with abandon. It was in the milieu of live performance that metal earned its nickname—cock rock. In the context of a burgeoning women's movement, it was a damning indictment, although in certain metal circles it probably would have been taken as a compliment. Heavy metal was a bastion of male dominance and privilege. There were no women in heavy metal. The only women who even came close to the genre were the Wilson sisters, Ann and Nancy, who rose to prominence as key members of Heart. Even though Heart's debut release, *Dreamboat Annie* (1976), pictured Ann and Nancy bare-shouldered on either side of a red heart, their combination of ballads and near-heavy metal rock propelled them past novelty status all the way to number seven on the pop charts. Subsequent hits like "Barracuda" confirmed the group's ability to rock with the best of them. In time, the group achieved a superstar status that carried them through the 1980s. In the 1970s, however, Heart was an anomaly.

If heavy metal was condemned, or more likely avoided, in progressive circles for its sexism, it was assaulted from the right for its fascination with the occult. The title of

Led Zeppelin IV appeared nowhere on the album's jacket, but one group of runes printed on the liner looked like it spelled Zoso, the name of the three-headed dog who guards the gates of hell. Armed with such evidence, fundamentalist groups accused Zeppelin of including satanic messages on "Stairway to Heaven" through backmasking, the process of recording passages backwards. Groups like Black Sabbath and Judas Priest (formed in 1974) attracted attention simply by virtue of their names. Album titles like *Sabbath Bloody Sabbath* and *Sin After Sin* only added fuel to the hell fire. Police agencies argued that Australia's AC/DC (also founded in 1974) stood for Anti-Christ/Devil's Children. Given metal's preoccupation with power, the more obvious reference to electric current might have been considered an equally likely acronym. In 1990, Zeppelin's Robert Plant chastised Americans for their inability to understand the British sense of irony and sarcasm. "There was . . . a lot of humor in the music," he explained in a retrospective interview. "Not all this glowering satanic crap. . . . it's very American. Nowhere else in the world has anybody ever considered it or been concerned or bothered at all about that."[85] Still, Black Sabbath's Ozzy Osbourne marketed the connection with satanism most effectively, particularly in his solo career in the 1980s, when it became an even more volatile issue.

Faced with a widespread lack of industry support, if not outright hostility, metal came to wear its outsider status like a badge of honor; part of its mission was to fly in the face of respectability. Blue Öyster Cult, a New York metal group in the Black Sabbath mold, used occult-style lyrics written by critic Richard Meltzer, who was also a vocalist for the group. They also sought to capitalize on the disreputable character of the music by adding Nazi paraphernalia to their metal regalia. Rush made a more considered nod toward fascism— or was it just pretension—with its recording of *2112*, which was based on right-wing novelist Ayn Rand's *Anthem*. Subsequent recordings led the group into the realm of platinum-selling bands. Some groups, for example Blue Öyster Cult and Motörhead, added gratuitous umlauts to their names to conjure up a more generic gothic horror, a practice that continued into the 1980s with Mötley Crüe and others.

Other heavy metal artists pushed the limits of decorum through performance and personal appearance. It was not just that the shows got harder and heavier or that strange animal rituals and awesome pyrotechnics were added, it was that heavy metal began to challenge the traditional concept of masculinity from within its exclusionary male environment. It was the last place one would have expected to find cracks in the facade of male sexuality. By the early 1970s, women and gays had become sufficiently vocal that gender roles and sexual preferences were no longer beyond question. While Mick Jagger had long played with androgyny, to find the beginnings of gender-bending in that area of

> It was not just that the shows got harder and heavier or that strange animal rituals and awesome pyrotechnics were added, it was that heavy metal began to challenge the traditional concept of masculinity from within its exclusionary male environment. It was the last place one would have expected to find cracks in the facade of male sexuality.

heavy metal that blossomed into glitter or glam rock was most unexpected. Among the weirdest acts was a group of white middle-class suburban athletes from Phoenix, Arizona, who named themselves after their leader, a minister's son who called himself Alice Cooper. Alice Cooper represented a clear break with the counterculture. "Even hippies hated us," Alice has said, "and it's hard to get a hippie to hate anything."[86] They made no pretense to authenticity or blues roots. Television was their main influence. Musically the group was as subtle as a train wreck; they simply plastered their fans against the wall with noise. The group's big break came the night they cleared the posh club Cheetah after only three songs. Frank Zappa was sufficiently impressed that he signed them to his label, which then brought them to the attention of its parent, Warner.

By 1976, the group had brought out eight gold or platinum albums, including the number one *Billion Dollar Babies* (1973) and a few memorable hit singles like "Eighteen" (1971) and "School's Out" (1972). Still, Alice Cooper's importance to rock history has much more to do with their outrageous stage antics than their music. These antics, which included cutting the heads off baby dolls, were invariably embellished by the press. The boa constrictor that Alice performed with became the biggest snake in the

Kiss played metal as heavy as anyone and were eminently successful at it. Their equally heavy use of make-up suggested a connection to the ascending glam rock movement that challenged traditional gender roles as never before.

world. When a chicken was trampled by the audience, it became, in the eyes of the press, Alice biting the heads off live chickens and drinking their blood. (There was a similar story about Ozzy Osbourne biting the head off a bat. The story simply fed the quest for evidence of Satanism.) Stranger yet, the group's members performed in spandex, high-heeled boots, and makeup. Forget that they looked about as feminine as Frank Sinatra; these guys wore makeup at a time when "real men"—especially a bunch of heterosexual ex-athletes from Phoenix—did not wear makeup. It was a perverse challenge to the security of fixed gender roles.

Kiss, a group that played metal as heavy as anyone with a posture that was just as macho, made makeup their trademark. As with Alice Cooper, the fact that Kiss racked up eight gold or platinum albums in the 1970s and were still going strong at the end of the following decade is less important to rock history than the image they presented. Members of Kiss did not just apply cosmetics, they donned whole personas. Bassist Gene Simmons (the one with the tongue) became a ghoulish monster, drummer Peter Criss, a cat, guitarists Paul Stanley and Ace Frehley, a clown and a spaceman. The group's gimmick of never being photographed without their makeup—to which they held fast until 1983—added measurably to their mystique.

All That Glitters Does Not Sell Gold

The success of Alice Cooper and Kiss proved that the limits of decorum and personal appearance could be pushed, and during the early 1970s, there was a short-lived movement in rock that pushed them over the edge. Glam, or glitter rock challenged traditional notions of masculinity and femininity as no other music had. As Iain Chambers has written, "'Glam' or 'glitter' rock's inroads into the public figure of male sexuality, in which the chameleon figure of David Bowie was seminal, seemed to crack an image brittle with repression."[87] In the United States, the focal point for the developing glitter scene was New York's Mercer Art Center, where groups like the Forty-Second Street Harlots, the Miamis, Teenage Lust, and the transvestite Wayne County held forth. It was here that the New York Dolls became local favorites. The New York Dolls played a brand of rock that would have placed the group somewhere near the Rolling Stones on the popular music continuum, but the music was tinged with the kind of informed cynicism that could only be bred in New York. Mostly burned-out, working-class dropouts, they performed in full drag—high heels, tights, mini-skirts, and bright red lipstick. Why they were surprised when people related to them as a "bunch of transsexual junkies or something" is baffling. Even with albums produced by Todd Rundgren (*New York Dolls,* 1973) and girl group veteran Shadow Morton (*Too Much Too Soon,* 1974), the Dolls never really got beyond cult status. Lead singer David Johansen did achieve some measure of pop success in the 1980s as Buster Poindexter.

The glitter scene in England was more developed, extending the music's reach to the rarefied atmosphere of art rock in one direction and teenybopper pop in another. When the tantalizing Marc Bolan shortened the name of his group from Tyrannosaurus Rex to T. Rex, he signaled a move to an electric hard rock style ("Bang a Gong (Get It On)," 1972) and brought the world of sequins and platform boots to teen fans. By the time of Bolan's death in 1977, many of his fans had switched their allegiance to The Sweet ("Little Willy," "Ballroom Blitz," "Fox on the Run," "Love Is Like Oxygen"). The portly Gary Glitter was another British star who excited teenagers with Elvis-styled sequined costumes and lackluster pounding rock. Alvin Stardust was similarly camp. Neither performer made a dent in the U.S. market.

The glam rocker who did and invested the music with its most lasting artistry and memorable theatrics was David Bowie. As Iain Chambers stated:

> His "feminine" pose and extravagant attire speak an indeterminate language, an androgynous code. But the narcissistic atmosphere this image invokes is in turn richly ambiguous. . . . Such a public display in self-fascination gestures towards the possibility of loosening the sexed male subject from previous, more predictable, moorings.[88]

Born David Jones, Bowie took his surname from the Bowie knife to avoid being confused with the Monkees' lead singer Davy Jones. When Bowie's early hard-rock style failed to capture a substantial following, he turned his attention to creating new personas for himself, mindful that such brazen artificiality represented a break with the rock authenticity he had once embraced. Drawing on influences as diverse as mime, the Beat poets, Dylan, the bohemianism of Oscar Wilde, and Warhol's pop avant-gardism, Bowie pointed the way to the future.

No artist marketed sexual ambiguity more successfully than Bowie did. Originally included in his 1969 album *Man of Words, Man of Music,* "Space Oddity," which became his first Top Forty hit when reissued in 1973, established Bowie as an extraterrestrial, an outsider looking in. The original cover of his follow-up album, *The Man Who Sold the World* (1970), pictured the artist in drag but it was withdrawn (at that point, it was ahead of its time) and a different cover was used. In addition to tributes to Dylan and Warhol, *Hunky Dory* (1972) contained "Changes" and "Oh! You Pretty Things," both of which celebrated

When David Bowie's early hard-rock style failed to capture a substantial following, he turned his attention to creating new personas for himself, mindful that such brazen artificiality represented a break with the rock authenticity he had once embraced.

the sexual subterfuge of glitter as a defining characteristic of the new counterculture and provided great copy for questions about Bowie's own preferences. His chiseled good looks offset by orange hair and platform boots presented a most androgynous package. By 1972, Bowie was more than ready to inhabit his alien alter ego Ziggy Stardust. The tour supporting the release of *The Rise and Fall of Ziggy Stardust and the Spiders from Mars* was a lavish glam rock extravaganza. It was during this period that Bowie announced his bisex-

With his androgynous good looks and flair for ambiguity, David Bowie elevated sexual subterfuge to an art form and provided critics with a seemingly endless list of questions regarding his own sexuality.

uality to the press. Never one to milk a persona for too long, he continued projecting sexual ambiguity through other protagonists on *Aladdin Sane* (1973) and *Diamond Dogs* (1974).

Credit for Bowie's marketing triumph was due, at least in part, to his manager Tony De Fries, who was also the manager for Lou Reed, Iggy Pop and the Stooges, and Mott the Hoople. This network not only placed Bowie in a line that led directly to punk, but it also drew the other artists into the orbit of glam. *Aladdin Sane* included "Jean Genie," a tribute that linked Iggy Pop with Jean Genet. In 1972, Bowie produced Iggy Pop's *Raw Power,* as well as Lou Reed's *Transformer,* which included his only hit single "Walk on the Wild Side," a darkly focused paean to sexual adventurism. That same year, Bowie produced Mott the Hoople's *All the Young Dudes,* the album that gave the group a new lease on life. The association with Bowie and the juxtaposition of the album's title cut with songs like "One of the Boys" and Lou Reed's "Sweet Jane" (about a New York transvestite), located the straight (in all senses) rock group in the middle of the "trendy gayness" of glam. The group was appreciative of Bowie's input, even if somewhat confused by its effects.

If in the construction of himself as an ever-changing media icon, Bowie took a lesson from Warhol's pop art manipulations, Bryan Ferry of Roxy Music was even more deliberate in his application of pop art principles. Ferry's early lyrics used "throwaway clichés and amusing phrases that you found in magazines or used in everyday speech— stylistic juxtapositions."[89] "Virginia Plain" (1972), the group's first hit single from their self-titled debut album, was a rambling pop narrative that took its title from a brand of cigarettes. As per the Warhol maxim that real art is commercial art, Ferry was also concerned with packaging, both of himself in the finest glam tradition and of his album covers. The cover for *For Your Pleasure* (1973) had seductive black satinlike surfaces. The cover for *Country Life,* the group's 1975 introduction to the American mainstream, originally pictured two scantily clad models.

Roxy Music's early sound resulted from the tension (musical and otherwise) between Ferry and Brian Eno. Armed with a Revox tape recorder, a VCS 3 synthesizer, and no musical training, Eno joined the group in 1971 as a "technical expert" rather than a musician. Eno's input moved the music in a direction that held sound and style to a higher value than musicianship per se. After leaving Roxy Music, Eno joined Bowie on a retreat to Berlin where the two collaborated on three albums of avant-garde synthpop. By this time, Roxy Music had had its only Top Forty single in the United States, "Love Is the Drug" (1976), and glam was about to be stripped naked by punk, a development Eno had anticipated on his solo single "Seven Deadly Finns" in 1974.

Between his Ziggy Stardust period and his Berlin reclusiveness, Bowie went through a number of changes. In embracing the artificial, Bowie had led the way from hippie idealism toward the eruption of punk. In 1975, he took another unexpected turn, swapping "the sci-fi future" of his glam period "for the uniform of white soul boy."[90] After *Diamond Dogs,* he decided to venture to Sigma Sound Studios in Philadelphia, the spiritual center of soft soul. There he recorded *Young Americans,* an album that Peter York would later describe as "avant-garde disco."[91] The title cut became a hit, and "Fame" provided Bowie with his first number one American single. Lou Reed had anticipated the move in *Sally Can't Dance* in 1974, but Reed's outing was sandwiched between other experiments in heavy metal and white noise and no one noticed. It was Bowie who became the first white performer of note to straddle both punk and disco.

David Bowie reinvents himself, straddles punk and disco

By the early 1970s, the established music industry had consolidated its hold over the rock and soul styles that grew out of the 1960s. In the fragmentation of popular music that ensued, audiences that might have overlapped in an earlier time were treated as discrete entities. This trend reached its zenith in the late 1970s in the emergence of punk and disco, whose audiences were viewed as mutually exclusive. Punk and disco were thus positioned as the two poles of pop that would define the extremes of a decade in which rock began to lose its status as outsider art.

NOTES

1. Michael Lydon, "Rock for Sale," in *The Age of Rock 2: Sights and Sounds of the American Cultural Revolution,* ed. Michael Lydon (New York: Vintage Books, 1970), 53.

2. Steve Pond, "The Seventies," *Rolling Stone,* 20 September 1990, p. 53.

3. For a detailed discussion of the merger movement, see Steve Chapple and Reebee Garofalo, *Rock 'n' Roll Is Here to Pay: The History and Politics of the Music Industry* (Chicago: Nelson-Hall, 1977), 82–87.

4. Peter Wicke, *Rock Music: Culture, Aesthetics and Sociology* (Cambridge: Cambridge University Press, 1990), 121.

5. Ben Fong-Torres, ed., *The Rolling Stone Interviews,* vol. 2 (New York: Warner Books, 1973), 292.

6. Wicke, *Rock Music: Culture, Aesthetics and Sociology,* 126.

7. Chapple and Garofalo, *Rock 'n' Roll Is Here to Pay,* 175.

8. Ibid., 109.

9. Ibid., 121.

10. Robert Draper, *Rolling Stone Magazine* (New York: Harper and Row, 1990).

11. Jann Wenner, "A Letter from the Editor." *Rolling Stone,* 9 November 1967, p. 2.

12. Michael Lydon, "The High Cost of Music and Love: Where's the Money from Monterey?" *Rolling Stone,* 9 November 1967, p. 1.

13. Jann Wenner, "A Letter from the Editor," p. 2.

14. Draper, *Rolling Stone Magazine,* 95.

15. Jann Wenner, "Musicians Reject New Political Exploiters," *Rolling Stone,* 11 May 1968, pp. 1, 22.

16. Jann Wenner, Introduction to "The Sound of Marching Charging Feet," by Michael Rossman, *Rolling Stone,* Special Insert: "American Revolution 1969," 5 April 1969, p. 1.

17. Draper, *Rolling Stone Magazine,* 157.

18. Jann Wenner, "A Letter from the Editor: On the Occasion of Our Fourth Anniversary Issue," *Rolling Stone,* 11 November 1971, p. 34.

19. *The Compleat Beatles,* video documentary, produced by Patrick Montgomery, 1982.

20. Ibid.

21. Joe Smith, *Off the Record: An Oral History of Popular Music* (New York: Warner Books, 1988), 242.

22. Simon Frith, *Sound Effects: Youth Leisure and the Politics of Rock 'n' Roll* (New York: Pantheon, 1981), 53.

23. *The Compleat Beatles,* 1982.

24. Ralph Gleason, "Perspectives: Changing with the Money Changers," *Rolling Stone,* 20 January 1968, p. 9.

25. Ralph Gleason, "Stop This Shuck Mike Bloomfield," *Rolling Stone,* 11 May 1968. p. 10.

26. John Pidgeon, *Eric Clapton* (London: Panther, 1976), 65.

27. Dave Morse, *Motown* (London: Vista, 1971), 108.

28. Jon Landau, "Soul," *Rolling Stone,* 24 February 1968, p. 18.

29. "The Rolling Stone Interview: Keith Richards," *Rolling Stone,* 19 August 1971, p. 24.

30. Wicke, *Rock Music: Culture, Aesthetics and Sociology,* 95.

31. Simon Frith and Howard Horne, *Art into Pop* (New York: Methuen, 1987), 86.

32. Ibid., 109.

33. Ibid., 108.

34. Ibid., 107.

35. Iain Chambers, *Urban Rhythms: Pop Music and Popular Culture* (New York: Macmillan, 1985), 114–115.

36. Robert Walser, *Running with the Devil: Power, Gender, and Madness in Heavy Metal Music* (Hanover, N.H.: Wesleyan University Press, 1993), 61–62.

37. Irwin Stambler, *Encyclopedia of Pop, Rock & Soul* (New York: St. Martins, 1977), 176.

38. Frith and Horne, *Art into Pop,* 98.

39. *Rolling Stone,* 28 May 1970, p. 17.

40. Chambers, *Urban Rhythms,* 118.

41. "Wexler Attributes Greater R&B Volume to Black Buyer," *Billboard,* 20 November 1971, p. 8.

42. Paul Ackerman, "Gortikov Scorches Whitey Trade in NATRA Speech," *Billboard,* 17 July 1969, p. 1.

43. "New Black Hope," *Billboard,* 17 May 1969, p. 34.

44. John Lombardi, "Kenny Gamble and Leon Huff and the Resurrection of Jerry Butler and Philly Soul," *Rolling Stone,* 30 April 1970, p. 39.

45. Nelson George, *The Death of Rhythm & Blues* (New York: Pantheon Books, 1988), 145.

46. Jim Miller, "The Sound of Philadelphia," in *The Rolling Stone Illustrated History of Rock & Roll,* ed. Anthony DeCurtis and James Henke (New York: Random House, 1992), 518.

47. Of course, not all veteran r&b groups were this lucky. The Dells, the model for Robert Townshend's film *The Five Heartbeats,* had been together since 1953. The group's biggest success, "Oh, What a Night" (1969), was a remake of an r&b hit the group had recorded thirteen years earlier. The Dell's last Top Forty hit was in 1973.

48. Jon Landau, "The Motown Story," *Rolling Stone,* 13 May 1971, p. 42.

49. *Billboard,* 20 November 1971, p. 8.

50. Ray Brack, "James Brown," *Rolling Stone,* 21 January 1970, p. 12.

51. Peter Guralnick, *Sweet Soul Music* (New York: Harper and Row, 1986), 391.

52. Robert Christgau, *Any Old Way You Choose It: Rock and Other Pop Music, 1967–1973* (Baltimore: Penguin Books, 1973), 217.

53. Ibid., 211.

54. Chapple and Garofalo, *Rock 'n' Roll Is Here to Pay,* 80.

55. Katherine Orloff, *Rock 'n Roll Woman* (Los Angeles: Nash Publishing, 1974), 11.

56. Gillian G. Gaar, *She's a Rebel: The History of Women in Rock & Roll* (Seattle: Seal Press, 1992), 123.

57. Orloff, *Rock 'n Roll Woman.* 133.

58. Christgau, *Any Old Way You Choose It,* 212.

59. Stephen Holden, "The Evolution of the singer-songwriter ," in *The Rolling Stone Illustrated History of Rock & Roll,* ed. Anthony DeCurtis and James Henke (New York: Random House, 1992), 489.

60. Robin Denselow, *When the Music's Over: The Story of Political Pop* (Boston: Faber and Faber, 1989), 180.

61. Ellen Willis, "Beginning to See the Light: or Rock & Roll, Feminism, and Night Blindness," *Village Voice,* 27 March 1978, pp. 21–22.

62. Christgau, *Any Old Way You Choose It,* 274.

63. Gaar, *She's a Rebel,* 138.

64. Ibid., 136.

65. Ibid., 139.

66. Cynthia M. Lont, "Women's Music: No Longer a Small Private Party," in *Rockin' the Boat: Mass Music and Mass Movements,* ed. Reebee Garofalo (Boston: South End Press, 1992), 242.

67. Gaar, *She's a Rebel,* 155–156.

68. Bill C. Malone, *Country Music, USA* (Austin: University of Texas Press, 1985), 386.

69. Stambler, *Encyclopedia of Pop, Rock & Soul,* 37.

70. Christgau, *Any Old Way You Choose It,* 269.

71. Anthony DeCurtis, "The Eagles," *Rolling Stone,* 20 September 1990, p. 92.

72. Malone, *Country Music, USA,* 404–405.

73. Deena Weinstein, *Heavy Metal: A Cultural Sociology* (New York: Lexington Books, 1991), 23.

74. Walser, *Running with the Devil,* 2.

75. Weinstein, *Heavy Metal,* 16.

76. Walser, *Running with the Devil,* 57–107.

77. Ibid., 10.

78. J. D. Considine, "Led Zeppelin," *Rolling Stone,* 20 September 1990, p. 59.

79. Stambler, *Encyclopedia of Pop, Rock & Soul,* 57.

80. Ibid.

81. Walser, *Running with the Devil,* 61, citing Mordechai, "Where There's Smoke . . . There's Fire." *Guitar World,* February 1991, 62.

82. Walser, *Running with the Devil,* 66.

83. Ibid., 68.

84. Christgau, *Any Old Way You Choose It,* 116.

85. Considine, "Led Zeppelin," 59, 109.

86. Smith, *Off the Record,* 273.

87. Chambers, *Urban Rhythms,* 113.

88. Ibid.

89. Frith and Horne, *Art into Pop,* 115.

90. Chambers, *Urban Rhythms,* 133.

91. Peter York, *Style Wars* (London: Sidgwick and Jackson, 1980). Cited in Chambers, *Urban Rhythms,* 138.

8 Punk and Disco: The Poles of Pop

When the U.S. music business passed the $2 billion mark in the early 1970s, many assumed that sales would continue to climb indefinitely. When the industry doubled in size between 1973 and 1978 and surpassed $4 billion in annual sales in 1978, years ahead of official growth projections, it appeared as if the assumption was correct. An era of mergers, it seemed, had consolidated the industry into a rationalized music machine. Industry marketing suggested that, with a generous expenditure of promotional dollars, sufficient exposure on radio, and a tour supporting his or her release, any proven artist could almost guarantee millions of dollars in return. As the country's leadership shifted from the lackluster and conservative Gerald Ford to the pleasant but largely ineffectual Jimmy Carter, it seemed to many that the rock 'n' roll rebellion that had begun in the 1950s was on the verge of being tamed. Popular music was becoming centrist, corporate, safe.

As the country's leadership shifted from the lackluster and conservative Gerald Ford to the pleasant but largely ineffectual Jimmy Carter, it seemed to many that the rock 'n' roll rebellion that had begun in the 1950s was on the verge of being tamed. Popular music was becoming centrist, corporate, safe.

If popular music could be drawn as a bell curve, the center of the curve would house a number of middle-of-the-road artists who borrowed soft-rock styles for pop-sounding lounge acts. Beginning with "(They Long to Be) Close to You" in 1970, the Carpenters, for example, parlayed a clever combination of rock covers and originals into twenty Top Forty hits in just over a decade. Barry Manilow, who began as the piano accompanist in the gay bathhouse where Bette Midler got her start, produced twenty-five Top Forty singles and became one of the industry's biggest stars. At the height of his career, he had three albums in a row—*This One's for You* (1976), *Barry Manilow Live* (1977), and *Even Now* (1978)—that sold more than 3 million copies each. Neil Diamond topped both of them. Between 1970 and 1986 he scored thirty-six Top Forty singles and twenty gold and platinum albums. It is a telling commentary on the state of popular music in the 1970s that the most popular singles of the year between 1974 and 1976 were "The Way We Were" by Barbra Streisand, "Love Will Keep Us Together" by the Captain and Tennille, and "Silly Little Love Songs" by Paul McCartney and Wings.

The pop rockers of the time were only slightly more adventurous. The album that dominated the charts in 1976 was Peter Frampton's *Frampton Comes Alive!* As a member of Humble Pie, Frampton had flirted with heavy metal; as a solo artist, he became a teen idol, more interested in melodic sweetness than volume. His first Top Thirty album, *Frampton* (1975), showcased the songs that would become his major hits ("Show Me the Way," "Baby, I Love Your Way," and "Do You Feel Like We Do") as melodic rockers with an acoustic feel. *Frampton Comes Alive!,* recorded live at the Winterland in San Francisco, made a nod toward his origins by including the same songs at hard-rock volume. The LP charted for nearly two years, selling more than 10 million copies.

Fleetwood Mac was a more mature version of these same rock tendencies. With their roots in John Mayall's Bluesbreakers, Fleetwood Mac really gelled when Britons Mick Fleetwood and John and Christine McVie added the acoustic/electric guitar stylings and sweet harmonies of Americans Lindsay Buckingham and Stevie Nicks to the group. The self-titled debut album of the reconstituted Fleetwood Mac hit number one in 1975, but it was *Rumours* (1977) that earned Fleetwood Mac a mythic place in rock lore. *Rumours* was a straight-ahead, upbeat pop-rock compilation that hit number one and generated four hit singles, including the number one "Dreams." The album sold 10 million copies in the United States and 25 million worldwide. When the group's follow-up album, *Tusk,* sold 4 million copies, there was a tendency to preface the accomplishment with the word "only." But then, in the mid-1970s, the music industry was basking in sales figures like these. Between Frampton's and Fleetwood Mac's hits, the Eagles released *Hotel California* which sold 11 million copies. Also released in 1976, Stevie Wonder's *Songs in the Key of Life*, Linda Ronstadt's *Hasten Down the Wind*, Boz Scaggs' *Silk Degrees*, and Boston's *Boston* all sold more than 3 million copies. The platinum releases that same year by Bob Dylan, Chicago, the Doobie Brothers, the Rolling Stones, Kansas, Ted Nugent, Rush, Foghat, Rod Stewart, and Elton John seemed almost routine by comparison.

As a gay man, Elton John added a bit of spice to the mainstream. With his Presleyesque glitter tendencies and wild array of custom-made eyeglasses, he was something of the Liberace of rock. Well before *Blue Moves,* his first platinum album, he was a bona fide rock star with seven number one albums to his credit, five of them in a row. With his long-time collaborator, Bernie Taupin, he was also a prolific writer whose compositions captured the spirit of vintage rock 'n' roll with a sense of humor. Early standout hits like "Rocket Man," "Crocodile Rock," "Goodbye Yellow Brick Road," and "Bennie and the Jets" celebrated the entertainment value of a well-crafted song without succumbing to the self-importance of art rock. Throughout the late 1970s, John produced hit singles and platinum albums, always remaining a cut above the formula

In mid-1970s, platinum record sales appear to be routine

mentality of the time. He brought something of the flair and showmanship of glam into the mainstream during one of rock's most colorless periods.

There were a few other artists who also had something to offer in the way of rock artistry during this period. Billy Joel, a piano man like Elton John, was an intensely personal songwriter who was able to muster a bit of John's flamboyance in concert. Like Bruce Springsteen, Joel added a rock edge to the craft of the singer/songwriter, but he projected more of a mainstream image. On *The Stranger* (1977) and *52nd Street* (1978), which rose to numbers two and one, respectively, he explored cultural themes and created portraits of everyday life with drive and sophistication, laying the groundwork for a career that would carry him past the next decade. Borrowing from jazz, r&b, and rock, Steely Dan introduced a level of instrumental sophistication that was rare in the mainstream market. Named after the dildo in William Burroughs' *Naked Lunch,* Steely Dan was essentially a studio band founded by quirky writer/instrumentalists Walter Becker and Donald Fagan who assembled different sidemen for various album projects. Although the group almost never toured, their fluid rhythms, cryptic lyrics, and exacting production generated sales. *Pretzel Logic* (1974), *Aja* (1977), and *Gaucho* (1980) all went Top Ten.

Aside from the occasional burst of creative energy offered by these artists, however, the center of rock had begun to take itself and its audience for granted. Beginning in the mid-1970s and continuing well into the 1980s, groups like Bob Seger and the Silver Bullet Band, Foghat, Styx, and Supertramp, followed by Foreigner, Journey, Air Supply, and REO Speedwagon, relied on tried and true music and business practices to produce guaranteed sales. It wasn't that their music was incompetent, it's that it was uninspired. It appeared that the mainstream music industry had become such a well-oiled music machine that, with precious little in the way of innovation and next to nothing approaching passion, any second-rate rock group could be assured of radio play, full stadiums, and platinum record sales. There were, however, other styles of music still in their formative stages, that were positioned at the periphery of the cultural continuum. There were initially few suitable venues for them and they were well beyond the pale of radio play. At one extreme there was punk, at the other, disco. In different ways and for different reasons, they would shake rock out of its complacency, at least for a time.

> It appeared that the mainstream music industry had become such a well-oiled music machine that, with precious little in the way of innovation and next to nothing approaching passion, any second-rate rock group could be assured of radio play, full stadiums, and platinum record sales.

Punk Versus Disco

There are, of course, a number of obvious distinctions between punk and disco. While disco was smooth, sleek, and sensual, punk was dense, discordant, and defiant. While disco depended on technological sophistication and studio production, punk's three chords could be hammered out by any garage band that could get its hands on an electric guitar. While disco dancers aspired to the controlled energy of the gymnast or the precision of group choreography, punks in the "pit" approximated the antics of a tag-team wrestling match. "[P]ogo dancing—jumping up and down and flailing one's arms," observed Charles M. Young, "is as far as one can get from the Hustle."[1] Disco proudly took its place among other black dance music styles. *Rolling Stone*'s Mikal Gilmore suggested that those "rock purists" who dismissed it as "a frivolous form of expression might do well to remember that rock & roll and rhythm & blues were dance styles, too, before they became art forms."[2] Punk, however, had a different agenda. Punk's aim was to deconstruct rock 'n' roll, bleeding it of its black rhythmic influences until only the elements of noise and texture remained. Robert Christgau noted that punk "differentiates itself from its (fundamentally black and rural) sources by taking on the crude, ugly, perhaps brutal facts of the (white and urban) prevailing culture, rather than hiding behind its bland facade."[3] Needless to say, these differences were mirrored in fashion statements that pitted the sheen of polyester leisure suits against the chill of black leather bondage gear and ripped T-shirts held together by safety pins. Fans of each viewed each other with surprise. "It was funny," Legs McNeil, cofounder of *Punk* magazine, has said. "You'd see guys going out to a Punk club, passing black people going into a disco, and they'd be looking at each other, not with disgust, but 'Isn't it weird that they want to go there.'"[4]

Differences as obvious as these tend to obscure the fact that there were certain similarities between the punk and disco cultures. Both were initially shunned by radio (albeit for different reasons) and forced to develop their own countercultural networks. Both were seen as contributing significantly to the destruction of Western civilization—punk with its nihilism, disco with its decadence. Both encouraged active—indeed, fanatical—participation among their audiences. Finally, both arose in reaction to the complacency of the music that preceded them. Compare, for example, Andrew Kopkind on disco with Simon Frith on punk. "Disco in the '70s is in revolt against rock in the '60s," Kopkind explained. "Disco is 'unreal', artificial, and exaggerated. It affirms the fantasies, gossip, frivolity, and fun of an evasive era."[5] Frith, describing the impetus for punk, told his readers that "the reason why teenage music must be *remade* is because all the original rock-'n'rollers have become boring old farts, imprisoned by the routines of show biz. . . . I'd rather listen to a good punk rock'n'roll band like the Jam or the Boomtown Rats than to either the old or new work of their original models, the Who and the Stones. But I'm still listening for the old reason—to feel good."[6] The motivation and effect of both genres was quite the same—to intensify the feeling of the moment in an otherwise uncertain world.

Still, most critics at the time decried disco as escapist and embraced punk as a political statement. According to Frith, "the return to rock'n'roll roots is, in itself, a radical rejection of record company habits and punk's musical simplicity is a political statement. The ideology of the garage band is an attack on the star system."[7] Although disco spawned its own multibillion dollar subindustry and punk barely registered a blip in sales, disco made no overt political statement. Herein lies the source of the distortion in the way in which the histories of punk and disco have been recounted. It was punk's political possibilities, real or imagined, that captured the attention of rock critics who had cut their teeth on the political movements of the 1960s. Never has so much been written by so many about so little. As Andrew Kopkind complained in 1979, "John Rockwell was still writing Hegelian analyses of the Sex Pistols in the Sunday *Times* when two-thirds of the city was listening to Donna Summer and couldn't tell Mr. Rotten from Mr. Respighi."[8]

Although disco was seldom intentionally political, in the long run it may have scored a larger political victory than punk. While a good deal of punk, particularly its British variant, was conceived politically, the conflict between its progressive urges and its flirtation with Nazi imagery often led to mixed results in its ability to pull people together. Disco, especially in the United States, brought people together across racial lines not to mention lines of class and sexual preference. It was disco that, as critic Abe Peck has noted, enabled "black artists [to] conquer the pop charts in a way they never did even during the height of rhythm and blues."[9] In such a context, anti-disco slogans like "Death to Disco" and "Disco Sucks" have to be regarded more as racial (and sexual) epithets than as statements of musical preference and the systematic avoidance of disco by the rock critical establishment can only be construed as racist, as Mikal Gilmore suggested in 1977:

A**nti-disco slogans like "Death to Disco" and "Disco Sucks" have to be regarded more as racial (and sexual) epithets than as statements of musical preference and the systematic avoidance of disco by the rock critical establishment can only be construed as racist.**

> [W]henever a phenomenon is given blanket dismissal, you can be sure something deeper is at work. And what's going on here is that rock fans, like the proverbial cake, have been left out in the rain. Disco's principal constituents have been gays, blacks, Hispanics . . . Then coincident with Saturday Night Fever, disco achieved anthem-like status with urban, working-class youth. So, in effect, disco had done what punk was supposed to accomplish. . . . rock pride was wounded. Somehow, an entire grassroots movement had passed us by: No wonder Clash fans cry, "Disco sucks!"[10]

By the time the decade had ended, disco had swamped the music business, and punk had imploded. While disco would collapse shortly thereafter, punk would be born again as new wave, incorporating such a wide range of influences, they included disco itself.

Punk: Rock as (White) Noise

If the history of punk has been distorted in favor of its political impact, there has been a corresponding tendency to emphasize its British origins because its arrival there coincided with right-wing advances and decaying social conditions, which gave the music a more critical political edge. In the United States, where the Carter presidency offered a brief, and ultimately fruitless, respite from the preceding eight years (and subsequent twelve) of conservative government, punk was less disruptive and more easily incorporated into the star-making machinery of the music industry once it got off the ground. Thus, in putting punk's best political foot forward, critics usually look first to the Sex Pistols, a British group that caused a political furor in their home country even before releasing their first single in 1976. While political impact is certainly one valid measure of the importance of a cultural form, it may not be the best way to trace its origins.

"It's the Before and After Sex Pistols debate," Caroline Coon wrote in *Melody Maker* in 1976. "'We saw Johnny Rotten and he CHANGED our attitude to music' (the Clash, Buzzcocks), or 'We played like this AGES before the Sex Pistols' (Slaughter and the Dogs), or 'We are miles better than the Sex Pistols' (the Damned)."[11] Comments like Coon's, which fail to mention a single U.S. group, limit discussion to the development of British punk and consign even British groups like the modish Jam (formed in 1974) to the category of "1960s revivalists." While there was something of a rivalry between London and New York in the competition for the punk throne, the emergence of U.S. punk does, in fact, predate its British eruption by nearly two years. While the Sex Pistols may have set the standard in England, they never registered on the Top Forty album or singles charts in the United States and broke up before completing their first and only U.S. tour. (Indeed, it was rare in the United States for a punk group to transcend cult status, much less to have a hit record.) The fact of the group's celebrity reveals one of the most important features of punk: its myth was always more powerful than its reality.

Central to the myth of the Sex Pistols is Malcolm McLaren, the group's manager. McLaren, who claimed he had managed the New York Dolls before returning to England to create the Sex Pistols, enjoyed picturing himself as a Machiavellian manipulator with a master plan to use the power of the music industry against itself, in the service of radical social change. In fact, he was never a committed activist. He was, however, fascinated by the 1968 student revolts in Paris (he even claimed to have been there) and intrigued by the tactics of the French situationists who created media-savvy situations as a way of transforming everyday life.

McLaren began as a sophisticated rag merchant with a keen eye toward youth fashion. He and his partner, Vivienne Westwood, had a shop at 430 Kings Road. In its first incarnation, it was called Let It Rock, and it appealed to impeccably attired teddy boys. When that fad began to fade, McLaren and Westwood changed the name of the shop to Too Fast to Live, To Young to Die and oriented its fashions toward leather-clad rockers. While in McLaren's myth he fashioned the Sex Pistols from nothing, in reality guitarist Steve Jones and drummer Paul Cook had already started the prototype group, the Strand (named after the Roxy Music song), before they began to frequent number 430. Bassist Glen Matlock joined later. It was Jones and Cook who went looking for McLaren to be their manager, not McLaren who went looking for them. Further complicating the picture was the addition of John Lydon (Johnny Rotten) as lead singer. Everyone knew that Lydon couldn't sing and had no sense of rhythm but, according to *Rolling Stone*'s Charles M. Young, he had three qualities to recommend him: "1) his face had the pallor of death; 2) he went around spitting on poseurs he passed on the street; and 3) he was the first to understand the democratic implications of punk."[12] While Lydon and McLaren would vie for control of the group until the end, at the time Lydon joined the group, McLaren and Westwood had reopened Too Fast to Live, To Young to Die as a shop called Sex, hence the group's name, Sex Pistols. At this point in their development, McLaren saw the group more as a vehicle for selling T-Shirts and trousers than as point men in an anarchist revolt.

McLaren's claim that he managed the New York Dolls was equally distorted. He had met the Dolls' guitarist Sylvain Sylvain, who had been a clothing manufacturer, in 1973 when he visited New York to exhibit clothing from Let It Rock. Through Sylvain, he met the rest of the group, which was then the toast of the underground. Having garnered the approval of the Dolls, McLaren was given the keys to the subterranean city: a room at the Chelsea Hotel, an invitation to meet Andy Warhol, and an interview in *Interview*.

McLaren became completely obsessed with the group, joining them on a tour of Europe later that year. It wasn't until the fall of 1974 that he revisited New York. By this time, the group was in trouble. The Mercer Art Center had physically collapsed a year earlier, leaving the Dolls without their major venue; the group's second album had stalled at number 167 on the charts; drummer Billy Murcia had died of a drug over-

Malcolm McLaren did more than anyone to promote the myth of punk and himself. As manager of the Sex Pistols, he transformed passing events into the stuff of legends.

dose; guitarist Johnny Thunders and drummer Jerry Nolan had serious heroin habits; and bassist Arthur Kane was well along the way to becoming a complete alcoholic. Finally, Marty Thau, the group's manager, dropped them. It was at this point that McLaren entered the picture. As a friend, he did right by the group, finding hospitals and drug treatment programs for those who needed them. As a manager, a relationship that was never formalized, he simply orchestrated the Doll's last gasp. Drawing on his interest in radical politics, he dressed the group in red patent leather with hammer and sickle flags for a backdrop and sent the press a manifesto rather than an invitation to their upcoming shows. "Out went Glam, in came Communism," said historian Jon Savage.[13] By most accounts, the band was tight, but, with no substance to their posture, their newest attempt at outrage had no beneficial effect. "You get beat up for being a fag," observed photographer Bob Gruen, "but you get killed for being a Commie."[14] Metaphorically speaking, this is exactly what happened to the Dolls, as their three-year run at celebrity abruptly came to a halt.

Born in the USA

During the descent of the Dolls, New York trash rock had gotten considerably more stripped down. As 1973 was crossing over into 1974, club owner Hilly Kristal was in the process of reopening his hangout for bikers and winos on the Bowery as a bar called Country Blue Grass and Blues (CBGB). Although Kristal expected country music to be the next big thing, Tom Verlaine and Richard Lloyd from the band Television convinced him to book underground rock acts. Within months, CBGB, the dingy Bowery bar, became the heart of the New York rock underground. Its only competition was Max's Kansas City. By the time McLaren returned to New York to preside over the Doll's demise, Hilly Kristal was already playing host to Television and the scene that would yield Patti Smith, Blondie, the Ramones, and the Talking Heads.

One thing that the first wave of punk rockers on both sides of the ocean had in common was a sense of rock 'n' roll history that recognized the importance of the Velvet Underground and Iggy Pop and the Stooges.

One thing that the first wave of punk rockers on both sides of the ocean had in common was a sense of rock 'n' roll history that recognized the importance of the Velvet Underground and Iggy Pop and the Stooges. At the poles of the Velvet Underground's creative axis were Lou Reed and John Cale. The Brooklyn-born Reed appeared to be your average college student. His tastes in music ran from doo wop and rhythm and blues to jazz. After graduating from college, he even became an assembly-line songwriter at Pickwick Records for a while. In 1965, however, songs like "Heroin" needed a more unorthodox vehicle than Pickwick could provide. Cale had a degree in classical music; his tastes ran more to the avant-garde sounds of Stockhausen, John Cage, and La Monte Young. The buzzsaw sound of Cale's modified electric viola became part of the early Velvet trademark sound and an inspiration to a generation of punks. The group's sound was rounded out by Sterling Morrison, a classically-trained bassist, and female drummer Maureen Tucker.

The Velvets' repertoire, instrumentation, and avant-garde excursions into feedback and white noise were in place before their fabled association with Andy Warhol began, providing an early model for McLaren's Sex Pistols myth. Warhol provided the group with a slot at the Factory (his umbrella for diverse multi-media projects), which was undoubtedly the best offer a band with material like "Heroin," "Venus in Furs," and "Black Angel's Death Song" could get in 1966. His only direct intervention was to install the striking Hungarian-born blonde singer Nico in the band as a more visually appealing focal point than the deadpan Reed. The new lineup was captured on the group's debut album, *The Velvet Underground and Nico,* in 1967. During this period, the group was incorporated into Warhol's touring multimedia show, the Exploding Plastic Inevitable.

Iggy Pop (born James Osterberg) was an uncultivated working-class kid from Ypsilanti, Michigan, who spent his high-school years playing in bands. It was at a performance of the Exploding Plastic Inevitable at the Ann Arbor Film Festival in 1966 that he was first exposed to the New York underground. His introduction to Warhol, affair with Nico, and subsequent induction into the art-rock scene must have been interesting for all concerned. In 1968, Pop founded the Psychedelic Stooges (later shortened to just Stooges) with the "unremittingly inept" Asheton brothers (Ron on guitar, Scott on drums). By this time he had already developed a style that, according to MC5 manager John Sinclair "had gone beyond performance—to the point where it was really some kind of psychodrama."[15] The group's material seldom included songs in the conventional sense; instead they were unstructured ramblings with titles like "The Dance of Romance," "Asthma Attack" and "Goodbye Bozos." Six months after the band was formed, the Stooges were signed to Elektra by a&r man Danny Fields. Fields had ventured to Detroit to sign the MC5 and, at the group's urging, had caught the Stooges' stage act. He was blown away by the group's "saber-toothed fury." Two weeks later he returned with Elektra's president Jac Holtzman and signed both groups. From Elektra's point of view, Iggy Pop must have seemed like a logical next step in the progression from the Doors to the MC5. Iggy's choice of John Cale as producer of his group's first album created a direct link between the Stooges and the Velvet Underground. Shortly thereafter Iggy was engaging in the acts of self-mutilation on stage (he once closed a New York date by making cuts in his chest with two drum sticks) that would earn him the title "Godfather of Punk."

By the end of the 1960s, the Velvet Underground had two more albums to their credit—*White Light/White Heat,* which included their classic seventeen-minute tale of horror, "Sister Ray," and *The Velvet Underground*—and Elektra had issued the Stooges' self-titled debut album. There were, however, so few venues that would book either act that it was almost impossible to promote their releases. Thus, they were frequently ignored. Only *White Light/White Heat* managed to scrape into the Top 200. By the early

1970s, the Stooges had disbanded and, of the original Velvet Underground, only Sterling Morrison remained. Two years later, David Bowie convinced the Stooges to reunite, but they could never keep it together for very long. By the time CBGB took off, the Stooges and the Velvets had more value as historical referents than as current practitioners. Still, the new generation of underground rockers who came to dominate the scene recognized their influence.

Punk usually followed the maxim: Whatever is popular, do the opposite. If hippies wore bell bottoms, punks would wear straight legs. If hippies ate brown rice and health food, punks would embrace fast-food, junk-food diets. If 1960s rock was inspired by psychedelic drugs (marijuana, LSD), punk's attitude and performance style would be defined by amphetamines (speed) on the way up and heroin coming down. If there was a politics to punk, it was the politics of refusal: the refusal to conform, the refusal to act with decorum, and in some cases, the refusal to learn how to play music. Aside from this fragile unity, the most distinctive thing about the early New York punk groups was just how different they were from each other. Consider, for example, Patti Smith's spoken-word rock poetry and mannish attire against Blondie's breathy pop and lead-singer Deborah Harry's peroxide persona; the Ramones' bikers-on-speed sound and image against the preppiness of the Talking Heads. The group that paved the way for all these opposites was Television.

> The most distinctive thing about the early New York punk groups was just how different they were from each other. Consider Patti Smith's spoken-word rock poetry and mannish attire against Blondie's breathy pop and lead-singer Deborah Harry's peroxide persona; the Ramones' bikers-on-speed sound and image against the preppiness of the Talking Heads.

Television, the first CBGB group to make a splash, was a ramshackle outfit that followed the Stooges' lead and pioneered the punk practice of learning on the gig. Although the group's guitarist Tom Verlaine cited John Coltrane and the free jazz of Albert Ayler among his influences and claimed that the Stones' "19th Nervous Breakdown" was his favorite rock 'n' roll song, an early review proclaimed that the group had "no musical or socially redeeming characteristics, and they know it."[16] At the time, this might have been taken as something of a backhanded compliment. Key to this endearing set of attributes was the presence of bass player Richard Meyers, a former poet, who took the name Richard Hell and lived up to it. Anticipating punk fashion, Hell supplied the look of Television—ripped T-shirts and close-cropped hair. The look was true to punk's maxim; it was as antiglam as it was antihippie. Hell also contributed the punk classic "Blank Generation"—an answer song of sorts to the Who's "My Generation"—to Television's early repertoire. While the song was taken as an early indicator of punk nihilism, Hell insisted that its message was misunderstood. "People misread what I meant by 'Blank Generation,'" he once told Clinton Heylin. "To me, 'blank' is a line where you can fill in anything. It's positive."[17] By the time Television had released its first independent single, "Little Johnny Jewel," tension between Verlaine and Hell had forced Hell out of the group. (Hell was also thrown out of his next group, the Heartbreakers.) It was not until 1977 that a reconstituted Television was able to follow "Johnny Jewel" with the album, *Marquee Moon,* one of the more interesting artifacts of the era. That same year, Hell committed "Blank Generation" to vinyl on an album of the same name with his new group, The Voidoids. By this time, punk was being called new wave.

Patti Smith was the first artist associated with CBGB to become famous. Smith attended Pratt Institute, an art school in Brooklyn, in the late 1960s. There she met her first mentor, photographer Robert Mapplethorpe, and became acquainted with the New York scene when she and Mapplethorpe took up residence at the Chelsea Hotel, which was then frequented by Andy Warhol and William Burroughs among others. While immersed in the Chelsea scene, she fell in love with playwright Sam Shepherd with whom she wrote *Cowboy Mouth* early in 1971. By this time, she was becoming known as a poet and had a burgeoning career as a rock journalist, writing primarily for *Creem* and *Rolling Stone.* Smith had already begun performing her work, accompanied by Lenny Kaye, a well-known rock journalist, on electric guitar when *Creem* took the unorthodox step (for a rock paper) of publishing a portfolio of her poetry late in 1971. One more boyfriend, Allen Lanier, keyboardist for Blue Öyster Cult, and an extended sabbatical in Paris where she visited Jim Morrison's grave took her several steps further in her journey toward the fusion of poetry and rock 'n' roll. Upon her return from Paris, she opened for the New York Dolls during the final days of the Mercer Art Center. After its collapse, she and Kaye began appearing regularly as a duo. However, it was not until they added pi-

anist Richard Sohl that they began to approximate the amalgam of free verse and improvisatory rock with which Smith would become identified. After attending a performance of Television at CBGB in the spring of 1974, the trio recorded their first single, "Piss Factory," which, with an assist from Tom Verlaine on lead guitar, was backed with "Hey Joe." "Piss Factory" was an

Patti Smith recorded the first punk album of note. Her androgynous attire, bohemian lifestyle, and successful fusion of rock and poetry suggested the possibility of new directions for music and new roles for women.

autobiographical account of the horrors of working in a New Jersey plant. The meaning of "Hey Joe" was transformed by an introductory poem about Patty Hearst's exploits with the Symbionese Liberation Army, which had created instant myth in 1974. By using an independent single to attract major label attention, Smith pioneered what would become the strategy of choice for punk groups from Television to the Sex Pistols. The release of the single coincided with Smith and Television sharing a memorable residency at Max's Kansas City. In the spring of 1975, this same double bill established CBGB as New York's premiere rock club. It was around the time of the CBGB residency that the Patti Smith Group was signed to Arista. By the time *Horses* was released in 1976, the group had added Ivan Kral on bass and Jay Dee Daughterty on drums. The ubiquitous John Cale served as producer. *Horses* was not only the first punk album of note, it was one of the few ever to enter the Top Fifty. Smith, whose trademark of a man's white shirt and tie also suggested possible new roles for women, was well on the way to stardom when she fell off a ten-foot stage while promoting the group's second album, *Radio Ethiopia,* and broke her neck. *Easter* (1978), the album that marked her return, included the decidedly unpunk hit single, "Because the Night," which was supplied by Bruce Springsteen.

While Television and Patti Smith were in residence at Max's in 1974, Blondie and the Ramones were making their debuts at CBGB. The Ramones were formed by a group of middle-class kids from Forest Hills, New Jersey. Jeff Hyman (Joey), John Cummings (Johnny), Doug Colvin (Dee Dee), and Tom Erdelyi (Tommy) each adopted Ramone (Paul McCartney's first pseudonym) as his surnom de punk. Unlike other punk groups, the Ramones played only original material. "We couldn't figure out how to play anybody else's songs," explained Johnny.[18] Stylistically, the group stripped rock 'n' roll naked with unadorned, rapid-fire guitar bursts, pneumatic drumming, and abrupt, minimalist lyrics. Lyrically, the group filled in the blank of Richard Hell's generation with a repertoire of refusal, including "I Don't Care," "I Don't Wanna Be Learned, I Don't Wanna Be Tamed," and "I Don't Wanna Go Down to the Basement." "We didn't write a positive song until 'Now I Wanna Sniff Some Glue,'" Dee Dee later quipped.[19] The group usually ran through a set with dizzying speed. Songs rarely lasted for more than two minutes and lyrics were seldom longer than eight lines.

Critical praise in the *SoHo Weekly, Rock Scene, Hit Parader,* and the *Village Voice* was not long in coming for the group. When London's *New Musical Express* did its first spread on the New York punk scene in 1975, the Ramones were the featured artists. It was the CBGB Festival of Unsigned Bands in the summer of 1975 that had prompted the spread. The festival also led Sire Records to sign the group, which became the second punk act after Patti Smith to secure a record contract. Seymour Stein of Sire played a pivotal role in developing punk, eventually signing not only the Ramones but also the Talking Heads, the Dead Boys, Richard Hell and the Voidoids, and the Pretenders.

Ramones' manic energy catches on in Britain immediately

The Ramones' eponymous debut album, released in 1976, delivered all the manic energy of the group's live performances. The album bombed in the United States, but in London, it was the talk of the town, at least in part because there was no similar domestic product. When the Ramones went to London to promote the album, they played the Roundhouse, an auditorium-sized venue. Reportedly, Malcom

Although the Ramones pointed the way for British bands, it was not until Rocket to Russia (1978) that the group finally broke into the U.S. Top 100 LPs. By this time, British punk/new wave was in full swing, and London had overtaken New York as the cutting edge of the new trend.

McLaren was thrown bodily down a flight of stairs by the concert's promoter for asking if the Sex Pistols could be the opening act. In the race to lay claim to punk, New York was well ahead of London at this juncture.

The Ramones played faster songs with shorter lyrics than anyone connected to the New York punk scene. Their rapid-fire delivery pointed the way for British punk.

Ramones' manic energy catches on in Britain immediately

The Ramones' second album, *Leave Home* (1977) did even more poorly in the United States than their first, but it cracked the Top Fifty in Great Britain and yielded a hit single there, "Sheena is a Punk Rocker." Although the Ramones, more than any other U.S. group, pointed the way for British bands, it was not until *Rocket to Russia* (1978) that the group finally broke into the U.S. Top 100 LPs. By this time, British punk/new wave was in full swing, and London had overtaken New York as the cutting edge of the new trend.

Blondie also found London to be the best launching pad for success in the United States. The group was formed by singer Deborah Harry and guitarist Chris Stein from the remains of their former group, the Stilettos. After recording with a forgettable folk rock group called Wind in the Willows in the late 1960s, Harry had done stints as a bartender and a Playboy bunny. As lead vocalist for Blondie (the name was taken from the comic strip character), she projected a Marilyn Monroe image. Stein had joined the Stilettos primarily because of his interest in Harry. As part of Blondie, he became more career directed, but the group's success was slowed by a number of early personnel changes. Between their debut at CBGB and the release of their first LP, bassist Fred "Sonic" Smith left to join Television, Ivan Kral was stolen by Patti Smith, and drummer Billy O'Connor quit to go to law school. The five-piece Blondie lineup that recorded the

Combining breathy pop vocals with a Marilyn Monroe persona, Blondie's Deborah Harry added disco and rap influences to punk.

group's self-titled debut album included only Harry and Stein from the original group. The album was issued on the small Private Stock label. The addition of Jimmy Destri on Farfisa organ gave the group a distinctive camp feel that harkened back to the pop sounds of the 1960s. Blondie had pop ideals from the beginning, but the group was still a good bit ahead of the mainstream. Although the album did not generate a ripple in U.S. sales, it brought the group to the attention of Chrysalis, which then purchased their contract for $500,000. The group's second album, *Plastic Letters,* also flopped, although it included a remake of Randy and the Rainbow's "Denise," changed to "Denis," which went to number two on British charts. For their third outing, Blondie switched producers to Mike Chapman, formerly of the sure-bet British bubblegum producer/songwriter team of Chinn and Chapman. *Parallel Lines* (1978) marked the group's breakthrough in the United States. It peaked at number six and yielded four hit singles in Britain.

Although the Talking Heads were formed in 1974 like other first-generation groups and achieved mass market success in the United States before either Blondie or the Ramones, they are considered part of a second-wave of CBGB groups. Unlike most of the first wave of punk groups, by the time Talking Heads took to the CBGB stage in the spring of 1975, they already knew how to play. From the group's live debut on, there was a structure, even rigidity, to a Talking Heads set that made them unlike all other CBGB groups. The group also embraced rhythm and blues as one strong element in what they envisioned as an otherwise pop-rock sound. Still, their presentation was sufficiently minimalist and self-conscious to earn them a place on the art rock side of punk.

The group had begun to take shape at the Rhode Island School of Design when guitarist and vocalist David Byrne and drummer Chris Frantz came together to form the Artistics in 1973. The following year, Byrne and Frantz and Tina Weymouth, Frantz's girlfriend, headed for New York to seek their artistic fortunes. It was the CBGB scene that reignited Byrne's desire to use music as his vehicle. Frantz also liked the idea, and the two rounded their rhythm section with the addition of Weymouth on bass. They were an instant hit. Hilly Kristal loved them; the press loved them; other groups were jealous of them. Within two months of their debut, they were headlining with the Ramones. The following year, they were signed to the Ramones' label, Sire. Before they recorded their debut single, "Love Goes to Building on Fire," in 1976, they added Jerry Harrison, a keyboardist from the proto-punk band the Modern Lovers, to the group. *Talking Heads '77,* the group's first album, made it into the Top 100. Although primarily a pop-sounding LP, singles like "Psycho Killer" showed an ironic punk edge. The group's next three albums were produced by Brian Eno who would see them through the punk era into the next decade. *More Songs about Buildings and Food* (1978) included a Top Thirty cover of Al Green's "Take Me to the River," that showcased the Talking Heads' affinity for African American music, which would become a cornerstone of their sound in the 1980s.

By the time the Talking Heads played their first CBGB gig, it was apparent that New York was not the only punk Mecca in the United States. There had been hints of

Talking Heads focus more on structure, musical elements

Even though the Talking Heads fashioned a minimalist arty sound, they never lost their affinity for African American music. This combination of influences served them well in the 1980s.

activity elsewhere when the New York well ran dry for the Velvet Underground in the late 1960s and a Boston club called the Boston Tea Party became their second home. In fact, it was Boston that had given birth to the first proto-punk band to embrace the Velvets fully—the Modern Lovers, led by Jonathan Richman. In 1972, however, the country was no more ready for the Lovers than it had been for the Velvets. After one album, the group sank without a trace, leaving keyboardist Jerry Harrison to resurface as a Talking Head. Cleveland, another city that provided an occasional respite for the exiled Velvet Underground, was also a burgeoning scene in the early 1970s. The Mirrors, the Electric Eels, and Rocket from the Tombs all began there. Peter Laughner of Rocket from the Tombs had done a stint with Television after arranging for the group to play Cleveland. While the Mirrors and the Eels went the way of the Modern Lovers, the Rockets split into two groups that earned a place in punk history: Pere Ubu and the Dead Boys. The Dead Boys' "Sonic Reducer" and Ubu's "Thirty Seconds over Tokyo," "Life Stinks," and "Final Solution" had been part of the Rockets' repertoire before the fracture.

   In Akron, Ohio, Devo (the name was a contraction for deevolution) was formed at Kent State University in 1972, two years after the National Guard had opened fire on student antiwar protesters. With inverted flowerpot hats and jerky robotic movements defining their image, the group found early acceptance in Britain. Devo was signed to Virgin in 1978, and Brian Eno was recruited to produce the group's first album, *Are We Not Men? We Are Devo!* The album's title was taken from the anthemic line from "Jocko Homo," one of the group's first singles. "Jocko Homo" and Devo's punk send-up of the Rolling Stones' "Satisfaction" were hits in Britain, but the group remained a cult item in the United States until the next decade.

Anarchy in the U.K.

CBGB showcased over thirty new groups at its 1975 Festival of Unsigned Bands months before the Sex Pistols played their first gig. But while punk developed earlier in the United States, the conditions to which it responded were more profoundly disturbing on the other side of the Atlantic. In Britain, a growing sense of foreboding accompanied the development of British punk bands. Unemployment had already reached record highs, and the country was plunged into its deepest recession since World War II. Although there was considerable labor unrest, the fascist National Front was growing stronger and the conservative Margaret Thatcher had become prime minister. The optimism of the postwar years was giving way to a knowing cynicism, and the consensus of values and behavior that had regulated social and political life was coming unraveled. In such a climate, even the name Sex Pistols, with its obvious connections to youth, violence, and sex, caused a stir. Thus, finding suitable venues for the group was a problem from the moment they started performing in 1975. The pub rock scene was already dominated by Dr. Feelgood, the Stranglers, and Eddie and the Hot Rods, groups that played loud, fast, aggressive rock, but who would never quite made it into the inner circle of punk. The Pistols' initial tour of Britain was staged mostly in college venues and attendance seldom reached triple figures. Still, by the summer of 1976, they had built a small following and were ready for slightly larger events. The most notable of these concerts occurred in Manchester where the group shared the stage with such local Manchester favorites as Slaughter and the Dogs and the Buzzcocks. It was at their second Manchester date that the Sex Pistols unleashed "Anarchy in the UK"—the call to arms that would establish them as the vanguard group in a nationwide movement. Manchester also led to an appearance on Granada TV's *So It Goes* where the Sex Pistols again performed "Anarchy," this time on national television.

It was at their second Manchester date that the Sex Pistols unleashed "Anarchy in the UK"—the call to arms that would establish them as the vanguard group in a nationwide movement.

Joe Strummer, a guitarist for a group called the 101ers, was positively inspired by this event. The 101ers, who had been playing the pub rock circuit, had taken their name from the number of the torture room in George Orwell's *1984*. With the guidance of manager Bernie Rhodes, a colleague of McLaren, Strummer teamed up with Mick Jones and Paul Simonon from a group called London SS to form the Clash. The group took its

In Britain, punk is a response to dire social conditions

name from the word most often used in tabloid headlines concerning class and race relations in Britain. If, as chronicler Jon Savage has suggested, "Punk's breakthrough was to unite people who saw pop in terms of social realism and those who viewed it as artistic expression," it was Clash, more than any other group, who took social(ist) realism to its artistic and political limits.[20] At the time, Simon Frith wrote that punk's message "comes most powerfully and most ambiguously from the Sex Pistols, but it comes most clearly from the Clash."[21] The group was the Sex Pistols' major competition and, in fact, outlasted the Sex Pistols by years.

Under the tutelage of Rhodes, the Clash seemed somehow more grounded in the real world than other punk outfits. While the Sex Pistols staked out the territory of nihilism with songs like "Pretty Vacant," "Seventeen," "Problems," and "Submission," the Clash appeared more socially engaged with material like the self-explanatory "London's Burning," "I'm So Bored with the USA," a searing commentary on popular culture, and "White Riot," which was inspired by the clashes between young blacks and police at the

Johnnie Rotten's painful engagement with his music captures the aesthetic of the Sex Pistols. The "destroy" T-shirt with the swastika juxtaposed against the Union Jack speaks to their contradictory politics.

The Clash had their sights set on nothing short of a socialist revolution through music. Not surprisingly, they were accompanied by heavy security whenever they arrived in the United States.

Notting Hill Carnival. In the spirit of punk, the Clash's "1977" proclaimed an end to Elvis, the Beatles, and the Rolling Stones. The group took on the issues of racism ("Police and Thieves") and unemployment ("Career Opportunities"), and cast the theme of youth identity in distinctly class terms ("What's My Name").

Another punk group of note that formed at this time were the Damned. The group as a whole was apolitical. Its members just liked speed and noise. Still, they were the first unmistakably punk group to land a record contract in Britain (Stiff Records) and the first to hit the Top Thirty ("New Rose," an amphetamine rush, ostensibly about the excitement of a new romance). The Vibrators were equally lacking in moral authority, but they also beat the Sex Pistols to the recording punch with the slightly off-color "We Vibrate," also on Stiff. Stiff had been founded in 1976 by two pub rock entrepreneurs, Dave Robinson and Andrew Jakeman, better known as Jake Riviera. Robinson had distinguished himself in rock lore earlier in the decade when he had flown 150 British journalists to New York's Fillmore East to catch Brinsley Schwarz, a pub rock group he was then managing. The grandiose scheme yielded nothing but bad press. Robinson had gone on to manage Graham Parker, whose intense r&b sound (*Howlin' Wind*, 1976) straddled the fence between pub rock and punk. Parker's backup group, the Rumour, was led by Brinsley Schwarz on guitar. Brinsley vocalist Nick Lowe became the house producer at Stiff and an artist in his own right. His "So It Goes" was Stiff's first release.

Lowe produced the Damned's first album and eventually supervised all of Elvis Costello's early work. Jake Riviera, Stiff's other principal, doubled as Costello's manager.

While McLaren knew that the Sex Pistols needed a record contract, he was grooming the group for the big leagues as part of his plan for worldwide subversion, and Stiff was a mere independent in his eyes. Hoping to capture the attention of the major labels, McLaren turned to the idea of a punk festival. It was an idea that always appealed to him. CBGB and Max's had benefited from their punk showcases and, even though a recent punk festival in the south of France had failed, McLaren felt he could pull it off in England. The Punk Rock Festival was staged at the 100 Club in September 1976. It featured, among others, the Sex Pistols, the Clash, the Buzzcocks, the Damned, the Vibrators, and Siouxsie and the Banshees, a group that was assembled at the last minute from the Bromley contingent of Sex Pistols hangers-on. Siouxsie and the Banshees originally included Sid Vicious, who later joined the Pistols, and Marco Pirroni, who joined Adam Ant. Billy Idol (later of Generation X) also agreed to be part of the group but disappeared before the festival. Vocalist Siouxsie Sioux was the group's focal point. At such a late date, the group saw no point in trying to learn any songs, so they debuted without a repertoire. Their set was a mess, but a memorable one.

The Punk Rock Festival as a whole was plagued by technical difficulties, professional rivalries, political differences, violence, and several arrests. In short, it was a roaring success.

The festival as a whole was plagued by technical difficulties, professional rivalries, political differences, violence, and several arrests. In short, it was a roaring success, especially for the Sex Pistols. In October, the group was signed to EMI; in November, "Anarchy in the UK" was released as a single. A tour with the Clash, the Damned, and Johnny Thunders' Heartbreakers was planned to promote the record. In December, however, the Sex Pistols were interviewed on Thames TV's *Today* show by Bill Grundy who goaded Steve Jones into calling him a "dirty fucker" and a "fucking rotter" on the air. In the ensuing scandal, deejays all across Great Britain (with the notable exception of John Peel) refused to play the song. Of the twenty-one dates booked for the Anarchy tour, the Sex

In the punk tradition, Siouxsie Sioux performed with the Banshees before the band had a repertoire. A testament to their staying power, Siouxsie and the Banshees went on to play the first Lollapalooza Festival in 1991.

Pistols were banned from all but three. Even so, with sales of more than 50,000, "Anarchy" entered the Top Twenty before Christmas, confirming that a good scandal can generate a great deal of free publicity.

In January 1977, amidst the fallout from the Grundy appearance, EMI dropped the Sex Pistols, which cost the company its £50,000 advance. A&M picked the group up in March for another £50,000 and dropped them a week later for an additional £25,000 buyout. Not bad for a group with only one single. The Grundy interview had finally put punk over the top, and the music industry was finally beginning to take notice of it. A new club called The Roxy became the CBGB of London. Manchester began to mirror Cleveland as punk's second home when the Buzzcocks had issued an EP called "Spiral Scratch" on their own New Hormones label and had sold 15,000 copies of it. Stiff signed a distribution deal with Island Records just in time to push the Damned's first album, *Damned Damned Damned,* into the UK Top Forty. United Artists had already signed the Stranglers, and Polydor had picked up the Jam. The biggest news, however, was that the Clash had been signed to CBS for an advance of £100,000.

The Clash's self-titled debut album was released in April 1977, a month after they had signed with CBS. It was a surprisingly accessible creation that clearly stamped punk with the imprint of social realism. It was, in the words of Jon Savage, "the first major Punk statement."[22] Unfortunately, it was not released in the United States. It wasn't until the beginning of the 1980s that the Clash did well in the U.S. market. *London Calling* (1980) and *Sandanista!* (1981) charted Top Thirty, and *Combat Rock* (1982) went Top Ten, yielding the group's only U.S. Top Ten single, "Rock the Casbah."

While CBS was promoting the Clash, McLaren was scrambling for a new contract for the Sex Pistols, eventually going with Virgin. By this time Sid Vicious had replaced Glen Matlock on bass. In 1977, Queen Elizabeth II's silver jubilee provided the perfect opportunity for the Sex Pistols to reassert their primacy. The record they planned to release was "God Save the Queen," which baldly accused the monarchy of being a "fascist regime." It was recorded immediately after the Virgin signing but proved difficult to get out. The CBS pressing plant held up production, the platemakers refused to make the plates for the liner notes, radio and television stations rejected advertisements, retail outlets refused to place orders, and the single itself was banned from the airwaves. Needless to say, all of this provided incredible publicity. "God Save the Queen" was finally released in late May (still a few weeks in advance of the planned celebrations) and was selected as the "Single of the Week" by all four British music weeklies. By the end of Jubilee Week, it had sold 200,000 copies. It would easily have gone to the top of the British charts except for some official tampering that resulted in listing a blacked-out song title and group name in the number one slot for the week of 18 June 1977. "God Save the Queen" was the only serious critique of the Jubilee. It uncovered cracks in the social facade that had been remarkably well papered over by official pomp and ceremony. The effectiveness of it, however, thrust the Sex Pistols' rhetoric up against the politics of the real world. Verbal attacks became physical, and the group, which had not even recorded an album yet, could only tour in secret. The Sex Pistols had definitely made rock 'n' roll "dangerous" again, and the movement they helped to set in motion had barely hit its stride.

If the Sex Pistols tended toward anarchism, the Clash headed straight for the far left. At different times, Strummer endorsed both Germany's extremist Baader-Meinhoff group and Italy's Red Brigades. Far more than any other punk group, the Clash took up the cry of the British working class. By the fall of 1977, they were announcing the apocalypse with slogans like "Hate and War," "White Riot," and "Sten Guns in Knightsbridge" stenciled on their new black jumpsuits. When CBS released a weak single called "Remote Control" without the group's permission, they retaliated with "Complete Control," an attack on CBS Records that was also a pronouncement of punk power. When Strummer screamed at the end of the song that taking control means "you," he was talking to his fans, his comrades-in-arms.

Flirtation with Fascism: The Underbelly of Punk

In their rush to shock, punks on both sides of the Atlantic often seized on any image that could be counted on to produce a strong reaction. No image filled that bill as well as the swastika. If 1960s rock had been marked by its associations with the leftist leanings of the counterculture, punk gravitated toward symbols at the other end of the political spectrum. For most punks, although certainly not all, flaunting the twisted cross was an exercise in confrontational art rather than a political endorsement of fascism per se. However, that fine distinction, which is rife in punk's recapitulations of itself, overlooked the importance of historical meaning.

It was Ron Asheton of the Stooges who pioneered the utilization of swastikas, iron crosses, and jackboots on stage. Asheton's fascination with the trinkets and jargon of Nazism was mirrored in other groups. One of the high points of the fledgling Cleveland scene in 1974 was an event entitled Special Extermination Night, which featured Rocket from the Tombs, the Mirrors, and the Eels. Swastikas adorned the poster advertising the event. Of the three groups, the Eels, whose members often appeared in ripped T-shirts with white power logos and swastikas, were easily the most offensive. The lyrics to "Spin Age Blasters," one of the group's songs, were taken from a slogan displayed at Cleveland's American Nazi Party Headquarters which read "Pull the Triggers on the Niggers." Even when these groups disbanded, the use of Nazi symbols did not disappear. After Pere Ubu rose from the ashes of the Rockets, the group released a song called "Final Solution" (the title taken, of course, from Hitler's plan to exterminate the Jews) as a single in 1976. The

> *For most punks, flaunting the twisted cross was an exercise in confrontational art rather than a political endorsement of fascism per se. However, that fine distinction, which is rife in punk's recapitulations of itself, overlooked the importance of historical meaning.*

Dead Boys showed up at CBGB's 1976 Festival of Unsigned Bands wearing Nazi uniforms. (It was at this event that Hilly Kristal agreed to manage the group, which led to a contract with Sire.)

After he left the Stooges, Ron Asheton went on to form his own band, The New Order. The Dictators, a group from upstate New York that formed about the same time as the early Cleveland groups, played a brand of rapid-fire rock that occupied a cultural space somewhere between the New York Dolls and the Ramones. In 1977, they released their first (of two) albums on Asylum. It was titled *Manifest Destiny.* The Ramones were packaged by Arturo Vega, a Mexican artist who made dayglo swastikas. Early song titles, "Blitzkrieg Bop" and "Today Your Love, Tomorrow the World," for example, contained explicit references to Nazism.

Per their situationist leanings, Malcolm McLaren and Vivienne Westwood had already noted that the swastika could be used quite effectively to disrupt the flow of everyday life. At one point, they had landed a commission to fashion the costumes for the film *Mahler,* which included an Aryan anima decked out in a leather miniskirt with a swastika emblazoned on her backside in brass studs. When the New York Dolls had toured Europe in 1973 with McLaren in tow, the group had added the occasional swastika to their trash drag queen attire. In Germany (of all places), a blathering Johnny Thunders had told the press that the Dolls wanted to play a benefit at Bergen-Belsen "for all the Nazis who gotta hang out in trees in fuckin' South America."[23] McLaren had observed the reaction and filed it away for future reference. In fact, McLaren and Westwood had a stock of Nazi memorabilia at their shop. The groups that arose from the Bromley contingent of Sex Pistols fans were heavily influenced by the fashion fare at Sex. Adam Ant was criticized early on for Nazi references in his lyrics. Sid Vicious wore T-shirts with swastikas. Siouxsie Sioux had a particular affinity for her swastika armband. The Clash, in fact, had objected strenuously to the Banshees' use of the swastika at the 100 Club festival. Nevertheless, these tendencies continued. In 1977, the Sex Pistols themselves started performing a song called "Belsen Was a Gas," which had been written earlier by Sid Vicious. The next generation of British groups included Joy Division, whose name was taken from concentration camp brothels; they evolved into New Order, a reference to Hitler's plan for the future.

The swastika, it should be noted, was only one of a number of disruptive symbols used by punks. For McLaren and Westwood in particular, fashion served as a part of their larger political strategy. When the Sex Pistols first performed the song that would become "Anarchy in the UK," McLaren and Westwood had designed a shirt to complement it. The "Anarchy" shirt combined small portraits of Karl Marx and flying swastikas with slogans like "Only Anarchists Are Pretty." The ensemble was completed with an armband that read "Chaos." "The intention was the group should not be politically explicit, but instead should be an explosion of contradictory, highly charged signs."[24] It was in this politics of confusion that punk irony became complicated.

Like the Sex Pistols, the Ramones did not limit themselves to fascist symbols in their attempts to outrage. Anyone with an intimate knowledge of the group's repertoire, which conjured up images across the landscape of the grotesque, could only interpret their antics as rock 'n' roll parody. As Robert Christgau has pointed out:

> Unless you think the Ramones identify with Charlie Manson, the Texas chain-saw killer, CIA men, SLAers, geeks, glue-sniffers, and electroshock patients—an absurd misreading as far as I'm concerned—then you must conclude that their intention is satiric, and the same applies when they turn to fascist characters.[25]

"The problem," Christgau noted, " is that irony is wasted on pinheads."[26] It was Lester Bangs who made one of the more cogent arguments against the use of the outrageous: "Another reason for getting rid of all those little barbs is that no matter how you intend them, you can't say them without risking misinterpretation by some other bigoted asshole; your irony just might be his cup of hate."[27] Bangs drove the point home by recounting the story of Miriam Linna of the Cramps who was quoted in a punk fanzine called *New Order* as saying: "I love the Ramones [because] this is the celebration of everything American—everything teenaged and wonderful and white."[28] She was pictured in leather and shades, brandishing a pistol in front of the Florida headquarters of the United White People's Party. In such a context, the intended irony of Patti Smith's "Rock & Roll Nigger" might well have been lost on many of her fans. Nico was being unmistakably clear when she told an interviewer that she "didn't like negroes" after performing "Deutschland Uber Alles" at CBGB.

The political climate of the 1970s further confused any punk attempts at irony. In the United States at this time, the curious concept of "reverse discrimination" began to come into popular usage. The logic of the Civil Rights Act of 1964 was turned on its head when the Supreme Court ruled in 1978 that Alan Bakke's civil rights as a white person had been violated by the University of California's affirmative action policy. The landmark decision signaled the

With the rise of the National Front in Britain, it did not take much to fan the flames of racial hatred. However, the most inflammatory statements by musicians came, not from the punks, but from within the ranks of the British rock aristocracy.

beginnings of a concerted attack on affirmative action and a tremendous resurgence of white supremacist organizations that would extend well past the next decade. In such a climate, any punk attempts to deconstruct racially loaded terms and symbols could only have unintended consequences. In Britain, the fascist National Front had already begun to make disturbing inroads into parliamentary elections. In response, a confused Paul Weller of the Jam, the group that had opened for the Clash on their White Riot Tour, told his fans that he would be voting Tory in the next election. Not even the Clash were above misinterpretation. "White Riot" had been intended as a statement that the white working class should stand up for its rights in the same way that blacks at Notting Hill Gate had. In the atmosphere of racially charged conservatism, however, it was sometimes taken as a racist rallying call to oppose such insurrection. The Sex Pistols, of course, traded on misinterpretation. The lyrics to "God Save the Queen," taken literally, could be (mis)heard as a call to save the "fascist regime." This is exactly what happened at an early Clash/Sex Pistols concert when the Student Union at Lanchester Polytechnic in Coventry refused to pay the groups, calling them "these fascists."

With the rise of the National Front in Britain, it did not take much to fan the flames of racial hatred. However, the most inflammatory statements by musicians came, not from the punks, but from within the ranks of the British rock aristocracy. In the spring of 1976, David Bowie was quoted as saying, "I think I might have been a bloody good Hitler."[29] He then staged his return from Berlin to London with what appeared to be a Nazi salute at Victoria station as he and his entourage piled into a Mercedes limousine. While Bowie later apologized for his flirtation with fascism, Eric Clapton did not. Clapton interrupted a concert in Birmingham in August 1976 to make a drunken speech urging support for Enoch Powell, the most rabid anti-black member of Parliament there was at the time. In response, a letter of protest signed "Rock Against Racism" was fired off to all the popular music weeklies, precipitating well over 100 enthusiastic replies in the first week alone.

Rock Against Racism: The Progressive Rejoinder

Rock Against Racism was organized as a broadly based mass movement that had as its sole purpose opposition to the National Front. According to RAR historian David Widgery, the organization had a multilevel strategy.

> On one level Rock Against Racism was an orthodox anti-racist campaign simply using pop music to kick political slogans into the vernacular. But on another level, it was a jail break. We aimed to rescue the energy of Russian revolutionary art, surrealism and rock and roll from the galleries, the advertising agencies and the record companies and use them again to change reality, as had always been intended. And have a party in the process.[30]

The energy and creativity for RAR came from graphic and fashion designers, photographers, actors, and punk and reggae musicians. Political direction was supplied primarily by the Socialist Workers Party, which later formed the Anti-Nazi League, which then merged with RAR.

At about the same time the Sex Pistols released "Anarchy in the UK" in late 1976, RAR began staging concerts. By the following year, the organization was producing major events that attracted hundreds of thousands of fans. RAR's anti-racist strategy of showcasing the new multicultural Britain in a positive light necessitated packaging black and white acts together. In doing so, a tilt toward reggae predominated. As Jon Savage has explained, "Any fascist ambiguity in Punk was fueled by the way that the style had bled Rock dry of all black influences; one way to overcome any taint of white supremacy was to affirm visible links with Reggae."[31] Thus, major RAR events paired reggae groups with punk bands: Aswad with the Adverts, the Cimarrons with Generation X, Steel Pulse with the Clash. Reggae was, of course, prevalent in Britain's West Indian enclaves, but it was also popular since the late 1960s with disaffected British white youth who were attracted to its hypnotic rhythms and unflinching "rude boy" stance. Its trajectory among white youth, however, was not always progressive. In the late 1960s, skinheads who were prone to racist attacks, adopted reggae as the marshall music to accompany their violent rages. By the time skinheads resurfaced in the media in the 1970s, they were adherents of punk. Some were racist Nazi sympathizers; others liked the music and opposed its fascist leanings. Thus, part of RAR's mission was to claim punk for the Left, thereby driving a wedge between racist skinheads who were drawn to the National Front and those with more progressive tendencies.

The skinhead affinity for punk and violence often put RAR in a delicate situation. Sham 69 was a sizzling punk band that performed a number of RAR benefits. But Sham also had a sizable skinhead following who wreaked havoc at their concerts by chanting "Sieg Heil," destroying property, and plastering Nazi emblems everywhere. Lead singer Jimmy Pursey was genuinely concerned about skinhead racism but sufficiently desperate to be a star that he was hesitant to cut himself off from his diehard fans. Rock Against Racism was able to turn the tables to some degree by booking Sham with a Southall reggae outfit called Misty, thus forcing skinheads to attend an antiracist benefit to see their favorite group. "I believe that black and white must live together," said an emboldened Pursey, who appeared wearing a Jamaican tam.[32] Sham and Misty then joined forces in a performance of an old Skinhead favorite, Desmond Dekker's "The Israelites."

The punk/reggae convergence projected a unique symbolic power that contributed significantly to the "black and white together" feeling of many RAR events. At one show in 1977, a member of Generation X and a member of the Cimarrons joined hands aloft while the entire audience chanted "Black and white. Black and white." Billy Idol remembered the experience as "one of the greatest nights of my life"[33]; the Cimarrons responded by recording a single called "Rock Against Racism."

Key to the widespread appeal of reggae was one Nesta Robert Marley. Bob Marley had already distinguished himself in his native Jamaica as an artist of genuine talent, moral authority, and political principle by the time Chris Blackwell signed him to Island in 1971. The decision to promote Marley as a rock star showed the quality of Blackwell's musical judgment and his intuitive grasp of marketing. Marley became the first black international superstar. Following in his wake, successful Jamaican reggae artists—everyone from the polemical Burning Spear and the anthemic Peter Tosh to the more pop-oriented Jimmy Cliff and Third World—contributed to a virtual subindustry of reggae influences that affected not only the music of black Britons but that of white punks as well. The Clash included a punk/reggae cover of Junior Murvin's "Police and Thieves" on their first album. For the reggae feel on "Complete Control," the group contracted Jamaican producer Lee "Scratch" Perry.

In the United States, where conditions favored the influence of rhythm and blues, reggae never had a terribly profound impact. Marley and the Wailers broke into the U.S. Top Thirty with two albums—*Rastaman Vibration* (1976) and *Exodus* (1977)—but no one else even came close. Although it might have been possible for Jimmy Cliff to have become a superstar before Marley because of his starring role in the cult classic film *The Harder They Come,* Cliff eschewed reggae in favor of undistinguished soul material after the film's 1973 U.S. release. Prior to this, the only Jamaican releases to crack the U.S. market had been Millie Small's "My Boy Lollipop" (1964), produced by Chris Blackwell, and Desmond Dekker's "The Israelites" (1969). In the late 1960s, Johnny Nash, a middle-of-the-road r&b singer from Austin, Texas, made a dramatic turn toward reggae and recorded Bob Marley's "Guava Jelly." Nash then hit number twelve on the U.S. charts with a version of Marley's "Stir It Up" in 1973. His own reggae-inflected "I Can See Clearly Now" (1972) went all the way to number one. For the most part, when U.S. white artists gravitated toward reggae, it was for a touch of exotica, as in Paul Simon's "Mother and Child Reunion" (1971). It was not until 1980 that Blondie embraced the style on "The Tide Is High," which became a number one hit. Throughout the 1970s, white British artists were more conversant with the style than their U.S. counterparts and often more successful using it than its Jamaican originators. It was a discouraging testament to the prevailing distribution of cultural resources that Eric Clapton's number one cover of Bob Marley's "I Shot the Sheriff" (1974) outsold the Wailers' original not only in England and the United States but also Jamaica. Clapton never repaid this debt by supporting RAR, preferring instead a safer charitable path that stretched from George Harrison's Concert for Bangladesh to his memorable appearance at Live Aid. Bob Marley, on the other hand, was sufficiently taken with RAR's reggae/punk alliance that he released "Punky Reggae Party" in solidarity.

As the RAR push to unite black and white met the reggae explosion, a number of integrated bands were formed. These bands delved into ska, the lighter, faster form of Jamaican dance music that had preceded reggae. From Coventry came Selecter and the Specials, from London, Madness, and from Birmingham, the English Beat. The groups recorded for a label called 2-Tone; its name was an obvious indicator of the interracial character of the bands and their music. UB 40, another ska-influenced band, came shortly thereafter, taking its name from the British unemployment form.

In attempting to build as broad a base as possible, RAR also reached across lines of gender and sexual orientation. It was a gay activist named Tom Robinson who unfurled the first "Rock Against Sexism" banner at an RAR concert. Robinson played it safe (and

> It was a discouraging testament to the prevailing distribution of cultural resources that Eric Clapton's number one cover of Bob Marley's "I Shot the Sheriff" (1974) outsold the Wailers' original not only in England and the United States but also in Jamaica.

Reggae has bigger impact in Britain, internationally than in U.S.

made the UK Top Ten) with his first single, "2-4-6-8 Motorway," but "Up Against the Wall," from his first album, captured the politics of punk as well as any song. At RAR concerts, he moved even straight audiences to tears with his heart-wrenching performances of "Glad To Be Gay." RAR's endorsement of progressive sexual politics dovetailed nicely with a potential that had been inherent in punk on both sides of the Atlantic from the beginning: the creation of new cultural spaces for women. When *Sideburns* magazine pictured an A chord, an E chord, and a G chord with the instructions, "This is a chord; this is another; this is a third; now form a band" in 1976 the message was almost as liberating for young women as it was for young men. Punk was aimed at destroying convention from its beginning; there was nothing that prohibited women from taking part. In New York, women began to appear in groups like DNA and Mars wearing black jeans, boots, T-shirts, and leather jackets, the same defiant image used by the men. They put out the same angry, dissonant sound as the men. It was christened "no wave" in opposition to new wave. "It was liberating," exclaimed Adele Bertei, organist for the Contortions, "we were just like the boys, finally, we could do what the fuck we wanted to, without any sexist bullshit."[34] X, a Los Angeles group, was led by a poet named Exene Cervenka and her husband, John Doe. Dissecting Los Angeles with a caustic wit and a rapid-fire beat, the group was able to make the jump to a major label, Elektra, and producer Ray Manzarek.

In London, there was Siouxsie Sioux and the Banshees and the Slits, an all-female band that translated a maelstrom of noise into a message of female power. Members of the Slits joined early RAR benefits. Poly Styrene, a portly biracial woman with braces and an acid wit, formed X-Ray Specs by placing an ad in *Melody Maker*. After only three performances, they released their first record, "Oh Bondage! Up Yours!" In 1978, as the group joined the Clash, Steel Pulse, the Tom Robinson Band, and others as headliners of RAR's biggest event at Victoria Park, "The Day the World Turned Dayglo" made the UK Top Thirty. By then, even Siouxsie and the Banshees had publicly distanced themselves from fascist icons. RAR had had its intended effect.

In the British general election of 1979, the National Front was soundly defeated. To be sure, Margaret Thatcher's exploitation of white Britain's worst racial fears ("this country might be rather swamped by people with a different culture") had a major impact on bringing the conservative vote back to the Tories, but the effect of RAR cannot be discounted. The Rock Against Racism movement provided a context that could nurture the more progressive impulses in punk. In return, punk and reggae musicians supplied the Left with the cultural politics needed to reach youth. It was one of the most successful marriages of music and politics ever to occur.

> The Rock Against Racism movement provided a context that could nurture the more progressive impulses in punk. In return, punk and reggae musicians supplied the Left with the cultural politics needed to reach youth. It was one of the most successful marriages of music and politics ever to occur.

Riding the New Wave

For the most part, the RAR movement coincided with the heyday of punk's first generation of performers. By the time there was a second generation, punk had been born again as "new wave." While the wit, irony, flair for the outrageous, and politics of the absurd that were a part of punk were never completely abandoned, the new artists were somewhat less oriented toward shock for its own sake, a bit more adept musically, and infinitely more successful commercially. In the United States, Blondie and the Talking Heads easily assumed the new label. The Clash made the transition while touring the United States so extensively they lost contact with their home base. In Britain, the new wave label was assumed by Elvis Costello, the Police, and the Pretenders, all of whom were connected in their own way to some form of political activism.

If there was any single performer who bridged the gap between punk and new wave and embodied all the contradictions contained therein it was Declan Patrick McManus, also known as Elvis Costello. When Costello started recording for Stiff, he was married, had a son, and had not given up his day jobs, the most legendary of which was as a computer operator for Elizabeth Arden, a company he skewered as a "vanity factory" on "I'm Not Angry." Costello combined the words of a poet with the temper of a madman. He told the press "revenge and guilt" were his primary motivations for his songs.

In 1977, Costello joined Nick Lowe, Dave Edmunds, and Ian Dury on a U.S. tour that Stiff sponsored for its artists. Edmunds and Dury, who were well into their thirties at the time, were too old to be punks and they had retained a good bit of rhythm and blues influence in their sound. Edmunds had cracked the U.S. Top Ten in 1971 with a cover of Smiley Lewis' "I Hear You Knockin'." Dury had experienced British success with the anthemic "Sex and Drugs and Rock and Roll" and had given Stiff its first number one UK hit with "Hit Me with Your Rhythm Stick." Nick Lowe would eventually hit U.S. number twelve with "Cruel to Be Kind" in 1979. The tour may have been a turning point for Costello who left Stiff in late 1977. His debut album, *My Aim Is True,* was issued on Columbia, as were all of his subsequent releases in the United States. Costello had genuinely catholic tastes in popular music. He released more than a dozen original homages to American r&b on *Get Happy!!* (1980) and packaged his favorite country songs on *Almost Blue* (1981). Only Joe Jackson, who was compared (unfavorably) to Costello on "Is She Really Going Out with Him" (1979), rivaled his eclecticism. Jackson explored reggae on *Beat Crazy* (1980), paid homage to Cab Calloway and Louis Jordan on *Jumpin' Jive* (1981), and delved into r&b, salsa, jazz, and funk on *Night & Day* (1982), which also yielded his biggest U.S. hit, "Steppin' Out." Costello generated hit after hit in Britain but managed only one Top Forty single, "Every Day I Write the Book" (1983), in the United States. His albums, however, usually garnered respectable chart positions, which placed him ahead of most of the British new-wave pack.

Elvis Costello, others bridge the gap between punk and new wave

There was no topic that was outside the reach of Costello's acerbic wit or immune to his incredible hostility. He bit the hand that fed his success on "Radio, Radio" and vented his misogyny on "Green Shirt." As he was no less contradictory than the punks who had preceded him, he was a staunch supporter of RAR. Inspired by RAR's punk/reggae fusion, his first big hit in Britain, "Watching the Detectives" (1977), was a lively reggae track backed by the Rumour. He contributed a number of songs about fascism to the RAR movement ("Less Than Zero," "Oliver's Army," and "Two Little Hitlers," among others) and shared the stage with Aswad at RAR's Brixton Carnival Two in 1978. None of this, however, kept him from getting into trouble in the United States the following year when Bonnie Bramlett belted him for muttering racial slurs about Ray Charles. Although his anger often got the best of him, he remained a darling of the critics throughout his career. At the end of the 1980s, he was still charting respectably in the lower reaches of the U.S. Top Forty.

Like Costello, the Police—Sting (bass and vocals), Andy Summers (guitar), and Stewart Copeland (drums)—rose from the punk scene, but unlike Costello, the group had little support in the punk community, which viewed them as too commercial. The

While the Police had little sympathy in the punk community, they achieved more commercial success than most groups in the punk/new wave category. After they peaked, they tended to go their separate ways with Sting remaining in the limelight as a solo artist.

Police were willing to appear in television advertisements. In fact, Sting's image was fashioned when he dyed his hair blonde for a chewing-gum commercial. The group was managed by Stewart Copeland's brother Miles, who owned a record company called Illegal. (The Copelands' father had worked for the CIA, which may or may not have some bearing on the name of the group and the record company, not to mention the group's biggest hit "Every Breath You Take" [1983], which has the listener being stalked by someone who was watching every move she or he makes.) Miles had been watching the New York and London punk scenes for some time and had signed a number of punk bands to one of his labels before the Police made their debut as the back-up band for Cherry Vanilla, a second-rate transvestite act from New York. The Police were thrown into the new-wave category primarily because of their nod toward reggae, which was then fashionable in Britain. A distant touch of reggae seasoning can be heard in such early hits as "Can't Stand Losing You" (a suicide threat) and "Roxanne" (about a prostitute). *Reggatta de Blanc,* the title of the group's second album, is patois for "white reggae."

Like Costello, the Police broke into the U.S. market by touring small clubs on a shoestring. But they were not parlaying an already solid British base into U.S. success. Instead, the Police entered both markets simultaneously, and when they hit, their success was immediately mainstream. Sting's rugged good looks were broadly appealing, and the group's white reggae style was sufficiently rock to be appreciated by the critics. Furthermore, the material the group wrote was good. "Message in a Bottle" and "Walking on the Moon" from *Reggatta de Blanc* and "Every Little Thing She Does Is Magic" and "Spirits in the Material World" from *Ghosts in the Machine* rank among the more engaging songs of the era.

In the early 1980s, the members of the group took time off to embark on a number of solo projects—Sting as an actor, Summers as a photographer, Copeland as his musical alter ego Klerk Kant. They reunited for *Synchronicity* in 1983, which remained in the number one slot for seventeen weeks and turned them into one of the biggest rock acts in the world. Since then, members have gone their separate ways, and Sting has drawn most of the attention. In the late 1980s, having missed the RAR movement, he became active in Amnesty International.

If members of the Police used the new cultural possibilities offered by the punk/reggae fusion to become successful, Chrissie Hynde walked through the door that punk had opened for women. Born in Akron, Ohio, Hynde attended Kent State (like Devo) for three years without becoming aware of the punk scene that was developing in her own backyard. In 1973, she headed to London to live out her rock 'n' roll fantasies. After stints as a writer for *New Musical Express* and as a clerk for McLaren and Westwood, she headed for Paris, thinking the new wave in music was going to break there first as it had in film. She returned to London as soon as the Sex Pistols took off, and there she formed the Pretenders. The group started with a cover of the Kinks "Stop Your Sobbing" and two moderate tempo singles, "Kid" and "Brass in Pocket." "Brass in Pocket" promptly went to number ten in Great Britain. The group was also an immediate success in the United States. "Brass in Pocket" made it into the Top Twenty, and the group's eponymous debut album entered the Top Ten with material ranging from aggressive, no-holds-barred rock ("Tattooed Love Boys," "Precious") to reggae ("Private Life") and ballads ("Lovers of Today"). *Pretenders II* also went Top Ten and was followed by the group's biggest single, "Back on the Chain Gang" (1983).

As the front woman for the Pretenders, Hynde projected a "tough-chick-in-leathers" image with uncommon grace and dignity. In 1983, she had her first child who then regularly accompanied her on tour. While her lifestyle owed a lot to the women's movement, Hynde's views on marriage and the family were quite conventional. As she later told an interviewer, "It's not sexist to say that a woman's place is in the home looking after children."[35] In 1985, she married Jim Kerr of Simple Minds and took time off to have another baby. Though feminism was not among her strongest motivations, Hynde did pursue vegetarianism and animal rights vigorously toward the end of the decade.

As new wave journeyed toward mainstream success, there were other artists who sought to retain the edge and anticommercialism of early punk. Prominent among them were Black Flag, X, the Minutemen, Fear, the Germs, and the Circle Jerks. These groups saw their mission as one of increasing punk tempos to the limits of human endurance while they railed against the conditions of everyday life. This was hardcore; the dance that accompanied it was called slamming. To the uninitiated, slamming could easily be mistaken for fighting, and indeed, fueled by their fans, many of the hardcore bands seemed more interested in concert brawls than in making records. Penelope Spheeris' 1981 documentary film, *The Decline of Western Civilization,* remains to date the best study of early hard-core bands. In addition to L. A., post-punk stalwarts also held forth from other locales, notably Minneapolis, where Hüsker Dü came from, San Francisco, home of the Dead Kennedys, and Washington, DC, which spawned Fugazi.

Key to the development of hardcore was SST, an independent label that was started by Black Flag in 1981. The label was also the musical home to the Minutemen and Hüsker Dü. Black Flag had been through a number of personnel changes before arriving at the line-up that featured Henry Rollins as lead singer. A bodybuilder and poet, Rollins unleashed a fury in his vocals that was well suited to the hard-core beat. On Black Flag's debut LP, *Damaged,* Rollins seemed to delight in celebrating depression and inflicting pain (mostly on himself). Before the group released its second album, *Slip It In,* Rollins left to form his own group.

Hardcore takes up where punk leaves off

Given the speed of their music, the Minutemen were aptly named. "On their first few recordings," Robert Palmer noted in the *New York Times,* "the Minutemen got through every song in under two minutes, many in under one, and still had time to sing each song through once, insert a manic guitar break and sing the song again."[36] Early Hüsker Dü was often compared to the Minutemen. On *Land Speed Record* (1982), one of their first releases, they more than lived up to the comparison.

The Washington D.C. variant of hardcore was no less hyper than its L. A. counterpart, but it was called straightedge because its adherents were encouraged to avoid drugs, alcohol, and promiscuous sex. If hardcore reacted against the overproduction of 1960s rock, straightedge also eschewed its freewheeling lifestyle. The straightedge philosophy was perhaps best captured in "Out of Step" by Minor Threat. After Minor Threat's founder, Ian MacKaye, disbanded the original group, a new group, Fugazi, was formed. Fugazi took hardcore in a more political direction, railing against racism, sexism, and environmental destruction.

The most politically oriented band in the hardcore scene was the Dead Kennedys. The group was founded in 1978 by Jello Biafra, the group's lead singer and a dedicated left-wing activist. On their first album, *Fresh Fruit for Rotting Vegetables* (1980), Biafra's biting satire was applied to issues ranging from poverty ("Kill the Poor") to U.S. involvement in Southeast Asia ("Holiday in Cambodia"). "California Uber Alles" skewered Jerry Brown, who was then governor, and other "zen fascist" devotees of the California lifestyle. For the group's second outing, *In God We Trust, Inc.* (1981), they rewrote "Über Alles" as "We've Got a Bigger Problem Now" to apply the same caustic wit to Ronald Reagan. According to punk enthusiast Vic Bondi, that song "defined the lyrical agenda of much of hardcore music, and represented its break with punk."[37]

While hardcore was pushing the boundaries of punk to the limit, new wave was incorporating other influences that pointed the music in an entirely different direction. Early punk had strayed as far from black music as one could get; new wave rebuilt the connection, primarily through reggae in Britain and rhythm and blues in the United States. The Talking Heads, for example, had always maintained a strong connection to rhythm and blues. It was, then, a logical extension of the group's sound to employ African drummers on *Fear of Music* (1979). Their unique synthesis of black and white reached its zenith on *Remain in Light* (1980), which featured Nona Hendryx (formerly of LaBelle) guesting on vocals and Bernard Worrell (formerly of Parliament) on keyboards. Some new wavers even began to make strange alliances with the dance craze that was threatening to swallow the music industry whole—disco. Blondie's breakthrough single in the United States, for example, was the disco-oriented "Heart of Glass" (1979). Blondie had always been based on a send-up of 1960s pop. "Heart of Glass" had, in fact, begun as a parody of disco, but in the hands of pop producer Mike Chapman, it became a genuine dance floor hit and a number one single. That same year, Third World released a full-fledged disco hit called "Now That We Found Love." One year later, Devo scored their only U.S. hit single with "Whip It," another dance floor favorite. Disco was what was happening and, at the beginning at least, the site of enormous creativity. "I'm cynical about rock music," said canny new waver David Byrne. "The innovations in popular music seem to be more often in disco and funk in the last ten years."[38]

Disco: The Rhythm without the Blues

"After 1970, when psychedelia gave way to a vogue for downers," Stephen Holden has written, "public dancing hit a low point. About the only people who didn't stop dancing were blacks and gays."[39] If one adds Latinos to Holden's list, it becomes more complete. The clubs frequented by the dancers were called discos from the French word *discothèque*. Discos had been around in the United States since the early 1960s, and many—New York's Peppermint Lounge, among others—booked live acts like Joey Dee and the Starlighters, whose forty-five minute versions of songs like "Shout" and the "Peppermint Twist" propelled patrons into a sweat-drenched dance frenzy. This was the defining element of disco. By the early 1970s, the discos had borrowed light shows from the psychedelic era; most featured records rather than live performances, primarily for economic reasons; and the dancers had added their own pharmacological embellishments to heighten the experience. Unlike the hallucinogens favored by 1960s rockers or the downers preferred by heavy-metal fans or the speed that fueled punk, the disco drugs of choice were cocaine and poppers (amyl and butyl nitrate). "It was about communal dance ecstasy," Tom Smucker has written of the disco craze. "A new brew of 1970s self-absorption and 1960s collectivity, mixing aerobics, the pick-up singles bar, drug highs and light shows . . . made the dance floor, rather than the concert hall, the locus of orgasmic revelation."[40]

Long before it became a genre unto itself, disco, the music, was whatever was played in dance clubs. "At the start, it was an amalgam of pirated songs," Barbara Graustark reported in *Newsweek* in 1979. "In black, Latino and gay all-night clubs on Fire Island, in New York City, and San Francisco, club deejays would create non-stop sequences of dance music by weaving together twenty minute medleys of tunes by Diana Ross, Barry White, The Temptations and Marvin Gaye."[41] Isaac Hayes and MFSB were also early favorites. At this point, disco was simply called "party music." As the sound began to evolve into its own musical genre, its sources of inspiration came from far and wide. "From Latin music, it takes its percolating percussion, its sensuous, throbbing rhythms; from the '60s 'funk' music of James Brown and Sly Stone, it borrows a kicky bass-guitar line; from Afro-Cuban music, it repeats simple lyric lines like voodoo chants;

and like early rock 'n' roll, it exploits the honking saxophones of black rhythm and blues," Graustark noted.[42] Often, nuances of musical taste indicated sexual preference. In the words of club deejay Danae:

> Straight disco is heavy-duty funk, the driving sound, that has all the power without much of the emotion. Gay's like to hear black women singers; they identify with the pain, the irony, the self-consciousness. We pick up on the emotional content, not just the physical power. The MFSB sound was gay, Barry White was a gay sound, so is Donna Summer, Gloria Gaynor.[43]

As has often been the case in this country where the language barrier can be as intractable as the race barrier, Latin music made itself felt primarily as an outside influence. Salsa was just coming into its own, and it developed as a separate subindustry with its own record labels (notably, Fania), distribution networks, and performance venues. Although Fania All Stars compilations like *Spanish Fever* and *Crossover* contained disco material, there was little direct crossover. Aside from Tavares from New Bedford, Massachusetts, a group that sounded distinctly pop, disco produced few Latino stars probably because of the difficulties of interacting with the mainstream culture, which were well documented after the fact in Reubèn Blades' poignant film *Crossover Dreams*.

Proto-Disco: The Funk Connection

The impact of funk was more direct but also limited. By the early 1970s, soul, not unlike the rest of popular music, had splintered. In the center, Stevie Wonder had a firm hold on the pop soul audience, just as the Jackson Five appealed to their younger brothers and sisters. At one end of the soul spectrum was the lavish, sweet sound of Philadelphia. At the other was funk, the more caustic, percussive sound descended from James Brown whose choppy, jagged rhythms interrupted the smooth forward motion of its Philadelphia cousin. Early on it seemed as if such self-contained funk bands as Kool and the Gang, the Ohio Players, and Earth, Wind, and Fire would make a major contribution to disco. Even a white funk band from Scotland, Average White Band ("Pick Up the Pieces," "Cut the Cake"), and a mixed unit from Oakland, California, Tower of Power ("What Is Hip"), appeared to be cutting a good bit of funk mustard. However, as the dance floor mania developed into a more and more upscale trend, the cruder sensuality of post-Sly, James Brown-inspired funk was eclipsed by the more polished sound associated with Philadelphia and the controlled, high-tech energy and propulsive (some would say relentless) 4/4 beat of what

> As the dance floor mania developed into a more and more upscale trend, the cruder sensuality of post-Sly, James Brown-inspired funk was eclipsed by the more polished sound associated with Philadelphia and the controlled, high-tech energy and propulsive (some would say relentless) 4/4 beat of what came to be known as Eurodisco.

came to be known as Eurodisco. In many ways, dance music was at its most creative when it combined elements of all these styles: the sweet soul tenor vocal over Earth, Wind, and Fire's funky instrumental on "Shining Star" or Donna Summer's soulful delivery over producer Georgio Moroder's clean, clear, driving synthesizer tracks on "Hot Stuff," which won a rock Grammy at the height of disco.

The funk sound had been a long time coming and was absorbed all too soon. Like a number of their Philadelphia soul mates, the Ohio Players had formed in the 1950s and labored for years before hitting the Top Forty in 1973 with "Funky Worm." Although they recorded five gold albums and a handful of hit singles—"Skin Tight," a dance-floor favorite, and "Fire" and "Love Rollercoaster," which hit number one—they disappeared from the Top Forty in 1976, even before disco peaked. Wild Cherry, another funk band from Ohio, picked up where the Ohio Players left off with "Play that Funky Music" in 1976. Following a similar, if more successful, trajectory, Kool and the Gang formed in the mid-1960s and first hit the Top Forty in 1973 with "Funky Stuff." Although the group seemed to be really taking off with two follow-up Top Ten singles ("Jungle Boogie" and "Hollywood Swinging") they also disappeared from the Top Forty in 1975. The inclusion of "Open Sesame" on the *Saturday Night Fever* soundtrack gave the group a new lease on life in 1978. At this point, Kool and the Gang came back strong with three Top Ten singles in a row—"Ladies Night," "Too Hot," and the classic "Celebration"—that took them successfully into the 1980s.

Earth, Wind, and Fire was formed later than either the Ohio Players or Kool and the Gang, but the group did better than its predecessors. Throughout the disco era, they turned out nothing but platinum-selling Top Ten albums. The group was founded in 1969 by Maurice White, but did not have a stable line-up until 1973, when Philip Bailey was added as colead vocalist. White had started as a session drummer at Chess records. By the 1970s, he had absorbed a catalogue of styles that ranged from American jazz and soul to African folk drumming. In 1975, the group released *That's the Way of the World,* their first number one album and the soundtrack to a documentary film about the band. The album contained all the musical elements that would wrestle for prominence in disco—funk guitar and horn licks punctuating African American and Latin rhythms, all providing a bottom for lavish strings and sweet harmonies with a James Brown tightness that could be rivaled only by the studio precision of Eurodisco. *That's the Way of the World* included the group's only number one single "Shining Star."

Under White's leadership, Earth, Wind, and Fire, who called themselves "the Creator's band," transformed their spiritual interests in Egyptology into a media-savvy image. (White had first become interested in Egyptology while touring with jazz pianist Ramsey Lewis in the late 1960s.) Pyramids and other Egyptian symbols became trademarks of the group. While they had a keen eye for commercial opportunities, they never lost sight of their funk roots. Their rendition of the Beatles' "Got to Get You into My

George Clinton's funk too extreme to be contained within disco

Life" from Robert Stigwood's film version of *Sgt. Pepper* was one of the few bright spots in an otherwise abysmal movie. The group was also one of the first African American acts to tour with theater sets and special effects. The band's 1979 world tour had Maurice White dueling on stage with a kind of Darth Vader character. Even at their most outrageous, however, Earth, Wind, and Fire seemed to be well within the bounds of soul orthodoxy when compared with George Clinton.

George Clinton was to funk what glam was to rock. His first group, the Parliaments (formed in 1955), had a straight soul hit called "(I Wanna) Testify" in 1967 on Berry Gordy's Revilot label. Following a contract dispute, Clinton found his way to white hippies, LSD, and the music of Jimi Hendrix and added these influences to his storehouse of sources. The new George Clinton (aka Dr. Funkenstein, Maggot Overlord, Uncle Jam) could be viewed as either a black Frank Zappa or a psychedelic James Brown. Attired in sequined jumpsuits and a blonde wig, he could rival any of David Bowie's science-fiction fantasies. At the same time, his express purpose was to "rescue dance music from the blahs."[44] In many ways, Clinton was the missing link between the 1960s focus

George Clinton is either a black Frank Zappa or James Brown on acid, depending on how you look at it. The mission of his P-Funk empire was to "rescue dance music from the blahs."

on consciousness expansion and the 1970s preoccupation with the body. An early album exhorted "Free Your Mind and Your Ass Will Follow."

   With a core of sidemen (Eddie Hazel, Gary Shider and Mike Hampton on guitars, Bernard Worrell and Junie Morrison on keyboards, and James Brown alumni Bootsy Collins on bass and Fred Wesley and Maceo Parker on horns), Clinton presided over an extensive and hopelessly complicated Parliament/Funkadelic empire. Funkadelic recorded Clinton's wild psychedelicized funk excursions for Warner. Parliament (essentially the same group) recorded shorter, if not simpler, material for Casablanca. Spin-off projects, which Clinton encouraged, were signed by any number of other labels. The Horny Horns, lead by Wesley and Parker, were signed to Atlantic, as were the Brides of Funkenstein. Worrell also issued a solo LP on Arista before joining the Talking Heads. Hazel recorded as a solo artist for Warner, who also signed Bootsy's Rubber Band. The P-Funk vocal chorus comprised Parlet, a group who recorded three albums on Casablanca.

All things considered, Parliament/Funkadelic had a prodigious output with reasonably impressive sales figures. At the height of the disco craze, six of Parliament's albums placed in the Top Thirty as did two of Funkadelic's. Still the music was not all that accessible to those who lived only for the dance floor. Disco was primarily a singles medium. Parliament/Funkadelic had only three Top Thirty singles—"Tear the Roof off the Sucker (Give Up the Funk)" and "Flash Light" as Parliament, and "One Nation under a Groove" as Funkadelic. By the late 1970s, their brisk album sales in the pop market stood more as an alternative to disco than as one of its formative influences.

Up from the Disco Underground

When disco first began to emerge as a genre, most of the initial releases were by black artists. In this sense, early disco was part of the continuing development of black dance music. Among the records that made the rare crossover from clubs to radio was "Soul Makossa" (1973), an obscure French import by a Cameroonian artist named Manu Dibango. Dibango thus became the first African musician to have an international hit. "Rock the Boat" by the Hues Corporation and "Rock Your Baby" by George McRae followed a similar path. B.T. Express had a couple of early hits with "Do It ('Til You're Satisfied)" and "Express," as did Tavares with "It Only Takes a Minute." By 1975, when Van McCoy and The Soul City Orchestra established the "Hustle" as the most important new dance craze since the twist, disco was already showing signs of respectability, but the music industry had not yet taken notice of it.

Perhaps the first disco hit to reach the charts as disco was Gloria Gaynor's "Never Can Say Good-Bye" (1975), reportedly one of the first records especially mixed for club play. Gaynor should have had a shot at the disco crown, but she was unable to follow up her first hit until 1979. In that year, her aptly titled "I Will Survive" went all the way to number one. "Six months ago," marveled her publicist, "we couldn't give Gloria Gaynor away."[45] Gaynor's mistake had been to record a dynamite disco hit before the music industry recognized disco as a trend. It was Donna Summer who became the first disco diva. Summer was a high-school dropout from Boston who fell into a fortuitous alliance with Europroducer Georgio Moroder when a part in the German production of *Hair* took her to Munich. Summer, who had done musical theater for years, could really belt out a vocal, but for what would become her first hit single in the United States, Moroder created a symphonic mix of drum machine rhythms and synthesized sounds and then cleared the studio so that Summer could repeat the song's one-line lyric over and over in a breathy whisper while simulating the sound of orgasm twenty-two times. While the widespread popularity of "Love to Love You Baby," which rose to number two early in 1976, moved disco closer to the surface, the established recording industry continued to ignore it. According to Andrew Kopkind of the *Village Voice:*

The record companies seemed bewildered by what they had, and promo people continued their quirky disregard of the disco category in their portfolios. Instead, they inflated passing fancies into seismic cultural events: Peter Frampton, reggae, and punk, for example. Not that some of those sounds or stars lacked merit; certainly Springsteen, Bob Marley, and the best of the New Wave deserve seats high in rock and roll heaven. But disco would soon swamp them all, and nobody was watching.[46]

With no promotional support forthcoming from the major record companies, disco was rarely heard on the airwaves. The one exception to this was New York's top black station, WBLS, where deejay Frankie Crocker (the Alan Freed of Disco) played many of the early disco hits from clubs. However, WBLS was clearly an exception. Forced to remain underground in this way, disco continued to receive its primary exposure in clubs, popularized only by the creative genius of the disco deejays who "prided themselves on psyching out a crowd and then programming them into an ecstatic frenzy, slip-cuing records into a continuous sequence and equalizing them for dancing by boosting the bass. The top DJs became taste-making alchemists-engineers with cults that followed them from club to club."[47]

Like the music they played, the disco deejays were initially shunned by record companies. To get records, they were expected to make the rounds to each label individually. Eventually, they organized themselves into "record pools" that served as central distribution points where new releases could be discussed and new tastes created. There were about fifty functioning pools in major markets scattered across the country as late as 1979. Much to the surprise of the mainstream music industry, which had not been taken by surprise since early rock 'n' roll, this network of record pools and nightclubs quickly became an alternative to the airplay marketing structure of the music business. Disco deejays were able to break out hits from the dance floor. Such hits were capable of selling upwards of 100,000 copies in New York City alone with virtually no radio play—no mean achievement in an industry which had committed billions of dollars to the airplay system of marketing. In the absence of sustained national exposure through radio play, many disco releases achieved hit status through regional sales. As late as 1979, one record company executive noted:

A year ago, we couldn't sell dance records outside the disco belt: New York, Boston, Philadelphia, Baltimore, Washington, and Miami. . . . With a group like the Trammps, who were one of the most successful disco groups, we would sell 100,000 to 150,000 LPs in New York, but only 5,000, say, in Detroit. Our total sales would be about 300,000.[48]

Such middling sales figures, however, demonstrated record company unwillingness or inability to promote disco more than they demonstrated the music's lack of commercial potential.

Disco deejays were able to break out hits from the dance floor. Such hits were capable of selling upwards of 100,000 copies in New York City alone with virtually no radio play—no mean achievement in an industry which had committed billions of dollars to the airplay system of marketing.

Disco initially ignored by radio, sells in regional markets

Disco's following was not just a fleeting, if dedicated, underground party culture; it was a significant record-buying public. As early as 1976, the year end pop charts were bursting with disco acts: Johnny Taylor ("Disco Lady"), Walter Murphy and the Big Apple Band ("A Fifth of Beethoven"), Silver Convention ("Fly, Robin, Fly," "Get Up and Boogie"), the Andrea True Connection ("More, More, More"), Sylvers ("Boogie Fever," "Hot Line"), Hot Chocolate ("You Sexy Thing"), K.C. and the Sunshine Band ("Shake Your Booty," "That's the Way I Like It"), Maxine Nightengale ("Right Back Where We Started From"), Rhythm Heritage ("Theme from S.W.A.T."), the Bee Gees ("You Should be Dancing"), and Vicki Sue Robinson ("Turn the Beat Around"). All of these artists' records were listed among *Billboard's* forty most popular of the year. Other disco acts, such as Candi Staton ("Young Hearts Run Free") and Brass Construction ("Movin'"), joined in the weekly Top Twenty.

Over the next couple of years, disco continued to swell its ranks on the pop charts with such acts as Brick ("Dazz"), and Dr. Buzzard's Original Savannah Band ("Whispering/Cherchez La Femme/Se Si Bon"), the Emotions ("Best of My Love"), Thelma Houston ("Don't Leave Me This Way"), Rose Royce ("Car Wash"), Hot ("Angel in Your Arms"), Chic ("Dance, Dance, Dance (Yowsah, Yowsah, Yowsah)"), Heatwave ("Boogie Nights") Peter Brown ("Do Ya Wanna Get Funky With Me," "Dance With Me"), and Taste of Honey ("Boogie Oogie Oogie"). Although as many of these acts were signed by major labels as were by independents, the majors neither promoted the music nor supplied any of its key innovations. When disco hit, the majors simply contracted with the independents for distribution or rode the disco wave with their own artists. By and large, then, disco's creative energy came from independent producers and upstart independent labels. Consider, for example, Richard Finch and Harry Wayne Casey, who made TK Records one of the premiere disco labels. Casey was a songwriter who worked for a record distributor in Miami, Florida, and he knew the club scene well. Finch was a bassist who worked as an engineer at TK Records in Hialeah. Together they wrote and produced George McRae's "Rock Your Baby" for TK, which gave the small independent its first entree to disco. Finch and Casey then went on to form KC and the Sunshine Band, an integrated (black, white, and Latino) ten-piece unit that established TK's position in disco. In 1975, the band released three singles that, like "Rock Your Baby," hit number one on both the pop charts and the r&b charts: "Get Down Tonight," "That's the Way (I Like It)," and "Shake Your Booty." By the end of the decade, Finch and Casey had turned out two more number ones—"I'm Your Boogie Man" and "Please Don't Go"—as well as a number of lesser hits. Their strong r&b feel, which came to be known as the "Miami Sound," contributed significantly to the funk side of disco.

When Georgio Moroder wanted to introduce Donna Summer to the United States, he took a three-minute demo of "Love to Love You Baby" to Neil Bogart, who had distinguished himself in the previous decade as "the Bubblegum King," producing groups like Ohio Express and the 1910 Fruitgum Company for Buddah. Bogart had recently founded

Donna Summer clutches one of her four Grammy awards. While she had the talent to rise above her disco queen image, the pressures of fame and fortune ultimately caused her to turn her back on disco altogether.

Casablanca Records with a roster that included two bands that had almost nothing in common: the heavy metal group Kiss and George Clinton's Parliament. The addition of Summer would point Casablanca in yet another direction. It was perhaps Bogart's inclination to take chances that attracted Moroder to his label. Summer, of course, became the Queen of Disco and a mainstay of Casablanca's financial health. At her peak she delivered three number one albums and eight Top Ten singles in a row, including "MacArthur Park," "Hot Stuff," and "Bad Girls," which reached the number one position. "Last Dance" from the film *Thank God It's Friday* earned her the first of four Grammies in 1978. Summer had trouble rising above her sultry disco seductress persona, but she had enough talent and persistence to seek more. In 1979, she duetted with Barbra Streisand on "No More Tears (Enough Is Enough)." Her ambition was also evident, if not fully realized, on her autobiographical disco mini-opera, *Once Upon a Time.* Under the pressures of fame and fortune (and a lawsuit against Casablanca), she became a born-again Christian in the early 1980s and turned her back on her disco queen image and the gay following who adored it.

Bogart continued to build his quirky roster with the addition of the Village People in 1978. The Village People were six gay men who costumed themselves as a cowboy, an Indian, a hard hat, a soldier, a cop, and a leather freak, respectively. The group was assembled by Jacques Morali, a French producer who parodied European perceptions of gay fantasy characters as "a protest against Anita Bryant," the notorious Florida orange juice queen turned antigay activist. Morali's upbeat, anthemic melodies and the group's animated, karate chop delivery were presented as camp disco to the general public. For those in the know, however, the irony of such hits as "Macho Man," "Y. M. C. A.," and "In the Navy" was not particularly subtle. With worldwide sales of 10 million albums, the Village People added measurably to Casablanca's fortunes. In 1978 alone, the fledgling company grossed $100 million.

If disco was largely a product of independent record companies, the independent producer was equally important to its creative drive, especially in Europe where producers like Cerrone and Alec Costandinos made such quasi-symphonic disco concept LPs as *Love in C Minor* and *Love and Kisses,* respectively. Costandinos also turned to literary sources to create *Romeo and Juliet* and *The Hunchback of Notre Dame.* There were, in fact, significant differences between Eurodisco and its U.S. counterpart. U.S. disco was more song-oriented and more r&b-based than Eurodisco. Disco albums produced by Freddie Perren in the United States, for example, contained ballads and dance cuts that varied in tempo and mood, with no segues between songs. Perren had begun as a staff producer at Motown, a label dedicated to the concept of crossover. As an independent producer, his first successes included the Sylvers' Jackson Five-ish "Boogie Fever" and Tavares' pop-oriented "Heaven Must Be Missing An Angel" and "Who Dunit." In the late 1970s, he produced Gloria Gaynor's "I Will Survive" and Peaches and Herb's disco hit "Shake Your Groove Thing." Still, neither Gaynor's nor Peaches and Herb's albums were all disco. In contrast, Georgio Moroder thought of himself as a composer. On Donna Summer's *Live and More* LP, "MacArthur Park" was followed seamlessly by "Heaven Knows," a song Moroder wrote expressly to complement the rhythm and feeling of "MacArthur Park," thereby maintaining the same tempo and emotional edge for the entire album side.

In some ways, the album-length compositions of the European producers attempted to do the work of the club deejays for them. In the United States where the success of disco depended on the dance-club environment and deejay creativity, the music developed as a singles medium.

In some ways, the album-length compositions of the European producers attempted to do the work of the club deejays for them. In the United States where the success of disco depended, at least at first, on the dance-club environment and deejay creativity, the music developed as a singles medium. In fact, a whole new subindustry of twelve-inch, 45 rpm singles (the so-called disco mix) opened to accommodate the specific needs of club deejays for extended play and heavy bass. It was this particular innovation that would provide the foundation for rap records in the next decade.

Mainstream Disco: The Bee Gees Boogie Down

In keeping with the popular music tradition of black innovation and white popularization, it was not until a white supergroup—the Bee Gees—came to dominate the scene that disco finally took on the mantle of respectability. According to Andrew Kopkind, the year 1978 saw

> several disco stars achieve the necessary "crossover" effect, bringing the music out of the subcultural ghettoes into mainstream life. The Bee Gees were crucial to that passage; they made disco safe for white, straight, male, young, and middle-class America. What Elvis Presley did for black rhythm and blues, . . . the Brothers Gibb have done for disco.[49]

Genius of independent producers is key to success of disco

By the time that Barry, Maurice, and Robin Gibb struck disco gold, they had already been through at least three musical incarnations. They began their hit-making career as a Beatles sound-alike act with "New York Mining Disaster 1941/Have You Seen My Wife Mr. Jones" in 1967. After a few more hits in the Beatles' style but lacking the Beatles' depth, the three brothers embarked on undistinguished solo careers. Their reunion in the early 1970s produced a few more hits ("How Can You Mend a Broken Heart" became number one) but still no distinctive voice of their own. It took Atlantic's producer Arif Mardin to help them create their disco-era Bee Gees persona. On *Main Course,* Mardin encouraged an r&b feel that is evident on cuts like "Jive Talkin'," a number one hit in 1975. On "Nights on Broadway" (later covered by Candi Staton), Barry unveiled the falsetto that would become the Bee Gees' disco trademark. The sound was perfected on "You Should Be Dancing," which rose to number one in 1976. Still, while they moved steadily up the ranks of the disco artists, they did not capture the disco crown until Robert Stigwood commissioned them to write the soundtrack for

The Brothers Gibb had been through a number of incarnations before achieving superstardom as top-selling disco artists. Their music crossed the dance fever over to the mainstream with a level of saturation that almost guaranteed a backlash.

Saturday Night Fever, a feature film starring John Travolta as Brooklyn disco king Tony Manero.

The Bee Gees had been associated with Stigwood from the start of their careers. In 1967, they were signed to a five-year management contract with Brian Epstein's NEMS company when Stigwood was its director. Reportedly, Stigwood paid $2,500 for a 51 percent interest in their publishing.[50] Beginning with *Main Course,* all Bee Gees recordings were released on Stigwood's RSO label. Stigwood was a master at what the industry was beginning to call "crossover media," a product in one medium that can sell a product in another. With the purchase of all the performance rights to the *Jesus Christ Superstar* album in 1970, he perfected a crossover media pattern that *Newsweek*'s David Ansen described as: "album sells theater ticket, play sells movie rights, soundtrack album sells movie, movie sells soundtrack album."[51] Stigwoood was involved in similar ways with the production of the film version of *Tommy,* the Who's rock opera, in 1975 and with *Grease, Evita,* and *Sgt. Pepper's Lonely Hearts Club Band* in 1978, months after he produced *Saturday Night Fever,* a film whose music he already owned.

As envisioned by Stigwood, the crossover media process was more than the popularity of a Broadway play or a Hollywood film generating sales for a subsequent soundtrack album. Stigwood consciously used each product as a marketing tool to sell the other. The plan was orchestrated to perfection with *Saturday Night Fever.* "How Deep Is Your Love" from the soundtrack album rose to number one about two months before the film's scheduled Christmas release. By the time the film broke in 504 theaters just before Christmas, "Stayin' Alive," the song that opens the movie, was in the number one position. "Every time the deejay announced 'Stayin' Alive'," crowed RSO Records president Al Coury, "he said, 'That's from the movie *Saturday Night Fever* starring John Travolta.' It was millions and millions of dollars of free publicity."[52] Two months later, "Night Fever," the song from which the film took its name, occupied the number one slot. This, of course, had the effect of keeping the film in circulation that much longer. This kind of marketing would become the rule in the 1980s, a decade dominated by video clips and movie tie-ins.

The success of *Saturday Night Fever* was unprecedented. The film grossed $130 million in its first U.S. run and the soundtrack of the same name sold 15 million copies in the United States and 30 million worldwide, becoming the best-selling record of all time. In addition to the Bee Gees' three number one hits, the LP generated hits for Tavares ("More Than a Woman"), the Trammps ("Disco Inferno"), and a number one single for Yvonne Elliman ("If I Can't Have You"), all within the film's initial run. The film even showcased the Latin side of disco with David Shire's "Salsation," the selection that accompanied the Latin couple who danced circles around Travolta. Under Stigwood, even the Bee Gees' younger brother Andy Gibb, also on RSO, tallied three number one singles in a row, peaking with "Shadow Dancing" in 1978. Midway through the year,

RSO estimated that its 1978 revenues would be somewhere between $300 million and $500 million. A generous Stigwood lavished cars, boats, even six-figure bonuses on his trusted employees without compromising his own insatiable taste for luxury in the slightest. The biggest winner of all, however, was Polygram, the Netherlands-based conglomerate that distributed both RSO and Casablanca.

After *Saturday Night Fever*, it became impossible to ignore disco. Artists of all persuasions jumped on the disco bandwagon. Cher's "Take Me Home" on Casablanca reached number eight on the charts. Dolly Parton contributed "Baby I'm Burnin'." Jazz flautist Herbie Mann had a disco hit with "Superman." Even the Rolling Stones and Rod Stewart became disco converts. The Rolling Stones' "Miss You" sold 2 million copies, and Rod Stewart scored the best selling single of his career with "Da Ya Think I'm Sexy?" (Stewart had actually turned his attention toward the disco market the previous year with "Hot Legs.") With such guaranteed hit-making artists as these on board, radio and television soon followed suit.

The commercial potential of disco came to full bloom when WKTU, an obscure, soft-rock station in New York, converted to an all-disco format. According to David Rapaport, the station manager, the conversion was simple: "We sent the program director out to a record store with a credit card Monday morning and he came back with 400 and some odd dollars worth of disco records. That night we changed our format from soft rock to disco."[53] Within months, WKTU went from a dreary 0.9 share of the market to an unbelievable 11.3 share, making it the most listened to station in the country. This was in December of 1978. By March 1979, there were some 200 disco stations broadcasting in almost every major market from Miami to Los Angeles, and syndicated television programs like *Disco Magic* and *Dance Fever* brought the dancing craze to the heartland. Of the fourteen pop Grammy awards in 1979, disco records captured eight. Some 36 million adults thrilled to the musical mixes of 8,000 professional deejays who worked just a portion of the estimated 20,000 disco clubs. Depending on the estimates one believed, disco accounted for 20 to 40 percent of *Billboard's* chart action. All in all, the disco phenomenon spawned an industry with annual revenues ranging between $4 and $8 billion.

Having seen the profits that disco could produce, the music business soon replicated the successful 120 beat-per-minute formula ad nauseam. The entire disco apparatus was harnessed in the service of industry profits. Record pools, first organized as a collective response to industry indifference, now served as indispensable marketing tools, supplying the record companies with crucial demographic data. Everything from Glenn Miller's "Chattanooga Choo-Choo" to the theme from "Star Wars" to Stravinsky's "Fire-

Disco takes over, popular artists jump on the bandwagon

The commercial potential of disco came to full bloom when WKTU, an obscure, soft-rock station in New York, converted to an all-disco format. Within months, WKTU went from a dreary 0.9 share of the market to an unbelievable 11.3 share, making it the most listened to station in the country.

bird Suite" fell prey to the relentless disco beat. Beethoven's "Fifth Symphony" was an early victim. Percy Faith even recorded a disco version of "Hava Nagila." In the hands of the industry, disco seemed to gobble up everything in its wake.

Of course, by this time, disco had come to symbolize all of the mindless overindulgence its critics had complained about in the first place. Even disco sympathizers had to acknowledge "its empty excesses, its superficiality, its desperate trendiness."[54] The disco underground, once a haven for the disenfranchised, had surfaced as affluent-chic. Disco "is the height of effete snobbery," snapped one observer, "the ultimate in mindless narcissism. Disco is Margaret Trudeau, Truman Capote, Cher, and all their vacuous Studio 54—*People* magazine cronies."[55] Many black artists began to complain that they had no alternative but to submit to the demand for disco. "We're in a period of the McDonald's of music, where it's mass-marketed like junk food," lamented Melba Moore, whose "You Stepped into My Life" was a disco hit. "I don't know what *good* is any more."[56] In a given week as many as forty of *Billboard's* Hot 100 were disco releases. With the market saturated to this degree, there was bound to be a backlash, and given disco's particular history, it was bound to have racial overtones.

The Hard-Rock Reaction

The most visceral antidisco reactions came from the hard rock/heavy metal axis of popular music. As John Travolta won the urban white youth market for disco, and scores of radio stations across the country converted to a disco format almost overnight, FM rock radio responded almost instinctively to its loss of audience share by initiating various antidisco campaigns. Dave Marsh writing in *Rolling Stone* explained their motivation in the following way.

> As competition becomes fiercer, each station must settle for a narrower demographic range. Right now the goal is males, ages eighteen to thirty-four . . . White males, eighteen to thirty-four, are the most likely to see disco as the product of homosexuals, blacks, and Latins, and therefore they're the most likely to respond to appeals to wipe out such threats to their security. It goes almost without saying that such appeals are racist and sexist, but broadcasting has never been an especially civil-libertarian medium.[57]

Marsh was not the first to note the racial dimension of these campaigns. Georgia Christgau had pointed out these tendencies in New York six months earlier.

> Three progressive FM rock stations in New York run anti-disco campaigns. It's not hard to do—radio is already segregated black from white. At a sellout show of Twisted Sister, a local group with a white following, a banner displayed from the balcony read, "We hate disco because it sucks." This isn't opinion, its willful ignorance, racism feeding on paranoia . . .[58]

The height of antidisco mania occurred on 12 July 1979 when Chicago deejay Steve Dahl staged a "Disco Demolition Night" for station WLUP (the "Loop") at a White Sox doubleheader. Drawn by the Loop's non-stop hype, 47,795 fans (more rock than baseball) paid their way into Comiskey Park while about half as many more either crashed the gate or swarmed around the streets and sidewalks outside. As soon as Dahl blew up a cache of disco records between games, hordes of rock crazies stormed the field, tearing up turf and chanting "disco sucks" at the top of their lungs. When Comiskey Park security was unable to restore order, the Sox were forced to cancel and subsequently forfeit the second game.[59]

In the frenzy of the antidisco campaigns, hard-rock fans generalized their antidisco feelings to include all black music. While rock radio could have demonstrated the connections between hard rock and black music for its listeners, it fanned the flames of racism instead. As Robert Hilburn has written:

> *Where young rock fans traditionally find identity or strength in the communal celebration of specific genres of rock (punk, heavy metal), much of the energy in the mid and late '70s was suddenly directed against something. "Death to Disco" became a rallying cry. In its enthusiasm, a large percentage of this white audience equated anything black with the dance-floor trend.*
>
> > *Rock-oriented radio stations could have educated this young audience on the historical link between rock and black music by programming classic Motown-Stax-Hendrix tracks or the rock-oriented tracks by such contemporary black stars as Stevie Wonder, Prince, Donna Summer, and Rick James. Eager to be culturally in tune with their listenership, however, the stations carelessly picked up on the anti-disco sentiment and fell into racist programming policies: They simply stopped playing all black records.*[60]

Although FM rock radio, which was called album oriented rock (AOR) at the time, viewed disco as a serious threat to its well-being, it was in no real financial danger. As originally developed by consultant Lee Abrams, AOR was programmed on the basis of sophisticated market research techniques that targeted the record-buying habits of the demographic population with the most disposable income. Needless to say, the use of these techniques meant that black music was usually excluded from programming. WKTU in New York may have been the most listened to station in the country in 1979, but with an estimated "annual pretax income of about $6 million on revenues of $9 million," AOR station KMET in Los Angeles was by far the most lucrative.[61] The economic reality for radio was that "disco pulled in an audience that was older, younger, more female or less affluent than desired. And it was easy to see that

As originally developed by consultant Lee Abrams, AOR was programmed on the basis of sophisticated market research techniques that targeted the record-buying habits of the demographic population with the most disposable income. Needless to say, black music was usually excluded from programming.

stations that had stuck to hard rock—KMET in Los Angeles, for instance—were prospering in just the demographic areas radio needed. So rock rose."[62]

As disco declined and rock radio reasserted its primacy, black-oriented radio stations were forced to adopt a new format—Urban Contemporary. Black radio had often had to attract a white listenership just to maintain respectable ratings. In the competitive environment of the 1970s, however, there was also pressure to appeal to a more affluent demographic. To do so, these stations retained those black artists in the soul, funk, and jazz idioms, for example, Stevie Wonder, Donna Summer, Rick James, Third World, Funkadelic, Quincy Jones and George Benson, who were central to their playlists and added white acts, for example, David Bowie or Hall and Oates, that fit the format. As the strategy began to show returns, bewildered black listeners called to ask why their stations were programming more and more white artists. While listeners were assured of the continuing commitment to the black audience, the stations continued to drift toward the mainstream market. According to Pablo Guzman: "To satisfy everyone in the spirit of the lowest common denominator and to appease big-budget advertisers who were still nervous about the 'black' tag, black references were dropped, music that was 'too funky' was abandoned in favor of white 'crossover' and UC was born."[63]

It must be admitted that the format Urban Contemporary was an interesting concept in that it was designed as a multiracial format. It was also quite successful, surpassing even AOR stations in many instances. Still, while Urban Contemporary programmers succeeded in providing greater access to white musicians on what had been black-oriented stations, black performers did not gain any greater access to rock radio. Thus, Urban Contemporary may well have been a net loss for black artists.

By the end of the 1970s, punk, which had been born again as new wave, had assimilated such diverse musical influences (everything from Jamaican ska to electronic music to disco itself) that it had expanded beyond categorization. Dance-oriented cuts like Blondie's "Rapture," the Clash's "Magnificent Seven," and Spandau Ballet's "Freeze" found their way into disco clubs, further blurring the line between genres. Concurrently, disco, as a distinct musical style, became so bloated that it began to collapse under its own weight, and black artists began to move in different musical directions. Such traditional soul artists as Smokey Robinson and Stevie Wonder began to reappear on the year-end pop charts. At the same time, a whole new style of black music known as rap was born. Artists like the Sugar Hill Gang, Kurtis Blow, and Grand Master Flash and the Furious Five transformed the street poetry of Harlem and the South Bronx into black popular culture. Other black artists—most notably Prince—moved in a rock-oriented direction. Indeed, the artist who dominated in the 1980s was Michael Jackson, the best-selling pop star in history. Jackson's ascent to superstardom was initially hampered by technological advances which allowed the transfer of radio's restrictive programming policies to the new medium of music television. As economic imperatives propelled the music industry toward a strategy of globalization, however, the 1980s witnessed a significant reshuffling of the musical deck. Even as the industry moved toward greater concentration, African American artists achieved superstar status in unprecedented numbers, and popular music became more politically engaged than any period since the 1960s.

NOTES

1. Charles M. Young, "Rock Is Sick and Living in London: A Report on the Sex Pistols." *Rolling Stone,* 20 October 1977, p. 68.

2. Mikal Gilmore, "Disco," *Rolling Stone,* 19 April 1979, p. 54.

3. Robert Christgau, "A Cult Explodes—and a movement is Born," *Village Voice,* 24 October 1977, p. 57.

4. Jon Savage, *England's Dreaming: Anarchy, Sex Pistols, Punk Rock, and Beyond* (New York: St. Martins Press, 1992), 138.

5. Andrew Kopkind, "The Dialectic of Disco," *Village Voice,* 12 February 1979, p. 11.

6. Simon Frith, "Beyond the Dole Queue: The Politics of Punk," *Village Voice,* 24 October 1977, p. 78.

7. Ibid.

8. Kopkind, "The Dialectic of Disco," 11.

9. Abe Peck, "Disco! Disco! Disco! Four Critics Address the Musical Question," *In These Times,* 6-12 June 1979, p. 20.

10. Gilmore, "Disco," 54.

11. Savage, *England's Dreaming,* 200.

12. Young, "Rock Is Sick and Living in London," 70.

13. Savage, *England's Dreaming,* 87.

14. Clinton Heylin, *From the Velvets to the Voidoids: A Pre-Punk History for a Post-Punk World* (New York: Penguin Books, 1993), 87–88.

15. Ibid., 38.

16. Ibid., 120.

17. Ibid., 123.

18. Ibid., 172.

19. Ibid., 174.

20. Savage, *England's Dreaming,* 202.

21. Frith, "Beyond the Dole Queue," 78.

22. Savage, *England's Dreaming,* 330.

23. Ibid., 63.

24. Ibid., 188.

25. Christgau, "A Cult Explodes," 70.

26. Ibid.

27. Lester Bangs, "The White Noise Supremacists," *Village Voice,* 30 April 1979, pp. 45–46.

28. Ibid, 46.

29. Savage, *England's Dreaming,* 242.

30. David Widgery, *Beating Time: Riot 'n' Race 'n' Rock 'n' Roll* (London: Chatto and Windus, 1986), 53.

31. Savage, *England's Dreaming,* 398.

32. Widgery, *Beating Time,* 80.

33. Ibid., 64.

34. Savage, *England's Dreaming,* 442.

35. Gillian G, Garr, *She's a Rebel: The History of Women in Rock & Roll* (Seattle, Washington: Seal Press, 1992), 277.

36. Robert Palmer, "New Rock from the Suburbs," *New York Times,* 23 September 1984, p. 23.

37. Vic Bondi, "Feeding Noise Back Into the System: Hardcore, Hip Hop, and Heavy Metal," (paper presented at the New England American Studies Association Conference, Brandeis University, Boston, Mass., 1 May 1993), 5.

38. Heylin, *From the Velvets to the Voidoids,* 314.

39. Stephen Holden, "The Evolution of a Dance Craze," *Rolling Stone,* 19 April 1979, p. 29.

40. Tom Smucker, "Disco," in *The Rolling Stone Illustrated History of Rock & Roll,* ed. Anthony DeCurtis and James Henke (New York: Random House, 1992), 562.

41. Barbara Graustark, "Disco Takes Over," *Newsweek,* 2 April 1979, p. 59.

42. Ibid., 58–59.

43. Kopkind, "The Dialectic of Disco," 14.

44. George Clinton quoted in Joe McEwen, "Funk," in *The Rolling Stone Illustrated History of Rock & Roll,* ed. Anthony DeCurtis and James Henke (New York: Random House, 1992), 521.

45. Graustark, "Disco Takes Over," 64.

46. Kopkind, "The Dialectic of Disco," 11.

47. Holden, "The Evolution of a Dance Craze," 30.

48. James Henke, "Record Companies Dancing to a Billion Dollar Tune," *Rolling Stone,* 19 April 1979, p. 46.

49. Kopkind, "The Dialectic of Disco," 16.

50. Russell Sanjek, *American Popular Music and Its Business: The First Four Hundred Years, Vol. 3* (New York: Oxford University Press, 1988), 514.

51. David Ansen, "Rock Tycoon," *Newsweek,* 31 July 1978, p. 41.

52. Ibid., 41.

53. Jay Merritt, "Disco Station Number One in New York," *Rolling Stone,* 22 March 1979, p. 11.

54. Kopkind, "The Dialectic of Disco," 11.

55. Don McLeese, "Anatomy of an Anti-Disco Riot," *In These Times,* 29 August–September 4 1979, p. 23.

56. Graustark, "Disco Takes Over," 58.

57. Dave Marsh, "The Flip Sides of 1979," *Rolling Stone,* 27 December 1979, p. 28.

58. Georgia Christgau, "Disco! Disco! Disco! Four Critics Address the Musical Question," *In These Times,* 6–12 June 1979, p. 21.

59. McLeese, "Anatomy of an Anti-Disco Riot," 23.

60. Robert Hilburn, "Musical Lessons From 1983's First Half," *Cape Cod Times,* 16 July 1983, p. 12.

61. N. R. Kleinfeld, "FM's Success is Loud and Clear," *New York Times,* 26 October 1979, p. Dl.

62. Marsh, "The Flip Sides of 1979," 30.

62. Pablo Guzman, "On the Radio, Part Two," *Rock & Roll Confidential,* January 1984, p. 2.

9 Music Videos, Superstars, and Mega-Events: The Eighties

The murder of John Lennon on 8 December 1980 put the big chill to any vestiges of 1960s idealism that had survived the Me Decade just as the election of Ronald Reagan one month earlier made it clear that the country was moving in a new political direction. Because of the faltering economy that had plagued the Carter administration, the Keynesian economic strategies of pump priming and deficit spending that had defined the fiscal policy of the Democratic Party since the 1930s no longer held sway among the electorate. Reagan's laissez-faire new federalism, which some labeled "voodoo economics," promised that deregulation of big business and supply-side manipulations would yield a balanced budget. Instead, this approach plunged the federal government into the worst deficit in its history.

At the time Reagan was elected, the music industry, like society as a whole, was already in a state of flux. Disco had fallen victim to the predictability of its own formula and the racist backlash of hard-rock fans. At the same time, punk had evolved into new wave, an umbrella category so diverse that it was virtually meaningless as a genre. As a result, the marketing categories of the music industry were temporarily thrown into disarray—a disturbing state

The murder of John Lennon on 8 December 1980 put the big chill to any vestiges of 1960s idealism that had survived the Me Decade just as the election of Ronald Reagan one month earlier made it clear that the country was moving in a new political direction.

of affairs for an industry that depends on targeting particular audience demographics. For a time, "new music" was used to describe everybody from Blondie to Michael

Jackson. Just to add to the confusion, in 1979, the U.S. music industry suffered its first major recession in thirty years. The phenomenal growth curve of the industry in the mid-1970s had led many to believe that it was virtually recession-proof. Between 1978 and 1979, however, revenues from the sale of recorded music in the United States declined by 11 percent, from an all-time high of $4.1 billion to $3.7 billion one year later.[1] Over the next few years, U.S. sales fluctuated, bottoming out at $3.6 billion in 1982. The international music industry followed a similar trajectory. International sales fell 18 percent in three years, from $11.4 billion in 1980 to $9.4 billion in 1983.[2]

Hardly the stock market crash of 1929, the decline in revenues was significant for an enterprise that had more than doubled in size in the preceding five years, and the industry was quick to respond. Within the first five months of decline, 700 record-company employees lost their jobs.[3] Between 1980 and 1986, CBS alone eliminated over 7,000 positions worldwide.[4] Production became more restrictive, making it harder for new acts to break into the business. One estimate suggests that record companies signed about 50 percent fewer artists during the recession than they had previously.[5] Accordingly, the number of new releases in the United States was cut nearly in half during this period, from 4,170 in 1978 to 2,170 in 1984.[6]

Any number of reasons were proffered for the slump. The industry itself favored home taping and piracy as the best explanations. Home taping (consumers illegally taping records instead of buying them) was, by far, the weaker of the two explanations as market research showed that the people who were buying blank tapes were precisely the people who were buying records. The introduction of portable cassette players in Walkmans, boom boxes, and car stereos had opened up new opportunities for listening to music. Consumers showed their preference for the new configuration by taping their own record collections. By 1983, the year the U.S. music business recovered from the recession, prerecorded cassettes surpassed record albums in unit sales. The figures on piracy were more convincing. In 1979, when the U.S. industry was plagued with returns because records were being shipped at 1978 levels, Al Coury, president of RSO, estimated that 20 to 40 percent of the returns to his company were illegal duplicates.[7] In 1982, the International Federation of the Phonographic Industry (IFPI) estimated piracy at 11 percent of the total market in the United States and Canada, 21 percent of the market in Latin America, 30 percent in Africa, and 66 percent in Asia.[8]

What the industry tended to leave out of its explanations, however, were the possibilities of a less than exciting period in music, a saturated market, and the failure of its own promotional apparatus. It also failed to note the diversion of its own investment capital into other profit-making ventures, including the burgeoning home video market for films and games. The introduction of the video cassette recorder (VCR) in the late 1970s had opened up the possibility of a home market for films on video. By 1980, *Billboard* had started its Video Sales chart, which was followed in 1982 by a Video Rentals chart. Having recognized the potential of films to promote music and Robert Stigwood's success with cross media marketing, many record companies, from such independents as RSO, Casablanca, and Island to such major conglomerates as Warner Communications and CBS, had developed film divisions and were betting that there would be stronger connections between film, video, and music in the near future. VCR penetration grew modestly at first but approached 75 percent by the end of the decade.

While the video-game market seemed to open a new path to profits for some in the industry, the market followed a boom and bust cycle that was even more dramatic than that of records. By 1982, the manufacture of arcade and home video games had become a $7 billion per year enterprise in which Warner Communications' Atari division (maker of Pac Man and other popular entries) led the way. In the first quarter of 1982, Atari's $400 million plus in sales accounted for two-thirds of Warner's total profits at the same time that its record and music publishing subsidiaries posted losses of over $100 million.[9] Noting this, the conglomerate staked its future on the development of video games but was completely unprepared for the intense competition and consumer backlash that occurred. A year later, Warner's Atari division faced losses in the hundreds of millions of dollars. During this same time, the pared-down record division rebounded significantly and was once again on its way to financial health.

If nothing else, the new leisure diversions of the late 1970s and early 1980s pointed up the importance of the technological advances that were about to transform the way in which music was produced and consumed. By the early 1980s, advances in satellite transmission had opened the door to the possibility of instantaneous national exposure for recording artists as well as the worldwide simultaneous broadcast of performances. At the same time, the global penetration of portable cassette technology provided for individualized reception anywhere in the world. In the United States, new transmission capability became apparent in 1981 with the creation of the most powerful music outlet ever to be developed—MTV.

> *B*y the early 1980s, advances in satellite transmission had opened the door to the possibility of instantaneous national exposure for recording artists as well as the worldwide simultaneous broadcast of performances. At the same time, the global penetration of portable cassette technology provided for individualized reception anywhere in the world.

Early Music Television: They Want Their MTV

While it is theoretically possible for music to exist as a solely auditory phenomenon, its presentation within some kind of accompanying visual context, be it dancing in a disco or attending a live concert, has long been seen as an indispensable part of its promotion. There is a sense in which a pop performance is a visual experience. Fans ask, "Have you ever *seen* Springsteen live?" not "Have you ever *heard* Springsteen live?" It is the visual impact of a performance, whether on film, stage, or television, that enables music to deliver its full measure of pleasure. This is a fact that the music industry has long recognized. Music played a prominent role in many of the first sound films. Louis Jordan, among others, made promotional music film clips in the 1940s that contributed measurably to his popularity and sales. For a brief time in the 1960s, there were even video jukeboxes (the Scopitone in France and the ColorSonics machine in the United States) that showed groups performing the selected record. Given the technological advances of the late 1970s, however, it was only logical that the visual context for music should become television.

Of course television had been used to promote popular music for quite some time. Rock 'n' roll stars had made regular appearances on family variety shows in the 1950s, and *American Bandstand* had provided national exposure for recording artists for years. In the 1960s, shows like *Shindig, Hullabaloo, The Monkees, The Archies,* and *The Partridge Family* were organized around rock. The Beatles' promotional film clips for "Penny Lane" and "Strawberry Fields" were, in fact, produced for television and anticipated some of the videographic techniques used in the 1980s. Indeed, the 1975 film clip for Queen's "Bohemian Rhapsody" is often remembered as the first music video. Still, music television in the 1980s ushered in a new era, an era in which the medium was used in new ways and video became the standard method for marketing popular music.

It was the deregulation of television at the start of the 1980s that encouraged an incredible expansion of cable services throughout the United States and a dramatic increase in the sheer number of available channels, all of which required new forms of programming. At the same time, technological developments enabled the hitherto unconnected media of television, film, and computer games to converge under the rubric of home video. It was only a matter of time before the home stereo would be added to the mix, which Robert Pittman, MTV's founding father, recognized when he announced the creation of MTV in 1981: "We're now seeing the TV become a component of the stereo system. What we're doing is marrying those two forms so that they work together in unison. . . . MTV is the first attempt to make TV a new form, other than video games and data channels."[10]

The U.S. music industry was fairly slow to warm up to the idea of music videos. They were a high-budget item, and it was not clear that there would ever be a substantial market for them. Indeed, music videos have never become consumer commodities in quite the same way as records, tapes, and compact discs have. Even in 1989, sales of music videos were a paltry $115 million in the United States, while the sales of sound recordings were $6.5 billion. Still, Pittman and his colleagues recognized that music videos, like sound recordings on the radio, could promote an interest in the music itself and deliver potential consumers to advertisers.

Thus, with an initial investment of $20 million, MTV, the first twenty-four hour music video cable channel, was launched on 1 August 1981 by Warner Communications and the American Express Company. The channel, described by Marshall Cohen, who was then vice president of marketing, as "the most researched channel in history," was devoted to the science of demographics or, to use Pittman's term, "psychographics." With 85 percent of its mostly white suburban viewers falling between the ages of twelve and thirty-four, MTV promised to deliver the perfect consumers for a tight economy.[11] In its first year of operation, 125 sponsors gambled that the channel would do just that, and the gamble paid off handsomely. With only 40 percent of the country wired for cable at the time, MTV expanded from an initial 2.5 million subscribers to 17 million in 1983, becoming the fastest growing cable channel in history. It was unquestionably the most effective way for a record to get national exposure.

In his book, *Dancing in the Distraction Factory,* Andrew Goodwin identified three historical periods in the development of MTV.[12] The first, 1981 to 1983, was characterized by a twenty-four hour continuous flow of music with little in the way of discrete programs. During this period, MTV was, in essence, a visual radio station with an AOR format, no news, and continuous music punctuated only by advertisements and the bland patter of the on-camera "veejays" (video jockeys). This is hardly surprising since Pittman had come to the cable channel from a career in radio. The second period, 1983 to 1985, marked a "second launch" as the channel became available in the New York and Los Angeles markets for the first time. During this period, a number of new music video outlets were created to fill in the gaps left by MTV's rock-oriented programming. Black Entertainment Television (BET) devoted about six hours per week to its *Video Soul* program, which was the primary outlet for video exposure for black artists. USA Cable Network's *Night Flight* played longer clips than MTV and showcased the work of some black and Latino acts. *The Nashville Network,* which went on the air in 1983, offered about eighteen hours of country music per day. WTBS inaugurated *Night Tracks,* a program that used a kind of Top Forty format. The networks also moved into the music video game with NBC's *Friday Night Videos* and ABC's *Hot Tracks.* Similar services, for example, MuchMusic in Canada and Music Box and the Power Station in Europe, soon began to appear elsewhere in the developed world.

MTV bested its U.S. competition at this time by entering into exclusivity arrangements with a number of major record companies. Under these arrangements, MTV had exclusive broadcast rights to certain videos for one month in return for cash payments in the hundreds of thousands of dollars annually. This period marked the beginning of a major commitment to heavy metal and the ascendancy of the "performance clip," essentially a video of a live performance in which the interaction between the band and their fans served as an indicator of metal authenticity. The third period saw a broadening of musical scope and a deeper commitment to youth culture. Videos aimed at those between the ages of twenty-five and fifty-four were transferred to the adult-oriented VH–1, a second MTV Networks music video channel. This period also witnessed the departure of Robert Pittman as MTV's auteur and the abandonment of the continuous flow of music format in favor of discrete programming that would eventually rival the cluttered schedules of the networks.

Goodwin has astutely pointed out that most studies of MTV have a postmodernist bent in that they focus disproportionately on the first period and Pittman's tenure. During the first period, according to Goodwin, the relatively small number of videos available to the channel contributed to a "high degree of repetition," and the continuous flow of music "blurred the categories of art-rock and pop, thus contributing toward a conflation of popular and high-cultural discourses."[13] The relatively small number of videos resulted from the reluctance of the U.S. music industry to enter the video market and forced MTV to rely on British music videos, which "tended toward the abandonment of narrative" as groups "eschewed the bland realism of performance videos."[14]

Music videos had developed earlier in Britain because the paucity of radio stations in Britain and throughout Europe had caused British record companies to seek exposure for their artists on television programs like Britain's *Top of the Pops*. With the coming of MTV, the videos, or promo clips, as they were called, offered a way of gaining entrance to the U.S. market that was more cost-effective than mounting cumbersome and chancy transatlantic national tours. Because the videos were conceived as a form of promotion, their producers and directors were drawn from the ranks of advertising. Thus, the videos were dominated by the aesthetic of advertising—fast cuts, ever-changing camera angles, eye-catching visuals, and a panoply of special effects. It is this aesthetic that is at the heart of the perception that postmodernism had arrived. The fact that Britain, at the time, was swept up in the new romantic movement, which, in its reaction to punk, combined black-influenced dance music, synthesizer pop, and a sense of disco glitz in a strikingly visual and unabashedly commercial package that was well suited to televisual presentation, has only added to this perception. Drawing on the repetitive electronic sounds of Can and Kraftwerk from Germany, British acts like Gary Numan and Ultravox made dance-oriented synth-pop safe for Spandau Ballet, Depeche Mode, Soft Cell, and other new romantics. While the movement itself was short-lived, MTV exposure contributed heavily to the success of Spandau Ballet's "To Cut a Long Story Short" and Depeche Mode's "Just Can't Get Enough." Indeed, Soft Cell's "Tainted Love" became a Top Ten hit at least in part because of its MTV exposure.

Throughout Pittman's tenure, MTV devoted a significant portion of its airtime to introducing white rock acts from other English-speaking countries. The channel's first video, appropriately titled "Video Killed the Radio Star," was by Buggles, a British group, and Australia's Men at Work owed their American success completely to MTV. In fact, beginning in 1982, the channel showcased so many English groups (Adam Ant, Billy Idol, Flock of Seagulls, New Order, After the Fire, Thomas Dolby, and ABC, among

Britain embraces music videos before U.S.

*B*ritain was swept up in the new romantic movement, which, in its reaction to punk, combined black-influenced dance music, synthesizer pop, and a sense of disco glitz in a strikingly visual and unabashedly commercial package that was well suited to televisual presentation.

many others) that it contributed significantly to what can only be described as a second British Invasion. In doing so, the channel propelled Human League's "Don't You Want Me?" to number one on the charts and prolonged the musical lives of the Kinks and the Hollies. It also rejuvenated the career of the supremely telegenic David Bowie when it placed his video of "Let's Dance" in heavy rotation (about half a dozen plays per day) in 1983, giving him his first Top Ten hit in seven years. Other British groups that were proponents of what was now called the new pop (Eurythmics, Culture Club, and Duran Duran, among others) also made their U.S. debuts in 1983 on MTV and parlayed their exposure into international superstardom. Annie Lennox of Eurythmics played with androgyny from a female point of view on the video of "Sweet Dreams" while Boy George of Culture Club performed gentle, soulful dance cuts like "Do You Really Want to Hurt Me?" "I'll Tumble 4 Ya," and "Karma Chameleon" decked out in heavy makeup and flowing female frocks. In both instances, the music was as satisfying as the visual images were striking. It was, however, the group Duran Duran that used the visual medium to greater advantage than any other act.

The physical attractiveness of the group, which was formed in 1978, was an early indicator of one of the prime requirements for video success. Shortly after the recruitment of the alluring, almost pretty, Simon Le Bon as lead vocalist in 1980, the group had become the favorite of the teeny bopper set in Britain. The group's first video, "Girls on Film," directed by former musicians Kevin Godley and Lol Creme, was so steamy/erotic/sexist (depending on one's perspective) that it was limited in its ability to

Eurythmics (Dave Stewart and Annie Lennox) look pleased with themselves after their performance of "Sweet Dreams Are Made of This" at the 1984 Grammy Awards. In challenging gender roles as she did, Lennox added an effective political statement to her considerable musical gifts.

get public exposure, which naturally identified Duran Duran as a group to watch, so to speak. The videos for "Rio" and "Hungry Like the Wolf," released in the United States in 1983, established them as international superstars. Though group members tried to defend their aesthetic choices as parody, in the eyes of the critics, Duran Duran was clearly eschewing the oppositional politics of punk in favor of jet-set images (yachts, sailboats) in exotic locations (Rio, Sri Lanka). The video of "Wild Boys," directed by ad-man Russel Mulcahy, was a surrealistic, science-fiction montage that epitomized the advertising technique of connecting disparate images formally, a common characteristic of early British music videos.

The second British Invasion was a fact of life in the music business by 1985, thanks in large measure to MTV. According to *Billboard*, the invasion "became a certifi-able matter of public record on 16 July 1983, upon which date no fewer than eighteen singles of British origin charted in the American Top Forty, topping the previous high of fourteen, set on July 18, 1965."[15] While it was true that a goodly number of British videos were visually more interesting than their U.S. counter-

If MTV executives claimed that few black artists recorded the kind of rock 'n' roll the channel played, how could they explain programming Phil Collins' note-for-note cover version of the Supremes' "You Can't Hurry Love" when Motown acts were getting no airplay? On what basis was Hall and Oates' r&b crossover music considered rock 'n' roll if the r&b crossovers of African American artists were not?

parts, it must be noted that MTV's selection process favored British groups at the expense of American artists and especially African American artists. Indeed, Britain's Thompson Twins ("In the Name of Love") was one of the few integrated groups to appear on the channel. A tally of *Billboard*'s MTV listings for the week of 16 July 1983 showed that, of nearly 100 videos aired that week, there were no African American artists in heavy rotation, none in medium rotation, and no new videos by African Americans had been added to the playlist. Needless to say, in the history of the channel, no concerts or specials by African American artists had been shown. Of the American videos shown, the only African American one was Donna Summer's "She Works Hard for the Money," which was in light rotation. Overall, there were only three black acts (all from other countries) in medium or heavy rotation.[16] The channel was roundly trashed in the popular press for its racism, which *People* magazine summed up in one line: "On MTV's current roster of some 800 acts, 16 are black."[17] MTV executives defended their prac-tices by claiming that few black artists recorded the kind of rock 'n' roll that the chan-nel's format required. The argument was, of course, circular. If the channel was format-ted according to extensive market research that targeted the tastes of a largely white suburban audience in the first place, then the format could not be used to explain away the racial bias. The format was the *cause* of the racial bias. Furthermore, if MTV execu-tives claimed that few black artists recorded the kind of rock 'n' roll the channel played, how could they explain programming Phil Collins' note-for-note cover version of the Supremes' "You Can't Hurry Love" when Motown acts were getting no airplay? On what basis was Hall and Oates' r&b crossover music considered rock 'n' roll if the r&b crossovers of African American artists were not? Indeed, in what sense was Rodney Dangerfield's rap record rock 'n' roll by anybody's definition? The channel's racism was exposed on the air when David Bowie caught veejay Mark Goodman off guard with a question about the lack of black artists on the channel. Replied Goodman: "Of course, also we have to try and do what we think not only New York and Los Angeles will appreciate, but also Poughkeepsie or the Midwest. Pick some town in the Midwest which would be scared to death by Prince, which we're playing or a string of other black faces, or black music."[18]

Perhaps the most blatant act of racial exclusion was MTV's rejection of five Rick James videos at a time when his album *Street Songs* had sold almost 4 million copies. An MTV spokesperson gave the standard reply: "We play rock and roll. We don't play Rick James because he's funk."[19] The response was particularly unconvincing because MTV was (perhaps reluctantly) playing Prince heavily at the time. While the case could certainly be made that James had a "blacker" sound than Prince, trying to set a rigid outer limit on rock 'n' roll somewhere between Prince's "Little Red Corvette" and James' "Superfreak" could only be considered an exercise in hair splitting. Of course, one possible explanation for this seemingly irrational distinction was the fact that Prince was signed to Warner, one of MTV's parent companies, while Rick James recorded for Motown. In any case, MTV steadfastly continued its refusal of Rick James videos at the time. "The tragedy," said Chris Blackwell of Island Records, "is that here's an opportunity to break down the barriers and they don't do it."[20]

It was Michael Jackson and the incredible success of *Thriller* that finally blew MTV's format argument out of the water. Jackson had already demonstrated his crossover appeal as a member of the Jackson 5 on Motown and as a solo artist on Epic. His first Epic album, *Off the Wall* (1979), produced by Quincy Jones, sold multi-platinum and yielded four Top Ten singles. Still, the album was only a warm-up for *Thriller*, which was number one for thirty-seven weeks in 1983 and generated an unprecedented seven Top Ten singles. It also accounted for a record twelve Grammy Awards in 1983, eight for Jackson himself and four more for Jones as producer. In fact, *Thriller* set so many records and was implicated in so many issues concerning the operations of MTV and the music industry that any consideration of its artistic merit can easily get buried under its impressive statistics. While there is no doubt that it was a marketing achievement of the highest order, the fact is that *Thriller* was a musical *tour de force.* Its songs and arrangements were well crafted, its production was crisp and uncluttered, its dance grooves were positively infectious, and Jackson's vocals were flawless. On *Thriller*, Michael Jackson demonstrated the versatility that might have earned him the title "King of Pop," but

*H*e launched into a dance routine that married the fluidity of Fred Astaire to the acrobatics of break-dancing, unleashing his now fabled "moonwalk" on millions of awestruck viewers for the first time. With a single performance, Michael Jackson boosted the sales of Thriller beyond all known records.

Because of criticism over reported physical alterations, charges of alleged child abuse, and unfavorable coverage of his failed marriage to Lisa Marie Presley, it is easy to lose sight of the fact that Michael Jackson once broke down racial barriers, set unimaginable sales records, and provided the inspiration and leadership for charity rock in the United States.

given the racial politics of fame, that was a throne he could only capture by crowning himself a decade later.

The album had something for just about everyone. Its first hit was "The Girl Is Mine," an upbeat pop duet with Paul McCartney that was guaranteed to pull in a middle-of-the-road, adult rock audience. It was followed by "Billie Jean," an exquisitely pulsing rocker with obvious dance floor appeal, that was number one for seven weeks. The song that displaced it was "Beat It," an overture to hard rockers that used Eddie Van Halen on guitar. As "Beat It" was beginning its descent from the number one slot, Jackson proved once and for all his televisual appeal in an appearance on *Motown 25,* a TV special celebrating Motown's twenty-fifth anniversary. The show, which was aired 16 May 1983, was intended to reunite such first and second generation Motown acts as Stevie Wonder, Marvin Gaye, the Supremes, the Temptations, the Four Tops, and the Jacksons, all of whom, with the notable exception of Stevie Wonder, had long since departed the label. For the most part, the celebration proceeded with spirit, although with twenty-five years of contract and royalty disputes, Flo Ballard of the Supremes dying on welfare, and bad blood between Jackson and his brothers, it would have been impossible for the show to be trouble free. Michael had agreed to appear on the condition that he be allowed to perform "Billie Jean," the only non-Motown song of the evening. The Jacksons' set went smoothly, and Michael even effected an on-screen reconciliation with Jermaine. Then, his brothers left the stage and he sheepishly introduced "Billie Jean." As the song's throbbing rhythms came up from the band and a black fedora appeared from nowhere, Jackson teased his audience to shrieks of delight. He then launched into a dance routine that married the fluidity of Fred Astaire to the acrobatics of breakdancing, unleashing his now fabled "moonwalk" on millions of awestruck viewers for the first time. With a single performance, Michael Jackson boosted the sales of *Thriller* beyond all known records.

Even with this kind of acceptance and obvious televisual charisma, MTV at first refused to air the videos of "Billie Jean" or "Beat It." On "Billie Jean," adman Steve

Barron portrayed Jackson as a shadowy figure who leads a private detective through a surreal street scene and vanishes into thin air just as he is about to be captured. Bob Giraldi, also from the world of advertising, shot "Beat It" as a straight ensemble dance number that reportedly used real Los Angeles gang members as well as professional dancers. Both videos made as good use of the medium as any of the British videos that were being aired, and their appeal should have been self-evident, but still MTV resisted. Whether it was the overwhelming popularity of the record or the widespread but officially denied rumor that CBS Records threatened to pull all of its videos from MTV unless they aired the Jackson videos, the fact is that MTV finally changed its mind and "Billie Jean" and "Beat It" proceeded to become two of the most popular videos the cable channel ever aired. "Billie Jean" is widely remembered as the video that broke the color line on MTV.

Having spent $150,000 on the production of "Beat It"—at a time when the cost of most videos was in the $35,000 to $45,000 range, Jackson went on to push production costs to the limit by hiring film director John Landis to shoot a $300,000, fifteen-minute version of "Thriller." Although the move threatened to price other artists out of the video market, Jackson recovered his investment when a long form documentary called *The Making of Michael Jackson's Thriller,* which included the video of the song, sold nearly one-half million copies, becoming the third best-selling video of 1984, behind *Jane Fonda's Workout* and *Raiders of the Lost Ark.*

While charges of racism provided MTV with its first controversy, it is the treatment of women and the portrayal of gender roles in music videos overall that have engendered the longest running debates. Particularly in its early years, the vast majority of videos aired on MTV were by white men trying to appeal to a similar audience demographic. Women appearing in these videos were used as visual hooks to encourage young male viewers to continue watching. Early examples of this practice include Duran Duran's "Girls on Film," David Bowie's "China Girl," the J. Geils Band's "Centerfold," ZZ Top's "Legs," Van Halen's "Hot for Teacher," and Robert Palmer's "Addicted to Love." Given the promotional nature of the videos and the fact that many of their directors came from advertising where it had long been considered axiomatic that sex sells, the sexism involved in these efforts cannot be attributed to the innocent experimentation of new art form. As Kevin Godley, codirector of "Girls on Film," has noted, "People are always accusing that video of sexism, and of course they're right. . . . We were very explicitly told by Duran Duran's management to make a very sensational, erotic piece that would be for clubs, where it could get shown uncensored, just to make people take notice and talk about it."[21]

It should be noted, however, that the objectification of women in music videos was neither uniform nor monolithic nor fixed. Madonna was routinely taken to task for objectifying herself in her early videos ("Like a Virgin," "Material Girl"). She defended the practice on the basis that she was in control of her image, and she has since been claimed by critics and her audience as a progressive rock star. "Material Girl," in particular, has been subjected to more scholarly (and mostly feminist) rereadings than any other video.[22] At the same time, male stars did not always exploit female images. Lionel Richie's "Hello" or Phil Collins' "One More Night," for example, displayed a respect for women. Furthermore, early music videos sometimes challenged the traditional images of men and women. Annie Lennox and Boy George played with androgyny. Girl-next-door Olivia Newton-John released one of the most popular, if overexposed, videos of the decade. "Physical" had middle-aged fleshpots in a gym metamorphosing into buff he-men as Newton-John fondled their muscles. At first glance, the video appeared to be little more than a shallow attempt on the part of the singer to spice up her image, but its ending had a touch of irony as the men left the gym arm-in-arm as gay couples. Diana Ross' "Muscles" included the muscles without the irony.

Cyndi Lauper, Donna Summer, and Pat Benatar tried different ways of giving a voice to women. The title of Lauper's debut album, *She's So Unusual* (1984), aptly described the singer with the extreme New York accent, rainbow-colored hair, and thrift-shop fashions, but it was her three-octave range that gave her four Top Ten hits in a row and propelled her to instant, if short-lived, superstardom. On the video of her first hit, "Girls Just Want to Have Fun," which was shot in her own home with her real mother, Lauper resisted the confines of traditional feminine roles and used imaginative computer graphics to make the point. Donna Summer's "She Works Hard for the Money" depicted a single working mother oppressed on the job and faced with the drudgery of housework and ungrateful kids at home. The bleakness of the mother's life is eased at the end of the video as women from all walks of life gather together to dance in the streets. Pat Benatar's "Love Is a Battlefield" took a similar line. In the video, Benatar portrays a young woman who is thrown out of her suburban home by unbending parents and forced to work in an urban brothel. She finds strength when she intervenes on behalf of a friend who is threatened by a surly patron. The video ends with the women dancing defiantly into the street, expressing both female solidarity and the pleasure of dancing together.

MTV was fraught with racist and sexist practices, but it went on line at exactly the right time for a music industry battling a recession. By late 1982, record companies could count on a 10 to 15 percent increase in sales for acts that made their debuts on MTV. Stray Cats sold about 2 million copies of *Built for Speed* (1982) on the strength of the videos accompanying "Rock This Town" and "Stray Cat Strut." Except for "The Breakup Song" in 1981, the Greg Kihn Band had been virtually hitless for eight years when an engaging video of "Jeopardy" shot the single to number two in 1982. By the week of 10 October 1983, seventeen of *Billboard's* Top Twenty albums had videos on MTV. Artists took the power of the

Radio took notice of MTV's power and often added new artists on the basis of video success. The music industry could have taken this trend as an indicator that breaking new artists could point the way out of the recession, but the major record companies perceived their growth potential to be tied to a different and far less democratic strategy.

Some artists challenge gender roles, give new voice to women

new medium very seriously. Stevie Nicks scuttled an elaborate Civil War drama shot for "Stand Back" at a cost of $85,000 because she thought she looked overweight in the video.

Given its impact, then, MTV could have had a major effect on the music industry's star system, particularly because it differed from radio in one significant way. "We play 80 percent new music, 20 percent old," boasted Robert Pittman. "Radio is just the opposite."[23] Radio took notice of MTV's power and often added new artists on the basis of video success. The music industry could have taken this trend as an indicator that breaking new artists could point the way out of the recession, but the major record companies perceived their growth potential to be tied to a different and far less democratic strategy.

Superstars: The Road to Economic Recovery

By 1983, the combination of the recession, the U.S. music industry's slowness in embracing music videos, and MTV's reliance on white British product and their unwillingness to air African American artists had resulted in U.S. pop charts that listed little U.S. music. Writing somewhat jingoistically in the Boston Globe Steve Morse noted, "The American pop charts these days have a shocking lack of true American music—especially country rock, blues, soul, rockabilly, folk and rhythm and blues. Or for that matter, black funk and rap music—two more recent styles that have been unable to transcend cult status."[24]

At the same time, as a result of the multiracial programming of Urban Contemporary stations and MTV's preponderance of new music, AOR radio, which was now the most conservative and segregated format in radio, experienced a significant decline. A resurgence of Top Forty radio in its new incarnation, Hot Hits, further hurt AOR. As Paul Grein explained in a five-part Billboard series on radio programming: "AOR used to be a broad-based no-holds barred format where you could play a wide variety of music and make it all work. But AOR got a little too structured and researched in the '70s and Top 40 took the ball and started playing the wide variety of music AOR once did."[25] Responding to pressures on all fronts, Lee Abrams, the founder of AOR, unveiled a new format called Superstars 83. By the end of the year, even the new format had been radically revised—ironically following MTV's reluctant and belated lead—to include black crossover acts like Lionel Richie, Donna Summer, Eddy Grant, Prince, and, of course, Michael Jackson. The appearance of black artists on AOR stations suggested some new developments in the music industry.

In 1978, five transnational music corporations—RCA, CBS, Warner, EMI, and Polygram—controlled through ownership, licensing, and/or distribution more than 70 percent of an international music market that was worth over $10 billion.[26] While both

CBS and RCA had reported in 1977 that more than 50 percent of their sales was coming from their international divisions, at the time there was still a marked division between artists who were aimed at the domestic market and those who were marketed primarily outside the United States. The surprisingly high international sales figures of the late 1970s were the result of international artists out-selling artists intended for the domestic market (Spanish balladeer Julio Iglesias, for example, barely made a dent in the U.S. market in the 1970s even though he lived in the United States and was the best-selling artist in the world at the time). Disco tended to transcend national boundaries, but it was, in many ways, a transnational music right from the beginning. Its global success was based more on the ubiquity of its international connections than the marketing strategies of U.S.-based record companies. While international sales provided a handsome source of additional revenue for U.S.-based record companies in the 1970s, the domestic market was still their main focus. The systematic exploitation of the world market as a condition of further growth did not become dominant until the 1980s.

> While international sales provided a handsome source of additional revenue for U.S.-based record companies in the 1970s, the domestic market was still their main focus. The systematic exploitation of the world market as a condition of further growth did not become dominant until the 1980s.

At this time, these companies developed a conscious strategy for internationalization that was based on the systematic exportation of Anglo-American popular music that was originally produced for the domestic market. Key to this development was the recognition, as reported in *Billboard*, that the economic recovery of the music industry that began in 1983 "was due more to the runaway success of a handful of smash hits than to an across-the-board pickup in album sales"[27] Of course, nothing better embodied this reality than the success of Michael Jackson's *Thriller*. By 1984 when total domestic sales of $4.4 billion indicated that the U.S. music industry had at least returned to its 1978 level of prosperity, Jackson's *Thriller* was well on its way toward earning a place in the *Guinness Book of Records* as the best-selling LP of all time, eventually reaching sales of some 40 million units worldwide. The success of *Thriller* signalled an era of blockbuster LPs featuring a limited number of superstar artists as the solution to the industry's economic woes. *Thriller* thus underscored the two most salient aspects of the industry's recovery: concentration of product and expansion into new markets.

Of course, the globalization of the music industry had implications for the treatment of artists at home. "Increasingly, the big record companies are concentrating their resources behind fewer acts," reported the *Wall Street Journal*, "believing that it is easier to succeed with a handful of blockbuster hits than with a slew of moderate sellers."[28] Accordingly, in 1984, Warner Records dropped over thirty artists from its roster, including Arlo Guthrie, Van Morrison, and Bonnie Raitt, who were not quite up to par in terms of sales. Some of these artists (for example, Raitt and Carly Simon, who left the label shortly after Raitt) went on to achieve their greatest successes at other labels. The major labels could have taken the push toward globalization as the occasion for scouring

Despite the fact that Prince projected a mysterious and seductive R-rated persona in the early 1980s, his music still took the mainstream by storm.

the world for new, exciting, and diverse talent, but instead, that became a research and development task for independent labels. In the cost-cutting fever generated by the recession, major companies looked to reap greater rewards from fewer artists.

If 1983 belonged to Michael Jackson, then 1984 was the year of Prince. Just as Jackson would become the (self-proclaimed) "King of Pop," Prince was the heir-apparent to Little Richard, Jimi Hendrix, and Sly Stone and synthesized funk and rock just as masterfully as Sly and the Family Stone had before him. As singer, guitarist, and producer, Prince was able to do all by himself what Michael Jackson needed Quincy Jones and Eddie Van Halen to do for him. Born of an interracial union in middle-class, middle-American Minneapolis, Prince Rogers Nelson, better known as Prince, was signed to Warner in 1978 and was granted an unprecedented degree of artistic autonomy for a teenager who used music as a vehicle for some very strange notions about sexuality and religion. His first albums were entirely self-written, played, sung, and produced. "Soft and Wet" from *For You* (1978), an album that was dedicated to "God," gave an early taste of the themes that would be included on *Dirty Mind* (1980), which contained odes to incest ("Sister") and oral sex ("Head") as well as other ditties that radio would not touch with the proverbial ten-foot pole. Still he seemed quite at home in concert appearing in black lace underpants, backed by the provocative female trio Vanity. For the double LP *1999* (1982), Prince moved closer to the rock mainstream, producing three major hits including "Little Red Corvette," which became one of the first videos by an African American artist to air on MTV. However, it was not until the release of *Purple Rain* (1984) that Prince was finally crowned. For *Purple Rain,* Prince assembled the Revolution, a new band that was integrated racially and sexually like Sly and the Family Stone. Released as both an album and a film of the same name, *Purple Rain* was the kind of triumph of cross-media marketing that Robert Stigwood would have envied. Parallels to the marketing of *Saturday Night Fever* abounded. Before the movie opened, "When Doves Cry," the first single from the album, had already reached number one. It was followed by "Let's Go Crazy," which hit number one shortly thereafter. Once Prince's sound and image were firmly implanted in the public mind, the title song was released and rose to number two. All in all, the album yielded five hit singles for Prince, and the film produced two more for the Time, the group that appeared as his musical competition in the film. *Purple Rain,* the album, sold some 14 million copies, while the video of the movie sold half a million units within six months of its release. Clearly, Prince and *Purple Rain* were more profitable for Warner than most of their other artists combined; not surprisingly, the release of the album coincided with the 1984 purge of the label's talent roster. Still, the artistry of *Purple Rain* should not be overlooked. The stark rhythms of "When Doves Cry" and the frenzied pace of "Let's Go Crazy" seemed to play fast and loose with the rules of pop, yet both reached number one. In the video, Prince unleashed some dance moves that approached Jackson's finesse and guitar playing that rivaled the best of the heavy metal virtuosos. It was Prince's finest hour.

Purple Rain's occupation of the number one position for twenty-four weeks delayed Bruce Springsteen's entrance into the top slot. *Born in the U.S.A.,* which was released about the same time as *Purple Rain,* ascended to number one and accomplished for Springsteen in 1985 what *Purple Rain* had done for Prince in 1984 and *Thriller* had done for Michael Jackson in 1983. *Born in the U.S.A.* tied *Thriller's* record of generating seven Top Ten singles and remained in the Top Forty for nearly two years, eventually selling some 11 million copies. In 1985 Springsteen was the hottest artist of the year.

Unlike many other superstars, Springsteen always felt more comfortable on stage than on video. An early clip for "Atlantic City" from his acoustic *Nebraska* album, was a black and white collage of mundane images of the Atlantic City boardwalk, parking lots, and casino scenes. Springsteen, himself, never appeared. "The music is left to speak for itself," observed *Newsweek's* Jim Miller, "a strategy that makes most other videos seem like garish distractions."[29] In his music and in his live performances Springsteen combined the image of a hard-driving, blue collar rock 'n' roller with that of a socially conscious 1960s romantic so effectively that

> **I**n his music and in his live performances Bruce Springsteen combined the image of a hard-driving, blue collar rock 'n' roller with that of a socially conscious 1960s romantic so effectively that he was able to project a "working-class hero" persona without pretense, even as he carried home tens of millions of dollars from the sale of Born in the U.S.A.

he was able to project a "working-class hero" persona without pretense, even as he carried home tens of millions of dollars from the sale of *Born in the U.S.A.* On *Born in the U.S.A.,* Springsteen brought together the unbridled energy of *Born to Run* and the sober portraits of everyday life that comprised *Nebraska.* In "Glory Days" he sang with passion about the trials and tribulations of a former high-school baseball star and a divorced prom queen. "My Hometown" was a thoughtful, searching ballad about the deindustrialization of small-town America. "Born in the U.S.A." was a wail about the racism and senselessness of the war in Vietnam and the cruel fate that befell its veterans. The song's hook line was so powerful (and so ambiguous) that both the Republican and Democratic candidates for president in 1984 (Ronald Reagan and Walter Mondale) tried to appropriate the song as a patriotic anthem, conveniently sidestepping the deeper issues it raised. Springsteen wisely avoided endorsing either of them, concentrating instead on the more grassroots approach of playing benefit concerts to raise money for food banks, soup kitchens, striking miners, and unemployed steelworkers.

Whitney Houston outsold Springsteen and set more industry sales records than he did, but she has never reached his heights as a political icon or culture hero. As the daughter of soul singer Cissy Houston and a cousin of Dionne Warwick, Houston came by her talent and gospel roots honestly. Because she had worked as an actress and a model before coming to the attention of Clive Davis at Arista Records, she was, in some ways, made for music television. Given the paucity of black acts, particularly black female acts, that were aired, however, her promotional clips were few and far between. Even so, the playful video for "How Will I Know" helped to maintain her 1985 self-titled debut album in the Top Forty for seventy-eight weeks, after it entered the charts at number one. By the time she released "Where Do Broken Hearts Go" from her second album, *Whitney,* she had tallied seven number one hit singles in a row, a feat that had not been accomplished since the Beatles.

Houston was capable of Aretha Franklin's range and power, but she tended to play it safe as an artist. Thus she emerged more as a pop entertainer than as a soul diva. "Saving All My Love for You" and "Didn't We Almost Have It All" were fairly standard pop ballads, as was her surefire remake of George Benson's "Greatest Love of All." "How Will I Know" and "I Wanna Dance with Somebody" were middle-of-the-road, if somewhat spirited, dance numbers. What made these songs work as well as they did was Houston's infectious delivery. In this, she was a lot like her cousin Dionne Warwick, who could transform the most vacuous pop material into something soulful. Among Houston's many number one hits, however, there was little that stretched her as an artist. Had she been a bit more adventurous in her choice of material she might have approached Aretha Franklin's stature as an artist, rather than just topping her sales figures.

Whitney Houston came from a family of rhythm and gospel giants. Although she has tended to play it safe musically, she is capable of combining Aretha Franklin's range and power with her cousin Dionne Warwick's ability to transform pop fluff into a thing of soulful beauty.

Needless to say, Jackson, Prince, Springsteen, and Houston were not the only superstars of the period. Lionel Richie had started as a founding member of the Commodores. He began by playing saxophone and then became lead vocalist and main songwriter. He was a versatile performer whose goal had always been maximum crossover. The Commodores' songs routinely registered in the upper reaches of the pop and r&b charts in the 1970s. "Three Times a Lady," a Grammy nominated number one hit, even earned Richie a country songwriter award from ASCAP in 1978. He went solo in 1981 under the tutelage of Kenny Rogers' manager, Ken Kragen. In 1983, Richie released *Can't Slow Down,* which went all the way to number one in the middle of Michael Jackson mania and remained in the Top Forty for seventy-eight weeks. The album generated five Top Ten singles, including "All Night Long (All Night)" and "Hello," which aided by videos on MTV, reached number one. Had it not been overshadowed by *Thriller,* the album, which sold more than 10 million copies, would have been the talk of the industry. Richie repeated his success with *Dancing on the Ceiling* (1986), which also went to number one. This time he capitalized on the popularity of the title song's video by issuing a "making of" documentary as Jackson had with "Thriller." After "All Night Long (All Night)," all of Richie's hits tended to be well within the bounds of pop convention, including those with movie tie-ins ("Say You, Say Me" from *White Nights,* 1985) and high-tech videos ("Dancing on the Ceiling," 1986). Richie wanted to crossover in a big way and he got his wish.

Madonna combined good promotion, danceable material, engaging choreography, and visual appeal into just the kind of superstar package that the industry wanted. Between 1984 and 1987, she had twelve Top Ten hits in a row. Nine of them came from two albums, *Like a Virgin* (1984) and *True Blue* (1986). Both albums hit number one and both remained in the Top Forty for a year. Madonna began her career as a

Throughout her career, Madonna has tested the limits of acceptable sexual expression. A talented dance/pop diva as well as a consummate businesswoman, she has always managed to turn controversy into record sales.

disco diva with such dance floor hits as "Holiday," Borderline," and "Lucky Star" and then used music videos to make the transition to rock star with "Like a Virgin" and "Material Girl." In her videos and live performances, she displayed an adult sexuality that inspired lust in teenage boys, emulation in young girls (dubbed Madonna-wannabees by the media), and outrage in their parents. Her penchant for Christian iconography sometimes recalls Prince's uneasy marriage of sex and religion. Over the years, she has continued to push sexual expression to the limit of public acceptability and sometimes beyond. Ambitious to the core and one of the most astute businesswomen in the industry, Madonna has always managed to use controversy to generate sales; all of her albums have been certified platinum.

There were a handful of other artists whose extraordinary chart runs generated similar mega-sales and rounded out the profile of a small group of superstars who could carry the entire music industry. In 1984, Wham! generated three number one singles in a row from the group's number one album, *Make it Big,* which remained in the Top Forty for more than a year. Between 1984 and 1985, Phil Collins also generated three number one singles in a row. Two of them—"One More Night" and "Sussudio"—came from the same album, *No Jacket Required* (1985), which was also number one and remained in the Top Forty for seventy weeks. Tina Turner's *Private Dancer* stayed in the Top Forty for seventy-one weeks; Steve Winwood's *Back in the High Life*, for sixty weeks; Billy Ocean's *Suddenly,* for over a year. Huey Lewis and the News had two number one albums in a row, *Sports* and *Fore!*. *Sports* remained in the Top Forty for seventy-one weeks. The two albums together generated nine Top Ten singles. The Pointer Sisters' *Breakout* stayed in the Top Forty for sixty-five weeks and yielded four Top Ten singles. By 1986, Janet Jackson and Anita Baker had also joined the list. Jackson's debut album, *Control,* hit number one, remained in the Top Forty for seventy-seven weeks, and generated five Top Ten singles. Baker's *Rapture* lasted seventy-two weeks. Needless to say all of these artists sold multi-platinum.

> In the 1980s, albums were carefully constructed repositories of quality material, designed not as single conceptual wholes like Sgt. Pepper but as time-release capsules, with individual cuts marketed to the public at precise moments, not to sell the single itself—singles had become largely promotional by this point—but to keep the album in circulation for months.

Such figures represented a dramatic statement of how concentrated the industry had become. During this period, the music industry realized a significant proportion of its revenues from about two dozen or so artists. Interestingly, for many of these artists—the Pointer Sisters certainly come to mind—the above releases contained some of their best work. In some respects the industry came full circle and returned to the days before rock became art when albums were aggregates of singles. In those days, however, LPs were crammed with filler because they were designed simply to sell the artist's current hit at a higher price. In the 1980s, albums were carefully constructed repositories of quality material, designed not as single conceptual wholes like *Sgt. Pepper* but as time-release capsules, with individual cuts marketed to the public at precise moments, not to sell the single itself—singles had become largely promotional by this point—but to keep the album in circulation for months on end. It was, of course, music television and cross media marketing, particularly movie tie-ins, that were crucial to this development. All of the superstar artists just discussed had music videos on MTV, and many of these were connected to first-run Hollywood films. Phil Collins had a number one hit with "Against All Odds (Take a Look at Me Now)," which came from the movie *Against All Odds.* Lionel Richie's "Say You, Say Me" came from *White Nights,* Madonna's "Live to Tell," from *At Close Range,* and Huey Lewis' "The Power of Love," from *Back to the Future.* Tina Turner's "We Don't Need Another Hero (Thunderdome)," from *Mad Max: Beyond Thunderdome,* went to number two, as did Billy Ocean's "When the Going Gets Tough, the Tough Get Going," which came from *Jewel of the Nile.* The Pointer Sisters hit the Top Ten with "Neutron Dance" from *Beverly Hills Cop.*

These examples, which barely scratch the surface, illustrate just how intertwined record companies and the film industry had become. As Chris Blackwell explained in 1986, "If you're in the entertainment business on the music side, you really need to be in films as well because I think they're really joining into one business."[30] Again, the industry had come full circle in some respects. Just as Tin Pan Alley had solidified its dominance through its relationship with Hollywood films in the thirties and forties, record companies now accomplished the same goal in the 1980s. As Simon Frith pointed out, "few hit films are released these days without an accompanying title song promotion."[31] Indeed, music had become so integral to films that it even effected how the films were made. In the 1970s, *Saturday Night Fever* had made it difficult to hear the Bee Gees' "Stayin' Alive" without imagining John Travolta strutting down the streets of Brooklyn. *Flashdance* and *Footloose* permitted similar associations in the 1980s, but it was the release of the 1987 sleeper hit *Dirty Dancing* that completed the fusion of music and film. In this film, the music that comprised the soundtrack actually became the focal point of the film. Bob Buziak, the RCA president who authorized the film and the soundtrack, noted at the time:

> I had a lot of experience with soundtracks and seen what worked and what didn't. The movie Back to the Future *grossed $150 million and had a No. 1 single with Huey Lewis; the soundtrack album only sold 600,000. That's because the music was "wallpapered" into the movie, and the songs were not an essential part of the emotional experience. For a soundtrack to be really successful—like* Top Gun *or* The Big Chill*—you have to hear what you see.*[32]

By harnessing all the technology and marketing tools at its disposal, the music industry created a small but internationally popular roster of superstars who were capable of generating unheard of profits. Revenues increased steadily from 1983 on even though total unit sales declined from 680 million units sold in 1984 to 618 million in 1986. In other words, the U.S. music business was making more money selling fewer sound recordings overall. This development was aided by another technological advance—the compact disc (CD), which was introduced simultaneously by Sony and Phillips in the late 1970s. As a digital configuration, the CD promised greater fidelity and ease of use than either records or tapes. Although CDs cost no more to produce than records or tapes, demand allowed record companies to charge more for them. In 1986, "the sale of 53 million CDs generated almost as much income ($930 million) as the 125 million LPs sold ($983 million)."[33]

Perhaps what was most striking about the star system that generated these profits was the fact that a significant number of the new international superstars—Michael Jackson, Prince, Lionel Richie, Tina Turner, Whitney Houston, Billy Ocean, the Pointer Sisters, Janet Jackson, Anita Baker, and to a certain extent, Stevie Wonder, Kool & the Gang, Luther Vandross, and Diana Ross—were African American. This may have been the first indication that the greater cosmopolitanism of a world market could produce some changes in the complexion of popular music at home. International acceptance, it appeared, gave access to the kind of promotional clout that could lead to superstardom at home. In 1985, nineteen of the Top Fifty albums of the year were by black artists. In 1986, eight of the twelve most popular hits of the year were by African American artists, four of whom were women. As *Billboard's* Paul Grein noted in 1986:

> *Black music has been setting the pace in pop for the past four years, with Michael Jackson, Lionel Richie, and Prince & the Revolution leading the way. . . . in 1986 . . . female artists came to the forefront. . . . The popularity of black female singers was dramatized in June, when "Whitney Houston," Patti LaBelle's "Winner in You" and Janet Jackson's "Control" held down the top three spots on the Top Pop Albums chart. It was the first time that black artists—or female artists, for that matter—had ever achieved that monopoly.[34]*

During this time, the talents of such African American producers as Quincy Jones, Nile Rogers, Narada Michael Walden, Jimmy Jam, and Terry Lewis also came to the forefront and paved the way for LA Reid and Babyface Edmunds toward the end of the decade.

Most of the white artists who achieved superstardom during this period were heavily influenced by black music. Madonna started as a disco artist and kept abreast of developments in the urban dance music scene throughout her career. Phil Collins had enjoyed a fruitful relationship with the Earth, Wind & Fire horn section since his earliest solo hits. Wham! evidenced a Motown influence even before George Michael left to launch a solo career that regularly crossed him over to the black music market. In 1989, he actually won the American Music Award for Best Black Male Vocal. Bruce Springsteen's on-stage interplay with sax player Clarence Clemmons foregrounded the r&b

roots of his music. Indeed, according to *Billboard,* the rest of the white rock scene was "in something of a sorry state. Urban/dance-oriented rock sounds seemed to garner the lion's share of chart success in 1986, with major names such as Robert Palmer, Peter Gabriel, and Steve Winwood all leaning more toward r&b than rock on their platinum releases."[35]

Record companies came to realize in the 1980s that the longevity of a particular product was the key to their financial well-being. If black artists could demonstrate that kind of staying power, then black artists would become superstars. Second in importance to longevity was to appeal to as broad a range of audience demographics as possible. Thus, the record companies adopted a deliberate strategy of appealing to different demographics simultaneously. This strategy became a virtual science with the release of a number of well-calculated cross-racial duets from 1984 on.

When Paul McCartney teamed up with Stevie Wonder in 1982 to record "Ebony and Ivory," with its transparent (and saccharine) appeal to racial harmony, the recording appeared to be something of a breakthrough and was discussed as such. McCartney then dueted with Michael Jackson on "The Girl Is Mine" in 1982 and "Say, Say, Say" in 1983. This recording was supported by one of the few interracial videos on MTV although one did have to wade through the trappings of minstrelsy in its staging, costuming, and blackface makeup to appreciate its significance. These projects can be viewed optimistically as attempts to break down the segregation of the music industry or cynically as two commercial giants cashing in on each other's superstar audiences. The James Ingram/Michael McDonald pairing on "Yah Mo B There" (1984) seemed to favor the optimistic view, but by and large, the companies were simply seeking to expose their major artists to new audiences. Julio Iglesias, for example, was introduced to the U.S. mainstream through two 1984 duets, one with Willie Nelson ("To All the Girls I've Loved Before"), to see if he might spark the country end of the market and one with Diana Ross ("All of You") to test his appeal among black listeners. Other cross-racial pairings seemed to be pop-oriented commercial gambits: Philip Bailey and Phil Collins ("Easy Lover"), Kenny Rogers, Kim Carnes, and James Ingram ("What About Me"), Patti LaBelle and Michael McDonald ("On My Own"), Aretha Franklin and George Michael ("I Knew You Were Waiting for Me"), and Linda Ronstadt and James Ingram ("Somewhere Out There"). These successes encouraged record companies to spread single acts around to multiple marketing categories. In 1985, Kool & the Gang released *Emergency,* which on the strength of three Top Ten singles, remained in the Top Forty for nearly a year. The group finished the year in the number one position on the black music charts and among the top twenty acts on the pop, adult contemporary, and dance charts. Madonna registered on the same four charts in that year, topping both the pop and dance categories. Stevie Wonder also found acceptance in these marketing categories when his "Part-Time Lover" reached number one on all four charts at various times during the year. As a whole, in their attempts to consolidate cross-racial markets, these efforts brought a new dimension to the very term "crossover." There were a few crossover projects that seemed to have a higher purpose. "Sisters Are Doin' It for Themselves" (1985), by Eurythmics and Aretha Franklin, included a video that portrayed women in a broader range of leadership roles than had ever been aired on music television. Proceeds from the sale of the number one single "That's What Friends Are For" by Dionne Warwick and Friends (Elton John, Gladys Knight, and Stevie Wonder) went to finance AIDS research. But these efforts had the benefit of hindsight, as they ventured down a trail that had been blazed some eight months earlier by the ultimate crossover recording— "We Are the World."

Charity Rock and Mega-Events: Who Is the World?

International superstars and technological wonders like satellite transmission and the incredible portability of cassettes had, by the mid-1980s, made popular music truly global. Perhaps nothing better illustrates this phenomenon than the string of socially conscious mass concerts and all-star performances, known as mega-events, that began in 1985 with Band Aid, Live Aid, and "We Are The World." Because these projects, which were somewhat cynically dubbed "charity rock," also aided transnational record companies in their quest to find new markets, construct new audiences, and deliver new consumers, they have sometimes been written off as politically irrelevant. More often than not, however, this judgment is too facile.

> In their relentless pursuit of higher profits, record companies have tended to relinquish artistic control and move farther and farther away from the creative process.

While it is true that a handful of major corporations have always been able to exercise tight economic control over the international music market, acquiring the lion's share of the market is not synonymous with determining the form, content, style, and impact of popular music. If anything, in their relentless pursuit of higher profits, record companies have tended to relinquish artistic control and move farther and farther away from the creative process. By the beginning of the 1980s, music, to the transnational corporate giants, was no longer limited to the manufacture and distribution of a fixed sound product. Instead, it had become a "bundle of rights" for things like television, movies, and advertising. Content to focus its energy on the development of these new sources of income for music, the industry evidenced little inclination to intervene in its content except when forced to do so (see Chapter 10). Thus, in the mid-1980s popular music tended to develop according to two opposing principles that correspond roughly to the extremes of the commercialism/authenticity continuum. On the commercial front, record companies discovered that their back catalogues were gold to filmmakers and advertisers. Ben E. King's "Stand By Me" was featured in a film of the same name and Levi used it to sell jeans in Britain. As a result, the 1961 r&b classic reentered the British charts and generated brisk sales in the United States as well. Cream's "I Feel Free" was used to sell cars, the Doors' "Riders on the Storm" to sell tires. The Beatles' "Revolution" turned up as the soundtrack for a Nike commercial. When the 1990s finally rolled in, even Bob Dylan's "The Times They Are A-Changin'" was used to promote an accounting firm. "What's new about the rock/ad agency tie-in," said Simon Frith, "is not the exploitation of stars' selling power as such (Coca-Cola has been using rock and pop idols that way for at least thirty years) but the use of anticommercial icons to guarantee the 'authenticity' of the product they're being used to sell."[36] If the meaning of authenticity was confounded by this commercial bent, it was recovered somewhat by the more humanitarian impulse of charity rock, which was colored, according to John Rockwell of the *New York Times*, by the left-leaning aura that had characterized popular music since the advent of rock 'n' roll.

> *Rock's leftist bias arose from its origins as a music by outsiders—by blacks in a white society, by rural whites in a rapidly urbanizing economy, by regional performers in a pop-music industry dominated by New York, by youth lashing out against the settled assumptions of pre-rock pop-music professionals.*
>
> *That bias was solidified by the 1960's, with its plethora of causes and concerns. . . . Rock music was the anthem of that change—racial with the civil-rights movement, and also social, sexual, and political.*[37]

Christmas in Ethiopia: The Advent of Charity Rock

The story of charity rock begins with the energy and imagination of Bob Geldof, leader of the Boomtown Rats, an Irish punk group. Inspired to action after seeing a BBC documentary on Ethiopian famine, Geldof, in collaboration with Midge Ure of Ultravox, wrote "Do They Know It's Christmas" and then organized the biggest names in British popular music to record the song as Band Aid, with all proceeds donated to famine victims. "Do They Know It's Christmas" became the biggest selling U.K. single ever, totaling 7 million copies worldwide. Based on its success, Geldof tried to organize a similar project in the United States but was stonewalled by some of the artists he contacted. "Look, they viewed me as a minor pop singer from England," he told *Rolling Stone*. "From their point of view, its like Joe Blow calling up. . . . But if Ken Kragen calls up, they know it's kosher. They know that Lionel [Richie] and Quincy [Jones] will be there and that you're gonna have a good show."[38] This is, of course, exactly what happened.

In the United States, charity rock was initiated by African Americans with Michael Jackson providing much of the leadership and musical direction. Although Jackson may have felt a growing ambivalence about his own "blackness," his career had opened doors for African American artists. The videos for "Beat It" and "Billie Jean" had played pivotal roles in breaking the color line on MTV, and *Thriller* pointed the way out of the recession for the music business. Jackson then enabled the industry to put its best international foot forward by taking the first American giant step in charity rock. "We Are the World" was cowritten by Jackson and Lionel Richie and produced by Quincy Jones with Jackson playing the role of music director. It was released by an all-star ensemble recording as USA (United Support of Artists) for Africa, which was also the name of the umbrella organization set up to administer the profits from the record. Organizational input came from Harry Belafonte and Ken Kragen, who, as manager for both Lionel Richie and Kenny Rogers, covered a broad range of pop terrain with the credibility that Geldof lacked. He was the perfect choice for president of USA for Africa.

"We Are the World" was an upbeat pop ditty structured around cameo appearances by the biggest names in U.S. popular music—Michael Jackson, Lionel Richie,

"We Are the World" brought together a range of artists who might not otherwise have appeared on the same stage. In so doing, the project opened the door to bolder undertakings like "Sun City."

Bruce Springsteen, Kenny Rogers, Billy Joel, Madonna, Cyndi Lauper, Diana Ross, Huey Lewis, Bob Dylan, Stevie Wonder, Ray Charles, and more. Because it fit promoter Bill Graham's description of 1980s rock as "the voice of corporate America," it proved to be an easy target for the critics. "With *We Are the World*, I know what they *meant*," said Jackson Browne, "But on the other hand, that's the problem with North America. We think we *are* the world!"[39]

When it was released, Greil Marcus argued that the song

> *sounds like a Pepsi jingle—and the constant repetition of "There's a choice we're making" conflates with Pepsi's trademarked "The choice of a new generation" in a way that, on the part of Pepsi-contracted song writers Michael Jackson and Lionel Richie, is certainly not intentional, and even more certainly beyond the realm of serendipity. In the realm of contextualization, "We Are The World" says less about Ethiopia than it does about Pepsi—and the true result will likely be less that certain Ethiopian individuals will live, or anyway live a bit longer than they otherwise would have, than that Pepsi will get the catch phrase of its advertising campaign sung for free by Ray Charles, Stevie Wonder, Bruce Springsteen, and all the rest.[40]*

There was also a distasteful element of self-indulgence in the "saving our own lives" line which follows in that the performers were proclaiming their own salvation for singing about an issue they would never experience on behalf of a people most of them would never encounter. Even so, "We Are the World" became for charity rock what "We Shall Overcome" was to the Civil Rights movement and helped to clear the way for Live Aid, the largest single event in human history.

Live Aid made Marshall McLuhan's global village something of a reality for at least sixteen hours. It was organized as an act of will by Geldof, who conned, cajoled, even resorted to what he called "moral blackmail" to convince more than sixty artists (not to mention promoters, ticket sales agencies, merchandising concerns, sponsors, satellite operators, and radio and television stations) to donate their time and/or money to the cause. The event, which capitalized on the international appeal of superstars, just as "We Are the World" and "Do They Know It's Christmas" did, was organized as a Band Aid project. USA for Africa did not participate as an organization, and neither Michael Jackson nor Lionel Richie appeared at the event even though the concert closed with an ensemble rendition of "We Are the World." The concert was staged simultaneously at Wembley Stadium in London and JFK Stadium in Philadelphia on 13 July 1985 and was broadcast either live via fourteen satellites or pretaped to more than 1.6 billion people in 160 countries.

Although the widely rumored Beatle reunion with Julian Lennon sitting in for John never happened, Live Aid had its share of classic rock 'n' roll moments. Keith Richards and Ron Wood of the Rolling Stones joined Bob Dylan for an all-star performance of "Blowin' in the Wind." Mick Jagger teamed up with Tina Turner for what one newsweekly called a "delightfully lascivious" version of "State of Shock." The Who played together for the first time in three years, and there were welcome Led Zeppelin and Crosby, Stills, Nash & Young reunions although time and other indulgences had taken their toll. Daryl Hall and John Oates joined former Temptations David Ruffin and Eddie Kendricks for some show-stopping choreography. Phil Collins managed to perform at both Wembley and JFK by zooming across the Atlantic on the Concorde, the supersonic jetliner that Geldof felt for some reason symbolized the potential triumph of technology over human suffering. Geldof's own magic moment occurred when he was hoisted onto the shoulders of Paul McCartney and Pete Townshend on stage for all the world to see.

In both the popular press and trade press, the concert was celebrated and criticized at the same time—celebrated for "weld[ing] together popular art and humane politics, for using the power, energy and invention of rock & roll to accomplish something of

Shared by 1.6 billion people in 160 countries, Live Aid was the largest single event in human history. The live concert was staged simultaneously at Wembley Stadium in London and JFK Stadium in Philadelphia.

"We Are the World," Live Aid become easy targets for critics practical social value,"[41] and criticized for its paucity of black and Latino artists and its trivialization of the issues. MTV, which carried the sixteen-hour telecast in its entirety, was the primary target for criticism in the United States because its vacuous veejays seemed more intent on displaying themselves than any knowledge of or interest in the issues at hand or the value of rock history. As the reunited Led Zeppelin launched into their seminal "Stairway to Heaven," the cameras cut to Martha Quinn looking enraptured. The performance of rap group Run-D.M.C., one of the few youth-oriented black groups booked for the event, was short-shrifted so that MTV could cover Sting's backstage arrival. If the veejays could not be blamed for directorial decisions, their commentary, which amounted to little more than the 1980s equivalent of "Wow!" and interview questions that never asked more than "What does Live Aid mean to you?," was no one's fault but their own. The event's hype, glitter, and industry gossip routinely took precedence over education, analysis, and a call to action.

Because Live Aid was a benefit, comparisons with other humanitarian events abounded. While the issue of starvation recalled George Harrison's Concert for Bangladesh, the most obvious comparison was to Woodstock. Indeed, Joan Baez opened the Philadelphia show with the words: "Good morning, you children of the 1980s. This is your Woodstock and it's long overdue." In point of fact, however, Baez's comments reflected wishful political thinking. To the extent that Woodstock helped usher in the big business/mass music/techno-culture of the 1980s, there was certainly a historical connection between the two events, but they had little else in common. Woodstock was the product of a bygone era; it was experienced as participatory, communitarian, and anticommercial. Live Aid was an unabashed celebration of technological possibilities in a period of yuppie conservatism. Live Aid made use of corporate sponsors—AT&T, Eastman Kodak, Chevrolet, and Pepsi—which would have been anathema to the Woodstock generation. "The politics of Woodstock were antiauthoritarian, antiestablishment, antiwar," said commentator Pete Hamill. "The American Live Aid audience was part of a new American generation that thinks Ronald Reagan is a wonderful president, Rambo a wonderful role model, and Grenada a wonderful war."[42]

Still, as Will Straw pointed out, "The most underrated contribution rock musicians can make to politics is their money, or ways in which that money might be raised," and although sometimes overlooked in the hype, the most important function of Live Aid had been that of fund-raising.[43] The actual take was $67 million. By anyone's fund-raising standards, that is a staggering amount of money to be generated from a single event. Even so, Geldof, who was nominated for the Nobel Peace Prize for his efforts, recognized its limitations: "I'm aware that a million dollars is a lot of money, but when 130 million people are affected by this problem, even $67 million is nothing."[44] Furthermore, there remained the question of the extent to which Live Aid served the issue at hand and the extent to which it served capital. At the 1986 ceremony of the British music industry's BPI awards, Norman Tebbitt of the Thatcher administration "extolled Live Aid as a triumph of international marketing."[45] On this side of the Atlantic, John Costello, vice president of Pepsi, said: "Live Aid demonstrates that you can quickly develop marketing events that are good for companies, artists, and the cause."[46]

Mega-Events: The Politics of Mass Culture

To many, charity rock was a contradictory phenomenon. While it provided activist musicians with a platform for political expression on a scale that was previously unthinkable, at the same time, it enabled the music industry to exploit a gold mine of untapped markets. Embedded in this contradiction, which went well beyond popular music and mega-events, was a new view of mass culture. Far from being considered a cultural wasteland that promotes mindless consumption, mass culture came to be seen as "contested terrain," an ideological cauldron in which new values could be forged.

Band Aid, Live Aid, and USA for Africa created a climate in which musicians from countries all over the world felt compelled to follow suit with African famine relief projects of their own. A partial list is sufficient to illustrate the point. Under the name of Northern Lights, Canada's top pop stars recorded "Tears Are not Enough," West Germany's all-star Band fur Ethiopia released "Nackt im Wind," as Chanteurs Sans Frontieres, thirty-six French singers offered

> "Sun City" urged musicians not to perform at the lavish Las Vegas-like entertainment complex that was located in one of the so-called South African homelands. Symbolically, it upped the political stakes of all-star recordings significantly.

"Ethiopie," Belgium contributed "Leven Zonder Honger," the Netherlands "Samen," Australia "E.A.T." (East African Tragedy), and fifty African artists, including Youssou N'Dour, Hugh Masakela, Manu Dibangu, and King Sunny Ade, recorded "Tam Tam Pour L'Ethiopie."[47] As politically cautious as some of these humanitarian efforts were, they created the cultural space for progressively bolder projects, including some that brought the issue of economic devastation closer to home. An offhand comment by Bob Dylan about the plight of the U.S. family farm made from the stage at Live Aid prompted Willie Nelson, John Cougar Mellencamp, and Neil Young to organize Farm Aid two months later. Nelson secured the use of the football stadium at the University of Illinois from Governor James R. Thompson and cajoled country artists from Kenny Rogers and Glen Campbell to Alabama and the Charlie Daniels Band to Merle Haggard and Loretta Lynn to perform. Young and Mellencamp pulled in rockers ranging from Billy Joel and Don Henley to Eddie Van Halen and Sammy Hager to X and the Blasters.

The concert brought together a unique coalition of rock and country artists who were uncommonly respectful of one another, raised $10 million in the process, and became an annualized event.

Other, more politicized ventures followed, including Sun City, the two Amnesty International tours, and two tributes to African National Congress leader Nelson Mandela. Using "We Are the World" as a model, guitarist Little Steven, fresh from Bruce Springsteen's E Street Band, assembled more than fifty rock, rap, r&b, jazz, and salsa artists to create the recording "Sun City," a politically charged anthem in support of the UN-sponsored cultural boycott of South Africa, which was then under white minority rule. "Sun City" urged musicians not to perform at the lavish Las Vegas-like entertainment complex that was located in one of the so-called South African homelands. Symbolically, it upped the political stakes of all-star recordings significantly.

In some ways, "We Are the World" was the logical extension of the crossover strategy developed in the mid-1980s. It was a pop-oriented tune that primarily utilized artists who, while drawn from the often mutually exclusive categories of rock, country, and r&b, had achieved mainstream acceptance. By including heavy metal acts like Judas Priest and Ozzy Osbourne, new wave groups like Simple Minds and the Boomtown Rats, r&b artists like Patti LaBelle and Ashford and Simpson, and rappers like Run-D.M.C., Live Aid had broadened the politicization of mass culture a bit more. "Sun City" pushed it even further. It was a forceful composition with an explicitly antiapartheid message. It included a broad range of artists (jazz great Miles Davis, salsa stars like Ray Baretto and Reubén Blades, rappers like Afrika Bambaataa and Run-D.M.C., and two South African groups, the Malopoets and Via Afrika, who risked personal reprisals as a result) as well as artists who were known to be politically outspoken, including Jackson Browne, Bonnie Raitt, Peter Garrett from Midnight Oil, and Bono from U2. Its video masterfully intercut scenes of the horrors of apartheid with cameo appearances of the performing artists. It climaxed with the ensemble cast singing the anthemic chorus at an actual divestment rally at CitiBank in New York and then segued seamlessly to a demonstration of black South Africans singing "Nkosi Sikelel' iAfrica," the (unofficial) black South African national anthem as the video faded, thus linking the participating artists with the antiapartheid movements in the United States and South Africa.

Not content with just presenting an antiapartheid message, the creators of "Sun City" also sought to encourage an activist audience response. The album jacket, for example, was filled with facts and figures about apartheid, and a teacher's guide showing how to use the record and the video in the classroom was issued. As part of its educational effort, the guide reported on numerous antiapartheid student projects that had been inspired by the recording. In creating a teacher's guide, the Sun City project was attempting to build on the familiarity of a mass cultural product to create exercises that could be tailored to local use.

U2 began their rock career as politically committed Christians from Ireland. By the late 1980s, they had also become one of the biggest rock acts in the world.

U2 encourages political activism for Amnesty International

The "Sun City" project was not the only one to encourage political activism on the part of its audience. In 1986, U2, then an up-and-coming Irish rock band from Dublin, headlined a U.S. tour, entitled The Conspiracy of Hope, for Amnesty International. As a group of politically progressive, devout Christians from strife-torn Ireland, U2 was the perfect choice to represent the organization that acts as an advocate for prisoners of conscience around the world. Formed in 1977, U2 first cracked the U.S. Top Forty in 1983 with *War,* which included "Sunday Bloody Sunday," the group's most poignant political commentary. With the release of *The Unforgettable Fire* (1984), which included the hit single "Pride (In the Name of Love)," they began their ascent to superstardom. By 1987, they were the hottest rock act in the world with millions of devoted followers including Bruce Springsteen. *The Joshua Tree,* which was released in 1987, went to number one and then charted in the Top Forty for more than a year, winning the 1987 Grammy Award for album of the year.

It was Jack Healy, then executive director of Amnesty International USA, who organized the Conspiracy of Hope Tour and engineered the connection between rock and the human rights movement. One of the tour's goals was to recruit new "freedom writers" who would participate in the letter-writing campaigns Amnesty uses to call attention to the plight of prisoners of conscience. Thus, as a part of the event, the tour targeted six political prisoners, three of whom were freed within two years as a result. In addition, Amnesty/USA added some 200,000 new volunteers to the organization. "Previous to 1986, we were an organization post forty," said Healy. "Music allowed us to change the very nature of our membership."[48] In 1988, Healy organized a world tour, called the Human Rights Now! Tour, that featured Bruce Springsteen, Sting, Peter Gabriel, Tracy Chapman, and Youssou N'Dour as headliners who were supported by a variety of local and national acts from host countries. Healy's choice of artists was well calculated. Sting, who had left the Police in the mid-1980s, was riding high from the success of *The Dream of the Blue Turtles* (1985) and . . . *Nothing Like the Sun* (1987), both collaborations with jazz saxophonist Branford Marsalis. Gabriel's *So* (1986), the best selling album of his solo career, had catapulted him to international superstardom, and he was already well respected in international circles as the prime mover of WOMAD, the international World of Music, Arts, and Dance Festival. Chapman's self-titled debut album hit number one in 1988, enabling Healy to add some diversity (musical and otherwise) to the bill. Youssou N'Dour was Senegal's most popular artist and a master of the African funk, rock, and jazz fusions that were becoming popular on the international stage. His presence conferred that much more credibility on the Human Rights Now! Tour. Springsteen was Amnesty's best selling artist, but the tour had as big an effect on him as he had on it. As Healy recalled:

> I remember Bruce Springsteen saying that he'd played to his first black audiences on the Human Rights Now! Tour in Zimbabwe and the Ivory Coast. We played to Shintos in Japan, Hindus in India, uptight Orthodox Christians in Greece, a mix of religions in Zimbabwe and a lot of Muslims in the Ivory Coast. And Bruce was loved by all of them; he rocked the stadiums everywhere.[49]

After the Human Rights Now! Tour, Amnesty boasted 420,000 members worldwide, with an average age of twenty.

There were also two massive international concerts staged at Wembley Stadium on behalf of Nelson Mandela. The first was held on 11 June 1988 to celebrate Mandela's seventieth birthday. The second was held on 16 April 1990 to celebrate the end of his thirty years of imprisonment. The eleven-hour Nelson Mandela Seventieth Birthday Tribute, as the first concert was officially named, featured a remarkably diverse roster of first-rate talent.[50] It was broadcast

Just as "Sun City" pushed against the limits of politicized pop, the Mandela shows eschewed charity in favor of structural change.

whole or in part to an estimated 600 million people in more than sixty countries. In calling for the release of the imprisoned leader of the African National Congress (ANC), an organization considered illegal by most of the countries that broadcast the concert, the Mandela Tribute raised the political stakes for mega-events once again. The stage was adorned by a thirty-foot scrim of Mandela's image perched tastefully atop the slogans "Isolate apartheid" and "The struggle is my life." The massive speaker columns were flanked by exact replicas of the late Keith Haring's "Free South Africa" poster. Just as "Sun City" pushed against the limits of politicized pop, the Mandela shows eschewed charity in favor of structural change.

Like all political events, the first Mandela tribute had found it difficult to balance the need to recruit stars who could insure the financial success of the event with the need to present those artists who had demonstrated commitment to the issue at hand. In the push to book name acts, lesser-known but politically more active artists like Billy Bragg and South Africa's Johnny Clegg were passed over for Whitney Houston and others. Houston was the biggest star booked for the event and thus attracted the most criticism, particularly because industry rumors suggested that her management had urged concert organizers to downplay the political aspects of the event as a condition for her appearance. For her part, Houston delivered the most animated performance of the day. While she was vulnerable to the charge of playing it safe both musically and politically, she was one of the first artists to commit to the festival. Her overwhelming popularity contributed significantly to making the event attractive to broadcasters all over the world, and she was a favorite of the imprisoned ANC leaders. Ahmed Kathrada, an ANC rebel who was serving a life sentence along with Mandela, sent a message that was distributed by the local Anti-Apartheid Movement and quoted in *Rolling Stone:* "You lucky guys. What I wouldn't give just to listen to Whitney Houston! I must have told you that she has long been mine and Walter's [Sisulu] top favorite. . . . In our love and admiration for Whitney we are prepared to be second to none!"[51]

Organizers of the second concert, An International Tribute for a Free South Africa, were in a particularly good position learned from the criticisms of the first tribute. With only fifty-four days to produce the concert, there were problems in booking artists. Still, with stars like Peter Gabriel, Tracy Chapman, Bonnie Raitt, Anita Baker, Neil Young, Natalie Cole, and Lou Reed, among many others agreeing to appear, an impressive lineup of artists was assembled on short notice. The 72,000 tickets for the live event sold out faster than any other event in the history of Wembley Stadium. Of course, the real headliner of the event was Nelson Mandela, and it was widely assumed that his presence, which without question gave the event political credibility, would make the concert irresistible to broadcasters the world over. That assumption turned out to be largely accurate; broadcasters from some 63 countries signed on to broadcast the four-hour concert. Even South Africa proposed to carry the show, a proposal that was eventually rejected by the ANC in support of the cultural boycott. It was, therefore, all the more shocking that not a single U.S. broadcaster could be persuaded to air the event. The only North American broadcast of the show was by MuchMusic, Canada's equivalent to MTV, which broadcast the concert in its entirety.

Using the international platform that the event offered, Mandela with his dignified but forceful demeanor and steadfast refusal to compromise his principles, drove home his antiapartheid message to hundreds of millions of people all over the world.

He indicated his understanding of the power of mega-events when he thanked the performing artists backstage for their efforts:

> Over the years in prison I have tried to follow the developments in progressive music. . . . Your contribution has given us tremendous inspiration. . . . Your message can reach quarters not necessarily interested in politics, so that the message can go further than we politicians can push it. . . . We admire you. We respect you, and above all, we love you.[52]

The international political agenda of mega-events was not limited to issues affecting only the African continent. Global environmental concerns were also important. Early in 1989, Geffen Records and cable music channel VH–1 teamed up to promote a project for Greenpeace, the environmental group. As its part of the project, VH–1 produced more than two dozen sixty-second spots, called "World Alerts," that featured celebrities discussing a range of environmental issues. Artists ranging from U2 and Talking Heads to John Cougar Mellencamp and Belinda Carlisle donated twenty-seven hit songs to a compilation album entitled *Rainbow Warriors,* which was released under the title *Breakthrough* in what was then the Soviet Union. It became the top selling record in there, with all proceeds split between Greenpeace and the Soviet Foundation for Survival and Development of Humanity. Our Common Future was another environmental extravaganza that was staged at Lincoln Center in the spring of 1989. Participants included Bob Geldof, Richard Gere, Sting, Midnight Oil, and Herbie Hancock, among others. In addition to entertainment, the show provided a platform for a number of scientists and world leaders to voice their concerns over global environmental decline. It was a little unnerving for some, however, to see Margaret Thatcher delivering a pretaped message about Britain's concern for the environment. It may be that the politics of the show were complicated by the sponsorship of multinational corporations, including Sony, Panasonic, and Honda, all of whom had their corporate logos prominently displayed during the syndicated telecast.

By the end of the 1980s, there was scarcely a social issue that was not associated in a highly visible way with popular music and musicians.

Critic Dave Marsh has been particularly critical of corporate involvement in mega-events, claiming that such involvement robs "charity-rock of one of its most important selling points: the selflessness of its motivation."[53] Given the scale of mega-events, however, most would be impossible without some kind of corporate sponsorship. Amnesty's Human Rights Now! tour would have gone bankrupt had not Reebok bailed it out at the last minute. Furthermore, the mega-events of the 1980s developed a kind of momentum that obliged corporations and world leaders to accommodate to initiatives that were essentially humanitarian or progressive. Indeed, this momentum exerted an effect on the culture of popular music in general. As Simon Frith and John Street have noted: "The paradox of Live Aid was that while in the name of 'humanity' it seemed to depoliticise famine, in the same terms, in the name of 'humanity' it politicised mass music."[54] There was a clear connection between John Cougar Mellencamp's involvement in Farm Aid and his "Rain on the Scarecrow," a song about the despair of modern rural life. Jackson Browne's interest in Central America led to "Lives in the Balance," a moving criticism of U.S. intervention in Central America. Likewise, there was a resonance between Sting's involvement with Amnesty International and his "They Dance Alone," a song about the widows of "disappeared" political activists in Chile, which became all the more poignant when he brought Chilean women out onstage to dance with him as he toured that country. With "Luka" (1987), singer/songwriter Suzanne Vega brought the issue of child abuse to the attention of many. A number of rap groups, including Public Enemy, Boogie Down Productions, and Stetsasonic, participated in "Self-Destruction," the anthem of the Stop the Violence movement, which protests black-on-black crime. In recording "Fight the Power" for Spike Lee's *Do the Right Thing,* Public Enemy contributed the soundtrack for the most powerful statement about racism in the 1980s. By the end of the 1980s, there was scarcely a social issue that was not associated in a highly visible way with popular music and musicians.

The mega-events of the 1980s also had an unintended but no less progressive side-effect on the music industry itself. In the United States, the formats for most music programs are designed to cater to the tastes of a fragmented audience. While these divisions ostensibly represent differences in musical taste, they correlate highly with divisions of class, race, age, and ethnicity. Because the artists who participated in the mega-events crossed a broad range of audience demographics and music programming formats, the media outlets that carried the performances contributed significantly to breaking down the apartheid of the music industry itself. "Whoever buys ['Sun City']," remarked coproducer Arthur Baker, "is going to be turned on to a new form of music, just as whoever sees the video is going to be turned on to an artist they've never seen before."[55] For a brief time in the 1980s, the internationalization of the music industry became a two-way process, albeit a limited one. While Anglo-American music may have been disproportionately broadcast to a worldwide audience, artists like Youssou N'Dour and Sly and Robbie did gain greater access to the world market. It was more than a coincidence that the emergence of world music (also known as world beat) in developed countries paralleled the development of charity rock. A greater awareness of world cultures, in turn, influenced the character of mainstream popular music at home. Peter Gabriel had long been credited with tasteful appropriations of African rhythms. Jackson Browne incorporated Central American sounds on *Lives in the Balance.* David Byrne of Talking Heads developed an interest in Brazilian music.

Perhaps the best-known—and most controversial—fusion of mainstream popular music and international music styles is Paul Simon's *Graceland,* which was in many ways a pivotal album of the 1980s. Released in 1986, the album was based primarily on South

African musical styles and incorporated an incredible diversity of cultural influences ranging, in the words of ethnomusicologist Steven Feld, from

> *quirky 1960's Long Island/Brill Building Simon lyrics, pedal steel guitar riffs from a Nigerian Jùjú band player via Nashville recordings, vocals from Senegalese Youssou N'Dour on break from recording projects with British pop star Peter Gabriel, and everything else from Synclavier samplers and drum machines to the Everly Brothers and Linda Ronstadt . . . with exemplars of zydeco . . . and East Los Angeles Chicano rock and roll. . . .*"[56]

Historically, the album has taken its place as one of the defining contributions to that amorphous category of world music or world beat. As such it has been at the heart of highly politicized discussions concerning musical appropriation and ownership on the one hand and cultural imperialism on the other.

On *Graceland,* Simon demonstrated his talent as a musician with a fine ear for exotic sounds. He was respectful of South African music and worked with such notable black South African artists as Ladysmith Black Mambazo and other first-rate studio musicians. He offered three times union scale for sessions and gave appropriate cowriter

Applying his ability as a singer/songwriter and fine ear for multicultural sounds, Paul Simon created one of the most celebrated and criticized albums of the 1980s. He is pictured with the late Joseph Shabalala, leader of Ladysmith Black Mambazo, who were among the featured South African artists to appear on Graceland.

credits on collaborative songs. The album also featured performances by Los Lobos and zydeco legend Rockin' Dopsie. The result was a hauntingly beautiful compilation that effectively linked South African rhythms with a range of regional ethnic U.S. influences. Still, as critics noted, most of the album was recorded in South Africa in violation of the UN cultural boycott. (This may explain why Simon agreed to appear as a soloist on "We Are the World" but refused to participate in the more radical Sun City project, which directly opposed violating the cultural boycott.) In using Linda Ronstadt, who had performed at Sun City without apologies, as a back-up vocalist, Simon simply added to the insult of his own violation of the cultural ban. If his purpose was to showcase black South African music, one had to wonder why he had named the album after the estate of a white American who had captured the rock 'n' roll crown by employing (some would say imitating) African American musical styles. Simon was also taken to task for writing the producer's credit and all the copyrights in his own name, which insured that he would receive any music awards that were given as well as the lion's share of subsequent royalty income. Contributing the lyrics for many of the songs, he was also vulnerable to the charge that he avoided political content. Under considerable international pressure, he added such explicitly antiapartheid performers as Miriam Makeba and Hugh Masakela to his 1987 Graceland Tour.

Because Simon considered himself to be antiapartheid (he did refuse to perform in South Africa), he and many others tended to dismiss the criticisms of *Graceland* out of hand, a position that receiving the 1986 Grammy Award for Album of the Year reinforced. The producer's Grammy Award for record of the year for the same album in 1987 seemed to be the final refutation of the criticisms. As a result, *Graceland* was variously celebrated, according to Feld, as "a melding of mainstream 'world' pop and African 'folk' musics; the major anti-apartheid consciousness-raising and publicity event of 1987; and a major international market breakthrough for the South African musicians."[57] Still, five years later, on the eve of Simon's 1992 South African tour—the first such tour by a major U.S. artist after cultural sanctions were lifted—the offices of the promoter and sound company were bombed by the Azanian National Liberation Army. While the tour was supported not only by the white minority government but also by two of South Africa's main black organizations (the ANC and the Inkatha Freedom Party), many in South Africa felt that the lifting of the sanctions was premature and Simon was considered an appropriate target because of the controversy that surrounded *Graceland*. In the international community, *Graceland* produced passionate responses on both sides of the political divide, reinforcing the notion of mass culture as contested terrain.

On the eve of Simon's 1992 South African tour—the first such tour by a major U.S. artist after cultural sanctions were lifted—the offices of the promoter and sound company were bombed. Simon was considered an appropriate target because of the controversy that surrounded Graceland.

Technology and the New International Music Industry

By the mid-1980s, the music industry had bounced back from the doldrums of world-wide recession and had resumed its pattern of more or less steady growth now tied to international sales. In 1990, according to *Billboard,* the United States alone boasted year-end sales of $7.5 billion in a world market worth well over $20 billion.[58] Given the reconfigurations of the global cultural economy, however, this recovery did not come without some profound structural changes in the ownership patterns of the transnational music industry which pointed to the beginnings of a decline in U.S. dominance. EMI Records, a division of the British electronics firm Thorn-EMI, also controlled Capitol, Chrysalis, IRS, and Rhino, among others. Japan's Sony Corporation had purchased CBS Records (renamed Sony Music) for $2 billion. The Netherlands-based Phillips Electronics Corporation owned Polygram, which included Polydor, Deutsche Grammophon, Mercury, and Decca, and acquired A&M and Island. The German publishing conglomerate, Bertelsmann, had purchased RCA Records and its affiliated labels from General Electric after GE had taken over RCA. In 1990, Matsushita purchased MCA, which included Geffen Records and Motown, for $6.6 billion. Thus, by the early 1990s, only one of the major transnational record companies—WEA (Warner Bros./Elektra/ Atlantic), a division of Time-Warner—remained in U.S. hands, and in 1991, Time-Warner entered into a $1 billion partnership agreement with Toshiba and C. Itoh. From the point of view of international capital, however, business was booming.

The internationalization of the music industry was also accompanied by some dramatic shifts in consumer preference for various playback configurations. By 1989, cassettes were outselling LPs in the United States nearly thirteen-to-one (446.2 million units against 34.6 million), as the vinyl configuration began its descent into virtual extinction. The reasons for the decline of vinyl were twofold. First, as a medium with recording, editing, and playback capabilities, cassettes were simply more versatile than LPs. Second, in the realm of sound quality, resistance to wear, and ease of use, CDs were far superior to LPs, which buyers quickly realized. While in 1987, unit sales for LPs and CDs were about equal, two years later the CD, which was sold for a higher price, was outselling the LP by a factor of six (207.2 million to 34.6 million units).[59]

Technology, of course, has played an indispensable role in the economic recovery of the music industry. But while technological advances have served to further the industry goals of expansion and concentration, music-related interests have not been monolithic in these developments. In the late 1980s, the introduction of digital audio tape (DAT), a digital tape configuration that held out the possibility of making studio quality recordings in one's living room, was threatening to record companies, whose primary task was to protect the "integrity" (i.e., financial viability) of the "artistic property" that was their economic lifeblood. A number of summit meetings were held between hardware manufacturers and record companies to try to arrive at a solution to the potential impact of DAT on record sales. This tension sometimes played itself out among different departments of the same corporation, for example, Sony, which made DAT recorders and owned CBS Records. The flap over DAT was but one small part of a larger historical pattern—that the electronic items that have caught the public's fancy have usually been those that delivered improved sound quality and offered consumers maximum flexibility and portability of use. In this sense, technology is a double-edged sword; its development has been rife with unintended consequences. In the words of Simon Frith:

> *The major disruptive forces in music in this century have been new devices, technological breakthroughs developed by electronics manufacturers who have very little idea of their potential use. The only lesson to be learned from pop history (besides the fact that industry predictions are always wrong) is that the devices that succeed in the market are those that increase consumer control of their music.*[60]

A similar pattern exists on the creative end. The same electronic innovations that have accompanied increased revenues in the music industry as a whole have encouraged decentralization in the creative process. As producer Nile Rogers has explained:

> *We're working out systems where if somebody who lives in England, say, has a system similar to what I have, and he's got a track and he wants me to play on it, well, he can send it to me over the satellite to New York. My system can then pick it up. It will go down on tape. I can listen to it, put my guitar overdub on it, send it back to him, and it'll all be digital information. It will sound exactly the same as when I played it. . . . I can play on your record if you're anywhere.*[61]

Technology, then, has altered the social relations of music production with the result of greater and greater degrees of artistic freedom. However, it leaves unanswered the question of whether or not a broad range of new cultural products will find acceptance in the marketplace.

If Michael Jackson's Thriller *represented the revitalization of the music undustry as an international cultural force,* Graceland *embodied all the contradictions involved in trying to manage the unequal distribution of cultural power. Technological advances had brought the cultures of the world closer together and, while these developments created possibilities for musical expression that were new and exciting, they also allowed the music industry to centralize its operations. In attempting to use the power of popular music to foster greater understanding and empathy among different cultures, mega-events politicized popular music and, at the same time, they provided the music industry with access to new international markets. In both instances, they generated considerable controversy. During this period in the United States, new developments in rap and heavy metal became the focus for controversy. By the late 1980s, rap and metal had become the defining elements of a new disaffected youth culture and, in the process, had precipitated the most concerted attempt to regulate popular music since rock 'n' roll's payola hearings.*

NOTES

1. Recording Industry Association of America (RIAA), *Inside the Recording Industry: A Statistical Overview, Update '86* (New York: Recording Industry Association of America, 1986), 4.

2. Michèle Hung and Esteban Garcia Morencos, *World Record Sales 1969–1990: A Statistical History of the World Recording Industry* (London: International Federation of the Phonogram Industry, 1990), 85.

3. Paul Grein, "Unemployment Lines: LA Industrial Personnel Face Major Challenges to Rebuild Their Careers," *Billboard,* 19 May 1979, p. 3.

4. Simon Frith, "Picking Up the Pieces: Video Pop." In *Facing the Music,* ed. Simon Frith (New York: Pantheon Books, 1988), 93.

5. "Record Business Sees Light Ahead—On Video Screen," *Chicago Tribune,* 26 April 1983, p. 5.

6. RIAA, *Inside the Recording Industry,* 5.

7. Russell Sanjek, *American Popular Music and Its Business: The First Four Hundred Years,* Vol. 3 (New York: Oxford University Press, 1988), 602.

8. Frith, "Picking Up the Pieces," 117.

9. Sanjek, *American Popular Music and Its Business,* 641.

10. Andrew Goodwin, *Dancing in the Distraction Factory: Music Television and Popular Culture* (Minneapolis: University of Minnesota Press, 1992), 133.

11. Eric Gelman, "Rocking Video," *Newsweek,* 18 April 1983, p. 98.

12. Goodwin, *Dancing in the Distraction Factory,* 132–139.

13. Ibid., 134.

14. Ibid.

15. Parke Peterbaugh, "Anglomania: America Surrenders to the Brits—But Who Really Wins?" *Rolling Stone,* 10 November 1983, p. 31.

16. *Rock and Roll Confidential,* July 1983, p. 6.

17. Rebecca Bricker, "Take One," *People,* 4 April 1983, p. 31.

18. Steven Levy, "Ad Nauseum: How MTV Sells Out Rock & Roll," *Rolling Stone,* 8 December 1983, p. 37.

19. Bricker, "Take One," 31.

20. Gelman, "Rocking Video," 98.

21. Michael Shore, *The Rolling Stone Book of Rock Video* (London: Sidgwick and Jackson, 1985), 86.

22. See, for example, E. Ann Kaplan, *Rocking Around the Clock: Music Television, Postmodernism, and Consumer Culture* (New York: Routledge, 1987); L. Lewis, *Gender Politics and MTV: Voicing the Difference* (Philadelphia: Temple University Press, 1990); and Susan McClary, *Feminine Endings: Music, Gender, and Sexuality* (Minneapolis: University of Minnesota Press, 1991).

23. Gelman, "Rocking Video," 97.

24. Steve Morse, "Can American Bands Beat the British Blitz?" *Boston Globe,* 1 January 1984, p. A4.

25. Paul Grein, "AOR Programmers Plan More Variety," *Billboard,* 14 January 1984, p. 66.

26. Laurence Kenneth Shore, "The Crossroads of Business and Music: A Study of the Music Industry in the United States and Internationally" (Ph.D. Diss., Stanford University, 1983), 248; Hung and Morencos, *World Record Sales, 1969–1990,* 85.

27. Paul Grein, "'83 RIAA Tally: Fewer Biggies," *Billboard,* 14 January 1984, p. 4.

28. Jeffrey Zaslow, "Music and Money," *Wall Street Journal,* 21 May 1985, p. 1.

29. Jim Miller, "State of the Art," *Newsweek,* 18 April 1983, p. 97.

30. Ted Fox, *In the Groove* (New York: St. Martin's Press, 1986), 322.

31. Frith, "Picking Up the Pieces," 97.

32. Stephen Holden, "Musical Odyssey," *New York Times,* 9 December 1987, p. C33.

33. Frith, "Picking Up the Pieces," 102–103.

34. Paul Grein, "Charts '86," *Billboard,* 27 December 1986, p. Y-4.

35. Steve Gett, "Rock '86," *Billboard,* 27 December 1986, p. Y-4.

36. Frith, "Picking Up the Pieces," 90.

37. John Rockwell, "Leftist Causes? Rock Seconds Those Emotions," *New York Times,* 11 December 1988, p. 23.

38. David Breskin, "Bob Geldof: The Rolling Stone Interview," *Rolling Stone,* 5 December 1985, p. 34.

39. Mark Coleman, "The Revival of Conscience," *Rolling Stone,* 15 November 1990, p. 71.

40. Griel Marcus, "Rock for Ethiopia" (panel presentation at the Third International Conference on Popular Music Studies, Montreal, Quebec, Canada, July 1985), 17.

41. Pete Hamill, "A Day to Remember," *Rolling Stone,* 29 August 1985, p. 28.

42. Ibid., 74.

43. Will Straw, "Rock for Ethiopia" (panel presentation at the Third International Conference on Popular Music Studies, Montreal, Quebec, Canada, July 1985), 28.

44. Breskin, "Bob Geldof: The Rolling Stone Interview," 28.

45. Simon Frith, "Crappy Birthday to Punk," *In These Times,* 23–29 April 1986, p. 20.

46. *Rock & Roll Confidential,* 1985 September, p. 1.

47. Stan Rijven, "Rock for Ethiopia" (panel presentation at the Third International Conference on Popular Music Studies, Montreal, Quebec, Canada, July 1985), 3–7.

48. Jack Healy, "Mass Concerts/Mass Consciousness: The Politics of Mega-Events" (panel discussion at the New Music Seminar, New York, 17 July 1989).

49. Coleman, "The Revival of Conscience," 80.

50. The bill included Whitney Houston, Sting, Stevie Wonder, Dire Straits, Tracy Chapman, Peter Gabriel, The Fat Boys, Jackson Browne, Natalie Cole, Little Steven, Eurythmics, Freddie Jackson, Phil Collins, UB40, Al Green, Midge Ure, Miriam Makeba, Hugh Masakela, Simple Minds, Sly and Robbie, Aswad, The Bee Gees, Youssou N'Dour, Salt-n-Pepa, and more.

51. Anthony DeCurtis, "Rock & Roll Politics: Did the Nelson Mandela Tribute Make its Point," *Rolling Stone,* 11 August 1988, p. 34.

52. Danny Schechter, "Why We Didn't See Wembley," *Africa Report* (July–August 1990): 66.

53. *Rock & Roll Confidential,* September 1985, p. 1.

54. Simon Frith and John Street, "Party Music," *Marxism Today* (June 1986): 29.

55. *The Making of Sun City,* MTV documentary produced by Steve Lawrence and Vinny Longabardo, Karl-Lorimar Home Video, 1985.

56. Steven Feld, "Notes on World Beat," *Public Culture Bulletin* (Fall 1988): 33–34.

57. Ibid., 32.

58. Susan Nunziata, "'90 Label Tally: Units Up 7.3%, $ Jump 14.6%," *Billboard,* 6 April 1991, pp. 1, 80.

59. Michèle Hung and Esteban Garcia Morencos, *World Record Sales 1969–1990: A Statistical History of the World Recording Industry* (London: International Federation of the Phonogram Industry, 1990), 60.

60. Simon Frith, ed. *Facing the Music (*New York: Pantheon Books, 1988) 129.

61. Ted Fox. *In the Groove* (New York: St. Martin's Press, 1986) 334–336.

10 Rap and Metal: Youth Culture and Censorship

In the mid-1980s, there was an interesting convergence of forces in popular music. Aided significantly by technological advances, mega-events politicized popular music to a greater extent than at any time since the 1960s. At the same time MTV—itself a product of new technology—launched a companion outlet, VH–1, aimed at an older audience and thus renewed its focus on youth culture. As in the 1960s, there emerged a connection between youth, music, and politics that soon became most apparent in the phenomenal expansion of rap and heavy metal. It was at this cultural moment that the Parents Music Resource Center (PMRC), a Washington-based pressure group that boasted Tipper Gore, wife of then Senator Albert Gore, as one of its founding members, launched its campaign against explicit lyrics in popular music. No sooner had the music industry recovered from the recession of the early 1980s than it found itself embroiled in a pitched battle with conservative forces over the values and principles that would guide the country into the next decade and perhaps the next century. The

> As in the 1960s, there emerged a connection between youth, music, and politics that became most apparent in the phenomenal expansion of rap and heavy metal.

PMRC initially targeted heavy metal as the prime offender of decency and decorum. As rap gained in prominence, however, it became the focal point of conservative wrath.

Technology, of course, has been a central factor in forging the connection between youth, their music, and its politics. As different as rap and metal may sound, both have enjoyed a particularly intimate relationship with the tools of their production. While it is safe to say that just about all successful popular recording artists make use of advanced technology, rap and metal artists, more than others, have incorporated advances in technology into the very essence of their music. In neither case have these advancements been appropriated straightforwardly. Rather, both styles have sought to turn the logic underlying technological advancement on its head. While the history of sound recording—from the acoustic recording horn to the digitization of sound—can be read as a quest to eliminate noise, both rap and metal have used this "cleaner" technology precisely to achieve a "dirtier" sound. Metal has used it in the service of volume and distortion; rap in the very organization of its disparate sonic elements.

Given the heavy metal preoccupation with power, technology has long been an indispensable tool in the continuing development of the music. The heavily distorted guitar sound that has become the most obvious sign of heavy metal power occurs when an amplifier is overdriven—that is, driven beyond its capacity to deliver a clean sound. In the 1960s, Jimi Hendrix achieved this effect through the creative use of feedback, using the operating noise of the amplifier to overwhelm the signal of the guitar. In the 1980s, Eddie Van Halen used a voltage regulator to increase power to his amp. Heavy metal vocalists often use vocal distortion boxes to create a menacing growl.

Both rap and heavy metal have used the power of noise to assault traditional musical conventions and to trace the boundaries of youth culture.

In the case of rap, dual turntable rigs were transformed into full-fledged musical instruments and boom boxes became localized radio stations, often to the dismay of nearby listeners. In the mid-1980s, rap artists began to use samplers, digital devices capable of recording, storing, and reproducing any sound in nature perfectly, and drum machines to construct the basic building blocks of a rap composition, the rumbling bass tones that can destroy car radio speakers, familiar beats looped into endless repetition, found sounds and prerecorded tracks reshuffled into an original sound collage.

If there is an aspect of rap that is analogous to power in heavy metal, it is the concept of noise. As rap has strayed further and further from middle-class conventions, it has come to be defined less by such traditional concepts as melody and harmony and more by the notion of organized sound or noise. In titling her definitive analysis of rap *Black Noise,* Tricia Rose has used the noun to explicate not only rap's relationship to technology but also a new development in the history of black orality and a cultural device for political resistance.[1] Public Enemy's "Bring the Noise," for example, assaults the listener with a dense mix of samples and synthesized noise. Borrowing from the gospel call-and-response style, Chuck D's vocal exhortation "Turn it up!" is answered by DJ Terminator X with furious record scratching (back cueing a record with the sound system turned on). As a whole, then, "Bring the Noise" mounts a defiant challenge to mainstream listeners through its intentionally aggravating use of noise.

Both rap and heavy metal have used the power of noise to assault traditional musical conventions and to trace the boundaries of youth culture. In doing so, they have provided highly visible, if fast moving, targets for the custodians of good taste. At the same time, however, both genres have their defenders. Once reflexive dismissals of metal's racism and misogyny—common during its first wave—have tended to give way to more complex rereadings of the music in an effort to understand the youth culture of the 1980s and 1990s. In a similar move, issues of violence and sexism in rap have become part of a heated dialogue concerning class, age, and gender differences within the black community and the relationship of black youth to the mainstream culture. As a result, both genres have become the arenas for what can be viewed as a battle for American values.

The Continuing History of Heavy Metal

After an initial surge in the early 1970s, it appeared as if heavy metal might be a short-lived phenomenon. First-generation fans began to move on to new styles and the succeeding generation of (white) youth gravitated toward punk. Still, metal never disappeared completely. Artists like Ted Nugent, Aerosmith, and Kiss had consistent runs of gold and platinum releases throughout the late 1970s. As the statement of a more or less coherent subculture, however, the music was in decline. Feminist dismissals of metal's misogyny had caused many thinking fans to reevaluate the music, and punk had supplanted metal's "empty virtuosity" with a more defiant political statement. But just when it appeared that metal might be destined for the dustbin of music history, a resurgence of the music beginning at the turn of the decade transformed it into the dominant expression of youth culture in the 1980s.

Heavy Metal: The New Wave

One key to this development was the cluster of groups that *Sounds* magazine dubbed and promoted as "the new wave of British heavy metal." These groups—Iron Maiden, Def Leppard, Motörhead, Saxon, Venom, Angelwitch, Diamond Head, etc.— filled the void that was left when first-wave British metal groups like Deep Purple and Led Zeppelin ceased touring or went into tax exile. Judas Priest, still in its ascent, had temporarily abandoned the British audience following the success of their U.S. tour as the opening act for Zeppelin in 1977. (They redeemed themselves partially with the release of *Stained Class* in 1978.) As a result, British fans were deprived of the opportunity to see their favorite artists in live performance, which was still the dominant mode of reception for heavy metal. It took a new generation of metal acts to fill this void. Two of the new groups—Iron Maiden and Def Leppard, which were formed in the midst of punk—went on to achieve worldwide success. AC/DC, which was formed in Australia in 1974 around a core of British ex-patriots, rode the new wave in the United States. The nucleus of AC/DC was brothers Angus and Malcolm Young on guitars and Bon Scott on lead vocals. Having achieved Australian and British chart success with such early releases as *Let There Be Rock* and outrageous stage shows, AC/DC broke into the U.S. Top Forty with the more occult-oriented *Highway to Hell* (1979), just before Scott died from alcoholism. With Brian Johnson as his replacement, AC/DC's momentum continued unabated with three Top Ten LPs in a row, climaxing with *For Those about to Rock We Salute You* in 1981, which went to number one. Def Leppard shared AC/DC's management. Their debut album, *On Through the Night* (1980), established the group as part of the new wave in Britain. Aided by MTV's broadcast of its promotional videos, Def Leppard's *High 'n' Dry* (1981) broke into the U.S. Top Forty. While Iron Maiden got a significant boost when they opened for Judas Priest, which helped push their debut album to number four in Great Britain, the group did not hit the U.S. Top Forty until 1982. At that point, Bruce Dickinson was installed as the lead singer on *The Number of the Beast,* another album that appealed to the U.S. fascination with the occult.

It should be noted that there was no particular brand of metal that dominated the British new wave. Motörhead was able to attract a punk following with pounding cuts, for example, "Overkill" and "Bomber," played at breakneck speed. This style aligned the group with the speed metal style that grew out of L.A. hardcore. The group continued in this vein throughout the 1980s, peaking early in the decade with *Ace of Spades* and the live album *No Sleep Till Hammersmith.* Iron Maiden, which was pegged by *The Number of the Beast* as a Satanist group, was more eclectic in its references and musical moods. In using Satanism as one of a number of biblical, occult, and mystical sources to explore a range of dilemmas involving morality, power, and chaos, however, the group leaned toward more traditional heavy metal. "Run for the Hills" addressed the plight of Native Americans; "Stranger in a Strange Land" and "Sea of Madness" spoke to the alienation of youth. Def Leppard guitarist and composer Steve Clark brought his classical training to bear on the group's music. On *High 'n' Dry,* producer Mutt Lange played up the melodic elements of Leppard's music, propelling the group toward a more pop sound, which has been described somewhat disparagingly by Philip Bashe as "metal pop" and by Deena Weinstein as "lite metal."[2] Even with such variation, however, there were elements that united the new wave groups under the heavy metal banner. "What all the new bands did share," Weinstein has written, "was a general heavy metal sensibility, along with youthfulness and a strong emphasis on visual elements."[3] According to Robert Walser, "the new wave of metal featured shorter, catchier songs, more sophisticated production techniques, and higher technical standards."[4] In the United States, Van Halen was the embodiment of these characteristics. Throughout the 1980s, the group turned out nothing but Top Ten, platinum albums. *1984* was on the charts for more than a year and yielded the number one single "Jump." Until he was replaced in the mid-1980s, lead singer David Lee Roth provided a striking, if vacuous, visual focus with his macho aerobic performances, and lead guitarist Eddie Van Halen had been, of course, the standard bearer of technical proficiency for years.

Among the standout guitar virtuosos of heavy metal, there was also Randy Rhoads. Like Van Halen, Rhoads was a classically trained guitarist who could claim influences that ranged from Alice Cooper to Vivaldi. He first made a name for himself as a member of Quiet Riot, a hard-rocking metal act from Los Angeles. He then became Ozzy Osbourne's lead guitarist, a move that promised to link the new virtuosity with traditional British heavy metal. Rhoads' classical influence can be heard on two 1981 recordings, "Goodbye to Romance" and "Mr. Crowley," and a live recording of "Suicide Solution," which was released on *Tribute* in 1987, five years after Rhoads' death in a plane crash. Following Rhoads' death, the torch of technical proficiency was picked up by Sweden's Yngwie Malmsteen. Although his debut release in 1984 led *Guitar Player* to name him Best Rock Guitarist in 1985, Malmsteen did not break into the U.S. Top Forty until three years later with *Odyssey*. More of a musician's musician than a commercial success, Malmsteen "adapted classical music with more thoroughness and intensity than had any previous guitarist, and he expanded the melodic and harmonic language of metal while setting even higher standards of virtuosic precision."[5]

Of course, virtuosity in heavy metal, indeed in the context of Western music generally, as Walser has astutely pointed out, "has always been concerned with demonstrating and enacting a particular kind of power and freedom that might be called 'potency.' Both words carry gendered meanings, of course; heavy metal shares with most other Western music a patriarchal context wherein power itself is construed as essentially male."[6] Walser allowed that some women might also be able to identify with this power as signifying "a more general sort of social capability," but in such instances, women would be forced to adapt a phenomenon coded as male in our society to suit their own needs and experiences.

There were precious few female fans who attended metal concerts. Those who did were accepted as subcultural equals only when they conformed to the masculinist codes of dress (jeans and black T-shirts) and evidenced the proper knowledge and love of the music.

Throughout its first generation, heavy metal was the exclusive province of young, white, males. There were no female heavy metal musicians to speak of unless the genre's boundaries are extended far enough to include the Wilson sisters from Heart. Indeed, there were precious few female fans who attended metal concerts. Those who did were accepted as subcultural equals only when they conformed to the masculinist codes of dress (jeans and black T-shirts) and evidenced the proper knowledge and love of the music. Women who appeared in "feminine" garb were usually regarded as groupies who were there to service the band sexually. It wasn't until 1980 that an all-female metal band released an album in the United States—*Demolition* by Girlschool, which emerged in Britain as part of the British new wave and achieved some measure of respect and chart success there after touring with Motörhead. U.S. success, however, never came their way.

Around 1983, the next wave of metal began to arrive from Los Angeles. Groups like Mötley Crüe and Ratt tended toward a glam rock appearance, harkening back to the New York Dolls, and a lite metal sound. "What happened in the punk rock days was that the girls looked very much like the boys," punk/metal documentary filmmaker

Penelope Spheeris has noted. "In the metal scene, the boys looked more like the girls, with the big poofy hair and the makeup and the plucked eyebrows."[7] Mötley Crüe ascended to national fame after opening for Kiss in 1983, which helped to push the group's *Shout at the Devil* album into the Top Twenty. Ratt first hit the Top Ten with *Out of the Cellar* in 1984. Other L.A. groups included Quiet Riot, Dokken, and W.A.S.P. Quiet Riot scored two hit singles from their *Metal Health* album, "Cum on Feel the Noize" (1983) and "Bang Your Head (Metal Health)" (1984), which was rare for a metal band at the time. Dokken's *Tooth and Nail* (1984) failed to crack the Top Forty but did earn the group a spot on *Hit Parader's* Top 100 Metal Albums, as did their Top Twenty *Back for the Attack* (1987), which promoted a consistent image of male victimization at the hands of the femme fatale, an oft-used misogynist device in metal. Though they had a hard core following, W.A.S.P. never had a major hit in the United States. The group's importance was blown out of all proportion when right-wing critics of heavy metal discovered "Animal (F**k like a Beast)," a song that was disturbing to many in its celebration of only the sheer physicality of sex.

The Los Angeles metal scene was given a boost by the U.S. '83 Festival, which was organized by Steve Wosniak, founder of Apple Computer. Originally envisioning a festival that would pay tribute to Woodstock, Wosniak took heed of the audience fragmentation that had occurred since the 1960s and organized the event around different genres on different days. The heavy metal day, which featured Ozzy Osbourne and Judas Priest from Britain, Scorpions from Germany, Triumph from Canada, and Van Halen, Quiet Riot, and Mötley Crüe from Los Angeles, drew the largest audience. The festival and the fact that the major U.S. groups were from Los Angeles prompted other metal acts, including Poison and Guns 'N' Roses, to relocate. Poison, in particular, was well suited to the glam look and the lighter sound that characterized much of the Los Angeles scene. The group's carefully tended, artfully moussed, blow-dried hair led it, along with Ratt and the lesser known White Lion, to be dubbed "hair" bands. Still, the Los Angeles scene created space for the emergence of female artists like Lita Ford and Vixen, who achieved a measure of metal fame in the late 1980s.

What was crucial to the growth of metal, particularly the Los Angeles variety, was its exposure on MTV. The genre had been largely excluded from radio since its beginnings. While some AOR stations had begun to program it in the late 1970s, it was significantly cut back in the early 1980s when these stations found themselves in ratings wars with other formats like urban contemporary (UC), contemporary hits radio (CHR) and adult contemporary (AC). Even MTV was reluctant to air heavy metal during its first phase of operation, preferring instead the cutting edge antinarratives of British newpop (see Chapter 9). During its second period, however, MTV "programmed heavy metal with a vengeance."[8] Among the more prominent metal groups which MTV aired were Mötley Crüe, Quiet Riot, Dokken, Twisted Sister, and Scorpions. MTV shifted its orientation, according to Andrew Goodwin.

The New Pop had gone out of fashion and . . . as MTV expanded from the main urban centers of the United States on the coasts into midwestern cities and towns, it needed to reach out with music that appealed to the rockist tastes of its new demographics. Furthermore, the network was no longer dependent on a relatively small number of clips originating in Europe. These factors colluded to generate MTV's embrace of heavy metal music.[9]

The success of heavy metal on MTV led to increased programming on radio, particularly AOR and CHR stations. The real payoff, of course, was in sales. In a special section on heavy metal, *Billboard* reported that the music's market share jumped after a year of heavy play on MTV from about 8 percent in 1983 to 20 percent in 1984.[10]

Metal's advance was slowed temporarily in 1985 when a loose confederation of right-wing Christian fundamentalist groups and various conservative civic, professional, and watchdog organizations pressured MTV into cutting back on its programming of the genre. Although MTV tried to explain away its action by claiming that it had cut back on metal to focus on more "cutting edge" product, according to Linda Martin and Kerry Segrave, "as most of the industry saw it . . . MTV was bowing to the pressure of various conservative watchdog groups who had been complaining."[11] This campaign—a prelude to the PMRC hearings held in Washington, D.C. later that year—had immedi-

For a music defined, in part, by transgression, increased acceptance into the mainstream of U.S. popular culture was a mixed blessing. The bonds of the heavy metal subculture had been forged in the cauldron of exclusion. Musicians and fans alike found strength in their outsider status.

ate results. In the first quarter of 1985, metal's market share dropped to 15 percent.[12] By this time, however, metal had begun to develop a momentum that could not be turned around. Gradually, it began to drift back into MTV's programming, and by the end of 1986, the demand for it had become so great that MTV created a weekly late-night program, Headbangers' Ball, devoted solely to metal, that gave the music its due and placed some of its more objectionable videos in an after-hours slot. Headbangers' Ball generated a weekly audience of 1.3 million viewers, becoming MTV's most popular show.

For a music defined, in part, by transgression, increased acceptance into the mainstream of U.S. popular culture was a mixed blessing. In many ways, the bonds of the heavy metal subculture had been forged in the cauldron of exclusion. Musicians and fans alike found strength in their outsider status. Prior to the beginning of mass acceptance, metal was free from the constraints of pop convention. Songs could be longer, instrumentals (favoring extended guitar solos) could be privileged over vocals (typically less prominent in the mix than in pop), the raw energy of live performance could be accorded a higher cultural value than the precision of studio production, and there was no need to produce hit singles. Mainstream acceptance brought with it pressure for higher "production values," sophisticated recording techniques, higher technical standards, and a more polished (commercial) sound. Thus, the expansion of the music beyond its original subcultural following paralleled the fragmentation of the genre.

Metal Fragments

By the late 1980s, the metal press became rife with distinctions between categories. Traditional or classic heavy metal was used to describe the original sound of wildly distorted guitar, heavy bass and drums, and raw, unadorned vocals; lite or pop metal emphasized sweeter vocals, even harmony; glam metal was defined by a particular look; thrash and speed metal featured faster tempos that were derived from punk; death metal, which was a subcategory of speed/thrash, focused on the issue of death; black metal focused on Satanic themes; and white metal was its Christian counterpart. For all these distinctions, however, there were really only two camps, each claiming their rightful place in a lineage that led back to the grand old groups of the genre, Led Zeppelin, Black Sabbath, and Deep Purple. At one end of the spectrum was lite metal and at the other were the groups lumped together as speed/thrash metal.

It was the lite metal of groups like Def Leppard, Quiet Riot, Van Halen, Mötley Crüe, and Bon Jovi that was favored by MTV, gained greater access to radio, and expanded the music into arena and stadium-sized venues. It was lite metal that initially transformed the metal audience from subculture to mass and altered its gender balance as well. As late as 1984, the metal audience was comprised primarily of male high-school teenagers. A year later, however, *Billboard* reported, "Metal music is no longer the exclusive domain of male teenagers. The metal audience has become older (college-aged), younger (pre-teen), and more female."[13] A number of lite metal album releases signaled the transition. Def Leppard's *Pyromania* (1983) reached number two and remained on the charts for more than a year. The album's three hit singles generated sales of 7 million units, a sure sign that metal was beginning to move beyond its subculture status. Quiet Riot's *Metal Health* and Van Halen's *1984* made similarly impressive showings, peaking at numbers one and two, respectively.

The lure of androgyny as a transgressive social practice was strong in metal, particularly among glam metal groups. It complicated metal's masculinist codes and, in conferring prestige on traditionally female signs, may have accounted for some of metal's positive appeal among young women.

These albums also mark the period when the performance clip came into frequent use on MTV. This was, according to Goodwin, "a direct result of the need for heavy metal acts to establish an 'authentic' (i.e., documentary rather than fictional) set of images and to display musical competence."[14] According to E. Ann Kaplan, these performance clips were typical of what she has called the "nihilist heavy metal video," in which

> the male body is deliberately set up as object of desire: zoom shots pick up male crotches and bare chests in an erotic manner and instruments are presented as unabashed phallic props. . . . these videos . . . adopt a challenging, aggressive stance toward the fans and spectators. . . . The camera often sways with the male bodies, and figures are filmed in slow motion, often jumping in the air, spread-eagled, as in Van Halen's "Jump."[15]

While Kaplan aptly describes metal's macho preoccupation with reinforcing an unstable and insecure masculinity, which was certainly a part of the heavy metal subculture, there was, as she acknowledges, "a more complicated set of discourses" involved in the way metal worked to shape identity. David Lee Roth, who was let go as Van Halen's lead singer shortly after "Jump" became the group's most popular single, argued that "a lot of what I do can be construed as feminine. My face, or the way I dance, or the way I dress myself for stage."[16] The lure of androgyny as a transgressive social practice was strong in metal, particularly among glam metal groups. It complicated metal's masculinist codes and, in conferring prestige on traditionally female signs, may have accounted for some of metal's positive appeal among young women.

Romance was another theme that was adopted in the mid-1980s, that clearly extended metal's appeal to females. Prior to the mid-1980s, themes of romantic love had been conspicuously absent from metal. This was one of the features of the music that helped maintain metal as a bastion of male bonding. Offering a broader analysis, Walser notes: "Until the mid 1980s one of these three strategies—misogyny, exscription, androgyny—tended to dominate each heavy metal band's 'aesthetic.' A fourth approach, increasingly important in recent years, 'softens' metal with songs about romance; this kind of music has drawn legions of female fans to metal."[17] The pivotal album in this regard was Bon Jovi's *Slippery When Wet* (1986).

Bon Jovi (named after lead singer Jon Bon Jovi) was formed in New Jersey in the early 1980s. In its first incarnation, the group sported many of the characteristics of

the standard heavy metal band—doom and gloom lyrics, macho performances, a leather/mascara look, and the powerhouse sound of distorted guitar. In keeping with metal's preoccupation with power and phallocentric imagery, the group's first Top Forty album, was named *7800° Fahrenheit,* the temperature of an erupting volcano. For *Slippery When Wet,* however, Bon Jovi reconstructed their image and their sound. In trading in their leathers and makeup for a more casual bluejean look, they

Jon Bon Jovi, leader of the group that bears his surname, started out as a leather-clad rocker who then drew legions of female fans to heavy metal with themes of romance and his vulnerable good looks.

consciously sought the broader appeal of rock authenticity. From pop they drew on a long tradition of songs about love and romance, which they could do effectively because Jon Bon Jovi himself projected a vulnerability that was rare among heavy metal artists. Put together, these new elements, which had been anathema to metal until this time, had enormous appeal for female fans and *Slippery When Wet* became one of the best-selling albums of the decade. It rose to number one on the charts and stayed in the Top Forty for well over a year, generating two number one hit singles. The album's biggest hit, "Livin' on a Prayer," was, as far as its content went, a classic love-conquers-all composition. How to position it musically was more complicated. In part because the group included keyboards, their inclusion in the heavy metal genre is controversial in certain circles. However, Walser has convincingly argued that "Features of heavy metal are evident in the timbres and phrasing of both instruments and vocals. . . . The sustained and intense sounds of heavy metal are channeled behind the romantic sincerity of pop, while smooth, sometimes poignant synthesizer sounds mediate the raw crunch of distorted guitar."[18]

Against this backdrop of upbeat, forward-looking pop crossover, speed/thrash metal, which had come into being in reaction to the perceived compromises of lite metal, turned inward, consciously seeking to position itself outside the parameters of mainstream acceptance in an attempt to forestall the further dilution of the genre. If lite metal was the expansionist wing of metal, seeking to broaden its audience base beyond the young, white, male demographic, speed/thrash metal was the preservationist side, seeking to fortify and defend the boundaries of an exclusionary male subculture. In the words of Deena Weinstein,

> *Speed/thrash can be understood as an attempt to reclaim metal for youth and especially for males by creating a style that is completely unacceptable to the hegemonic culture. Speed metal represents a fundamentalist return to the standards of the heavy metal subculture. But like all forms of fundamentalism, speed metal is at least as much a new beginning as it is a continuation of what it seeks to revive.*[19]

Speed/thrash metal began as a West Coast phenomenon (primarily in Los Angeles and San Francisco) with groups like Metallica, Slayer, Testament, Megadeth, Exodus, and Possessed, which eschewed the glamour and popularity of lite metal in favor of an underground club scene where the subculture could be maintained more easily for white male teenagers. They were later joined by other groups, including Anthrax, Nuclear Assault, Suicidal Tendencies, Annihilator, and Sepultura. The creators of speed/thrash metal were influenced as much by hard-core punk as by earlier forms of heavy metal. From punk came speed/thrash metal's faster tempos, more hostile posture, and menacing vocals; from heavy metal came sheer volume and ensemble virtuosic precision. Lyric

If lite metal was the expansionist wing of metal, seeking to broaden its audience base beyond the young, white, male demographic, speed/thrash metal was the preservationist side, seeking to fortify and defend the boundaries of an exclusionary male subculture.

Speed/thrash metal defends the music against further compromise

content, according to Weinstein, "specializes in chaos. Sex is rarely mentioned, alcohol and drugs are judged to be bad rather than pleasurable . . . Themes of lust and romance are ceded to lite metal."[20] The resultant fusion, according to the *Boston Globe,* was "ugly, nasty, angry."[21] Still, while it is true that speed/thrash metal tended to focus on the darker side of life, as evidenced in the growth of death metal, it was not, as many of its detractors have claimed, simply empty nihilism. Themes of justice and environmental concern ran through the music and tended to resemble the content of protest songs: "Environmental destruction has almost become as standard a theme for this subgenre as sex is for lite metal."[22] Nuclear Assault's "Inherited Hell," Testament's "Greenhouse Effect," and Metallica's "Blackened" all raised environmental issues. Metallica's *. . . And Justice for All* expressed a concern for justice.

Metallica became the best-known speed metal group. Formed in Los Angeles in the early 1980s, the group, had been influenced by the speed of L. A. hardcore. They began by playing covers of British new wave metal bands at breakneck speed. Among the practitioners of speed metal, Metallica parlayed its outsider status into greater sales than any other group in the category. *Masters of Puppets* (1986) became the first platinum-selling speed/thrash album, which suggests significant crossover success. Still, in the eyes of most fans and critics, Metallica remained loyal to the subculture. "Remaining true to a tough identity incompatible with MTV, AOR, or even college radio," wrote one critic, "Metallica are the first in years to build a big career in American rock disregarding the

Like most heavy metal groups, Metallica enjoys an intimate relationship with power and technology. What is rare is that they have been able to achieve official artistic recognition and overwhelming commercial success without losing subcultural credibility.

dictates of all three. They've called their own shots, kept their integrity, and rallied their support on the strength of their music and non-image."[23] True to form, . . . *And Justice for All* (1988) achieved Top Ten status and platinum sales with virtually no radio play.

By this time, metal's popularity had exceeded all expectations. In 1987, Bon Jovi's *Slippery When Wet* became the most popular record of the year, and after its success, as *Billboard* reported, "five more metal bands cracked the top five: Cinderella, Poison, Whitesnake, Mötley Crüe, and Def Leppard. At one point in June, five of the top six albums were by metal-leaning acts."[24] These included the Ozzy Osbourne/Randy Rhoads *Tribute* LP, Mötley Crüe's *Girls, Girls, Girls,* Poison's *Look What the Cat Dragged in,* Bon Jovi's *Slippery When Wet,* and Whitesnake's *Whitesnake.* In 1988, metal accounted for eleven of the fifty best-selling albums of the year and in 1989 ten of the top forty most popular albums were metal. At this level of success, the genre was impossible to ignore. Accordingly, in 1988, the National Academy of Recording Arts and Sciences (NARAS) established a new Grammy Award for Best Hard Rock/Metal Performance. Metallica delivered a sizzling performance of "One" at the awards telecast and was widely expected to be the recipient of the new Grammy. By including hard rock in the category, however, NARAS was able to appease its conservative elements and award the prize to the largely irrelevant Jethro Tull. Metal was not given its full due until the following year when NARAS separated hard rock from heavy metal and Metallica finally walked off with a Grammy.

Among the ten most popular albums of 1989 were two LPs by Guns 'N' Roses, a new Los Angeles group. *Appetite for Destruction,* the group's Top Forty debut, rose to number one and remained on the charts for seventy-eight weeks, generating three Top Ten singles. The album was aptly titled, as G 'N' R showed a strong propensity for stirring up trouble wherever they went. In record time, they became the new bad boys of heavy metal. Rising as they did from the ranks of the L.A. street scene, their raw emotion resonated with the experiences of many alienated white young people. As *Rolling Stone* put it, "You didn't have to be a runaway to relate to the feelings of dislocation, terror and excitement that mingled in the likes of 'Paradise City' or 'Welcome to the Jungle.'"[25] At the same time, however, on "One in a Million" the group tapped into (or exploited) the racial/sexual fears, insecurities, and hostilities of some of their fans when lead singer Axl Rose spoke of African Americans and homosexuals as "niggers" and "faggots." While the group incurred the wrath of the more progressive elements of the rock critical establishment, its popularity continued unabated into the next decade. *Use Your Illusion I* and *Use Your Illusion II* both finished among the twenty most popular albums of 1992.

By the end of the 1980s, metal had become so expansive that there was even space for a handful of African American and female artists. Most prominent among African American groups was Living Colour, which was led musically and spiritually by guitar virtuoso Vernon Reid. Reid was a founder of New York's Black Rock Coalition, which had as its express purpose the reclamation of the black roots of rock 'n' roll. Living Colour was the perfect articulation of the organization's position. Reid and company drew on every major movement in black music, from the blues and jazz to hip hop, from Jimi Hendrix and Sly Stone to James Brown and George Clinton, to fashion their brand of metal. At the same time, they paid tribute to the British contributions to the genre by choosing the British spelling of "color" for the group's name. Living Colour first hit the Top Ten with *Vivid* in 1989 and finished on the year-end pop charts for that year just a couple of notches below Guns 'N' Roses. That same year, the group received the Hard Rock Grammy for "Cult of Personality."

Living Colour's metal success made the absence of other African Americans that much more conspicuous, especially since most heavy metal musicians had found their way into the genre through the blues and nearly all of them cited Hendrix as an important influence.

Living Colour's metal success made the absence of other African Americans that much more conspicuous, especially since most heavy metal musicians had found their way into the genre through the blues and nearly all of them cited Hendrix as an important influence. From Thin Lizzy in the 1970s to King's X in the 1980s, even the number of racially mixed groups could be counted on one hand. Historians of the genre have tried to explain the absence of black musicians in various ways. While Walser has pointed to the music's history as a British working-class style, Weinstein has argued that it is the result of black "cultural self-segregation."[26] Weinstein's argument, in particular, contradicts the founding principle of Living Colour, and does not adequately account for why the group had so much difficulty in getting signed to a label or why their label had so much trouble marketing them afterwards. In the end, the group was assigned to a new marketing category called funk metal, as were other black metal artists who, according to Weinstein, "brought the contribution of their separate musical culture to metal, grafting themselves onto it."[27]

In assessing the significance of racism in heavy metal, it is important to note that, except for isolated examples such as Guns 'N' Roses' "One in a Million," explicitly racist themes, as Walser has observed, seldom show up in the content of the music.[28] Still, one must wonder how much the antidisco campaigns of hard rock radio stations in the late 1970s served to widen the already existing racial divide. Racial tensions flared between Living Colour and Guns 'N' Roses when the groups opened for the Rolling Stones in Los Angeles in 1988. Both groups traded harsh, racially charged barbs on and off stage, which given the pattern of racial exclusion in metal, created the impression that metal was foreign territory for black artists.

For female artists, the road to metal success was almost impassable, a reality that has been amply documented in most accounts of the genre. While the explosion of lite metal and the inclusion of romantic themes contributed significantly to creating more gender-balanced audiences, they opened few doors for female performers. Even at the height of metal mania, there were few women in the genre. In the second half of the

Living Colour achieves metal success, reclaims rock as black

Lita Ford is one of the only women artists who has achieved any measure of success or respect within heavy metal. To get to that point she paid her dues for far more than a decade.

1980s, Heart had a run of LPs that reached numbers one, two, and three respectively and scored with a number of singles, beginning with "What about Love" (1985), that ap-proached the sound of a power ballad. Joan Jett and the Blackhearts also hit the Top Twenty in 1988 with *Up Your Alley,* but the inclusion of either group in heavy metal would be hotly contested among most fans.

There were only two female acts that were incontrovertibly metal and achieved national recognition—Lita Ford and Vixen. Ford had performed with Joan Jett as a mem-ber of the Runaways in the mid-1970s. After years as a solo artist, she released her first album, *Out for Blood,* on Polygram in 1983, but she did not garner national attention until she changed labels and managers. She felt the switch to RCA and Sharon Os-bourne, manager of husband Ozzy Osbourne, allowed her the freedom to be herself. *Lita* (1988) brought her into the Top Thirty, and its hit single, "Close My Eyes Forever," which was cowritten with Ozzy Osbourne, entered the Top Ten. When Ford said in a *Rolling Stone* interview, "I wear my balls on my chest," she spoke volumes about the con-tradictory demands placed on a female performer in a masculinist subculture.[29] Vixen worked as an unsigned performing ensemble for years before landing a contract with EMI. The group's eponymous debut album, released in 1987, was among the most pop-ular albums of 1989, eventually selling more than 1 million copies. By 1990, there was a glut of metal bands in the marketplace, and metal sales experienced something of a slump. By this time, the pop charts were dominated by black pop, and rap had begun to push metal aside as the cutting edge statement of youth culture.

Hip Hop, Don't Stop

Rap music must be understood historically as one cultural element within a larger social movement known as hip hop which also included break-dancing and, to some extent, graffiti art. The movement was nothing short of a whole way of life. As Tim Carr has noted:

Hip Hop is to funk what bebop was to jazz . . . a new strain of an old form, stripped down and revved up, rejuvenated. The Young Turks challenging the old masters. Just as bebop replaced stiff collared swing orchestras with Zoot-suited combos . . . so has hip hop emerged as a musical style with a brand new way of walking, talking, dancing, and seeing the world.[30]

Hip hop, which has its roots in the gang cultures and ghetto communities of the South Bronx and Harlem, originated at the same time as disco but developed for more than five years in almost complete isolation. According to David Toop, "Since nobody in New York City, America, or the rest of the world wanted to know about the black so-called ghettos—the unmentionable areas of extreme urban deprivation—the style was allowed to flourish as a genuine street movement."[31]

Old School Rap

The early culture heroes of hip hop, like those of disco, were the disc jockeys, or as the hip hop movement called them, DJs. Following the norms of gang culture, certain DJs dominated particular geographical territories. As early as 1973, pioneer Bronx-style DJs like Kool Herc, who was soon followed by Afrika Bambaataa and Grandmaster Flash, had already begun to distinguish themselves from their disco counterparts. The new DJs played hard-core funk such as Jimmy Castor's "It's Just Begun," the Incredible Bongo Band's "Apache," and James Brown's "Get on the Good Foot." More importantly, they developed a new way of handling records. While disco deejays concentrated on segueing smoothly from one cut to the next, hip hop DJs experimented with different ways of playing records. Kool Herc, for example, played only a record's hottest, most percussive portion, known as the "break." These sustained peaks of dance beats created a musical collage that came to be called break-beat music, and the young "b-boys" and "b-girls" who danced to it came to be known as break-dancers. As this was happening in New York, on the West Coast, the Original Lockers, a dance troupe, introduced the robotic movements known as popping and locking that would help to rejuvenate hip hop dancing in the 1980s.

These sustained peaks of dance beats created a musical collage that came to be called break-beat music, and the young "b-boys" and "b-girls" who danced to it came to be known as break-dancers.

Hip hop DJs tried to outdo each other by spinning outrageous combinations of records. One of Afrika Bambaataa's sets, for example, might include the theme from the *Pink Panther*, the Beatles, the Rolling Stones, Grand Funk Railroad, Kraftwerk, and the Monkees in addition to James Brown, Sly and the Family Stone, and the Jackson Five. "Hip hop," David Toop has noted, "was the new music by virtue of its finding a way to absorb all other music."[32] By 1976, the DJs had transformed records and turntables from mere sound carriers into full-fledged rhythm instruments through the introduction of such technical innovations as scratching.

As their popularity increased, the best Bronx-style DJs outgrew the small house parties they worked and moved into clubs, community centers, and finally into auditoriums, some of which could accommodate up to 3,000 people. In these larger venues, the DJs began to use members of their crews as "MCs" who could provide some sort of vocal entertainment as a means of crowd control. Like break-dancing, "MCing" as it was first known, started as a solo art; there would be one DJ and one MC. Like DJs and break-dancers, MCs soon developed their own unique styles, which eventually came to be known as rapping. Among the first solo MCs were Eddie Cheeba, DJ Hollywood, and later Kurtis Blow, all of whom used a disco-oriented style. The first Bronx-style MC was, again, Kool Herc. It was Grandmaster Flash who expanded the idea to include whole groups of MCs. Soon rap groups were popping up all over the Bronx and Harlem, using names like Double Trouble, The Treacherous Three, and The Funky Four Plus One. One of the best-known rap groups, the Furious Five, was started by Flash. Afrika Bambaataa worked with a number of rap groups, including the Jazzy Five, the Cosmic Force, and finally, the Soulsonic Force. By around 1978, MCs had begun to surpass DJs in cultural importance.

Although the style of these early rap groups evolved spontaneously, it is important to note that the roots of rap can be traced through various traditions of the Caribbean islands back to the griots of West Africa. In the United States, the ancestors of rap include field hollers, work and prison songs, competitive urban word games like "signifying" and the "dozens," scat singing, the rhymes of Muhammed Ali, the politically potent verse of the Watts Prophets and the Last Poets, and, finally, the lyrics of such artists as James Brown and Gil Scott-Heron. While the development of rap clearly followed an African American progression, there was also a strong Latino presence in the hip hop movement. Early hip hop sources, for example, Jimmy Castor, routinely included Latin influences in their music. DJs like Kool Herc and Afrika Bambaataa incorporated Latin music into their mixes just as Puerto Rican DJs like Charlie Chase played funk at block parties that combined disco and hip hop. Graffiti artists spanned all racial/ethnic groups. Taki 138

Out of his love of music and his experiences as a South Bronx gang member and a follower of the Black Panther, Afrika Bambaataa, a pioneer hip hop DJ and leader of the Soulsonic Force, fashioned the Zulu Nation as an inclusive hip hop posse.

was of Greek lineage; Julio 204 was Chicano; the internationally known Lee Quinones was Puerto Rican. The most famous of the breakdance crews, the Rock Steady Crew, was predominantly Puerto Rican.

Although Bronx-style rapping had been around since 1976, it was not recorded commercially until 1979. Prior to then, rapping existed only in live performance or on the homemade cassettes that blared from boom boxes in the South Bronx. It is surprising, therefore, that the first two rap records did not come from that neighborhood. "King Tim III (Personality Jock)" was recorded by the Fatback Band, which was from Brooklyn, and "Rapper's Delight" was made by the Sugar Hill Gang, which was based in New Jersey. Edging into the lower reaches of the pop Top Forty, "Rapper's Delight" utilized classic hip hop rhymes recorded over "Good Times" by Chic, and eventually sold some 2 million copies.

Given its lineage, it was inevitable that rap would include topical themes. The first recorded rap to deliver a serious message was "How We Gonna Make the Black Nation Rise" (1980) by Brother D and Collective Effort. The style and political priorities of message rap had been anticipated by two earlier albums, *Hustler's Convention* and *Rappin' Black in a White World*. *Hustler's Convention* was recorded in New York by Lightnin' Rod, a pseudonym for Jalal Nuridin, who had been the leader of the Last Poets. His powerful prison poetry over tracks by members of Kool and the Gang inspired many early MCs. *Rappin' Black in a White World* was recorded by the Watts

Flashdance *made it appear as though break-dancing techniques were invented by Jennifer Beals or, to be more accurate, her uncredited body double. The only hints of historical accuracy in the film were the brief scenes in the park in which Beals looks on as the Rock Steady Crew performs to Jimmy Castor's "It's Just Begun."*

Prophets, the Los Angeles analog to the Last Poets. Though the Prophets and the Poets were unknown to each other until 1969, both had come to the attention of the FBI's infamous COINTELPRO operation and neither received their artistic or commercial due at the time. Two decades later, samples of their work could be found on albums by Def Jeff, Too Short, Tim Dogg, and A Tribe Called Quest.

It was the phenomenal success of "Rapper's Delight" that first alerted the mainstream media to the existence of hip hop. More than five years after the subculture had come into being, hip hop was discovered by the music business, the print media, and the film industry in turn. Camera crews and print journalists scoured the South Bronx in search of untold stories, and Bronx DJs entered the downtown New York club scene. Afrika Bambaataa was invited to spin at the Mudd Club, the Ritz, the Peppermint Lounge, Negril, Danceteria, and finally the Roxy, where, on a good Friday night, he would host crowds of up to 4,000 people. Films like the low-budget *Wild Style,* the blockbuster *Flashdance* and *Breakin'* and *Beat Street* soon followed, bringing hip hop to the attention of a mass audience. Unfortunately, the mass media have a way of ripping any cultural phenomenon out of its historical context. *Flashdance* made it appear as though break-dancing techniques were invented by Jennifer Beals or, to be more accurate, her uncredited body double. The only hints of historical accuracy in the film were the brief scenes in the park in which Beals looks on as the Rock Steady Crew performs to Jimmy Castor's "It's Just Begun." Similar disjunctures were evident on vinyl. The first so-called rap record to reach number one on the pop charts was "Rapture" by Blondie. Although lead singer (rapper?), Deborah Harry tried to be respectful of hip hop, there was simply no way her musical roots could be traced to the Last Poets, let alone the Yoruba. That same year, Chris Frantz and Tina Weymouth of Talking Heads formed Tom Tom Club and recorded "Wordy Rappinghood," which was followed by the hip hop-influenced "Genius of Love." During this same time, however, some of the most enduring Bronx-based rap records were also produced. "Planet Rock" by Afrika Bambaataa and the Soulsonic Force and "The Message" by Grandmaster Flash and the Furious Five were released in 1982 and showcased all the innovations of hip hop culture. Borrowing freely from Kraftwerk's "Trans Europe Express," "Planet Rock" utilized a Roland TR 808 drum machine and rhymes that were, according to Steven Hager, "a dreamy, utopian throwback to the 1960s" to create a formidable dance floor and retail hit.[33] "The Message" heralded greater lyric sophistication and a tilt toward topical themes. It was quickly followed by "Problems of the World" by the Fearless Four and "White Lines (Don't Do It)" by Grand Master Melle Mel and the Furious Five.

Shortly after these releases, critics began to debate whether or not rap would continue. In the final analysis, these debates were irrelevant. Hip hop had already infected everything from ballet and modern dance to fashion design and studio art, to pop, rock, funk, soul, and jazz. As critic Stephen Holden noted:

> Last season's synthesizer-pop has been dressed up and rhythmically charged with elements of "hip hop," the New York-originated dance music style that embraces rapping, scratching, breakdancing, and harsh, electronic sound effects. In fashion industry terms, the mood of these records might be described as one of elaborate severity, in which high technology meets the streets.[34]

David Toop's description of Herbie Hancock's "Rockit" illustrates the ubiquity of rap's sources: "In among the Fairlight, Chroma, Emulator and alphaSyntauri, the bata drums and the DMX, the Led Zeppelin guitar chord and the Vocoder, Grandmaster D.ST is featured cutting in rhythmic fills with turntable scratching of a record of the Ketjak Balinese Monkey Dance."[35] More straightforwardly, Chaka Khan used Grandmaster Melle Mel to deliver a rapid-fire rap introduction on "I Feel for You," which hit the Top Ten in 1984.

Hip Hop: The Next Generation

By this time there was a second generation of New York rap artists, including Whodini, The Force MDs, The Fat Boys, and Run-D.M.C. There was also a fledgling hip hop scene developing in Los Angeles. A crew of mobile DJs called Uncle Jam's Army (after the Funkadelic album *Uncle Jam Wants You*) played music at street parties while such clubs as Radio served the downtown crowd. Prominent among the local DJs were Dr. Dre and Yella from the World Class Wrecking Cru, the group that would eventually metamorphose into N.W.A. Also on the scene were Ice-T and Kid Frost. Ice was a New York transplant who rapped harder than most of his contemporaries at Macola Records. He had been the star of the documentary *Breaking and Entering,* a West Coast version of *Wild Style.* Kid Frost was hip hop's first Chicano nationalist. Both Ice and Frost at first played to predominantly Chicano audiences. In 1984, station KDAY made a significant commitment to hip hop when, through the efforts of Greg Mack, the station's program director, all the popular New York groups performed in Los Angeles.

The growth of New York hip hop moved rap from the twelve-inch single, the industry standard for dance music since disco, to the album. Key to this transition was the success of *Run-D.M.C.* (1984), which was the first gold rap album. The group that gave its name to the album represented a departure from first-generation rappers in a number of ways. Joseph Simmons (Run), Darryl McDaniels (DMC), and Jason Mizell (Jam Master Jay) came from the lower middle-class neighborhood of Hollis in Queens. They were college educated, and they had their sights set on nothing short of conquering both the rock and rap markets. On their second album, *King of Rock,* they proclaimed their conquest and backed it up with hard, boastful rapping complemented by the Hendrix-like live guitar of Eddie Martinez. While hip hop DJs had always used rock tracks in their mixes, Run-D.M.C.'s use of live guitar was novel. The presence of Martinez, who also appeared on "Rock Box" from the group's first album, served as a bridge to rock and a reminder of the Latino presence in hip hop. The Latin connection was further emphasized on *King of Rock* in the use of mixes by Tony Torrez and the Latin Rascals.

Run-D.M.C. represent the beginnings of a second generation of rappers. Their hard, boastful rhymes combined with rock influences helped bring rap to the attention of the mainstream audience.

In 1986, Run-D.M.C. released *Raising Hell,* which went to number three on the charts and sold 3.5 million copies. The album contained, among other things, an interesting version of "Walk This Way." Like other hip hop DJs, Jam Master Jay, had long used rock cuts in the mixes he created for the group. One of his favorite selections was Aerosmith's 1977 hit "Walk This Way." For the album, producer Rick Rubin suggested remaking the song as a duet between Run-D.M.C. and Aerosmith's Steven Tyler and Joe Perry, who were just returning to music from an extended bout with drugs and alcohol. The video of the song is a metaphor for all the contradictions inherent in crossing over. It opens with Run-D.M.C. and Aerosmith performing to audiences on opposite sides of a brick wall. As Run-D.M.C. becomes intrigued by the noise on the other side, they crash through the wall and end up performing with Aerosmith, leaving their own audience behind.

The only album to rival the sales of *Raising Hell* was *Licensed to Ill* by the Beastie Boys, a group of white bohemians from Manhattan who were branded as rap's first major affront to human decency because of their on- and off-stage antics and the content

> *The Beastie Boys, a group of white bohemians from Manhattan who were branded as rap's first major affront to human decency, were the first significant white performers in rap. They did not, however, become its kings.*

of their first hit single, "You've Got to Fight for Your Right to Party." Signed to black-owned Def Jam, the Beasties were the first significant white performers in rap. They did not, however, become its kings. Over the next few years, such East Coast rap releases as UTFO's *Lethal,* L. L. Cool J's *Bigger and Deffer,* Whodini's *Open Sesame,* Heavy D. & the Boyz' *Living Large,* Eric B. & Rakim's *Paid in Full,* Salt-N-Pepa's *Hot, Cool & Vicious,* and the Fat Boys' *Crushin'* continued to make significant inroads into the album and cassette markets. Eight of *Billboard*'s Top Thirty black albums for the week of 28 November 1987 were rap albums.

By this time, the Los Angeles rap scene, which featured harder rhymes set to the slower pace of L. A. cruising was beginning to come into its own. In 1986, Ice-T recorded "Six in the Morning," which spoke of early morning police raids and threw in a bit of gratuitous misogyny for male posturing. The recording led to a six-year association with Warner that produced *Rhyme Pays* (1987), *Power* (1988), *Iceberg* (1989), and *OG* (1990). It was also in 1986 that a sixteen-year-old Ice Cube wrote "Boyz N the Hood." It was recorded with Eazy E providing the vocals over a grinding, bass-heavy rhythm track created by Dre and Yella. It was this association that led to the formation of N.W.A. (Niggas With Attitude) and the music that has come to be called gangsta rap. Although Los Angeles is usually considered home to gangsta rap, the style can be traced to earlier artists, including Philadelphia's Schoolly-D and the single "PSK," which projected a chilling image of gang membership, and New York's KRS-One and Scott La Rock of Boogie Down Productions and the album, *Criminal Minded,* which included cuts like "South Bronx" and "9mm" that employed the gangsta vocabulary.

As the Los Angeles rap scene began to bloom, Public Enemy, the group responsible for the most politically advanced lyrics in rap, was formed in New York. The group, which hailed from Long Island, or Strong Island as they called it, was an extended posse that included leader Chuck D, MC Flavor Flav, DJ Terminator X, a production team (affectionately called the Bomb Squad) composed of Bill Stephney, Hank Shocklee, and Eric "Vietnam" Sadler, Professor Griff as minister of information, and a paramilitary troop of bodyguards known as Security of the First World. Public Enemy sought to advance the cause of black nationalism and Afrocentricity with tracks as compelling and technically advanced as they were controversial. After cutting their teeth on *Yo! Bum Rush the Show*, the group hit its stride with *It Takes a Nation of Millions to Hold Us Back* (1988) and *Fear of a Black Planet* (1990). Writing of *Nation of Millions*, David Toop has said, "The droning loops, screams and word-blitz of [this] album . . . elevated the art of rap onto a level that was simultaneously abrasive and seductive; the texture of its noise and the polysemic, labyrinthine maze of imagery were relentless."[36] On the album, PE positioned themselves among a host of black leaders, including Marcus Garvey, Rosa Parks, Steven Biko, Martin Luther King, Malcolm X, and Nelson and Winnie Mandela. "This literal act of insertion by Public Enemy into the tradition of black resistance," Brian Cross has written, "collapses the boundary between popular culture and politics."[47]

As 1988 continued, it became clear that message rap had embarked on a course that would raise the consciousness of its fans and the blood pressure of its enemies in equal measures.

As 1988 continued, it became clear that message rap had embarked on a course that would raise the consciousness of its fans and the blood pressure of its enemies in equal measures. The cover for *Nation of Millions* had included a logo that pictured a bereted silhouette caught in the cross hairs of a rifle sight. That same year, KRS-One, who was recovering from the shooting death of his partner Scott La Rock, released *By Any Means Necessary.* Invoking the famous Malcolm X photograph, the cover of the album pictured KRS-One looking out the window with a gun. Thus, by the time N.W.A. released *Straight Outta Compton* in 1988, hip hop culture had already become highly politicized and controversial. N.W.A. added to the controversy by portraying the seamier side of Los Angeles gang life without any distance or moral judgment. Brian Turner, president of Priority, the label that distributed N.W.A., defended the group, saying,

> What impressed me about N.W.A. and Eazy-E was that these guys lived the things they talk about. All I was hearing on the news was the perspective of the police and outsiders—you never get the perspective of the actual guy they're talking about. When I saw what these guys wrote, it really hit me that their side of the story is important to tell.[38]

While Turner may have felt it was important to tell the other side of the story, it seemed that not everyone agreed with him. Even a cursory look at rap's audience made it clear that something of a generation gap had developed in black music. Nowhere was this gap more apparent than in the programming on black radio. At the time, *Billboard* maintained charts which distinguished between sales and airplay for the Top Forty black singles. Of the twenty-eight rap songs that reached *Billboard*'s Top Forty sales chart in the first forty-six weeks of 1988, only sixteen registered on the magazine's airplay chart.[39] Clearly, rap was not receiving airplay commensurate with its sales. Tony Gray, the program director at WRKS in New York, tried to explain the reasons for this:

> Those records appeal to a specific demographic, primarily 12- to 18-year-olds, or perhaps 12- to 24-year-olds. The battle that [black] radio stations have is that they do need to play popular music, but for marketing reasons they have to be concerned with the 25-plus listeners as well. You don't want to alienate those listeners because that's where the bulk of your revenue comes from.[40]

Although black radio had often been caught between rock and a hard place in the struggle for a viable listenership, in the case of rap, black stations were exhibiting a reluctance to play cuts that were clearly outselling other selections on their lists. To some, it seemed that the split between rap and other forms of black popular music was more than a generation gap. It was an indicator of class divisions within the black community. Bill Adler, publicist for Run-D.M.C., L. L. Cool J, and Public Enemy, among others, put it rather starkly: "Black radio is run by 'buppies' [black urban professionals]. They've made a cultural commitment to a lifestyle that has nothing to do with music on the street. . . . This music very rudely pulls them back on the street corner, and they don't want to go."[41] Artists themselves often identified "bourgeois blacks" as the main source of resistance to rap.

Of course, rap's detractors had no lack of issues to point to. From different quarters, rap was roundly chastised for bigotry, sexism, and/or violence. The cries of anti-Semitism

As one of the original gangsta rappers, Ice-T was controversial from the start. Still, he has been able to fashion a credible film career and make a bridge to heavy metal with Body Count. While some of his political decisions may be open to debate, his business sense has been unerring.

that were directed at Public Enemy's Professor Griff reached a peak when he claimed in an interview with the *Washington Times* that Jews were responsible for "the majority of wickedness that goes on in the world."[42] (Griff was subsequently fired and then rehired as liaison to the black community.) At the time, critic Jon Pareles berated Professor Griff for his misguided prejudices in the *New York Times* but also noted that Public Enemy's "overall message is one of self-determination for blacks."[43] As to rap's sexist tendencies, Harry Allen noted:

> When Ice-T releases a record called "Girls, Let's Get Buck Naked and Fuck" ("Girls, L.G.B.N.A.F." on the album cover), when 2 Live Crew on a cut called "S & M" calls to women to bring their "d _ _ k-sucking friends," when Ultramagnetic M.C.'s Kool Keith on "Give the Drummer Some" talks about smacking up his bitch in the manner of a pimp, sisters understandably scream.[44]

"Hip-hop is sexist," Allen concluded, but he added "It is also frank."[45] One wonders if rap would have been so upsetting if it had not been so frank. Still, while it should be noted that sexism has never been a stranger to any genre of popular music or any aspect of life in America, rap's sexism should not be excused.

Evidence of a change in the sexual politics of hip hop started to become apparent in 1985 when Roxanne Shanté's "Roxanne's Revenge," the answer track to "Roxanne Roxanne," UTFO's insult song, beat the original at its own game. It was, however, the overwhelming commercial success of Salt-N-Pepa's double platinum debut LP, *Hot, Cool & Vicious* (1988), that finally convinced some rap labels to promote female rappers, many of whom had been part of the hip hop underground for years.

> After six years of releasing records, Def Jam finally recorded Nikki D's "Daddy's Little Girl," their first track by a female rapper, and Public Enemy recruited Sister Souljah to the ranks. In Los Angeles, Ice Cube put his support behind Yo Yo, co-producing her scorching Make Way for the Motherlode. . . . Yo Yo, who had already showed her capacity for fightbacks on Ice Cube's "It's a Man's World," founded the Intelligent Black Woman's Coalition, hoping to reverse the low status and self-esteem that women were clearly suffering in the face of such a concerted shut-out by men.[46]

By the end of the decade, women had added a new public voice to hip hop. With releases like "Paper Thin" (MC Lyte), "Independent Woman" (Roxanne Shanté), and "Ladies First" (Queen Latifah), critics tended to portray women rappers as a female corrective to adolescent male sexual ranting. However, such a portrayal was not entirely accurate.[47] After all, not all male raps were sexist. Consider, for example, "Date Rape" by A Tribe Called Quest. Furthermore, trying to shoehorn groups like Hoes with Attitude or Bitches with Problems into a feminist mold is obviously problematic. In fact, even

> *Even the most progressive female rappers resisted the feminist tag, perceiving it as a label for a white middle-class movement that existed in tension with their commitment to racial solidarity.*

the most progressive female rappers resisted the feminist tag, perceiving it as a label for a white middle-class movement that existed in tension with their commitment to racial solidarity. It was perhaps this commitment more than a tacit approval of male sexism that made most female rappers reluctant to speak out publicly against their male counterparts.

The woman who best managed this conflict between racial solidarity and feminism was Queen Latifah. Projecting a powerful and dignified image, Latifah developed "a forthright rapping approach that sidestepped the dissing clichés."[48] Through cuts like "Dance for Me" and "Come into My House," she was able to establish herself as a rapper whose talent was commensurate with that of her male counterparts. She released her first album, *All Hail the Queen,* on Tommy Boy in 1989. On the video for the album's most popular cut, "Ladies First," which was performed as a duet with her "European sister" Monie Love, Latifah positioned herself as a military strategist in the company of such historical black women activists as Sojourner Truth, Angela Davis, and Winnie Mandela and offered a pro-female version of the predominantly male lineage portrayed in other political rap videos. Still, these gains were offset by the continuing objectification and exploitation of women, expressed most straightforwardly by the Miami-based 2 Live Crew on *Move Something* (1988) and *As Nasty as They Wanna Be* (1989).

Queen Latifah is one of the most intelligent and articulate women in rap. Her forceful rhymes added measurably to the chorus of female voices that began to emerge in the late 1980s. In the 1990s she went on to star in the television sitcom Living Single.

Violence was the third issue that rap's critics frequently decried. The confrontational stance and uncompromising lyrics of Public Enemy ("Fight the Power") and N.W.A. ("_ _ _ _ tha Police") and skirmishes at rap concerts fueled the notion in the minds of some that rap promoted violence. Violence had occurred at some rap concerts, but that, in and of itself, did not distinguish them from rock concerts or, for that matter, soccer matches in Britain. Furthermore, rappers themselves addressed this problem head-on. Following the leadership of critic Nelson George, a number of rap groups—Stetsasonic, Boogie Down Productions, and Public Enemy, among others—initiated a campaign called Stop the Violence in 1989, which was aimed specifically at black-on-black crime. As one of their projects, these groups contributed their time and talent to "Self-Destruction," the all-star rap recording that became the anthem of the movement. The following year, West Coast rappers followed suit with "We're All in the Same Gang."

> *While the press frequently decried gangsta violence and hip hop misogyny, the fact remains that a good deal of rap spoke positively to real issues.*

Ironically, the West Coast effort occurred amidst bitter splits among the N.W.A. posse. Following the success of *Straight Outta Compton,* Ice Cube left the group over disputes about creative control and money. Looking toward the Public Enemy orbit for support and inspiration, he "sought to bring the gangsta style of rhyming from the west to the apocalyptic beats of the Bomb Squad."[49] The result was the Top Twenty *Amerikkka's Most Wanted,* one of the best selling albums of 1990. The album launched Cube on one of the most successful solo careers in rap and led to his best selling LPs *Death Certificate* (1991), *Predator* (1992), and *Lethal Injection* (1993). N.W.A. responded with *Efil4zaggin* in 1991, after which Dr. Dre also left the group. He returned as a solo act the following year with *The Chronic* (the term for a particularly strong strain of marijuana). The N.W.A. split made it clear that gangsta conflicts in the music community were as likely to be resolved in lawyers' offices as on the streets.

While the press frequently decried gangsta violence and hip hop misogyny, the fact remains that a good deal of rap spoke positively to real issues. "Any examination of rap's lyrical content," wrote David Nathan in *Billboard,* "reveals a very high percentage of anti-violent, anti-drug messages, many aimed at improving self-esteem, encouraging the youth of the 80s to continue their education and approach adulthood with a positive approach."[50] Unfortunately, this side of rap, which stood in sharp contrast to the lyric vacuity of most other forms of black pop at the time, tended to get lost in the controversy. "Self-Destruction" sold nearly 500,000 units and never even registered in the black airplay Top Forty. Writing for a *Billboard* special on "The World of Black Music" in the summer of 1989, Dan Stuart pointed out, "Today it's virtually impossible to find a non-rap song in the black top 40 that contains lyrical content that deals with any topic besides dancing and romancing."[51]

The turmoil surrounding rap may have presented a problem for the population at large and black radio in particular, but major record companies were quick to recognize the financial potential of the sound. While few majors signed rap acts directly, buy-ins and distribution deals with successful rap indies soon became commonplace. The first to make a move was Columbia Records, which concluded a custom label deal with Def Jam (L. L. Cool J, Oran 'Juice' Jones, the Beastie Boys, Public Enemy) in 1985. Jive Records (Whodini, Kool Moe Dee, Steady B., D.J. Jazzy Jeff & the Fresh Prince, Boogie Down Productions) entered into distribution arrangements with both RCA and Arista. Cold Chillin' Records (Marly Marl, Roxanne Shanté, Biz Markie, M. C. Shan) signed a distribution deal with Warner in 1987. Warner also bought a piece of Tommy Boy (Stetsasonic, Force MDs, De La Soul, Queen Latifah, Black by Demand, Digital Underground). Delicious Vinyl (Tone Loc, Def Jef, Young M. C.) concluded a national distribution deal with Island. National distribution for Priority (N.W.A., Eazy E, Ice Cube) went to Capitol. By and large, these majors left creative functions at street level and simply provided the rap independents with superior distribution, which increased rap's access to mainstream outlets. As a result, rap tended to get more support on pop radio than on black radio. Even MTV initiated a rap show. Although at first buried in a late-night weekend slot, *Yo! MTV Raps* soon moved to a daily afternoon slot and became one of the channel's most popular programs. By 1988, rap had so entered the mainstream that NARAS added a rap category to the Grammy Awards. However, the academy refused to include the first rap award in its live telecast, which led four of the five nominees, including the winners, D.J. Jazzy Jeff & the Fresh Prince, to boycott the show. Shortly thereafter, *Billboard,* unceremoniously and with no editorial comment, added a rap chart to its pages.

As usual, entrance into the mainstream led to exposure in other media, such as television and film. Following the award of the first rap Grammy, Will Smith (the Fresh Prince) received a starring role in the prime-time sitcom, *The Fresh Prince of Bel Air.* Rappers also began to show up on other African American sitcoms, including *A Different World* and *Cosby*. The poignant comedy/variety show, *In Living Color,* which was clearly grounded in a hip hop aesthetic, featured regular appearances by

There appeared a rash of black-directed films about life in the "hood." These films were far more realistic in their portrayal of urban life and far more demanding in their political analysis than either the break-dance movies of the mid-1980s or the "blaxploitation" films of the early 1970s.

such artists as Monie Love and Queen Latifah, who later landed a starring role in her own television sitcom, *Living Single.* Quincy Jones, producer of *Fresh Prince*, also attempted "to bridge generations and traverse musical boundaries" in the production of his award-winning 1989 LP, *Back on the Block,* which brought together such diverse musical talents as Sarah Vaughn, Ella Fitzgerald, Siedah Garrett, Al Jarreau, Bobby McFerrin, Take 6, Ray Charles, Chaka Khan, Al B. Sure, James Ingram, and Barry White with rappers like Ice-T, Melle Mel, Big Daddy Kane, and Kool Moe Dee.

Major labels view rap as a viable commercial product

It was in film, however, that rap made some of its most powerful statements. When Kid N Play parlayed their LP *Funhouse* into the film comedy *House Party* (and a sequel as well as a Saturday-morning cartoon show), they only hinted at the connections between rap and topical film. It was Spike Lee's *Do the Right Thing,* powered by the hip hop force of Public Enemy's "Fight the Power," that tied rap and topical film tightly together. Following the success of Lee's devastating treatment of race relations, there appeared a rash of black-directed films about life in the "hood," including *Straight Outta Brooklyn, Juice, New Jack City,* and *Boyz N the Hood.* The latter two of these starred Ice-T and Ice Cube respectively and featured their music. As a group, these films were far more realistic in their portrayal of urban life and far more demanding in their political analysis than either the break-dance movies of the mid-1980s or the "blaxploitation" films of the early 1970s.

In 1990, rapper/dancer Hammer (then M.C. Hammer) scored another first for rap with his album *Please Hammer Don't Hurt 'Em,* which logged twenty-one weeks at number one on the pop charts and became the best selling rap album ever. With sales of more than 10 million copies, it outdistanced its nearest competitor by a factor of two. Ambitious to the core, Hammer set his sights on nothing short of toppling Michael Jackson. Roundly "dissed" by the hip hop nation for playing to mainstream sensibilities, Hammer enlisted the services of no less a figure than James Brown to bolster his credibility. In the long-form prologue to the "2 Legit to Quit" video, Brown anoints Hammer as his "godson" and directs his heir apparent to "bring back the glove," an obvious reference to Michael Jackson and, therefore, to the pop crown.

Ironically, Hammer's pop tendencies may have created cultural space for his main competition, Vanilla Ice. After touring as Hammer's opening act, Ice's LP, *To the Extreme,* skyrocketed to number one on the pop charts and multi-platinum certification, temporarily displacing Hammer himself. At this point, however, Ice ran into credibility problems when it was discovered that part of his biography had been falsified to make him look more "street." This drive "to appear more 'authentic,'" according to Kristal Brent Zook, "demonstrates that an increasing sense of African-American solidarity seems to inspire an increasingly blatant demand for inclusion among (some) white people who now sense themselves uncomfortably shifting from center to margin."[52] Another group of white rappers, called Young Black Teenagers actually included a song called "Proud to be Black" in their debut album, pushing the identification with black culture to the limit. Other white rap groups, such as Third Base, were taken at face value. Their acceptance by other rappers seemed to be based on a certain repudiation of white skin privilege in their own lifestyles.

Los Angeles gangsta rap tended to push rap toward harder rhymes, and its success led both Hammer and Vanilla Ice to follow up their earlier successes with harder images— Hammer looking like a gangsta, Ice wearing dreadlocks and publicly embracing marijuana. However, gangsta rap was also home to an incredible diversity of rappers. In 1989,

In 1990, Hammer (formerly known as M.C. Hammer) recorded the best selling album in rap and promptly earned the wrath of the hip hop community for selling out. While his raps were not the strongest, there may also have been a certain amount of jealousy in the reaction.

Kid Frost, a Chicano veteran of Los Angeles hip hop, recorded the bilingual *Hispanic Causing Panic.* He was joined in short order by Cubanos Melloman Ace and Skatemaster Tate. Named after the discharge of a shotgun, the Boo Yaa Tribe, a group of Samoans who grew up among blacks and Chicanos in southeast Los Angeles, were a formidable looking group of ex-gang members. Toop notes their "raps are written in hardcore prison slang, with joy, pleasure, identity and emergence expressed in metaphors of death, violence, intimidation, fear and imprisonment."[53] Against this background, the members of the group have talked openly about respect for women in their culture. The most diverse posse in the Los Angeles hip hop scene were the groups associated with the Soul Assassins. At the center of the Soul Assassins posse was Cypress Hill with Grandmixer Muggs, an Italian, B-Real, a Chicano, and Sen Dogg, a Cuban. Known for their "old school" hook lines and harmony approach to rap and B-Real's characteristic nasal whine, Cypress Hill's debut single, "How I Could Just Kill a Man" (1991), propelled the group to national recognition. Songs dealing with such hot-button issues as drugs ("I Wanna Get High") and violence ("Cock the Hammer") brought further recognition. Their second album, *Black Sunday* (1993), debuted at number one on the pop charts. Following the group's initial success, Muggs set up the Soul Assassins as a production company that included FunkDoobiest and House of Pain. Among the members of FunkDoobiest were Puerto Rican and Sioux MCs and a Mexican DJ. House of Pain was Irish with a Latvian DJ. With the release of the 1992 single "Jump Around" and the LP, *Fine Malt Lyrics,* House of Pain achieved national fame, bringing something of the Irish experience to hip hop.

By the early 1990s, then, hip hop had become, in the words of Brian Cross, "a voice for many different subjectivities—women, Chicano, Cubano, Asian, Irish, gay, and all the variants covered by black, Jamaican, Dominican, etc."[54] According to Cross, far from detracting from the African American cultural priorities that determined the trajectory of rap, the expansion of the music "brings the struggle of African-Americans to many new ears, thereby providing a new perspective on one's own problems."[55] From an isolated street culture, hip hop expanded in less than twenty years into a global phenomenon. It is perhaps because of this that it has been the focus of a ferocious backlash.

Popular Music and the Politics of Censorship

Popular music has never been a stranger to controversy or opposition. Herman Gray has noted three periods of particularly strong opposition: the response to jazz in the early part of the century, the reaction against rock 'n' roll in the 1950s and 1960s, and the most recent wave of controversy associated with heavy metal and rap.[56] No matter what the genre, certain themes such as a fear of the connection between music and sexuality tend to run through all three periods. Such concerns may be expressed either as the fear that sensual rhythms can overcome rationality or that lyrics that push the boundaries of decorum can undermine moral values. Because of these fears, each genre has been linked at various times to drug abuse, lawless behavior, and general moral decline. In turn, all of these problems have been projected to some degree onto race.

These conservative groups are not monolithic, but rather linked by common themes, such as an adherence to a narrow interpretation of the "Christian way of life," and certain sound-bite concepts, such as "family values," that have become media codes for conservatism.

Lawrence Grossberg has ascribed the most recent round of attacks on popular music to the new conservatism espoused, in his view, by Christian fundamentalists, conservative elitists, and organizations like the PMRC.[57] His view is shared by Nan Levinson, a Tufts University professor and correspondent for the *Index on Censorship* journal. "Though usually played as revolts of the fed up," Levinson has said, "these skirmishes are likely to be nurtured or orchestrated by organizations of the extreme moralist right."[58] Both Grossberg and Levinson believe these conservative groups are not monolithic, but rather linked by common themes, such as an adherence to a narrow interpretation of the "Christian way of life," and certain sound-bite concepts, such as "family values," that have become media codes for conservatism.

Picking up on the initiatives of the new conservatism, the popular press began to cast music as a social irritant and its detractors as defenders of a decent society. It should also be noted that the shift in the political center of gravity toward the right during the Reagan-Bush years made essentially conservative arguments that much more persuasive to many would-be liberals. The assumption—often made tacitly—was that popular music communicated an intentional message, usually through its lyrics (although visual images, hypnotic rhythms, subliminal suggestions, and sheer volume were also mentioned), to an impressionable young audience with little will or inclination to resist, thus producing a direct and uniform effect on human behavior. Of course, the way in which popular music communicates is far more complicated than this. As Susan McClary and Robert Walser have pointed out:

> [M]usic relies on events and inflections occurring on many interdependent levels (melody, rhythm, harmony, timbre, texture, etc.) simultaneously. Each of these has something of a syntactical dimension—a grammar of expectations, normal continuity, etc.—and also a wide-open semiotic dimension. . . . When all these levels are operating at the same time, whether reinforcing or contradicting one another or both, we are dealing with a tangle that pages and pages of words can only begin to unpack.[59]

Add to this the visual dimension of music video, which frequently eschews narrative organization altogether, and the complexity of communication increases significantly. Popular music is polysemic; it communicates on many levels at once. Its meaning may be different for different people in different places, and that meaning may change over time. This is not to suggest that popular music has no effects. In its association with the social movements of the 1960s, popular music was certainly related in some way to the social transformations of the era. Today, however, that same music is used to sell beer, cars, and running shoes. During the mega-events of the 1980s, popular music clearly served as a vehicle for mobilizing masses of people toward particular political ends. At the same time, it opened new markets for and delivered new consumers to transnational corporations. The proposition that lyrics and images glorifying violence or the degradation of women contribute to those same proclivities in the society as a whole must be taken seriously. However, it must be considered in proportion to all of the forces that bear on the problem. In other words, the lyrics and images of popular music would have to be considered as one of a number of variables, including such things as class, age, race, gender, ethnicity, sexual orientation, employment status, housing, education, religion, drug laws, obscenity standards, health status, nutrition, the availability of social services, the state of the economy, and the prevailing political climate. In the 1980s and 1990s, however, as in the jazz era and the hey day of rock 'n' roll, the reaction to popular music seemed to lack such a sense of proportion. Indeed, there seemed to be a compelling drive to treat popular music as if it were solely responsible for (and actually more harmful than) the social problems it referenced. The signal event for this treatment was the high-profile government investigation that was initiated by the PMRC in 1985.

The Parents Music Resource Center

The PMRC was founded in early 1985 by a group of prominent women in Washington, D.C. Founding members included, in addition to Tipper Gore, Sally Nevius whose husband had chaired the city council, Pam Howar, and Susan Baker whose husband, James Baker, was then secretary of the Treasury. Indeed, of the twenty original members, seventeen were married to influential Washington politicians.[60] They were immediately dubbed "the Washington wives" by the press in recognition of their access to political clout. Concerned, as they said, "about the growing trend in music toward lyrics that are sexually explicit, excessively violent, or glorify the use of drugs and alcohol"—as evidenced in the lyrics to songs like Prince's "Nikki Darling" and Madonna's "Like a Virgin"—these women decided to exploit their personal connections to "educate and inform parents about this alarming trend as well as to ask the industry to exercise self-restraint."[61] The PMRC consistently maintained that it was in favor of voluntary measures, not censorship, and that it was not opposed to all forms of popular music.

With a cash contribution from Mike Love of the Beach Boys and office space donated by Coors Beer, a company already well known for its anti-union tactics and conservative funding practices, which included contributions to the Contras and the Heritage Foundation, the group set up shop and formed an alliance with the national Parent/ Teacher Association (PTA). Having gained through this alliance instant access to the PTA's base of 5.6 million members, the PMRC then set about trying to convince the music industry to publish the lyrics to all new releases and institute a rating system similar to the one used for movies ("X" for explicit lyrics, "V" for violence, "O" for occult, and so on). In August 1985, Stan Gortikov, then president of the RIAA, offered a compromise generic warning, "PARENTAL ADVISORY/EXPLICIT LYRICS," in response to the PMRC's demand. Acknowledging the legitimacy of the PMRC's concerns, he cited only legal and logistical problems as the reason for the compromise.

Whatever one's position on labeling, there were, as Gortikov pointed out at the time, a number of legal and logistical problems with the PMRC's original proposal. "Unlike the motion picture industry, which rates about 325 films a year," Gortikov noted, "the recording industry releases 25,000 songs annually, which would require a process for rating 100 tunes a day."[62] He then went on to point out that publication of lyrics without the permission of the publisher would violate the copyright laws. Beyond such mechanical problems, however, there were the more pressing difficulties of interpretation. Popular music often resists a single, fixed meaning that can be read off its surface. As Simon Frith asserted long ago, "different consumers *use* rock differently,"[63] which is to say that different consumers may attach a range of competing meanings to their experience of music. Such meanings might be based on a knowledge of subcultural codes, mediations in fanzines and the music press, and/or individual subjective judgments and emotional responses. The use of such recording practices as echo, distortion, and "backward masking," the process of recording passages backwards, which has lead to charges of subliminal messages, makes any discussion of meaning still more complex. The mind boggles at the thought of a committee trying to make definitive cultural sense out of all of this in a timely fashion, especially given some of the confusion over meaning that the music industry itself reported during the hearings. Frank Zappa recalled one record company executive who forced his group to excise the phrase "And I still remember mama with her apron and her pad/ Feeding all the boys at Ed's Cafe" because he thought that the word *pad* referred to a sanitary napkin.[74]

As the leader of the Mothers of Invention, Frank Zappa was as creative and idiosyncratic as he was uncompromising and disciplined. In 1985, he played a prominent role at the PMRC hearings as an outspoken defender of First Amendment rights.

To the average onlooker, Gortikov's compromise suggested that the music industry had surrendered to minimal pressure. Gortikov's willingness to compromise, however, began to make some sense when the PMRC rejected his suggestion and decided to unleash its full powers, or, more accurately, the powers of their mates. In September, the Senate Committee on Commerce, Science, and Transportation held public hearings on the PMRC's charges. Among the members of the committee were John Danforth, who was its chairman, Fritz Hollings, and Albert Gore. Their wives were members of the PMRC. Gortikov immediately saw that the industry faced the dual threats of legislation and regu-

The character of the 1985 PMRC hearings was reminiscent of the payola hearings of 1959. Once again, morally high-toned critics advocated protecting innocent children from the evils of popular music. Testimony from the young people allegedly affected was notably absent.

lation if it did not cooperate. Adding further impetus to the industry's desire to cooperate was the home taping bill (H.R. 2911), which the record companies wanted passed. The bill would have levied a tax on blank tape, enabling record companies to recover millions of dollars in revenues presumably lost because of home taping. Representative Thomas Downey was an early sponsor of the bill and a past recipient of the RIAA's culture award. His wife was a member of the PMRC. When hearings on the bill were stalled, the industry looked to the Senate for help. Charles Mathias, Chairman of the Senate Subcommittee on Copyright Laws, had authored a bill (S. 1739) similar to the House version. The cosponsor of the Mathias bill was Albert Gore.

The character of the 1985 PMRC hearings was reminiscent of the payola hearings of 1959. Once again, morally high-toned critics advocated protecting innocent children from the evils of popular music. Testimony from the young people allegedly affected was notably absent. Unlike the 1959 payola hearings, however, the players did not fall into neatly defined interest groups, such as major record labels and independent record labels or liberal and conservative artists and politicians. Important labels, including MCA, A&M, and Geffen, initially broke ranks with the RIAA and joined a group of smaller labels to form an anticensorship group called the Musical Majority. While Smokey Robinson and Mike Love spoke out against so-called porn rock, artists ranging from Frank Zappa and Dee Snider of Twisted Sister to John Denver and Donny Osmond denounced the rating system.

Denver testified about the dangers of being overly literal in the interpretation of lyrics, recounting how some radio stations had refused to broadcast his "Rocky Mountain High" because they thought it was about drugs. PMRC cofounder Susan Baker had attempted to anticipate any warnings about overly literal interpretations by pointing out earlier that Cole Porter's "The Birds Do It, The Bees Do It" could hardly be compared to the heavy metal group W.A.S.P. singing "F-U-C-K like a Beast."[65] However, Baker neglected to mention that the W.A.S.P. song had never been released in the United States, or that the Porter classic could be compared to the Captain and Tennille's "Do That To Me One More Time," which, according to Zappa, had appeared on the PMRC's original hit list.[66] Omissions like these left many openly suspicious of the proceedings. "Beneath the 'save the children' rhetoric," editorialized *Rolling Stone*, "is an attempt by a politically powerful minority to impose its morality on the rest of us."[67]

In November 1985, shortly after the hearings, a compromise was hammered out between the RIAA and the PMRC and announced publicly. Essentially, the PMRC ended up agreeing to Gortikov's original proposal. With a "voluntary" rating system now in place, the question remained as to what was considered offensive and how serious it was. It was in this area that the PMRC scored its greatest victories in terms of framing the issues and capturing public attention.

The Issues: Sex, Drugs, and Rock 'n' Roll Revisited

In 1988, the PMRC produced *Rising to the Challenge,* a video in which the group outlined "five major themes" in popular music that were of concern to them. The themes were:

1. Abuse of drugs and alcohol
2. Suicide
3. Graphic violence
4. Fascination with the occult
5. A sexuality that is graphic and explicit[68]

The PMRC claimed that the five themes listed above "occurred consistently in some rock music and especially in heavy metal."[69] While they would later add rap to their list of music to be watched, at the time the organization maintained that heavy metal was "the most disturbing element in contemporary music," claiming that "much of it dwells on themes that glorify rape, sado-masochism, violence, and suicide."[70] According to Robert Walser, however, "heavy metal lyrics dealing with these topics are uncommon. For example, examination of eighty-eight [heavy metal] song lyrics reprinted by *Hit Parader* reveals relatively little concern with violence, drug use, or suicide."[71]

To bolster its claims in their video, the PMRC drew attention to the unsavory lifestyles of certain heavy metal groups like Mötley Crüe, using lead singer Vince Neil's conviction in a drunk driving accident that took the life of another musician as an example. While Neil certainly projected the image of a profoundly irresponsible person, such behavior is hardly limited to heavy metal artists, and the vast majority of incidents surrounding heavy metal artists were far less dramatic. While the PMRC argued that times had worsened since Elvis ground his pelvis into the consciousness of an adoring generation, the fact was that Elvis could match drug habits and violent outbursts with the best of the heavy metal artists. As to the music itself, *People* magazine reminded its readers that "Cole Porter's 'Love for Sale' was considered so 'blue' that it could be broadcast only in instrumental form. . . . Duke Ellington's 'The Mooche' was considered so provocative that some blamed it for a national rise in incidents of rape."[72]

While the PMRC themes have, to a large degree, defined the terms of debate over popular music since they were issued, the fact is that, from Shakespeare's *Romeo and Juliet* to Dante's *Inferno,* sex, drugs, violence, suicide, and the devil have always been compelling themes in Western art and common obsessions in the lives of its practitioners, whether they are painters, sculptors, writers, or musicians. "Berlioz made no bones about his use of opium," Walser has noted, "his program for the *Symphonie Fantastique* explicitly connects opium use with the rhetorical splendor of his music. Abuse of alcohol is well documented for composers such as Schumann, Schubert, and Mussorgsky."[73] Mozart was also no saint; his depiction in the movie *Amadeus,* while somewhat caricatured, was well within the bounds of historical accuracy. Wagner's music has long been associated with imperialism and violence. It is no coincidence that director Francis Ford Coppola selected Wagner's "The Flight of the Valkyries" to accompany the destruction of the Vietnamese village in *Apocalypse Now.* The composition, which tells of warrior maidens who preside over battles and transport fallen heroes to Valhalla, effectively made the statement Coppola wished to make about U.S. involvement in Vietnam.

In targeting heavy metal and, later, rap to the extent that they did, the PMRC and their allies were drawing a line between themselves and youth.

In targeting heavy metal and, later, rap to the extent that they did, the PMRC and their allies were drawing a line between themselves and youth. In so doing, they made it clear that other forms of music—even other forms of popular music—would not be subjected to the same scrutiny. Country music, for example, remained largely untouched by the PMRC, even though it has often dealt with themes of sex, violence, and alcohol. Critic Dave Marsh noted this double-standard when he wrote, "Imagine how the rapper

Ice Cube would be denounced for a song about drunkenly disrupting an old girlfriend's wedding and threatening the groom, then setting out on a bender with his crew. That is exactly the story line of Garth Brooks' 'I've Got Friends in Low Places'."[74]

In some ways, the country music industry relished the attacks on rap and heavy metal. "Every morning when they play that stuff," said Jimmy Bowen, head of Nashville's Liberty Records, "people come running to us."[75] Frank Zappa went so far as to suggest that the rating system would "have the effect of protectionist legislation for the country music industry."[76] Occasionally, there were explicit political connections between country music and the new conservatism, as with Randy Travis' 1990 hit "Point of Light," written expressly for Bush, but the real payoff for country music was in expansion and sales. Albums by country artists like Randy Travis, George Strait, Clint Black, and Garth Brooks began to appear regularly among the best selling pop albums of the year, historically a rare occurrence for country product. In 1992, Garth Brooks alone had five albums among the year's most popular, including *Ropin' the Wind* at number one, the first time a country album had ever been cited as top pop album of the year.

This is not to suggest that the increase in the appeal of country music was only the result of the reaction to other forms of popular music or that the PMRC had not identified some real issues. However, in the selective application of their research to rap and metal, the PMRC raised serious questions about their commitment to freedom of expression. The logic of the First Amendment suggests that it is the most unpopular ideas and expressions that are most in need of protection. In his testimony at the PMRC hearings, Stan Gortikov—easily the most cooperative industry spokesman—had expressed the "fear that the only acceptable translation of the wishes of the PMRC will somehow constitute a de facto first stage form of censorship."[77] Since the creation of the rating system in 1985, many retail record outlets had, in fact, refused to carry stickered product, fearing organized consumer protest over them. These stores included department stores like Sears and J. C. Penney as well as music chains like Record World, Disc Jockey, and Camelot Music, the second largest chain in the country. The influential Wal-Mart chain took the practice one step

> If the warning label was designed simply to alert parents to controversial material, as the PMRC contended, why was it being used as a basis for criminalization?

further, refusing to carry a growing list of non-stickered records as well.[78] (Wal-Mart had distinguished itself prior to this by refusing to stock thirty rock magazines, including *Rolling Stone, Creem,* and *Tiger Beat,* on the basis that they were "pornographic."[79] This policy was implemented while the giant warehouse chain was still selling guns.) By 1990, as many as nineteen states had considered legislation requiring lyric labeling, and some of them, Louisiana for example, used the appearance of a stickered product in a store as grounds for criminal liability.[80] (There was at the same time a spate of proposed legislation aimed at regulating live concerts and volume levels on boom boxes.) In 1992, the police chief of Guilderland, New York, sent a letter to local music stores, warning about the legality of selling stickered records even though selling stickered records was not illegal.[91] That same year, four record outlets in Omaha, Nebraska, were actually charged with violating the state's harmful to minors law when they sold stickered LPs to teenagers.[82] If the warning label was designed simply to alert parents to controversial material, as the PMRC contended, why was it being used as a basis for criminalization? The fact is that the 1985 PMRC hearings marked the beginning of an intensified effort to put popular music on trial.

Shortly after the 1985 hearings, singer Ozzy Osbourne was sued by the parents of a California teenager, when it was alleged that Osbourne's song, "Suicide Solution," had caused their nineteen-year-old son, John McCullom, to shoot himself. The case became a cause célèbre for the PMRC, and the song and McCullom's death were highlighted in *Rising to the Challenge* a few years later. Because the lyrics, which referred to suicide as "the only way out," were admittedly ambiguous, Osbourne's claim that "Suicide Solution" was actually an antisuicide song whose lyrics were inspired by the alcohol-related death of a friend did not convince the public at large, although the lawsuit was thrown out of court. The arguments over the meaning of the lyrics of "Suicide Solution" simply underscore the fact that the way in which popular music communicates is complex. As Walser has pointed out, "music does not simply inflict its meanings upon helpless fans . . . indeed, the evidence suggests that only a tiny minority of fans found 'Suicide Solution' depressing rather than sobering and thought-provoking."[83]

A late 1980s broadcast on the impact of heavy metal by ABC's *20/20* corroborated Walser's view. The show addressed a suicide case involving Metallica's "Fade to Black," another song that had caught the PMRC's attention when two Chicago teenagers, Nancy Grannan and Karen Logan, were found dead clutching a note that contained the lyrics to the song. The PMRC blamed the song for encouraging suicide. The *20/20* segment included

Since he began his career as lead singer for Black Sabbath in the late 1960s, Ozzy Osbourne has been a target of conservative religious groups and watchdog organizations. Still, he has managed to turn his demonic glare into pure gold.

interviews with students from a New Jersey high school and journalist Charles M. Young. Said Young, "Heavy metal speaks to the anger and despair of teenagers today the same way the blues used to speak to the despair and anger of black people in the South. Without heavy metal, there would probably be more suicides because metal and certain other forms of rock give teenagers something to believe in that they get no place else."[84] While Metallica acknowledged the tragedy of the case in an interview in *Parade* magazine, bassist Jason Newsted also said, "I wish you could hear all the kids that come up to us and say, 'If it weren't for "Fade to Black" . . . I'd be dead now.' Or, 'You guys helped me through those times, to want to continue my life.' And there's hundreds of those."[85]

The most celebrated suicide case was the 1992 lawsuit in which it was alleged that subliminal messages on Judas Priest's *Stained Class* caused Ray Belknap and Jay Vance of Reno, Nevada, to kill themselves with a shotgun. Because lyrics about suicide had already been ruled as protected speech in the Osbourne trial, the plaintiffs built their case around subliminal commands to "do it" and backward messages exhorting "try suicide," "suicide is in," and "sing my evil spirit," which they claimed were part of the LP. When it was revealed that Vance and Belknap came from severely troubled backgrounds that could have accounted for their self-destructive behavior easily, Judas Priest was cleared of all charges. The judge found that whatever subliminal messages were on the album were neither intentional nor necessary to explain the suicide pact. He did, however, leave the door open to future law suits in ruling that "subliminal messages and 'backmasking' . . . are not protected speech under the First Amendment."[86]

Subliminal messages and backmasking also figured heavily in charges of Satanism, an issue that clearly reveals the affinity between the PMRC and the religious right. Prominent among the Christian fundamentalists who were attempting to link popular music and Satanism were James Dobson, leader of Focus on the Family, Dan and Steve Peters, two ministers in St. Paul, and the Reverend Donald Wildmon, head of the Mississippi-based American Family Association, which claimed to have 380,000 members at the time. In the late 1980s and early 1990s, Focus on the Family campaigned vigorously to remove "objectionable" records from stores. At the time, the PMRC's Susan Baker was a member of their board of directors. The Peters brothers, who lectured widely on the evils of popular music, were endorsed by PMRC cofounder Sally Nevius, who said, "It was guys like them who got the rock & roll wrecking ball rolling in the right direction."[87] While there was no structural connection between Wildmon's group and the PMRC, a 1990 *Time* magazine article, entitled "No Sympathy for the Devil," suggested an ideological one, describing the campaigns of both groups in similar terms.[88]

There have been wildly divergent estimates as to how widespread and how dangerous Satanism is. In 1985, Darlyne Pettinicchio, a consultant on gangs for police agencies who worked at the Back in Control center, a counseling program that advocated, among other things, "deprogramming" youth who had fallen under the spell of heavy metal, estimated that there were approximately 135,000 covens of nine to thirteen people each in the United States, bringing total occult membership to well over 1 million.[89] In contrast, David Alexander, writing in *The Humanist*, placed the number of actual Satanists in the United States at fewer than 1,000. Alexander also pointed out that Satanists were members of a religion protected by the First Amendment and that none of them had been charged in any ritual crimes.[90] Law enforcement agencies, in particular, have tended to view Satanism as dangerous. Writing in *The National Sheriff*, Robert J. Barry maintained that "Satanism is on the rise in America. Hardly a day passes without reports of violent acts conducted by Satanists. Across the country law enforcement organizations are receiving reports of homicide, mayhem, assault, suicide, child abuse and animal mutilations that are linked with the satanic occult."[91] Barry went on to claim, "One of the major contemporary movements exploiting Satanism is the music industry and its punk rock and 'heavy metal' productions."[92] However, there is little to validate Barry's claim other than the sensational arrest of Richard Ramirez, the alleged "Night Stalker," who was described by the press as "an AD/DC fan who had apparently been obsessed by Satanism."[93]

Even without corroborating evidence the issue of Satanism in popular music continued and reached fever pitch in 1990 when New York's Cardinal John J. O'Connor warned his flock that "diabolically instigated violence is on the rise."[94] The cardinal's message came three weeks after J. Gordon Melton, head of the Institute for the Study of American Religion in Santa Barbara, California, reported that "press reports of satanic activities showed no increase and that upon investigation many of the most dramatic reports turned out to be without basis."[95] Nevertheless, in his sermon, the cardinal said that "some kinds of rock music" were a tool of the devil and singled out Ozzy Osbourne's "Suicide Solution" as an example.[96] "The Cardinal's observations on rock music," reported the *New York Times*, "followed closely those of Tipper Gore."[97]

If one were looking for any religious connections between popular music and violent crime, one would do well to look at white supremacist organizations that espouse some form of Christian fundamentalism rather than Satanism. The White Aryan Resistance (WAR), for example, consciously used a variant of punk rock called oi to recruit skinheads. In 1989, Tom Metzger, a former Ku Klux Klansman and leader of WAR, and his son John organized an "Aryan Woodstock" for their skinhead followers. A year later, the Metzgers and two skinheads were found liable for the 1988 beating death of an Ethiopian student named Mulugeta Seraw in Portland, Oregon. The crusaders who attacked heavy metal, however, seemed to overlook problems of racism and bigotry. Where, for example, was the PMRC and the religious right when Jon Pareles, music critic for the *New York Times*, took Public Enemy to task for their anti-Semitism and challenged Guns 'N' Roses for their use of "nigger" and "faggot"?[98] Because neither the religious right nor the PMRC had included

The crusaders who attacked heavy metal, however, seemed to overlook problems of racism and bigotry. Where, for example, was the PMRC and the religious right when Jon Pareles, music critic for the New York Times, *took Public Enemy to task for their anti-Semitism and challenged Guns 'N' Roses for their use of "nigger" and "faggot"?*

racism or bigotry in their list of concerns, these incidents were largely unmentioned in their campaigns. They did not begin to speak to such issues until after Pareles' criticism forced a partial reframing of the issues.

Clearly, then, the way in which a problem is framed can determine the response. Nowhere is this more apparent than in the PMRC's concern over "a sexuality that is graphic and explicit." In phrasing its concern in this way, the PMRC made sexuality itself the concern. While this may have appealed to conservative fundamentalists, it permitted no distinctions between a sexuality that is violent and degrading to women and a sexuality that is gentle and sensuous. In this phrasing, it matters not whether a woman is a passive victim or actively in control of her sexual choices. The only thing that matters is that sex has taken place. Within this all-inclusive scattershot approach, the PMRC, of course, hit some worthy targets. But, their inability to make distinctions led only to the conclusion that "sex is bad," a message that is disorienting and repressive to teenagers at a crucial stage in their own sexual development.

Madonna, of course, was the main target of the PMRC's concerns about sexuality. Susan Baker said that it was Madonna's "Like a Virgin" that moved her to become a founding member of the PMRC. Pam Howar expressed the concern that Madonna was teaching young girls "how to be porn queens in heat."[99] Madonna had expressed her sexuality consistently and boldly in her musical performances and videos. She had also been forthright in her promotion of safe sex, speaking out publicly on the issue, performing at AIDS benefits, including informational materials in her albums, and distributing condoms at her concerts. In so doing, she had become a major source of irritation for the PMRC and the religious right. Transforming the role of undergarments in fashion and taking liberties with Christian iconography in her visual presentations only added to the ire of her detractors.

It was her "Justify My Love" that was, for some, the final straw. The video presented the viewer with graphically implied, but not quite explicit, sex, which was made more complicated by insinuations of homosexuality and group sex. Its artful black and white cinematography recalled Fellini's *La Dolce Vita.* Madonna was aware that she was pushing the boundaries on the video. Still, its sexuality was soft and gentle, and it forced her fans to grapple concretely with the complexities of sex that her critics would sooner have avoided by preaching abstinence. There was certainly room for discussion concerning her choice of images, but in the PMRC's conception of the problem, the issue was closed before any questions could be raised. "Justify My Love" earned the singular distinction of being the first video ever to be officially banned by MTV, a status that quickly turned it into the best selling music video in history. Rather than take on the more complex questions of sexuality, the battles over sex in popular music tended to pit First Amendment defenses against fundamentalist dismissals of all provocative material as obscene.

In December 1985, shortly after the PMRC's hearings, a young girl from Los Angeles purchased the Dead Kennedys' *Frankenchrist* album, which also included the poster "Penis Landscape" by the award-winning Swiss artist H. R. Giger. Her parents were so horrified at the graphic portrayal of ten male appendages that they called the California Attorney General's office to complain. In April, 1986, Jello Biafra, the leader of the group, was arrested for distributing harmful material to a minor. Criminal charges were also leveled at his record company, his distributor, the Los Angeles wholesaler, and even the sixty-seven-year-old owner of the pressing plant that manufactured the record. The retail outlet that actually sold the record was not charged because, according to the police, "They were cooperative and took the record off the shelves."[100]

The Dead Kennedys bust had all the markings of a test case. The police may have thought that Biafra and his label, Alternative Tentacles, would be an easy target because the label was a small, self-managed and self-supported company that could ill afford a protracted legal battle. Biafra quoted a police official as saying: "We feel this is a cost-effective way of sending a message that . . . we are going to prosecute."[101] Biafra, however, decided to fight. Defending his artistic choices as political speech, he argued that the Giger poster resonated with themes that ran through the *Frankenchrist* album. Whatever the courts may have thought of the wacky, activist history of the Dead Kennedys, it had to be admitted that Jello Biafra was a serious political figure. In 1979, he had actually run for mayor of San Francisco and placed fourth in a field of ten candidates. The case ended with all defendants cleared, but the legal battle, which dragged on for a year and a half at a cost of tens of thousands of dollars, bankrupted Alternative Tentacles and ended the career of the Dead Kennedys.

The Biafra obscenity case was followed by several others that received nationwide coverage. In June 1988, Tommy Hammond, the owner of a small record store in Alabama, was arrested on obscenity charges for selling 2 Live Crew's *Move Something* to an adult undercover agent. At the time of his arrest, the album had not been declared obscene in any court of law. In fact, Hammond kept the album behind the counter and refused to sell them to minors because they carried a warning sticker, as did all of 2 Live Crew's albums. Nevertheless, four months after his arrest, Hammond was fined $500 by a municipal court judge who declared the album obscene on the spot. While Hammond appealed and, after several postponements, was acquitted, neither 2 Live Crew nor sellers of the group's albums were done with obscenity charges.

Henry Louis Gates, Jr., testified that 2 Live Crew's risqué rhymes were part of the venerable tradition of "signifying" and "playing the dozens" and that judging the legal status of 2 Live Crew's work, therefore, required a familiarity with "black codes," which had been absent in the original determination of obscenity.

In 1990, 2 Live Crew's LP, *As Nasty As They Wanna Be,* became the first recording to be declared legally obscene in a federal district court. After Judge José A. Gonsalez handed down the ruling, the group was arrested for performing some of the material from the album at an adults only nightclub. Charles Freeman, an African American record-store owner from Fort Lauderdale, was also arrested for selling the LP. Like the

Dead Kennedys, 2 Live Crew was thought to be an easy target. Cuts like "Me So Horny" from an album which detailed sex in every imaginable position, were bound to be considered offensive by many, and the record was produced by a small independent label (Luke Records, owned by group leader Luther Campbell), which did not have the financial resources for an extended legal battle.

The 2 Live Crew case is important not only because it tested the strength of the First Amendment, but also because it confronted all the racism associated with the application of the obscenity laws. There is at present a three-pronged test for the legal determination of obscenity. To be judged obscene by a court of law, a work must (1) lack serious literary, artistic, political, or scientific value; (2) when taken as a whole, appeal to prurient interest; and (3) be patently offensive, as judged by community standards.[102] Given this third standard, what the Supreme Court has called the "dim and uncertain" line separating obscenity from constitutionally protected speech can change from one locale to another. A work that has been judged obscene in Florida may be perfectly legal in New York, which was, in fact, the case with the 2 Live Crew recording. It is, of course, the determination of community standards in a multicultural community that has made obscenity rulings questionable, and it was this ambiguity that served as the basis for 2 Live Crew's defense. Appearing as an expert witness for the defense, eminent African American scholar Henry Louis Gates, Jr., testified that 2 Live Crew's risqué rhymes were part of the venerable tradition of exaggeration found in such competitive African American word games as "signifying" and "playing the dozens" and that judging the legal status of 2 Live Crew's work, therefore, required a familiarity with "black codes," which had been absent in the original determination of obscenity.[103] The defense prevailed, and the obscenity ruling was overturned in May 1993. Although there was strong sentiment that Gates' eloquence had papered over some deficiencies in both the quality of 2 Live Crew's production and their treatment of women, the question of obscenity was finally laid to rest when the U.S. Supreme Court refused to challenge the appellate decision.[104] Unfortunately, in their ecstasy over 2 Live Crew's acquittal, civil libertarians hardly noticed that Charles Freeman, the record-store owner, was convicted and fined $1,000 for selling the group's album two months later.

Charges of obscenity in rap have been second only to charges of violence. These charges of violence became particularly loud in the 1992 election year, primarily because of the political fallout surrounding the uprising in Los Angeles that followed the not guilty verdict given to the police who had beaten Rodney King. In that charged atmosphere, the righteous anger that had led to the uprising ran head first into political expedience that required candidates to respond to what was said and done. Cultural and political differences between speakers resulted in a considerable distortion of what was actually being said. When President Clinton characterized Sister Souljah's comments about the situation in Los Angeles as being "full of hatred," David Mills, the *Washington Post* reporter who had interviewed her, noted in an article for *Essence*, "Clinton really *did* take her comment out of context. Souljah was describing the attitude of the L. A. rioters, not prescribing future action."[105] Far from being easy target, Souljah turned out to be a formidable opponent, trading blows with the likes of Bryant Gumbel, Larry King, and Phil Donahue, and eventually landing on the cover of *Newsweek.*

A few weeks later the rap/metal song "Cop Killer" from Ice-T's *Body Count,* which he had been performing for more than a year, sparked further national debate over rap's seeming encouragement of violence. To some, the song captured all the outrage and dissatisfaction associated with the Rodney King verdict. At the same time, its violent imagery prompted others, including dozens of police agencies all over the country, to call for a boycott of Time Warner, then the parent company of Ice-T's record label. In the ensuing controversy, public figures ranging from George Bush and Dan Quayle to Mario Cuomo jumped on the bandwagon to denounce the record. Sixty congressmen wrote to Time Warner about the song. Oliver North joined forces with Jack Thompson, the Florida attorney who had gone after 2 Live Crew, to try (unsuccessfully) to have the record declared illegal under federal sedition laws. Charleton Heston, a member of the Time Warner board, read the lyrics aloud at a board of directors meeting. Among the directors, Beverly Sills was publicly critical of the company while others proposed "screening" future releases. "Maybe I underestimate my juice," said a bewildered Ice-T, "but there's people out there with nuclear bombs, people with armies, and the president has time to sit up and get into it with me?"[106]

While in some ways, the furor over "Cop Killer" was similar to the furor over N.W.A.'s "_ _ _ _ tha Police" a few years earlier, the environment was quite different. Most of the world had seen the video of Rodney King's beating by the police and knew the outcome of the subsequent trial. These events recontextualized the messages of both songs. Although the album had long since peaked in sales, the publicity surrounding the song in the aftermath of the riots boosted *Body Count* from number seventy-three back up to number twenty-six on the pop charts. While it is easy to understand why some police officers found the song unsettling, it is interesting that the National Black Police Association denounced the Warner boycott, noting that "Cop Killer" "did not happen in a vacuum. People have always expressed their feelings and opinions through songs, and they are talking about how African-American people have been victimized by police brutality. And that is very real. Where were those organizations when Rodney King was beat up and when that verdict came in."[107] The association was disappointed when Ice-T agreed to pull the song from future pressings of the album. Like many other groups, it feared that the action would send "a negative message to other artists."[108]

No sooner had this controversy begun to subside than three more rappers made headlines for allegedly crossing the line into violence in real life. In August 1993, Snoop Doggy Dogg was charged in connection with the fatal shooting of Philip Woldemarian in Los Angeles. In October, Tupac Shakur was arrested for aggravated assault in the shooting of two off-duty Atlanta police officers. Three weeks later he was arrested again with two friends on charges of sexual assault. Public Enemy frontman Flavor Flav was arrested for attempted murder and criminal possession of a firearm.

Flavor Flav had confronted his girlfriend's alleged lover with a gun. In a jealous rage, he had fired one shot into the ground. Fortunately, he had enough presence of mind to check himself into the Betty Ford Clinic for crack abuse. Still, his irresponsible behavior compromised the effectiveness of Public Enemy, which had consistently put forth a message of self-determination for African Americans. For Tupac Shakur, both incidents initially seemed out of character. Described by others as quiet and shy, Shakur was a formally trained actor who had received an NAACP Image Award nomination for his role in the film *Poetic Justice.* His hit single, "Keep Ya Head Up," according to Havelock Nelson, "speaks urgently and respectfully about the struggles of black women."[109] Thus, many observers of the hip hop scene found Shakur's behavior troubling. The NAACP deflected criticism by giving the Image Award to Denzel Washington. Havelock Nelson took a harder line, arguing that "Shakur . . . is endangering more than just his own career. He and other rappers who can't get a grip are also helping set the stage for hip hop's last blast. With their buck-wild actions, these artists are unwittingly playing into the hands of forces fed up with heightened levels of black achievement."[110]

*R*ap had been roundly criticized when its art simply imitated life. The media blitz following these incidents seemed to suggest the more disturbing possibility that there was no difference between the two.

Although Snoop Doggy Dogg was only indirectly involved in violence, his case received more publicity than the others because he had just made music history. On 11 December 1993, his debut album, *DoggyStyle,* became the first debut album ever to enter the *Billboard* pop charts at number one. In its first week of release, the LP sold more than 800,000 units. Snoop Doggy himself entered the music business as a protégé of rapper/producer Dr. Dre, formerly of N.W.A. A veteran of the Los Angeles streets, Snoop was no stranger to gang violence. In the incident in question, it was Snoop Doggy Dogg's bodyguard who actually shot Woldemarian; Snoop was driving the car. The rapper pleaded not guilty, claiming the shooting was in self defense.

One of the things that distinguished Snoop from other rappers was his style, which was described in the *New York Times* as "gentle"; "where many rappers scream," said *Times* reporter Touré, "he speaks softly." Touré then added, "While Snoop delivers rhymes delicately, the content is anything but."[111] Snoop's work on Dr. Dre's rap hit "Deep Cover" from the film soundtrack of the same name supports this assessment. On this cut, Snoop's laid-back vocal drawl smoothed the edges from what had been perceived as the song's chilling refrain, "cuz it's 1-8-7 on a undercover cop." The number referred to the California police code for homicide, which, of course, prompted a number of comparisons between "Deep Cover" and Ice-T's "Cop Killer." None of the comparisons appearing in the media, however, mentioned that the line in the movie was delivered in sympathy for a good cop who was tragically slain at the end of the film.

Rap had been roundly criticized when its art simply imitated life. The media blitz following these incidents seemed to suggest the more disturbing possibility that there was no difference between the two. According to this logic, rap could be held responsible for all social disintegration. As David Toop has pointed out, however, "children carry automatic weapons like Uzis and sell crack in the streets. Babies are born with AIDS and teenagers are shot dead for their shoes. Music may be powerful and influential but no music is strong enough to create this kind of social decay."[112] When James Brown ran afoul of the law, he went to jail, but no one said funk was to blame. The fact that Tupac Shakur served jail time for some of his actions should be no different. Such instances cannot be used legitimately as the occasion for indicting a whole genre of music.

Following these incidents, media outlets began falling over themselves to outdo each other's antiviolence policies. Black radio station WBLS in New York banned violence and profanity from its broadcasts. The rap magazine *Rap Sheet* stopped carrying advertisements that pictured guns. Black Entertainment Television (BET) instituted a policy of no guns in the videos they aired. The Box, a pay-to-view channel, initiated a "guns suck" campaign that exhorted: "Wake up and smell the roses before they toss 'em on your grave."[113] These moves coincided with an escalation of protests against gangsta rap from within the black community. In late December 1993, the National Political Congress of Black Women (NPCBW), which boasted a membership of 2,500, staged demonstrations in Washington D.C. against two record retail outlets, Nobody Beats the Wiz and Sam Goody. The organization was joined in civil disobedience by activist Dick Gregory and endorsed by the National Council of Negro Women, the NAACP, and Jesse Jackson's National Rainbow Coalition, among others. In addition to direct action, the NPCBW took the well-worn path of advocating government hearings. Beginning in February 1994, both the House and Senate scheduled hearings to gather testimony on gangsta rap. In some ways, these proceedings recalled the 1985 PMRC hearings. Senator Carol Moseley Braun, who chaired the Senate committee, proposed a rating system like the one used for movies—the same idea that was abandoned in 1985 as too unwieldy—

The question is not why some rappers are so offensive, but rather, why do so many fans find offensive rappers appealing?

"to prevent records from getting into the hands of children."[114] In the first round of hearings, no rappers were invited to offer testimony. Instead, the hearings relied on comments from people like Dr. C. DeLores Tucker, national chairwoman of the NPCBW, and entertainer Dionne Warwick, thus raising questions of class and age divisions within the black community. At the time, Darryl James, the founder of *Rap Sheet,* said: "Frustrated men and women like the Rev. Jesse Jackson and Dr. C. DeLores Tucker, who misrepresent themselves as representatives of the masses, only serve to fan the flame of controversy."[115] There was one aspect of the hearings that differed significantly from the PMRC hearings. While none of the participants who criticized rap—most of whom were African Americans—condoned violent or misogynist lyrics, nearly all recognized the legitimacy of black rage and placed their comments in the context of societal disintegration. "The issue is not whether to spurn, regulate, restrict, segregate, or otherwise curb the distribution of hip hop music," said David W. Harleston of Rush Associated Labels. "Rather, the issue is whether we, as a community and nation, are prepared to address the very issues that have given rise to the lyrics that some find so troubling."[116] In framing the issue as he did, Harleston put a rather different spin on the problem than was the case in 1985. The question that follows logically is not why some rappers are so offensive, but rather, why do so many fans find offensive rappers appealing? It is this question that suggests a consideration of popular music as one variable among the myriad of social forces that affect the quality of life.

Against the odds, metal had risen from the embers of a dying 1970s subculture. Rap emerged from one of the most dispossessed communities in the country. By the late 1980s, they had become the primary musical expressions of youth culture. Working from the bottom up, these styles seemed to thrive on the indifference of the music industry. They engendered fanatical devotion among their fans and a ferocious backlash among their detractors. In this sense these styles were decidedly political, whether they intended to make an overt political statement or not. The intensity of feelings generated by rap and metal resonated with the profound rethinking of American values that characterized the period. In the 1990s, a new sound that was labeled alternative began competing for national attention among youth. For many, alternative was the fulfillment of the political promise of punk a decade later. Alternative emerged as an intensely personal music with a discordant sound and its artists initially adopted a doggedly anti-commercial posture. Paradoxically, the music became wildly successful.

N O T E S

1. Tricia Rose, *Black Noise: Rap Music and Black Culture in Contemporary America* (Hanover, N.H.: University Press of New England, 1994).

2. Philip Bashe, Heavy Metal Thunder: The Music, Its History, Its Heroes (Garden City, N.Y.: Doubleday, 1985). Deena Weinstein, *Heavy Metal: A Cultural Sociology* (New York: Lexington Books, 1991).

3. Weinstein, *Heavy Metal,* 44.

4. Robert Walser, *Running with the Devil: Power, Gender, and Madness in Heavy Metal Music,* (Hanover, NH: Wesleyan University Press, 1993), 12.

5. Ibid., 94.

6. Ibid., 76.

7. Gillian G. Garr, *She's a Rebel: The History of Women in Rock & Roll* (Seattle, Wash.: Seal Press, 1992), 415.

8. Andrew Goodwin, *Dancing in the Distraction Factory: Music Television and Popular Culture* (Minneapolis: University of Minnesota Press, 1992), 135.

9. Ibid., 135.

10. Greg Ptacek, "Majors Return to Nuts and Bolts of pre-MTV Metal Marketing Days," *Billboard,* 27 April 1985, p. HM 15.

11. Linda Martin and Kerry Segrave, *Anti-Rock: The Opposition to Rock 'n' Roll* (New York: Da-Capo Press, 1993), 232.

12. Ptacek, "Majors Return to Nuts and Bolts," HM 3.

13. Ibid., HM 15.

14. Goodwin, *Dancing in the Distraction Factory,* 136.

15. E. Ann Kaplan, *Rocking Around the Clock: Music Television, Postmodernism, and Consumer Culture* (New York: Routledge, 1987), 102–103.

16. Roberta Smoodin, "Crazy Like David Lee Roth," *Playgirl,* August 1986, p. 43 quoted in Walser, *Running with the Devil,* 129.

17. Walser, *Running with the Devil,* 111.

18. Ibid., 121.

19. Weinstein, *Heavy Metal,* 48.

20. Ibid., 50.

21. Jim Miller, "It's Not Only Rock 'N' Roll." *Boston Globe,* 23 August 1991, p. 94. There were parallel developments in post-punk. Thrash metal was to classic metal what the hard-core sound of Black Flag and SS Decontrol was to new wave. By the time Black Flag leader Henry Rollins left to form his new group, the Rollins Band, its music was defined by yet another fusion category called thrashcore, which included a group called Suicidal Tendencies.

22. Weinstein, *Heavy Metal,* 51.

23. Sue Cummings, "Road Warriors," *Spin,* August 1986, quoted in Weinstein, *Heavy Metal,* 160.

24. Paul Grein, "The Year in Charts," *Billboard,* 26 December 1987, p. Y-4.

25. J. D. Considine, "Metal Mania," *Rolling Stone,* 15 November 1990, p. 104.

26. See Weinstein, *Heavy Metal,* 66; Walser, *Running with the Devil,* 17.

27. Weinstein, *Heavy Metal,* 67.

28. Walser, *Running with the Devil,* 17.

29. Laurel Fishman, "Lita Ford," *Metal,* May 1988, quoted in Walser, *Running with the Devil,* 132.

30. Tim Carr, "Talk That Talk, Walk That Walk," *Rolling Stone*, 26 May 1983, p. 22.

31. David Toop, *The Rap Attack 2: African Rap to Global Hip Hop* (London: Serpent's Tail, 1991), 14.

32. Ibid., 154.

33. Steven Hager, *Hip Hop: The Illustrated History of Break Dancing, Rap Music, and Graffiti* (New York: St. Martin's Press, 1984), 91.

34. Stephen Holden, "Pop Records Turn to Hip Hop," *New York Times*, 23 September 1984, p. 78.

35. Toop, *The Rap Attack 2,* 149.

36. Ibid., 179.

37. Brian Cross, *It's Not about a Salary: Rap, Race and Resistance in Los Angeles* (New York: Verso, 1993), 50.

38. Alex Henderson, "Active Indies," *Billboard,* 24 December 1988, p. R-16.

39. Ibid., R-8.

40. Dan Stuart, "Black Radio," *Billboard,* 17 June 1989, p. B-12.

41. Henderson, "Active Indies," R-21.

42. Jon Pareles, "There's a New Sound in Pop Music: Bigotry," *New York Times,* 10 September 1989, Arts and Leisure, 1.

43. Ibid., 33.

44. Harry Allen, "Hip Hop Madness: From Def Jams to Cold Lampin', Rap Is Our Music," *Essence,* April 1989, p. 117.

45. Ibid.

46. Toop, *The Rap Attack 2,* 200.

47. For an excellent discussion of this complexity, see Rose, *Black Noise,* pp. 146–182.

48. Toop, *The Rap Attack 2,* 201.

49. Cross, *It's Not about a Salary,* 55.

50. David Nathan, "Rap," *Billboard,* 24 December 1988, p. R-5.

51. Stuart, "Black Radio," B-12.

52. Kristal Brent Zook, "Reconstructions of Nationalist Thought in Black Music and Culture," in *Rockin' the Boat: Mass Music and Mass Movements,.* ed. Reebee Garofalo (Boston: South End Press, 1992), 262.

53. Toop, *The Rap Attack 2,* 185.

54. Cross, *It's Not about a Salary,* 58.

55. Ibid.

56. Herman Gray, "Popular Music as a Social Problem: A Social History of Claims Against Popular Music," in *Images of Issues,* ed. Joel Best (Hawthorne, NY: De Gruyter, 1989).

57. See Lawrence Grossberg, *We Gotta Get Out of This Place: Popular Conservatism and Postmodern Culture* (New York: Routledge, 1992). For an abbreviated treatment of this discussion, see Lawrence Grossberg, "The Framing of Rock: Rock and the New Conservatism," in *Rock and Popular Music: Politics, Policies, Institutions,* ed. Tony Bennett et al. (New York: Routledge, 1993), 195.

58. Nan Levinson, "Shut Up," *Boston Globe,* 20 February 1994, p. 79.

59. Susan McClary and Robert Walser, "Start Making Sense: Musicology Wrestles with Rock," in *On Record: Rock, Pop, and the Written Word,* ed. Simon Frith and Andrew Goodwin (New York Pantheon Books, 1990), 278.

60. Linda Martin and Kerry Segrave, *Anti-Rock: The Opposition to Rock 'n' Roll* (New York: DaCapo Press, 1993), 292.

61. U.S. Congress, Senate, Committee on Commerce, Science, and Transportation, *Record Labeling,* 99th Cong., 1st sess., 1985, 11, quoted in Herman Gray, "Rate the Records: Symbolic Conflict, Popular Music, and Social Problems." *Popular Music and Society* (Fall 1989): 6–7.

62. Steven Dougherty, "Parents Vs. Rock," *People,* 16 September 1985, p. 50.

63. Simon Frith, *Sound Effects: Youth, Leisure, and the Politics of Rock 'n' Roll* (New York: Pantheon Books, 1981), 175.

64. Dougherty, "Parents Vs. Rock," 50.

65. Gray, "Rate the Records," 9.

66. Frank Zappa, "The Porn Wars," *Penthouse,* May 1989, p. 78.

67. Editorial, *Rolling Stone,* 7 November 1985, p. 10.

68. PMRC Video, *Rising to the Challenge,* produced by Teen Vision, Inc., 1989.

69. Ibid.

70. Ibid.

71. Walser, *Running with the Devil,* 139.

72. Dougherty, "Parents Vs. Rock," 52.

73. Walser, *Running with the Devil,* 140.

74. Dave Marsh, "What's Being Sold in Country?" *New York Times,* 24 May 1992, p. 20.

75. Ibid.

76. Robin Denselow, *When the Music's Over: The Story of Political Pop* (Boston: Faber and Faber, 1989), 267.

77. U.S. Congress, Senate, Committee on Commerce, Science, and Transportation, *Record Labeling,* 99th Cong., 1st sess., 1985, 11, quoted in Gray, "Rate the Records," 10.

78. David Thigpen, "Up Against the Wal," *Rolling Stone,* 24 February 1994, p. 16.

79. Jello Biafra, "The Far Right and the Censorship of Music," *Harvard Law Record* (17 April 1987): 11.

80. Marjorie Heins, *Sex, Sin and Blasphemy: A Guide to America's Censorship Wars* (New York: The New Press, 1993), 90.

81. Ibid., 89.

82. Ibid., 92.

83. Walser, *Running with the Devil,* 150.

84. ABC, *20/20,* Segment on heavy metal, produced by Danny Schechter, 1987.

85. Lynn Minton, "Is Heavy Metal Dangerous?" *Parade,* 20 September 1992, p. 12.

86. K. Zimmerman, "Priest Ruling Gives Unclear Message," *Variety,* 3 September 1990, p. 8, quoted in Steve Jones, "Ban(ned) in the USA: Popular Music and Censorship," *Journal of Communication Inquiry* (Winter, 1991): 77.

87. The editors of *Rock & Roll Confidential, You've Got a Right to Rock* (Los Angeles: Duke and Duchess Ventures, Inc., 1990), 6.

88. Richard N. Ostling, "No Sympathy for the Devil," *Time,* 19 March 1990, p. 56.

89. Robert J. Barry, "Satanism: The Law Enforcement Response," *The National Sheriff,* February/March 1987, p. 40.

90. David Alexander, "Giving the Devil More Than His Due," *The Humanist,* March/April 1990, quoted in Walser, *Running with the Devil,* 199–200.

91. Barry, "Satanism," 39.

92. Ibid., 41.

93. Dougherty, "Parents Vs. Rock," 46.

94. Ostling, "No Sympathy for the Devil," 56.

95. Peter Steinfels, "Surge in Satanic Activity Alarms O'Connor," *New York Times,* 6 March 1990, p. B6.

96. Reuters, "Of Hard-Rock Demons: A Cardinal Speaks Out," *Boston Globe,* 6 March 1990, p. 23.

97. Steinfels, "Surge in Satanic Activity Alarms O'Connor," B6.

98. Pareles, "There's a New Sound in Pop Music: Bigotry," 1, 32–33.

99. Dennis Wharton, "D.C. Bluebloods Want X Rating for Porn Rock," *Variety*, 22 May 1985, quoted in Martin and Segrave, *Anti-Rock,* 293.

100. Biafra, "The Far Right and the Censorship of Music," 12.

101. Ibid.

102. Heins, *Sex, Sin, and Blasphemy,* 22–24.

103. Henry Louis Gates, Jr., "2 Live Crew, Decoded," *New York Times,* 9 June 1990, A23.

104. Brechner Center for Freedom of Information, *The Brechner Report* (Gainesville: University of Florida, 1992), 2.

105. David Mills, "Rap as Politics: The Sayings of Sister Souljah," *Essence,* September 1992, p. 20.

106. Alan Light, "Ice," *Rolling Stone,* 20 August 1992, p. 30.

107. Charlene Orr et al., "Texas Police Pursue 'Cop Killer'," *Billboard,* 27 June 1992, p. 79.

108. Greg Sandow, "Fire & Ice," *Entertainment Weekly,* 14 August, 1992, p. 32.

109. Havelock Nelson, "Music and Violence: Does Crime Pay?" *Billboard,* 13 November 1993, p.109.

110. Havelock Nelson, "The Rap Column," *Billboard,* 4 December 1993, p. 30.

111. Touré, "Snoop Dogg's Gentle Hip Hop Growl," *New York Times,* 21 November 1993, p. 32.

112. Toop, *The Rap Attack 2,* 170.

113. Phyllis Stark et al., "Gangsta Rap under the Gun," *Billboard,* 18 December 1993, p. 141.

114. Bill Holland, "Senate Hearing Examines Gangsta Lyrics," *Billboard,* 5 March 1994, p. 10.

115. Ibid., 89.

116. Ibid., 10.

11 Alternative to What?

The success of rap and metal at the turn of the decade reminded many of precisely that aspect of rock 'n' roll that had so distressed the moral guardians of the 1950s: that the music of the most disenfranchised elements of society—angry blacks and irreverent working class whites—could be the most compelling culturally, politically, and economically. Accordingly, *Rolling Stone*'s Mikal Gilmore remembered 1990 as "the year in which rock & roll was reborn."[1] There was also something of a postmodern twist to this particular rebirth that became apparent as the major market breakthrough of what had been called alternative music brought about a further disintegration of the barriers between cult and mass, margin and mainstream, underground and commercial, and, ultimately, serious art and popular culture.

Prior to rock 'n' roll, there had been an attempt to separate rhythm and blues from pop and country (the other two major marketing categories of the music industry) along racial lines. At first, rap and metal developed according to this division, but as was the case with rhythm and blues, fissures in the race barrier began to occur when rap artists laying hard-edged urban rhymes over hot rock tracks began to cross over to the mainstream audience. Still, joint efforts like the now classic Run-D.M.C./Aerosmith collaboration on the remake of Aerosmith's "Walk This Way," were rare. Except for their respective commitments to technology and transgression, the genres developed in fairly distinct ways—rap based on technologically sophisticated electronic beats and def(t) linguistic juxtapositions; metal based on guitar virtuosic precision and sheer volume. Beneath these two main youth cultural trends, however, lay an underground of post-

The success of rap and metal at the turn of the decade reminded many of precisely that aspect of rock 'n' roll that had so distressed the moral guardians of the 1950s: that the music of the most disenfranchised elements of society—angry blacks and irreverent working class whites—could be the most compelling culturally, politically, and economically.

punk, alternative sounds in which genre boundaries were not always so clear or well defended.

Cross-genre influences were starting to become more conspicuous as the 1990s dawned. According to Gilmore, Living Colour's second LP, *Time's Up,* "fused punk rhythms and speed metal leads with a complex harmonic architecture derived from the avant-garde sensibility of legendary jazz saxophonist Ornette Coleman."[2] Living Colour's mission was to reclaim rock 'n' roll as black music, less in the interest of cultural separatism than historical accuracy. Cuts like "History Lesson" (reminiscent of Keith LeBlanc's "No Sell Out"—the Malcolm X rap record) and "Pride" drove the point home. At the same time, Faith No More, an all-white post-punk band, released *The Real Thing,* which Gilmore noted "took a personalized, raplike delivery and intercut it with hard-edge metallic textures."[3] Faith No More had been knocking around the San Francisco underground for more than eight years with two previous albums to their credit—*We Care a Lot* (1985) and *Introduce Yourself* (1987). Bolstered by MTV support for the single "Epic," *The Real Thing* went gold. "Between these two bands," Gilmore said, "the face of modern rock was virtually overhauled this last year."[4]

Both Living Colour and Faith No More ended 1990 among the best selling pop artists of the year and enjoyed substantial sales in the mainstream market. What is interesting is that the label "alternative" was applied to both groups, although for different

reasons. That same year, Sinéad O'Connor, another mainstay of alternative music, released her second album, *I Do Not Want What I Haven't Got,* which, propelled by her heart-wrenching video of Prince's "Nothing Compares 2 U," entered the *Billboard* pop charts at number twenty-four and logged six weeks at number one, achieving double platinum certification within months of its release. Combining as it did Irish pathos with punk rage, O'Connor's

Sinéad O'Connor displays the Video of the Year, Best Female, and Post-Modern video awards she won for "Nothing Compares 2 U" in 1990. It was that kind of recognition that began to collapse alternative into the mainstream.

1987 debut album, *The Lion and the Cobra,* had won her a devoted following in the alternative category. With even more challenging material, *Do Not Want* sold millions of copies. This level of success begs the question: Alternative to what?

In her book, *Manic Pop Thrill,* Rachel Felder has recognized the inadequacy of the term "alternative," and argued against a strictly economic definition of the term, favoring instead a formulation that draws on Fredric Jameson's conception of a postmodernism that encourages "specific reactions against the established forms of high modernism" and erodes "the old distinction between high culture and so-called mass or popular culture."[5] In applying Jameson's conception to a particular moment of theoretical development and cultural history, Felder posits Nirvana's raspy vocals and guitar sludge as the alternative to the "high modernism" of the latter-day George Michael, Eric Clapton, or Elton John. Jameson himself had noted the punk explosion of the late 1970s as an alternative to mainstream rock that had begun to collapse the boundaries between high art and popular culture. Similar applications of Jameson's concept could be made throughout the contemporary era. There is a sense in which loud, grainy-voiced, rhythm-based rock 'n' roll could be considered an alternative to melodic Tin Pan Alley pop smoothness even after rock 'n' roll had succeeded in outselling the music it displaced. The best selling music of the 1960s can also be considered to signify an alternative to mainstream values. In this sense, the term "alternative" connotes opposition or resistance to established norms, a countercultural lifestyle. In addition, Dylan and the Beatles, among others, mounted a challenge to the high art/popular art division.

It is clear that there has been a war of cultures going on since the appearance of rock 'n' roll and that most often the battles have been fought in the arena of popular music. There have been different responses from the music industry at different times. In the 1950s, the major record companies aligned themselves for the most part with the more conservative elements of society in resisting rock 'n' roll. The writers, performers, deejays, and independent record companies that produced and disseminated the music were essentially in competition with the established powers of the industry. Thus, the victory of rock 'n' roll has been perceived as a victory for independent production, and there has been a continuing tendency to depict independent labels as heroic underdogs even though the structural relationship between independents and majors has long since been transformed. The beginnings of this transformation lie in the mid-1960s when the majors realized that rock and soul were key to the future success of the industry. Far from fighting the independents, major companies began to rely on them for research and development. Today, independent labels do the groundwork of ferreting out niches of unsated consumer demand and/or test-marketing new musical forms. If this activity becomes successful, the majors are there to buy the independents, distribute their product, or sign their most successful artists. This

The idea that alternative music can only retain its integrity when it is produced by small independent labels leads to the tendency to lionize artists when they are least successful and to dismiss them precisely at the moment of their greatest impact.

was the pattern with punk and disco in the 1970s, and it was the pattern with rap and metal in the 1980s. The only thing that has changed in the 1990s is the speed and efficiency with which the mainstream music industry is able to incorporate new trends.

Still, while the mainstream music industry can control the marketplace economically, this is not synonymous with determining the message or blunting the effects of the music. Content to focus on the revenue-generating aspects of popular music production, the major record companies have long since chosen to distance themselves from the creative process. As a result, popular musicians enjoy a greater degree of artistic autonomy than most other popular artists. It is the failure to understand this fact that is at the heart of our inability to grasp the contradictions that are inherent in the notion of alternative music. The idea that alternative music can only retain its integrity when it is produced by small independent labels leads to the tendency to lionize artists when they are least successful and to dismiss them precisely at the moment of their greatest impact.

Strange Bedfellows: Alternative and the Mainstream

In the 1980s, the music that usually was labeled alternative had its roots in the punk movements of the 1970s and their 1980s post-punk (as opposed to new wave) variants. Still, it should be noted that the label was applied in one way for African American artists and in another for white artists. The fact that African American artists as diverse as the metallic Living Colour, the folk-oriented Tracy Chapman, bluesman Robert Cray, and soul singer Terrence Trent D'Arby were labeled alternative speaks more to race-based marketing strategies than to a shared aesthetic among the groups in question. Chapman outgrew the confines of the label quickly when her self-titled debut LP went to number one on the pop charts, but as a black female acoustic folksinger, she was still in a class by herself. Her search for a musical home led her to headliner status on the Amnesty International tours and eventually to Farm Aid V, where she shared the stage with Living Colour's Vernon Reid. It was fitting that she should collaborate with Reid (and Bobby Womack) on her third album, *Matters of the Heart* in 1992. In 1991, Reid and his group, still falling through the cracks of conventional industry marketing categories, could be found among the headliners of the first Lollapalooza tour, adding breadth to the alternative festival. When Living Colour first previewed their 1992 lineup, which featured Doug Wimbish on bass, they chose CBGB, the legendary New York punk club, to do so, again challenging the limitations of forced racial confinement.

While white groups labeled alternative also sounded different from one another, they derived from a more coherent lineage of forebears, including those groups associated with the hardcore SST label (Black Flag and the Minutemen from Los Angeles, Sonic Youth from New York, Dinosaur, Jr., from Massachusetts, and Hüsker Dü from

Minnesota), the Dead Kennedys from San Francisco, Fugazi from Washington, DC, and R.E.M. from Athens, Georgia. Felder has lumped the latter three groups together with Depeche Mode and the Cure in the safe, if admittedly "oxymoronic," category "the alternative establishment."[6] Athens and Minneapolis had established the viability of regional alternative scenes, but it was Seattle that put the music over the top.

If Seattle seems like an unlikely place for a guitar-based post-punk explosion, one has only to remember that the city had earlier spawned those fathers of guitar-based instrumental rock 'n' roll, the Ventures, and the greatest psychedelic guitarist of them all, Jimi Hendrix. In fact, Seattle had a thriving, if isolated, alternative scene for years. At its center was Sub Pop records, which was founded by Bruce Pavitt, a former deejay and local promoter, and Jon Poneman, who published a fanzine called *Sub Pop* in the early 1980s. Among the groups that got their start on Sub Pop were Soundgarden, Nirvana, Pearl Jam, Alice in Chains, Screaming Trees, Smashing Pumpkins, Mud Honey, L7, and the Afghan Whigs (actually from Cincinnati). These groups were supported by Seattle's radio stations KCMU and KJET early on and by a developed alternative press that included the now-defunct *Backlash* and the *Seattle Rocket*. Prior to the 1990s, all the groups lived in and around Seattle and played to local audiences. In 1991, however, Nirvana released *Nevermind,* an album that announced alternative to the mainstream with a vengeance. Aided significantly by MTV's decision to push the video of the album's haunting single "Smells Like Teen Spirit" to anthem-of-a-generation status, *Nevermind* managed to displace Michael Jackson's *Dangerous* from the number one slot on the pop charts, if only for a week. Nirvana's album sold 3 million copies in four months and thereafter continued to sell at the rate of 100,000 copies a week. If the connection between the title of the Nirvana LP and the Sex Pistol's historic *Never Mind the Bollocks* seemed striking, it is important to note that just as the Pistols recorded for the major label EMI, *Nevermind* marked Nirvana's major label debut on David Geffen's DGC imprint. Like the Sex Pistols, Nirvana embodied all the contradictions of alternative music, but whereas the Pistols embraced the tension until they self-destructed, Nirvana fell victim to its pressures early on. The beginning of the end began with the group's inexorable ascent to rock superstardom once Seattle was discovered.

Although Nirvana is the group that most readily comes to mind when considering the collapse of alternative into the mainstream, the Seattle gold rush actually began with the signing of Soundgarden to A&M in 1988. Soundgarden had contributed three tracks to a 1986 compilation album called *Deep Six*. It is this album that marks the rise of the Seattle scene. Before signing with A&M, Soundgarden had recorded two EPs for Sub Pop and a full-length, Grammy-nominated LP for SST entitled *Ultramega OK*. Kim Neely has described the album as "a pastiche of psychedelia, blistering hardcore and wrecking-ball blooze wrapped up with odd tunings and time signatures [that] was a sonic fuck-you to

*L*ike the Sex Pistols, Nirvana embodied all the contradictions of alternative music, but whereas the Pistols embraced the tension until they self-destructed, Nirvana fell victim to its pressures early on.

the candy-ass poodlehead bands that were clogging the charts at the time."[7] Due to a number of personnel changes, a poorly timed European tour, and the death of a close friend of the band, Soundgarden's A&M debut, *Louder Than Love* (1989), failed to set the music world ablaze. The group did better with *Badmotorfinger* (1991) and *Superunknown* (1994). Still, it was the promise of Soundgarden in the late 1980s that prompted a slew of major label a&r men to descend on Seattle in search of the next big thing. Columbia signed Alice in Chains; Pearl Jam went to Epic, and Nirvana eventually signed with DGC.

It was the promise of Soundgarden in the late 1980s that prompted a slew of major label a&r men to descend on Seattle in search of the next big thing.

On the surface, the story of Nirvana, especially that of the late Kurt Cobain, the group's leader and spiritual center, seems quite out of proportion with the impact the band made. As rock 'n' roll hard luck tales go, Nirvana's was not atypical. The group originally hailed from Aberdeen, Washington, a dying lumber town that passed on to its inhabitants depression, disillusionment, and dysfunction. Cobain was a product of all three. The group played around Olympia, Tacoma, and Seattle before coming to the attention of Sub Pop, which, as it usually did, issued a test single (now a collector's item), "Love Buzz" backed with "Big Cheese" in 1988. That same year, the group contributed one obscure cut, "Spank Thru," to a sampler called *Sub Pop 200,* an early anthology of the dark, brooding guitar-based sludge that came to be known as grunge. The following year, Sub Pop released Nirvana's first full-length LP, *Bleach.* The album was a shoestring production but had respectable regional sales and showcased the promise of Cobain's songwriting. On the strength of this run-of-the-mill track record, Nirvana was signed by DGC. By this time, Cobain and bassist Krist Novoselic had settled on Dave Grohl as the band's permanent drummer. It was this lineup that recorded *Nevermind* and its hit single, which, in the words of Anthony DeCurtis, captured "a defining moment in rock history." As DeCurtis argued in his eulogy for Cobain, "Nirvana announced the end of one rock & roll era and the start of another. In essence, Nirvana transformed the '80s into the '90s."[8] The impact of *Nevermind* was a huge burden to Cobain, who was ill at ease with fame and ill-equipped to handle the responsibility that accompanies success. He knew his fans would be suspicious of any kind of fame; indeed, he himself was suspicious of it. How could he be the spokesperson for a generation when he could barely keep his own life together? Under the pressure, which manifested itself most acutely in his agonizing stomach pains, the singer often resorted to what he euphemistically called "medicating myself," which included taking heroin and a range of tranquilizers. He was also something of a gun nut, who was photographed at one point with the barrel of an M-16 in his mouth. Drugs and guns could not have been a healthy combination for someone who always seemed too close to the edge. Like many of his grunge comrades, Cobain was preoccupied with integrity. Upset by *Rolling Stone*'s use of "Smells Like Teen Spirit" as the headline for a cover story about the television series *Beverly Hills 90210,* Cobain appeared on the magazine's cover two months later wearing a T-shirt that read "Corporate

Seattle, Nirvana become central focus of alternative music

With the release of Nevermind, Nirvana introduced alternative to the mainstream with a vengeance. Kurt Cobain shrinks at the prospect of fame while Krist Novoselic sports a T-shirt advertising Sonic Youth, their labelmates at DGC.

Magazines Still Suck." It was a feeble attempt at bolstering his alternative identity. Cries of sell out had accompanied the mainstream success of Faith No More in 1990, and he was sure they would soon be applied to Nirvana.

Following the runaway success of *Nevermind,* alternative bands, particularly those from Seattle, began to enter the mainstream as never before. Pearl Jam's debut LP, *Ten,* went straight to number two and, with sales upward of 7 million copies, could still be found among the top 100 albums three years later. The group's follow-up LP, *Vs.* (1993), entered the charts at number one. Alice in Chains enjoyed similar success. In October 1992, with their 1990 debut *Facelift* still on the charts, the group's second LP, *Dirt,* entered the *Billboard* 200 at number six. That same week Pearl Jam's *Ten* held the number seven slot, and the soundtrack to Cameron Crowe's *Singles,* the film that put Seattle on the big screen, was at number ten. If Seattle had any smell at this point, it was the sweet smell of success, and for a fleeting moment, it looked as if Cobain might enjoy it. With the 1993 release of *In Utero,* Nirvana's long-awaited studio follow-up to *Nevermind,* Cobain tried his level best to portray his life as one worth living. "I've never been happier," he told *Rolling Stone,* this time appearing on the cover of the magazine in a suit and tie and embracing his mass following. Why? "Pulling this record off. My Family. My child. Meeting William Burroughs and doing a record with him."[9] This, of course, was the other side of Cobain: the brilliant singer/songwriter who tried to exorcise his demons through his art; the genuine misfit who longed for the normalcy of love and family, which he tried to find in his marriage to Courtney Love, leader of the female-dominated punk band Hole, and the co-parenting of their child Frances Bean. Ultimately, however, the picture he tried to paint for *Rolling Stone* was the forgery of a man in serious denial. His relationship with Love was a tumultuous and well-publicized foray into co-dependency, complete with guns, drugs, domestic violence, overdoses, detoxes, and police interventions. Neither were things much rosier on the artistic front. The release of *In Utero* had been fraught with last minute title and track changes. Cobain had originally wanted to title the album *I Hate Myself and Want to Die* after a song he had written for the LP, but he pulled the song just prior to release because he feared no one would get the joke. (The prophetic single subsequently appeared as the lead track on the otherwise lackluster *The Beavis and Butt-Head Experience.*) After the album's release, he authorized Geffen to make changes that appeared uncharacteristically compromising. First, the record company removed the collage of fetuses from the back cover of the album that had caused chains like Kmart and Wal-Mart to refuse to stock it. Then, they changed the title of "Rape Me," the album's most controversial song, to "Waif Me." Because Cobain equated compromise with selling out, these changes must have eaten away at his artistic soul.

On tour in Europe in the spring of 1994, Cobain nearly died from what was initially described as an accidental overdose. It was later disclosed that the singer had ingested fifty pills and left a suicide note. That Cobain was prone to suicide came as a surprise to no one. For years, his interviews had been peppered with references to ending it all, and if one thing is clear from the research on suicide, it is that people who talk a lot about doing it are more likely to succeed. Nirvana's repertoire also contained similarly dark, if more ambiguous, pronouncements. Even so, people were unprepared for what they discovered on 8 April 1994. Cobain had apparently barricaded himself in the greenhouse above his garage a couple of days earlier, pressed the barrel of a 20-gauge shotgun to his head, and pulled the trigger. He could be identified only by his fingerprints and the wallet he left open showing his driver's license.

Commentators spoke of Cobain's death with a profound sense of loss. At the same time, however, they did not pass over lightly or excuse the suicide. Aware that his actions might be seen as something to be emulated by troubled teens, at a time when teen suicide had reached epidemic proportions, Courtney Love repeatedly called her late husband an "asshole" as she read his suicide note aloud. Donna Gaines, author of *Teenage*

Wasteland, a superb book on teen suicide, took a more analytic perspective in an article for *Rolling Stone.* "Despite his compassion, he wasn't an altruist who died for anybody's sins," she wrote. "His suicide was a betrayal; it negated an unspoken contract among members of a generation who depended on one another to reverse the parental generation's legacy of neglect, confusion and frustration. Cobain broke that promise. He just walked."[10] Thus was cut short Nirvana's contribution to the chapter of popular music history that bore their imprint. What makes the whole sorry story sadder is that there were role models, Sonic Youth and R.E.M., among others, that could have pointed the way for Nirvana and, perhaps, Cobain.

In some ways, Sonic Youth was to 1990s alternative what the Velvet Underground had been to 1970s punk—a formative influence with a distinctly New York posture and avant-garde tendencies. The group was formed in the early 1980s, and two of its members, guitarists Thurston Moore and Lee Ranaldo, had previously played with avant-garde musician Glenn Branca's group. From Branca's group they learned to use unconventional tunings to bend otherwise standard pop songs completely out of shape, a trademark of Sonic Youth that, in Seattle, resonated as well as the dark side of their musical vision. Sonic Youth recorded a number of albums for independent labels before being signed by DGC later in the decade. Nirvana's respect for the group was, in fact, one of the factors that made DGC attractive to them.

> In some ways, Sonic Youth was to 1990s alternative what the Velvet Underground had been to 1970s punk—a formative influence with a distinctly New York posture and avant-garde tendencies.

Sonic Youth's vocals were split between Moore and bassist Kim Gordon, who can best be described as something of a female Lou Reed with, as Rachel Felder has put it, "a deadpan combination of attitude, confidence, and an 'I dare you' mix of balls and femininity."[11] On cuts like "JC" and "Swimsuit Issue" from *Dirty* (1992), the group's second DGC album, Gordon combined an overt sexuality with uncompromisingly feminist lyrics about women's issues. In her seemingly contradictory mix of femininity and feminism, she served as a role model for many other post-punk female bands, including Babes in Toyland, L7, and Hole. "These bands . . . reject the stereotype of women as demure and innocent," Felder has noted. "Often dressed in little girls' dresses paired with 'don't-fuck-with-me' Doc Martens unisex boots, these guitar bands bolt with an intensity that never makes concessions to being female."[12] Just as it had for 1970s punk, the rules-don't-apply attitude of the alternative scene created a cultural space for women to experiment with new roles and sounds. At the time of Cobain's death, Sonic Youth had just released *Experimental Jet Set, Trash and No Star,* the group's third DGC album. At the time, Gordon and Moore were also expecting their first child, which prevented the band from touring in support of the LP. The decision to put family ahead of fame and fortune was one that Cobain should have been able to relate to, but he acted otherwise.

R.E.M. was another group Cobain could have looked to for help. Just prior to his death, he had been in regular contact with Michael Stipe, R.E.M.'s enigmatic leader.

Indeed, the two had talked about collaborating. Stipe had enormous respect for Cobain, and Cobain was an unabashed R.E.M. fan. In fact, R.E.M.'s career was the model that Cobain would have liked for Nirvana. R.E.M. had mainstream success at a pace that could be handled without the abandonment of artistic or personal integrity. At the time of Cobain's death, R.E.M. was at work on their ninth and most abrasive album, *Monster,* which was dedicated to River Phoenix, the rising young actor who had recently died of an accidental drug overdose. The group's 1992 outing, *Automatic for the People,* had already logged seventy weeks on the pop charts, after peaking at number two. R.E.M. had been formed in Athens, Georgia in 1980 as a jangly inaccessible folk rock unit, as beholden to 1960s era Byrds as to any punk influences. It might have been possible to anticipate their future success when *Rolling Stone* selected their first full-length album, *Murmur* (1983), as album of the year over Michael Jackson's *Thriller.* The *Village Voice* lavished similar "best of" praise on the LP. At the time, however, *Murmur* had only sold 150,000 copies. R.E.M. built their career slowly from the bottom up, broadening their fan base through live performances and support on college radio. From *Murmur* on, most of R.E.M.'s albums sold slightly better than the one before. In 1987, *Document* became the band's first million seller, prompting a move from independent IRS to major Warner. *Green,* the group's 1988 major label debut, occasioned their first arena level tour. *Out of Time* (1991) became their first album to reach number one, making it, along with *Nevermind,* one of the releases that pushed major labels into taking alternative acts more seriously. *Out of Time* actually beat out *Nevermind* in 1991 for the Grammy Award for Best Alternative Music.

R.E.M. has enjoyed success at a pace they could handle without compromising their artistic or personal integrity. If Kurt Cobain could have done likewise, it might have changed the course of his life.

The band also received nominations for Album of the Year, Record of the Year, and Song of the Year, the recording industry's highest pop honors, which further erased the distinction between alternative and mainstream. In all, R.E.M., which had never been nominated for a Grammy before, tallied seven nominations in 1991, more than any other performer, and walked away with additional trophies for Best Pop Performance and Best Short-Form Video for "Losing My Religion," *Out of Time*'s hit single.

Throughout their career, R.E.M. have kept their personal lives out of the limelight and have tried to be musically and politically progressive. Michael Stipe, for example, has been involved with environmental causes, animal rights, and antinuclear campaigns. He also founded his own nonprofit film company, C-00, which has produced public service announcements about AIDS, homelessness, and racism. A number of the group's songs have had explicitly political themes. For example, "Fall on Me" (from *Life's Rich Pageant,* 1986) deals with acid rain, *Document*'s "Welcome to the Occupation," protests U.S. intervention in Central America, and "Ignoreland" is an anti-Republican anthem from *Automatic for the People.* Other songs, such as "The One I Love," which deals with opportunism in love, "Losing My Religion," which was banned in Ireland, and "I Took Your Name," which concerns relationships that can breed resentment, have leaned more toward the politics of the personal.

For a group with the longevity and achievement of R.E.M., their career has been remarkably trouble free. Of course, there have been a few bumps on the road to success. While members proclaimed early on that they would never play arenas or lip sync, to the dismay of some diehard fans, they broke both vows with the *Green* tour and the video for "Losing My Religion." Still, on the cooptation scale, these were fairly minor infractions. Overall, it has been a testament to the strength of the group's fan loyalty and artistic staying power that, some fifteen years later, R.E.M. was still being reviewed as a model of musical integrity.

Marketing Categories and Monster Contracts

The mainstream acceptance of alternative bands was music to the ears of major record company executives who smacked their corporate lips at the prospect of dozens of small regional scenes with the potential to go national. In the fractured world of fringe music, however, it could be difficult to find one's way without a road map. Thus, by the early 1990s, genre mapping had become something of a journalistic cottage industry as the mainstream press tried to chart a course to the next big thing. These attempts provided uninitiated consumers with some kind of tool, however nonsensical, for positioning a new group that may have been the product

> The mainstream acceptance of alternative bands was music to the ears of major record company executives who smacked their corporate lips at the prospect of dozens of small regional scenes with the potential to go national.

R.E.M. could have been role models for Cobain, Nirvana

of a local or regional scene and gave record companies a marketing hook upon which to hang a promotional campaign.

As early as 1991, the *Boston Globe* organized the hip popular music landscape as:

- Post-Punk (XTC, the Cure)
- Hardcore-Punk (Black Flag, SS Decontrol)
- Punk-Folk (Billy Bragg)
- Power-Pop (Material Issue)
- Thrash/Speed-Metal (Metallica, Megadeth, Slayer)
- Goth-Rock (Bauhaus)
- Doom-and-Gloom (Joy Division)
- Art-Metal (Public Image, Ltd., Jane's Addiction)
- Punk-Funk/Funk-Rock (Red Hot Chili Peppers, Faith No More, Living Colour)
- Neo-Psychedelic (Jesus Jones)
- Acid-House (no stars)
- Dancehall-Reggae (Shabba Ranks, Yellowman)
- Hip-Hop (Public Enemy, MC Hammer)
- Gangsta Rap (Ice T, N.W.A., Ice Cube)
- Hard-Alternative (Fishbone, Primus, King's X)
- Psychobilly (Cramps)
- Glam-Rock (Poison)
- Space-Rock (Kraftwerk, Guru Guru)
- Cyber-Rock (Rush, Voivod)
- Shock-Rock (GWAR)
- Bar-Band Rock (Bruce Springsteen, Stompers, Beaver Brown)
- Garage-Rock (Lyres)
- Arena-Rock (Bon Jovi, Cinderella, Scorpions)
- World Music (Kassav, Fela Kuti)[13]

Two years later, the *Globe* embellished current dance styles:

- Hip-Hop (Queen Latifah)
- House (C+C Music Factory)
- Hippy House (Charlatans [UK])
- Techno (808 State)
- Industrial (Ministry)
- Gothic (the Cure)[14]

In 1992, an *Entertainment Weekly* cover story on the new rock weighed in with the following categories:

- Dream Pop (the Cure, The Jesus and Mary Chain)
- Death Metal (Death, Cadaver, Carcass)
- Alternative Rap (De La Soul, P. M. Dawn, Jungle Brothers)
- Goth (the Cure, Sisters of Mercy)
- Grunge (Nirvana, Sonic Youth, L7)
- Industrial (Ministry, Skinny Puppy, Nine Inch Nails)

- Jangle Pop (R.E.M., the Smithereens)
- Pranksters (Butthole Surfers, GWAR)
- Thrashcore (Rollins Band, Soundgarden)
- Funk and Roll (Red Hot Chili Peppers, Jane's Addiction, Living Colour)
- U.K. Dance Pop (EMF, Soup Dragons)[15]

For groups that did not fit into any of these categories, there was still the catchall term "alternative," but the speed with which alternative forms were absorbed into the mainstream increased as quickly as the number of categories. The success that it took R.E.M. twelve years and seven albums to build and Nirvana four years and three albums came to Pearl Jam on their first outing. By the time the Seattle-based grunge explosion had made its full impact, "alternative" had virtually become its own mainstream marketing category.

By the time the Seattle-based grunge explosion had made its full impact, "alternative" had virtually become its own mainstream marketing category.

Interestingly, the success of groups ranging from Living Colour to Nirvana did not cause the music industry to alter its marketing strategies in the least. "Instead of investing in and nurturing a wide range of new talents," observed Anthony DeCurtis in 1992, "record companies are betting wildly like drunks at the roulette table, hoping that one big score—whether by an old favorite or a new lucky number—will cover all past debts."[16] Ever since the success of Michael Jackson's *Thriller* in the early 1980s, the music industry had clung to a conception of artist development that demanded eventual superstardom. Consequently, even with the acceptance of a rather broad range of genres pointing toward a decentralized grassroots strategy, record companies continued to hang on to the concept, ponying up millions for contracts in the 1990s that were surely unprecedented, perhaps unrecoverable.

Janet Jackson started the ball rolling when she switched from A&M to Virgin in 1991. With only two albums (admittedly both were number one on the charts) and one tour, she scored a reported $30 million deal. At the time, Richard Branson, chairman of Virgin Records, compared the signing to buying a Rembrandt. Columbia's Don Ienner put it more honestly (if more crassly) on the eve of Mariah Carey's platinum debut. "We don't look at Mariah Carey as a dance-pop artist," he said. "We look at her as a franchise."[17] (According to this logic, her subsequent marriage to label head Tommy Mottola must have been a corporate merger.) Columbia also saw new value in Aerosmith. When Aerosmith had left Columbia for Geffen in 1985, the band was broke. In 1991, they signed a new deal with Columbia worth upwards of $30 million. That same year, Mötley Crüe renewed their agreement with Elektra for a $25 million guarantee to be paid over four albums. ZZ Top scored $30 million at RCA. The Rolling Stones topped all of these with a $40 million, three-album deal with Virgin. As large as these contracts may seem, they paled in comparison with the deals that were eventually offered to Madonna, Michael Jackson, and Prince, all of which were reportedly worth more than $60 million in guarantees.

Mariah Carey was considered a hot property at Columbia from the moment she was signed. She lived up to expectations when her multi-platinum self-titled debut album brought her the Best New Artist and Best Pop Vocal Performance, Female, Grammys in 1990.

Interestingly, the biggest superstars failed to sell like superstars. New releases by Madonna and Prince (who, after his adoption of an unpronounceable name, was called "the artist formerly known as Prince") rose and fell on the charts as never before. Prince sustained himself with three greatest hits packages; Madonna, with a fifty dollar "art" book (*Sex*) of suggestive photographs of herself. Pearl Jam outsold Michael Jackson. In fact, the huge contracts had little to do with the current sales figures of any one artist; they were instead the result of changes in the industry as a whole.

In 1993, according to the International Federation of the Phonogram Industry (IFPI), the international music business topped $30 billion in worldwide sales. The largest percentage of these sales was generated by U.S.-based but, with the exception of Time-Warner, no longer U.S.-owned record companies. Beginning in the late 1980s, record companies were bought and sold in a speculative atmosphere that pushed their value beyond reason. Big record companies bought smaller ones at prices that started at astronomical and increased galactically. In 1988, MCA bought Motown for $60 million. A few years later, Polygram purchased A&M and Island for more than $300 million each. Then MCA shelled out an inexplicable $545 million for Geffen Records. These huge recording combines were, in turn, bought by larger multinational electronics firms in a trajectory that was even more unbelievable. When Sony bought CBS Records in 1988 for $2 billion, it was the biggest record company sale in the history of the industry. Only two years later, however, Matsushita forked over a whopping $6.6 billion for MCA and its affiliated labels. Figures like these had a significant effect on the way that major artists negotiated their contracts. "When you hear that your record company has been sold for 20 or 30 times its earnings," said Tim Collins, Aerosmith's manager, "you think, 'I want a piece of that.'"[18] The sale of so many record companies for such incredible sums of money led artists to begin to think of themselves as major factors in the overall profitability of a company, a thought that had not been factored into contract negotiations prior to this. A new realization of the value of catalogue sales simply added to the performer's awareness of their role in profitability.

Back catalogue has always been a valuable commodity because when an artist has a hit record, it often boosts the sales of his or her previous recordings. Following Kurt Cobain's death, Sub Pop reaped an unexpected windfall when sales of *Bleach* jumped from 150,000 copies to 800,000. With the advent of the compact disc, the industry had slowly shifted to a new standard, and back catalogue became even more important as consumers began buying recordings they already owned in the new configuration. In the early 1990s, catalogue sales were estimated to be as much as 40 percent of all album sales. Thus, for many artists, back catalogue was their most valuable asset. Aerosmith, for example, had recorded seven Top Forty albums on Columbia before switching to Geffen. According to the group's original contract with Columbia, the rights to previous recordings reverted to the group after twenty years. Had Columbia not managed to pull them back from Geffen, it would have lost not only earnings from the band's current popularity but also any interest in previous recordings. Knowing this, Aerosmith managed to negotiate a very good deal.

For both artists and companies, a second and perhaps more attractive aspect of back catalogue came from the practice of linking particular groups and songs with particular films or products. The success of *Singles,* both the movie and the soundtrack, again demonstrated the value of cross-media marketing and the symbiotic relationship between film and popular song. Advertising proved to be even more lucrative. If the Beatles' "Revolution" could be used to sell sneakers and Dylan's "The Times They Are A'Changin'" could jazz up the image of an accounting firm, it was hard to imagine that Nirvana's "Smells Like Teen Spirit" would not be used to sell something at some point.

Country and R&B: The Other Alternatives

All the talk about big contracts, all the time and energy spent in policing rap and heavy metal, and all the column inches devoted to alternative music tended to obscure the biggest commercial breakthrough of the 1990s—country music. If the early part of the 1990s belonged to any one artist, it was Garth Brooks of country music fame. *Billboard* listed Brooks as Top Pop Album Artist and Top Country Album Artist for the years 1991, 1992, and 1993. In 1992, NBC aired a Garth Brooks special opposite a CBS Michael Jackson special. Jackson placed sixty-sixth in the ratings while Brooks finished among the ten highest rated shows. In

All the talk about big contracts, all the time and energy spent in policing rap and heavy metal, and all the column inches devoted to alternative music tended to obscure the biggest commercial breakthrough of the 1990s—country music.

1993, all six of his albums—*Garth Brooks, No Fences, Ropin' the Wind, In Pieces, Beyond the Season,* and *The Chase*—could be found among the 100 most popular albums of the year. By the end of the year, *No Fences* and *Ropin' the Wind* had sold about 10 million copies each. It was Brooks' *Ropin' the Wind* that caused the industry to stand up and take notice. Released in September 1991, *Ropin' the Wind* went straight to number one (the first country album to do so in ten years) and remained there for eight weeks despite challenges from Hammer and Guns 'N' Roses. U2's *Achtung Baby* unseated the album for one week, Michael Jackson's *Dangerous* held the position over Christmastime, and Nirvana hit the top slot for a week in January 1992, but following that, *Ropin' the Wind* regained the number one position for another ten weeks.

Brooks was neither your average superstar nor your average country singer. A paunchy, slightly balding singer from Yukon, Oklahoma, he made it big with no major tale of woe to hang his considerable hat on. While there is no question that he was exposed early on to country greats like Merle Haggard and George Jones, his tastes ran as far afield as Kiss, Kansas, ELO, and Styx. His music is to be distinguished from the music of such "new traditionalists" as Ricky Skaggs and Emmylou Harris, both of whom achieved a certain amount of crossover appeal in the early 1980s by updating honky-tonk heroes like Hank Williams and Lefty Frizzell, as well as from the embarrassment of country riches that followed the success of *Urban Cowboy*. Brooks came from a generation of country artists whose blend of folk, country, and rock 'n' roll ran the gamut from the songs of singer/songwriter James Taylor to the mellow country rock of the Eagles to the raucous southern boogie of Lynyrd Skynyrd. His performance style was steeped in the arena rock aesthetic, including theater smoke, fireworks, and sophisticated lighting effects. Teenagers wearing Megadeth and Cinderella T-shirts have been known to attend his shows.

Garth Brooks, more than any other artist, dominated the early 1990s and turned country music into the biggest commercial breakthrough of the decade. With his roots in the country tradition, he packs his live performances with all the glitz of an arena rock show.

Needless to say, Brooks' fame caused a shake up in Nashville and highlighted a generation gap in country music. Not only was he a best selling country artist under the age of forty (indeed, the ten best selling country artists of 1992 were all under the age of forty), but his material challenged some of country music's most sacred cows. In 1991, The Nashville Network (TNN) refused to air the video of "The Thunder Rolls," which ends with a woman shooting her abusive husband. "We Shall Be Free" was written as a response to the Rodney King beating and includes lines supportive of gay rights. After completing the video for the single, Brooks played two benefits that raised $1 million for South Central Los Angeles and shrugged off any criticism of his actions as "Garth-bashing." He also defended his music as real country. "No one could doubt that we did country music," he told one interviewer in 1993. "One thing was who I surrounded myself with: two guys from Kansas, three from Oklahoma. Out in front you've got steel guitar, fiddle, you got hats, we're all wearing Wranglers and Ropers." While he acknowledged the arena rock mentality of his shows ("I got guys smashing guitars, I got guys doing leads while running across the stage"), he came back to what, for him, was the bottom line, the fact that he and his band were "just a bunch of country bumpkins who got lucky. And *know* that they got lucky."[19]

Brooks' crossover triumph opened up unprecedented space on the pop charts for other country artists. Between 1991 and 1994, Clint Black, Reba McIntyre, Travis Tritt, Vince Gil, Trisha Yearwood, Dwight Yoakam, Mary Chapin Carpenter, George Strait, and Billy Ray Cyrus could all be found among the best selling pop artists of the year. By 1992, country radio had become the second most listened to music format in the country. It had an 11.6 percent share of the market, which was second only to adult contemporary's 18.1 share. TNN's 1.6 cable channel share of the market may not have set any records, but it was higher than MTV's 0.6 percent piece of the action.

Rounding out the musical preferences of the early 1990s were r&b vocal styles that combined the smooth balladry of Luther Vandross (a consistent pop best seller) with the hip-hop harmonies of groups like Boyz II Men, Color Me Badd, Jodeci, and Silk. Thus, the pop landscape of the early 1990s offered a surprising diversity. In addition to the predictable pop of such artists as Mariah Carey and Michael Bolton and the continuing in-your-face presence of rap and heavy metal, there was also a country boom and something of a resurgence of r&b, as well as an explosion of a whole range of alternative sounds. Still, if music had become more diverse than ever, the barriers separating the fans from one another seemed to be quite intact. At the end of 1992, Anthony DeCurtis lamented that "no one was truly able—or much interested in making the effort—to reach across

> *T*he pop landscape of the early 1990s offered a surprising diversity. In addition to the predictable pop of such artists as Mariah Carey and Michael Bolton and the continuing in-your-face presence of rap and heavy metal, there was also a country boom and something of a resurgence of r&b, as well as an explosion of a whole range of alternative sounds.

boundaries and address what many people have come to envision as the new multicultural America. Some people believe that a coming together of the tribes may not even be possible anymore."[20]

Lollapalooza: Countercultural Sensibilities, Mainstream Clout

One enterprise that did make the effort with some success was Lollapalooza, an annualized alternative festival of cutting-edge music, media, and culture that began in 1991. From a certain point of view, rap, metal, and alternative developed separately at least in part because the industry that produced them, like society at large, was divided along lines of race and culture. It could easily be argued that the fans who listen to rap, metal, and alternative had a fair amount in common, including, certainly, their age and alienation from the establishment. After all, these styles were themselves united in their commitment to transgression—transgression of musical conventions, transgression of societal values, transgression of behavioral norms. If rap, metal, and alternative were already individually threatening and controversial, what could be more upsetting than putting them all together? No doubt these thoughts crossed the mind of Perry Farrell, the leader of Jane's Addiction, when he organized the first Lollapalooza festival.

If rap, metal, and alternative were already individually threatening and controversial, what could be more upsetting than putting them all together? No doubt these thoughts crossed the mind of Perry Farrell, the leader of Jane's Addiction, when he organized the first Lollapalooza festival.

The idea of Lollapalooza came to Farrell and booking agent Marc Geiger in 1990 while they were in Europe marveling at the routine success of annual multi-act summer music festivals like the Reading Festival in England. While these types of festivals had never caught on in the United States in any big way, Farrell and Geiger felt certain they could pull one off and joined forces with Ted Gardner and Don Mullen to do so, picking the worst concert season in recent memory to launch the event. Jane's Addiction, who had recently broken into the Top Twenty with their album *Ritual de lo Habitual*, headlined the event. It was, in fact, the group's farewell tour (or, perhaps, parting shot) as Farrell moved on to begin work with his new group, Porno for Pyros. Other acts included Living Colour, Nine Inch Nails, Ice-T and Body Count, the Henry Rollins Band, the Butthole Surfers, and Siouxsie and the Banshees. In a summer when mainstream acts flopped or lost money on multiple dates, the seven-act, twenty-one city tour—assault, really—played to a total of 430,000 people and grossed $10 million. "Lollapalooza became," as *Boston Globe* critic Jim Sullivan wrote, "the surprise smash summer tour of 1991, an artistic success and a substantial moneymaker in a recession-plagued season."[21]

To capture the unifying element that seemed to run through the tour, The *New York Times* titled Jon Pareles' review, "Howls of Rage." Henry Rollins delivered the vein-popping punk fury that had characterized his stage demeanor since fronting Black Flag in the early 1980s. The Butthole Surfers bashed away at acid-induced, punk-influenced three-chord garage rock. Over a mechanized industrial beat, Trent Reznor continued the nihilistic rants that had pushed Nine Inch Nails' *Pretty Hate Machine* to platinum sales. Siouxsie and the Banshees, the only female-fronted act, carried forward the punk spirit of an earlier generation. (The tour boosted the group's new LP, *Superstition,* into the weekly Top 100 albums.) Living Colour delivered messages about everything from racism to the environment and their music was as scorching as ever. Jane's Addiction matched them in fury and multicultural influences, drifting, in Pareles' words, "from heavy metal stomps to scrabbling funk to finger-picking folk rock. . . . Mr. Perkins added a touch of Latin Timbales to rock rhythms, while Morgan Fichter on violin brought hints of country and Arabic music to some songs."[22] In many ways, however, it was Ice-T who put the show over the top, both musically and politically. After rapping for half his set, he brought out his new thrash metal band Body Count for the second half. It was at Lollapalooza that he first performed "Cop Killer," the song that got him in so much political hot water one year later. Like the Butthole Surfers, he openly brandished firearms on stage, vowing to avenge police brutality. In Atlanta, he tested the limits of racial tolerance when he teamed up with Farrell for a provocative version of Sly Stone's "Don't Call Me Nigger, Whitey." "That was really intense," remarked an awestruck Henry Rollins.

Perhaps more than its music, what made Lollapalooza "alternative" was the continual projection of political messages concerning everything from censorship to the Gulf War and the presence of many left-leaning activist organizations. Among the organizations present at the festival, which occurred in the midst of the Bush administration, were the National Abortion Rights Action League; Refuse and Resist; the Hyacinth Foundation; an AIDS group; and Handgun Control, Inc. (apparently Ice-T and the Surfers did not get the message of that organization). The tour may well have been an early harbinger of the slight shift to the left that accompanied Clinton's election the following year (a shift that was more than undone in the Republican landslide in the midterm elections of 1994). The potential for making an impact at the polls in an election year was not wasted on festival organizers the following year. "We got a lot of people registered [to vote] last year," Don Mullen said, "and this year signing people up is even more important."[23] The political booths for Lollapalooza '92 included Rock the Vote and College Democrats as well as the more radical gay activist organization ACT-UP, the militant environmental organization Greenpeace, the controversial animal rights group PETA (People for the Ethical Treatment of Animals), the Cannabis Action Network, and the Coalition for the Homeless.

Because the first festival had been such a success, the production group for Lollapalooza '92 initially tried to land bigger (and more mainstream) headliners like Neil

> *Perhaps more than its music, what made Lollapalooza "alternative" was the continual projection of political messages concerning everything from censorship to the Gulf War and the presence of many left-leaning activist organizations.*

Young and R.E.M. and expanded the festival from a twenty-one city tour to a thirty-six city tour. In some ways, organizers felt like they had to settle for a lineup that included the Red Hot Chili Peppers, Pearl Jam, Soundgarden, Ice Cube, Ministry, The Jesus and Mary Chain, and Lush. In the five months it took to put the show together, however, the vagaries of pop stardom smiled on the event. By the time the tour hit the road, Pearl Jam's *Ten* and the Chili Peppers' *Blood Sugar Sex Magik* were both riding the Top Ten, peaking at numbers two and three respectively. At that moment, either group could have sold out shows the size of Lollapalooza. Furthermore, Soundgarden's *Badmotorfinger* had already gone Top Forty, and Ice Cube's *Death Certificate,* which had peaked at number two, was still riding the charts. The festival nearly doubled its audience (to 800,000) and its take (to $19 million) and propelled Ministry's *Psalm 69* into the Top Thirty. The 1992 festival also featured a second stage for lesser known acts like Cypress Hill, the Boo Yaa Tribe, and Sharkbait.

The Red Hot Chili Peppers provided some of the most interesting music on the tour, its sound recalling at times early hip-hop sources like Jimmy Castor and Parliament-Funkadelic grafted onto heavy metal. Lead singer Anthony Kiedis hovered somewhere between rapping and singing. Formed in the early 1980s, the group had been a part of the Los Angeles underground for years. "Loved and scorned in equal measure as tattooed punk-funk loons obsessed with the horizontal rumba," David Fricke has said, "the Chili Peppers are skateboard-culture heroes, recognized even by their detractors as early pioneers of the mosh-pit marriage of funk, rap, and thrash that Living Colour and Faith No More took to the bank."[24] Following their self-titled debut LP in 1984, they recorded *Freaky Styley* and *The Uplift Mofo Party Plan* before hitting pay dirt with *Mothers Milk* in 1989. During this period, the band struggled through the death of guitarist Hillel Slovak, which was caused by a heroin overdose, and Kiedis' own heroin addiction. *Blood Sugar Sex Magik* marked the group's Warner debut in 1991. "Under the Bridge," the unlikely hit single that kicked them into the Top Ten, detailed Kiedis' ordeal with drugs.

In terms of musical range, Lollapalooza '92 was similar to its predecessor. Although there were differences between them, Pearl Jam and Soundgarden carried the banner of Seattle grunge. Pearl Jam was a safer, more straightforward blend of heavy metal and psychedelic rock. The group's lead singer, Eddie Vedder was dark and brooding as he agonized over questions of sanity and personal existence. Soundgarden was more dissonant with irregular tempos and time signatures. Lead singer Chris Cornell segued from angry growls to high piercing tones. Concerned about Ice-T's removal of "Cop Killer" from *Body Count,* Soundgarden performed the song. Ice Cube, the reigning king of gangsta rap, supported the sentiment with a new rap line, "Rappers don't kill people. Cops do." Ministry dispensed industrial rock with as many as four guitars pounding frenzied riffs. The Jesus and Mary Chain played nihilistic Ramones-derived punk. Lush supplied the only female voices of the day, offering ethereal introspective punkish folk rock.

By the time Lollapalooza '92 hit the road Pearl Jam was so well known that the alternative festival was well on its way to becoming a mainstay of the summer concert circuit. Lead singer Eddie Vedder is held aloft by the crowd as he explores the darker side of life.

As varied as the music was, however, there was already a kind of formula mentality setting in. Anthony Kiedis, in particular, was critical of the 1992 lineup, insisting it was "way too male" and, especially on the main stage, "way too guitar-oriented."[25] By 1993, the festival had become an institution. Headline positions on the main stage became slots to be filled. Alice in Chains replaced Soundgarden, just as Dinosaur Jr. occupied Pearl Jam's slot. (Nirvana spurned the event.) Arrested Development, with their multi-platinum 1992 debut album, *3 Years 5 months & 2 days in the Life of . . .* , still on the charts, represented rap as Ice Cube and Ice-T had done in years past. Fishbone, from Los Angeles, was the West Coast ska to gospel to heavy metal answer to New York's Living Colour. Front 242 took over the industrial niche vacated by Ministry and Nine Inch Nails. Primus closed the show, although not as successfully as the Red Hot Chili Peppers, with snappy, quirky, quasi-funk. Again there was only one female act, Babes in Toyland, a group from Minneapolis. With Perry Farrell playing a lesser creative role, Lollapalooza '93 became, in the words of critic Steve Pond, "the year Lollapalooza doesn't like to talk about."[26]

> **A**s varied as the music was there was already a kind of formula mentality setting in.By 1993, the festival had become an institution. Headline positions on the main stage became slots to be filled.

By 1993, Lollapalooza had become so successful that other artists began to develop alternatives to the alternative festival, the most notable of which was called Alternative Nation. The tour featured the Spin Doctors, Soul Asylum, and Screening Trees. By tour time, the Spin Doctors' 1991 debut *A Pocket Full of Kryptonite* had gotten a second wind, which propelled it to platinum status. Soul Asylum's *Grave Dancer's Union* had already gone platinum. The group's video for the single "Runaway Train" featured listings of missing children and led to a gig at the White House as President Clinton signed the youth service bill. Screening Trees' *Sweet Oblivion* album and "Nearly Lost You" single from the *Singles* soundtrack announced the group's arrival after eight years and six albums. Like Lollapalooza, Alternative Nation was a summer-long tour that played to hundreds of thousands of fans in sold-out shows across the country. It was dubbed by *Rolling Stone* "the Little Lollapalooza that Could." Cute!

In 1994, Farrell again played an active role in planning, and Lollapalooza regained its artistic footing. Nirvana had agreed to play, but the commitment was derailed by Cobain's suicide. Still, the festival featured Smashing Pumpkins, the Beastie Boys, George Clinton and the P-Funk All Stars, the Breeders, A Tribe Called Quest, L7, Green Day, and others. Because Smashing Pumpkins' *Siamese Dream* was already double platinum and the Beastie Boys' *Ill Communication* entered the charts at number one before the tour began, the festival was as vulnerable as its predecessors had been to the criticism of being too mainstream. However, the fact is that all the Lollapalooza tours crossed lines of class, race, and gender in ways that most tours would have avoided like the plague. On the whole, each festival has presented a reasonably representative cross section of what was going on musically in youth culture, and each has done so with far more heart and spontaneity than the festival held on the twenty-fifth anniversary of Woodstock. Because Woodstock '94 performances were broadcast only on pay-per-view, MTV was temporarily reduced to the rock equivalent of the Home Shopping Network with its incessant merchandising schemes. It was the ultimate corporate extravaganza.

Because Woodstock '94 performances were broadcast only on pay-per-view, MTV was temporarily reduced to the rock equivalent of the Home Shopping Network with its incessant merchandising schemes. It was the ultimate corporate extravaganza.

In the final analysis, it is unrealistic to expect any alternative to remain alternative for long within a market economy. A market economy depends on the presentation of something new to stimulate consumer demand. Thus, there is a constant need to absorb and mass market anything that appears fresh, which, over time, deadens its appeal. In the absence of lasting structural realignments that would change this situation, the best that can be expected is a continual dialectic of renewal and incorporation. In popular music, the recording industry has learned to absorb innovative sounds and images with remarkable speed and efficiency.

Those who would seek to create an alternative must stay one step ahead of this process as they search for longer term solutions to the problem of incorporation. In the meantime, the music that rock 'n' roll sired continually folds in upon itself as innovative artists try to marry old sources to new forms and thereby breathe new life into the music that has mattered so much to so many for so long. In 1990, Living Colour tried to revisit rock history by including in Time's Up a single titled "Elvis Is Dead," which included a guest rap by Little Richard, one of the African American rock 'n' rollers who might have been king. In 1994, the circle was completed in a gesture that was as wildly symbolic as it was culturally unlikely: Michael Jackson, the African American superstar who had usurped the title "King of Pop" through the arduous process (both artistic and cosmetic) of trying to erase the distinctions between black and white, married Lisa Marie Presley, the daughter of the dead white rock 'n' roller who had been crowned king of rock 'n' roll at the very moment that countless unsung black artists were ushering in the era that would define popular music for the second half of the twentieth century. That the marriage would not last only made it a more appropriate metaphor for the ephemeral nature of popular music. After all, it was only rock 'n' roll, but we liked it.

NOTES

1. Mikal Gilmore, "The Year in Music." *Rolling Stone,* 13–27 December 1990, p. 13.
2. Ibid., 17.
3. Ibid.
4. Ibid.
5. Rachel Felder, *Manic Pop Thrill* (Hopewell, N.J.: Echo Press, 1993), 3.
6. Ibid., 69.
7. Kim Neely, "Into the Unknown," *Rolling Stone,* 16 June 1994, p. 117.
8. Anthony DeCurtis, "Kurt Cobain, 1967–1994," *Rolling Stone,* 2 June 1994, p. 30.
9. David Fricke, "Kurt Cobain," *Rolling Stone,* 27 January 1994, p. 36.
10. Donna Gaines, "Suicidal Tendencies: Kurt Did Not Die for You," *Rolling Stone,* 2 June 1994, p. 67.
11. Felder, *Manic Pop Thrill,* 77.
12. Ibid., 78.
13. Jim Miller, "It's Not Only Rock 'n' Roll," *Boston Globe,* 23 August 1991, pp. 93–94.
14. Michael Saunders, "Getting Hip to Pop," *Boston Globe,* 9 May 1993, p. B1.
15. David Browne, "Turn That @#!% Down: The Complete (Idiot's) Guide to the Future of Rock & Roll," *Entertainment Weekly,* 21 August 1992, pp. 16–25.
16. Anthony DeCurtis, "The Year in Music," *Rolling Stone,* 10–24 December 1992, p. 26.
17. "1990 Yearbook," *Rolling Stone,* 13–27 December 1990, p. 72.
18. Fred Goodman, "Big Deals: How Money Fever Is Changing the Music Business," *Musician,* January 1992, p. 42.
19. Anthony DeCurtis, "Ropin' the Whirl Wind," *Rolling Stone,* 1 April 1993, p. 35.
20. DeCurtis, "The Year in Music," 24.

21. Jim Sullivan, "Lollapalooza: The Sound of Success," *The Boston Globe,* 2 August 1992, p. B25.

22. Jon Pareles, "Howls of Rage, Nine Hours Worth, at Waterloo Village," *New York Times,* 13 August 1991, p. C13.

23. Peter Watrous, "Good Things Happen to Lollapalooza," *New York Times,* 5 August 1992, p. C13.

24. David Fricke, "Red Hot Chili Peppers' Naked Truth," *Rolling Stone,* 25 June 1992, p. 29.

25. Ibid., 29.

26. Steve Pond, "The Trick Is to Be Loved but Not Embraced," *New York Times,* 26 June 1994, sec. 2, p. 28.

Bibliography

Ackerman, Paul. "Gortikov Scorches Whitey Trade in NATRA Speech." *Billboard,* 17 July 1969.

Alexander, David. " Giving the Devil More Than His Due." *The Humanist* (March/April 1990).

Allen, Harry. "Hip Hop Madness: From Def Jams to Cold Lampin', Rap Is Our Music." *Essence,* April 1989.

"American Revolution 1969. "*Rolling Stone,* special insert, 5 April 1969.

Ansen, David. "Rock Tycoon." *Newsweek,* 31 July 1978.

Archer, Gleason L. *History of Radio to 1926.* New York: American Historical Society, 1938.

"ASCAP Defied." *Business Week,* 16 November 1940.

Bangs, Lester. "The White Noise Supremacists" *Village Voice,* 30 April 1979.

Barlow, William. "Cashing In." In *Split Image: African Americans in the Mass Media, Second Edition,* ed. Jannette L. Dates and William Barlow. Washington, D.C.: Howard University Press, 1993.

Barnouw, Erik. *The Golden Web: A History of Broadcasting in the United States, 1933–1953.* New York: Oxford University Press, 1968.

Belz, Carl, *The Story of Rock.* 2d ed. New York: Harper Colophon, 1971.

Bennett, Tony, et al., eds. *Rock and Popular Music: Politics, Policies, Institutions.* New York: Routledge, 1993.

Berry, Robert J. "Satanism: The Law Enforcement Response." *The National Sheriff,* February/March, 1987.

Biafra, Jello. "The Far Right and the Censorship of Music." *Harvard Law Record* (17 April 1987).

"The Birth of Our Popular Songs." *Literary Digest* (7 October 1916).

Bondi, Vic. "Feeding Noise Back into the System: Hardcore, Hip Hop, and Heavy Metal." Paper presented at the New England American Studies Association Conference, Brandeis University, Boston, Mass., 1 May 1993.

Brack, Ray. "James Brown." *Rolling Stone,* 21 January 1970.

Brackett, David. "The Politics and Practice of 'Crossover' in American Popular Music, 1963 to 1965." *The Musical Quarterly* (Winter, 1994).

Breskin, David. "Bob Geldof: The Rolling Stone Interview." *Rolling Stone,* 5 December 1985.

Bricker, Rebecca. "Take One." *People,* 4 April 1983.

Broven, John, *Rhythm and Blues in New Orleans.* Gretna, La.: Pelican Publishing Co., 1988.

Browne, David. "Turn That @#!% Down: The Complete Idiot's Guide to the Future of Rock & Roll." *Entertainment Weekly,* 21 August 1992.

Carr, Tim. "Talk That Talk, Walk That Walk." *Rolling Stone*, 26 May 1983.

"To Censor Popular Songs." *Literary Digest,* (24 May 1913).

Chambers, Iain. *Urban Rhythms: Popular Music and Popular Culture.* New York: Macmillan, 1985.

Chapple, Steve, and Reebee Garofalo. *Rock 'n' Roll Is Here to Pay: The History and Politics of the Music Industry.* Chicago: Nelson-Hall, 1977.

Christgau, Georgia. "Disco! Disco! Disco! Four Critics Address the Musical Question." *In These Times,* 6–12 June 1979.

Christgau, Robert. *Any Old Way You Choose It: Rock and Other Pop Music, 1967–1973.* Baltimore, Md.: Penguin Books, 1973.

———. "A Cult Explodes — and A Movement is Born." *Village Voice,* 24 October 1977.

Clarke, Donald, ed. *The Penguin Encyclopedia of Popular Music.* New York: Viking, 1989.

Coleman, Mark. "The Revival of Conscience." *Rolling Stone,* 15 November 1990.

Considine, J. D. "Led Zeppelin." *Rolling Stone,* 20 September 1990.

———. "Metal Mania." *Rolling Stone,* 15 November 1990.

Cripps, Thomas. "Film." In *Split Image: African Americans in the Mass Media, Second Edition*, ed. Jannette L. Dates and William Barlow. Washington, D.C.: Howard University Press, 1993.

Cross, Brian. *It's Not about a Salary: Rap, Race and Resistance in Los Angeles.* New York: Verso, 1993.

Cummings, Sue. "Road Warriors." *Spin*, August 1986.

Dates, Jannette L., and William Barlow, eds. *Split Image: African Americans in the Mass Media, Second Edition.* Washington, D.C.: Howard University Press, 1993.

Dawson, Jim, and Steve Propes. *What Was the First Rock 'n' Roll Record.* Boston: Faber and Faber, 1992.

DeCurtis, Anthony. "The Eagles." *Rolling Stone,* 20 September 1990.

———. "The Year in Music." *Rolling Stone,* 10–24 December 1992.

———. "Ropin' the Whirl Wind." *Rolling Stone,* 1 April 1993.

———. "Kurt Cobain, 1967–1994." *Rolling Stone,* 2 June 1994.

DeCurtis, Anthony, and James Henke, eds. *The Rolling Stone Illustrated History of Rock & Roll.* New York: Random House, 1992.

de Forest, Lee. *Father of Radio.* Chicago: Wilcox and Follett, 1950.

Denisoff, R. Serge and Richard A. Peterson, eds. *The Sounds of Socila Change: Studies in Popular Culture.* New York: Rand McNally, 1972.

Denselow, Robin. *When the Music's Over: The Story of Political Pop.* Boston: Faber and Faber, 1989.

Dexter, D. "1935–1945, Disk Jockey: Origin of the Species." *Billboard, 27* December 1969.

Draper, Robert. *Rolling Stone Magazine.* New York: Harper and Row, 1990.

Eisen, Jonathan, ed. *The Age of Rock.* New York: Vintage Books, 1969.

Ennis, Philip. *The Seventh Stream: The Emergence of Rocknroll in American Popular Music.* Hanover, N.H.: Wesleyan University Press/University Press of New England, 1992.

Farrar, Richard. "Da Doo Ron Ron." *Rolling Stone,* 11 May 1968.

Feld, Steven. "Notes on World Beat." *Public Culture Bulletin* (Fall 1988).

Felder, Rachel. *Manic Pop Thrill.* Hopewell, N.J.: Echo Press, 1993.

Fong-Torres, Ben, ed. *The Rolling Stone Interviews.* 2 vols. New York: Warner Books, 1973.

———. "The Rolling Stone Interview: Ray Charles." *Rolling Stone,* 18 January 1973.

Fox, Ted. *In the Groove.* New York: St. Martin's Press, 1986.

———. *Showtime at the Apollo.* New York: Holt, Rinehart and Winston, 1983.

Fricke, David. "Kurt Cobain." *Rolling Stone,* 27 January 1994.

———. "Red Hot Chile Peppers' Naked Truth." *Rolling Stone,* 25 June 1992.

Frith, Simon, ed. *Facing the Music.* New York: Pantheon Books, 1988.

———. "Crappy Birthday to Punk." *In These Times,* 23–29 April 1986.

———. *Sound Effects: Youth, Leisure and the Politics of Rock 'n' Roll.* New York: Pantheon Books, 1981.

———. "Beyond the Dole Queue: The Politics of Punk." *Village Voice,* 24 October 1977.

Frith, Simon, and Andrew Goodwin, eds. *On Record: Rock, Pop, and the Written Word.* New York Pantheon Books, 1990.

Frith, Simon, and Howard Horne. *Art Into Pop.* New York: Methuen, 1987.

Frith, Simon, and John Street. "Party Music." *Marxism Today,* June 1986.

Gaar, Gillian G. *She's a Rebel: The History of Women in Rock & Roll.* Seattle, Wash.: Seal Press, 1992.

Gaines, Donna. "Suicidal Tendencies: Kurt Did Not Die for You." *Rolling Stone,* 2 June 1994.

Garofalo, Reebee. "Setting the Record Straight: Censorship and Social Responsibility in Popular Music." *Journal of Popular Music Studies* (Vol. 6 1994).

———. "Crossing Over, 1939–1992." In *Split Image: African Americans in the Mass Media, Second Edition,* ed. Jannette L. Dates and William Barlow. Washington, D.C.: Howard University Press, 1993.

———, ed. *Rockin' the Boat: Mass Music and Mass Movements.* Boston: South End Press, 1992.

———. "Understanding Mega-Events: If we Are the World, The How Do We Change It?" In *Technoculture,* ed. Constance Penley and Andrew Ross. Minneapolis: University of Minnesota Press, 1991.

———. "Nelson Mandela, the Concert: Mass Culture as a Contested Terrain." *In Re-Imaging America: The Arts of Social Change,* ed. Mark O'Brien and Craig Little. Philadelphia: New Society Publishers, 1990.

———. "The Impact of the Civil Rights Movement on Popular Music." *Radical America* (March 1989).

George, Nelson. *The Death of Rhythm & Blues.* New York: Pantheon Books, 1988.

Gett, Steve. "Rock '86." *Billboard,* 27 December 1986.

Gillett, Charlie. *The Sound of the City: The Rise of Rock and Roll.* New York: Outerbridge and Dienstfrey, 1970.

Gilmore, Mikal. "The Year in Music." *Rolling Stone,* 13–27 December 1990.

———. "Disco." *Rolling Stone,* 19 April 1979.

Gitlin, Todd, *The Sixties: Years of Hope, Days of Rage.* New York: Bantam Books, 1993.

Gleason, Ralph. "Stop this Shuck Mike Bloomfield." *Rolling Stone,* 11 May 1968.

———. "Perspectives: Changing with the Money Changers." *Rolling Stone,* 20 January 1968.

Goldberg, Michael. "Bill Graham: The Rolling Stone Interview." *Rolling Stone,* 19 December 1985.

———. "The Spending Begins." *Rolling Stone,* 24 October 1985.

Goodman, Fred. "Big Deals: How Money Fever Is Changing the Music Business." *Musician,* January 1992.

Goodwin, Andrew. *Dancing in the Distraction Factory: Music Television and Popular Culture.* Minneapolis: University of Minnesota Press, 1992.

Graustark, Barbara. "Disco Takes Over." *Newsweek,* 2 April 1979.

Gray, Herman. "Popular Music as a Social Problem: A Social History of Claims against Popular Music." In *Images of Issues,* edited by Joel Best. Hawthorne, N.Y.: De Gruyter, 1989.

———. "Rate the Records: Symbolic Conflict, Popular Music, and Social Problems." *Popular Music and Society* (Fall 1989).

Grein, Paul. "The Year in Charts." *Billboard,* 26 December 1987.

———. "Charts '86." *Billboard,* 27 December 1986.

———. "'83 RIAA Tally: Fewer Biggies." *Billboard,* 14 January 1984.

———. "AOR Programmers Plan More Variety." *Billboard,* 14 January 1984.

———. "Unemployment Lines: LA Industrial Personnel Face Major Challenges to Rebuild Their Careers." *Billboard,* 19 May 1979.

Grossberg, Lawrence. "The Framing of Rock: Rock and the New Conservatism." In *Rock and Popular Music: Politics, Policies, Institutions,* ed. Tony Bennett et al. New York: Routledge, 1993.

———. *We Gotta Get Out of This Place: Popular Conservatism and Postmodern Culture.* New York: Routledge, 1992.

Grossman, Jay. "Let There Be Dancing in the Streets." *Rolling Stone,* 23 May 1974.

Guralnick, Peter. *Sweet Soul Music: Rhythm and Blues and the Southern Dream of Freedom.* New York: Harper and Row, 1986.

———. *The Listener's Guide to the Blues.* New York: Facts on File, 1982.

———. *Feel Like Going Home: Portraits in Blues and Rock 'n' Roll.* New York: E. P. Dutton, 1971.

Guzman, Pablo. "On the Radio, Part Two." *Rock & Roll Confidential,* January 1984.

Hager, Steven. *Hip Hop: The Illustrated History of Break Dancing, Rap Music, and Graffiti.* New York: St. Martin's Press, 1984.

Hamill, Pete. "A Day to Remember." *Rolling Stone,* 29 August 1985.

Hamm, Charles. *Yesterdays: Popular Song in America.* New York: W. W. Norton, 1983.

Hammond, John. *On Record.* New York: Penguin Books, 1981.

Heilbut, Tony. *The Gospel Sound: Good News and Bad Times.* New York: Simon and Schuster, 1971.

Heins, Marjorie. *Sex, Sin, and Blasphemy: A Guide to America's Censorship Wars.* New York: The New Press, 1993.

Henderson, Alex. "Active Indies." *Billboard,* 24 December 1988.

Henke, James. "Record Companies Dancing to a Billion Dollar Tune." *Rolling Stone,* 19 April 1979.

Hersey, Gerri. *Nowhere to Run: The Story of Soul Music.* New York: Penguin Books, 1984.

Heylin, Clinton. *From the Velvets to the Voidoids: A Pre-Punk History for a Post-Punk World.* New York: Penguin Books, 1993.

Hilburn, Robert. "Musical Lessons from 1983's First Half." *Cape Cod Times,* 16 July 1983.

Hill, Trent. "The Enemy Within: Censorship in Rock Music in the 1950s." *South Atlantic Quarterly* (Fall 1991).

Holden, Stephen. "Musical Odyssey." *New York Times,* 9 December 1987.

———. "Pop Records Turn to Hip Hop." *New York Times,* 23 September 1984.

———. "The Evolution of a Dance Craze." *Rolling Stone,* 19 April 1979.

Holland, Bill. "Senate Hearing Examines Gangsta Lyrics." *Billboard,* 5 March 1994.

Holloway, Joseph E., ed. *Africanisms in American Culture.* Bloomington: Indiana University Press, 1990.

Hung, Michèle, and Esteban Garcia Morencos. *World Record Sales 1969–1990: A Statistical History of the World Recording Industry.* London: International Federation of the Phonogram Industry, 1990.

Jacobs, Norman, ed. *Culture for the Millions? Mass Media in Modern Society.* Princeton: D. Van Nostrand, 1959.

Jones, Hettie. *Big Star, Fallin' Mama.* New York: Viking Press, 1974.

Jones, Leroi [Amiri Baraka]. *Blues People.* New York: William Morrow, 1963.

Jones, Steve. "Ban(ned) in the USA: Popular Music and Censorship." *Journal of Communication Inquiry* (Winter 1991).

Kaplan, E. Ann. *Rocking around the Clock: Music Television, Postmodernism, and Consumer Culture.* New York: Routledge, 1987.

Kleinfeld, N. R. "FM's Success Is Loud and Clear." *New York Times,* 26 October 1979.

Kopkind, Andrew. "The Dialectic of Disco." *Village Voice,* 12 February 1979.

Landau, Jon. "The Motown Story." *Rolling Stone,* 13 May 1971.

———. "Soul." *Rolling Stone,* 24 February 1968.

Lax, Roger, and Frederick Smith. *The Great Song Thesaurus.* New York: Oxford University Press, 1989.

Lederman, Minna. "Music and Monopoly." *The Nation,* 28 December 1940.

Levinson, Nan. "Shut Up." *Boston Globe,* 20 February 1994.

Levy, Steven. "Ad Nauseum: How MTV Sells Out Rock & Roll." *Rolling Stone,* 8 December 1983.

Lewis, L. *Gender Politics and MTV: Voicing the Difference.* Philadelphia: Temple University Press, 1990.

Light, Alan. "Ice." *Rolling Stone,* 20 August 1992.

Lipsitz, George. *Time Passages: Collective Memory and American Popular Culture.* Minneapolis: University of Minnesota Press, 1990.

———. *Class and Culture in Cold War America: "A Rainbow at Midnight."* South Hadley, Mass.: J. F. Bergin, 1982.

Lombardi, John. "Kenny Gamble and Leon Huff and the Resurrection of Jerry Butler and Philly Soul." *Rolling Stone,* 30 April 1970.

Lont, Cynthia M. "Women's Music: No Longer a Small Private Party." In *Rockin' The Boat: Mass Music and Mass Movements,* ed. Reebee Garofalo. Boston: South End Press, 1992.

Lydon, Michael, ed. *The Age of Rock 2: Sights and Sounds of the American Cultural Revolution.* New York: Vintage Books, 1970.

———. *Rock Folk: Portraits from the Rock 'n' Roll Pantheon.* New York: Dell, 1968.

———. "Smokey Robinson." *Rolling Stone,* 28 September 1968.

———. "The High Cost of Music and Love: Where's the Money from Monterey?" *Rolling Stone,* 9 November 1967.

Malone, Bill C., *Country Music U. S. A.* Rev. ed. Austin: University of Texas Press, 1985.

Marcus, Greil. "Is This the Woman Who Invented Rock & Roll? The Deborah Chessler Story." *Rolling Stone,* 24 June 1993.

———. "Rock for Ethiopia." Panel presentation at the Third International Conference on Popular Music Studies, Montreal, Quebec, Canada. July 1985.

———. *Mystery Train: Images of America in Rock 'n' Roll.* New York, Dutton, 1975.

Marsh, Dave. "What's Being Sold in Country?" *New York Times,* 24 May 1992.

———. "The Flip Sides of 1979." *Rolling Stone,* 27 December 1979.

Martin, Linda, and Kerry Segrave, *Anti-Rock: The Opposition to Rock'n'Roll.* New York: DeCapo Press, 1993.

Maultsby, Portia K. "Africanisms in African-American Popular Music." In *Africanisms in American Culture,* ed. Joseph E. Holloway. Bloomington: Indiana University Press, 1990.

McClary, Susan. *Feminine Endings: Music, Gender, and Sexuality.* Minneapolis: University of Minnesota Press, 1991.

McClary, Susan, and Robert Walser. "Start Making Sense: Musicology Wrestles with Rock." In *On Record: Rock, Pop, and the Written Word,* edited by Simon Frith, and Andrew Goodwin. New York: Pantheon Books, 1990.

McLeese, Don. "Anatomy of an Anti-Disco Riot." *In These Times,* 29 August–4 September 1979.

Merritt, Jay. "Disco Station Number One in New York." *Rolling Stone,* 22 March 1979.

Miller, Jim. "It's Not Only Rock 'n' Roll." *Boston Globe,* 23 August 1991.

———. "State of the Art." *Newsweek,* 18 April 1983.

———, ed. *The Rolling Stone Illustrated History of Rock 'n' Roll.* New York: Rolling Stone Press, 1976.

Mills, David. "Rap as Politics: The Sayings of Sister Souljah." *Essence,* September 1992.

Minton, Lynn. "Is Heavy Metal Dangerous?" *Parade,* 20 September 1992.

Mooney, H. F. "Popular Music Since the 1920s: The Significance of Shifting Taste." In *The Age of Rock,* ed. Jonathan Eisen. New York: Vintage Books, 1969.

Moore, Jerrold Northrop. *A Matter of Records: Fred Gaisberg and the Golden Era of the Gramophone.* New York: Taplinger Publishing Co., 1976.

Morse, Dave. *Motown.* London: Vista, 1971.

Morse, Steve. "Can American Bands Beat the British Blitz?" *Boston Globe,* 1 January 1984.

Nathan, David. "Rap." *Billboard,* 24 December 1988.

Neely, Kim. "Into the Unknown." *Rolling Stone,* 16 June 1994.

Nelson, Havelock. "Music and Violence: Does Crime Pay?" *Billboard,* 13 November 1993.

"New Black Hope." *Billboard,* 17 May 1969.

Nunziata, Susan. "'90 Label Tally: Units Up 7.3%, $ Jump 14.6%." *Billboard,* 6 April 1991.

Odum, Howard W., and Guy B. Johnson. *Negro Workaday Songs.* Chapel Hill: University of North Carolina Press, 1926.

"Of Hard-Rock Demons: A Cardinal Speaks Out." *Boston Globe,* 6 March 1990.

O'Neil, Thomas. *The Grammys for the Record.* New York: Penguin Books, 1993.

Orloff, Katherine. *Rock 'n Roll Woman.* Los Angeles: Nash Publishing, 1974.

Orr, Charlene, et al. "Texas Police Pursue 'Cop Killer.' " *Billboard.* 27 June 1992.

Ostling, Richard N. "No Sympathy for the Devil." *Time,* 19 March 1990.

Palmer, Robert. "The Church of the Sonic Guitar." *South Atlantic Quarterly* 90, no. 4, (Fall 1991).

———. "The Fifties." *Rolling Stone,* 19 April 1990.

———. "New Rock from the Suburbs." *New York Times,* 23 September 1984.

———. *Deep Blues.* New York: Viking Press, 1981.

Pareles, Jon. "Howls of Rage, Nine Hours Worth, at Waterloo Village. *New York Times,* 13 August 1991.

———. "There's A New Sound in Pop Music: Bigotry." *New York Times,* 10 September 1989.

Passman, Arnold. *The Deejays.* New York: Macmillan, 1971.

Peck, Abe. "Disco! Disco! Disco! Four Critics Address the Musical Question." *In These Times,* 6–12 June 1979.

Perry, Steve. "Ain't No Mountain High Enough: The Politics of Crossover." In *Facing the Music,* ed. Simon Frith. New York: Pantheon Books, 1988.

Peterbaugh, Parke. "Anglomania: America Surrenders to the Brits—But Who Really Wins?" *Rolling Stone,* 10 November 1983.

Peterson, Richard A. "Why 1955? Explaining the Advent of Rock Music." *Popular Music* (January 1990).

Peterson, Richard A., and David C. Berger. "Cycles in Symbol Production: The Case of Popular Music." *American Sociological Review* (April 1975).

Pond, Steve. "The Trick is to Be Loved but Not Embraced." *New York Times,* 26 June 1994.

———. "The Seventies." *Rolling Stone,* 20 September 1990.

Pruter. Robert, *Chicago Soul.* Urbana: University of Illinois Press, 1992.

Ptacek, Greg. "Majors Return to Nuts and Bolts of pre-MTV Metal Marketing Days." *Billboard,* 27 April 1985.

Reagon, Bernice Johnson. "Songs That Moved the Movement." *Civil Rights Quarterly* (Summer, 1983).

"Record Business Sees Light Ahead—On Video Screen." *Chicago Tribune,* 26 April 1983.

Recording Industry Association of America. *Inside the Recording Industry: A Statistical Overview, Update '86.* New York: Recording Industry Association of America, 1986.

Rijven, Stan. "Rock for Ethiopia." Panel presentation at the Third International Conference on Popular Music Studies, Montreal, Quebec, Canada. July 1985.

Roberts, John Storm. *The Latin Tinge: The Impact of Latin American Music on the United States.* Tivoli, N.Y.: Original Music, 1985.

Rockwell, John. "Atwater's Other Hat: Stealing an Inaugural Show." *New York Times,* 23 January 1989.

———. "Leftist Causes? Rock Seconds Those Emotions." *New York Times,* 11 December 1988.

Rose, Tricia. *Black Noise: Rap Music and Black Culture in Contemporary America.* Hanover, N.H.: University Press of New England, 1994.

Roxon, Lillian. *Lillian Roxon's Rock Encyclopedia.* New York: Grosset and Dunlap, 1971.

Sanjek, David. "Can a Fujiyama Mama be the Female Elvis? The Wild Wild Women of Rockabilly." In *Sexing the Groove,* ed. Sheila Whitely. New York: Routledge, 1996.

Sanjek, Russell. *American Popular Music and Its Business.* 3 vols. New York: Oxford University Press, 1988.

———. "The War on Rock." In *Downbeat Music '72 Yearbook.* Chicago: Maher Publications, 1972.

Saunders, Michael. "Getting Hip to Pop." *Boston Globe,* 9 May 1993.

Savage, Jon. *England's Dreaming: Anarchy, Sex Pistols, Punk Rock, and Beyond.* New York: St. Martin's Press, 1992.

Scaduto, Anthony. *Bob Dylan.* New York: Signet Books, 1973.

Schechter, Danny. "Why We Didn't See Wembley." *Africa Report* (July–August 1990).

Schicke, C. A. *Revolution in Sound: A Biography of the Recording Industry.* Boston: Little, Brown and Co., 1974.

Schipper, Henry. "Dick Clark." *Rolling Stone,* 19 April 1990.

Schuller, Gunther. *Early Jazz: Its Roots and Musical Development.* New York: Oxford University Press, 1968.

Seldes, Gilbert. *The Seven Lively Arts.* 1924. Reprint. New York: A. S. Barnes, 1957.

Shapiro, Nat. *Popular Music: An Annotated Index of American Popular Songs: 1940–1949.* Vol. 2. New York: Adrian Press, 1965.

Shaw, Arnold. *Black Popular Music in America.* New York: Schirmer Books, 1986.

———. *Honkers and Shouters: The Golden Years of Rhythm and Blues.* New York: Collier Books, 1978.

———. *The Rockin' '50s.* New York: Hawthorne Books, 1974.

Shore, Laurence Kenneth. "The Crossroads of Business and Music: A Study of the Music Industry in the United States and Internationally." Ph.D. diss. Stanford University, 1983.

Shore, Michael. *The Rolling Stone Book of Rock Video.* London: Sidgwick and Jackson, 1985.

Small, Christopher. *Music of the Common Tongue: Survival and Celebration in Afro-American Music.* New York: Riverrun Press, 1987.

Smith, Joe. *Off the Record: An Oral History of Popular Music.* New York: Warner Books, 1988.

Southern, Eileen. *The Music of Black Americans: A History.* New York: W.W. Norton, 1971.

Stambler, Irwin. *Encyclopedia of Pop, Rock & Soul.* New York: St, Martin's Press, 1977.

Stark, Phyllis, et al. "Gangsta Rap Under the Gun." *Billboard,* 18 December 1993.

Steinfels, Peter. "Surge in Satanic Activity Alarms O'Connor." *New York Times,* 6 March 1990.

Straw, Will. "Rock for Ethiopia." Panel presentation at the Third International Conference on Popular Music Studies, Montreal, Quebec, Canada, July 1985.

Stuart, Dan. "Black Radio." *Billboard,* 17 June 1989.

Sullivan, Jim. "Lollapalooza: The Sound of Success." *The Boston Globe,* 2 August 1992.

The editors of *Rock & Roll Confidential. You've Got a Right to Rock.* Los Angeles: Duke and Duchess Ventures, Inc., 1990.

Thigpen, David. "Up Against the Wal." *Rolling Stone,* 24 February 1994.

Toop, David. *The Rap Attack 2: African Rap to Global Hip Hop.* London: Serpent's Tail, 1991.

Tosches, Nick. *Country: Living Legends and Dying Metaphors in America's Biggest Music.* New York: Charles Scribner's Sons, 1985.

Touré. "Snoop Dogg's Gentle Hip Hop Growl." *New York Times,* 21 November 1993.

Townshend, Charles R. *San Antonio Rose: The Life and Music of Bob Wills.* Urbana: University of Illinois Press, 1976.

Walser, Robert. *Running with the Devil: Power, Gender, and Madness in Heavy Metal Music.* Hanover, N.H.: Wesleyan University Press, 1993.

Warhol, Andy, and Pat Hackett. *POPism: The Warhol '60s.* New York: Harcourt Brace Jovanovich, 1980.

Watrous, Peter. "Good Things Happen to Lollapalooza." *New York Times,* 5 August 1992.

Weinstein, Deena. *Heavy Metal: A Cultural Sociology.* New York: Lexington Books, 1991.

Wenner, Jann. "A Letter from the Editor: On the Occasion of Our Fourth Anniversary Issue." *Rolling Stone,* 11 November 1971.

———. "Musicians Reject New Political Exploiters." *Rolling Stone,* 11 May 1968.

———. "A Letter from the Editor." *Rolling Stone,* 9 November 1967.

"Wexler Attributes Greater R&B Volume to Black Buyer." *Billboard,* 20 November 1971.

Wharton, Dennis. "D.C. Bluebloods Want X Rating for Porn Rock." *Variety*, 22 May 1985.

Whitburn, Joel. *The Billboard Book of Top 40 Albums.* New York: Billboard, 1991.

———. *The Billboard Book of Top 40 Hits.* 3rd. ed. New York: Billboard, 1987.

Whitcomb, Ian. *After the Ball: Popular Music from Rag to Rock.* Baltimore, Md.: Penguin Books, 1974.

Wicke, Peter. *Rock Music: Culture, Aesthetics and Sociology.* Cambridge, England: Cambridge University Press, 1990.

Widgery, David. *Beating Time: Riot 'n' Race 'n' Rock 'n' Roll.* London: Chatto and Windus, 1986.

Wilkinson, Francis. "More Washington Show Talk." *Rolling Stone,* 9 December 1993.

Willis, Ellen. "Beginning to See the Light: or Rock & Roll, Feminism, and Night Blindness." *Village Voice,* 27 March 1978.

Wolfe, Tom. "The First Tycoon of Teen." In *The Kandy-Kolored Tangerine-Flake Streamline Baby.* New York: Farrar, Straus, and Giroux, 1965.

Work, John W. *American Negro Songs.* New York: 1960.

York, Peter. *Style Wars.* London: Sidgwick and Jackson, 1980.

Young, Charles M. "Rock Is Sick and Living in London: A Report on the Sex Pistols." *Rolling Stone,* 20 October 1977.

Zappa, Frank. "The Porn Wars." *Penthouse,* May 1989.

Zaslow, Jeffrey. "Music and Money." *Wall Street Journal,* 21 May 1985.

Zimmerman, K. "Priest Ruling Gives Unclear Message." *Variety,* 3 September 1990.

Zook, Kristal Brent. "Reconstructions of Nationalist Thought in Black Music and Culture." In *Rockin' the Boat,* ed. Reebee Garofalo. Boston: South End Press, 1992.

Zwick, Edward. "An Interview with the Father of Hi-Fi: Dr. Peter Goldmark." *Rolling Stone,* 27 September 1973.

Index